Miscellaneous State Papers

ANECDOTE   HISTORY

J. Stuart inv.   Published according to Act of Parliament Feb. 1. 1778. by W. Strahan & T. Cadell   B. Caldwell sculp.

MISCELLANEOUS

STATE PAPERS.

From 1501 to 1726.

IN TWO VOLUMES.

VOL. I.

VETUSTIS NOVITATEM DARE, NOVIS AUCTORITATEM,
OBSOLETIS NITOREM, OBSCURIS LUCEM, DUBIIS FIDEM, &c.

PLIN. HIST. NAT.

LONDON:

LONDON:

PRINTED FOR W. STRAHAN; AND T. CADELL, IN THE STRAND.
MDCCLXXVIII.

PREFACE.

AS the Public muſt ultimately decide on the merits of every work, and their opinion is neither to be corrupted by flattery, nor biaſſed by prejudice, the Editor thinks nothing elſe neceſſary, by way of Introduction, than to open the plan of the Collection, and to aſſign a few reaſons, for adding one more to the numerous publications of this kind, which the world is already poſſeſſed of.

The principal idea which has prevailed in the choice of the materials, has been, not to dwell too long on any one ſubject, or any one period ; and to ſelect ſuch papers, as mark moſt ſtrongly the characters of celebrated Princes and their Miniſters, and illuſtrate ſome memorable æra, or remarkable ſeries of events. It ſeems ſuperfluous to obſerve, that the introductions prefixed to moſt of the articles will connect (as far as was practicable) the different diviſions of the work with general hiſtory, and lead the reader's attention to ſuch points as he may think deſerve it beſt. Notes are occaſionally inſerted at the bottom of the page, with the ſame view : and it is hoped they will not be thought either tedious or trifling.

The

PREFACE.

.The Editor is well aware of the difguſt which often ariſes to a delicate taſte, from the antiquated ſtyle and ſtiff phraſeology, which unavoidably occur in theſe publications of hiſtorical documents. It is preſumed, however, that many nervous and able diſpatches will be found here, of a remote date, which do credit to the compoſitions of thoſe early times, on topics of buſineſs. And it may be fairly aſſerted, that new lights are thrown on the conduct and characters of ſome eminent perſons; as Burleigh, Walſingham, Leiceſter, and Charles I.; notwithſtanding that part of our hiſtory may appear to ſuperficial readers to have been already exhauſted.

Some facts and incidents of ſmall importance may, indeed, be pointed out, in the courſe of the papers, as languid and uninterelting. But it is to be confidered, that in every picture there muſt be ſome ſhades; and that it was impoſſible to avoid this objection but by giving broken extracts; by which mode the connection and arrangement of the writer's narrative and ſentiments would have been greatly diſturbed. The reader will confult his taſte, and turn over thoſe pages, where nothing attracts him: though the Editor flatters himſelf that many ſuch will not be met with. He will not attempt to recommend himſelf at the expence of thoſe who have gone before him;

him; and therefore declines giving any reasons why the plan he has adopted may deserve the preference.

-· Whoever looks into these Volumes will be better prepared for his future entertainment, if he pleases to consider the work before him as an historical picture gallery, where the different modes and fashions of upwards of two centuries are exhibited in regular succession. The politics and sentiments of Henry VIII. and Elizabeth's time, differ as much from those of William III. and of George I. as the ruff and fardingale in the habits of the former, from the hoop petticoat, and long pockets of the latter. There may be pieces of inferior masters in the gallery; but, doubtless, some Titians and Vandykes will be distinguished.—The relation of the Princess Catherine's reception, with which we open, and of the late Queen of France's marriage, with which we conclude, as they represent the fashions and ceremonial of the respective times, may be thought good companions to the picture of the *Champ de Drap d'Or*, in Windsor Castle.

The Editor cannot conclude, without acknowledging the useful assistance which he has received from the Rev. Dr. Douglas, Residentiary of St. Paul's. It is difficult to say, whether the zeal of that gentleman on every occasion, where a friend is concerned, or the judgment and ability which he exerts in serving him, are most conspicuous.

Nothing

P R E F A C E.

Nothing remains but to submit this Collection, with proper resignation and deference, to the judgment of the Public. Their information and amusement have been the only objects in view; and, it is hoped, the endeavour will be attended with some success.

CONTENTS

OF THE

FIRST VOLUME.

No. I.

Certain Notes taken out of the Entertainment of Katherine, wife of Arthur, Prince of Wales, Oct. 1501. Page 1
[From the Harleian Collection.]

No. II.

Original Letter of Thomas Leigh, one of the Visitors of the Monasteries, to Thomas Cromwell, Lord Privy Seal, dated from the Monastery of Vale Royal, August 22, 1536. — — — 21
[From the Harleian Collection.]

No. III.

The Privy Council to the Duke of Norfolk, the Marquis of Exeter, and Sir Anthony Brown, Knight. Instructions for the levying men to go against the Rebels in the North, 1536. — — 23
[From the Harleian Collection.]

The Privy Council to the Duke of Norfolk, and the Marquis of Exeter, being in their march toward Doncaster, against the Rebels, October 20, 1536, — 25

The

CONTENTS.

The Privy Council to the Duke. Inftruftions about dealing with the Rebels, and offering them pardon, Dec. 2, 1536, Page 27

The Privy Council to the Duke of Norfolk, December 6, 1536, — — 30

The Privy Council to the Duke, Feb. 4, 1536-7, 33

The Privy Council to the Duke, Feb. 4, 1536-7, 35

The Privy Council to the Duke, Feb. 25, 1536-7, 37

The Privy Council to the Duke, March 3, 1536-7, 38

The Privy Council to the Duke, March 12, 1536-7, 39

The Privy Council to the Duke, March 17, 1536-7, 41

The Privy Council to the Duke, April 7, 1537, 43

The Privy Council to the Duke, April 8, 1537, 46

No. IV.

Roger Afcham's communication with Monfieur d'Arras, at Landau, October 1, 1552. To Sir Richard Moryfon. — — 48

[From the Paper Office.]

Sir Richard Moryfon to the Lords of the Council, October 7, 1552, — — 51

No. V.

The Journey of the Queen's Ambaffadors unto Rome, Anno 1555. The Reverend Father in God the Bifhop of Ely, and Vifcount Montague, then Ambaffadors; who fet out of Calais in Picardy, on Wednefday, being Afh Wedday, the 27th of February. — 62

[From the Harleian Collection.]

No. VI.

Letters concerning Calais.   —   Page 103
            [From the Paper Office.]
    The Council of Calais to the Queen, May 23, 1557,   ibid.
    Lord Wentworth, Lord Grey, &c. to the Queen, December
        27, 1557,   ——   ——   104
    Their consultation, Dec. 27, 1557,   ibid.
    The Lord Wentworth, Deputy of Calais, to the Queen, January
        1, 1557-8,   ——   ——   107
    Lord Wentworth to the Queen, Jan. 2, 1557-8,   109
    Lord Grey to the Queen, Jan. 4, 1557-8,   113
    Mr. Highfield's account of the siege and loss of Calais,   114

No. VII.

Letters from Sir Nicholas Throkmorton, Ambassador in
    France.   —   ——   121
            [From the Paper Office.]
    To Secretary Cecil, Oct. 28, 1560,   ——   ibid.
    To Secretary Cecil, Oct. 31, 1560,   ——   124
    To the Queen, Nov. 17, 1560,   ——   125
    To Secretary Cecil, Nov. 17, 1560,   ——   144
    To Secretary Cecil, Nov. 18, 1560,   ——   146
    To the Queen, Nov. 28, 1560,   ——   147
    To Secretary Cecil, Nov. 28, 1560,   ——   153
    To the Queen, Nov. 28, 1560,   ——   155
    To Secretary Cecil, Nov. 29, 1560,   ——   157
    To the Queen, Nov. 29, 1560,   ——   159
    To Secretary Cecil, Dec. 1, 1560,   ——   161

CONTENTS.

No. VIII.

Mr. Jones to Sir Nicholas Throkmorton, Ambassador in France. — — Page 163

[From the Original, in the possession of the Earl of Hardwicke.]

No. IX.

Letters from Sir William Cecil, and from the Earl of Bedford, to Sir Nicholas Throkmorton, Ambassador in France. — — 170

[From the Originals, in the possession of the Earl of Hardwicke.]

From Sir William Cecil to Sir N. Throkmorton, May, 1561, ibid.

From the Same to the Same, July 14, 1561, 172
Earl of Bedford to Throkmorton, July 8, 1561, 175
From Cecil to Throkmorton, Aug. 26, 1561, 176
From the Same to the Same, Dec. 22, 1561, 177

No. X.

A note of consultation had at Greenwich, primo May 1561, by the Queen's Majesty's commandment, upon a request made to her Majesty by the King of Spain's Ambassador, that the Abbot of Martinengo being Nuntio from the Pope, and arriving at Bruxells, might come into the realm with letters from the Pope and other Princes to the Queen. — — 180

[Copied from the Advocates Library at Edinburgh.]

No.

No. XI.

Henry Earl of Huntingdon, to the Earl of Leicester, April 1563. — — Page 187
[From the Original in the British Museum.]

No. XII·

Letters from the Queen of Scots to the Duke of Norfolk, 189
[From Dr. Forbes's Collection, in the poffeffion of the Earl of Hardwicke.]

From the Queen of Scots to the Duke of Norfolk, Jan. 31, 1569-70,	190
From the Same to the Same, March 19, 1569-70,	191
From the Same to the Same, May 17, 1570,	192
From the Same to the Same, June 14, 1570,	193
From the Same to the Same, — —	194

No. XIII.

Letters from Sir Edward Stafford, Ambaffador in France.
[From the Originals in the Paper Office.]   196

Sir Edward Stafford to the Queen, Dec. 1, 1583,	197
Sir E. Stafford to Secretary Walfingham, Dec. 1, 1583,	204
Sir Edward Stafford to the Queen, Dec. 10, 1583,	208
Sir Edward Stafford to Lord Burleigh, Dec. 19, 1583,	212
Copy of a private letter to Mr. Secretary, about the Anfwer of that he writ to me of my Lord Paget, —	213
Sir Edward Stafford to the Queen, —	215

No. XIV.

From the Queen of Scots to Charles Paget, May 20, 1586.
[From Dr. Forbes's Collection, in the poffeffion of the Earl of Hardwicke]   218

CONTENTS.

No. XV.

Evidence against the Queen of Scots.   Page 224
[From a Copy of the Trial in the poffeffion of the Earl of Hardwicke]

No. XVI.

A Letter from Sir Edward Stafford, Ambaffador in France, to the Queen, with one to Lord Treafurer Burleigh, inclofing it. —   —   251
[From the Original in the Paper Office.]
Sir Edward Stafford to the Queen, Feb. 25, 1587-8,   ibid.
Sir Edward Stafford to the Lord Treafurer, Feb. 26, 1587,   264

No. XVII.

A brief Difcourfe, containing the true and certain manner how the late Duke of Guife, and the Cardinal of Lorraine his brother, were put to death at Blois, the 14th of December 1588, for fundry confpiracies and treafons practiced by them againft their Sovereign the French King; wherein is farther declared the imprifonment of fome other of the confpirators and leaguers, with divers other circumftances and matters happening thereupon. Written unto our late Queen Elizabeth, by Sir Edward Stafford, at that time her Ambaffador in the court of France.   266.
[From the Harleian Collection]

No. XVIII.

Letters to and from Lord Leicefter, in the Low Countries.
[From the Originals in the Cotton Library.]   297

Lord

Lord Burleigh to Lord Leicester, Feb. 7, 1586, · Page 297
Mr. Thomas Duddeley to Lord Leicester, Feb. 11, 1586, 298
Mr. Davison to the Earl of Leicester, Feb: 17, 1586, 201
Earl of Leicester to Sir Francis Walsingham, Feb. 8, 311
Earl of Leicester to the Lords of the Privy Council, Feb. 8,
1585-6, ——— ——— 315
Earl of Leicester's letter to Mr. Davison, expostulating with
him, and Mr. Davison's notes in the margin upon it, March 10,
1585-6 ——— ——— 318
The Answer of the Council of State to the Queen of England's
Letter of the 13th of February 1585, ——— 321
Earl of Leicester to the Lords of the Council, March 27,
1586, ——— ——— ibid.
Extract of my Lord of Leicester's letter of the 5th of April,
1586, ——— ——— 323
Lord Burleigh to the Earl of Leicester, ——— 324

No. XIX.

Letters from Sir Philip Sidney to the Earl of Leicester. 330
  [From the Originals in the Cotton Library.]
  Sir Philip Sidney to Lord Leicester, Feb. 2, 1586, ibid.
  The same to the same, Feb. 2, 1586, 332

No. XX.

Papers about a private Treaty with Spain. 334
  [From the Originals in the Cotton Library.]
  Lord Burleigh to Andreas de Loo, ——— ibid.
  Earl of Leicester to Lord Burleigh, Sept. 30, 1587, 340
  Earl of Leicester to Lord Burleigh, Oct. 30, 1587, 346
  Earl of Leicester to the Lords of the Council, Nov. 6, 1587, 351

CONTENTS.

Sir Francis Walsingham to the Earl of Leicester, Oct. 9, 1587,
Page 357
Sir Francis Walsingham to the Earl of Leicester, Nov. 12, 1587,
359

No. XXI.

Letters from Sir Francis Walsingham to Sir Edward Stafford, Ambassador at the court of France. 361
[From the Originals in the Paper Office.]
Sir Francis Walsingham to Sir Edward Stafford, Sept. 8, 1588, ————— ibid.
Sir Francis Walsingham to Sir Edward Stafford, Sept. 30, 364
Sir Francis Walsingham to Sir Edward Stafford, Oct. 19, 365
The same to the same, Oct. 20, ————— 367
Sir Francis Walsingham to Sir Edward Stafford, Nov. 10, 368
Sir Francis Walsingham to Sir Edward Stafford, Nov. 28, 369
Sir Francis Walsingham to Sir Edward Stafford, Dec. 10, 370

No. XXII.

Letter of Henry Cuffe, Secretary to Robert Earl of Essex, to Mr. Secretary Cecil, declaring the effect of the instructions framed by the Earl of Essex, and delivered to the Ambassador of the King of Scots, touching his title to the crown of England; which letter was written after Cuffe's condemnation. ————— ————— 372
[From a Copy in the possession of the Earl of Hardwicke.]

No. XXIII.

No. XXIII.

Two Letters of Sir Dudley Carleton, afterward Viscount Dorchester, concerning Sir W. Raleigh's plot; inclosed in the following letter from Mr. Dudley Carleton to Philip Lord Wharton. — Page 377

[From the Wharton Papers.]

Mr. Dudley Carleton to Lord Wharton, Feb. 14, 1651, .ibid.

Sir Dudley Carleton to Mr. John Chamberlain, Nov. 27, 1603, — 378

The same to the same, Dec. 11, 1603, — 387

No. XXIV.

Mr. Chamberlain to Sir Dudley Carlton at Turin, March 15, 1614. — 394

[From the Paper Office.]

No. XXV.

The Earl of Buckingham to Mr. Secretary Winwood, March 28, 1617. — 398

[From a Copy taken by Mr. Sawyer.]

No. XXVI.

Papers relative to the Spanish match. — 399

[From the Harleian MSS. in the British Museum.]

King James to the Prince and Duke of Buckingham, Feb. 26, 1622-3, — ibid.

The Prince and Duke to King James, March 10, 401

The Prince and Duke to King James, — 403

King James to the Prince and Duke, March 15, 404

King James to the Prince and Duke, March 17, 406

The Prince and Duke to King James, March 17, 408

The

Duke of Buckingham to King James, — Page 410
King James to the Prince and Duke, March 25, 1623, 411
The Prince and Duke to King James, March 27, 413
King James to the Prince and Duke, April 10, ibid.
The Prince and Duke to King James, April 22, 414
The Prince and Duke to King James, April 27, 416
Prince Charles to King James, April 29, — 417
Duke of Buckingham to King James, April 29, 418
King James to the Prince and Duke, May 11, 419
The Prince and Duke to King James, June 6, ibid.
King James to the Prince and Duke, June 14, 421
Prince Charles and the Duke to King James, June 26, 422
Prince Charles and the Duke to King James, June 27, 423
Duke of Buckingham to Secretary Conway, June 29, 425
Prince Charles and the Duke to King James, June 29, ibid.
Prince Charles and the Duke to King James, July 15, 426
King James to the Prince and Duke, July 21, 428
Secretary Conway to the Duke of Buckingham, July 23, 429
Prince Charles and the Duke to King James, July 29, 432
Duke of Buckingham to King James, July 30, 433
Secretary Conway to the Duke of Buckingham, Aug. 5, 436
Secretary Conway to the Duke of Buckingham, Aug. 6, 444
King James to the Prince and Duke, Aug. 5. 445
Secretary Calvert to Secretary Conway, Aug. 8. 446
King James to the Prince, Aug. 10, — 447
Prince Charles and the Duke to King James, Aug. 20, 448
Prince Charles and the Duke to King James, Aug. 30, 449
The Infanta to King James, Aug. 30, — 450
Duke of Buckingham to King James, September 1, 451
Prince Charles to the Pope, — — 452
Duke of Buckingham to King James, — — 454

Prince

Prince Charles to the Duke of Buckingham, April 26, 1624,

Page 455

Prince Charles to the Duke of Buckingham,		456
King James to the Duke of Buckingham,	——	457
Prince Charles to the Duke of Buckingham,	——	458
Duke of Buckingham to King James,	——	460
Duke of Buckingham to King James,	——	461
Duke of Buckingham to King James,	——	463
Duke of Buckingham to King James,	——	465
Duke of Buckingham to King James,	——	466
Duke of Buckingham to King James,	——	468
Duke of Buckingham to King James,	——	469
Duke of Buckingham to King James,	——	470
Duke of Buckingham to King James,	——	471

No, XXVII.

The Spanish match continued ; the Earl of Bristol's Letters.

[From the Original in the Paper Office.] 473

Earl of Bristol to Secretary Calvert, Oct. 24, 1623,		ibid.
Earl of Bristol to the King, Aug. 29,	——	476
The Same to the Same, Sept. 9,	— ——	479
The Same to the Same, Sept. 24,	——	481
The Same to the Same, Oct. 24,	——	483
The Same to the Same, Nov. 26,	—— ——	488
Earl of Bristol and Sir Walter Aston to the Same, Dec. 26,		490

*The Answer to the Earl of Bristol to certain interrogatories in-
tended for his Majesty's private satisfaction, with a reserve
for a permission of making recourse to such other things as may.
be farther necessary to his clearing,* —— 494

No. XXVIII.

Papers relative to the French match. 523

'[From the Original in the possession of the Earl of Hardwicke.]'

CONTENTS.

*From Secretary Conway to Lord Carlisle and Lord Holland,
Aug.* 12, 1624, —— —— Page 523
From Walter Montague to the Earl of Carlisle, 526
From Lord Carlisle to the Duke of Buckingham, Oct. 2, 528
—— *In the Earl of Carlisle's hand-writing,* —— 531
From Secretary Conway to the Ambassadors, Oct. 5, 532
From Lord Carlisle to the Prince, Oct. 7, 535
From Lords Carlisle and Holland to Secretary Holland, Oct. 18,
536
From Mr. Lorkin to the Lords Carlisle and Holland, Oct. 11, 542
From the Same to the Same, Oct. 21, —— 545
*Copy of the Secret Escrit presented by the French Ambassadors,
and avowed to be the same agreed on between them and his
Majesty's Ambassadors in France, Nov.* 18, —— 546
From Secretary Conway to Lords Carlisle and Holland, Dec. 23,
547
From Lords Carlisle and Holland to Secretary Conway, 549
From Lord Carlisle to the Duke of Buckingham, Feb. 16, 1624-5,
551
From Mr. Thomas Lorkin to the Lords Carlisle, &c. Feb. 12, 555
From Secretary Conway to Lord Carlisle, Feb. 24, 559
The Duke of Buckingham to Lord Carlisle, March 15, 561
From Secretary Conway to the Same, March 16, 562
From the Same to the Same, March 24, 564
From the Same to the Same, March 24, 565
From the Same to the Same, April 12, 1625, 567
From the Same to the Same, April 28, 568
From the Same to Lords Carlisle and Holland, May 5, 570
*Account of the vastly rich Clothes of the Duke of Buckingham,
the number of his Servants, and of the noble Personages in
his Train, when he went to Paris, A. D.* 1625, *to bring
over Queen Henrietta Maria,* —— —— 571

7 APPEN-

A P P E N D I X.

No. I.

Letter of Richard the Third to the Bishop of Lincoln.
[From the Harleian Library.] Page 573

No. II.

The Earl of Leicester to Queen Elizabeth, July 27, 1588.
[From the Originals in the Paper Office.] 575

No. III.

*Letters from the Commanders of the Fleet, about the Spa-
nish Armada.* —— —— 579
[From the Originals in the Paper Office.]

*From Sir Francis Drake to Secretary Walsingham, from aboard
the Revenge, June* 24, 1588, ibid.
From the Lord Admiral to the Same, July 6, 1588, 580
Sir Francis Drake to the Lord Henry Seymour, July 21, 583
From the Same to Secretary Walsingham, July 31, 1588, 584
From the Same to the Queen, Aug. 8, 1588, 585
From the Same to Secretary Walsingham, Aug. 10, 1588, 586

E R R A T A.

Most of which are Mistakes of the Transcriber of the Original MSS.

Page 46. line 23. *for* blotted out, *read* bolted out.
  50.   23. *for* Roan, *read* Rhine.
  69.   30. *for* Chenevy, *read* Geneva.
  86.   22. *for* Sunday, *read* Saturday.
  94.   7. *for* not unpunished, *read* unpunished.
  95.   11. *for* which marble, *read* white marble.
         24. *for* pledges, *read* pages.
 113. &c. *for* Newhavenbridge, *read* Newnambridge.
 118.   15. *for* both, *read* loth
 121.   15. *for* remarkable, *read* remarkably.
 131.   24. *for* move, *read* give.
 350.   10. *for* told, *read* bold.
 353.   7. *for* defend, *read* offend.
 399.   15. *for* though a man of Honour, *read* in the main a man of Honour.
 409.   5. from bottom, *for* come, *read* Rome.
 433.   7. *for* to cast ourselves, *read* to part ourselves.
 555.   8. *for* 'tis inflexible, *read* us inflexible.
 556.   20. *for* promised, *read* premised.
 558.   *for* From the Same to Lord Doncaster, *read,* From the Same to the Same.

MISCELLANEOUS

STATE PAPERS,

&c. &c. &c.

No. I.

Certain Notes taken out of the Entertainment of Katherine, Wife of Arthur, Prince of Wales, Oct. 1501.

Harleian
Collection,
69. 25.

[This is printed * as a curious specimen of State ceremonial during
times, when the pomp, order, and magnificence of Courts were
kept up to the height. The Princess too, who was the occasion
of it, was innocently, but unfortunately for herself, the source
of great events.]

IT is ordained, that my Lord Steward †, and the other persons
thereto appointed, be attending upon the Princess in their barks,
somewhat before she come to Gravesend, and there hail and salute
in the best manner they can; and that the minstrels fail not to do
their parts as accordeth to them, and as soon as her ship shall be
fallen to an anchor, the said Lord Steward and all other Nobles shall
go into the ship wherein the said Princess shall be, and after the

---

* In the fifth volume of the last edition of
Leland's Collectanea, p. 352, &c. is a narrative of the Princess Katherine's *arrival and
reception*, &c.; but it differs entirely from what
is here laid before the public; containing only
her journey from Plymouth, where she landed,
to Kennington near Lambeth, where she continued till every thing was prepared for her
public entry; the particulars of which, never-
before printed, are the subject of the present
article. A *Narrative of the justs, banquets,
and disguisings,* after the marriage, may be
seen in the above volume of the Collectanea,
from p. 356, to p. 373.   † Lord Brooke.

HENRY VII.

King's commendations made by my said Lord Steward; the Queen's by her Chamberlain, and the Prince's, by his Chamberlain, in such form as they shall be by them commanded; the Prior of Canterbury shall say the proposition, after the which, my said Lord Steward shall shew, or cause to be shewed to the said Princess, that the King's Grace, tenderly considering her great and long pain and travel upon the sea, would full gladly that she had landed and lodged for the night at Gravesend: but forasmuch as the plague was there of late, and that is not yet clean purged thereof, the King would not that she should be put in any such adventure or danger, and therefore his Grace hath commanded the bark to be prepared and arrayed for her lodging: wherefore he shall on the King's behalf desire her, for her more ease and relief, to depart out of her own ship into the said bark; declaring to her also, that in the same she shall be conveyed to the city of London: and if it shall please the said Princess so to do, my said Lord Steward shall see that she shall be well and honourably entreated and entertained, in every behalf, and that she be served in the said bark of her diets, as appertaineth; and though the said Princess will not in any wise depart out of her ship into the said bark, before such time as she shall be strait conveyed into the city, the King's commandment yet is, that she have the said diets and all such victuals and wines as be provided for her, sent her in her ship, and there served with the same.

· Item, That there be certain Ladies appointed by the Queen's Grace, to give their attendance upon the said Princess, that is to say, the Dutchess of Norfolk and six women: the Countess of Kent and four women: the Countess of Salop and four women: the Lady Hungerford and two women: the Lady Grey, wife to the Earl of Kent's son, and two women: the Lady Abergavenny and two women: the Lady Cobham and two women: Dame Catherine Grey and one woman: Dame Jane Guilford and one woman: Dame Elizabeth Vaux and one woman: Dame Elizabeth Darcy and one woman: Dame Margaret Poyntz and one woman:

Dame

Dame Ann Tyrrel and one woman: Dame Eleanor Wyndham and one woman: Dame Tomazin Rifte and one woman: Dame Ifabella Poynings and one woman: Dame Sibill Scott and one woman: Dame Jane Darrell, wife to Sir Edward Darrell, and one woman: Dame Mary Lewis, wife to Sir Richard Lewis, and one woman: Dame Beautrix Tyrrel, wife to Sir Thomas Tyrrel, and one woman: Mrs. Hungerford, wife to the fon and heir of Sir Walter Hungerford: Mrs. Wynham: Mrs. Fettyplace: Mrs. Ruffel: Mrs. Katherine Griffith, wife to the fon and heir of Sir Rice ap Thomas: Mrs. Elizabeth Calthrop: and letters of the fame intent forthwith to be fent by the Queen's Grace to the faid Ladies, and all other Ladies, that fhall give any attendance, or do any fervice at this feaft, be forthwith written out to prepare them for their attendance: and that they be advertifed by the fame letters, to be ready upon an hour's warning, to come at fuch time, and at fuch place as fhall be affigned unto them by the Queen's fecond letters: and that William Hollibrand, one of the Cuftomers of London, for the caufe following, be then attending the faid Dutchefs: and that the Queen's Chamberlain call diligently upon the faid letters to be fent out unto the faid Ladies, and give unto them warning at their coming, how they fhall order themfelves for the faid intent in every behalf.

Item, That the faid Dutchefs and Ladies in their barges, be attending upon the faid Princefs, in the faid place where fhe fhall lie at anchor, by the fpace of one   at the leaft, before fhe depart thence; whereof they fhall have the more certain knowledge by my faid Lord Steward: and at their coming thither, they fhall go to the faid Princefs, to whom William Hollibrand, in as humble manner, and with as good fpeech as he can ufe, fhall fhew that the faid Dutchefs of Norfolk, and the other Ladies there, being prefent by the King's commandment, be come to vifit and welcome her to the realm, to give her their attendance, to do her the fervice that may be to them poffible, and convey her to her lodging: wherefore the

B 2   faid said Dutchefs and Ladies moft humbly befeech her, thus to accept her and them, and to command them her good pleafure: and my Lord Chamberlain hath the charge to give inftruction to Hollibrand for the ordering of himfelf according to the premifes.

Item, That certain Lords, fpiritual and temporal, be in likewife the fame time attending at the fame place, to receive and convey the the faid Princefs by water, in their barges, to London : that is to fay, Bifhop of Norwich and Rochefter, in one barge : the Earl of Arundell and the Lord Maltravers, in another : the Earl of Effex, and my Lord Montjoy, in another : my Lords of Abergavenny, Delawar, and Clinton, in another : the Lords Howard, Berneis, and Dacres, in another : the Abbots of St. Auftin, and Battle, in another : and that the fame Lords, in the company of the faid Dutchefs, vifit the Princefs in her fhip. My Lord Chamberlain hath taken upon him the warning of thofe Lords.

Item, That femblable letters, as the letters that the Queen's Grace fhall write to the Ladies, whereof is mention made before, be forthwith fent by the King's Grace, not only to the faid Lords and Nobles, but alfo to all others that fhall give attendance or do any fervice at this feaft; and as foon as the King's Grace fhall have certain knowledge of the place, port, and time, that the faid Princefs fhall be tranfported to, then both his Grace and the Queen with all diligence fend forth the faid fecond letters: and that in the faid fecond letters, the time and place when and whereunto, the Lords, Ladies, and others fhall come, be fpecially expreffed, and that every Bifhop and Abbot be advertifed to bring with them their pontificals; and of thefe both firft and fecond letters, and the fending of them forth, fhall have the charge, the King and Queen's Secretaries.

Item, The faid Princefs fhall alfo be met about the Black-Wall, with the ftates following: that is to fay, the Duke of Bucks in one barge: the Bifhop of Bath in another: the Bifhop of Exeter in
another:

another: the Earl of Northumberland in another: the Earl of Kent in another: the Lords Saintmound and Stourton in another: the Abbot of Glaſtonbury in another: the Abbot of Abingdon in another. My Lord Chamberlain ſhall advertiſe them of their attendance.

Item, The Mayor and Crafts of London ſhall meet her, in their ſeveral barges, after their manner accuſtomed, at Deptford, and every of theſe barges ſhall hail and ſalute her in the beſt manner they can, and row about behind, and upon the ſides of her ſhip, and of this attendance to be given by the Mayor and others, my Lord Chamberlain hath the charge to give warning unto them, and when they ſhall come upon the water, then they to be ordered by my Lord Steward.

Item, That for the more ſurety of the ſaid barks and barges, and to make the more ſpace and room for the paſſage of the ſame upon the Thames, it is ordained that Mr. Robert Rydon, Under Admiral, ſhall take ſuch proviſion, that all the ſhips that ſhall fortune to be then in the Thames, be laid as nigh unto the ſhore, as they may be on the one ſide of the Thames, whereof my Lord Chamberlain ſhall advertiſe the ſaid Mr. Rydon.

Item, That the Lords, Ladies, and all others, order them with their barges, about the bark of the ſaid Princeſs, in the manner following: that is to ſay, my Lord of Bucks, and all that come in his company, to keep them upon the right hand of the ſaid Princeſs: and the Lords that meet her firſt, upon the left ſide, and all the Ladies and ſhip boats, to come after her, and the Mayor and Crafts of London, to go before her: and that they have warning thereof by my Lord Steward: and at the coming of the ſaid Princeſs in the wharf of the Tower of London, ſhe ſhall be ſet on land on the weſt-ſide of St. Thomas's Tower, as it is 1co feet from the Tower-gate, and there ſhe ſhall be received with my Lord of Yorke, the King's ſecond ſon, accompanied with the Lords and

† Nobles

Nobles following: that is to fay, the Archbifhop of York, the
Bifhop of Durham, the Earl of Suffolk, the Earl of Shrewfbury,
the Lord Harrington, the Lord Strange, the Lord Haftings, the
Lord Willoughby, the Lord Zouch, the Lord William of Devon,
the Lord William of Suffolk, the Abbot of Weftminfter, the Abbot
of St. Albans : Sir Edward Stanley, Sir Edward Daniel, Sir Nicholas
Vaux, Sir Thomas Cheney, Sir Thomas Green, Sir William
Terwitt, Sir Thomas Brandon, Sir John Longueville, Sir Marma-
duke Conftable, Sir John Saville, Sir William Gafcoigne, Sir John
Huffey, Sir Henry Heydon, Sir William Boleine, Sir Robert
Broughton, Sir Hugh Conway, Sir John Rainford, Sir Henry
Marney, Sir Richard Lewis, Sir Pierce Edgcumbe, Sir John Pafton,
Sir Philip Calthrop, Sir Robert Brandon, Sir Thomas Wentworth,
Sir John Ferris, Sir Thomas Rotheram, Sir John Audley of Suffolk,
Sir Thomas Bryan, Sir Edward Rawley, Sir John Verney, Sir
John Digby, Sir Robert Cleie, Sir Henry Willoughby, Sir Edward
Stanhope, Sir John Wingfield, Sir Robert Paynton, Sir Thomas
Bawde : and all thefe, with their fervants waiting upon them, fome
upon the one fide, and fome upon the other, after their honor and
degree, fhall be ranged in an order upon the wharf of the Tower,
by Sir Thomas Lovell, calling unto him the King's Marfhal, and
the Officers of the Marfhalfea, and to call all the faid Lords and
Nobles together, and advertife them of that, to them is appointed,
and to caufe them to order them accordingly to the fame. The
Bifhop of Durham and Sir Thomas Lovell have taken the charge
upon them.

It is to be remembered that no barge attending upon the faid
Princefs, take upon them to land in any place, neither upon the
one fide, nor upon the other of the Thames, but always to hover
till the Princefs be landed, and then depart to their lodgings at
their pleafure, except the Ladies, the Duke of Bucks, and the
Earls, which fhall land with her, and convey her to her lodging ;

2   and

and that my Lord Steward give unto them warning and charge of the fame.

It is appointed that the gate of the wharf of the faid Tower towards St. Katherine's at the one end, be fpied all the day, that the Princefs fhall arrive, and the other gate at the other end of the faid wharf toward London, be kept by Officers of the Marfhalfea, and the King's Bench, that no man enter by the fame, but fuch only as fhall attend upon my Lord of Yorke, and fuch honeft perfons as fhall be thought convenient by the difcretion of the faid Sir Thomas Lovell; and that the fame Officers of the Marfhalfea and King's Bench keep all the faid wharf, that no man land there by boats, and that the bridge over the Tower-ditch be furely made of a meet largenefs, and fufficiently railed on both fides, and the ward-houfe before the gate taken away, or fet apart: and afore the time the faid Princefs fhall lodge in the Tower, her company fhall lodge in the City at the *Harbigage* of the Mayor and his Officers, as nigh the Tower as conveniently may be done, or with their acquaintance lodging within the Tower, and then depart to their lodgings at their pleafure, if they fhall fo like; and the faid Sir Thomas Lovell hath taken upon him the whole charge and execution of this article.

Item, It is thought convenient that the faid Princefs fhall lodge in the Tower in the King's lodging, the fame to be apparelled by my Lord Chamberlain, and there to reft two days or more, as fhall pleafe the King's Grace, and as the cafe fhall require.

Item, The Queen's lodging, and fix more of the beft chambers within the Tower, be apparrelled and dreffed for the Ladies of the faid Princefs; and that this be done by Sir Charles Somerfet, and Sir Thomas Lovell.

Item, At the coming of the faid Princefs to the Tower of London, and for the time of her refting there, it is thought that my Lord Steward fhall provide for the diets of the faid Lady, under the

form

form following: that is to fay, for a chamber for herfelf, a chamber for her Ladies, a chamber for her Lords and other Nobles, and that the gates being kept, that as few enter in the fame, except only fhangers and honeft perfons, as may be, but only the officers and purveyors for the houfehold, and fuch as fhall be commanded by the King, or appointed to do fervice or attendance for the time, and during the feaft, at Paul's and Weft-minfter, and alfo for the time that the King fhall afterwards be at his manor of Richmond, or his caftle of Windfor, or any other place, till the Spaniards have taken their leave: the Lords and Ladies with their menial fervants to have free refort at every meal to the King's houfe.'

Item, When the Princefs fhall diflodge out of the Tower, it is appointed, that then my Lord of Yorke, and all the other Lords and Nobles that have given their attendance fince fhe was firft met, be ready at the faid Tower on horfeback, to convey her to the weft door of the church of St. Paul's, and that no perfon but only the faid Lords, and fuch gentlemen as fhall await upon them, be on horfeback, and that no Lord or other have any more fervants attend-ing upon him on foot, but only as followeth: that is to fay, my Lord of Yorke 12, the Archbifhop of Yorke 4, the Duke of Bucks 4, every Bifhop and Earl 3, every Baron 2, and every Knight and Efquire 1; and that they, and every of them have thereof adver-tifement by my Lord Chamberlain, and that two of the King's fervants appointed by my Lord Chamberlain, give their attendance upon the faid Lords and Nobles, to caufe them to keep this ordinance: and my faid Lord of Abergavenny, having attending upon him for this time the officers of arms, hath taken upon him to put into due order the faid Lords and Nobles, as appertaineth to their degrees and eftates, and in the fame order to keep them from their departing out of the Tower, to their coming to the faid weft door.

Item,

Item, That a rich litter be ready to receive and convey the said HENRY VII. Princess to the weft door of the church of St. Paul's.

Item, That three horsemen in side-saddle and harness, all of one suit, be arrayed by the Master of the Queen's Horse, to follow next to the said Princess's litter.

Item, That a fair palfrey with a pillion, richly arrayed, and led in hand, for the said Princess, do follow next unto the said Horsemen.

Item, That 11 palfreys in one suit, be ordained for such Ladies, attending upon the said Princess, as shall follow next unto the said pillion.

Item, That 5 charres diversely apparelled for the Ladies and Gentlewomen, be ready the same time at the said Tower, whereof, one of the chief must be richly apparelled and garnished for the said Princess, and the other four to serve such Ladies as shall be appointed by the Queen's Chamberlain, and that the same follow in such order as the said Chamberlain shall appoint.

Item, That betwixt every of the said charres, there be 5 or 6 palfreys of such Ladies, as shall come to the feast, for the attendance given upon the Queen's Grace.

Item, That the same Chamberlain have also the ordering of the said palfreys, as well as of the charres, and if there fortune any more charres to come than above is assigned, then the same to be ordered by the said Chamberlain.

Item, It is to be remembred, that some wise and expert person or persons be assigned by the King and the Queen for the purveyance of the said litter, palfreys, charres, and the apparels that shall be necessary for the same, and that this be done with all speed, for the case it requireth.

Item, That the Mayor, Citizens and Crafts attend upon the said Princess at the Cross in Cheap, in such manner, and in such solemn pageants and ceremonies as they have devised for the honor of

C   the

the City, and of the feaft, whereof my Lord Abergavenny hath the charge.

Item, That the faid Princefs be conveyed thro' the high ftreets of London, in fuch cafe accuftomed, ftrait to the weft door of Paul's, where fhe fhall be received with proceffion, by the Archbifhop of Canterbury in pontificalibus, accompanied with a good number of fuch Prelates, all likewife in pontificalibus, as he fhall call to him: and from the faid door, with the choir of the church, proceffionally to bring her to the high altar, and there to do fuch ceremonies as in fuch cafe is accuftomed; and after her offering, to be conveyed to the little door againft the confiftory that leadeth into the palace, and fo forth brought to her chamber within the faid palace. And for her long travel and labor, it is thought that fhe fhould tarry in the faid palace one day, at the leaft before the day of her marriage, and more as the cafe fhall require, and as it fhall pleafe the King.

Item, That her Ladies and Gentlemen be lodged in the Dean's and Canon's lodgings, and other honeft houfes adjoining to the faid palace, by Whiting and Trefry Gentlemen Ufhers, by the overfight and ordering of my Lord Chamberlain and Sir Charles Somerfet, and that a confideration be had that they be lodged after their honours and degrees.

It is appointed that after the faid Princefs hath refted her in her chamber by the fpace of an hour or thereabouts, that then the faid Princefs in her litter accompanied with the Dutchefs, of Norfolk in her litter, and certain other Ladies, fome of the Queen's, and fome of the faid Princefs's at the Queen's nomination, and alfo certain Lords to be appointed by the King for the attendance given upon the Lords of Spain, fhall be conveyed by Paul's chain, down Lambert's hill, to the King and the Queen being at Baynard's Caftle: and that my Lord of Oxford receive her at her lighting which fhall be within the court, and bring her into the

King's

King's great chamber, and my Lord Chamberlain hath the charge of giving advertifement to the Earl of Oxford.

Item, That Lambert's hill fhall be fanded by the Mayor of London againft the fame time, whereof my Lord Abergavenny fhall give him advertifement, and that the Serjeant Porter be warned, that no manner of perfon enter the gate in charre, neither on horfeback, but only the faid Princefs and fuch other Nobles and Ladies as fhall accompany her: my Lord Chamberlain hath the charge of the execution of this article: and Sir Charles Somerfet is to forefee that the King's guard be there well apparrelled, ranged, and ordered, at the entry of the faid Princefs.

Item, Afore the day of the marriage, it is thought that for the more folemnity of the feaft, it fhould be on the Sunday, or fome Holiday, and that the faid Princefs be going out of her chamber towards the church, fomewhat before 9 of the clock, whereof my Lord Chamberlain fhall advertife the Duchefs of Norfolk.

Item, It is ordained that the Bifhops of Exeter, Hereford, Bath, Lincoln, Sarum, Chefter, Rochefter, and Norwich, and the Abbots of Weftminfter, Bury, St. Albans, Glaftonbury, Abingdon, and Reading, all in pontificalibus, give their attendance the day of marriage upon the faid Archbifhop of Canterbury, executor of the faid marriage.

And afore the Princefs's coming to the City, it is thought that he fhould be there four days before the coming of the faid Princefs to the Tower, and that he fhould lodge in the Bifhop of Sarum's Place, till the night next before the marriage day; and that night, for his more readinefs for the bufinefs of the next day, to lodge in the wardrobe, and the next day to make his entry into the church fomewhat before the Princefs's coming thither, which entry is devifed to be at the fouth door next weftward to our Lady of Grace in the body of the church; and the Princefs's houfehold fervants to give their attendance and

convey

convey him to the hault place to be made before the confiftory, in the faid body of the church, fomewhat before her coming thither. Sir Richard Poole hath taken upon him the charge of this article.

Item, The faid Princefs, accompanied with the greateft eftates of the Lords and Ladies, go out of the palace at the great gate, and enter by the Weft door of the faid church, and fo go to the faid hault place led by my Lord of York; whereof my Lord Chamberlain fhall give advertifement, as well to the Lords as to Sir John Rifley, for that that toucheth my Lord of York, and the Queen's Chamberlain fhall advertife the Ladies.

Item, For the more eafy coming of the faid Princefs, it is devifed that barrs fhall be made from the faid palace gate, unto the faid weft door of the church, and fo from thence to the foot of the gallery, whereof Sir Charles Somerfet and Mr. Comptroller hath the charge.

And as for the hault place, it is devifed to be fet in the nave and body of the church, even annenft the confiftory, to the intent that the King and the Queen may fecretly go out of the Bifhop's palace into the fame confiftory, whereof Mr. Comptroller and Sir Charles Somerfet have the charge.

Item, The fafhion of this hault place is devifed to be made like unto the hault place at the chriftening of the King's child, with broad and large greeces and fteps, and with a good large fpace all on high one loft, to the intent that the executor of the office of the marriage, and the minifter of the church neceffary for to do that act, and the Prince and the Princefs may be together, and no more above, in the faid fpace all on high, than be neceffary: and the Bifhops, Abbots, and other Prelates and Officers, may ftand lower upon the faid fteps of the hault place, fo as thereby grow no impediment to the fight of the people, and that from the faid hault place to the choir door, there be made a ftage of five feet high, with a rail upon either fide: and Sir Charles

Somerfet

Somerfet and the Comptroller of the King's houfe have taken upon them, that the faid work fhall be made fure and fubftantial.

Item, That the trumpets ftand aloft over the fame weft door, and blow continually after the firft coming of the faid Princefs out of the great gate of the faid palace, till the time fhe be in the church upon the hault place, and then forthwith when fhe fhall be there, the trumpets to ceafe : and the ordering and guiding of the faid trumpets and minftrels for the time of the feaft, is committed to Thomas Lovell, Yeoman Ufher of the King's chamber.

And when the faid Prince and Princefs fhall be on the faid hault-place on loft, and the banes afked them, that Mr. Secretary object openly in Latin againft the faid marriage, that it cannot be lawful, for fuch reafons as he fhall exhibit there, fuppofed to be grounded on the laws of Chrift's Church; whereunto Mr. Dr. Barnes fhall reply, and declare folemnly, likewife in Latin, the faid marriage to be good and effectual in the law of Chrift's Church, by virtue of a difpenfation which he fhall have there, to be openly read, and thereupon forthwith to deliver it to the Executor Officii, and the fame Executor to command his Chancellor to read it; the fame objections made, or any other to be made againft the fame, notwithftanding. and for advertifement of the Archbifhop of Canterbury in all fuch things as fhall be executed by him at that folemnity, the King's Secretary hath taken upon him the charge.

And in cafe it be requifite after the manner of Spain, as it is after the cuftom of England, that fome man fhall give the efpoufe, then the greateft Perfonage that fhall come with the faid Princefs, fhall give her. The charge of this article refteth in my Lord Chamberlain.

Item, When all fhall be finifhed that is to be done on the faid hault-place for the matrimony, then fhall the Prince and. Princefs go together upon the faid gallery hand in hand, all along the body

2   of

of the faid church, ftrait after hede upon the fame gallery ftrewed
with rufhes, herbs, and flowers up to the choir, and through the
choir to the high altar to their places appointed there: and that the
ordering, rufhing, and apparrelling of the faid gallery, be provided
for by Sir Charles Somerfet and Mr. Comptroller.

Item, As foon as the Prince and Princefs fhall begin to depart
from the faid hault-place, then fhall all the minftrels, every man
after his faculty, one after another, being all on high in the vaults
of the church, do their parts in mufic continually, as fhall come in
their courfe, till the Prince and Princefs fhall be before the high
altar, and then all the minftrels to ceafe. And the ordering of all
the faid minftrels is committed to Lovell, Ufher of the King's
Chamber.

And to the intent that the faid Prince and Princefs may have always fome place fecretly to refort unto, for fuch cafualties that may
fall during the high mafs of the marriage: It is to be forefeen that
the Prince fhall have a traverfe made and fet on the north fide
the choir near the high altar in place convenient, with a running
curtain to ferve when need fhall be: fo as the minftrels about the
high altar, and thofe in the vaults, fhall not now fee what fhall be
done in the faid traverfe: and femblably, another traverfe to be made
likewife, and to be fet on the South fide of the choir, alfo in
place convenient for the faid Princefs to refort into, if any occafion
fo demand. My Lord Chamberlain hath taken upon him the provifion and making of thefe traverfes.

Item, As for the carr-cloth, it fhall be of white baukin, and provided by my Lord Chamberlain, and by him delivered to the Prince's
Chamberlain; and the fpices and wines to be provided by my Lord
Steward, and delivered to the Prince's Chamberlain and his officers,
they to have the ordering of the fame; and that the carre-cloth be
holden by two Lords to be affigned by my Lord Chamberlain.

Item,

Item, After the folemnity of matrimony fhall be fully done, the Prince fhall firft, and before the Princefs, depart with his company, down all along the North fide of the church, and make his entry at the door of the palace of the Bifhop, that is next unto the faid con- fiftory, far within the faid palace, at her chamber door to receive the faid Princefs.

Item, The faid Princefs, foon after the departing of the faid Prince, led by my Lord of York fhall return the fame way fhe went, that is to fay, through the choir down upon the faid gallery, all along the body of the church, out of the great Weft door of the fame, and in at the great gate of the Bifhop's palace, and fo to her chamber, where, at the door thereof, the Prince fhall receive her, as the cuftom of England is.

Item, That firft, the minftrels, and after, the trumpets, every man after his courfe and faculty, do their parts when the Princefs fhall return towards the palace of the Bifhop, as they did at her going from the fame.

Item, It is thought good, that, fomewhat befide the great Weft door of the church, in the South fide thereof, there fhall be a folemn conduit, well and pompuoufly devifed for to run divers forts of good wines, and the faid conduit to begin to run as foon as the Princefs fhall be entered into the faid palace, and fo to run continually all that day, and part of the pipes to run till midnight following: whereof Sir Charles Somerfet and Mr. Comptroller hath the charge.

Item, It is thought convenient, that fuch head officers as fhall have charge of the feaft, the day of the faid marriage, do provide amongft other things, that the hall of the Bifhop of London's palace as well in the   of the boards, tables, and forms thereof, and in hanging of the houfe, as in making of cupboards, as well in the chamber where the faid Princefs fhall dine, as alfo in the hall, and otherwife, thought neceffary, be well and honourably garnifhed and dreffed, fo as it fhall be beft devifed for the honour

of

of the faid feaft: the charge of the execution of this article is committed to Worley, to be done by the advice of Sir Charles Somerfet
and Mr. Comptroller.

Item, After the feaft, that matter is remitted unto the Steward,
Comptroller and the head officers of the King's moft honourable
Houfhold, and the Cofferer to fee for the payment thereof.

Item, The third day after the day of marriage, the faid Prince
and Princefs to depart from the faid palace, towards Baynard's caftle,
to go to Weftminfter with the King's Grace; and that the faid
Princefs fo departing, fhall ride in her litter, or on her fpare horfe,
with the pillion, behind a Lord to be named by the King, and eleven
Ladies upon palfreys after her; and that certain convenient number
of the faid Lords and Nobles be named, and warned by my Lord
Chamberlain, then alfo to await on her on horfeback, with the fame
number of their fervants with them on foot, that they had betwixt
the Tower and the church of St. Paul's, keeping company with the
Lords of Spain, as they did before accompany the faid Princefs to
Baynard's caftle, where the King and the Queen fhall be: and fo
forth to go with the King by water to Weftminfter: and for this to
be well done, two things are behoveful, the one is, that the ftrects
from Paul's chain down Lambert's hill, between the Earl of Derby's
Place on the one fide, and the Under Treafurer's lodging, to the
faid Baynard's caftle, be well gravelled, and fubftantially caft with
fand, by the Mayor of London, for the horfes more furety to keep
themfelves upright in the great defcent of the hill aforefaid: the
other is, that the faid Princefs diflodge the faid third day, from the
Bifhop's palace at fuch good hour, as fhe may come to the King
and Queen, to depart, if the King fo be pleafed, the fame day at time
convenient from the faid Baynard's caftle, to the King's palace of
Weftminfter: the care of the ordering of fuch things comprifed in
this article, my Lord Chamberlain hath taken the charge.

Item,

Item, That-the great bridge at Weftminfter be amended by the Treafurer of England, and the King's arms be renewed and new painted, whereof he fhall have warning by Mr. Comptroller.

Item, The floor of Weftminfter-hall be alfo new repaired, and the windows of the fame glazed; whereof Mr, Comptroller and Worley have the charge.

Item, That the Woolbridge at the fame Weftminfter be alfo new repaired at the King's coft, the charge whereof is committed to Mr. Comptroller and Worley.

Item, That all the gates and doors be fhut, fo that there be none enter except only through the great hall of Weftminfter and the White hall.

Item, For the more royalty of the going of the King and the Queen, of the Prince and of the faid Princefs, unto Weftminfter by water, it is accorded that the King and Queen and Prince have their barges apart, well and pompoufly rigged and dreffed; for the King's barges, the Lord Chamberlain hath the charge; and for the Queen's, and Prince's, the Chamberlain of both the Queen and Prince have charge.

Item, That, likewife, all the Lords fpiritual and temporal that have given their attendance at the feaft, accompany the King in their barges and great boats to the faid Weftminfter; and as for the faid Princefs, it is thought that fhe fhould be with the Queen's Grace in her barge.. The Lord Chamberlain hath the charge to advertife the Lords of the premifes, and the Queen's Chamberlain to provide for the Princefs's conveyance with the Queen.

Item, Befides this provifion, that the King's great and little boats be purpofely prepared and kept for fuch ftrangers as fhall come with the faid Princefs, whereof my Lord Chamberlain hath taken charge.

Item, When all thefe barges and boats of the Lords fpiritual and temporal, fhall be thus appointed and ready upon the Thames, to fet forward towards Weftminfter, then the faid Lords fpiritual and

D   temporal

temporal fhall attend, every man in his barge, or boat, in the river, upon the King's barge, and when the King in his barge fhall fet forth from the faid Baynard's caftle, then all the other barges and boats, to row by the King, after the King, and about the King, as the fpace of the river with the ebbe or flow, and good order, fhall lead them, till the time his Grace fhall be landed at the great bridge of Weftminfter; and that the Queen's Grace and all the Ladies and certain Lords, to be appointed by the King's Grace to attend upon her, follow the company of the King: and when fhe fhall come to the great bridge at Weftminfter, that then fhe, her Ladies and Lords attending upon her, paufe and reft in their barges till fuch time that the King with his company be landed and entered into the palace. The charge of the ordering and appointing of the Lords to give attendance upon the King's Grace and the Queen, in their barges, is committed to the Lord Chamberlain; and for the ordering of the Queen, with the appointing of the Ladies to give attendance upon her Grace, the charge is committed to the Queen's Chamberlain.

And for jufts, tourneys, and other ceremonies, they be remitted to the faid Mr. Comptroller, ferjeant of the King's armoury: and as for provifion of the fcaffolds, and all other things belonging to the faid jufts, Mr. Comptroller and Worley have taken upon them the charge.

Item, It is ordained, that the morrow after the King's coming to Weftminfter at afternoon, in the evening, the King fhall make the Knights of the Bath, and the day next enfuing fhall begin the tourneys and jufts to endure at the King's pleafure.

Item, It is thought fitting and honourable, that every Lord fpiritual and temporal that fhall give their attendance at the time, keep his houfe during the faid feaft, and till the King depart from Weftminfter.

Item, That my Lord Chamberlain fend certain of the Ufhers of the King's chamber, to take up Heron's houfe within the fanctuary,

and

and to fearch all the lodgings that be within the Abbey and the Chanon Row, and caufe the owners of them to drefs and furnifh them with ftuff, and to make their report of every of the fame by writing.

Item, My Lord Steward and Mr. Comptroller, to caufe fix of the beft furnifhed lodgings of the Sanctuary, and the town of Weftminfter, to be referved and kept for ftrangers.

Item, That Mr. Robert Southwell, and Sir William Pampage, fhall have either of them a whole copy of this book, to the intent they may often overfee and perfectly perufe the fame, and not only to advertife every man that hath any charge committed to him to be ready, and to do their offices, but alfo to call upon them for the execution of the fame.

Item, That Jaques Hault, and William Pawne, be appointed to devife and prepare difguifings and fome morifques, after the beft manner they can, whereof they fhall have warning by my Lord Chamberlain.

Item, Whereas my Lord Steward is now fick, if it fortune that he continue in his ficknefs fo long, that he fhall not now attend to fuch charges as be committed to him by divers articles of this book, Mr. Comptroller hath taken upon him to do, perform, and execute all the faid charges by the faid articles appointed to my faid Lord Steward, and in manner and form as my Lord fhould have done, if he had not been letted by his faid ficknefs, forefeeing always there be fome noble Perfonage appointed to occupy the place and room of the faid Lord Steward, touching the receiving and conducting the Princefs, which Perfonage is thought fhould be my Lord of Surrey.

Item, The Bifhop of Durham hath taken upon him to make an abftract out of this prefent book, of every man's charge, as it is comprifed in the fame, and the fame abftract divided into feveral

articles

articles as the matter toucheth every man apart, to deliver in writing to Mr. Secretary, which fhall inclofe the faid articles feverally in as many letters as there fhall be articles, and the fame direct and caufe to be fent to fuch perfons, as be named in the heads of the faid articles, defiring them by the fame letters, to do and perform for their parts as is expreffed in the fame articles.

No. II.

Original Letter of Thomas Leigh *(one of the Vifiters of the Monafteries) to* Thomas Crumwell, *Lord Privy Seal. Dated from the Monaftery of* Vale Royal, *the 22d of Auguft,* 1536.

HENRY VIII.

Harleian Library, 604.

[This is a curious but authentic picture of Country Manners about the time of the Reformation: It is no wonder that Vifiters, making fuch reports, were unpopular.]

IN my moft humble manner I commend me unto your good Lord-fhip, evermore thanking you of your munificency, and great goodnefs, at all times fhewed unto me. Advertifing your Lordfhip, that whereas I have hitherto, according to your commandment, vi-fited the archdeaconries of Coventry, Stafford, Derby, and part of Chefhire; for that I can perceive accordingly, as I heretofore have written unto you, there laketh nothing but good and godly inftruc-tion of the rude and poor people, and reformation of the heads, in thefe parts. For certain of the knights and gentlemen, and moft commonly all, liveth fo incontinently, having their concubines openly in their houfes, with five or fix of their children, and put-ting from them their wives, that all the country therewith be not a little offended, and taketh evil example of them. Wherefore hitherto I have given and fent commandment to them (forafmuch as I could not fpeak with them all, by reafon they were at the affizes), to put from them immediately fuch concubines, as they have hi-therto notorioufly and manifeftly occupied and kept, and to take again

again their wives; or elfe to appear before your Lordſhip, to ſhew a caufe why they ſhould not be compelled; and if your Lordſhip will command any other thing to be done in the premiſes, I ſhall be ready to accompliſh the ſame. And feeing my Lord of Norfolk is come to the court, I ſhall moſt humbly deſire you to have me in remembrance. And thus God preſerve you, and have you in his moſt firm tuition, with much increaſe of honour, according to the contentation of your Lordſhip's moſt noble good heart's deſire.

From the monaſtery of Vale Royal, the 2ed of Auguſt.

Your Lordſhip's humble at

commandment,

THOMAS LEIGH.

No. III.

The Privy Council to the Duke of Norfolk, the Marquis of Exeter, and Sir Anthony Brown, Knight. Inſtruc- HENRY VIII.
tions for the levying Men to go againſt the Rebels in the Harleian Collection, No. 6989.
North, 1536.

[This formidable Rebellion is not very fully related by our Hiſtorians, and ſtill leſs the Intrigues which produced it; had more of
the Nobility and Men of Property joined in it, the Throne of
Henry VIII. and his Church Eſtabliſhments would have been
ſhaken, if not overturned.]

Ctober 19th, 1536.

AFTER our right hearty commendations, Theſe ſhall be to
advertiſe you, that this morning arrived here a poſt with the
letters herein incloſed, directed to you my Lord Norfolk, and others
to the K. Highneſs, the copy alſo whereof you ſhall receive herewith, which was commanded, as by the ſaid letters you ſhall perceive, to have firſt paſſed by you, and ſo after to have come hither.
For anſwer to the contents of which letters, the King's Majeſty
hath commanded us to ſignify unto you, that firſt his pleaſure is,
you ſhall, with all poſſible diligence, ſend unto my Lord Suffolk all
ſuch munitions as in his letters to you my Lord of Norfolk be contained. Second, that you Sir Anthony Brown, ſhall with your
number
S

number of 560 men, in his Grace's laft letters mentioned, and with 440 men on horfeback more, to make up a full thoufand, if they may poffibly be there gathered, advance fpeedily to my Lord of Suffolk, taking alfo with you the ten pieces of ordnance that were before appointed unto you, with powder, fhot, and all things convenient for the fame. And if the faid 440 men, to make up the full thoufand men on horfeback, or within an hundred at the uttermoft of the fame, cannot be there levied, then his honour's pleafure is, that you fhall take the 560 men on horfeback before prepared, and with them alfo 1000 footmen, or very near that number, to be in like manner conveyed with you, or after you, to my faid Lord of Suffolk with all poffible diligence. And his Grace's inftant defire is, that you my Lord of Norfolk and Exeter, fhall, with the band of 5000 men in all, limited unto you, make your addrefs with the like fpeed to my * Lord Steward. And that you fhall take certain order, that the pofts may be laid furely for the fpeedy conveyance of letters, both between Lincoln and Windfor, and between the places where you fhall fortune to be, and the fame. Finally you fhall underftand, the King's Highnefs hath at the writing hereof prefently difpatched to Mr. Cofferer by Dr. Leighe †, and Dr. Leighton †, for your good furniture, now at your fetting forth, and in your journey towards my Lord Steward, the fum of two thoufand pounds, having alfo appointed, that a fpecial and certain Treafurer fhall, for the faid journey only, with the fame wait upon you. And therefore his Grace defireth you to fear no want of money; for this day there

---

* The Earl of Shrewfbury, who was the King's Lieutenant againft the rebels in Yorkfhire.

† Thefe by the Lord Cromwell's means had lately been fent abroad by commiffion from the King, to vifit the abbeys, and to take account of the enormities there committed. And there is a letter wrote by one of them, viz. Leighton, to Cromwell, concerning the nuns and friars of Sion, extant in Fuller's Church Hiftory. In the diffolution of the abbies, thefe men had the fingering of the revenues thereof for the King's ufe, which made them fo odious, that thefe rebels among their demands at Doncafter made this, that Leigh and Leighton fhould be imprifoned for bribery and extortion.

is also difpatched to Mr. Goftyck above ten thoufand marks, and more fhall come after. And befides, if any bruit or noife fhall be of any want of money, it might greatly difcourage men, and fo hinder much the King's affairs at this time, which by all means would be fet forth and advanced. And thus moft heartily fare you well.

From Windfor the 19th of October.

Your loving friends,

THOMAS AUDELEY, Chancellor,
THOMAS CRUMWELL.
ROBERT SUSSEX.
EDWARD HEREFORDE.

The Privy Council to the Duke of Norfolk and the Marquis of Exeter, being in their march towards Doncafter againft the Rebels. Anno 1536.

1536.
October 20.

AFTER our right hearty commendations. Forafmuch as by letters fent from my Lord Steward, and my Lord of Suffolk, with others to the King's Highnefs, it appeareth, the number of rebels groweth and increafeth daily; his Grace's pleafure is, that for the better furniture of your forces, as well you, my Lord of Norfolk, fhall take with you the reft of your band, over and above the number appointed, which you wrote was 1500 men or thereabouts : as that you, my Lord Marquis, fhall femblably take all the reft of your band, over and above the number agreed upon with you, if you fhall together think it fo expedient; hafting yourfelves to my Lord Steward with all poffible diligence. Advertifing you furthermore, that for the more perfect keeping of Lincolnfhire in quiet,

E

HENRY VIII. quiet, his Grace hath commanded my Lord Chamberlain (Lord Sands). Mr. Poulet, and Mr. Kingston, with the residue of the Gloucester-shire men, not being of the thousand going with you, and others to furnish on horseback, and on foot, if they can there at Ampthill levy so many good men, and the number of 2000 persons, and the same with speed to send to my Lord of Suffolk; signifying further unto you, that because this matter seemeth to be so hot and dangerous, his Grace desireth you, my Lord of Norfolk, to advertise him by this bearer, whether you shall think it expedient, that his Grace should levy an army to attend upon his person, and so advance towards the said rebels; and what you think else expedient to be considered touching the same. And to this said bearer to give firm credence, for his Highness hath declared his full mind and pleasure in that behalf. And thus most heartily fare you well; the 20th day of October, 1536.

THOMAS AUDELEY, Chancellor.

JOHN OXYNFORD.

EDWARD HEREFORDE.

THOMAS CRUMWELL.

ROBERT SUSSEX.

RICHARD CICESTER.

Endorsed thus, *In secundo exitu versus* Doncaster *:

* For the rebels had already taken Hull and Pomfret, and were advanced southward before Doncaster, 30,000 strong, lying there. divided into three bodies. And hither the Duke was now hastening to meet and fight them.

*The Privy Council to the Duke. Inſtruĉtions about deal-
ing with the Rebels, and offering them Pardon.* Anno
1536.

AFTER our right hearty commendations to your Grace. The
ſame ſhall herewith receive the double of a letter ſent to the
King's Highneſs from my Lord of Suffolk, upon the arrival with
him of a ſervant of Sir William Muſgrave's; by the contents thereof,
with the credence of the ſaid Muſgrave's ſervant, it appeareth, that
Tyndeſdale, and Riddeſdale be of a good ſort, and have rather done
diſpleaſure to the rebels, than ſhowed themſelves any thing toward
to condeſcend to their traiterous faĉtion. And that the parties of
Cumberland and Weſtmoreland be not of ſo evil diſpoſition as hath
been ſuppoſed. And further, the ſaid Muſgrave's ſervant hath declared to the King's Highneſs, that the Lord Clifford, the ſaid Sir
William Muſgrave, Aygleby and others do keep peaceably the town
and caſtle of * Carliſle, with the parts about the ſame: and that
Sir William Muſgrave has been with the Earl of Cumberland at
Skipton †, and found him ſo viĉtualled and furniſhed in every condition, that he eſtceemeth not much the malice of his enemies. Which
things weighed and conſidered, his Majeſty thinketh, if you ſhall
for the firſt brunt fortify the paſſages of Doonne with ditches, according to his device, the Yorkſhire men, and thoſe that ſhall take
their parts, will be, within ſhort ſpace, eaſy enough to deal withal.

---

* But ſoon after it was beſieged by one
Nich. Muſgrave and 8000 men. But they
were repulſed by the city. And in their
return encountered by the Duke, who cauſed
all the Captains (except Muſgrave who
eſcaped), and ſeventy perſons beſides, by
martial law to be hanged on Carliſle walls.

† Skipton was a caſtle belonging to the
Earl, which the rebels, in Oĉtober, had attempted, and he reſolutely defended againſt
them; though 500 gentlemen retained at his
coſt, had deſerted him.

For

For being the parties before rehearfed brought to fome ftay, wherein
his Grace will travail, my Lord of Suffolk, with the Lincolnfhire
men of the one fide, you, my Lord Steward, my Lord of Rutland,
my Lord of Huntingdon, and others there, with the forces of thofe
parts, on the other fide, and my * Lord of Derby on the third pârt,
with fuch preparation as his Grace can fhortly make, fhall be able
enough to conftrain the rebels to fuch conformity and obedience, as
appertaineth.

Wherefore his Majefty defireth you, confidering it fhould not be
honourable for him to grant the free pardon, but a mean to encourage the offenders, and others alfo, to the enterprifing of like
attempts, to ufe all the dexterity to you poffible, to induce them to
receive the firft † pardon, and to ftay with them long, before you
fhall proceed to the other degree, which his Highnefs would by no
means come unto, if fudden extremity fhall not enforce the fame.
And, good my Lord, ufe in this matter all your wifdom, to fatisfy his
Grace's princely courage and defire.   For it is much to his Grace's
regret to receive from you fo many defperate letters, and in the fame
to hear no mention of the remedies.   Infomuch as his Grace making
a difcourfe of the whole progrefs of the matter, upon the letters
written lately, that he fhould be deceived if he trufted to the paffages, faid, thofe words agreed but fhrewdly with the letters written
unto him from Cambridge, wherein you defired fo much that my
Lord Steward fhould not have paffed Trent, before your coming to
him, as though you had known the country and rivers fo well,
that you had been then able at your will, in manner to have put the
rebels to difcomfiture.   Which matter not fucceeding according to

---

* This Earl had raifed forces out of Lancafhire and Chefhire, to ftop another army of
rebels, that were coming fouthward through
Lancafhire, to join thofe that were up in
Yorkfhire.

† Wherein ten were excepted, fix named,

and four unnamed, but the four unnamed
concerning every body, it was declined   The
free pardon was without any exception at
all, on condition they would lay down their
arms, and make their fubmiffion to the King's
Lieutenants.

your

your defire, you did after much lament. And yet his Highnefs faid, that unlefs my Lord Steward had indeed marched forward contrary to your mind, there had been more loft, than percafe would have been recovered again in a good time, befides the difhonour that fhould have enfued of the fame. Surely his Highnefs is your good and gracious Lord; and therefore we all befeech you eftfoons now to fhow all your wifdom to conduce thefe things to that end, that may be to his Grace's fatisfaction: for we affure you, his Highnefs thinketh his honour fhall be much touched, if he fhall grant them the free pardon.

Your Grace fhall herewith receive letters from the King's Highnefs privately written to yourfelf; but we affure your Grace, whatfoever is contained in the fame, his Majefty is as good and gracious Lord unto you, as ever he was in his life; and we all be your affured friends, defiring as much that fuccefs in this matter, that may be to your honour, as yourfelf can defire the fame, which we fhall alfo advance to our poffible powers; knowing right well, that whatfoever is written touching the flay for the free pardon, you will no further ftrain them to take the firft pardon, than your wifdom fhall think meet for the quieting of the matter, which is moft to be regarded. And thus we befeech our Lord, fend your Grace no worfe to fare than we would ourfelves. From Richmond the fecond of December. Your affured loving friends,

THOMAS AUDELEY, Chancellor.
JOHN OXYNFORD.
ROBERT SUSSEX.
THOMAS CRUMWELL.
RICHARD CICESTER.
WILLIAM POULET.

Endorfed at Hatfield. From the King's Council, 4th December.

The Privy Council to the Duke of Norfolk.

AFTER our right hearty commendations to your Grace.
These shall be to advertise you, that yesternight about six of
the clock we received your letters written from Welbeck on Saturday, upon certain others from us, before to you addreffed, touching our hope that the King's Majesty would condescend to your
desires * made by Sir John Ruffel, rather than the matter should grow
to a further extremity. The contents of which letters, when we had
perused, we signified to his Highness, being the same, both to his
Grace, and all us, very pleasant and comfortable; as well for that
we perceive thereby the good inclination and loyal disposition of
the Gentlemen, with your certain intelligence † with the same, as
for that the said Gentlemen being so well disposed, it is not to be
doubted, but though the cankered Commons would attempt any
further enterprizes, the said Gentlemen and their servants and friends,
with your advice and counsel, and the aid of such force as you have,
and may easily prepare there, shall be able to stay their fury and
traiterous madness. And his Majesty giveth unto your Grace and
your colleagues ‡ there, his most hearty thanks, that by your wis-

---

* Viz. That the King would yield to a
general pardon, and a Parliament to be held
in those parts, which were some of the things
the rebels required, and which being granted,
he thought it might be a means to quiet all.
This the Duke desired, that he might be in a
better readiness for the treaty, which was to
be by the King's allowance on the 6th of
December between the Duke and the Earl of
Shrewsbury on the King's part, and 300 of
the rebels at Doncaster. Which request the
King granted, leaving the whole to the Duke's
discretion.

† For the rebels had compelled all the nobility and gentry they could get into their
hands, to go with them, making them swear
to an oath they administered to them; and
some did willingly join with them   With
some of these the Duke held a secret corre-
spondence, of which he made good use.
Among these were the Lord Scroop, the Lord
Lumley, Lord Latimer, &c.

‡ Earl Shrewsbury, Marquis of Exeter,
Earls of Huntingdon and Rutland, &c.

                                        doms

doms you have conduced this great matter to fo good a towardnefs
of the clear finifhing of the fame. And whereas your Grace's opinion is, that growing to an end with the rebels at this meeting, it
fhould be meet you fhould forthwith enter into the country, and fo
fwear the fame from place to place, as you fhould travel, and that
you fhould in that cafe be furnifhed with fome good company of
nobles and gentlemen, as well for the better advancement and fhowing of the King's honour, and for your furety in all events and
chances; which noblemen and gentlemen would look for their cofts
paid in that journey. His Grace doth right well allow and approve
your device therein. Neverthelefs his defire is, that you fhould firft
fignify unto him, what noblemen and gentlemen, and what the
grofs number of all the train, fhould be, that you would have with
you. And thereupon his Highnefs will fend you your commiffion,
and take fuch further order for the entertainment of you and your
train, that you fhall have caufe to be contented. Trufting that you will,
in the advertifement hereof, confider the great charges his Majefty hath
been at, and devife for the alleviation of the fame, as much as you can
poffible. And upon that advertifement, his Highnefs will alfo write
to the Earl of Northumberland * for his coming hither, if nothing
chance unto him in the mean feafon; not doubting but your Grace
will have fuch refpect unto his brethren, that they fhall not be able
to do any difpleafure, though they would malicioufly practife any
evil purpofe.

Now there refteth but only one thing to be confidered, which the
King's Majefty hath much at heart, and we fhall no lefs defire, that
is, the prefervation of his Grace's honour, which his Highnefs and
we all think, fhall be much touched, if there be no man referved to
punifhment, for the example of others hereafter. Wherefore albeit
the King's Majefty hath referred all to your difcretion, yet if your.

* Who had been Lord Warden of the Marches, but lately fufpected and difcharged, and
now about to be fent up.

‡   Grace

Grace could, by any good means, or poffible dexterity, referve a very
few perfons to punifhment, you fhould affuredly adminifter the greateft
pleafure to his Highnefs that could be imagined, and much in the
fame advance your own honour. And amongft a few vile perfons,
becaufe he is notable and moft wilful, if you could referve * Sir
Robert Conftable, we be not able to exprefs how much the fame
would tend to his Majefty's fatisfaction. Wherein we fhall not need
to defire your Grace to travail, knowing. that you will leave no
means unattempted, that your wifdom fhall think may accomplifh
his Highnefs moft fervent defires in that behalf, only grounded upon
the prefervation of his honour, which, without the fame, he thinketh,
and fo do we alfo, fhall be much touched.

We fend unto your Grace alfo, certain of the † letters addreffed
to the Bifhops, with divers copies of the ‡ articles agreed upon by
the clergy : and for the more plain declaration to the people of the
truth of the fame, you fhall receive one copy, whereunto the Bifhops
and Clergy.did at the beginning fet their hands, which we require
you to referve for his Highnefs. And thus moft heartily fare you
well. From Richmond the 4th of December. Your affured friends,

THOMAS AUDELEY, Chancellor.	WILLIAM POULET.
ROBERT SUSSEX.	JOHN OXYNFORD.
THOMAS CRUMWELL.	RICHARD CICESTER.
EDWARD HEREFORD.	WIILLIAM KYNGSTON.

Endorfed at ‖ Hatfield from the King's Council, 6th Dec.

* He, upon the rebellion foon after breaking out again, with the Lord Darcy, Sir
Thomas Percy, Afk, and divers others, was
fent up to London by the Duke, and afterwards executed.

† Thefe letters were, I fuppofe, certain
injunctions, in number eleven, fent under
the name of Crumwell, the King's Vice-
gerent, to be obferved by Deans, Parfons,
Vicars, Curates, &c. which may be feen in
Lord Herbert's life of King Henry, p 472

‡ Thefe articles may be read in the fame
Author, p. 467, 468, which were figned by

Crumwell and eighteen Bifhops, forty Abbots and Priors, and fifty Archdeacons and
Proctors of the Clergy at their convocation.
Several copies of thefe articles were fent to the
Duke on purpofe to be difperfed in thofe
parts, for the better exercife of the ftudies
and thoughts of the clergy, who had been
the chief inftruments in thefe commotions.

‖ The Duke was now at Hatfield in his return back to the North, whence he had come
lately up to Court, upon this occafion He
found the rebels number far to exceed the
King's army, which was not above 5000. So to

gain

The Privy Council to the Duke.

AFTER our right hearty commendation to your good Lordſhip. This morning arrived here your letters unto us on
Candlemas-day, with the copies ſent with the ſame; containing
as well your advice and proceeding touching the ſtay of the
retainder of certain perſons, whoſe names you have ſent in one
of the ſaid copies, as the ſtate of the country there, with certain
other things therein contained, which we have ſhowed unto the
King's Highneſs. And albeit his Majeſty ſeemed to approve
the plain declaration of your mind in that behalf; yet in the
reading of that part of the letter, he ſaid, he ſomewhat marvelled,
that you ſhould be more earneſt in the diſſuaſion of the retainder
of them that have been put, murderers and thieves (if they have
ſo been), than you were that his Grace ſhould not retain thoſe
that have been rebels and traitors. Theſe men have rather done
good than hurt, in this troublous time, tho' they did it not with
a good mind and intent, but for their own lucre. What the
other did, no man can better tell than you. If theſe men may
be made good men, with this advancement, his Highneſs may
think his money well employed. If they will nevertheleſs continue evil, all the world ſhall think them the more worthy
puniſhment, for that they have ſo little regarded the great
clemency and goodneſs of his Majeſty, calling them from their
evil doings to honeſt preferment, to the intent they ſhould the

gain time till more forces came in, he put the
rebels upon petitioning, which advice they
took, and ſent up a petition by two gentlemen that they had compelled to yield to them.
And the Duke promiſed to accompany them

up to forward their petition, and that brought
him into theſe parts But he ſoon returned
again to his charge, and was now gotten as
far as Hatfield.

F   rather

rather leave and forfake the fame. And his Grace may all times
punifh them according to their demerits, when · he fhall think
meet, if they fhall eftfoons offend. And yet his patents of their
annuities be no pardons, nor they by the fame changed into
another ftate than they were before. And therefore his Majefty's
pleafure was, we fhould not only fignify unto you, that he would
have his determinations accomplifhed in that behalf, but alfo,
that with all poffible fpeed after the receit hereof, you fhall write
to Sir Anthony Browne to proceed therein without ftay, according to his former commiffion, any thing by you written to the
contrary notwithftanding; as by the copy of the letters fent to
the faid Sir Anthony, which you fhall receive herewith, you
fhall perceive. And thus moft heartily fare you well. From
Greenwich, the 4th of February.

> THOMAS AUDELEY, Chancellor.
> ROBERT SUSSEX.
> RICHARD CICESTFR.
> CHARLES SUFFOLK.
> THOMAS CRUMWELL.
> EDWARD HEREFORD.
> WILLIAM FITZ-WILLIAMS.
> WILLIAM POULET.
> J. RUSSEL.

The Privy Council to the Duke.

AFTER our right hearty commendations to your good
Lordſhip, theſe ſhall be to advertiſe the ſame, that by this
bearer you ſhall receive the King's Highneſs's letters, which his
Grace doubteth not but you will put in execution with ſuch
dexterity as the ſame may be a ſpectacle of the end of ſuch
abominable treaſons; and a mean to reduce that country to a
perfect quietneſs. You ſhall alſo underſtand that ſince your
departure, the King's Majeſty hath received ſundry letters from
my Lord of Wincheſter and Maſter Wallop, declaring as well a
general communication had between the French King and them,
of the matter of my Lady * Mary, which yet remaineth in the
ſame terms you left it, as an heap of lies which have been ſpread
abroad there, touching our ſtate, and the late buſineſs here. Whereunto, when anſwer was made, the Ambaſſador of France here re-
ſident, made requeſt for acceſs to the King's preſence, and obtaining the ſame, on the French King's behalf, required his Grace's
favourable licence for the young † Queen of Scots' paſſage through
his realm into Scotland ; preſenting therewith a letter from the
Great ‡ Maſter, importing that the King of Scots would be content
to do the ſame. The ſtrangeneſs of the demand whereof, being ſo

---

* A propoſal was made by Pomeray, the
French King's ambaſſador, for a match between the French King's ſon, the Duke of
Orleans, and the Lady Mary the King's
daughter. But that Ambaſſador did little in
the affair. Yet it ſeems Wincheſter and
Wallop, the King's Ambaſſadors with the
French King, had communicated with him
concerning it.

† King Francis of France had lately beſtowed his daughter Magdalen upon the Scots
King, which King Henry took very ill, becauſe he ſaw hereby that King deſigned a
more ſtrict friendſhip with the Scots, which
the Engliſh King was very jealous of, and
therefore made a boggle of letting her paſs
through his kingdom.

‡ Duke Montmorency

F 2   divided

HENRY
VIII.
divided into parts, and commenced in the name of the French King and the Great Mafter, and nothing at all at the interceffion, or in the name of the King of Scots, moved the King's Majefty to ftay in his anfwer. And we upon confultation thereupon had, as yet think it in no wife to be granted, for many great refpects, befides the manner of requeft *. Neverthelefs, as we fhall therein conclude, we fhall from time to time, of that, and fuch other occurrents as be here, advertife you. Requiring you by your next letters to fignify your opinion and good advice unto us, touching this matter, with fuch reafons as, on either part, fhall move you in the fame. And thus moft heartily fare you well. From Greenwich; the 4th of February.

Your affured Friends,

CHARLES SUFFOLK.

HE. EXETER.

RICHARD CICESTER.

ROBFRT SUSSEX.

WILLIAM FITZ-WILLIAMS.

THOMAS CRUMWELL.

EDWARD HEREFORD.

WILLIAM POULET.

Endorfed, *Rec. Feb. 9. Ebor. a Regis Confilio.*

---

* I believe this requeft was denied For Queen came together by fea to Edinburgh I find the King of Scots and his new-married about Whitfuntide.

The Privy Council to the Duke of Norfolk.

AFTER our hearty commendations to your Lordfhip. Whereas the King's Majefty, having eftablifhed an order upon his Grace's eaft and middle marches, as by the device thereof, which we fent unto you, the fame hath perceived, doth intend to frame a like order for his weft marches. Albeit, there hath been a femblable device made for fuch officers and penfioners as fhall be retained upon the fame, the copy whereof we fend unto you herewith; yet knowing as well your great experience in thofe parts, as confidering that it fhall be meet your Lordfhip fhould have the direction of it, we have fufpended the giving of our fentences to the device, which, as is aforefaid, you fhall receive thereof, with thefe our letters, till we fhall from you hear again, how you like the fame. Requiring you therefore to weigh and confider it with your accuftomed wifdom, and to fignify your opinion therein unto us, with as much fpeed as you may conveniently; to the intent the King's Highnefs may thereupon finifh his purpofe therein, as fhall appertain, and be moft for his Grace's honour and furety. And furely we be all as glad of your profperous proceedings in the reducing of that country to good quiet and obedience, and that it hath pleafed God to preferve you in health to the fame, notwithftanding the fear you were in of ficknefs, as any man may be, or as your own noble heart could defire. And thus moft heartily fare you well. From Weftminfter this 25th of February.

Your Lordfhip's affured Friends,

THOMAS CRUMWELL, &c.

*** We require your Lordfhip to keep this matter to yourfelf.

Endorfed, *Newcaftle, ultimo Feb. a Regio Concilio.* With the device for the Weft Marches made by the King's Highnefs.

HENRY
VIII.

1536-7.
March 3.

The Privy Council to the Duke.

AFTER our right hearty commendations to your Lordſhip. Theſe ſhall be to advertiſe the ſame, that foraſmuch as the King's Majeſty hath lately addreſſed his letters to Sir Robert Con-ſtable for his repair unto his preſence, the bearer whereof found him removed to   which is thirty miles from the place where he commonly lieth; and that, upon the delivery of the ſaid letters, he neither uſed any reverend behaviour, nor made any ſuch convenable anſwer for his acceſs, as might have any thing tended to his Grace's ſatisfaction: his Majeſty, conſidering that the ſaid Sir Robert Con-ſtable could, either for his commodity, or for his further intent and purpoſe, remove to a place ſo far diſtant from his habitation and common dwelling-place, ſtanding the ſame alſo upon the ſea-ſide: and on the other ſide, that he could, neither in reſpect of his duty towards his Highneſs, nor in reſpect of his late offences, make any ſeemly anſwer, or of that behaviour in the receit of the ſaid let-ters, and that appertained, and conceiving ſome marvel thereof; hath commanded us to ſignify unto you, that his pleaſure is, you ſhall not only have a ſpecial eye upon him, but alſo that you ſhall of yourſelf adviſe him in ſuch wiſe as you ſhall think moſt conve-nient, with acceleration to make his repair hither. Which, by all likelihood, he may eaſily do, in accompliſhment of his duty, which for his pleaſure could remove thirty miles. And if he ſhall not thereupon addreſs himſelf hitherwards with diligence, then his Grace's pleaſure is, you ſhall cauſe him to be ſent up with a ſerjeant at arms, and with further aſſurance, if you ſhall ſo think meet. And alſo his Highneſs would, that you ſhall ſecretly make Sir Ralph Merker the younger, and Sir Ralph Evers, privy to this matter,

com-

commanding them to take such order in the ports of Hull and Scar- HENRY
borough, and the creeks thereunto belonging, that in cafe he would VIII.
fteal into any outward parts, he may be apprehended, and fo conveyed up unto his Grace in convenient furety, with all diligence:
. Finally you fhall underftand, that his Majefty taketh all your proceedings there in good part, and doth in every condition as thankfully accept the fame, as your own heart could defire. Which we
affirm unto you upon our honefties, becaufe you fhall not doubt in
the fame. And fo moft heartily fare you well. From Weftminfter
the 3d of March.

Your Lordfhip's loving Friends,

Thomas Crumwell, &c.

Endorfed, *Newcaftle, 6th March. A Regio Confilio.*

The Privy Council to the Duke of Norfolk. 1536-7.
March 12.

AFTER our hearty commendations to your good Lordfhip.
We have received your letters of the 7th of this month. And
forafmuch as the King's Majefty hath made anfwer to the greater
part of the principal points contained in the fame, we fhall not
trouble your Lordfhip with the repetition thereof; only we fhall, at
fome length, fignify our minds frankly unto you, touching the matter of the direction of the Borders: wherein you have written your
opinion upon our letters, for that purpofe before addreffed to you.

You write, that you, and other the wife men of thofe parts, think,
that fuch a multitude of wild folks as be upon thofe borders, fhall
not be contained in fuch order as were to be wifhed, by fo mean
men as fhould have the direction of the fame. But that for that
refpect,

refpect, it fhould be meet fome man of great nobility fhould have
the rule thereof.

Firft, my Lord, we have learned by experience, that when the
Earl of Northumberland was for fundry refpects removed from the
office of the Wardenry of the Eaft and Middle Marches, being the
fame offered in manner to two Noblemen that were thought meet
to receive it, they did both, as they might, refufe it. So that for
thofe parts, the King's Majefty was enforced, in a manner, to take fuch
to ferve him therein, as he might, when thofe to whom he minded
it, were not willing to receive it. And thereupon a device was
made, which you feemed much to approve, faving for a few perfons whofe offences and converfation was fuch, as you thought them
not meet in any wife to be advanced. Second, We have by experience feen, that the King hath been much the worfe ferved upon
the Weft Marches, by the reafon of controverfy and variance depending between the great men, that lie upon the fame. And if the
King's Majefty fhould remove the Earl of Cumberland, and eftfoons
prefer into the room of his Warden there, the Lord Dacres, we fee
not but the pique between them fhould be rather augmented than
taken away. Again, if it fhall pleafe his Majefty to appoint the
meaneft man that for fuch a purpofe could be thought on, to rule
and govern in that place, is not his Grace's authority fufficient to
caufe all men to ferve his Grace under him, without refpect of the
mere eftate of the perfonage not having that authority?

We defire to know the names, with the reafons of thofe wife men
that think his Grace fhall not be ferved there with fuch men, whatfoever they be, as he fhall appoint to have authority under him.
How his Highnefs hath been ferved with thofe fuch as have had that
room, what by want of good qualities meet to fupply the places that
fome of them were in, and what by reafon of their difcords, we all
know. And to be fhort with your Lordfhip, we think, that his
Majefty, retaining all the Gentlemen and head-men, as he doth,

7   fhall

ſhall not be evil ſerved. At the leaſt we think it ſhall not be evil, that his Majeſty ſhall eſſay this way, and it were but only to ſee who would not as gladly ſerve him under another, as he would do, if he had the beſt place himſelf. For it importeth no neceſſity of continuance, but as his Majeſty ſhall think, with the proof thereof, expedient. And thus moſt heartily fare you well. From Weſtminſter the 12th of March.

Your Lordſhip's loving Friends,

T. Cantuarien.

Thomas Audeley, Chancellor, &c. &c.

The Privy Council to the Duke.

AFTER our right hearty commendations to your good Lordſhip. Theſe ſhall be to advertiſe the ſame, that debating the effect of your letters of the 12th of this month addreſſed to me the Lord Privy Seal, with the King's Highneſs; his Grace amongſt other things ſaid, he marvelled much, that you and the reſt of his council ſeemed ſo certainly to reſolve, that his Majeſty could not be ſerved upon his marches, but by Noblemen. When I would (quoth his Highneſs) have preferred to the Wardenry of the Eaſt and Middle Marches my Lord of Weſtmoreland, like as he did utterly refuſe it, ſo my Lord of Norfolk noted him a man of ſuch heat and haſtineſs of nature, that he could not think him meet for it. When he would (quoth his Grace) have conferred it to my Lord of Rutland, he refuſed it alſo; and my Lord of Norfolk noted him a man of too much puſillanimity, to have done us good ſervice in it, if he would have embraced an overture in it. And we think (quoth his Highneſs)

G

nefs) he would not advife us to continue in it my Lord of Northumberland.   Now if we fhall prefer none of thefe three to that room,
we would be glad (quoth his Grace) that my Lord of Norfolk fhould
name the Nobleman that he thinketh meet for that office.   For
gladly we would have fuch a one in ftore to appoint it unto, if we
fhould hereafter alter our device, which we be not yet determined
to do, nor fhall apply to that fentence, till we have better experiment what fhould enforce us unto.

Now touching the Weft Marches, my Lord of Norfolk himfelf
(quoth his Grace) thought it not meet that the Earl of Cumberland
fhould be avoided out of the Wardenry thereof, and the Lord Dacres
eftfoons thereunto preferred.   For it fhould but engender mortal
feud between their houfes.   Again, we think, (quoth his Majefty)
that it were unfeemingly to remove him, that hath fo well preferved
himfelf from our rebels in this troublous time, and hath fo well kept
our town and caftle of Carlifle, and in his place to put him, that
hath been taken as his enemy.   If then having determined, for the
withdrawing of heart-burning from them both, to remove them
both from that office, which in either of their hands could have
been no mean of amity between them, we would for thofe Marches
alfo have my Lord of Norfolk name unto us a third Nobleman, not
meddling with any before named.   Which communication we thought
convenient to fignify to your Lordfhip, that you may perpend it
accordingly.   Not doubting but that your wifdom fhall the better
perceive, that, like as his Grace could not be furnifhed with any of
thefe men conveniently before named, for the refpects fpecified, fo
his Highnefs thinketh there will no man refufe, or be flack to ferve
immediately under him, that could be content to ferve under a
Nobleman and his deputies, being all but fubjects.   And this we
write only unto you, to the intent your Lordfhip may perceive the
whole difcourfe of the faid conference and communication, and for
no purpofe of ourfelf, either utterly to impugn your opinion, though
                                                                      the

the contrary by experience may prove right well, or to pique you therein, which, in the utterance thereof, the King's Majefty nothing minded. And fo moft heartily fare you well. · From Weftminfter the 17th of March.

Your loving Friends, ·

· THOMAS CRUMWELL, &c.

u ·   Endorfed, *Holden, 20th March.* · *A Confilio Regis.*

The Privy Council to the Duke.

AFTER our right hearty commendations to your Lordfhip. Forafmuch as not only upon the matter of William Levenyngs, being with the Lord Darcy, Sir Robert Conftable, and Robert Afk, after his attemptate in the new rebellion, which you fignified to me the Lord Crumwell, Privy Seal; but alfo upon the examination and knowledge of fundry other great matters revealed againft them, the fame Lord Darcy, Sir Robert Conftable, and Robert Afk, be this day by the King's Highnefs's commandment, committed to the Tower of London, there to abide till they may be juftified according to the law; his Highnefs's pleafure was, we fhould thereof advertife your Lordfhip, to the intent you may divulge the caufe of their captivity to the people of thofe parts, that they may the rather perceive their miferable fortunes, that being once fo gracioufly pardoned, would eftfoons combine themfelves for the attempting of new treafons, to the great peril of his Grace's perfon, and the danger of his whole realm: which thing his Grace doth alfo defire your Lordfhip to caufe to be publifhed by others, in all parts there, with fuch dexterity, as his fubjects, perceiving the truth thereof, conceive

G 2   not

not, that any thing is done for their former offences, done before the pardon, which his Grace will in no wife remember or fpeak of; but for thofe treafons which they have committed again fince, in fuch deteftable fort, as no good fubject would not wifh their punifhment for the fame.

And whereas your Lordfhip hath eftoons written to the King's Majefty for your repair hither, we do all require you to think, that in cafe his Highnefs will not grant it, the fame is not delayed upon any decay of his favour unto you, or for want of good will in any of us to have had you fatisfied therein; but upon the neceffity of his Grace's laft letters unto you fpecified, and for fundry other refpects and caufes, the particularities whereof you fhall perceive by his Grace's next letters to be addreffed unto you. Wherewithal we truft you will repofe yourfelf in that behalf.

And finally you fhall underftand, that I, the Lord Privy Seal, have fued out your pardon for fuch money as you have defrayed in the wars, and fhall likewife fue out your broad feal thereof, with diligence.

Moreover your Lordfhip fhall underftand, that whereas you wrote lately of one Rochefter, a monk, who by his letters inclofed in a letter of yours, directed to me, declareth himfelf to be a rank traitor, the King's Highnefs's pleafure is, you fhall fend for him to fome fuch place as you fhall think meet, and in cafe he will abide by his opinion, to caufe him to be juftified there, and executed according to the laws.

And as concerning Sir Stephen Hamerton and Nicholas Tempeft *, whom you write will be ready to come up, upon privy feals to be fent for them; his Grace is content that you fhall command them to come up at liberty, if you fhall think they will fo do, without fuch fear as fhould caufe them to ftart. But if you fhall have any doubt in them, his Grace requireth you to fend them up, according

* Who were both after found guilty of treafon, and executed.

to the tenor of the former letters, written for that purpofe. And albeit we doubt not, but your Lordſhip doth think, that we be not fo light to fend for any men in fuch fort, as was lately written for Gregory Conyers *, unlefs there were pregnant matter detected againſt them; yet the King's Highnefs, at the contemplation of your letters, is content that you ſhall fuffer the faid Conyers to come up at his liberty, if you think he will fo do, or elfe that you ſhall fend him up, as was before prefcribed. And to conclude, his Grace doubteth not, but your Lordſhip will caufe this matter of the apprehenfion of the Lord Darcy, Sir Robert Conftable, and Afk, to be fet forth in fuch a general fort, upon their treafons committed fince the pardon, as there be no fpecialty touched or fpoken of, till they may be fo conveyed in a mafs together, as all men may perceive the fpecialties and effects of the fame. And thus moft heartily fare you well. From Chriſt Church † in London, the 7th of April.

Your Lordſhip's affured, &c.

Endorfed, *Durefme,* 10 *Aprilis. A Confilio Regio.*

---

* Who I believe was cleared.
† A monaftery within Aldgate, that upon the diffolution, came to Audeley the Lord Chancellor, where he and the *Privy Council* now fat, and from him to the Duke of Norfolk, who had married Audeley's daughter and heirefs, and fo was afterwards called *Duke's Place.*

The Privy Council to the Duke.

AFTER our right hearty commendations to your good Lordſhip.
By this bearer your ſervant, the ſame ſhall receive the King's
Highneſs's letters, containing his Grace's reſolution upon your ſuit,
for acceſs unto his preſence, (which we doubt not but your wiſdom
will take in good part : conforming yourſelf to that thing that may be
moſt to his contentation. and to the advancement of his affairs)
with certain other things in the ſame letters contained. which we be
aſſured you will ſee accompliſhed, as ſhall appertain. And foraſmuch as we did lately write unto you, the King's Highneſs's reſolution touching the borders, with ſuch cauſes as his Grace did alledge
for the ſame ; and that we have received no anſwer thereunto, his
Highneſs deſiring to hear your farther opinion in that matter, which
he doubted not, but you have ere this time well digeſted, and
thoroughly debated, hath commanded us by theſe letters, to require
your anſwer in that behalf, which we deſire you we may receive by
the next meſſenger.

And whereas your Lordſhip doth write, that in caſe the conſcience
of ſuch perſons, as did acquit Levyning, ſhould be examined, the
fear thereof might trouble others in the like caſe; the King's Majeſty conſidering his treaſon to be moſt manifeſt, apparent and confeſſed, and that all offenders in that caſe be principals, and none
acceſſaries, doth think it very neceſſary, that the means uſed in that
matter may be blotted out, as a thing which may reveal many other
matters worthy his Highneſs's knowledge : and doth therefore deſire
you not only to ſignify their names, as was before written unto you,
but alſo to travail all that you can, to beat out the myſtery thereof.
Wherein we ſuppoſe alſo, you ſhall do unto his Majeſty, high and
acceptable ſervice. And becauſe you write, that the conveyance up
of

of all the prifoners that be written for, fhould require a great number of perfons for the furety of the fame, which fhould fomewhat
disfurnifh you, his Grace is content you fhall caufe as many of them
to come up at their liberty, by your command, as you think will
obferve the fame: which fhall alfo alleviate the charges his Highnefs
fhould be at in that journey. And thus moft heartily fare you well.
From the Rolls *, the 8th of April.

Your Lordfhip's affured Friends.

Endorfed, *Durefme*, 11 *Aprilis.*

* Here the Council fometimes met at the Lord Crumwell's lodgings, who was Mafter of
the Rolls.

No. IV.

[The two following letters from Roger Afcham, and Sir Richard Moryfon, containing fome minute particularities of the Emperor Charles V. are thought worthy to be publifhed. Sir Richard Moryfon was a good fcholar, and we are told, read over Herodotus and Demofthenes in his journey with his Secretary, Roger Afcham, the famous Grammarian, and one of the Revivers of Polite Literature in England.]

Roger Afcham's communication with Monf. D'Arras, at Landau, Oct. 1, 1552. To Sir Richard Moryfon.

AFTER your hearty commendations done, according to your inftructions, I defired his Lordfhip in your name, to take in good part, this my coming to the Court, trufting, that he would confider, that the defire of doing your duty to the King's Majefty, did move you to fend me to him at this time. For now, when you had learned, that the Ambaffador of Portugal was in the Court, and that you were fent from a greater Prince than he was, you trufted his wifdom would confider, that you could not make a good reckoning at home, of your duty abroad, except you might be both in the Court and in the Camp as well as he. Therefore your fuit was, that you might alfo forthwith come thither; for his Lordfhip might be well affured, that he of Portugal, nor the King his mafter, could be more glad the one to write, and the other hear, of the Emperor's moft profperous fuccefs, in all this journey, than you were, both prefently

here,

here, and alfo to write it diligently home; nor no Prince nor country more in daily expectation of the Emperor's Majefty's lucky proceedings, than is the King's Highnefs our Mafter, and all his whole realm of England ; and here I paufed.

Monf. D'Arras's anfwer was,—As concerning the Ambaffador of Lufitania. (for fo he named him always) I pray you defire your Mafter not to think much, that the Emperor at this time hath given order to the Ambaffador, and to Secretary Grofs, to intreat for the convey of his daughter to her hufband, the King of Lufitane's fon, which is the only caufe of the abode of that Ambaffador in this Court. And fo likewife, if your Ambaffador had any matter of intreaty betwixt the two Princes, he may come or fend at his pleafure. Likewife I truft he will confider, that it ftandeth the Emperor much in hand to be well affured that under the pretence of the Ambaffador's retinues, the enemies have not too open means to look into his Majefty's matters and doings. Therefore, except fome fpecial matter of the Emperor and the Princes whom they ferve, do require otherwife, all Ambaffadors muft be content that his Majefty, for his own private affairs, do, as his wifdom fhall lead him thereunto. And concerning the King your Mafter's glad expectation for the profperous fuccefs, his Majefty thereof is moft affured. And here the Bifhop with a friendly countenance faid unto me, ye know thefe matters do belong not a little to the King your mafter, for ye are not ignorant how this year the Frenchmen have robbed England above 150,000l.; and befide all old fpites of France done unto England, we truft the King's Majefty, his honourable Council, and realm, cannot forget how unjuftly not long fince the French King hath dealt with him, in his younger years, even when he was troubled with ftirs at home, *nec id ratione jufti belli, fed potius injufti latrocinii, ut alias confuevit facere,* (thefe were his words) as the Emperor's Majefty was always England's Friend, as his anceftors have been, and will continue unto his life's end. His words were

H   earneftly

EDWARD earneftly fpoke in thefe matters, which being too deep for me to
VI. wade in, I thought not good to enter into them; but thus much I
thought it meet to fay, that I knew the King's wifdom and his
Council, did fo weigh, he his honour, and they the fafety of his
perfon and wealth of his realms, as neither wrong would be
borne, nor benefits be forgotten, which were done to his Grace and
his realm, and fo turned to my errand again and faid,

Seeing the Emperor's Majefty will not have the Ambaffadors
with their retinue in his camp, yet becaufe my Mafter knoweth,
that certain agents be fuffered to tarry in the Court, at leaft it might
pleafe your Lordfhip, that John Bernardin the King's Majefty's fervant, may attend likewife there, who might without fail
there fpeedily write home, his Majefty's good proceeding in this
journey.

His anfwer was, Indeed certain agents belonging to cities and
Princes under his Majefty, as from F. Gonzaga Pietro di Toledo,
Piacenza, &c. remain in this Court to ferve the Emperor's own purpofes for thefe places, but all other muft be content to follow his
order; for affure yourfelf, no agent, fecretary, or man of any Ambaffador fhall be fuffered to write or tell out, what is done here, but
if they be taken, they muft fuffer fuch order as is appointed by the
Emperor's Majefty. And John Bernardin lefs than any other. For
when I was on the other fide of the Roan, Bernardin came unto me,
as he faid, to take his leave of me, for on the next morrow he would
take his journey into England, faying he could not agree with my
Lord Ambaffador, purpofing, belike, *hoc fermone me capere*, which
thing I was not content to hear, but fo difmiffed him. And furely
if he come any more to this Court, *jubebo illum apprehendi et com-
prehendi vinculis*, and I pray you tell him fo for me, if it be your
chance to fee him hereafter. And I pray you commend me heartily
to my Lord Ambaffador, and tell him, he fhall, of all Ambaffadors,
be the firft certified of our affairs, and in his private matters he

I   muft

muſt be content to ſend neither you, nor no other of his men, but write by ſome belonging to this Court, and I will friendly and ſpeedily diſpatch his requeſts. And thus I, having ſpeedy acceſs at my coming, and gently diſmiſſed at my parting, came my way.

R. A.

Sir Richard Moryſon to the Lords of the Council.

PLEASE it your good Lordſhips. The King's Majeſty's inſtruc- tions, with letters from your honours, bearing date the 24th of September, I received at Spires, the 4th of this month; which as ſoon as I had well peruſed, and learned the King's Highneſs's plea-ſure, then I forthwith made towards the Court, where I found ſuch favour, as I had acceſs to his Majeſty, almoſt as ſoon as I came; for I ſent my Secretary from me, which had ridden half the way, to ſhow Monſ. D'Arras * that I was coming to the Court, with letters from the King my Maſter to the Emperor, and ſomewhat I had alſo to ſay by word of mouth from his Highneſs unto his Majeſty, truſt-ing that foraſmuch as Ambaſſadors might not long bide nigh the camp he would help ſhortly that I might have audience. And becauſe ſuch good will as D'Arras ſhowed at this my coming, may give your honours the better to judge of the Emperor's gladneſs from mine arrival, I will orderly touch what he did. At my Secretary's com-ing, D'Arras was with the Emperor, and ſo finding Mr. Adrian of the Emperor's chamber, Aſcham made him the means that D'Arras came to him ſtrait, who learning the cauſe of his coming, went in, and told the Emperor the matter, and forthwith bad Aſcham go home with him, for I ſhould ſtraitway be provided of a lodging. By chance I went into the town, when D'Arras was going home to his houſe, who very gently willed me to go home with him, for I ſhould ſhift me in his lodging, and do what

* Biſhop of Arras, afterwards Cardinal Granville.

H 2   I would

EDWARD
VI

I would, till the Emperor had word, that I was now come, or till
the Fourriers had provided me a houfe of mine own; and forthwith he
fent for Anwerpe the harbinger, to whom he gave commandment,
in the Emperor's name, that he fhould fee me well lodged. I faid,
to be lodged was enough for a night or two; well lodged was not
to be fought for, of fuch as would follow camps. I rode a good way
in the town at his right hand, he ufing me with great humanity,
and being come to his houfe, he brought me into his bed-chamber,
to the which he willed me in any wife to fend for my mail, and fo
to fhift me there. While it was coming, he afked me, what news?
I told him, I had brought with me none but good, and, as I thought,
would much content the Emperor's Majefty. He afked me, how
the King's Highnefs did; and after I had faid what I thought, both
of his Majefty's health, increafe of ftrength, virtues, &c. he afked
me, how we did with France, whether the French made reftitution
of fuch goods, as they had violently taken from us, or not. I faid,
I could not tell, but I heard, that there was good and large promifes
that all fhould be reftored, and the injury might be thought the lefs,
that in time of war, and in time of peace, pirates and fuch robbers
and freebooters act without laws. He replied, faying, they were a
fhrewd fort of pirates that had taken 200,000 l. from our merchants.
Whereunto I anfwered, it were too much, if it were a good deal
fhort of that fum, and yet I heard the French King had promifed
reftitution of all that could be juftly demanded; and with this my
mail came, and the Bifhop faid, he would let me alone till I had
changed my apparel. While my men brought me fuch things as I
did mind to wear, his fervants did fetch me a brufh, water for my
hands, and after this, they caft a couple of napkins upon the table,
and brought in a pafty of red deer, and faid, there was a couple of
partridges at the fire, and would ftraitway be ready. I told them,
I had dined at Spires, and yet the Bifhop, now knowing that my
men had done with me, came again, and willed me to tafte of the

4   venifon,

venifon, that I might tafte of his wine. I faw a difh of olives, and
fo did eat one of them, and brought him good luck in a cup of wine,
which he would needs I fhould tafte. His kindnefs was very great,
in comparifon of any that ever I received in this Court, and I thought
my good lucks came together, for Bernardine was gone that morning
towards England, as he told divers, and I was thus cockered of the
Bifhop at afternoon, which both were fuch news to me, and fo
welcome, that I wift not whether I was gladder, that Bernardine
was gone from this Court, or of this my rare entertainment with
D'Arras; but I muft go on in order with my matter. I, for that I
had more lift to talk than to eat, would no venifon, and therefore
the pafty was carried to my men, and they much made of. He and
I fell to talking again, he groping to know mine errand, and I keeping it for the Emperor. He afked me, whether the ports were fhut
in England, as he had word from Flanders, or no? I faid, I neither
knew of any caufe why they fhould be kept, or heard of any keeping
of them, more than that he had faid. And whilft we thus talked,
his Chamberlain came from the Court, and told him, that the Emperor did now look for me. D'Arras feeing my horfe without a
foot-cloth, did offer me his mule. But I gave him thanks, and,
faving your honours, in bufkings and fpurs, and other fhort apparel, made my horfe ferve me well enough. And in going I
faid, I knew well mine errand would now not be long hid from him.
He brought me forth of his houfe, and tarried abroad, till I was
on horfeback, then alfo courteoufly with his cap in hand, taking
leave of me; and thus being come to the Court, I found Adrian of
the chamber waiting for me, who was fo ready to bring me in to
the Emperor, that I was fain to intreat him, to give me leave to
breathe me a little, for that I had come apace up a long pair of ftairs.
Upon this fhort paufe, I followed Adrian, and found the Emperor
at a bare table without a carpet, or any thing elfe upon it, faving his
clock, his brufh, his fpectacles, and his picktooth. At my coming
in,

EDWARD in, I offered to ſtand upon that ſide of his Majeſty, which was next
  VI.   :to the door, but it being on his left hand, he willed me to go almoſt
round about the table, that I might ſtand on his right ſide, perhaps
for that he heareth better on the one ſide than on the other; but as
I took it, he did it to honour the King my maſter. Here, after the
delivery of the King's Highneſs's letters, which his Majeſty received
very gently, putting his hand to his bonnet, and uncovering the
better part of his head, I did efforce myſelf with as good a countenance as I could, and with as good words as my wit would ſerve
me to deviſe, in the riding almoſt of twenty. Engliſh miles, to ſhow
the gladneſs of the King my Maſter, for that his Majeſty, in ſo long
and painful a journey, either had his health continually, or was by
being ſometime indiſpoſed, ſoon brought to perfecter health. I did
ſay beſides much more, there could be few that did more rejoice
at his Majeſty's ſo honourable and fortunate approaching towards the
Low Countries, than did the King my Maſter, who did repute all
his Majeſty's good ſucceſſes, to be as his own, and as glad as of any
that could happen to himſelf; beſeeching his Majeſty to believe me
in this, I added nothing of mine own, but faithfully did ſay in
Italian, that the King's Majeſty had, word for word, appointed me in
Engliſh, and ſaid the King's Majeſty even in theſe years, did con-
tend with his noble father either in loving the Low Countries of
Flanders, or in deſire to ſhow pleaſure to his Majeſty, Lord of them.
He did not ſuffer me to go on, but with the leaſt pauſe that I could
make, he did utter unto me in gentle words, that he took the King
his good brother's letters in very thankful part, and took his ſa-
lutations, and ſending of me to him with ſuch a friendly meſſage, as
they did right well deſerve, ſaying, as well as he could (for he was
newly rid of his gout and fever, and therefore his nether lip was
in two places broken out, and he forced to keep a green leaf within
his mouth, at his tongue's end, a remedy as I took it, againſt ſuch
his dryneſs, as in his talk did increaſe upon him), ſaying therefore
                                                              as

as well as he could, he neither had nor could forget the King's Majefty's Father's love, at fundry times fhewn unto him, nor deceive that truft, which at his death he did put him in, recommending unto his truft, the King his fon. He would not forget the amity, that fo many years had lafted between the realm of England and the houfe of Burgundy; he trufted the King his good brother had in thefe his young years, found friendfhip and no hurt at his hand, and that he had feen a defire in him perpetually to preferve this antient amity, ufing this fentence, that old amities which had been long tried, and found good, are to be made much of; and this he fpake a little louder than he did the reft, as though he would, indeed, have me think that he did earneftly mean, that he faid. And yet hath he a face, that is as unwont to difclofe any hid affection of his heart, as any face that ever I met withal in my life; for there all white colours, which, in changing themfelves, are wont in others to bring a man certain word, how his errand is liked or mifliked, have no place in his countenance; his eyes only do bewray as much as can be picked out of him. He maketh me oft think of Solomon's faying, Heaven is high, the earth is deep, a King's heart is unfearchable; there is in him almoft nothing that fpeaketh, befides his tongue, and that at this time, by reafon of his leaf, and forenefs of his lip, and his accuftomed foftnefs in fpeaking, did but fo fo utter things to be well underftood, without great care to be given to his words; and yet he did fo ufe his eyes, fo move his head, and order his countenance, as I might well perceive, his great defire was, that I fhould think all a good deal better meant, than he could fpeak it; and as I dare in fo weighty a matter, I do furely think, he meant the moft of what he faid. Sure I am, he is too wife not to wifh the King's Majefty to be fully his.

When he did paufe, and that I had licence to fpeak again, I entered into the Turk's matter, faying as much therein, as might both fhow, in what peril Chriftendom is and what praife the King's Majefty's good nature did worthily deferve, which being fartheft off of

all.

all Chriftian Princes from the danger, is the firft and readieft of them all, to think upon the remedy. And in this his Majefty's great zeal did appear, that he offered his aid, only for pity borne to the miferable ftate of Chriftendom; not defired to it, but moved rather by the harm like to light upon his friends, than upon himfelf, although by courfe of nature his Majefty was like enough to live while part of the mifery might be felt even in England, if the Turk fhould do his will in Hungary, and in thefe coafts of Germany, which two years together he had very cruelly affaulted; making the King's offer, I did fay, when his Majefty fhould fee it expedient, he was fully bent to accord with him and other Chriftian Princes and Eftates for the abafing of fuch a cruel and common enemy, not only to the Chriftians, but to Chrift himfelf. And here he faid, my good brother meaneth this his aid, only againft our enemy the Turk. I faw he liked this offer as it were well enough, but he made not much of it, thinking in very deed, as I might perceive, to have heard fomewhat of joining of forces againft another enemy of his, to whom he beareth as little good-will as he can do to the Turk, as at whofe hands he hath received more difpleafures, than at the Turk's. And here, he having fo good an occafion to have faid fomewhat of the French King, whether it was for that he fpake with fome pain, or whether he would that I fhould fpeak firft againft him, did not fo much as once name him; howbeit, I do guefs, he looked for fome direct anfwer of the fuit which the Regent* made to the King's Majefty, as concerning the aid for Luxemburgh, wherein I would have made a foul error, if, the Emperor faying nothing, I would have fought redrefs thereof. For how could I have found his grief but I muft have granted there was juft caufe of his grief? and therefore he hiding the fore, it was not my part to complain. And for this caufe, the more he feemed indifferent to prefs me, the more lay I in wait not to pafs my commiffion, being content to reftrain my talk,

* The Regent of the Netherlands, the Emperor's fifter.

and

and to think he meant to anfwer me by D'Arras, úfing in very deed feldom to determine his pleafure out of hand, where D'Arras hath brought the matter to him before. And yet I faid fo much to him herein, that his Majefty faid, he did very much rejoice to hear the zeal in fo young a King to find fo good a will, fo great a defire, to mean good to fo many, and prayed me to give to his good brother from him, his hearty thanks, for this his good and princely offer. And when I had promifed his Majefty to do both it, and any thing elfe that might pertain to the duty of a good Minifter, he gave me his hearty thanks, but I did perceive he looked for better news at my hands, and thought all thefe the leaft part of mine errand. It may be he had heard, before my coming, how the French fhips were ftayed in England, which news were fo brim in the Court at mine arrival, that while I was with the Emperor, Secretary Bane was in hand with Afcham, to know whether I had brought with me the confirmation of thefe news or not, faying he was the Emperor's Secretary, and therefore he might truft him with news, which he fhould fhortly know, though he did not tell him the fame. Yea, they had alfo bruited it in the Court, before my coming, that our Ambaffador in France, had faid in exprefs terms to the French King, that if he did not forthwith make reftitution of fuch goods as were wrongfully taken from our merchants, he had commandment from the King our Mafter, to denounce him cruel war. It was alfo reported and allowed in Court, for true news, that our ports were kept fhut, and that none might pafs out of England to any place, that perchance he that looked to hear all thefe good news, and more too at my coming, thought I had told him very little, having but a meant aid againft the Turk to tell him. For men do fooner find a lack when they mifs that they hoped for, than take thankfully that they think on. I feeing no occafion to fpeak of any man to be fent into England, did as I was bidden, in ending my meffage, leave the confideration thereof to his Majefty's wifdom, not miftrufting

I   but

but I fhould have good occafion to make the offer to D'Arras, if
the Emperor fhould feem earneftly to mind the matter.   Whereupon
I paufing, the Emperor faid, he would fhew his whole pleafure to
D'Arras, as touching this his good brother's offer.   And putting his
hand, as he could, to his cap, feemed to me to crave an end of this
talk.   Whereupon I, after I had looked, if there were any thing
elfe that his Majefty would fay to me, and found he had no more
to fay, I with an humble manner as I could, took my leave of his
Majefty.   I was not fo foon gone out of the Court, but I found the
Bifhop's Chamberlain waiting for me, who brought me to my houfe,
which was where the Palfgrave lay, all the time he was at Court.
Perhaps, if D'Arras had known mine errand before, I might have
been worfe lodged, and have found no man to conduct me to my
lodging.   The Chamberlain had commiffion to will me to fend to
my Lord his Mafter, for wine, and what I wanted befides, which I
did, and had birds and fowl offered my man, with a pafty of red
deer, but he brought me nothing but a flaggon of his wine, and four
or five caft of his manchets.   I was in mine houfe an hour and more,
before it was time to fupper, and thought D'Arras would have fent
for me to talk to him; but whether it were that he looked that I
fhould make him offer, or whether it were for that he had other
bufinefs, he fent not for me, till it was nine o'clock in the morning
after; at which hour, his Chamberlain came for me, and I went
ftraight way to him.   He faid, the Emperor's Majefty had fent to him
to know, whether I had been with him or no, and hearing that I
had not been with him fince my talk with his Majefty, he fent again,
willing him to talk with me, and to require of me, whether I had
any particular matters touching the prefent occurrents, and to pray
me that I would declare them unto D'Arras.   Mine anfwer was,
if I had been commanded to fay more to his Majefty than I had faid,
I would be loth to live, while I might be juftly charged with it.
I had kept no jot from his Majefty that I was willed to fay unto

9   him.

him. I thought the news good as they were, and was glad I might bring them hither, as well for that they did both fhow a great good nature in the King my Mafter, and alfo a great care in him toward the fafety of the Emperor's ftate, honour, and dominions. I thought if other Princes might be by long intreaty, as well perfuaded to fet upon fo noble an enterprife, as the King of England was bent to it out of his own good nature, the Turk fhould be driven to do hurt fomewhere elfe, or to do none to Chriftendom from henceforth. D'Arras told me, if I had no more, he would go to the Emperor, and fay, his Majefty had heard as much as I had commiffion to fay. It feemeth they would fain have given me a new commiffion. Mine anfwer was, he fhould do well fo to do, for I was a Minifter, and could not appoint myfelf, to fay any thing in my Mafter's name, without a warrant for it; from myfelf I could fay fomewhat, not as Ambaffador, nor one bidden to fay it, but as one that, with the King my Mafter, did earneftly wifh a fafety to all the Emperor's things; and if he would give me leave to lay afide mine office, mine Ambaffadorfhip, and privately to talk with him, as a poor friend might fpeak with an Emperor's great Counfellor, I would tell him what I thought; marry, I would fay it to hear no more of it. By the way from Spires hitherward, I thought I faw I might be bold with the Emperor's Majefty, to have faid unto him, that he fhould do well to fend fome fpecial men both to the King's Majefty, and alfo to other Princes, devifing with each of them, how this league againft the Turk might be well made; and if you think as I do, let me fit out, and make the devife your own; if ye like it not, I fhall better bear it to be counted unwife, than unwilling to help forward that which I take to be fo beneficial to all Chriftendom. For what hurt can the Turk do to Chriftendom, if Chriftians do not back him? And here D'Arras faid enough againft the French King, and faid he would fhow me a pretty way of writing news, and going to a coffer of his, he brought out a couple of

blanks

blanks fent by Darramont from Conftantinople to the French King, wherein might be written fuch news as might beft ferve the French King's purpofe, and be taken for news come from the Turk's Court, becaufe Darramont had fubfcribed both the blanks with his hand and name. I faw both the blanks, but whether they were Darramont's or like to be his, I know not. After this and much other talk, I took my leave of him, and he faid he would to the Emperor. At four o'clock his Chamberlain cometh to me again, and prayeth me to take fo much pains as to come again to his Mafter. When we were both fet, he told me he had fhewed the Emperor, that what I was commanded to fay, I had faid it all, who once again told me, he thought I might of good confideration, for not troubling his Majefty long, who was as yet not well recovered, have kept fome particularities in ftore; but faith he, feeing you have nothing elfe to fay unto him, he faith thus to you, that ye muft render his moft hearty thanks unto his good brother, and fay that his Majefty maketh great account of this his kind and friendly offer, and therefore will forthwith addrefs his letter unto the Regent, that fhe for her nighnefs may both underftand the prefent occurrences of England, and alfo know further the King's Majefty's mind, touching the offer which ye have in his Majefty's name made unto him, and ufe it as fhe fhall fee caufe. And, faid he, as I told the Emperor, ye could not enlarge your commiffion, fo I alfo told him, what ye thought as of yourfelf, for the which your honeft and friendly advice, he gives you his moft hearty thanks, not miftrufting, but ye that thus carefully do think of things, will fo fet out his good will, favour and love, to the King his good brother, as the amity may daily increafe. The Emperor you fee is no catcher up of other men's things, but could be well content to lack a good portion of that he hath, if without impeachment to his honour, he could let go his juft inheritance. And here, he faid, the Emperor did wifh the like godly mind in the reft of the Princes, that he found in the King, his good brother, and

did

did truft he fhould be a King of as great honour as hath been in England many hundred years. This, and an hundred times as much, he fpake with fuch affection, as, if words may be thought to mean what they fay, there can be no more wifhed for, than is to be hoped for. The reft I leave to your wifdoms to weigh, more I cannot fay in this matter. For occurrents here, there be no more than I fent your honours in my laft letters. It may be, Wefton may meet with fome by the way, for that every hour we look to hear, that the Duke of Alva, and Marches Albert have bickled together. At the Court, there is no talk of the Emperor's going from Landau. Monfieur D'Arras has promifed to write them unto me, when there come any good news, and if there had been any ready made, I do not doubt but I fhould have had fome. And thus I take me leave moft humbly of your Lordfhips.

From Spira, the 7th of October, 1552.

Your Lordfhip's, &c.

RICHARD MORYSON *.

* This letter and R. Afcham's were tranfcribed from the originals in the Paper Office.

No. V.

The Journey of the Queen's Ambaſſadors unto Rome, anno
1555. *The Reverend Father in God the Biſhop of Ely,
and Viſcount Montagu, then Ambaſſadors ; who ſet out
of Calais in Picardy, on Wedneſday, being Aſh-Wed-
neſday, the 27th of February.*

[This Journal, though not writ by one of the moſt diſtinguiſhed
perſons in the train of the Ambaſſadors, contains many curious
particulars of the face of the country, the appearance of the great
towns, and the cuſtoms of Italy at that time. Some minutiæ and
inaccuracies muſt be overlooked. This is the laſt embaſſy which
went from England to pay public homage to the See of Rome.
Lord Caſtlemain, ſent by King James, could only addreſs the
Pope in the name of his Maſter, and of the Engliſh Catholics;
not that of the nation.]

FROM Calais to Boulògne, ſeven leagues, paſſing by Sandy-
forde Abby, and through Morgyſon, which were both de-
ſtroyed by Henry VIII.

From Boulogne to Monſtrueil, ſeven leagues, paſſing by Hardito
caſtle, which ſtandeth upon a great marſh, and a wood on the one
ſide of it. Monſtrueil ſtandeth high as Boulogne doth, Boulogne
having on the north-eaſt and ſouth ſide of it, a marſh. At our being there, they were fortifying and enlarging of the town. It was
better manned by much than Boulogne.

From Monſtrueil to Abbeville, ten leagues, leaving a town on the
right hand. This town ſtandeth very ſtrongly, by reaſon of marſh
grounds about it, and the river of Somme paſſing by it.

From

From Abbeville to Amiens, ten leagues, paffing by a caftle of MARY
Monf. de Rion's of Flanders, and a bridge named Pont de Remy, 1555.
and by a houfe of the Vidames Pequigny, leaving always on the left
fide of us, the river of Somme. Amiens ftandeth on the river of
Soane, in a marvellous even ground, the town being walled about,
and fome few Englifh miles in circuit; the water of Soane runneth
in feven ftreets of the town. In this town we faw the reliques of
St. John's head, very richly enclofed in gold, and many precious
jewels. The church very beautiful, and adorned with cunning
workmanfhip. The Ambaffadors were lodged in the Duke of Ven-
dofme's houfe. There is alfo a place called St. Dennis church-yard,
which is thicker befet with fundry fafhioned croffes, than any man
can well number; and very good devotion there cuftomably fhewed,
of all forts.

From Amiens to Breteuil, feven leagues. In our way we faw the
firft vineyards.

From Breteuil to Clermont, feven leagues. There we faw fix
pictures of Gentlemen hanged upon the gibbets, ftanding in the
midft of the market-place; but the gentlemen themfelves, were fled
away. There is very good wine at Clermont.

From Clermont to Luzarche, feven leagues, paffing through a
town, St. Leu. We paffed alfo over the river Oife, in a ferry-
boat. This river parteth Picardy and France.

From Luzarche to Paris, fix leagues, leaving on our left hand, the
Conftable's houfe, called Chantilly, with a very great poole a digging
to it. We faw alfo another houfe, which the faid Conftable had but
lately built, called Ecouen; which was praifed for the faireft houfe
in France. This houfe ftandeth upon a pleafant large hill, yet in
the middle of a great plain; the one fide is employed to corn, and
the other full of vineyards. The hill is full of wood on every fide,
faving the top, where the houfe ftandeth; yet is there no tree but
beareth fruit; the greateft fort, chefnuts, wallnuts, pine or fir trees.

The

The fmaller, figs, cherries, almonds, peaches, and others, which was to the beholders a marvellous fight and pleafure. This houfe is built in a quadrant form, to the height of two ftories plain, and the roof with gable windows caft out for a third; the forefaid gable windows being of a marvellous greatnefs, anfwering to the others beneath, in number, fafhion, and quantity. The whole houfe is of free ftone, fo white, fo great and fair as may be feen; the covering is of blue flate; the roof (as through all France) more raifed up, than our buildings, the which giveth much beauty to their houfes. The gate is made extant with pillars, and thrice vaulted, and in the uppermoft vault ftandeth St. George on horfeback, wrought alfo in free ftone, to a marvellous greatnefs, the pillars likewife being Tufcan work. In the infide of the faid gate, two of the loweft pillars are of blue fair marble, anfwerable to a like couple right over againft them on the fartheft fide, there being a   like front and   to that galleries before. Of the four fides of this quadrant, the gate fide, with that over againft it, are appointed to two galleries, the other couple to chambers. The galleries of the gate are of a lower roof than the other three, and therefore hath but his gallery above of a high vaulted roof, and his terrafs beneath, open to the court and quadrant. This gallery is twenty-one feet broad, and eighty in length: the pavements are very broad, and like even, ftained with the arms of the Crown and Peers of France, the King's poefy being *Donec totum impleat orbem.* The roof within is gilt, the ridge tiles without are alfo gilt. The cieling within is of walnut. The other gallery was hanged with rich arras, where was alfo a chart of the Holy Land, made of divers woods, and of natural colours, fet in fmall pieces, as the demonftration of the faid places required, and feemed rather to have been done with the pencil, than otherwife. At the end of the gallery, under the fame roof, is the chapel, the cieling whereof is like workmanfhip to the chart afore-named, of Brazil, furric, walnut tree, and other like woods, joined in the

figures

figures of the apoftles, and other curious works. The table of the altar, with the images thereabout, be of white marble, with two pillars of fine jett. The chambers are not great, but very well conveyed, having a narrow gallery to convey you to every one of them apart; but the gallery is clofe, and appears not outward to them that be in the court. The chimneys ftand two feet off the wall into the chambers, and yet feem not to hurt the room, nor the fight thereof, becaufe they be raifed in the midft of the fide of the chamber, having a fide light of the window; and again, they keep even largenefs to the roof of the chamber; all above the marble, planted with pleafant works, and in oil coloured. In the court ftandeth an huge great horfe of copper, which fhall be fet upon the gate, with the image of the King upon the back of him.

Within two leagues of this houfe is St. Dennis, where all the Kings of France be buried, and fometimes crowned. But the appointed place of coronation is at a city called Rheims in Champagne.

The town of St. Dennis is neither fair nor large, but the church is great, and the treafure alfo. In this church we faw the fhrine of St Dennis made of filver, and gilt, and a great roode of clean gold, lacking but one arm, the which Francis the French King took away to maintain his wars; adjoining inftead thereof, for recompence, one of filver, and gilt. There is alfo one whole unicorn's horn, which was almoft two ells long grown taper wife, and wreathed, as we fee it commonly painted. This horn is but flender to the length, yet notwithftanding maffive and heavy. There was alfo St. Dennis's head (*ut dicitur*) richly enclofed in gold, and befet with precious ftones and orient pearl. Likewife a piece of the holy crofs, and one of the nails wherewith Chrift was nailed thereto, fet in gold. We were alfo brought into the treafury there, where we faw reliques in another place with ornaments of the King and Queen's coronation. And firft I faw thefe reliques, a piece of the holy crofs, in a crofs of gold; the finger of St. Thomas that he put into the wound of our

K Lord;

Lord; a griffin's claw trimmed with filver, as great as a hunter's horn of the middle fort; St. Benedict's head; St. Dennis's Penner and Inkhorn; a cup was Solomon's, and one other made of an Agather, of a marvellous greatnefs and riches. I faw alfo the crowns of the King and Queen: upon the King's crown, a ruby as big as a wallnut, and on every part fet with ftones. Alfo the fword and fcepter of the Kings, fet with maffy gold, the knob thereof being fet with diamonds and pearl. Alfo the King's fpurs of gold, and the portraitures of Nero, Charlemayne, and other Emperors.

Between St. Dennis and Paris, there are divers croffes, much like to churching croffes, but not fo big altogether, nor fo high; where (as it is faid) St. Dennis refted after he was beheaded.

Thus rode we towards Paris where Monf. le Bois Dauphin met the Ambaffadors in the highway to Paris, which city ftandeth fomewhat low upon the river of Seine, which divideth the univerfity from the town, compaffing round about the city, which lieth between them both as an ifle, yet is Paris altogether of a round form. It is very fair and great, and full of merchants; but the ftreets be very foul, by reafon their houfes be very high and the ftreets very narrow. The city alone hath nineteen churches in it, with the great church of Notre Dame, in the fteeple whereof, hangeth a bell, weighing 33,000 lb. The French King hath a houfe there called Louvre.

I faw in Paris the wonderful inftrument of Oroncius, then alive; therein was to be feen the courfe of the feven planets prefently moving, with afpects the one to the other. I alfo faw the coining houfe, with the new coins fo perfectly ftamped, that in my judgment no man is able to conterfeit the fame. The mill that ftandeth in the midft of Seine, ferveth to ftrike the bullion, and the work is fo fpeedy, that putting in a lathe of metal an inch thick, and a foot long, he bringeth it quickly to the thinnefs of a French fous, and the thicknefs fufficient to the ftamp is, when the lathe will enter in a little notch,

that

that is in a fteel . We tarried there the feventh, eighth, and ninth day.

From Paris to Melun, feven leagues, leaving on the left hand, one league from Paris, a caftle of the King's, built by King Henry V. King of England, named Bois de Vincenne, where all the prifoners taken in the wars againft the Emperor, do lie in hold; and fo paffing through two towns, the one called Pont Charenton, and the other Ville Neuve St. George. At Pont Charenton there meeteth two rivers, Marne and Seine, and fo runneth to Paris. Almoft at the gate we went out of, ftandeth the caftle, called the Duke of Bedford's caftle, and the Baftellion, without the gate, where the Frenchmen now build a pace. In Melun ftandeth a caftle environed with the river of Seine, built by Englifhmen.

From Melun to Fountainbleau, four leagues, where the French King's Court lay. Two miles off the Court, certain gentlemen of the King's houfe met our Lords, and courteoufly entertained them, and brought them the neareft way to the Court, where they lovingly received them, and led them into a gallery, where they had every one of them prepared a very fair lodging, coftly hanged, and fet forth with as rich beds as might be feen. The houfe is called Fon-·tainbleau, for the goodly fountain it hath in the houfe, and the fair-nefs of the water. This houfe is both beautiful and larger than any I had before feen in France or England. I may refemble the ftate thereof to the honour of Hampton Court, which as it paffeth Fon-tainbleau, with the great hall and chambers, fo is it inferior in outward beauty and uniformity, which praifeth all kind of building moft, for the covering thereof is blue flate, and all the reft of free ftone.

There is an out court or quadrant, whereof one fide is a gallery, to walk in, being in length fix hundred feet. There is alfo on the fouth fide a garden, having in it a gieat pond, the walks and allies fhadowed with pine and cyprus trees. At the end of one of the allies is a vault curioufly counterfeited as out of the rock natural,

whither

whither they do repair to refresh themselves in hot weather. · There
is another garden more privy, set full of antiquities of copper. In
the face of the great lodging, riseth a great fountain, as I have said,
spouting with five spouts upright, out of a natural rock, or else, very
naturally wrought. This house standeth in a valley, compassed
about with rocky hills, but not very great; and the country is forest,
full of deer, wolves, and wild boars. The name of the forest is
Barre, the house standeth three leagues within it every way. The
Lords came to the Court about four o'clock, and within one hour

Henry II.
after were brought to the King's presence, who received them very
genteelly, and embraced as many gentlemen of the train as came
unto him. After the Lords had some talk with the King, they
were brought into the Queen's chamber of presence, where the

Catherine de Medicis.
French Queen, accompanied with the Queen of Scots, and two of
her own daughters, were ready to receive them. From thence they
departed to their lodgings, where were ready to wait upon them,
divers of the French King's gentlemen, being appointed to attend
them dinner and supper during their abode there. The next day
after, being the 11th day, the rest of the train that could not be
lodged at the Court came thither, and desired certain Scottish gentlemen, that they might see the Queen of Scots; who being told of
their desire to see her, immediately she very courteously came forth
out of her privy chamber into her chamber of presence amongst us
all, and said unto us, she was very glad to see us, calling us her
countrymen. About four o'clock this afternoon the French King
came from hunting the wild boar, and then the Lords went and took
their leave of him, and the King embraced them, and as many of
their gentlemen as came unto him. That done, the same night they
departed from the Court, and rode to St. Mathurin's. The King is a
goodly tall gentleman, well made in all the parts of his body, a very
grim countenance, yet very gentle, meek, and well beloved of all
his subjects.

We

·We remained all this, the 12th day, at St. Mathurin's. This St. Mathurin (as they faid) is a holy man, that can help mad men and women, within nine days fpace, if they do this that follows. The Prieft, when Mafs is done, muft call for the madmen or women, to come and kneel before the altar, and when he had faid certain prayers, he muft come and lay flannel upon their heads, and, making the fign of the Crofs, fay certain words over them ; that ended, they rife, and go round about the altar four times, and at every time, kifs the four brazen pillars that ftand about the altar. Then muft they offer up unto St. Mathurin, a pottle-pot full of wine, three loaves of bread, and a French fous in money, which in value in our Englifh money is ijd. oh. q. and doing this for the fpace of nine days together, they fay they fhall have their right wits again.

From St. Mathurin to Montargis, eight leagues, this town ftandeth fo well for wood, water, and meadow, as I have not feen the like in all France before. There ftandeth a caftle, fair for all lodgings ; but of no force, the which fometime (as they fay) was in the keeping of my Lord Talbot. The houfe is of great receit, and very ftately. The hall hath a pair of ftairs fifty-fix fteps going up to, it hath alfo fix chimnies in it, fixty-five paces long, and twenty paces broad. There is both a guard chamber and a chamber of prefence, the which I have not feen in other places in that country.

From Montargis to Briare, nine leagues. By this town runneth the greateft river in France, called Loyre, leaving it always upon our right hand. It parteth the dutchy of Berry from Nyvernoys, and from Barboys.

From Briare to Cone, eight leagues, through a town called Bony. From Cone to la Charité, eight leagues, leaving on the right fide of us, over the river of Loyre, a town called Sancer, with a caftle in it of great force, which town of late is called young Chenevy, of divers men, becaufe of their religion.

From La Charité to Nevers, five long leagues. As we rode by the river of Loyre, we faw water mills ftanding upon boats in the

main

main river, to be removed by the millers to any other place they like better, as they lift. At Nevers is a bridge twenty-five fcore paces over, upon the which we paffed the river of Loyre, and there left it.

From Nevers to St. Pierre le Monafter, five long leagues. This is a little walled town, where the Juftices of the country ufe it, and keep their feffions.

From St. Pierre le Monafter to Moulins, through a town called Villeneuve, leaving the river Allier on our right hand, the which runneth into Loyre. This town of Moulins, is the chiefeft town in Borbonnois, where is a great and ancient houfe of the Duke of Bourbon's, commodious conduits and gardens. There is a conduit having out of the midft of the ftem an artichoke bearing four ripe as it were, and one feeded, and out of the leaves fpringeth water, as rain, very artificially wrought in copper and gilt. Here we faw oranges, lemons, pomegranates, growing by labour and diligence of men; for the trees be growing with barrels filled with good earth, and in the winter be removed, under terraffes and houfes made of purpofe, and are ever brought out again the fpring, into the garden again. In the garden be two goodly banqueting houfes, the one of them hath water about it, and the other a great many of finging birds in it, of divers forts, and at every corner of it, a great hart's head ftanding, with many other goodly commodities.

There is a bone of a man to be feen, whofe length was fixteen feet, and found in Vienne in Dauphine. Furthermore I faw there the proportion of divers cities, with the walls, churches, and bulwarks, carved in wood very curioufly.

From Moulins to la Palice, ten leagues. This town ftandeth upon a hill, the country round about it, being foreft and heath.

From la Palice to Roanne, fix long leagues, paffing a fmall mountain. There we paffed the river of Loyre, as we go out of the town towards Italy.

From

From Rouane to Tarare, fix long leagues. This town ftandeth in a deep bottom, the hills hanging over.on every fide, and is watered with a narrow ftream, but fo fwift, that within the fpace of two hundred yards, four mills are driven, two for corn, one to faw timber, and another to beat the hemp. The corn mill grindeth with a flat wheel, the water being forced to one fide of it. The faw mill is driven with an upright wheel; and the water that maketh it go, is gathered whole into a narrow trough, which delivereth the fame water to the wheels. This wheel hath a piece of timber put to the axletree end, like the handle of a broch, and faftened to the end of the faw, which being turned with the force of the water, hoifteth up and down the faw, that it continually eateth in, and the handle of the fame is kept in a rigall of wood from fwerving. Alfo the timber lieth as it were upon a ladder, which is brought by little and little to the faw with another vice. The hemp mill is much like the cyder mills we have in England, where a ftone is rolled about in a vault or veffel, where the hemp lieth.

From Tarare to Lyons, fix long leagues. Lyons is a goodly city, and a ftrong, by means of the rocks on the one fide of it, and the waters on the other fide. We came into the town on Lyons fide, a mile before we came to any bridge, and then we paffed a bridge over the river Saone, and going out of town, we went a long mile in Dauphine fide, and paffed a long bridge over the river Rhone. The greateft part of the town, is as it were an ifle. At the end thereof, both the rivers being joined together. Upon the north fide of the town is the new fortification, and the caftle upon the very rock. Upon the fouth fide is the church of St. Henry, his corpfe and fepulchre; the pillar whereunto Chrift was bound, of blue marble, with white veins; and on the eaft fide, a valley or plain, very fruitful. It is evil dwelling there for thofe that will perjure themfelves, for they fhall be burned with a fire called St. Anthony's fire.

5

fire. We tarried two days at Lyons. Here we had great entertainment of Madame Lacheveriere, a great Lady in Lyons.

From Lyons to Burgoin, five leagues. This town ftandeth under a great hill, having a good foil, with wood and water enough.

From Burgoin to 'Pont Beauvoifin, five leagues, through a town named La tour du Pin, paffing a great wood of chefnuts. Through this town runneth the river of Giers that cometh from the mountains. The one fide of the water is Dauphinois, and the other is Savoy. There is alfo a mill to make oil of walnuts.

From Pont Beauvoifin to Chamberry, five long leagues, where, by the way we paffed by Mount Aiguberte, a great mountain, and very dangerous, one league high and more, all upon rocks, and a very narrow paffage. Here, mafter White, whofe father was Mafter of the Requefts to Queen Mary, and a gentleman of

Ambaffador Leger to Rome, taking hold of his horfe's head, to pull him nearer the rock fide, to keep him from falling down the hill, his horfe going back pulled his mafter after him, and both together tumbled down the hill a great way, and there ftaid, and yet neither of them hurt. This is the chiefeft town of all Savoy, and hath a great fair caftle in it, but of no force; it ftandeth in a valley full of corn, woods and pafture, plenty of fruits, as figs, almonds, &c. We being almoft at the foot of the hill, and thinking we had but one Englifh mile to the town, we found it five long miles before we came at it, and the way very ftrait.

From Chamberry to Aigubelle, five long leagues, through Mount Melian, a pretty town, in which ftandeth a notable ftrong caftle upon a rock, that keepeth the paffage between the mountains, the which is thought impregnable but by famine or treafon. By this town runneth the river Lyzore, and through Aigubelle, the river Arte is called Aqua Bella of the Fountains, but the river is exceedingly foul.

The

The church of Aigubelle was founded by a Bifhop of Harteforde, called Petrus de Acqua Bianca.

From Aigubelle to St. Jean de Morienne, fix long leagues, riding betwixt the mountains of a very great height, all that journey; upon which mountains was plenty of corn and vines, with very many dwelling houfes and cottages, as we call them, and fome of them ·thought to be a league high. That day we paffed over the river of Lyzere four times. This town ftandeth very barrenly upon the river of Arte, the which falling from the mountains, is fo fwift, and makes fo great a noife, that it is able to make a man deaf, and hath no fifh in it. We rode along this river five days journey. In thefe mountains be wild boars; their hogs are all black; their fheep great and long legged, with crooked fnouts; and very many goats.

From St. Jean de Morienne to St. Andre, four long miles, ftill between the mountains, and thofe higher to my feeing than the other. There was fuch a noife of water beating upon the rocks, and fuch monftrous mountains to behold, of a huge height, being always in danger of fome ftone falling upon us, that it feemed rather a hell than a highway to pafs in. Upon the right hand on the other fide of thofe mountains, all the way is Dauphiny. At St. Andre, I coming into a church, about four o'clock in the afternoon, fpied a young child lying dead upon a board before the image of our Lady, and an old woman fitting watching and praying by it, having alfo a tallow candle burning, and a great many peafe and beans in a little tray, the which fhe had offered unto our Lady. I afked her in French what fhe meant to do? And fhe anfwered, that the child was born dead, and that fhe looked for the life of it, or at leaft to burft out a bleeding in fome place of the body; and thus they do for the fpace of fifteen days together till it ftinked. If it be fo that it bleed, although it receive no life, it is chriftened, if not, then it is caft into the river. In this town news came for certainty, that Pope Julius Tertius died at Rome, the 25th of March.

L   From

From St. Andre to Lanebourg, five long leagues, paffing by a town called Trefignon, over a great mountain, yet there accounted as none, by reafon of the ineftimable height of the other mountains. This day we had great rain and fnow, and coming under the fteep of a clift, a great gulf of water-fall, as great as the throw of a mill, fell down, in falling down fuddenly from the clift was turned into fnow, and had made there a mighty heap, on which we trod, the fnow falling continually thick, and yet the fpace from the fall to the ground cannot be judged above twenty fathom. Among thefe mountains we faw on the 26th of March a young partridge. I being among thefe mountains, was drawn in a fledge a great part of the way for the value of ijd.

The way is made out of the rocks and mountains by men's hands; the diet there of the common people in Lent, is nothing elfe but peafe and hearts, oil and chefnuts, and yet they be very fat withal.

From Lanebourg to Sufa, fix long leagues; paffing over the great mountain Cenis, the which is two leagues to the top, and when we are come to the top, then we have a great plain to go, which is two long leagues and a half; then had we three feet of the mountain (as they call it) to go down, that were half leagues a-piece, two of them, and the third was a whole league; we all paffed without dangers, thanks be to God, to the great admiration to all the country, and no lefs I affure you to them that fhould hear the truth.

After we got to the top of the mountain, which we came, but with great pain, for I was faln to hire one to lead my horfe up before me and I to come after him holding by the tail, for fear of falling backwards, it was fo fteep to the top; by the way I did fee a poor man lie almoft drowned in the fnow, making round balls of fnow, and eating of them for very hunger.

After we came at the top of the mountain, going the way towards the chappel, named La Chapelle de Trancizes, to wit, the Chappel of the Dead, being half a league: this chappel lieth full of dead

9   men's

mens fculls that have died upon the mountain for extreme cold and other misfortunes, and there feemeth to be more than one thoufand perfons; whereof fixteen Launceknights were thrown in there, in March before.

From thence we went to the Poft Houfe, called La Tavaro, an Inn, being half a league off. We had no other ground to go but only fnow, that was but two feet broad, and hardened with the continual froft that is there almoft always. So that in this way, the fnow was thought to be at the leaft a fpear depth and more, the which doth, if there be any heat at all, fink every two horfes. The very fame day that we paffed over this mountain, there were four perfons drowned by going a little out of their way; we were in the more hazard, by reafon of the great wind that blew, and the abundance of fnow that fell fo faft from the elements, that one of us could not fee another, being but a fmall way afunder, and fuch was it all the way of the plain of the hill. Defcending of the plain, we turned upon the way, as though we had been going down a pair of ftairs, having at every corner under us vallies of fnow, fome ten fathom deep, and fome more. In my going down, I fell willingly above a dozen times, only to ftay myfelf. What the Knights faid it was, I will not write, left I fhould be counted a lyar; but the truth is, no man will believe the danger of the hill but fuch as know it; and in this wife did we turn at every ten or twelve fathoms, for half a league, until we came to a place called the Hofpital; then turned we in like cafe upon the rocks half a league, until we came to a town called Feriere, and the firft town of Piedmont, and from thence to another town named Nova-lefe, the which payeth twenty-two Crowns to the French King monthly; from thence to Sufa all the way upon good ftone, but not fo evil as before. This town Sufa payeth in like cafe monthly unto the French King one hundred Crowns. The 26th of April, five men drowned upon this mount Cenis, and three weeks before that, were three of the Prince of Salerne's men drowned in fnow. The fame

L 2

day

day that we went over mount Cenis, it was told us, that the number that have been drowned there within this half year, is above
fifty perfons, by report of the inhabitants thereabouts, and yet in
the months of July and Auguft the fnow is melted quite away from
the plains of the mountain, befides fome other; fo that you fhall fee
as good ground there as in all Savoy. Furthermore, the town of
Sufa is not ftrong, but yet kept with a garrifon of men, to keep the
paffage between Savoy and Piedmont. Dr. Bennet, fome time Arch-
deacon of Salifbury, and Ambaffador from King Henry to the Pope,
lieth buried in Sufa. Upon the north fide Sufa is a mountain called
Rochemelune, by eftimation ten leagues high, upon the top whereof
ftandeth a chappel of our Lady of Niges, the which was built by a
Jew, that made his vow, he would build a chappel upon the top of
the higheft mountain in Europe, this being the higheft mountain
of all others. The Duke of Bourbon went thither before he went
to the facking of Rome, to offer up his harnefs to our lady of Niges.
It was fo high, that he made three days journey to the very top of it.
We remained at Sufa two days, the third and fourth. Upon mount
Cenis there appeareth the way that was cut out of the rock by
Hannibal when he entered into Italy.

From Sufa to Avigliana, five long leagues, through three towns,
the one called Buffolin, the fecond St. Ambrofe, and the third St.
George. This town ftandeth very pleafant; it hath a caftle of great
force in it, the which payeth monthly to the French King five hundred Crowns.

From Avigliana to Porcin, ... miles, leaving Turin on the
right hand of us, which is the chiefeft town of Piedmont. It feemeth to be very fair and ftrong, and ftandeth upon the river Po; it
was our right way to have gone through it, but we could not be fuffered to come within it, becaufe their enemies lay fo near unto it.
There, the wars were fet between them, the French King and the
Emperor; they fkirmifhed every day through a town named Rivole,
                                                                which

which payeth fix hundred Crowns a month to the French King, and by a fort of the French King's, called Mount Calcar, a very ftrong fort, over the river Po, the which is the greateft river (as they fay) in all Italy. We left alfo on the right hand of us, as it were a league from us, a very ftrong town, named Chieri, a town of war of the French King's; alfo Porcin hath been a very ftrong town but decayed by the wars, and is now a neuter town. There, for lack of lodgings, we were fain to lie in barns and ftables all the night, in our hoods.

From Porcin to Afti, twelve miles; the which being the march, or frontier town of . . . . and we being to pafs by the holds and caftles of either party, who had daily fkirmifhes together, we were conducted by a French trumpet and a Spanifh drum, by a town called Villa Nova D'Afti, French, and another called Villa Franca, Imperial, the towns round about us being all fpoiled and burnt. Half a mile on this fide the town of Afti, the Captain of the town, accompanied with three thoufand men of arms, met the Lords and brought them to the town with great rejoicing, and they fo curvetted their great horfes, that fome of them, horfe and men, lay in the ditches; and when we came to the town, they gave the Lords a great volley of fmall fhot, and fome great ordnance fhot off the walls, as my Lord North's younger fon was in danger of killing; but there went one galloping to tell my Lords coming, and it was known they were Englifhmen, fo that they were glad. For about four o'clock in the afternoon, there was a general proceffion in the town, in token of rejoicing, as it feemed at our coming, fuppofing the Lords journey had been, as well to have treated a peace betwixt the Emperor and the French King, as for any matter befides. In this proceffion there were thirteen croffes, and fuch a number of Friars, as I never faw in all my life before, and above two thoufand people I am fure. The women went ftrangely apparelled, fitter for mafkers and players than women. This is the firft town of the Emperor's. Here the Lords had very

great

great prefents given them. The town of Afti is not very ftrong of itfelf, but it is well guarded with men of war. The Frenchmen gave alarum to the town this night, we lying there. The next day the Captains and men of arms conveyed the Lords in like manner, out of the town, as they brought them in, and with as much bravery as they could devife; for in three feveral places as we departed out of town, all the foldiers of the town made a guard in very good order, and gave the Lords a volley of fhot to the number of two hundred. Then, when we came out of the gate, we faw two hundred fhot marching before us in good array, which went along with us a good mile out of the town, and when the Lords came nigh to them, they blew off their pieces, and took their leave of the Lords, and fo departed back to the town, and went in like manner as they came out.

From Afti to Alexandria, twenty miles; paffing by the caftle of Nonven, which when we came over againft it, fhot off, very friendly; and as we paffed through fmall towns they rung the bells, in token of rejoicing. At the gates of Alexandria, the Captain of the town, with a great number of Gentlemen, came and entertained the Lords very courteoufly, and brought them to their lodging, the faireft houfe of the town. As we entered the houfe, there was a great peal of fquibs fhot off with a train, which made a very great report, that to our thinking we took them for great pieces of ordnance. That night there came to the Lords from the Emperor's camp, a Gentleman of Spain, called Signior Andrea Rodovico, with a great troop of horfemen, and lay that night in the town to keep the Lords company; the Emperor's camp being but eight miles off the town. Here the Lords and all their train were clearly defrayed at the Knight's coft and charges for all things, for not eight days before our coming thither, the Captain of the town was taken prifoner of the Frenchmen. The French King had then taken Cafal and the whole ftate of Mount Ferrat, which is the inheritance of the

Duke

Duke of Mantua, enjoining five hundred holds and small towns to them. There runneth a goodly river on the west side of Alexandria, with a fair bridge over it, and divers mills.

From Alexandria to Voghera, twenty miles; being accompanied with Rodovico, before named, and his troop of horsemen. Passing over the river at the town's end in a boat, there met us a small number of horsemen, but excellently well appointed, which went forward with us; riding two or three miles further, we were met with a great garrison of soldiers, which brought us through a town called Tortona, with trumpets blowing as they rode; and as we were passing through the town, the castle played with great shot. When they had brought us through the town, many of the horsemen returned to the camp. Then, when we came within a mile of a town called Ponterook, soldiers of another garrison came to attend the Lords, and went forward with us, and being within half a mile of Voghera, a Gentleman of the town, well accompanied, met the Lords, and brought them to their lodgings, where they, and all the train, were defrayed by the King. I never saw better horse, nor better appointed, than those that met the Lords by the way this day.

From Voghera to Pavia, fifteen miles; ferrying over the river of Po. Within a mile of Pavia, being over the river, the Lords and Gentlemen of the town met our Lords, and brought them to the city; passing a bridge at the town over the river Tessin, or Ticinium; upon which bridge stood a great number of soldiers in good order, and well appointed, and among them three thousand shot, which gave the Lords a brave volley. And so, after they had brought them to their lodgings, being the house of Signior Hyeroleino Sacco, there the state of Milan defrayed the Lords charges and train, and appointed divers to attend upon them.

All the foot bands of the garrison came marching to the Lords lodgings in the afternoon, five in a rank, passing bravely armed and appointed as ever I saw. Here the Lords were very sumptuously feasted

and

and entertained at the King's charges. · Pavia is an old ancient city, and a county, and was in times paſt a kingdom.   Lombardy is a goodly plain country, and very rich.   Pavia is an univerſity, and very pleaſant for gentlemen to lie in.   In the great church there, we ſaw the lively image of St. Auguſtine, and his tomb of white marble very rich; the tomb alſo of Leofranda, the laſt King of Pavia. The tomb of Boetius Severinus; and the tower of Fazen the lawyer. At our going out of the city, to give the Lords their farewel they ſhot off their great ordnance, and ſmall ſhot gave the vollies.

From Pavia to Milan, twenty miles.   Five miles from Pavia, we were brought to La-certoza de Pavia, where the Lords dined, and were greatly feaſted.   It is the goodlieſt and beſt houſe in all Europe. It was founded by Giovanni Galezzo, Duke of Milan, who lies there interred in a tomb of white marble; the two coffins and the table of the altar are all of ivory, with ſuch workmanſhip, that it is a ſpectacle to all Lombardy.   There is a cloyſter forty feet quadrant; the doors, deſks, and ſtools be ſo garniſhed with ſuch notable hiſtories, all of cut work, of divers kinds of woods, that no man poſſibly can paint them out more finely and lively.   The marvellous works that be there, as well of the elephant's tooth, as of all kinds of wood, I think there be no where elſe to be found in Europe; howbeit it is not yet all finiſhed.   By the way we ſaw the field, where the French King was taken priſoner.   Betwixt Pavia and the Charter Houſe, the Duke encloſed a piece of ground with a great high wall, four ſquare, and fifteen miles in compaſs about.   This is called his garden, having within it divers ſeveral encloſures, for bears, wild boars, red and fallow deer, wolves, and all other kind of beaſts of venery; which garden, at the battle when the French King was taken priſoner, was ſpoiled by divers breaches that he had made into the ſame.   All the Monks of this Charter Houſe be nobly born and deſcended.   The revenues of the ſaid Charter Houſe per ann. is fifteen thouſand
Crowns.

Crowns. The Lords were very honourably received in Milan, and
lodged in a Nobleman's house, called Il Signor Constantio, where
they were highly feasted at the charge of the King. Thither came,
to salute the Lords, Il Conte l'Andriano, divers Nobles, and divers
gallants of the city. Here the Lords had all the pleasure that could
be shewed them, as well by instruments of music as otherwise.
The city is by estimation seven or eight miles about. The form
thereof, is like unto a heart, and hath six gates, and to every
gate, two noblemen of the city appointed, and every gate is bound
to marry twelve poor maidens yearly, being at certain charges in
their bridals and apparel. Upon Easter Tuesday we saw twelve
maids married, every one of them led with two Noblewomen,
they themselves being clad in white. When they are married,
there is given each of them a purse, with twenty ducats in it, one
suit of apparel, besides that on their backs, and their dinner. The
walls of the city are exceeding strong, but not altogether finished; and the castle also, for provision and strength, is to be wondered
at; as for artillery, munition, corn, wines, oil, bacon, powdered
beef, and Parmesan cheese. They make great store of armour in the
castle; but no townsman may come in at the gate. This castle is of
such force, as none in all Europe is comparable unto it. The church
is an huge thing all of white marble, growing within their own
dutchy, at a place called Lago di Como. They bore us in hand,
that the covering shall be also of marble, but is not likely to be
finished in our time, notwithstanding they have daily one hundred
labourers upon it.

There is an hospital that may dispend 25,000 Crowns a year, the
provision whereof passeth all other; for at that present, we saw one
hundred fat oxen in a stable, one hundred vessels of wine, every one
containing five tons, in one cellar; the diet so cleanly and daintily
prepared for the sick as can be, by the recourse of surgeons and phy-
sicians, that it is a goodly thing to see. In this hospital are five

M   hundred

hundred nurfes to look to the fick, and to bring up children. Many hofpitals more there are, fome for men and fome for women, and fome for children, befides a houfe built without the town, for fuch as fhall be infected of the plague, having three hundred and fixty-five chambers feveral. This city is notably rich, and full of merchandize, and artificers, very wealthy; for there is almoft no artificer's wife but fhe weareth a chain of gold about her neck or middle. The Noblemen and Gentlemen of Italy lie always in the great towns, and never in the country. The Lords tarried at Milan fix days, viz. the 12th, 13th, 14th, 15th, 16th, and 17th.

From Milan to Lodi, twenty miles; paffing through a town called Marignano, where the Marquis hath a goodly houfe, and the Lords were made a great banquet there, the Marquis Marignano himfelf being at that time General for the Emperor, and lay before Siena, befieging the town againft the French King. All the way betwixt Milan and Lodi, we rode as between gardens; and to fpeak truth, my eyes never faw any foil comparable to it for beauty and profit. They make hay there thrice a year. Their ground for tillage, beareth them alfo vines and fuel; for their vines are grown up by certain trees called Oppie, that are of a quick growth, therefore . . . . . . every three years from one of thefe trees to another, they pull the main branches of the vines, as ftiff and ftrait as a cord, fo that they hurt not the ripening of their corn. And thus their vines and their trees growing in order, there is a fpace left to the plough, and fo intermix the corn with the ranks of the vine. There are no woods of fuch timber as we have, but thefe only, willows, white hafels, and poplars, all fet by line, in their meadows, paftures, and grounds for tilling, &c. fo that you cannot fee any way from you half a quarter of a mile. They bring their water in every ditch, round about their enclofures, and make them run continually like little rivers of either fide of the way, and have none other defence but that: and for their commodity, they make their waters so to run one over another and contrary to each other, because the evenness of the ground helpeth them much thereto. Their kine be great and good, and they eat a meat called Latimel or Forita. Their cheese is the best in the world, and also veals. Marignano is a pleasant castle, but of no force; it standeth upon the river of Olon. The Lords were received into their lodging very honourably, with shot, both great and small. They were lodged in the house of the most noble Lodovico Vestarino, then General of the camp in Piedmont in Novara. This Lodi standeth upon a hill, very strongly, and hath a castle in it of great force.

From Lodi to Piacenza, twenty miles; passing by a little pile where was shot off ordnance both great and small; the Lords had a banquet in this pile; and after, passed the river of Po with boats; being all over the river, the Lords were received as before, and so passed by the town walls a long while ere ever they came to their lodgings. They being lodged in the house of Signior Francisco Baratiero, in the street called Santo Nazaro (la Signora. Hippolita sua moglie. Signior Cesare et Hercole suoi figliouli. Signior Alberico, Alessandero, et Camillo Baratiero nepoti del detto Francisco Baratiero). This city is very strong, and a castle of great force, but not fully finished yet. This town did belong to the Church of Rome. Paulus Tertius being a Roman born, of the noble house of the Farnesi, and Pope, who willing to advance his own blood, created his son Peter Aliege Duke of Piacenza and Parma, who, for his cruelty and rigour towards his subjects, was slain in his own house; and because he that did kill him was afraid of the Pope, the townsmen delivered their town into the Emperor's hands, the which he hath exempted unto the Dutchy of Milan. This Peter Aliege, the first Duke of Piacenza and Parma, married the base daughter of the French King, and had by her three sons and one daughter; his daughter is married to the Duke of Urbine, and his eldest son named Octavio, is now Duke of Parma; the other two

brethren

brethren be Cardinals, the one called Cardinal Farnefe, who is now Chancellor of Rome, and the other, Cardinal St. Angelo, they both being in great eftimation with the Pope Paulus Quartus, that now is; fo that it is thought that they will procure and ftir up war againft the Emperor, for recovery of Piacenza for the Duke of Parma. Here the Lords remained two days, the 20th and the 21ft.

From Piacenza to Cremona, eighteen miles, where we paffed over the river of Po. This city is great and rich, and payeth yearly to King Philip of Spain (now our King), without tax, fifty thoufand Crowns. There is an high fteeple in the town, from whence this proverb arifeth, "Una Torre in Cremona, uno Porto in Ancona." They make excellent good knives at Cremona. Being paffed over the river Po, the Lords were received and feafted as before. It is the leaft city of the Dukedom of Milan, and is a great circuit about; a fair town, and rich of merchandife, but of no great force. It hath a notable caftle in it. There is no ordnance in any town through the whole Dukedom, as we rode, but all in the caftle as I could perceive. The Lords viewed this caftle, but no Italian was fuffered to go in with them, three or four of the chief only excepted, that did accompany them. At their going out, the caftle fhot off their fmall and great pieces. We tarried here the 23d day. This day Il Conte Defpefiano Porzenno married the fifter of Signior Camillo Stanga, a very honeft gentleman. Divers of the Lords Gentlemen were bidden thither by this young Count to dinner and fupper, and there danced with the Ladies. This country and Dukedom is wonderful pleafant, and fo replenifhed with corn, vines, fruit, pafture and meadow, all the ground being fo level, and fo well watered, that the like is not to be feen in any one country again, fo long together. In this town is a notable ftrong caftle. The Lords viewed this caftle, and at their coming out, there was ftore of great and fmall fhot, to give the Lords an honourable farewel.

From

From Cremona to Caneto, twenty-two miles, through a town named Salra Terra, paffing over the river Oglio by boat. This river parteth the Dukedom of Milane, and the Dukedom of Mantua; in this town the Lords lay at the Duke's charges.

From Caneto to Mantua, twenty miles; over the river of Chiçfe, through a town called Aqua Negra, where we faw men whip themfelves with chains, going after a proceffion. • We paffed through a town called Andadefco, and by our Lady of Mantua her chapel, where is the greateft offering in thofe parts of Italy. There they fhew pictures of men, which fhe preferved (as they fay), that were ftricken into brains and hearts, and in at the backs, with fwords and daggers; and where is alfo fuch wonderful works of wax, as I never faw the like again. Mantua is a notable ftrong city, environed with great lakes and marfhes. The Duke met with the Lords in the city, and brought them to their lodgings, which was in an old palace of the Duke's. This Duke is very young, and looketh a little afquint. Here the Lords were greatly feafted at the Duke's charge. After fupper, they went to the Court to deliver the Queen's letters, and there we faw the Duke's grandmother, his mother's fifter, the wife of Gonzaga, and his daughter, and one other lady called Hippolita, one of the faireft ladies in the world. After compliments of falutation, the Lords had a banquet, in the which were green almonds, the firft that ever I faw; we were brought into the Dutchefs's jewel houfes, which exceeded in rich jewels, as agates, fapphires, diamonds, an unicorn's horn, a tree of red coral an ell long; here we faw alfo a beaft called the tyger.

From Mantua to Oftia, twenty miles; over a bridge at Mantua, a quarter of a mile long, paffing by the end of the river of Mewfe, which runneth into the river of Po, upon the which, this town ftandeth. On the other fide of the river ftandeth a fair town of the Duke of Ferrara, called Renache.

From

From Oftia to Ferrara, thirty miles; riding twelve miles by the river Po, and then paffed it in a boat, and dined that day in a poft-houfe, being ten miles of this fide of Ferrara. After dinner towards Ferrara, within two miles of it, an Earl of the country met with the Lords, and brought them within the city. Then the Prince met with them, and brought them to their lodgings, to a fair houfe of the Duke's, richly furnifhed and hanged. The pavements of the houfe were of fuch curious works, of white marble, red, and black, that it is impoffible to find fairer. The borders of the chambers and chimnies, of fuch jafper ftone that they might be . There is alfo a clofet, wherein are fuch curious works of all kind of marble, and other ftone, and all of the Duke's father's doings, as they cannot be mended. This city is very ftrong, for they may drown the country round about them. The town walls are very thick, and the ramparts twenty-five yards broad. There be two caftles in the city, the one in the midft of the town, and the other ftanding upon the river of Po, both of great ftrength. The town ditch is one hundred yards over. There are three thoufand Jews in the city and above, having a temple and fchool, after their own laws. They keep the Saturday for their Sabbath. Their market is kept upon the Sunday, with fifh, herbs, and other things, till twelve o'clock at noon. Upon the Sunday they eat nothing but fifh, and that which was dreffed the day before; neither do they touch any money that day. Here the Ambaffadors were honourably feafted, at the Duke's charges, and lodged in his palace, the Prince keeping them company all the time, the Duke himfelf was at Rome at the confecration of the Pope. The ftreets of this town be very wide, and full of excellent good building: there was a camel in this town to be feen. That day before dinner, the Lords and Gentlemen being mounted upon the Duke's horfes, excellently well trimmed, the Prince and Gentlemen rode about one part of the wall, fhewing them the commodities of the town. After dinner, they were brought about the other

9 .part

part of the walls, where they faw fuch wonderful pleafures, and
ftrange things, that it was wonderful to behold; after the which,
they had a very notable banquet; the heavenly noife that was there,
as well with ftrange inftruments of mufic, as otherwife, I cannot declare. The truth is, our entertainment here, did far exceed the beft
entertainment the Lords had other where. The Duke's name is
Hercules d'Efté, and the other Prince his fon, Alphonfo, who is as
worthy a Prince as may be feen, and of as goodly a perfonage.
Here we faw a tortoife a yard long and more, and half a yard broad.
We met the Duke coming homewards to Ferrara, who, when he
met the Lords, faluted them very lovingly, and faid, he was forry
he was not at home, to make them better cheer. The Lords ftaid at
Ferrara the 26th day.

From Ferrara to St. Petro in Cafale, twenty miles; over the river
of Po, riding about fix miles within the Duke of Ferrara his liberties.
After that, we came into the Pope's dominions, where the Vicelegate
fent a gentleman to provide for the Lords and their train at his
charges. It is but a fmall town, infomuch that the train was difperfed this night into three feveral places, fome two miles, fome
three miles off, the lodgings there were fo fcant. Pope Marcellus
Secundus was then alive.

From St. Petro to Bononia, ten miles, being met with feveral
trains of Noblemen and Gentlemen, with trumpets and drums, and
fo brought into the town; but before we could recover the town
gates, a mighty tempeft of rain poured down upon us. At the gates
of the town, the Vice Legate and the Bifhop of Bononia, with a great
company of horfemen, met the Lords, and brought them to the Vice
Legate's houfe, where they were lodged. Notwithftanding this extreme fhower of rain, the trumpeters ftood over the gates of the
Vice Legate's houfe, and blew a long time, until we were all alighted:
And when the Ambaffadors went to fupper, there was excellent
mufic of lower inftruments. The next day being the firft of May,
there was in the morning brought in a brave May, with a number
of

of fhot and pikes, well appointed, marching into the market place, all being the Vice Legate's men, to the number of fixty.

About ten o'clock this forenoon, there was an officer brought in, according to the cuftom of the town, who is, as it were, the Prefident of the Council there. There are twenty-four of the Council, whereof the Prefident is chofen at the end of twenty-four days, and entereth not into his office, till the end of forty-fix days. You fhall under-ftand, that when he entereth into his office, he is fetched from his own houfe very honourably, by him that occupied the place before him, with all the reft of the Council, as alfo with the Vice Legate's guard, and fo brought into the palace, where he is put into a cham-ber, having but two men waiting upon him, and to abide there to the end of two months without coming out, and in all that time, neither his wife, his children, friends, nor fervants may fpeak with him. He is largely allowed for his diet, and keepeth a good table, being as well ferved, as lodged, as if he were in his own houfe.

The fecond day a poft came from Rome, that brought the Lords word, of the death of Pope Marcellus Secundus, and that he died the laft of April. A fight of worfhipful relicks to be feen in Bo-nonia. The body of St. Dominick, the body of St. Rutherin, and a piece of the crown of thorns, wherewith Chrift was crowned. To this town cometh a fmall river called Rheno; the town is great, and hath thirteen gates in it. It is fair built, and with fuch vaults, that in the greateft rain and fouleft weather, men go dry, and are alfo defended from the heat of the fun. The Vice Legate is Bifhop of and hath a guard of Launceknights * well appointed for his guard; other foldiers there be none in the town, except when it is Sedia Vacante, (that is to fay) when there is no Pope. The Pope being dead, ten of the gates are kept fhut, and eight hundred fol-diers appointed, to watch and ward, in divers places of the town; for at that time mifdoers and offenders think themfelves without a

* German Infantry,—the proper term is *Landfknecht*, from whence the French *Lanfquenet*, and our Englifh corruption of the word, as in the text.

law.

law. As for example, when Julius Tertius died, there came a ba- MARY.
niſhed man to the city with four hundred ſoldiers, and to have done 1555.
much miſchief there. He was let into the town, himſelf taken and
beheaded, and all his men taken and ſlain. The Lords were very
greatly feaſted at the Pope's charges all the time they lay in Bononia, Bologna.
and ſo were they invited to Noblemen's houſes of the city, and were
greatly entertained by them. Two noblemen of the town (Rillades
and Mallvachall) were at deadly war. We remained at Bononia thirteen days together.

From Bononia to Imola, twenty miles; over the river of Quaderno
leaving St. Pietro, a town on our right hand, which hath a caſtle
in it, but of no great ſtrength. The Lords, viz. the Biſhop of Ely,
and Lord Montagu, they took their journey to ſee Fiorenza. Dr.
Kearne, the Leger Ambaſſador from Rome, he with all the carriage,
and the greateſt part of the train, departed from the Lords, and took
his journey through la Romagna, to Rome.

From Imola to Faenza, ten miles; over the river Amone, which
keepeth no ceitain courſe, but ſometimes very great, another time
very ſmall, paſſing the caſtle Eologneſe, an old walled town. The
Lords of the town met my Lord Ambaſſador two miles without the
town, and brought him to the Pope's palace, where he was lodged,
with trumpets and drums before him. The town defrayed him,
and all the train, at their chaiges. The commodity and profit of
this town ſtandeth by making of cotton, and making many ſundry
things in fine mell and earth *.

From Faenza to Forli, ten miles; being met without the town as
before, and lodged in the palace at the town's charge. In the market place, when the Ambaſſador came unto it, there were harque-
buſſes of crocke, and other ſhot, diſcharged. There is a very ſtrong
caſtle in the town, ſtanding upon the river of Montone, the which
cometh from the mountains. The caſtle hath great lodgings in it,

* Earthen ware called *Fayence* in French, as being made at Faenza The word *mell*,
means enamell. See Dict. de Trevoux, *mail & email.*

N   and

and store of great ordnance. It was built by Julius Cæsar, and is called after his name, Castello Julio.

From Forli to Cesena, ten miles; passing over the river Ronco with a boat, and by a castle named Framole, leaving a strong town standing on the right hand upon the side of a hill, with a castle on the top of it called Bartinore. The Leger Ambassador was received into this town as before, and lodged at the palace at the town's charges. There is a castle in this town, situated upon a hill adjoining to the palace: there cometh a river called Rubicon: the boys of the town being a great number, met my Lord Ambassador without the town gate, crying Viva Inghilterra (as much as to say) God save England; every one of them brought an olive branch in their hands.

From Cesena to Rimino, twenty miles; leaving a town called Archangelo on the right hand. Here the Ambassador was received and lodged as before, at the palace, at the charge of the town. It standeth upon the sea named Il Golpho di Venetia, and hath a small haven pertaining unto it; the town itself is of no force, but the castle in it is very strong.

From Rimino to Pesaro, the chiefest town of the Dukedom of Urbino, twenty miles. The young Prince (the Duke of Urbin's son) was determined to have met the Ambassador, but being prevented by his sudden coming, he met with him at the stairs feet in the hall, and then received him very honourably, and brought him up to his lodging, which was very richly hanged, and there we were notably feasted, all at the Duke's charges. After dinner, the Dutchess his mother sent for all the Gentlemen of our train, into a withdrawing chamber, where we found her sitting in a rich chair, the Prince her son standing by her, and a great number of Ladies and Gentlewomen sitting about her. After we had all humbly done our duty unto her Grace, as many of us as could speak Italian, or French, went to entertain these Ladies and Gentlewomen. The rest of us, that had no language to entertain them with, yet sat down amongst
them,

them, to behold (as *fpectatores formarum*) the glory of their furpaffing beauties. This heavenly and angelic troop of Ladies being thus accommodated, and we greatly graced by their honourable prefence, on the fudden they were prefented with the mufic of the virginals, lute and viol. Then the young Prince took one of his play-fellows by the hand, and danced the *paven* with him, and afterwards a galliard; which being ended, the Prince entreated our Gentlemen that could dance, to take out a Lady or Gentlewoman to dance withal, and fo they did. The dancing ended, we departed out of the chamber, and there left the Dutchefs with the Ladies. This young Prince is not paft ten years of age, but he is well favoured, and excellently made in all his parts of his body. The town is not ftrong, but yet wanting no ordnance; of fmall circuit, but very well built, and paved with brick throughout. It ftandeth upon the forenamed fea, having a pretty haven, and a pleafant country joining unto it.

From Pefaro to Foffembrone, twenty-fix miles, leaving Fano, a fair town on the left hand, by the fea-fide. The Ambaffador was lodged at the Duke's palace, and there defrayed by the Duke. The town ftandeth betwixt the mountains. Betwixt Fano and Foffembrone, there runneth a river caled Il Metro, where is a goodly plain, and there was a great battle fought betwixt the Romans and the Africans, where were flain 53,000 Africans, and 9000 Romans.

From Foffembrone to Cantiano, twenty miles, through a park of the Duke's, with fallow deer in it, three miles from Foffembrone, which was the firft park we faw in all Italy before: from the park to Furlo, two miles, paffing through a rock fmoothly cut out, and clofe over our heads, made by man's hand, for Hannibal to bring his army that way againft Scipio Africanus; fo to Acqualagna, and thence to Caglie, through the town, and fo to Cantiano, all the way of an huge height, between mountains and rock, twenty miles. This town is but little, ftanding amongft the mountains, here all our charges were defrayed by the Duke.

N 2

From Cantiano to Sigillo, twelve miles, over great mountains, paſſing by Schiecoia, the laſt town of the Duke of Urbine's, two miles from Sigillo. This town is the Pope's, there we tarried the 23d and 24th day.

From Sigillo to Perugia, twenty-two miles, very ill and dangerous way. Here the Lords met all three together again. The Pope's Vice-Legate there, more for ſhame than for any good-will he bare to the Lords, met them without the town gates, and brought them to the abby of St Auguſtine's without the town, where they were lodged. The town is very great, and hath a marvellous ſtrong caſtle in it, built by Pope Paulus Tertius. The people be all French in their hearts. For three nights together fires were made, as well upon the walls of the caſtle, as in other places in the town, only for joy of a new Pope * Paulus Quartus. The great pieces of ordnance, and ſmall ſhot, ſhot off, brave and great fireworks beſides in the air. The cauſe of this their great joy was ſuppoſed to be, becauſe the Pope was French in heart, and enemy to the emperor, notwithſtanding he was a Neopolitan before born. Here we remained the 26th day: on this day all the trumpeters and drummers came to viſit the Lords, and began to play; but anſwer was ſent from the Lords, that with what friendſhip they were received and lodged, with the like they ſhould receive their reward. Then they departed in gieat ſpite and anger, ſtriking upon their drum heads as hard as they could lay on, they being twelve drums in number. That day, at five o'clock at night, the Vice Legate ſent a preſent to the Lords, viz. three dozen and a half of capons, ſix dozen of rabbets, fifteen weathers and lambs, a veal, and thirty-two ſacks of barley, and oats for their horſes; but forafmuch as it was known to the Lords that the Legate had intelligence of their departure the next morning following, and conſidering how ungenteelly they had been uſed before, they refuſed the preſent, rendering few thanks. This evening, the Vice Legate ſent the ſoldiers

* Caraffa.

of

of the town, being fix hundred, marching in rank to the Lords lodging, and there to honour them; they gave three feveral vollies of fhot, and fo departed, without reward given them.

Here we faw a fpecial relick forfooth of our Lady's, a ring, the firft (they ftick not to fay) that ever fhe did wear, which is not fhewed, I tell you, without great ceremony. This ring is a great ring, all of black horn, and hangeth in a pix within a tabernacle, being clad with two or three fold of lawn: that is feen in myftery as all other relicks be. When it is fhewed to any body, there is a wonderful much bleffing, kiffing, kneeling and knocking; and upon either fide of the tabernacle is a great bafon, in the which two or three children of five or fix years old, do fit, and are let down in the bafon; then the ring is to be fhewed to any body. They make us believe forfooth, that thefe children are not by meat or drink, but are marvelloufly fed by the Holy Ghoft.

From Perugia to Foligni, eighteen miles; leaving a town on our left hand, called Affifi. There was a great market fair at that time we were there. The town of Foligni ftandeth in a fair plain, having great mountains on both fides of it.

From Foligni to Spoleto, twelve miles, leaving a town named Trevi on the left hand. Spoleto hath a caftle in it, ftanding upon a hill, which commandeth the town and the people. Here the Lords remained five days, even till the third of June, on which day they went from thence.

The 29th, the Lords received letters out of England, dated the 14th of May. This town ftandeth between the mountains, as far eaft as can be travelled that way. The Cardinal of Perugia is Governor of this town. The people are very proud and beggarly, and of no civility; great boafters, but of no activity; and much given to fecret murther, and privy f——y. The villany is fuch, and they fo much born and maintained in it, that a boy being, as they term it, difhonoured

noured by his like, he will ever after feek the death of his difhonourer. As for example, at our being in the town, two fchool boys, one of them bearing malice to the other, coming into the fchool, and finding there the other boy his enemy, that had difhonoured him, he fuddenly caft a ball of lead at him, and hit him over the head, that he amazed him, and having brought a dagger, he ftabbed the boy to the heart, fo that he died: the fact was not unpunifhed, as I did learn afterwards of certain. O 'what good juftice is executed in this town, and offenders punifhed to the uttermoft, as ye may hear, to the good example of other !'

From Spoleto to Narni, eighteen miles; through a town named Terni, twelve miles on the way. A mile without the town, the Bifhop of Sullino met the Lords with four hundred foldiers, who was fent of purpofe to bring them to the place where they fhould dine, at the Pope's charge; there the foldiers blew off their pieces and departed. After dinner the Lords were brought out of the town in the like manner as they were received into it. The river of Nera runneth on the fouth fide of the town. This town is well ftored with great ordnance and fmall fhot; the caftle in it ftandeth upon a very high hill, and the town upon the fide of a hill, and a goodly plain on the one fide, and great mountains on the other fide. When we came near to Narni, the Legate met the Lords a mile without the town, as before, and brought them to their lodgings, lying at the Pope's charges, and had a prefent fent them from the Legate of the town. In the time of *fedia vacante*, which is when there is no Pope, Narni and Terni be at great wars together.

From Narni to Rignano, twenty miles, paffing over the river of Tyber with a boat, to a town named Borgetto, where the Lords dined at the Pope's charges. The Lords train were lodged in field inns, and could not be fuffered to come within the town gates; but the reafon of it, I could never yet learn.

From

From Rignano to Rome, twenty-two miles; paffing through a
town called Caftello Novo, eight miles from Rignano, and fo forth to
La Prima Porta 7. M. where the Lords dined at the Pope's charges,
and thence to Rome, being feven miles. This Prima Porta, hath
the name of the firft old gate in Rome, when Rome flourifhed, as
appeareth by the old ruins of the walls. After dinner, within a
mile of Rome, we paffed over a bridge called Ponte Mole, over the
river of Tyber, and rode to a houfe without the city, which Pope
Julius Tertius built, where the Lords refted themfelves, and had a
banquet. This houfe is of an excellent building, and hath fuch a
notable commodity in it, all of which marble, fo curioufly wrought,
fo replenifhed with ftrange fruits, and furnifhed with antiquities,
that be daily digged up in the ruins of old Rome, and fome found
in the river of Tyber, in fuch fort, that it doth far exceed all the
buildings that ever I faw, except the Charter Houfe befide Pavia.
Amongft which antiquities there are two marble pillars, of fuch
mixture of colours, white and black, being five cubits long, and a
yard about in the greateft part, which two pillars, Pope Julius
Tertius would not have given for one million of gold, and are of
many men efteemed at a 100,000 crowns. After that the Lords had
refted themfelves in this vineyard three or four hours, there came
now one nobleman, then another, and fometimes five or fix together,
fo that there were fixteen Bifhops. The Cardinals they fent their
pledges, riding upon their mules, having their mafter's   hanging
behind them on their backs, their mules being bravely furnifhed, and
they were in number thirty-five. The Pope fent alfo the officers of
his Court, to bring in the Lords into the city, befides his guard to
wait upon them: and laft of all came a Bifhop that reprefented the
Pope's Holinefs, who was accordingly honoured of the Lords: fo
about fix o'clock at night, the Lords were brought into Rome in very
good order, and fo conveyed to their lodgings, with trumpets and
drums before them, in a fair palace, having in train 1000 horfes and
mules,

†

mules, where Cardinal Pigio lay, which rented of the D. of Parma, and removed himfelf, leaving it unto the Lords. Here the Lords lay at their own charges. This palace was of old time the bath or thermes of Julius Cæfar, as in William Thomas's book of the defcription of Italy ye may read of thermes and baths *.

The two former Popes, Julius Tertius, and Marcellus Secundus, had made great provifion for the Lords in the palace of St. Mark; the which provifion this new-created Pope, Paulus Quartus, did fpend and eat himfelf. The eighth day at night, the Lords were fent for, and had fecret audience, but no Englifhman fuffered to come into the chamber. The 9th day in the morning, Cardinal Caraffa, the Pope's Nephew, newly made Cardinal on the 7th day, fent the Lords a prefent, three veals, three great Parmefan cheefes made in Rome, three dozen of capons and chickens, fifty-two fpades of bacon, and torches of virgin's wax, twenty-four pounds of candles of virgin's wax, ten fugar loaves, fix tons of wine, fifty quarters of barley, and oats for their horfes.

The 10th day, the Lords went to the Court, accompanied with divers Bifhops, Noblemen and Gentlemen, and there had open audience. As they paffed by the caftle of St. Angelo, the Lords were faluted with a great peal of ordnance.

The Pope fat in a conclave, where he was chofen, in a great high chair, having a very rich cope upon him, and a mitre of a wonderful price upon his head. The place where he fat was railed in, that the people might not come and trouble the Orator. The Cardinals fat in benches, within the rails, round about the Pope's Holinefs; the Bifhop underneath them, and the Pope's fervants lay upon the ground. After my Lord my Mafter, the Lord-Bifhop of Ely †, had ended his oration made to the Pope, then all the Englifhmen of the Lords train were called for, and let come within the rails, to kifs the Pope's

* The Editor has feen this defcription, which is very inferior to later accounts, and curious only as the hint.

† Dr. Thirlby.

Holinefs's

Holinefs's foot, who had a crimfon velvet flipper on, that had a crofs of filver laid upon it. That done, the Pope blefled them, and fo they departed fanctified.

The 11th day, the Lords invited divers Cardinals, and at the Cardinal of Pifa's houfe, I faw a live oftrich, and plucked a white feather from it.

The 12th day in the morning, the Lords heard a dirge mafs, at the Spanifh church, for the Emperor's mother, where we had every one of us a taper given us, to hold all mafs time in our hands. This day dined with the Cardinal Caraffa, at a place called Belvedere, as much as to fay, fair to look on, fo called, becaufe it ftandeth in fo good an air, and hath the moft pleafant profpects of all the palaces which are in Rome. After dinner, the Lords went to vifit other Cardinals which lay in the Pope's Court, and fo went up to the chamber of prefence, to wait upon the Pope, that came out to even-fong. When they came firft into the prefence, they found but one Cardinal there, who very curioufly entertained them. Afterwards there came two of the Cardinals together, and fometimes three, and fo came till they made the number of thirty: and ever as they came over the bridge of St. Angelo, whether it were one, two, or three Cardinals together, fo many as they were, fo many pieces of ordnance were fhot off the caftle for an hour. That the Pope is bound to obferve to his well beloved brethren, whenfoever they pafs the bridge, whether they come to the Court or no. Alfo, as the Cardinals do come to the outer gates of the Pope's palace, a drum and fife do give warning of their coming. Within half an hour after the Cardinals were come into the prefence chamber, there came the Pope's Holinefs out of his privy chamber among them. They all rifing up at the fight of him, bowed themfelves, ducking friar fafhion, and the Pope likewife to them again. Then he being led by two Cardinals to a little fide table in the chamber, they both did help him to put on his robes, pertaining to his Holinefs. His robes being put on him, he went on this manner

O   towards

towards the chapel to Even-fong, attended upon as followeth : Firft, the officers of his houfhold, being a great number, before him, all in fcarlet gowns. After them followed two, carrying each of them a mitre, and two officers next them with filver rods in their hands. Then the Cardinals having a crofs borne before them, and every Cardinal his feveral pillar borne next before himfelf. After them cometh the Pope's Holinefs in a chair of crimfon velvet, wrought with gold, having fixteen more fpare men waiting upon the chair. Thus going to the chapel, two fervants going before him, crying ftill Abaffo, Abaffo (which is to fay, kneel down, Mafters), he fitting, bleffing all the way as he went to Even-fong ; which being done, the Pope returned, in like manner, to his chamber again.

The next day, being the 13th, his Holinefs went through St. Peter's church to Mafs, to the chapel of St. Peter, in like manner as before, faving that he had two triple crowns borne before him, of an ineftimable value, which he had not before. So Mafs being faid, he went in proceffion, in this order following : Firft, went the Friars, and every parifh by themfelves with their crofs, all having white torches in their hands. Next to them followed the Pope's officers all in fcarlet gowns and black velvet coats ; then the Priefts and finging men of the Pope's chapel ; then Bifhops, to the number of fifty-eight, all of them having mitres of white linen cloth on their heads, and copes on their backs. After them followed the Cardinals, having mitres of white damafk, and tunicles upon their backs, with their croffes and pillars borne before them, as above faid. Then came the Pope's Holinefs, and next before him went the guard, being a great number, the Pope being carried in his chair as before mentioned, having a little table before him, whereupon ftood the facrament, and two men going before him with great broad fans made of peacocks tails, to keep the fun and flies from his holy face. The moft part of his Cardinals had alfo the like fans before them. After the Pope, followed a troop of light horfemen, to the number

of

of fixty-four, well armed and appointed. And thus was the order
of the Pope's going in proceffion. Now, at the Pope's fetting out of the gates of his palace with the proceffion, all the Pope's trumpeters ftood there and founded. Then was there a warning piece fhot off to the caftle of St. Angelo, whereupon the caftle gave a great peal of ordnance, which continued a long time.

To write any thing of the antiquities of Rome, I thought it needlefs, confidering they are truly and notably fet forth in William Thomas's book, of the Defcription of Italy. We remained at Rome fourteen days.

The fixteenth day the Lords dined and fupped with the Pope at the palace of St. Mark. After dinner they went to vifit the Cardinals they had not fpoken with before, and the fame night they took their leave of the Pope, who gave my Lord Montague a table diamond, with a ring, efteemed at 2000 crowns; and my Lord of Ely my mafter, a crofs of gold. They made great bonfires in Rome, becaufe we were reconciled to the church of Rome, and the caftle fhot off much ordnance. We faw a world of relicks, very ridiculous and incredible, viz. the picture of Chrift, called La Sudaria, lively as he was upon the earth. One of the nails that Chrift was nailed with to the crofs. The ftairs Chrift went up on going to be examined and judged of Pilate; upon which ftairs he had a fall; and with his elbow, to fave himfelf, he made a great hole in the ftairs, the which is covered over with a grate of filver; unto the which there is made a great offering. The table that Chrift made his laft fupper upon with his difciples. The crown of thorns wherewith Chrift was crowned, upon the crofs, *cum multis alus quæ perfcribere longum eft.*

Note here, the whole number of miles from London to Rome. Accounting the leagues in France two Englifh miles a league, and thofe in Savoy and Piedmont, at three every league, though fome miles in Savoy be more; yet becaufe the Italian miles be fhorter

than

than the Englifh, I let them borrow of the leagues in Savoy, accounting all as Englifh miles; by which account, all together make up
one thoufand one hundred and fifty-eight miles.

The End of our Journey to Rome.

Our Journey from Rome, through Germany, and fo to London.

FROM Rome to Rignano, twenty miles. From Rignano to
Narni, twenty miles. From Narni to Spoleto, eighteen miles.
From Spoleto to Foligni, twelve miles. From Foligni to Sigillo,
twenty-four miles; to Nocera to dinner, twelve miles. From Sigillo
to Urbino, twenty-two miles; and to Caglie to dinner, feventeen
miles.

This town is the principal town of the Duke's, and ftandeth
upon the top of a high hill, but of no great ftrength. The Duke
was in the town at our coming thither.

There we faw Polydore Virgilius' grave, who died not paffing a
month before we came thither. Here they all remained one day,
which was the 26th.

From Urbino to Rimino, twenty-four miles, calling at Montefiore,
to dinner, twelve miles. From Rimino to Cefena, twenty miles.
From Cefena to Imola, thirty miles. From Imola to Bononia,
twenty miles; where we ftaid the firft day of July. From Bononia
to Crocetta, fourteen miles, by a caftle named St. Zunan, of great
force, and well watered. From Crocetta to Concordia, twenty-five
miles, paffing over the river of Panaro upon a bridge in a little village called Bonporto, riding a long time the river of Secchia, which
cometh to this town, and meeteth the Po ten miles from Concordia.
This town belongeth to the Principality of Mirandula, and was
burnt three years paft by the Pope Julius, with others   for
difpleafure.

From

From Concordia to Mantua, twenty-two miles, paffing the river of Secchia, riding through a town called St. Benedetto, where we paffed the river of Po. There we inned at the Black Morian.

THe Duke of Mantua his revenue by year, was but one thoufand ducats, but afterwards the Duke his father increafed it thirty thoufand ducats more, by marriage with a Nobleman's daughter in Italy, an heirefs. The Duke that is now, was but the fecond brother. He is very uncomely of perfon, fquint-eyed, crook-backed, and but fifteen years old.

His elder brother was drowned by misfortune, being a fifhing in a boat, in the lake that is about the town. The third brother was put to the King's Court to learn French; but the French King will no more let him come home as yet; fome think he will marry to one of his daughters, that after the deceafe of the Duke his brother, he being the next heir, might enjoy the Dukedom of Mantua. The fourth brother is a Bifhop. The Duke's uncle being Cardinal of Mantua, is Governor of this town. Here I faw a mill to wind filk, which was a notable piece of work.

From Mantua to Bofolingo, twenty-two miles, through a town called Villa Franca, a ftreight, by which they muft pafs that come from Mantua to Venice by land, or from Mantua to Trent; in the which ftreight are fuch exceptions as I have not known before; for no man can pafs that way, but he muft pay the value of an Englifh penny, and yet is it not gathered for the repairing of an high-way or bridges. There be two men that farm this ftreight of the Venetians yearly, for one hundred and fifty crowns. By this town runneth the river of Adige, the fwifteft river that ever I faw, which falleth into the gulph of Venice.

From Bofolingo to Paw, twenty-two miles, paffing over the river of Adige, and riding through two towns, Sereigne and Bergetto, ftanding both between mountains, upon the river of Adige. At Sereigne is a ftreight called La Chiufa, having notable locks on the one fide

of

of it, and the river on the other fide, being well fortified with
ordnance and munition, as the Venetians have all their ports for
the moft part, fo that there is very hard paffage without licence.
Thefe two towns Bergetto and Paw, belong to the King of the Romans.   The Cardinal of Trent is Governor of them.

From Paw to Trent, twenty-two miles, riding all the way by
the river of Adige, and between mountains, paffing through a
goodly town of the King of the Romans, called Roveredo, where we
dined at the fign of the Star.   It hath in it a very ftrong caftle ftanding upon a rock.   Trent ftandeth upon the river of Adige, but it is
of no force, neither great, nor much fair building in it, his own
palace or caftle excepted, which is wonderful beautiful, and very
richly furnifhed.   The Cardinal is abfolute Lord and Governor of
the town; he hath a guard of fifty men to wait upon him, befides a
great number of gentlemen and other fervitors.   He is a Dutchman
born, and cometh of a very noble houfe; but in his houfe-keeping
he fheweth himfelf an Italian, to keep bare cheer, and a mean table;
notwithftanding this Cardinal is more honourably ferved in his houfe,
for the cheer he keepeth, than any other that I have feen, and is very
rich.   I faw two oftriches at his houfe, the one ruffet, the other black.
Here we faw a child, whom the Jews had martyred many years paft,
all his body pricked with needles.   We inned at the fign of the
Rofe, and remained there three days, the 8th, 9th, and 10th.

The reft of the journey homewards is omitted as not material.

No. VI.

Letters concerning Calais.

[Queen Mary faid, during her laft illnefs, that after fhe was dead, they would find Calais lying at her heart.—It appears from the papers contained in this article, which have been thought to deferve publication, that the lofs of it, which happened foon after, was owing to the negligence of her Council, in not fupplying that place and Guifnes, with fufficient garrifons and ammunition.]

The Council of Calais to the Queen.

1557.
May 23.

IT may pleafe your Highnefs to underftand. That where, upon circumfpect confideration and view of your Majefty's ftore here of munition and other habiliments for war, there is prefently found not only a great want in many kinds thereof, but alfo fuch a decay in divers other things, as the fame are not ferviceable, and will be utterly loft if they be not with fpeed repaired and put in better eftate; as this bearer, Mr. Highfield, mafter of your ordnance here, can declare more amply the particularities thereof, either unto your Majefty, or unto fuch of your Council, as fhall pleafe your Highnefs to direct him; we have thought it our bounden duties to be moft humble fuitors unto your Majefty, that it would pleafe the fame to give immediate order, as well for the fupplement of the faid lacks, as alfo for your warrant to be addreffed hither, for the repairing of all other things requifite to be done within his office.

And thus we continually pray Almighty God for the long prefervation of your Highnefs in moft profperous eftate. From your town of Calais the 23d of May 1557.

I   Your Majefty's, &c.

Lord Wentworth, Lord Grey, &c. to the Queen.

OUR bounden duties moſt humbly remembered unto your High-neſs; Upon the receipt of the intelligences ſent unto your Majeſty this other day, from me your Grace's deputy, I forthwith diſpatched to my Lord Grey, requiring his Lordſhip to repair to this town, that we might together conſult of the ſtate of your Highneſs's places and country on this ſide. So his Lordſhip coming hither, we have conferred together our ſeveral intelligences, and finding the ſame in effect to agree, it hath very much augmented our ſuſpicion, that this train now meant by the enemy ſhould be made towards your High-neſs's country or places. Whereupon we all together have conſi-dered the ſtate of the ſame, and ſaid our opinions therein, as it may appear unto your Highneſs by theſe articles we ſend herewith to your Majeſty, which we have thought our duties to ſignify unto you. Moſt humbly beſeeching your Highneſs to return unto us your pleaſure therein. So we pray Jeſu grant your Majeſty long and proſperous reign. At your town of Calais, 27th Dec. 1557.

Your Highneſs's, &c.

Our Conſultation made the 27th Decem. 1557.

FIRST, Having no ſupplement of men other than is preſently there, we think it meeteſt, if the enemy ſhould give the attempt, to abandon the town (which could not be without very great danger of the caſtle), and defend the turnpike, which is of the more import-ance, becauſe that way only, in neceſſity, the relief to the caſtle is to be looked for.

Item, There is great want of wheat, butter, cheeſe, and other victuals.

Item,

Item, It is requifite to have fome men of eftimation and fervice to be there, that might be able to take the charge in hand, if either ficknefs or other accident fhould fortune to me the Lord Grey; which I the faid Lord Grey the rather require by reafon of Sir Henry Palmer's hurt, being of any other perfon at this prefent utterly unfurnifhed.

HAMPNES CASTLE.

Item, We think the, fame fufficiently furnifhed of men for the fudden; albeit, this hard and frofty weather, if it continue, will give the enemy great advantage, yet we put in as much water as is poffible.

Of victuals, that place is utterly unprovided, except the Captain's flore.

It is alfo thought meet to have there fome man of eftimation and fervice, for the refpects contained in the article of Guifnes, which alfo the Lord Dudley requires.

NEWNAMBRIDGE.

Item, We think it meet, upon the occafion to withdraw the bands from the Caufeway thither; and then are of opinion, the fame to be fufficient to defend that place for a feafon, unlefs the enemy fhall get between this town and the bridge.

It is clean without victuals other than the Captain's own provifion.

RYSBANK.

Becaufe that place ftandeth upon the fea, and by the fhore fide may the enemy come in a night to it, we think it meet to appoint thither a band of the low country under the leading of Capt. Dodd. It is altogether unfurnifhed of victuals, other than for the Captain's own flore.

P   CALAIS.

CALAIS.

Whereas all your Majesty's places on this side make account to be furnished of victuals and other necessaries from hence; it is so, that of victuals your Highness hath presently none here, and also this town hath none, by reason that the restraint in the realm hath been so strait, as the victuallers as were wont to bring daily hither good quantities of butter, cheese, bacon, wheat, and other things, might not of late be suffered to have any recourse hither, whereby is grown a very great scarcity of all such things here.

Finally, forasmuch as all the wealth and substance of your Majesty's whole dominion on this side, is now in your low country, a thing not unknown to the enemy, and if with this his great power coming down (as the bruit goeth), for the victualling of Arde, he will give attempt upon your Highness's country, we do not see that the small number here (in respect of their force) can by any means defend it. And if we should stand to resist their entry into the country, and there receive any loss or overthrow, the country should nevertheless be overrun and spoiled, and besides it would set the enemy in a glory, and also be the more peril to your Highness's places. We therefore upon the necessity, think it meet to gather all our men into strengths, and with the same to defend your places to the uttermost; notwithstanding all the power on this side is far insufficient to defend the places, in case the enemy shall tarry any space in the field.

WENTWORTH, GREY, &c.

The Lord Wentworth, Deputy of Calais, to the Queen.

IT may pleafe your Highnefs. Having retired the Bands from the Caufeway the laft night, and placed them at the bridge, and within the brayes; this morning early I returned them to the faid Caufeway, to defend that paffage in cafe the enemy would attempt to enter there, and alfo to offer fkirmifh to take fome of them, and to learn fomewhat of their power. Between nine and ten the enemy fhowed in a very great bravery about fix enfigns of footmen, and certain horfemen, and came from the chaulk pitts down the hill towards the caufeway. Whereupon fome of ours iffued and offered the fkirmifh, but the enemy would in no wife feem to meddle. During this their ftillnefs, they caufed about two hundred Harque-bufiers to cut over the marfhes from Sandgate, and get between ours and the bridge, and then to have hotly fet on them on both fides. In this time alfo, at a venture, I had caufed your Majefty's Marfhall with the horfemen to go abroad, and maintain the fkirmifh with the footmen, and by that the Marfhall came there, the enemy's Harque-bufiers that paffed the marfhes were difcovered, and ours fuddenly took a very honeft retire, which the enemies on the land fide per-ceiving, came on, both horfemen and footmen, marvellous hotly; to whom ours gave divers onfets, continually fkirmifhing till they came to the bridge, and there repofed themfelves. The bridge beftowed divers fhot upon the enemy, and hurt fome. Of ours, thanked be God, none flain nor hurt, but a man at arms ftricken in the leg with a currior. The alarm continued till one o'clock in the after-noon, before the end whereof our enemy's number increafed; for eleven enfigns more of footmen came in fight, and three troops of horfemen; befides, the alarm went round about our country at that inftant, even from Sandgate to Guifnes, and bands of the enemy at

every paſſage. They have gotten Froyton church, and plant themſelves at all the ſtreights into this country. The bulwarks of Froyton
and Neſle have this day done their duty very well, to whom I have
this afternoon ſent aid of men, and ſome ſhot and powder. Howbeit
I am in ſome doubt of Neſle this night.

I am perfectly advertiſed their number of horſemen and footmen
already arrived, is above 12,000, whereof little leſs have come in
ſight here. The Duke of Guiſe is not yet arrived, but hourly looked
for with a more number. This evening I have diſcovered five hundred waggons laden with victual and munition, and have further perfect intelligence, that thirty cannons be departed from Boulogne
hitherwards. They are ſettled at Sandgate, Galley Moat, Cauſe-
way, Froyton, Calkewell, Neſle, and Syntrecaſe. At one o'clock
after midnight, I look for them, being low water at the paſſage over
the haven. Thus having ſet all things in the beſt order I can, I
make an end of three days work, and leave your Majeſty to conſider
for our ſpeedy ſuccour. Beſeeching God to grant your Highneſs
victory, with long and proſperous reign. At your town of Calais,
this New Year's Day, at nine in the night, 1557.

I have received your Majeſty's letter by the Maſter of the Ordnance, who came in this morning. The contents whereof I will
follow as near as I can.

Your Highneſs's moſt

humble and obedient

ſervant and ſubject,

WENTWORTH.

Lord Wentworth to the Queen.

AFTER my humble duty remembered, it may pleafe your Highnefs, this laft night our enemies lay ftill, without any thing
attempting in the places mentioned in my laft letters, as we did well
perceive during the whole night, by great fires made in the fame
places.

This morning early, I put out frefh footmen to the bridge, to
relieve the watched men. About nine o'clock, the enemies in very
great number approached the bridge, and offered the fkirmifh;
whereupon iffued out fome of our Harquebufiers and Bowmen, and
kept them in play, with the help of the fhot from the bridge, more
than an hour; and in the end, being overmatched with multitude,
made their retire within the turnpike without any lofs or hurt. The
enemies fhadowing themfelves under the turnpike wall, with their
curriors (which affuredly fhot very great bullets, and carry far) kept
themfelves in fuch furety, as our pieces of the bridge could not
annoy them, till at eleven o'clock, certain of ours bored holes with
auger through the turnpike, and with harquebuffes beat them out
into the fhot of ordnance, and fo made them retire to the Caufeway.

This forenoon certain Swiffes and Frenchmen, to the number of
five hundred, got within the marfhes between Froyton and Nefle
bulwarks; and the men of the bulwarks feeing themfelves to be
compaffed on all fides, and feeing alfo that time yet ferved them
well to depart, and fearing they fhould not fo do, if they tarried till
they were affailed on both fides (as they could not indeed) forfook
their bulwarks, and right manfully, notwithftanding the enemies between them and home, faved themfelves through the marfhes. In the

9   retire

retire of the enemies, one Cookfon, a man at arms, and few other foldiers, with the countrymen, refcued moft part of the booty (which was certain kine) and took three prifoners of the Captain of Abbeville's band. The report of this enterprize of the enemy being brought to me, fearing Colham Hill, I forthwith appointed your Majefty's Marfhal with the Horfemen, and two hundred footmen, to repair thither, and as they fhould fee their match, fo to demean themfelves. Ere thefe men had marched a quarter of a mile, the enemies were retired out of the country, upon occafion, that wading as they entered in up to the girdle ftead, and perceiving the water to increafe, thought good to make a fpeedy return: and neverthelefs, for all their hafte, went up to the breaft, and if they had tarried a little longer, I had put in fo much water, as I think would have put them over head and ears; and God willing, at the next tide I will take in more. This afternoon they have been quiet, and we the mean time be occupied in cutting up of paffages to let in more water about the bridge, and that part of the marfhes, whereby the enemies fhall have very ill watering. I would alfo take in the falt water about the town, but I cannot do it, by reafon I fhould infect our own water, wherewith we brew, and notwithftanding all I can do, our brewers be fo behind-hand in grinding and otherwife, as we fhall find that one of our greateft lacks. I therefore make all the hafte and provifion I can there, and howfoever the matter go, muft fhortly be forced to let in the falt water.

The three men taken to-day be very ragged, and ill appointed. In examining, they confefs that there is great mifery in their camp, and great want of money and victuals. They fay, and I partly believe it, becaufe it almoft appeareth to me, their number to be 25,000 footmen, whereof 10,000 Swiffes, and 10,000 horfemen. The Duke of Guife is already among them, and the only devifer and leader of this enterprife. They fay alfo, a fhot from the bridge to the Caufe-

way

way yesterday, struck off the Master of the camp's leg, called Captain Gourdault. I am also perfectly advertised, both by these men and otherwise, that they have no great ordnance yet come, but look for it daily by sea; it is eighty pieces, whereof thirty be cannons, and are laden, with munition and victuals, in vessels, which shall land at Sandgate, or rather I think at Boulogne, and to be taken out of the great ships, and so again embarked to Sandgate in lesser vessels, as they have done most part of their victuals and carriage that they have hitherto occupied. And surely if your Majesty's ships had been on this shore, they might either have letted their voyage, or at the least very much hindered it, and not unlike to have distressed them, being only small boats. Their ordnance that comes shall be conveyed in the same sort, it may therefore please your Majesty to consider it. I have also now fully discovered their enterprize, and am (as a man may be) most sure they will first attempt upon Ryfbanke, and that way chiefly assail the town. Marry I think they lie hovering in the country, for the coming of their great artillery, and also to be masters of the sea. And therefore I trust your Highness will haste over all things necessary for us with expedition. Under your Majesty's reformation, I think, if you pleased to set the passage at liberty for all men to come that would, bringing sufficient victuals for themselves for a season, I am of opinion here would be enow, and with more speed than can be made by order. Marry then must it well be foreseen to transport with expedition victuals hither.

I have written to the King's Majesty, of the enemy's being here, and was bold humbly to beseech his Majesty to give commission to the Governors of his frontiers, I might, in necessity upon my letter, have three or four hundred harquebusiers Spaniards, that now be placed about St. Omer's, whereof I thought it my duty to advertise your Majesty for your pleasure, whether I may write to the Governors to that effect, upon his Majesty's answer, and take them or not.

I, with

I, with the reſt of your Council here, are forced to put your Majeſty to ſome charges; for having taken in a confuſed number of countrymen, we muſt needs reduce them into order, and the commoners alſo, and have therefore called them into wages, and appointed Captains of the fitteſt men that preſently be here.

I have placed Dodd with his band in Ryſbanke, and the reſt of the extraordinary bands be at the bridge, and in the brayes of this town.

As I was making this diſcourſe, ſix Enſigns of footmen, and certain bands of horſemen, came from Sandgate by the Downs, within the ſight of Ryſbanke, on whom, that place and this town alſo, beſtowed divers ſhots.

This evening, they have made their approach to Ryſbanke, without any artillery, and as far as I can perceive, do mind to make the aſſault with ladders, herdy, &c. and other things, and that ways get it. At Calais the 2d of January, at ten in the night, 1557.

As I was in communication with your Mayor and Aldermen, touching the ſtate of this town, whom I find of marvellous good courage, and moſt ready to live and die in this town, I received letters from my Lords of the Council, of your Majeſty's aid provided for us.

I fear this ſhall be my laſt letter, for that the enemy will ſtop my paſſage, but I will do what I can tidily, to ſignify unto your Majeſty our ſtate.

Your Majeſty's, &c.
WENTWORTH.

Lord Grey to the Queen.

MY moſt bounden duty humbly premiſed to your Majeſty; whereas I have heretofore always in effect written nothing to your Highneſs but good, touching the ſervice and ſtate of your places here; I am now conſtrained with woful heart to ſignify unto your Majeſty theſe enſuing. The French have won Newhaven-bridge, and thereby entered into all the Low country, and the marſhes between this and Calais. They have alſo won Ryſbank, whereby they be now maſter of that haven. And this laſt night paſt, they have placed their ordnance of battery againſt Calais, and are en-camped upon St. Peter's heath before it; ſo that now I am clean cut off from all relief and aid, which I looked to have both out of England and from Calais, and know not how to have help, by any means, either of men or victuals. There reſteth now none other way for the ſuccour of Calais, and the reſt of your Highneſs's places on this ſide, but a power of men out of England, or from the King's Majeſty, or from both without delay, able to diſtreſs and keep them from victuals coming to them, as well by ſea as by land, which ſhall force them to levy their ſiege to the battle, or elſe drive them to a greater danger. For lack of men out of England, I ſhall be forced to abandon the town, and take in the ſoldiers thereof for defence of the caſtle. I have made as good proviſion of victuals as I could by any means out of the country, with which, God willing, I doubt not to defend and keep this place as long as any man, whatſoever he be, having no better proviſion, and furniture of men and victuals than I have; wherein your Grace ſhall well perceive, that I will not fail to do the duty of a faithful ſubject and Captain, although the enemy attempt never ſo ſtoutly, according to the truſt repoſed in me. I addreſſed letters preſently to the King's Majeſty by this

Q   bearer,

bearer, moft humbly defiring aid from him, according to the effect aforefaid. I might now very evil have fpared this bringer, my fervant and trufty officer here, in this time of fervice. Howbeit confidering the great importance of his meffage, I thought him a meet man for the purpofe, defiring your Majefty to credit him fully, and to hear him at large, even as directly as your Grace would hear me, to open my mind in this complaint of imminent danger. Thus trufting of relief and comfort forthwith from your Majefty for the fafeguard of Calais, and other your places here, I take my leave moft humbly of your Grace. At your Highnefs's Caftle of Guifnes, moft affured Englifh even to the death, the 4th of January 1557, at feven of the clock in the morning.

> Your Majefty's moft humble
>> Servant, and obedient Subject,
>>> GREY.

To the Queen our Sovereign Lady.

PLEASETH your Highnefs to underftand the declaration of your humbleft and faithful fervant, John Highfield, concerning the befieging and lofs of your Grace's town of Calais.

Firft, being appointed by your moft honourable Council to repair into England, I came. And after fome intelligence that the French army drew towards the Englifh pale, I was commanded to return with diligence unto my charge at Calais, and I arrived there on New Year's Day in the morning. The enemy being then encamped about Sandgate; the faid morning, after I had delivered letters to my Lord Deputy, from your Grace's faid Council, the faid Lord Deputy told me how the alarm was made the night before, and alfo what he thought meet for me to be done, for the better furniture of
thofe

thofe fortreffes which were in moft danger, as the bulwarks of the
High Country, Guifnes, Newhavenbridge, and Ryfbanke, and alfo for the Defence of the Low Country, becaufe his Lordfhip thought their enterprife had tended only to the fpoil thereof. Then I fhowed that there was fufficient ftore of all munitions, and that I would fend to all places as need required, which was done.

Item, On Sunday following, we perceived the French ordnance was brought to their camp; whereby appeared that the enemy meant to batter fome place. And thereupon there were two mounts repaired for the better defence. At the fame time, I defired to have fome pioneers appointed to help the cannoneers (who were not forty in number) for the placing and entrenching of our great ordnance, which pioneers I could never get. The fame day, the enemy forced our men to forfake the bulwarks of the High Country, and then it was moved to my Lord Deputy, that the fea might be let in, as well to drown the caufeway beyond Newhavenbridge, as alfo other places about the town; wherein was anfwered, not to be neceffary without more appearance of befieging; and becaufe that the fea being entered fhould hinder the paftures of the cattle, and alfo the brewing of the beer. The fame day my Lord took order that victuals and other neceffaries fhould be fent to Newhavenbridge for fix days, which was done.

Item, On Monday in the morning, my Lord Deputy with the reft of the Council there, perceiving that the enemy intended to approach nearer, were in doubt whether they might abandon the Low Country; and by advice, my Lord gave order, that the Bailiff of Marke fhould appoint the fervants and women of the Low Country, with their fuperfluous cattle, to draw, if need happened, into the Flemifh pale, and the faid Bailiff with his beft men to repair to Marke church, and there to abide further order. The fame morning before day, the enemy had made their approaches, and did batter both Newhaven-bridge and the Ryfbanke, which was given up before nine of the clock.

The

The Captain of Newhavenbridge had word fent him, that if he faw no remedy to avoid the danger, that then he fhould retire with his company into the town.   The Captain of Ryfbanke did about the fame time furrender, becaufe (as he told me fince) his pieces were all difmounted, and the foldiers very loth to tarry at the breach, wherein I know no more.   But after the enemy were entered, I caufed the faid Ryfbanke to be battered, and when my Lord faw how little it profited, he commanded to ceafe,   The fame day the paffages being both loft, the enemy planted their ordnance on the Sand-hill, to batter the north fide of the town ; and then I moved my Lord to call in as many countrymen as he could, and to appoint them Captains, and their feveral quarters, for the relief of thofe which did moft commonly watch and attend on the walls, who anfwered, that he had determined already fo to do.   Howbeit the women did more labour about the rampart than the faid countrymen, which, for lack of order in time, did abfent themfelves in houfes and other fecret places.

The fame evening, Captain Saligues came into Calais, whereupon the people rejoiced, hoping fome fuccour, but after that time, it was too late to receive help by land, becaufe the French horfemen were entered the Low Country.

Item, On Tuefday in the morning, the enemy begun their battery to the town, on which fide 1 had placed fourteen brafs pieces. Howbeit, within fhort time, the enemy having fo commodious a place, did difmount certain of our beft pieces, and confumed fome of the gunners, which flood very open for lack of mounds and good fortification. · For if the rampart had been finifhed, there might divers pieces have been brought from other places, which were above fixty in number, ready mounted, but lacking convenient place, and chiefly cannoneers and pioneers, it was hard to difplace the French battery; which counter-battery could not have been maintained for lack of powder.   For at the beginning, having in ftore four hundred

dred barrels, I found that there was fpent within five days, one
hundred.

Item, On Wednefday the enemy continued their battery on the town without great hurt done, becaufe they could not beat the foot of the wall, for that the contremure was of a good height, and we reinforced the breach in the night, with timber, wool, and other matter fufficiently, and we looked that the enemy would have attempted the affault the fame evening, whereupon I caufed two flankers to be made ready, and alfo placed two bombards, by the help of the foldiers, appointing weapons and fireworks to be in readinefs at the faid breach. At which time my Lord commanded the foldiers of the garrifon to keep their ordinary wards, and Mafter Grimfton to the breach with the refidue of the beft foldiers. And then my Lord exhorted all men to fight, with other good words, as in fuch cafe appertaineth. And my faid Lord told me divers times, that although there came no fuccour, yet he would never yield, nor ftand to anfwer the lofs of fuch a town.

Item, On Thurfday began one other battery to the caftle, which being a high and weak wall without rampart, was made faultable the fame day. Whereupon the Captain of the caftle defired fome more help, to defend his breach, or elfe to know what my Lord thought beft in that behalf. Then after long debating, my Lord determined to have the towers overthrown, which one Saulle took upon him to do, notwithftanding I faid openly, that if the caftle were abandoned, it fhould be the lofs of the town. The fame night my Lord appointed me to be at the breach of the town with him; and about eight of the clock the enemy waded over the haven at the low water, with certain harquebufiers, to view the breaches, and coming to the caftle, found no refiftance, and fo entered; then the faid Saulle failed to give fire unto the train of powder. Then my Lord underftanding that the enemy were entered into the caftle, commanded me to give order for battering the caftle, whereupon incontinent

there

Z

there were bent three cannons, and one faker before the gate, to
beat the bridge, which being in the night did not greatly annoy.
The same time, Mr. Marſhall with divers ſoldiers came towards the
caſtle, leſt the enemy ſhould enter the town alſo. And after we
had ſkirmiſhed upon the bridge (ſeeing no remedy to recover the
caſtle), we did burn and break the ſaid bridge; and there was a
trench immediately caſt before the caſtle, which was only help at
that time. Within one hour after, upon neceſſity of things, determined to ſend a trumpet with a herald, declaring, that if the French
would ſend one gentleman, then he would ſend one other in gage.
Whereupon my Lord ſent for me, and commanded that I ſhould
go forth of the town for the ſame purpoſe, wherein I deſired his
Lordſhip, that he would ſend ſome other, and rather throw me over
the walls; then he ſpoke likewiſe to one Windebanke, and to Maſ-
ſingberd (as I remember), which were both to go unto ſuch ſervice.
Then my Lord ſent for me again into Peyton's houſe, and being
eftſoons commanded by the Council there, I went forth with a trumpet,
and received in a French Gentleman, who, as I heard, was brought to
my Lord Deputy's houſe, and treated upon ſome articles, which were
brought within one hour by one Hall, merchant of the Staple. Then
Mohſieur D'Andelot entered the town with certain French Gentlemen, and the ſaid Hall and I were brought to Monſ. de Guiſe, who
lay in the Sand-hills by Ryſbanke, and there the ſaid Hall delivered a
bill, and we were ſent to Monſ. D'Eſtree's tent. The Friday after,
Monſ. D'Eſtrees told me, that my Lord Deputy had agreed to render
the town with loſs of all the goods, and fifty priſoners to remain.
On Saturday he brought me into the town, willing me to tell him
what ordnance, powder, and othei houſes did belong unto my office,
becauſe he would reſerve the ſame from ſpoiling by the French ſoldiers. And after he had knowledge that all my living was on that
ſide, he was content that I ſhould depart into Flanders. Notwithſtanding, I was driven off until Wedneſday; then he ſaid, he would
                                                               ſend

fend me away, if I would promife him to make fuit, that his fon might return in exchange for the Captain of the caftle, who being prifoner, defired me alfo to travail in it, for he would rather give 3000 crowns than remain a prifoner. Whereupon I promifed to enquire and labour in the fame matter to the beft of my power. At my faid return into the town, I found my wife, which fhowed me that in my abfence, fhe had beftowed my money and plate to the value of 600 *l.* which was found before my coming, faving one bag with 350 crowns, which I offered to give unto the faid Monf. D'Eftrees, if he would promife me on his honour to difpatch me on horfeback to Graveling, which he did. And there I met with Monf. de Vandeville, to whom I told, that I thought the enemy would vifit him fhortly ; and among other things, I enquired of him where Monf. D'Eftrees's fon did he, who told me that he was at Bruges.

Then at my coming to Dunkirk, there were divers Englifhmen willing to ferve, whereupon I fpake to the Captain of the town, who advifed me to move it to the Duke of Savoy. Then I rode to Bruges, befeeching him to confider the poor men, and how willing they were to ferve the King's Majefty if they might be employed. Then he anfwered, that he thought my Lord of Pembroke would fhortly arrive to Dunkirk, and then he would take order. Further, the faid Duke afked me, after what fort the town was loft ? I anfwered, that the caufe was not only by the weaknefs of the caftle, and lack of men, but alfo I thought there was fome treafon, for, as I heard, there were fome efcaped out of the town, and the Frenchmen told me, that they had intelligence of all our eftate within the town. Then I put the Duke in remembrance of Guifnes, who told me, that he would fuccour the caftle, if it were kept four or five days. Then I took leave to depart from him, and when I was going out of the houfe, he fent the Captain of his guard to commit me to prifon, where I have remained nine weeks, without any matter

3   laid

MARY.
1557-8.
laid to my charge, faving he fent to me within fourteen days after, to declare in writing, after what fort the town was loft, which I did as nigh as I could remember. And at the Duke's next return to Bruges, I fent him a fupplication, defiring, that if any information were made againft me, that I might anfwer it in England, or otherwife at his pleafure. Whereupon he took order to fend me hither without paying any part of my charges, which I have promifed to anfwer. Moft humbly praying your Highnefs to confider my poor eftate, and willing heart, which I bear, and am moft bounden to your Grace's fervice, befeeching God to conferve your Majefty in all felicity.

No. VII.

Letters from Sir Nicholas Throkmorton, Ambaffador in France. From the Originals in the Paper Office.

[This fuite of Letters from Throckmorton is publifhed by way of addition to what Dr. Forbes has already printed, of the negociations of that able and well informed Ambaffador. He was then on the moft confidential terms with Cecil; but on his return home, not meeting with the reward he expected and deferved for his fervices, he ftruck in not only with the Leicefter faction, but with the Queen of Scots' party, and did the worft offices in his power to the Secretary; he had likewife quarrelled in France, and was at the eve of fighting with Sir T. Smith, his colleague, and the intimate friend of Cecil, and it is probable that the latter who went by plain ways to direct ends, difliked his intriguing fpirit, and dreaded his abilities. There is an original picture of him at Wobourn, which has a remarkable fubtle look.]

Sir Nicholas Throkmorton to Secret. Cecil.

SIR,

THE 25th of October, in the night, I received the Queen's Majefty's packet, with the letters and writings mentioned in the fame, by my fervant Davis; and alfo a letter from you, which amongft other things containeth your advice to have me write to her Majefty, to move the fame for order to be taken in the better difpatch of her affairs, which, you fay, are too much neglected. For anfwer whereunto, I fay, I know not where to begin: I looked by your laft to be fomewhat fatisfied and refolved, touching the greateft matter of all, I mean the Queen's marriage. I know not what to think, nor how to underftand your letter in that point. And the bruits be fo brim, and fo malicioufly reported here, touching the marriage of the

R   Lord

Lord Robert, and the death of his wife *, as I know not where to turn me, nor what countenance to bear. Sir, I thank God I had rather perish and quail with honefty, than live and beguile a little time with fhame.

And therefore I tell you plainly, until I hear off, or on, what you think in that matter, I fee no reafon in the advifing of her Majefty. Marry, to you I fay in private, that albeit I do like him for fome refpects well, and efteem him for many good parts and gifts of nature, that be in him, and do wifh him well to do; yet the love, duty, and affection, that I bear to the Queen's Majefty, and to the furety of herfelf, and her realm, doth, and fhall, during my life, take more place in me, than any friendfhip, or any particular cafe. And therefore I fay, if that marriage take place, I know not to what purpofe any advice or counfel fhould be given; for as I fee into the matter, none would ferve. If you think, that I have any fmall fkill or judgment in things at home, or on this fide, or can conjecture fequels, I do affure you, the matter fucceeding, our ftate is in great danger of utter ruin and deftruction. And fo far me-thinketh I fee into the matter, as I wifh myfelf already dead, becaufe I would not live in that time. I befeech you, like as I deal plainly with you, fo to fignify plainly unto me, not only what is done in that matter, but what you think will be the end. Thereupon you fhall perceive, that I will write unto her Majefty my poor advice, in fuch fort, as becometh a true and faithful fervant. And if the matter be not already determined, and fo far paft, as advice will not ferve, I require you, as you bear a true and faithful heart to her Majefty and the realm, and do defire to keep them from utter defolation, & in vifceribus Jefu Chrifti, I conjure you to do all your

---

* The daughter of Sir J. Roberfet; fhe died in a lonefome houfe in Berkfhire, belonging to a tenant of Lord R Dudley; her death was attended with fuch odd circumftances, as gave occafion to many unfavourable reports, and Lord Burleigh, in a note of his printed in the 1ft Vol. of the Hatfield Papers, takes notice of it, as affording juft grounds of fcandal

endeavour

endeavour to hinder that marriage. For, if it take place, there is
no counfel nor advice, that can help. Who would be either patron
or mariner, when there is no remedy to keep the fhip from finking?
As we begin already to be in derifion and hatred, for the bruit only,
and nothing taken here on this fide more affured than our deftruction ; fo if it take place, we fhall be *opprobrium hominum et abjectio*
plebis. God and religion, which be the fundaments, fhall be out of
eftimation ; the Queen our Sovereign difcredited, contemned, and
neglected ; our country ruined, undone, and made prey. Wherefore
with tears and fighs, as one being already almoft confounded, I
befeech you again and again, fet to your wits, and all your help to
ftay the commonwealth, which lieth now in great hazard.

Let us remember what this noble wife man faid, when he ufed
thefe words: " Ego enim exiftimo melius agi cum civibus privatim,
" fi tota refpublica fortunata fit, quam fi per fingulos cives felix
" fit, publicè vero labefactetur. Nam quum evertitur patria, is,
" cui privatim bene eft, nihil tamen minus et ipfe evertitur ; cui
" autem malè, is in illa profperè agente, multo magis incolumis eft."
For your letters, they be as fafe in my hand as in your own, and
more fafe in mine than in any meffenger's. Think it affuredly,
I am as jealous of your fafety and well doing, as yourfelf; and fo
conceive of me.

If you will be pleafed to write unto me fooner than you fhall have
occafion to fend a poft, my coufin H. Middlemore, my fteward,
can, I fuppofe, convey your letters fafely unto me. I am much
beguiled, if he be not an honeft and faithful young man; I pray you
deal with my letters as I do with yours; for all is not gold that
glitters, and that you may well perceive by fome men's new haunts.
It may like you to fhew this bearer fome favour for my fake, in his
fuit. I pray you alfo, let my Lord of Creigh find courtefy at your
hands. The man is well affected to you, for the bruit that

R 2   runneth

runneth of you. Thus I humbly take my leave of you. From Paris
the 28th of October, 1560.

Yours, &c.

N. THROKMORTON.

Sir Nicholas Throkmorton to Secret. Cecil.

Mr. SECRETARY,

BY letters which I wrote to you by the Lord of Creigh, of the 28th of this prefent, I fignified, that I minded not to depart out of this town, till Du Bois, mafter of the camp, were paffed by; now I am advertifed, that the 30th of this month, he went along here, and hath brought with him out of the places and forts of Picardy, one thoufand footmen, who marched together, by this town and Roan, towards Anjou, as it is told me; but the very truth, whither they fhall go, is not known but to himfelf and to the Duke of Guife, and to never a Captain of his company.

Their kind of marching is very ftrange. They keep together ftrong, as if it were in the enemy's country.

I am advertifed, that after thefe thoufand, come five hundred more; the places from whence thefe be taken, are filled up again with the Legionaires. Anjou is not far from Nantz, where the gallies lie; and therefore the matter is to be looked to, and the more, if there be any fhips or bottoms in rigging there, or near unto. And therefore it fhall not be amifs to have an eye thither, by fuch as trade that way from England, or by fuch other means, as you can devife, wherein I will alfo travail the beft I can. Hereof I thought good to advertife you: and alfo, that I am now upon my departure towards Orleans, the faid Du Bois being paffed by.

I fend

I send you herewith the last order that was taken for the assembly of the men at arms, to be at Orleans, as you shall perceive. You shall also receive a new almanack and prognostication of Nostradamus; but I think he never saw it.

I cannot perceive that the King of Navarre is yet come to the Court. This Scottish Gentleman, bearer hereof, is named Alexander Forster, laird of Torwood. I pray you let him have your favour, by your favour and your means, for his good usage, and quiet passing into his country, whither he repaireth presently. And thus I take my leave of you, wishing you in health your heart's desire. From Paris the last of October 1560.

Your's, &c.

N. THROKMORTON.

Sir Nicholas Throkmorton to the Queen.

IT may please your Majesty to be advertised, that since the sending of my letters unto the same the 28th of October, by my Lord of Creigh, upon knowledge given me, that the master of the camp, De Bois, was coming forward out of Picardy with 1500 men, I staid somewhat longer at Paris than I minded to have done, to understand what way he would take; wherein I signified somewhat to Mr. Secretary by my letters of the last of October, sent by the Laird of Torwoodhead, of Scotland, and as the said De Bois being passed by towards Angiers and Nantz, giveth cause of suspicion; and, therefore, considering what advertisement your Majesty hath of preparation there (which I know not), and his coasting that way greatly to be doubted, and that the galleys be at Nantz, which have lately been victualled; the worst is to be feared: so I thought not convenient to stay longer at Paris, but took my way towards Orleans, where I arrived

arrived the 4th of this prefent; and for my better proceeding, touching your Majefty's inftructions given unto me, immediately upon
my coming thither, I ufed means to fpeak with
the 6th of this prefent at night,   where
                            had proceeded with this King and Queen,
and their Council, fince his arrival here. Of the particularities of
whófe doings, the bearer hereof, your Majefty's fervant, whom I
have therein inftructed, fhall be able to inform your Majefty, to
whom it may like you to give credit.

                            that he had not, as they had, any com-
modity, either to fhew his commiffion, or to demand the ratification,
and that the 6th of this prefent, he was appointed to fhew his commiffion, and thereupon minded to demand the faid ratification. And
forafmuch as the chief caufe alleged by the King for the ftay of
the ratifying of the treaty between your Majefty and him, when it
was laft demanded, depended upon the priority (as this King took it)
of the Scottifh treaty, and that hitherto the faid Ambaffador was at
no point, nor could not tell whereupon to truft; albeit your Majefty
commandeth me by your letters of the 19th of October, to require
audience, and to demand the ratification eftfoons at this-King's
hands; yet becaufe I would the more groundly proceed in my charge,
by as much knowledge as I could get of the anfwer to be given to
the Scotch Ambaffador, I ftaid my demanding of audience, till I
might be informed, how he had proceeded, touching his charge.

    Having thus ftaid to fee what would fucceed the 6th of this pre-
fent, of the faid Ambaffador's doings, and perceiving the 7th of the
fame, that there was nothing done touching the ratification of his
treaty between France and Scotland, but that he had very good
words and promifes for his fatisfaction; I fent your Majefty's fervant
Mr. Somers, the fame night, to fpeak unto the Cardinal for audience,
who made anfwer, that the next day the King was determined to go
on hunting, fo as I could not that day fpeak with him; but he faid,
                                                                    that

that if I would the next morning fend unto him, he would fend me more particular word of the King's pleafure; whereupon the 8th of this month, I fent again unto him for that purpofe, and he fent me anfwer that I could not have audience before Monday the 11th of this prefent.

Notwithftanding the Cardinal his laft anfwer, the 10th of this prefent, about dinner time, he fent unto me a Gentleman to advertife me, that the King was fet to dinner, and was pleafed in the afternoon to give me audience; and therefore prayed me (if I would) to come to dinner to him.

After I had ftaid a little while at my lodging, being fet at dinner before his coming, he returned the fame Gentleman again unto me, to tell me that the King and he had dined and tarried for me; whereupon I repaired to the Court, and firft fpeaking with the Cardinal, and after with the King, I declared to either of them that part of your Majefty's inftructions given me, touching the demanding of the ratification. I received of them both one anfwer, which was, (they faid) that the Mafter of St. John's of Scotland was indeed come; but forafmuch as the King was greatly impeded through his own affairs, and could not have time to underftand his charge, and to give him audience, they had not as yet thoroughly confidered thefe things which he had to do with them; notwithftanding the King would fpeak with the faid Mafter of St. John's the next day (which was the 11th of this prefent) and then give him anfwer; whereupon, if I did fend my Secretary unto the Cardinal, I fhould know when I fhould eftfoons have accefs to the King, and then underftand his further pleafure.

The Lord of St. John's having been with the King's Council the 11th of this prefent, I looked to hear from the Cardinal (as he promifed) touching my charge; and ftaying two days without knowledge from him, I did, the 13th of this prefent, fend Mr. Somers to the Cardinal, to put him in remembrance, that I might know the King's pleafure,

touching

touching the ratification, feeing the Lord of St. John's had already been two days before with the Council. The Cardinal made him anfwer, that the King had been fo bufied, as he had no time, fince my being at the Court, to confider the matter. Mr. Somers told him, that I faid that with thefe delays the time paffed, and that your Majefty would both think it long, and judge a great fault in me, that there was no better expedition therein; the Cardinal faid hereunto, that the King had caufe to think the time as long as your Majefty did; but there was no remedy, and therefore I muft be contented.

After I had received this anfwer from the Cardinal, I did underftand, by good means, that fuch of the French King's Council, as had the fcanning and difcuffion of the treaty of Scotland in their hands, found divers faults and imperfections (as they expounded it), whereby the French King and Queen may have good reafon to refufe the ratification thereof, as (I am indeed advertifed) they mind to do. Whereupon weighing that it would be a long time before the Lord of St. John's could be anfwered, and that, in the end, the treaty fhould not be ratified, I thought not meet to ground my proceedings further upon the faid Ambaffador's delays, but to proceed more roundly to the demanding of the ratification of your Majefty's faid treaty. And becaufe the Cardinal had fent me two dilatory anfwers before, touching the fame, the 14th of this prefent in the forenoon, I fent Mr. Somers to the Cardinal to tell him, that I had received fince my being with him, other letters from her Majefty, and therefore prayed him to fignify unto me, when I might have audience (for I feared left that if I had fpoken of the treaty, he would further have delayed me). The Cardinal as then made him anfwer, that if he would come again in the afternoon, he would fend me word what I fhould do, which Mr. Somers did, and the Cardinal thereupon made anfwer, that the next day, the 15th of this prefent, I fhould have audience, and that he would fend a Gentleman unto me to advertife me of the time, and to conduct me to the Court.

The

The 14th day the Lord of St. John's (as I am informed) was earneft with the Cardinal, and preffed him for fome refolution, touching his charge. The Cardinal anfwered him, that the King's
Council had confidered the affairs he was fent for, and found, that
the King and Queen's fubjects of Scotland, fought to deprive the
King and Queen of the right of pre-eminence of the realm of Scotland, and to reduce it to the form of a republic; which he faid the
King and Queen could in no wife endure, as they fhould right well
perceive. The Lord of St. John's ufed as good means as he could
to perfuade the contrary to the Cardinal, who faid, Ufe no more
words to perfuade me in the matter, for we fee too thoroughly into
it, and (quoth he) what meaneth this dealing, that they fend you
hither in poft, and fend a great legation to the Queen of England,
with great fhow and pomp? I fpeak it not becaufe we take exceptions to you, as though you were not meet enough to take the charge
of the matter, but we do fee the little reverence they have towards
their Sovereigns, and the great eftimation they have of the Queen
of England; and it appeareth by their doings, that they defire all
the world fhould fee it. But my Lord, quoth the Cardinal, you
fhall not need to trouble yourfelf any more with the matter, for you
fhall have your difpatch the 17th of this month, and the King and
Queen mind to fend two Gentlemen into your country fhortly, who
fhall declare on their behalf, the reafons why the King and Queen
refufe to ratify your treaty.

The 15th of this prefent, after the King had dined, the Cardinal
fent a Gentleman unto me, to accompany me to the Court, where
being arrived, Monf. de Lanfac, a Knight of the Order, entertained
me a while, in the chamber next to the King's chamber, until the
Cardinal of Lorrain came unto me, out of the King's chamber (after
I had paufed with the faid de Lanfac), unto whom I faid, Monfieur
Cardinal, you do well remember, that upon Sunday laft at my laft
audience, renewing on the Queen my Miftrefs's behalf to the King,

S   the

the demand for the King and Queen's ratification of the treaty concluded and accorded in Scotland, by the deputies of both their Majesties, the King and you answered me, that when his Majesty and his Council had thoroughly considered the matters of Scotland, which should be within three or four days, I should have my answer, and for that now five days be past, and I hear nothing of the King's pleasure, and also I being, by late letters from her Majesty, commanded to renew again the demand for the ratification, have desired audience, to put the King in remembrance thereof.

The Cardinal answered, that the King was a little impeached, and therefore I must a while take patience; but, quoth he, as unto the ratification of the treaty, the King being a Prince of honour, meaneth to proceed thereafter, and will promise nothing but he will perform, and therefore he will look well to what he promiseth. The Princes, quoth he, be equal, and the King doth not mean so to derogate from himself, as to begin to do an act first, thereby to abase himself. In these cases the Princes must execute together, and, quoth he, you must not take it, that the King doth look for any pre-eminence at the Queen, your Mistress's hands. The King and his Council, quoth he, have seen all that the Master of St. John's hath brought; and otherwise also understandeth the truth of their proceedings in Scotland, which is so far out of order, as if your Mistress were arbiter, she would not think meet, that the King should ratify the treaty, as we shall give her to understand by such Ministers, as the King doth mean presently to send into Scotland, through England.

I said unto the Cardinal, Monsieur, doth not the King mean to ratify the treaty?

You shall anon, quoth the Cardinal, know the King's pleasure therein. I said unto him, the Queen my Mistress will find it very strange, if there be any more delays used in that behalf, and because you are, quoth I, the King's principal Counsellor, I will declare

unto you the occasions that the Queen my Mistress hath to find Her- ELIZA-
self grieved, and very strange handled of a Prince, that pretendeth BETH.
to bear her amity.

Firft, I will pafs over all the evasions that have been hitherto used,
touching the ratification of the treaty, which you know have been
many, and I will remember you, that contrary to the exprefs words
of the treaty, the King doth the Queen my Miftrefs this injury, as
to bear yet her arms quartered with his, as hath been moft manifeftly feen, at his entry at St. Dennis, and laftly at this town, where
they hang yet openly upon every gate, and here at the court-gate
very notoriously.

Moreover, the Queen, my Miftrefs's fubjects, be daily fpoiled at
the fea, either by the King's fubjects, or by pirates of this nation;
and no reftitution can be had by any means, fo as there is no difference between your peace and war.

Thirdly, The Queen my Miftrefs, doth underftand, that in fundry
ports of this realm, as at Havre de Grace and in other places, there
be fhips prepared to do either fuch like enterprifes or worfe, and it
is not alfo unknown that all along the coaft, there is preparation to
make a navy to the fea.

Her Majefty doth alfo underftand of the amaffing of forces by
land, as well in this realm as elfewhere in Almain and Switzerland;
and now laftly, confidering, after fo many promifes, thefe new delays to be ufed for the ratification of the treaty, will move the Queen
my Miftrefs, together with thefe former injuries, and caufes of fufpicion, occafion to hold the King's meaning greatly fufpected.

And finally, the Queen is advertifed, that your galleys, which
lately arrived at Nantz, there to winter, be now victualled, and fhall
fhortly be brought into the narrow feas; and albeit, quoth I, your
force gathered by land, may feem to have fome colour reafonable,
for the appeafing of the tumults in this realm; yet there is no caufe

S 2   why

why the preparing of an army by fea, fhould ferve to any fuch purpofe.

The Cardinal anfwered, as unto the ufing and bearing of the arms of England, the King and the Queen did ufe them, as you know of long time before, and not without reafon and title, as it is thought. We fee no reafon why the King fhould leave his right, until others do that which they are bound to do: for where you allege for your purpofe the treaty, we fay it is no treaty until it be ratified, and then there is no reafon why the King and Queen fhould in that behalf more fatisfy your Miftrefs than fhe fhould fatisfy them, nor we begin before fhe begin.

I told him, your Majefty had performed all things on your part, that was required by the treaty, and further, had fhewn great kindnefs and pleafures to fundry of the King's Minifters, as in lending them money, in tranfporting their people forth of Scotland, in retiring your force from thence, and difarming your navy; and in recompence hereof, there was nothing done on their behalfs.

The Cardinal faid, I will tell you frankly; the Scots, the King's fubjects, do perform no point of their duties; the King and the Queen hath the name of their Sovereigns; and your Miftrefs hath the effect and the obedience. They would bring the realm to a republic, and fay in their words, they be the King's fubjects. To tell you of the particular diforders, quoth he, were too long; every man doth what he lift: all this is too far out of order, and when fault is found with them, they threaten the King with the aid of the Queen your Miftrefs: let your Miftrefs either make them obedient fubjects, or let her rid her hands of them; for rather than they fhall be at this point, the King will quit all. They have made a league with the Queen your Miftrefs, of themfelves, without us. What manner of dealing is this of fubjects? Thereupon it is they bear themfelves fo proudly. What conveniency is there in their

3   doings?

doings?: They have fent hither a mean man in poft to the King and
Queen, their Sovereigns, ànd to the Queen, your Miftrefs, a great
and folemn legation. To be plain with you, quoth he, the King
cannot like thefe dóings. As I told you the King meaneth to fend
two Gentlemen; firft, to the Queen your Miftrefs, to inform her
of the things where the King is offended, and the caufe why he
refufeth the ratification of the treaty; and they fhall pafs into Scotland, to declare unto them the King and Queen's pleafure. And
where you fay your Miftrefs hath in all things performed the treaty,
we fay the Scots do by her countenance perform no point of the
treaty; and moreover fhe hath broken the old treaty, in giving
paffport and licence to the King's fubjects of Scotland, to come into
England; and for that purpofe neither motion hath been made by
our Ambaffador, nor letter from the King nor Queen, their Sovereigns, granted them in that behalf.

: As to the fpoiling, quoth the Cardinal, of your Miftrefs's fubjects
at the fea; this complaint is too general; you have made but one
complaint unto us particularly, and what fpeedy and favourable difpatch the plaintiffs had, I report me to yourfelf, and to them. We
could remember you of divers particular matters, whereof we have
but cold redrefs. If you inform·us of the depredations, and the
offenders, and then can get no redrefs, then you have caufe to complain, and to charge us.

: As to the equipage of the fhips, quoth he, at Havre de Grace,
and in other places, true it is, the Admiral doth fet forth four or
five, fome for Brazil, and fome for Mina *. Of thefe there is no caufe
why you fhould be jealous. The Ambaffador of Spain was in hand
with us for the fame purpofe. The Admiral hath afcertained him
with his own hand, that they are for thefe voyages, and if there be
any other matter in it, it will coft him his head. We are not fo

---

* On the Guinea coaft.

jealous

jealous of your preparations of five or fix ships, which be ready to come forth of Thamife.

As to the affembling of our forces by land, quoth the Cardinal, we have brought them from Picardy hither into the midft of the realm, you had more caufe to fufpect them being at Picardy than where they be, I am fure you know as well as we where they be.

For Almain and Switzerland, I affure you of mine honour, we levy not a man; indeed, our Commiffaries be gone to warn our Colonels, to be ready when we fhall have need of them.

As to the galleys, quoth he, we cannot fuffer our men to be unvictualled; but they be in no readinefs to make a voyage; for many of our chief men be gone to Marfeilles, there to winter; but what and the King do remove them to fome other place, will you be jealous if the King do remove his fhips or galleys, from one port to another upon his own coaft, as his affairs requireth, or the more commodious harbour for them? we be not fo quarrelling nor jealous when your fhips go from one place to another.

This great legation forth of Scotland, quoth he, goeth for the marriage of the Queen your Miftrefs with the Earl of Arran, what fhall fhe have with him? I think, quoth he, her heart too great to marry with fuch one as he is, and one of the Queen's fubjects.

But to conclude with you, quoth the Cardinal, the King will fee the obedience of his fubjects, and their duties better performed, before he ratify the treaty. I will now, quoth he, go tell the King that you have long tarried for him; and fo he departed from me.

Shortly after, I was brought to the King, whom I put in remembrance what paffed betwixt us the 10th of this month at my laft audience; and that I was now come to demand his ratification of the treaty again.

The King anfwered, that the Scots, his fubjects, had in no point obferved their duty, nor no part of the treaty; and for that caufe,

he

he could not ratify your Majesty's treaty. I told him that your Majesty would find it strange, that after so many delays, the matter was now so answered; and therefore your Majesty had given me in charge to tell him on your part, and so declared unto him all your griefs, which I did as I had done unto the Cardinal, and set forth unto him all the good parts used on your behalf towards him, the Queen his wife, and all their Ministers and subjects.

His answer was, that he had not failed on his part to do the like; and he would send two of his Gentlemen to your Majesty, to inform you of all; and, quoth he, I am sure mine uncle the Cardinal hath answered you to all those points that you complain of; and so he dismissed me.

The Duke of Guise did accompany me from the King, to whom I did reiterate this strange manner of dealing, and recited unto him those your Majesty's causes of misliking the King's usage and proceedings towards you, as I had done to his brother.

The Duke answered me as the Cardinal did, to every point; and added further, in answering the complaint of the depredations, and slow restitution, that they had a great deal more cause to complain, as well for sundry spoliations made upon the King's subjects, by your Majesty's subjects, as also for the taking of his brother's goods, the Marquis D'Elbeuf, as corn of the King and other munition, with sundry other spoils, whereof they had but slow amends.

I told him those matters (if there were any such) were done before the treaty was made; and so the Cardinal and Monf. de L'Aubespine called him from me.

I desired to speak with the Queen mother, and so I was brought to her by Monf. de Lanfac.

The said Queen was accompanied with the Marshal Brisac. I did repeat unto her all your Majesty's proceedings; since the making of the treaty, at good length, all the office that I had used in the demanding the ratification; and lastly the answer I had received of the King

King and his Council, together with the declaration of injuries and caufes of offence offered fundry ways unto your Majefty. I fet forth unto her, as I could, the good opinion your Majefty had always of her, and of her good affection and inclination to maintain the King her fon, and you in good amity and intelligence.

For anfwer, fhe thanked your Majefty for your good opinion of her; and faid, you were therein nothing deceived; and it fhould always appear by her doings. As unto the ratification, fhe knew the King and his Council had declared reafons unto me, for the ftay of it; which your Majefty fhould know fhortly by exprefs men from the King her fon.

As unto the injuries and fufpicions, fhe faid, fhe was fure the Cardinal and the Duke of Guife had opened enough unto me, to hold myfelf contented; ending, that for her part, fhe would do the beft fhe could, to keep both your Majefties, your realms, and fubjects, in good terms and amity.

Whilft I was talking with the Queen Mother, the French Queen came in, unto whom, after the communication ended with the Queen Mother, I faid, Madame, it is not unknown to you, how the ratification of the treaty lately made in Scotland, hath feemed hitherto to have been deferred, becaufe the nobility and people of your realm of Scotland did not fend hither to the King and you, to do their duties, and now that the Queen my Miftrefs doth underftand, they have in that part, and in the name of them all, fatisfied their duty, by fending hither the Lord of St. John's to the King and you; her Majefty hath commanded me to demand of your Majefty the ratification of the treaty, accorded and concluded by both your deputies at Edinburgh.

The Queen anfwered, Such anfwer as the King my Lord and hufband, and his Council, hath made you in that matter, might fuffice to anfwer you; but becaufe you fhall know I have reafon

to

to do as I do, I will tell you what moveth me to refuse to ratify the E L I Z A-
treaty; my fubjects of Scotland do their duty in no thing, nor have
not performed one point that belongeth to them. I am, quoth fhe,
their Queen, and fo they call me, but they ufe me not fo; they
have done what pleafeth them, and though I have not many faithful
there, yet thofe few that be there on my party, were not prefent
when thefe matters were done, nor at this affembly. I will have
them affemble by my authority, and proceed in their doings after
the laws of the realm, which they fo much boaft of, and keep none
of them. They have fent hither a poor Gentleman to me, who I
difdain to have come in the name of them all, to the King and me,
in fuch a legation. They have, quoth fhe, fent great perfonages to
your Miftrefs. I am their Sovereign, but they take me not fo:
They muft be taught to know their duties. In this fpeech the Queen
uttered fome choler and ftomach againft them.

I faid, as to the Lord of St. John's, I know him not; but he is
great Prior of Scotland, and you know by others, what rank that
eftate hath, equal to any Earl within your realm.

The Queen anfwered, I do not take him for great Prior, for he
is married; I marvel how it happeneth, that they could fend other
manner of men to the Queen your miftrefs.

I faid, Madame, I have heard, that if your Majefty proceed gracioufly with the Lord of St. John's, in obfervation of all that which
was by the Bifhop of Vallence and Monf. de Randan promifed in
the King and your names; the Nobles and State of Scotland doth
mind to fend hither unto the King and you, a greater legation.

Then the King and I, quoth fhe, muft begin with them.

Madame, quoth I, I am forry that the ratification of the treaty is
refufed for that matter, together with other injuries offered to the
Queen my Miftrefs, as (contrary to the exprefs articles of the treaty)
the King and you do bear openly the arms of England, which will

T   give

give the Queen my Miſtreſs occaſion greatly to ſuſpect your well meaning unto her.

Mine uncles, quoth ſhe, have ſufficiently anſwered you in this matter: and for your part, I pray you do the office of a good Miniſter betwixt us, and ſo ſhall you do well; and ſo the Queen diſmiſſed me, and Monſ. de Lanſac brought me to my horſe.

Thus your Majeſty may perceive my negociation with this King, the Queens, the Cardinal, and the Duke of Guiſe, touching the ratification, the 15th of this preſent.

The Duke of Guiſe told me, that it was determined that Meſſrs. de Noailles, late Ambaſſador with your Majeſty, and de Croc, were they whom the King would ſend into Scotland.

As touching the occurrents of this Court, it may pleaſe your Majeſty to be advertiſed, that the King of Navarre being on his way to this Court, hath had letters, as I am informed, written unto him, of great good opinion conceived of him by this King, with all other kind of courteſies, to cauſe him to repair thither. Nevertheleſs, upon his coming, being accompanied with his brethren the Cardinal of Bourbon, and Prince of Condé, after they have done their reverence to the King and Queens, the Prince of Condé was brought before the Council, who committed him forthwith priſoner to the guard of Meſſrs. de Breſy and Chauveney, two Captains of the guard, and their companies of 200 archers. He remaineth cloſe in a houſe, and no man permitted to ſpeak with him; and his proceſs is in hand. And I hear he ſhall now be committed priſoner to the caſtle of Loches, the ſtrongeſt priſon in all this realm.

The King of Navarre goeth at liberty, but as it were a priſoner, and is every other day on hunting, and lieth out of the town at his pleaſure, and as it is judged, and as it ſeemeth indeed, beareth and alloweth his brother's handling.

The ſaid King hath ſince his coming hither, ſent one in poſt to Rome, to acknowledge his obedience to the Pope.

He

He fhall, as it is faid, forego his Governorfhip of Guyenne, and the fame fhall be beftowed upon Monf. de Termes.

Madame de Boy, the Admiral of France his fifter, mother to the Princefs of Condé, is taken and conftituted prifoner.

It is faid, that the Vifdame of Chartres fhall come to Orleans, where the Knights of the Order fhall be affembled; and he thereupon is like to fee the end of his procefs

I am informed, that the Prince of Condé, his * procefs being in the hands of the Parliament of Paris, the Prefident and Council of the fame have anfwered, that the Prince may not be judged by them, but by his Peers, becaufe he is of the blood Royal.

The Dutchefs of Ferrara, mother to the Duke that now is, according to that I wrote heretofore to your Majefty, is arrived at this Court, the 7th of this prefent, and was received by the King of Navarre, the French King's brethren, and all the great Princes of this Court.

Monf. de Martigues hath of late been at Paris, and there committed himfelf to juftice for manners' fake, for the late outrage committed there by him. He had his pardon in his hands; he is now returned to the Court, very much made of, and waited upon, with above twenty of the braveft and beft Captains of France.

The French King mindeth to keep his eftate here at Orleans, where all the armour is taken from the townfmen.

The Marfhal Termes is at Poiâiers, with divers companies of men at arms; where alfo the townfmen be ufed, as they be at Orleans.

The Cardinal of Tournon being Legate for the Pope in France, is arrived here at Orleans, and is of the King's Privy Council.

At Bourdeaux, and in all places between this town and that, all is very quiet, notwithftanding divers bruits to the contrary, and (as

* About the confpiracy of Amboife.

one

ELIZA-
BETH. one Swanne, a fubject of your Majefty's, informeth me, who came
directly thence in poft) all the fea coafts are furnifhed with men at
arms, and foldiers, to what end no man knoweth.

The houfe of Guife practifeth, by all the means they can, to make
the Queen Mother Regent of France at this next affembly; fo as
they are like to have all the authority ftill in their hands, for fhe is
wholly theirs.

It is faid, that the French King mindeth, with the time, to convert all his Abbeys into Commandaries of divers Orders, as there be
in Spain.

It is faid, that Ferdinand of Auftriche levieth men in Almain;
but to what end I cannot learn

The Rhinegrave remaineth ftill in Almain, and goeth from one
Prince to another. His being there is diverfly difcourfed upon, confidering the time of the year is unmeet for paftime.

The Sophy is dead; his fon hath conjoined himfelf with Bajazet
the Turk's fecond fon, who having their forces together, are about
to deprive the Turk and his eldeft fon of the empire, which news
was fo difpleafing to the Turk, as it is thought he is thereupon
dead; and it is advertifed from Venice, that he was in very great
danger of his life, and could hardly efcape.

The French King and his Court do remove hence the 19th of
this prefent towards Semmceau, the Queen Mother's houfe, and
mindeth not, as it is faid, to return hither before his eftates be affembled.

Two fons of Oconer, who have been in France thefe eight years,
are lately difpatched hence into Ireland, as I am informed. I doubt
not but that there is good order, that they fhall be able to do no
hurt.

It is fecretly talked here, that there is fomewhat in hand, touching the ifles of Guernfey, Jerfey, and Scilly.

There is an advertisement come hither, from the French Agent in
Flanders, that the Dutchess of Parma hath put to death, for the cause of religion, either two of your Majesty's subjects, or else denizens being of Flanders, Whether it be true or not, I am not assured; but these men seem to be very glad of it, as I am well informed.

There is here arrived an Ambassador from the Duke of Savoy, named Monf. de Moreto, who, as I understand, shall shortly repair into England, to speak with your Majesty from the said Duke.

De Lignerol is also upon his dispatch, if he be not already arrived in England before this bearer.

I am informed, that Charlebois shall come away from Dunbarre, and that Croc shall remain there in his stead.

The King of Spain hath kept divers of his Cortes, and is still in following the same. He maketh ready one hundred galleys, as I am informed, and a good number of ships, and withal maketh preparation for an army. It is said to be to renew his enterprize of Tripoli; but many do doubt, that they be for some other purpose.

The said King oweth twenty-one millions of Ducats, as it is judged; and were it not, as it is said, for his new Minister, he had been brought very low for money.

The Pope hath granted to the said King, licence to sell 50,000 Crowns of Spiritual Revenue, the profit whereof will rise to, at the least, two millions of crowns.

The said King hath sent in present to the French King, as I am informed, six very beautiful Jennets of Spain of his own; and hath suffered his servants to buy in Spain fifteen others of the most principal pieces that could be found.

The General Council is, by the order and consent of the Pope, the Emperor, the Kings of France and Spain, appointed to be at Trent, where not only the said Princes will assist by their Ministers, but also the Kings of Portugal, Poland, and Navarre, with the States of Italy.

Monsieur

Monfieur de Ferme, a Secretary of this Court, who went with Monfieur de Bourdezieve to Rome, is returned with the Pope's grant for the taking of an 100,000 Crowns of the Spiritual Revenues to be fold. The confideration of which grant, and the like to the King of Spain is (as I am informed) to the end, that the money made thereof be employed againft the Proteftants and heretics, as they term them.

Notwithftanding the late treaty, your Majefty's arms have been fet up quartered, when the French King made his entry in St. Dennis, and were alfo in like fort fet up at the King's entry here, upon the town and Court gates, where they do ftill remain in open fhew to the world.

I am well informed, that the French King maketh reckoning to have of his fufpect towns and fubjects, about three millions of franks, and his charge in going up and down, to punifh his fubjects, borne.

I am alfo credibly informed, that there be four fhips of war in fetting forth at Newhaven, which are faid to be for the voyage of Brafil, and that there be four others in Brittany, which are bruited to be for Peru.

A great Perfonage of this Court hath faid (as I am right well informed) that if the King had not thus been conftrained to feek to chaftife his fubjects, your Majefty's realm had ere this felt him.

I am informed, that the French King mindeth to make a citadel at Calais, which fhall ftretch to St. Peter's church, and that the haven fhall be conveyed into the town.

I am alfo well advertifed, that there is order given to Monf. de Trez, Mafter of the Ordnance here, to convey to Calais both munition and artillery; and that the galleys fhall be brought about, and remain there.

I am alfo informed, that becaufe the galleys fhall be the better able to fight with fhips, and to turn in their fight, that they have here
devifed

devifed to make a part of them fhorter, and to make a new mould ELIZA-
of galleys.

I am informed, that one Hector Wentworth, an Englifhman,
who hath been here in France thefe twelve years, and fpeaketh good
French, being withal a proper man with an auburn beard, hath of
late robbed (as it is reported by him) Capt. Boys, mafter of the
camp, who was his mafter; and that he is thereupon fled into England.   He lately before ferved Charlebois, and was in Leith when
it was befieged.   I have not before heard of him; but if none of
your Majefty's fubjects heard of him at Leith, his being in England
is much to be doubted; and therefore good heed is to be taken of
him, if he may be found.

I am by very fecret and credible means informed, that the French
King hath taken up in Auvergne and Brittany, eight hundred oxen,
which be part of them already in Normandy at feeding.   This
provifion of victual in fo great quantity in one place, giveth a
fhrewd likelihood, that they do in all places together make greater.

The Earl Bothwell fhall be (as I am informed) difpatched hence
forthwith; he hath promifed them here to do great things in Scotland, from whence he hath received lately great comfort by one who
is come thence with great diligence by fea.

I am advertifed, that de Noailles, and de Croc, who, as it was
told me, fhould be fent out of hand, fhall not now be difpatched
of long time, if they be fent at all; and that this matter is to no
purpofe, but to abufe your Majefty and the Scots both together.

I do alfo underftand, that the French King hath fent order to Marfeilles for the bringing about of eight galleys more.

Since the writing of this before, I underftand that the Earl Bothwell is ftaid from going into Scotland, and hath a prefent given him
of fix hundred Crowns, and is made Gentleman of the King's
chamber, with the fee thereto belonging.

And:

And thus having none other occurrents to write prefently unto your Majefty, I befeech God long to preferve the fame, in health, honour, and all profperity.

From Orleans, the 17th of Nov. 1560.

Your Majefty's, &c.

N. THROKMORTON.

Sir Nicholas Throkmorton to Secretary Cecil.

1560.
Nov. 17th.

SIR,

I WISH, that others would, as you will, weigh thefe mens proceedings and my advertifements, to be of more importance than news, and of more danger than not to be cared and provided for in time. Make your reckoning, thefe men will effay their fortune, and the King of Spain can be contented to fuffer her Majefty to fall into fuch terms, as you muft be driven to pray him to do with that ftate and realm, what pleafeth him: he accounteth you muft needs come to that point, fince you difpleafe all, and fatisfy no party. I truft there fhall be fuch feafonable counfel given in time, as your enemies and fufpected friends fhall be beguiled of the expectation they have of our calamity. The Lord of St. John's of Scotland, in his negociation, hath behaved himfelf very difcreet and (as he is taken to be) like a fincere gentleman. His behaviour hath been fuch in his charge, as his country hath had good caufe to be pleafed with him, and the Queen's Majefty no lefs, for her own particular affair. I pray you be a mean, that her Majefty may allow well of his doings; and that he may find the fame, when he cometh
into

into England. . I underſtand by letter that I lately received from Sir Thomas Chamberlain, of the 2d of this month, that he can obtain of the King of Spain as yet little favour, to keep one of his ſervants from the inquiſitor's apprehenſion. I ſay, that amity will prove to us worſe than enmity. Aſſuredly I fear him more than the French, and he will occaſion more inconveniency amongſt us. Let not her Majeſty be deceived, for ſurely he meaneth not well, whatſoever his Miniſter there doth make ſhew of. I think, notwithſtanding that theſe men did promiſe to ſend their Miniſters to ſatisfy her Majeſty for the ſtay of the ratification forthwith, you ſhall not hear of them theſe twenty-days, as I have intelligence. Peradventure Monſ. de Sevre * ſhall ſay ſomewhat to retain you longer in hope, that the Spring may be advanced before you think of the matter. I am ſure this refuſal of the ratification doth trouble you there at home; but, will you know how it cometh to paſs? I will be ſhort in it. Firſt, to ſave their honour and intereſt, whereupon I know they were egged by the Spaniſh practice and Miniſters. Theſe occaſions did grow from themſelves; but theſe were not ſufficient. From thence they were to do thus by theſe reaſons animated; your haſty diſarming, and ſpecially of your navy; her Majeſty's great inclination to live in pleaſure and quietneſs, which they ſay they did many ways copy; that neither Counſellor nor conductor was rewarded; that all men, which did at this time ſervice, were diſpleaſed; that her Majeſty would do her own pleaſure in all things, ſo as there was none to take the ſpecial care of her affairs. And laſtly and chiefly, that they take it for truth and certain, that her Majeſty will marry the Lord Robert Dudley; whereby they aſſure themſelves, that all foreign alliance and aid is ſhaked off, and do expect more diſcontentation thereby amongſt yourſelves. Thus you ſee your ſore; God grant it do not with rankling feſter too far and too dangerouſly. Thus I

* French Ambaſſador in England.

U

humbly

humbly take my leave of you. From Orleans the 17th of November, 1560.

Your's, &c.

N. THROKMORTON.

    Sir Nicholas Throkmorton to Secretary Cecil.

Mr. SECRETARY,

THIS Gentleman, bearer hereof, is fent prefently from his
Mafter, the Duke of Savoy, in legation to the Queen's Majefty, to congratulate with her Highnefs for her happy avenement
to the Crown. He faith, the unquietnefs in his Mafter's country,
and his raw-coming thither, after the late accord, have been caufes,
that this office hath been done no fooner; his name is Monf. de
Morette, nephew and heir to old Morette, that hath been Ambaffador from late King Francis, to King Henry VIII. well known to my
Lord of Pembroke, and my Lord Marquis of Northampton, and
to my Lord Admiral, and my Lord Chamberlain, and both to Mr.
Wotton. This man was, in the late French King's days, Gentleman
of his chamber, and fince retired and fettled at home in Piedmont.

Befides this kindnefs of congratulation, he hath to break with her
Majefty, in the Duke his Mafter's name, for marriage with the
Duke of Nemours, which, I perceive by communication paffed betwixt us, he mindeth to fet forth, if the matter be not too far paffed
at home, as all the bruit is here, that it is. For this Gentleman
was told by the Pope's Ambaffador here, that he fhould come into
England in good time to her Highnefs's marriage, with the mafter
of her horfes. In cafe this Gentleman fhall find her Majefty at
liberty

ELIZA-
BETH.

liberty from any such thing, and that her Highness do shew any inclination to hear of this his overture; I perceive by him, as he said, that the King of Spain and this King too, are so desirous to have it take effect, that they will both travail, what they can, to bring it to pass. Hereof I thought good to advertise you, as I have done the Queen's Majesty, by my letter now unto her.

This Gentleman's good usage, and good entertainment by all good means, I recommend unto you; he is a very good Courtier, and therefore knoweth what belongeth thereunto, and so will report as he findeth. And so I take my leave of you. From Orleans the 18th of November, 1560.

Your's, &c.

N. THROKMORTON.

Sir Nicholas Throkmorton to the Queen.

1560.
Nov. 28th.

IT may please your Majesty, since my letters to the same of the 17th of November, sent by your servant, Mr. Jones, and others from me, of the 18th of the same, sent by Monf. de Morette, Ambassador from the Duke of Savoy to your Majesty; I do understand that the Bishop of Limoges, Ambassador from this King to the King Catholic, hath of late insinuated to the said King, that the Nobility and States of Scotland have very evil accomplished the late treaty accorded at Edinburgh, betwixt the said King's Deputies and the States of Scotland; and much less performed their duties and obedience, which doth belong to good subjects: whereupon the said Ambassador hath, on his Master's behalf, required the King of Spain to give the French King, his good brother, advice and counsel, how

U 2

he

he fhall intreat the faid Scots his fubjects, and in what wife he may
beft by his counfel proceed with them.   The King of Spain anfwered, doth the King my brother mean in this matter fincerely?
and doth he demand mine advice, as one, that would be by me advifed? or doth he move this matter to prove what I would fay to
it? It was anfwered by the faid French Ambaffador, that the King
his Mafter meant fincerely, and as one that defired to have his good
brother's advice and counfel in that matter.   Then the King of
Spain faid, I will fend to mine Ambaffador, refident in France, to
know of the King my brother, how he mindeth of himfelf, to
proceed with them, whether by force and reftraint, or by other
means.

Agreeable whereunto, Monf. de Chantonet, Ambaffador, refident
here, for the King Catholic, the 18th of this prefent, had audience
of the French King, and did on his Mafter's behalf defire to know,
how and after what fort this King did mind to proceed with his
fubjects of Scotland.   It was anfwered by the French King and his
Council, that he the French King did not mind to ufe force againft
them, if he might otherwife have them well ordered, and obedient
fubjects.

The 19th of this prefent, Monf. de Chantonet, after his audience,
did advertife me of the premifes by his Secretary.

What this brotherly participation betwixt thefe Princes, of the
Scottifh affairs, doth mean; and to what end this kind communication of thefe matters will tend, I know not.   But becaufe your
Majefty did, by your letters of the 19th of October, command me to
advertife Sir Thomas Chamberlain, your Highnefs's Ambaffador in
Spain, what fpeed I fhould receive of thefe men, touching the
ratification of the treaty, and of fuch other things as fhould feem
to me meet for your Majefty's further fervice; I have advertifed Sir
Thomas Chamberlain, by my letter of the 20th of November, how

                                                          I have

I have proceeded with these men, and how I am by them answered; **ELIZA-BETH.** whereby my whole doings may appear unto him at good length, with such other things, as I thought convenient for him to know, meet for your Majesty's service; the copy of which my letter to the said Sir Thomas Chamberlain, I have herewith sent to your Majesty, whereby the same may perceive at good length the particularities of this my whole dispatch to your said Ambassador in Spain.

It may like your Majesty to be further advertised, that I have intelligence, that the King of Spain hath in great haste given order to flay the five thousand Spaniards in the Low Country; yea, though they be embarked, and upon the sea, to revoke them, if it be possible, who should have gone to Sicilia.

The Prince of Spain is still sick of his quartan, and judged not to be long lived. It is now said that he shall be fianced to the Dowager of Portugal, his father's sister, who (some think) shall come to be Regent in Flanders, after she is so fianced.

The posts do come apace and often of late, betwixt the French King and the King of Spain. Of late, (whatsoever the matter meaned) Monf. de Chantonet would not suffer Gamboa, your Majesty's pensioner, to speak with me, who came to this town the 17th of this month, from Spain, in post, to pass into Flanders, for so the said Gamboa sent me word.

Whereas in my letters of the 17th of this month, I did advertise your Majesty, that the Earl Bothwell did not so soon return to his country; since that time the said Earl is departed suddenly from this Court, to return into Scotland by Flanders, and hath made boast, that he will do great things, and live in Scotland, in the despite of all men.

He is a glorious, rash, and hazardous young man; and therefore it were meet his adversaries should both have an eye to him, and also keep him short.

This

This King, by an indifpofition, that he hath found in himfelf, within thefe three or four days, fince my laft letters to your Majefty, of the 18th of this month, hath refolved, at the difpatch hereof, not to ftir from this town, until the Affembly of the Eftates be paft.

I have herewith fent to your Majefty, a letter that Sir Thomas Chamberlain, your Ambaffador in Spain, did lately fend to me.

The Lord Seton had his difpatch from hence the 22d of this month, and had eight hundred franks paid him of the arrearages of his penfion due to him, for being Gentleman of the King's Chamber; and for the fatisfaction of his money difburfed by him for their provifions at Leith, and for fuch other neceffaries as he did then furnifh them of, he hath affignation upon the Queen's domain in Scotland. This King and Queen hath alfo given him in reward, an abbey in the north part of Scotland, which is thought, if he may enjoy it, will be worth to him yearly four thoufand Crowns of the Sun. When the faid Lord Seton did take his leave of the French King, the King thanked him for his good and faithful fervice done unto him, and did affure him to reward him liberally for it; and fo hath the faid King affured him, that fuch in Scotland as have, from the higheft to the loweft, offended him, and the Queen his wife, fhall know and feel what it is to be difobedient fubjects to fuch a great Prince.

The Lord of St. John's weighing the refufal of the ratification, the ftate and maniment of the affairs of his own country, and confidering thefe men's determinations, together with fuch intelligences, as he hath of the French's intents towards them in Scotland, did lately require me to recommend unto your Majefty the fpecial care and order of their affairs in Scotland. For, faid he unto me, unlefs the Queen your miftrefs do order and manage our matters, confidering the time and terms that we ftand in, we be utterly undone; and confequently great danger and peril will after enfue to her realm.

6   For,

For, said he, unless her Majesty direct us, and put substantial order amongst us, we shall among ourselves fall asunder, and so bring upon us great confusion; and such is our case and danger, as it requireth no delay.

The Lord Seton hath a letter from the French Queen to your Majesty, and hath also in charge to present unto your Highness the said Queen's picture, as I hear.

These men do much depend, among others, upon the advice of one Henry Sencler in Scotland; for the Lord Seton hath letters from hence to the said Sencler.

It may please your Majesty to be further advertised, that the state of the Prince of Condé his process, at the dispatch hereof, was in these terms: The King had sent his Chancellor and sundry Presidents, together with others of his learned Council, to the said Prince, to examine him, three or four times. The Prince would never answer them to any interrogations, but refused them all, as insufficient to examine him; saying, that the knowledge of his cause did not appertain to men of their quality; for being a Prince of the blood, he said, his process was to be adjudged either by the Princes of the blood, or by the twelve Peers; and therefore willed the Chancellor and the rest to trouble him no further.

The King of Navarre's Chancellor is taken prisoner, and is looked for to be brought hither every day. Monf. de Jarnac did take him in the said Chancellor's own house in Guyenne; whereat many do much marvel, the said Jarnac being always esteemed well affected to the King of Navarre.

The Abbot of St. Saluce returned from Bruffels by this Court to Rome; he had conference with the Cardinal of Lorrain of your Majesty; and, as I understand, made here a very lewd discourse of your Majesty, of your religion, of the fruits thereof, and of your proceedings. He tarried here eight days, and departed hence towards Rome the 20th of this present.

I am

..I am credibly advertised, that one named Villemort, servant to the late Dowager of Scotland, hath advertised hither, that Inskeith in Scotland must be better manned, that it may be upon all events, and in despight of all men kept, and rather than fail, to put the soldiers of Dunbar into the said Inskeith, if they cannot otherwise furnish it with men; for the keeping of that isle is of such moment, as having that, the French may, when it pleaseth them, take what place they like, upon either side of the Firth.

Whereas I have written above, that the Lord Seton should bring a letter to your Majesty, from the French Queen, and therewith her picture; the said Lord Seton departing hence the 22d of this month, left his servant behind at the Court, to bring after him his dispatch to Paris. In the end his servant hath been answered, that the said French Queen will neither write at this time to your Majesty, nor send her picture, excusing that the same is not yet made; which the said Lord Seton taketh in very evil part, and will cause him to be a worse Frenchman, and a better Scottishman.

· I am well advertised, that the 25th of this month, assignation was given out, for the payment of twenty-five thousand franks, for the use of the galleys at Nantz.

It is said that the Duke of Savoy hath fortified a place in Savoy named Salviano; and hath with certain Protestant Cantons in Swisse made a league, which doth somewhat offend these men. But in the mean time the Duke doth that which is meet for him.

. The Lord of St. John's had his dispatch here the 26th of this month; he took not his leave of the King by reason of his indisposition, but of the Queen and Cardinal of Lorrain, he had very good words, and was required to use the part and office of a good Minister towards the estates of Scotland, and of a good subject towards his Sovereigns. He hath a letter from the King and Queen to the said estates; the copy whereof I send your Majesty herewith.

with. And fo I pray God long to preferve your Majefty in health, honour, and all felicity. From Orleans the 28th of November, 1560.

ELIZA-
BETH.

Your Majefty's, &c.

N. THROKMORTON.

Sir Nicholas Throkmorton to Secretary Cecil.

1560.
Nov. 28th.

SIR,

THIS bearer, Alexander Clarke, Gentleman of Scotland, of whom you have heard often in my letters, and not fo often as he hath deferved, hath gotten leave to go into his country, for fuch purpofes as he will declare unto you: fomewhat I have written to her Majefty thereof by him; his fervice done to the Queen's Majefty hath been fuch, as I am forry to mifs him for that refpect. But I am the lefs forry, for that his being in Scotland cannot but be to very good purpofe, as the occafions of thefe men's practices be offered prefently. I am fure you fhall be made privy of that I have written to her Majefty, and therefore need not reiterate it again. As for other particularities, he is fufficient, and inftructed to fatisfy you at large. I do moft heartily recommend him unto you; his deferts have been great, and his intent and means to deferve more, is worthy to be liberally confidered, and well looked on. I have alfo befought her Majefty to confider him both for the paft, and for his and others better encouraging to continue. It may pleafe you to help forth the matter, fo as he may know and feel whom he hath ferved; and alfo that my recommendation in his behalf doth work for him, as he may of good right challenge at my hands. Indeed

X   this

ELIZA-
BETH. this journey of his at this time doth more rife of my device, than of his particular motion; albeit, I am contented if it be otherwife coloured. There fhall hardly be any thing there by the French faction practifed, but he fhall know it. His further ordering I refer to your good judgment. If it pleafe the Queen's Majefty to fpeak with him, it muft be done with great fecrecy, left the French there know of it. He accompanieth thither the Lord Seton, and meaneth to make the court to the French Ambaffador with fhew of offers and fervice to be done to their Prince, for fo he muft go to work; and yet his nature is fo honeft, as he can very hardly diffemble. I have at his requeft given him a memorial of my opinion, how to will the Lords in his country to proceed prefently, confidering the time, the ftate, and the terms of their affairs, which I have willed him to fhew you, to be ordered and altered as you think good. Sir, at the difpatch hereof I had not heard from the Court fince the 19th of October. This Prince is fick, and very cafual; and thereupon dependeth great matter, and here affure you the difcourfe is made thereafter. Thus I humbly take my leave of you. From Orleans the 28th of November, 1560.

Your's, &c.

N. THROKMORTON.

Sir Nicholas Throkmorton to the Queen.

IT may pleafe your Majefty, this bearer, Alexander Clarke, Gentleman of Scotland, one of the archers of the guard of corps, of whom your Majefty hath oftentimes; by my letters, and by others credit, fent from hence, heard of, having gotten leave to return into Scotland, I cannot but moft humbly recommend to your Majefty. He hath ftood me in fuch ftead for your Majefty's fervice (as partly Mr. Kyllegrew doth well know); that I could not well have been without him, nor your Majefty well fpared the fervice that he hath here done; the fame hath been no common fervice. His diligence and painfulnefs, without regard of hazard to himfelf, hath well tried his faithfulnefs to the advancement principally of your affairs, and the liberty and benefit of his own country. I can more and better teftify of him, than I can write in his commendation. He goeth now into Scotland, and partly being vehemently fufpected, as a prin-cipal doer in thefe late ftirs here (and therefore the worfe looked on), and fo mindeth not to hazard himfelf in that fufpicion, but by his abfence for a time, if it may be, to bury it, and partly being by me procured fo to do, for the better fervice of your Majefty in thofe parts, doth at this time make this voyage. The caufe thereof is, the French I perceive intend, and are in hand with great practices there, to work their purpofe, as to win fome and to fow difcord be-twixt others, fpecially to breed diffenfion betwixt the Earl of Arran and the Lord James * and his favourers, by means whereof he fhall be able to do much good betwixt them: he is alfo in good credit with Lord Seton, and fo fhall he fee always into his doings and practices, and likewife by that means into the French faction's workings: he fhall be able to overfee more of their doings than another of more appear-ance: the colour he hath to return with the Lord Seton, is to good

* Afterwards Earl of Murray, and Regent.

X 2. purpofe

purpofe for many refpects, fo as thereby your Majefty may be
from time to time truly advertifed of all the fecret workings of the
French Minifters in Scotland, in having order and means how to
fend. Such a Minifter of truft is to be made of. I humbly befeech
your Majefty to have confideration of him and of his deferts, that
he may know and feel whom he hath ferved, and alfo with the better will to continue his good heart and devotion towards your Majefty, which your goodnefs, I truft, fhall be well employed. It may
pleafe your Majefty, I being determined to make this difpatch the
23d of this month, was occafioned to ftay the fame until the date
hereof; fince which time I underftand this King's ficknefs doth fo
fucceed, as men do begin to doubt of his long lafting. The conftitution of his body is fuch, as the phyficians do fay he cannot be
long-lived: and thereunto he hath by his too timely and inordinate
exercife now in his youth, added an evil accident; fo as there be
that do not let to fay, though he do recover this ficknefs, he cannot
live two years; whereupon there is plenty of difcourfes here of the
French Queen's fecond marriage; fome talk of the Prince of Spain,
fome of the Duke of Auftrich, others of the Earl of Arran.

Thus Almighty God long preferve your Majefty in health, honour,
and all felicity. From Orleans the 28th of November, 1560.

The Duke of Florence arrived at Court the 5th of this month;
his train is faid to be eight hundred horfe. Of that his fo fudden
voyage, here be very many and fundry difcourfes.

Your Majefty's, &c.

N. THROKMORTON.

Sir Nicholas Throkmorton to Secretary Cecil.

S I R,

HOWSOEVER others be inclined to give ear to thefe mens delays, and to be pleafed to be brought into fome expectation by their new fending of new Commiffioners thither firft, and from thence into Scotland, there to affemble a new Parliament; I truft you be too wife to be with fuch toys fo carried away, or to be advifed by thofe dealings; but I am fure you fee fo far into the matter, as there is no caufe why any body ought to look for a better iffue now, than at the laft affembly, which was done by this King and Queen's authority, as appeareth by exprefs words in the laft accord made with the eftates of Scotland. And I am fure you be too well experimented to think that Noailles, late Ambaffador in England, one of the Mafters of the Requefts, and the fame in no great grace here, and Le Croc, a Gentleman, fervant to the King and Queen, fhould have a greater truft and authority committed to them, to proceed abfolutely in this matter, or that more truft, credit and expectation of promife-keeping, and ratification of the treaty, fhould be looked for at their hands, or by their means, than there was at the end-making, by a Bifhop of this King's Privy Council (as Monf. de Vallence * was), or of Monf. de Randan, then Gentleman of the Chamber, and Captain of fifty men and arms, and now Knight of the Order. And befides the ftate and circumftances of the caufe and handling of it, which I truft you do thoroughly confider; I will at this time fay no more to perfuade you to do that; which is in this cafe meet to be done; but tell you, that thefe men do all with fecrecy, fpeed, and policy, give order by hook or by crook, to man, victual, and reinforce the places they hold in Scotland. Sir,

* Monluc.

I pray

ELIZA- I pray you difpatch H. Middlemore, my fteward, unto me with the next
BETH. letters; for I may very evil be fo long without him. The Lord James,
the baftard of Scotland, would be in time there in his own country
fomewhat recompenfed either of fome Abbey or of fome penfion, fome
ecclefiaftical promotion, in recompence of his penfions here reftrained, for the which he hath of late made means here. This old faying is a true faying, *Munera faevos illaqueant duces:* if the allotment
of his recompence might be fo ufed, as the Earl of Arran might be
feen to be the principal doer thereof, it would in my opinion do no
harm. Thus I humbly take my leave of you, From Orleans the
29th November, 1560.

                                        Yours, &c.

                                        N. THROKMORTON.

'After my fimple judgment, her Majefty and her Council muft be
as careful for the well ordering of Scotland at this prefent, as the
fame and they be for the well governing of Ireland or Wales.
And upon all events, that matters may be fo managed, as England
may make their*

      * The concluding part of this fentence is not decyphered.

Sir Nicholas Throkmorton to the Queen.

IT may like your Majesty to understand, That since the date
and dispatch of my letters of the 28th of November to your
Highness, I have been credibly ascertained, that the French King
hath dispatched two from hence suddenly for Scotland, with charge
to use all their best means with the King's assured there; and other,
that by practice, disguising, and whatsoever devices may best serve
for that purpose, to put out of hand, and with great secrecy, as
much victuals, as many men, and necessaries belonging thereunto,
into Dunbar and Inskeith in Scotland, as may be done. What their
names are, I cannot yet learn; whether they all go by sea, or pass
through England, or embark by Flanders, I know not. But it is
told me, that two ships are ready at Dieppe, to go thither, as merchants laden wares, and go without shew, and yet not unprovided
of as much munition as may be carried without open knowledge.
It is, like enough, that these two may go that way. This matter
being worthy the looking unto; I refer to your Majesty's good and
grave judgment, to be considered, whereof I thought necessary to
advertise the same.

Whereas the Lord James, Bastard of Scotland, had, out of a
Bishopric and Abbey of this country, a yearly pension of 2,500
crowns; he hath made suit to this King and Queen, to have not
only the arrearages of the same, since it hath been staid, but also the
continuation thereof. The Queen hath made him answer, that like
as this his falling from his duty hath been cause of the stay thereof,
and deserveth his exemption from the same; so his demerits again
towards her is the only way to purchase her favour, and the said
pension, which, if he accomplish according to the trust she hath of

2   him,

him, he fhall not only be fure of his fatisfaction, but alfo of all the good favour that may be fhewed him, befides his penfion, whether he difpofe himfelf to be ecclefiaftical or temporal.

The name of one of them, that is now fent into Scotland, is named Pellegrin. At the difpatch hereof I underftand, that there is great lamentation at the Court, for the French King, of whofe recovery they begin to miftruft. In my fimple opinion, it fhall not be good to make any of the Scots privy to the danger that this King is in. And thus I pray God long to preferve your Majefty in health, honour, and all felicity. From Orleans the 29th of November, 1560.

Your Majefty's, &c.

N. THROKMORTON.

1560.
Decem. 1ft.

Sir Nicholas Throkmorton to the Queen.

IT may like your Majefty, fince my letters of the 29th of November to your Majefty, wherein I advertifed your Highnefs, of the French King's ftate in his ficknefs, I underftand, that he is fomewhat amended, but yet very weak, and fo feeble, as he was not able to keep the feaft of the Golden Fleece, on St. Andrew's day, whereof he is Knight; and now the phyficians miftruft no danger of his life for this time.

And whereas in the fame letter I wrote to your Highnefs, that the French Queen was not then minded to fend your Majefty her picture, nor letter, which fhe had erft promifed, as I advertifed your Highnefs by my letter of the 28th of the laft; I underftand now, that fhe hath given order, that my Lord Seton fhall both

bring

bring a letter from her to your Majesty, and also her picture. Whether it come of her better mood, or by the said Lord Seton's importune suit, to have the carrying thereof to your Highness, I know
not. I understand, that the French King hath pressed two and thirty
captains, they to be ready with their bands upon the next warning.
And thus I pray God long to preserve your Majesty in health,
honour, and all felicity. From Orleans the 1st of December,
1560.

Your Majesty's, &c.

N. THROKMORTON.

Sir Nicholas Throkmorton to Secretary Cecil.

SIR,

GOOD accord and unity to be had among all the States of Scotland, is to be maintained and conferved. But if the Devil will
cast a bone among them, the Earl of Arran's amity, and his friends,
be most fit for England, for many respects; and he, in mine opinion,
if he be wise, or well counselled, must needs be English again; for
if he see deeply into the world, and into his own case, that must be
his best reckoning; and therefore at all events, if the Scots do now,
upon the refusal of the treaty, resolve to seize into their own hands
and custody Infkeith and Dunbar, and to put out all the Frenchmen from thence (as methink of reason and necessity they ought
to do), then the custody of the same two places would be committed
to the guard of some wise and fit men of the country, and such as
be wholly at the Deputy of Edinburgh's devotion; for thereby if

Y   some

fome turn their coats, and fall to catch that catch may, the faid
Earl being ours, we fhall not make the worft end for ourfelves. For
all the country on this fide the rivers of Clyde and Firth, fhall be at
the Queen's Majefty's devotion, which if you will confider, is no
evil frontier, and thereby alfo may the better order her realm of
Ireland; but thefe matters muft be cunningly handled. This bearer
Alexander Clarke, will difclofe untol you, if the Lord Seton keep
promife with him, fome folk, that are to be looked to, who are
the intelligence givers to the French.

From Orleans the 1ft of December, 1560.

Yours, &c.

N. THROKMORTON.

No. VIII.

Mr. Jones to Sir Nicholas Throkmorton, Ambaffador in France.

[This is an extremely curious letter, and, together with the others, in which the Queen's marriage with Lord Robert Dudley is men-tioned, plainly fhews the general opinion, both at home and abroad, of her inclination that way. Indeed Elizabeth herfelf does not difclaim it.]

SIR,

W ITH all the diligence I could make, I arrived not at the Court here till Monday at night, the 25th of November, at what time I delivered my letters to Mr. Secretary, and attending all the next day upon him, I fpake not with the Queen's Majefty till Wednefday at night at Greenwich, whither fhe came to bed from Eltham, when fhe dined and hunted all that day with divers of my Lords.

I had declared unto Mr. Secretary, before I fpake with her, the day after my arrival, the difcourfe of the Lord of St John's, and your Lordfhip's opinion, touching the declaration in French, which he willed me to put in writing, as I did; Mr. Secretary fhewed both the fame to the Queen's Majefty, as her Highnefs in my talk with her told me, and a third perfon knew the fame, but how, I know not. I will tell your Lordfhip the ftory, and then you may guefs at it. There was occafion, as your Lorfhip knoweth, in the

From the Original in the Poffeffion of the Earl of Hardwicke.

Y 2   difcourfe,

difcourfe, to fpeak of the delivery of the letters to the French King
and Queen in the favour of the Earl of Arran, and of that the
French Queen faid, the Queen's Majefty would marry the Mafter of
her horfes.   The 26th of November all my Lords of the Council
dined at the Scotch Ambaffador's lodging, where they were very
highly feafted.   I repaired thither to fhew myfelf to my Lords,
where, after I had attended half dinner time, my Lord Robert rofe
up, and went to the Court, and in the way fent a gentleman back
to will me to repair thither after him, as I did, after I had declared the meffage to Mr. Secretary.   Being come unto him, he afked
me, whether the French Queen had faid that the Queen's Majefty
would marry her horfe-keeper, and told me he had feen all the difcourfe of your Lordfhip's proceedings, together with the intelligence, and that Mr. Secretary told him, that the French Queen had
faid fo.   I anfwered, that I faid no fuch matter.   He laid the matter
upon me fo ftrong, as the author thereof being avowed, I would not
deny, that the French Queen had faid, that the Queen would marry
the Mafter of her horfes.   This was all he faid to me, and he willed
me, that I fhould in no cafe let it be known to Mr. Secretary, that he
had told me thus much, as I have not indeed, nor mean not to do;
whereby I judge, that Mr. Secretary did declare it only to the
Queen, at whofe hands my Lord Robert had it.   The fame night
I fpake to Mr. Killigrew, and having delivered your Lordfhip's letter
and told him of the intelligence; he faid in the end unto me, with,
as it were, a fad look, I think verily, that my Lord Robert fhall
run away with the hare, and have the Queen; to whom I anfwered
nothing.   Thus much I thought good to write before I came to
fpeak of my proceeding with the Queen's Majefty.

The 27th, I fpake with her Majefty at Greenwich, at fix o'clock
at night, and declared unto her the talk of the Ambaffadors of Spain
and Venice, and the Marquis *, and your advice, touching the General

* Of Northampton.

Council.

Council *. When I had done with the firft point of my firft tale, By my troth, faid fhe, I thought it was fuch a matter, and he need not have fent you hither, for it had been more meet to have kept you there ftill. I faid, that if it had been written in cypher, it muft have come to the knowledge of fome others. Of nobody, faid fhe, but of my Secretary; or elfe he might have written it in my own cypher. When I came to touch nearer the quick, I have heard of this before, quoth fhe, and he need not to have fent you withal: I faid, that the care you had was fo great, as you could not but advertife her Majefty of fuch things † as might touch her, and that you took this to be no matter to be opened, but to herfelf. When I came to the point that touched his race ‡, which I fet forth in as vehement terms as the cafe required, and that the Duke's ‖ hatred was rather to her than to the Queen her fifter; fhe laughed, and forthwith turned herfelf to the one fide and to the other, and fet her hand upon her face. She thereupon told me, that the matter § had been tried in the country **, and found to be contrary to that which was reported, faying that he was then in the Court, and none of his at the attempt at his wife's houfe; and that it fell out as fhould neither touch his honefty nor her honour. Quoth fhe, my Ambaffador knoweth fomewhat of my mind in thefe matters. She heard me very patiently, I think the rather becaufe I made, before I fpake unto her Majefty, a long proteftation, as methought I had need to do, confidering that my Lord Robert knew thereof as much as he did. Her Majefty promifed me *fidem, taciturnitatem, & favorem,* the laft whereof I found towards myfelf, but as for your Lordfhip, fhe not once made mention of you unto me, unlefs that

* That the Queen fhould fend thither.
† Of the talk in France of her marriage.
‡ Lord Robert Dudley's.
‖ Of Northumberland.
§ This relates to the report of Lord Robert's having his wife privately murdered.
** Probably Coroner's Inqueft.

† once

ELIZA-
BETH.
once or twice fhe afked, whether your Lordfhip willed me to declare this matter unto her, as I affirmed you did. Thus much have I thought good to write, touching the Ambaffador of Spain's talk. For * the Venetian Ambaffador's talk, fhe protefted, that fhe never to any Ambaffador or other, difclofed any   and nobody but Mr. Secretary knew of thefe matters; who was, fhe faid, wife enough. When I rehearfed the terms of *veneficii & maleficii reus*; fhe caufed me to repeat the fame twice or thrice, which methought did move her more than that I faid touching the Ambaffador of Spain's talk. For the Marquis, fhe believed the firft part, touching his affection towards her; and for the laft of that he reported, touching her Majefty's difcourfe with him for the not marrying of any other fubjects, fhe affirmed unto me, that it was never fpoken unto him, touching any fuch matter.

Touching the Council at Trent, and the confederation, and therein touching the Scots and Almains, fhe faid, that the Scots were *populus fine capite*, but the *others* † and her Majefty heard one from another, and that fhe did make affured account of them. Neverthelefs there was none named unto me; but how fecret that matter is made, it may appear by the Italian fool, who, upon provocation, talked openly of the fame, and devifed upon the means of fending, even as I had debated the fame with the Queen's Majefty. I did recommend unto the Queen's Majefty fuch as fpake with me before my departure thence, and fuch others as your Lordfhip commanded me, the fervices of whom her Majefty took in right gracious part, as her Majefty faid, fhe would wifh to be known. I mean Mr. Cavalcanti; and for Mr. Clarke, I fet out as much his fervice in France, as ability to ferve in Scotland; though I did not prefs the fame, being moved to it by that I perceived fomewhat, the Queen's Majefty's difpofition for Scotland very cold. She faid, fhe did not know him, but

* It fhould feem, that all thefe talks related to Lord Robert.   † The Germans.

2   that

that she was glad to hear of his service. I spake unto her Majesty, ELIZA-BETH. touching Noailles; of the strait league between the French King and the King of Spain; and of the practice of their division of the two realms between them.

And as for Calais, I had good reason to persuade the Queen's Majesty that it should never be restored; for Mr. Bourdin hath 700 acres of ground in the country, and will build there; and one hath built already without the town as much as hath cost 3000 crowns; and they mind to perfect their huge fortifications out of hand; with divers other matters, which I learned by reason of my long tarrying there against my will, by want of wind and good passage.

The Queen's Majesty looketh not so hearty and well as she did, by a great deal; and surely the matter of my Lord Robert doth much perplex her, and it is never like to take place, and the talk thereof is somewhat slack, as generally misliked, but of the setters forth thereof, who are as your Lordship knoweth.

My Lords, for the most part, as Pembroke, Clinton, Bedford, Northampton (who have told me so much themselves), do like well your Lordship's letters and advertisements at this time, and seem to be careful for the due consideration of them, and yet none of them have questioned with me, to know any further of them. I doubt, pleasure and pastime, with their attendants, and the folly of some who seem to make court to them whom they mislike, will either mar all, or hinder all.

I have declared unto Mr. Secretary, what your Lordship thinketh of the General Council, who wished I had not told the Queen's Majesty a matter * of such weight, being too much he said for a woman's knowledge.

I told him also, in whose behalf I had spoken to the Queen's Majesty, and of all other matters, saving of the two Ambassadors talk. He heareth what I have to say very favourably, but asketh

---

* It was probably about sending to the Council of Trent from hence.

me

me-no further touching any matter. I am forry to fee how he is troubled; and as if, mefeemeth, overwhelmed with bufinefs; but all lighteth upon him without any affiftance. He looked for more, and afked me, whether I had not brought him any other letters from your Lordfhip.

Mr. Secretary was in hand with me to know, whether I brought not two letters to the Queen's Majefty; for, he faid, the letter he received from the Queen's Majefty back again, was not fo thick as when he delivered it: I told him I knew not, for I made not up the packet.

Mr. Treafurer * received your Lordfhip's letter very thankfully; but when I went from him, and he had read it over, he was clean changed, and not over-courteous. He fell fick the next day, fo as I could not fpeak unto him, and I do well know that letter and the matter of the other were the occafion of his evil. He is half afhamed of his doing for the Lord Robert.

My Lord Admiral is very diligent in his charge; two new fhips be now making of great burden, and other veffels fhall be made to meet with the gallies.

Religion is neglected; all men difcontented; no man confidered; Captains fell their harnefs; and every man is for himfelf.

The Queen's Majefty ftayeth the creation. The bills were made for the purpofe, at the day appointed. When they were prefented, fhe with a knife cut them afunder. I can by no means learn, and yet I have talked with fuch as know much, that my Lord Robert's matters will not go, as was looked for; and yet the favours be great which are fhewed him at the Queen's Majefty's hands.

The Scots Lords have been feafted fumptuoufly at my Lord of Pembroke's, where I dined among them. They have been alfo at my Lord of Bedford's. As far as I can learn among the Scottifh

* Sir Thomas Parry.

men,

men, if their alliance be not more eftablifhed than fome here would, that favour the Lord Robert, which be very ⸻ and lefs honeft, they fhall be conftrained, to fave their necks, and to win the French favour again, to turn their coats, which doth not a little grieve them. The Scotch caufe doth like well, fo far as I can learn, my Lords of the Council, and the doings there in France bring the matter to a neceffity. I dare not advife your Lordfhip to do any thing; but I judge that thofe things confirmed of every hand, may work a miracle, and I can fee no other, but that we here ftay much upon your Lordfhip's judgment; and though the confideration of things be great, yet undoubtedly there is great want; and will fay no more. Mr. Middlemore, as Mr. Secretary fhewed me, fhall be difpatched before me. I truft not to be long after, rather to fatisfy my duty, than for any hope I have to be otherwife confidered. I humbly befeech your Lordfhip to excufe me that I have written no fooner; for it was fo long ere I could fpeak with the Queen's Majefty, and I fpake with none before her; but Mr. Secretary, as I could not write how I had proceeded, and your Lordfhip to be affured, that I have not paffed my commiffion in any one point of my charge. The laft of November, 1560.

E L I Z A-
B E T H.
1560.

Your's, &c.

R. J. JONES.

Letters

E L I Z A-
BETH.
1561.

No. IX.

From the
Originals in
the Possession
of the Earl of
Hardwicke.

Letters from Sir William Cecil, and from the Earl of Bedford, to Sir Nicholas Throckmorton, Ambassador in France.

[In the letters from Cecil, the reader will have ample proofs of his wisdom, integrity, and moderation. It is impossible, at this distance of time, to explain the cause of the dissatisfaction of this great Statesman. The Queen his Mistress (as Sir Robert Cecil truly says of her, in a letter printed in *Nugæ antiquæ*) " was " sometimes more than a man, and sometimes less than a woman." But the defects in her character and temper, though considerable, should not detract from her real merit; and she will deservedly remain one of the greatest Sovereigns that ever filled the English throne.]

May, 1561.   *From Sir William Cecil, to Sir N. Throckmorton.*

S I R,

WE shall now shortly see whether my Lady your wife's journey, shall be to fetch you home or no; for upon answer made to Dr. Somer by the Scotts Queen, you may boldly write to the Queen's Majesty for your return according to her Majesty's former answer. But, to say the truth, who shall succeed, for your service of the Queen's Majesty? Mr. Knolles hath been much spoken of; but two things may yet be required in him, although he have good furniture of the best, that is outward hability of wealth,

and

and acquaintance, in such public affairs, so mixed with divers practices as these be. Here hath been no small ado to refuse this Popish Messenger; not that any counsellor was outwardly unwilling, but no man was found so earnest and bold as to adventure the advising of such as were of other minds. This Bishop of Aquila * had won more with former preludes than was easy to overtake; but in the end, thanked be God, he findeth all his conceptions and practices unjointed, and under foot. What he will do to recover them I cannot tell. My Lord of Suffex is ready to depart into Ireland, and shall, I trust, proceed with a posting against Shane Oneyle. The Earl of Kildare is now here, and hath his friends also here, as you know; and, I think, for understanding of the truth, there will be some coupling betwixt them in argument, the Irish Earl to deprave the other's governance; and the other (if he be so pressed) to charge those last in service.

I find that I am taken to be drawn against the Earl of Ireland; but, surely, I confess to you, I will know both, before I stand to any side. Although I see no cause but to lean with our English governance against such as always have fought, and of course will seek, to shake off from their necks our regiment.

The Consuls of Hamburgh have written to the Queen's Majesty touching the stay of her armour, and affirm it to be done by commandment of the Princes, in respect of an information given that it was to be sent into Muscovia; and therefore upon her Majesty's assertion that it is not so, they will deliver it. Whereupon her Majesty hath written thanks to them, with blaming such slanders of her, and avowed her property and meaning.

I understand that this was a malicious practice of this Bishop here, by means of Lazarus Vanfwenden; such is their hollow meaning towards us. If the marriage that way hath pass, we must

* The Spanish Ambassador in England.

enter

enter a reciproque amytye that ways, wherein I would ye fhould
bethink yourfelf.   To end; the Queen's Majefty, I affure you,
taketh your laft writing in right good part, and willed me to require
you that fome goldfmith there might be induced indirectly to come
hither with furniture of agrets, chains, bracelets, &c. to be bought
both by herfelf, and by the Ladies here, to be gay in this Court,
towards the progrefs. What is meant in it I know not; whether
for that which many look for, or for the coming in of the Swede;
but, as for me, I can fee no certain difpofition in her Majefty to any
marriage; and any other likelihood doth not the principal here find,
which caufeth him to be perplexed.

     May 1561.   Your's, ye know,

                                W. CECIL.

From the Same to the Same.

SIR,

ALTHOUGH this may feem an unlooked-for refolution to you, confidering the courfe of your writing, to have all courtefy fhewed
to D'Oyfel, and fo confequently the Scottifh Queen better fatisfied,
yet it hath fo fallen out here, that, although in all other things
D'Oyfel hath been well and gently ufed, yet fo many reafons have
induced us to deny the principal requeft,* that I think it fhall be
both of the wife allowed, and of our friends in Scotland moft
welcome.

The very noife of D'Oyfel's coming had ftirred fome maze in
fundry heads, and the expectation of the Queen's coming had erected

* The principal requeft was, that the Queen of Scots might crofs the feas into Scotland,
upon Elizabeth's fafe-conduct.

                                                 up

up Huntly, Bothwell, Hume, and others, that it could not be
agreeable for us to feed them ·in their humours; and by this our denial, our friends in Scotland fhall find us to be of their difpofition, and fo ftop them in their humours.

.. I think plainly the longer the Scottifh Queen's affairs fhall hang in an uncertainty, the longer will it be ere fhe fhall have fuch a match in marriage as fhall offend us. Your advertifement of the offer of the Portugal, feemeth fo acceptable, as the Lord Admiral will fend a veffel of his own, of almoft one hundred tons, and the Mayor and Mr. Garrett will venture one thoufand pounds, &c. *

Sir, where you would have me advertife you my own mind, whether you fhould write to the Queen's Majefty of fuch things as you hear worth to be known to her Majefty; only two things move me to incline to a ftep. The one is my friendly care of you particularly; the fecond is, the regard that I have to preferve the eftimation of proteftants in the Queen's Majefty's judgment, which is already not increafed; and if your fharp reports fhould come from fuch, I fear the mifliking would be turned to them. And yet, comparing both thefe with the good that I know the reporters meant her Majefty, I dare not conclude either to forbid you, or to promife you as much as toucheth yourfelf. You can confider, *jaéta curam fuper Dominum, et ipfe te enutriet.* It ferveth me fometimes to adventure, but yet I will never have my friend adventure fo far as myfelf.

Sir, I moft heartily thank you for my fon, in whom as ye fhall fee faults rife up, fo, I pray you, root them up by fharp advertifement; for I fee that long fufferance of any thing, maketh the removing of it harder; and fpecially one fault engendreth another in our corrupt natures.

I cannot certainly write unto you of the King of Sweden's coming, His Chancellor being not of acquaintance with Englifh conditions, doth his purpofe more hurt than he thinketh.

* This relates to a projeét of a voyage to the coaft of Guinea.

The

The Queen's Majefty hath plainly written to this King, that, confidering fhe is not as yet difpofed to marriage, fhe doubteth that in coming, and not obtaining his fuit, he fhould change his love into offence; and therefore I think, upon the receipt of thofe lines, he will ftop. I am moft forry of all that her Majefty is not difpofed ferioufly to marriage; for I fee likelihood of great evil both to this State and to the moft of the good particular perfons, if fhe fhall not fhortly marry. There hath been a matter fecretly thought of, which I dare communicate to you, although I mean never to be an author thereof; and that is, if an accord might be made betwixt our Miftrefs and the Scottifh Queen, that this fhould, by Parliament in Scotland, &c. furrender unto the Queen's Majefty all matter of claim, and to the heirs of her body; and, in confideration thereof, the Scottifh Queen's intereft fhould be acknowledged in default of heirs of the body of the Queen's Majefty. Well, God fend our Miftrefs a hufband, and by time a fon, that we may hope our pofterity fhall have a mafculine fucceffion. This matter is too big for weak folks, and too deep for fimple. The Queen's Majefty knoweth of it, and fo I will end. I have advertifed the Lords of Scotland of the Queen's Majefty's anfwer to D'Oyfel. De Sevre faid yefterday privately, that he looked for fuch an anfwer as this was. Yefternight, I thank the Queen's Majefty, fhe took a fupper at my rude new cottage, wherein I thought my cofts well beftowed for her gracious acceptance of all my offers. Sir Thomas Challoner is putting himfelf in order to go into Spain to take Mr. Chamberlain's place, and now it refteth to compafs your coming home. I am had here in continual jealoufy, and you in like miftruft. Commend me to my good L dy Throckmorton. The Queen's Majefty thinketh long for the Paris goldfmith: he fhall be free of cuftom for all that he fhall not fell. God be with you. From London the 14th of July 1561.   Your's affuredly,

2   W. CECIL.

Earl of Bedford to Throckmorton.

AFTER my very hearty commendations to your Lordſhip; by your laſt letter that I received from you, for the which and all others I give moſt hearty thanks, I underſtood moſt chiefly of your good health, and for occurrence little or none, being referred to Mr. Secretary's advices and diſcourſes to him written; of whom, becauſe I aſked not, neither did he tell me any thing thereof, your letter ſeemed to be as good as if it had come from Brigſtock park. Mr. Killigrewe your great friend, one of no ſmall eſtimation and credit with Lord Robert, can and doth, I doubt not, as well as other your agents and friends here, write unto you how things paſs; to whom I muſt deſire you to be referred, for as much as I have taken my leave of the Queen's Majeſty, and bidden the Court farewell, and am now, to-morrow, going to Woborn in Bedford-ſhire, and ſo further into Northamptonſhire to hunt this ſummer; from whence you know nothing can be written but that which might make you wiſh yourſelf there alſo; and ſo would I you were, at ſuch idle times as you could pick out, to diſport yourſelf after your great buſineſs.

From London this 8th of July 1561.

Your Lordſhip's right aſſured,

F. BEDFORD.

From Cecil to Throckmorton.

S I R,

YOUR fervant Davis hath lingered now longer than I thought
he fhould in the beginning, upon this Court, to come with
fome intelligence of the Scots Queen's return home. The 19th of
this prefent, in the morning early, fhe arrived at Leith with her two
gallies, her whole train not exceeding fixty perfons of meaner fort.
The Lords of Scotland were not nigh, being warned only againft the
laft of this month; only there was at Holyrood-houfe the Lord
Robert, to whofe houfe fhe went and there remained, and gave
orders with fpeed to affemble her Lords. This was the whole I could
learn, being fo written in hafte at the fame inftant. The Queen's
Majefty's fhips that were upon the feas to cleanfe them from pirates,
faw her, and faluted her galleys; and ftaying her fhips, examined
them of pirates, and difmiffed them gently. One Scottifh fhip they
detain, as vehemently fufpected of piracy.

Since the laft conflict in Ireland, whereof I wrote of late to you,
Shane O'Neyle hath made new requeft to come hither, but he addeth
fome conditions to it not palatable; as, to have a new garrifon planted
at Armagh this laft July, to be removed. Sir William Fitzwilliams
hath been here to declare the fame, and to require the Queen's
Majefty's pleafure. Indeed I fee fuch various events of thofe wars,
that, fo furety be feen to that he come, I regard lefs of opinion of
eftimation. If he come, the matters may furely and honourably
fall out; if he come not, howfoever account is made of honour,
I doubt of furety. Upon him dependeth the whole weal or lofs of
Ireland; if ye yield, all is the Queen's Majefty's at prefent; if contrary, the reft will be in danger. He hath unluckily, in June laft,
                                                              taken

taken Callogh O'Donell and his wife the Countefs of Kildare, and
keeping him in chains, committeth the country to Collogh's brother Hugh O'Donell, 'fifter's fon to Shane, and fo hath at his will all Tyrconnel, a matter of no fmall confequence if James M'Onell fhould be won to him.

Though Lady Catherine * is in the Tower, and near the time of delivery of child; though herfelf remain prifoner, nobody can appear privy to the marriage †, nor to the love, but maids, or women going for maidens. The Queen's Majefty thinketh, and fo do others with her, that fome greater drift was in this; but for my part I can find none fuch.

From Stortford the 26th of Auguft 1561.

Your's always affured,

W. CECIL.

From the Same to the Same.

S I R,

SINCE this bearer Killigrew came over, I thought beft to ftay
him all this time, thinking that fome matter fhould have happened worth his tarrying and return; but feeing no fuch chanceth, knowing his defire to return, I have thought to difpatch him with thefe my own letters. I do my uttermoft to procure Mr. Dannett to come thyther, but he fo grunteth thereat, partly for ficknefs hanging upon him though not poffeffing him, partly for poverty inclofing him round about, that, if it were not for your fatisfaction, furely I would not thus deal to offend him as I do. I perceive her Majefty will not be induced to relieve his laft difeafe,

* Lady Catherine Grey, whofe mother (Duchefs of Suffolk) was niece to Henry VIII.
† With the Earl of Hertford.

A a otherwife

otherwife than his ordinary wages. I might lament my place that I hold, being, to outward appearance, becaufe of frequentation with her Majefty, of much credit; and indeed, of none at all. But my remedy is only to leave the place; wherein my only grief is, to fee likelihood of fuch fucceffors, as I am fure fhall or will deftroy all my good purpofes. I may not write, but yet I may lament. What is my credit to help any body, may appear in myfelf, that have been forced to fell off the land which I had when I came to this place with the Queen; one hundred and fifty pounds of good known lands *; and, at this inftant, I am with burden of debt compelled to afk leave of her Majefty to fell away my office in the Common Pleas, that hath been the only ftay of my living thefe fifteen years, and her Majefty doth licence me fo to do. But fo that I might be able to procure furniture for others to ferve her Majefty, I cared not for myfelf; and in this term doth ftand the fending away of Mr. Dannett.

I have carried in my head, with care, means how her Majefty fhould from time to time conduct her affairs. I fee fo little proof of my travels, by reafon her Majefty alloweth not of them, that I have left all to the wide world. I do only keep on accounts for a fhow, but inwardly I meddle not; leaving things to work in a courfe, as the clock is left when the barrel is wound up. It is time to end thefe complaints to you who cannot remedy them; but yet becaufe you write to me divers times of matters worthy your confideration, thinking that you have beftowed them well on me, in hopes that I will fafhion them and put them forth, when you fee I have no comfort fo to do, I thought not inconvenient to note thus much to you of my imperfection.

Here be no fmall practices in forging, fome think, of the fuccef-fion, if her Majefty fhould not marry or leave iffue. This fong hath

* However the cafe might be then, it is notorious that Cecil raifed a very confiderable fortune out of his long courfe of fervice.

                                                                      many

many parts; but, for my part, I have no fkill but in plain fong. Others be devifing how to hinder religion, the rather for that her Majefty feemeth eafy therein; and if I do any good, I am fure therein I do no hurt; and in refpect thereof, principally, do I the reft of all my fervice.

I find a great defire in both thefe Queens to have an interview; and knowing the diverfity of both their intents, although I wifh it, yet I know it dangerous to be any fingular doer therein.

Shane O'Neyle cometh over with my Lord of Kildare under a protection, though thereof is not meet to ufe fpeech. He will complain of my Lord of Suffex; but my Lord of Suffex hath, for the Queen, more caufe to complain of them, as he fayeth. Howfoever it is, authority muft be favoured. My Lord of Suffex hath licence to come hither; who fhall fucceed him I know not, if it be not Sir H. Sidney. I think my Lord Ambrofe * at length fhall be, on Chriftmas day, Earl of Warwick, a matter often promifed, and often broke off. From Weftminfter, December 22d, 1561.

Your affured Friend,

W. CECIL.

* Dudley, brother to Lord Robert.

A a 2　　　　A Note

STATE PAPERS.

No. X.

*A Note of Confultation had at Greenwich, primo May
1561, by the Queen's Majefty's commandment, upon a
requeft made to her Majefty by the King of Spain's Ambaffador, that the Abbot of Martinengo being Nuntio
from the Pope, and arriving at Bruxells, might come
into the realm with letters from the Pope and other
Princes to the Queen.*

PRESENT.

The Lord Keeper of the Great Seal of England,
William, Marquis of Northampton,
Henry, Earl of Arundell,
Edward, Earl of Derby,
William, Earl of Pembroke,
Edward Fines, le Admiral,
William Howard, Lord Chamberlain to the Queen,
Sir Edward Rogers, Comptroller,
Sir Francis Knolles, Vice Chamberlain,
Sir William Cecil, Secretary,
Sir Ambrofe Cave,
Sir William Petre,
Sir John Mafon,
Sir Richard Sackvyll,
Mr. Wotton, Dean of Canterbury.

IT

IT was devifed and accorded by all and every one of the faid
Counfellors, without any manner of contradiction made by
any, that the Nuncio fhould not come into any her Majefty's dominions; and fo by fpecial fpeech of every Counfellor expreffed;
raifing therefore divers fundry and good reafons; whereof thefe
that follow were the chief, although in utterance much more earneftnefs, and length of fpeech was ufed by divers of the faid Council,
for more confirmation of their arguments, than is here ufed.

Firft, It is both againft the ancient laws and late laws of this realm,
that he fhould enter into the fame, or into any the Queen's Majefty's
dominions; for, by the ancient laws, yea when the Pope had moft
credit in this realm, no Legate or Nuncio might come into the fame;
for both he fhould have licence before, and alfo make a folemn oath
on the other fide the feas, that he fhould bring nothing with him,
nor attempt any thing in this realm, to the derogation of the King
of this realm, and liberties thereof; and of this there be many
examples of ancient time remaining of record; as well of the denying and refufing of the Pope's Nuncio, to come into this realm; as
alfo it is manifeft by act of Parliament. It is enacted, that no
foreign Prelate fhall ufe any power fpiritual or ecclefiaftical within
this realm, and if any fhall, by word or deed, fet forth or maintain
the power or jurifdiction fpiritual of any foreign Prelate or perfon
hereafter claimed and ufed within this realm, or fhall put in ufe any
thing for fetting forth the faid pretended power; that then every
fuch perfon fhall be punifhed for the fame, as further appeareth by
the ftatute; and therefore it is not only againft the laws of this realm
that any fuch Nuncio fhould come hither, but alfo that any perfon
fhould, by word or deed, allow his coming.

Secondly, although it were lawful, and without danger for pain
of forfeiting, as it is not, yet having regard to the Queen's Majefty's Crown and royal eftate as Queen of England, by the Laws
and acts of Parliament of this realm and in the time of Henry VIII.

her

her Majefty's noble father, to which all the fubjects of this realm have been fworn, it is manifeft, that allowing the authority of the Pope, according to fuch jurifdiction as he claimeth, there will follow one great peril to the furety and truth of the Queen's undoubted title to the Crown of England: the which at prefent ftandeth, both by the laws of God and this realm, fo fure and firm, that no true fubject can, without evident fufpicion of evil and traiterous meaning, allow the Pope's jurifdiction in this realm to any purpofe; efpecially being contrary to the truth of the Queen's Majefty's intereft and right; as, amongft other things, evidently appeareth by the travel that her Majefty's adverfaries have made to difprove her title by colour of the Pope's laws, being contrary to the laws of God; a matter of greater confequence, than can be expreffed in few words.

Thirdly, the great perils and inconveniences which are likely to follow, are fuch, that no man which loveth quietnefs, can confent to his coming in.

For whereas in winter-time the only found of coming of a Nuncio hath wrought, in fundry evil-difpofed perfons, fuch a boldnefs and courage, as they have not let both to break the laws with great audacity, and difperfe abroad falfe and fcandalous reports of the Queen's difpofition to change her religion and government of this realm; a thing very falfe; but alfo in fome places have conjured with the devil, and caft figures to know the continuance of her Majefty's life and reign, which God long continue; how may it be thought, without great and evident danger, to have the faid Nuncio come hither after thefe preparations, and againft Summer, in which time the Devil hath moft opportunities to make trouble and tumults? And as the evil fort, which defire alteration and change, might receive comfort hereby, and be encouraged by the fequel to attempt great enterprizes, with a face of fome other purpofes, as always rebellions have cloaks; fo, on the contrary part, the true quiet and faithful fubjects might have caufe to forbear to
                                                                            fhew

shew openly their affection and duty to the service of the Queen and realm. And in this matter it is to be considered, that as in a man's body after long sickness, being nearly well recovered, and the good humours quieted, and the evil overcome; if the good humours be troubled, and the evil fed and cherished, and so error committed, the peril would be greater to the body than the first sickness was: even so the common weal being so late, so well recovered, settled and quieted, and the evil members thereof, if any were, either reformed and put to silence by law and order, and the good quieted by law and order, if this coming of the Nuncio, being already looked for, should be permitted; thereof should come such a disquietness and change to the body of the common weal, as thereof the peril would be greater than it was at the first, or than presently can be understood. For nothing doth more damage to a commonwealth than changes against law or opinions, or hopes of changes, whereby do daily grow great dangers, both to the estate of the Prince, and also of the good subjects, and in the end ruin to the whole common weal; whereof examples past, too many and too lamentable to be remembered.

Now to answer them that would have the Pope's Nuncio to come in. It may be said, that the Nuncio will swear, that he will do nothing prejudicial to the Crown and estate of this realm; and yet it may be doubted whether he will swear: but howsoever he may be induced to swear for his advantage, he cannot observe his oath, except he would come into the realm, and neither speak nor deliver any letters from the Pope: or else he may presume, that it is not perjury to break promises with such as he is taught to repute as heretics. If he should swear, and afterwards break his oath, what peril might ensue, is easily to be seen, to them which should assent to his coming in.

And although the Queen's Majesty might dispense with the pains, yet no man of honesty would be willingly content to be reputed in the common weal a breaker of a weighty law, that was made so

lately

lately by a universal consent of the, whole realm in Parliament, in
the which law also all the, whole realm hath interest at this day, and
namely every such inheritor and possessor as hath any thing by the
law of this realm, but contrary to the laws and constitution of
Rome. What man in the late time of Queen Mary saw not, what
peril was toward the subversion of the policy of this realm? So that
we might be noted of great folly, if at any time hereafter we
should adventure the like danger. But to answer the truth of the
matter, what an abuse is this to bear us in hand, that no harm is
meant by the Pope, when he had already done as much as in him
lieth to hurt us? The Pope, even at this instant, hath his legate in
Ireland, who is already joined with certain traitors there, and occupied in stirring a rebellion; having by open acts deprived the Queen of
her title there, as much as in him lieth, although that the power that
her Majesty hath there, as well of public Ministers as of a number of
good subjects, do little esteem such attempts, as things whereof
shortly revenge shall be made. And why should we not believe that
this man would do the like, as much as in him lieth, in this realm?
It cannot be denied, but the last year, when the Abbot St. Salute
was sent from the said Pope, of the same errand and, tour, to Brussels, where the Nuncio now is, about this time also of the year,
it was purposed he should have done his best to have raised a rebellion here in this realm, under colour of religion; and why hath not
this Abbot the like sweet errand? There is no reason to be shewn;
but contrarywise more reason is now to prove it likely in this man,
than was then for the other; especially such preparations being used
before-hand, this present year, to prepare the hearts of discontented
subjects, as have by divers means been used otherwise than the
last year, and it is notoriously known and discovered. It hath also
been said, if he come, he shall not lodge with any Ambassador, but
be lodged apart by himself; forsooth it is a simple offer, and so to be
weighed, and not worthy the answering.

                                                                    But

But that which for the coming of this Abbot maketh more, is this, and very meet to be truly anfwered; that this Nuncio cometh, as is pretended, only to move the Queen to fend to a General Council, as other Chriftian Princes (as it is fayd) have been moved. To this may well and truly be anfwered, that indeed nothing can better pleafe her Majefty, than to hear of a General Council: and among all worldly things that might happen unto her, no one thing could be thought more happy, than that fhe might live to hear of fuch a General Council, as might tend to make a unity in Chriftendom in the matters of religion; to the furtherance whereof her Majefty will fpare neither travel, treafure, nor any thing moft dear to her: And therefore her Majefty, when fhe fhall underftand a Council to be called in fuch a fort, and meeting at fuch a place, and at fuch time, and with fuch conditions of freedom, for all Chriftian Princes and eftates to come thither, as may apparently tend to make concord and unity, and not to maintain faction; will of her own mere motion, and devotion toward the unity of Chriftendom; as being one of the principal Monarchs thereof, and not fubject to any Potentate fpiritual under God; fend thither fuch meet perfons, as fhe doubts not fhall declare the fincerity of her mind, and the earneftnefs of her affection to have one unity of all matters in Chrift's religion.

But for that as yet her Majefty cannot underftand that the Council now mentioned is fo called, nor her Majefty fo orderly admonifhed thereof, as might feem, by the fame mind of concord, in truth of Chriftian religion, but rather to the contrary; her Majefty cannot make prefently a refolute anfwer to fend thither. For if it be called by the Pope's authority only, and begun as a continuation of the laft fummoned Council at Trent, as by the printed examples of certain libels, publifhed this laft month of November and December, appeareth, and that it be not a Council for any perfon to have any right decifion, but fuch as be already fworn to the maintain-

B b

ance

ance of the Pope's authority, then fhall her Majefty be very forry,
finding therein no direction, meaning to concord by confultation,
but either to maintain affection by cover and name of a General
Council, as former examples have declared.   And in this part her
Majefty will conceive fome doubt and lack of fuch good meaning
towards her as is pretended : for if other Chriftian Princes, as the
Emperor, the French King, and King of Spain, have been long paft
fent unto, and their opinions firft required for the place and time of
this Council, and their confents defired before it was appointed ; in
the day alfo now paft, then, at the laft, to prefent to the Queen,
being a Prince of Chriftendom, and having intereft in the well
thereof, fuch a meffenger as this, to admonifh or to exhort to fend
to that Council, without requiring her opinion therein as well as of
other Princes ; her Majefty and her whole realm may juftly think,
that there hath been no fuch honourable nor juft confideration
had of her eftate, and of her realm, as was meet, nor that fhe
may hope of any other thing but a determination, as much as in
the Pope fhall lye, to prejudice her Majefty and her realm, and all
other eftates of her poffeffions, and to eftablifh and confirm the authority of the Pope with all his abufe and errors.

No. XI.

Henry, Earl of Huntingdon, to the Earl of Leicester.

From the
Original, in
the British
Muſeum.

My Honourable good Lord,

I AM ſorry that my preſent diſeaſe is ſuch, as there are left me 1563. April. but theſe two remedies, either to ſwallow up thoſe bitter pills lately received, or to make you a partner of my griefs, thereby ſome- thing to eaſe a wounded heart. At my wife's laſt being at Court, to do her duty as became her, it pleaſed her Majeſty to give her a privy nippe, eſpecially concerning myſelf, whereby I perceive ſhe hath ſome * jealous conceit of me, and, as I can imagine, of late digeſted. How far I have been always from conceiting any great- neſs of myſelf, nay how ready I have been always to ſhun applauſes, both by my continual low ſail, and my carriage, I do aſſure myſelf, is beſt known to your Lordſhip, and the reſt of my neareſt friends; if not, mine own conſcience ſhall beſt clear me from any ſuch folly. Alas, what could I hope to effect, in the greateſt hopes I might imagine to have in the obtaining the leaſt likelihood of that height? Will a whole commonwealth deprive themſelves of ſo many bleſ- ſings preſently enjoyed, for a future hope uncertain, in favour of one inferior to many others, both in degree, and any princely quality? Will they forſake a Prince, both for excellent qualities, and rare virtues of nature, and of great hopes of an ineſtimable bleſſing by her princely iſſue, in reaſon of her youth, for a poor ſubject in years, and with- out any great hope of iſſue? No, no, I cannot be perſuaded they would, if I ſhould be ſo fooliſhly wicked to deſire it, or that my

---

* The ſuppoſed title of Lord Huntingdon   jealouſy about her ſucceſſion is well known; to the Crown came, through a female, from   and a ſtrong inſtance of it has been already George, Duke of Clarence, youngeſt brother   given in the impriſonment of Lady Catherine to Edward IV. Queen Elizabeth's extreme   Grey.

mind

mind were fo ambitioufly inclined. I hope her Majefty will be perfuaded of better things in me, and caft this conceit behind her. And, that a foolifh book, foolifhly written *, fhall not be able to poffefs her princely inclination, with fo bad a conceit of her faithful fervant, who defires not to live, but to fee her happy. What grief it hath congealed within my poor heart (but ever true) let your Lordfhip judge, whofe Prince's favour was always more dear unto me, than all other worldly felicities whatfoever. This I am bold to make known to your Lordfhip, humbly defiring the fame, when you fee your opportunity, to frame a new heart in her Majefty's princely breaft, whofe power I know is not little in effecting of far greater matters than this; for never fhall there be a truer heart in any fubject, than I will carry to her Majefty, fo long as I breathe. And fo I reft

Your poor Servant and Brother,

H. Huntingdon.

April   1563.

* John Hales's, in which fome confiderable perfons were concerned.

No. XII.

Letters from the Queen of Scots to the Duke of Norfolk.

From an in-
correct Tran-
fcript in Dr.
Forbes's
Collection,
now in the
poffeffion of
the Earl of
Hardwicke.

[Thefe political love-letters (for they can pafs under no other de-
nomination), from a very artful woman to a very weak man,
are, from the characters of the parties, and the confequences of
their intimacy, thought to deferve publication. It is fingular,
that, with all the commendation beftowed on the beauty of Mary
Queen of Scots, there are no two portraits of her which refemble
each other; that by Ifaac Oliver, in the King's poffeffion, and
that in the Duke of Devonfhire's at Chifwick, by Zuccero, are
undoubtedly more advantageous to her than any others we
know of. Brantome commends her perfon and her wit; and
Sir Nicholas White, Mafter of the Rolls in Ireland, fays of her to
Secretary Cecil, "She hath an alluring grace, a pretty Scotch
"fpeech, and a fearching wit clouded with mildnefs. Then, joy
"is a lively infective paffion, and carrieth many perfuafions to
"the heart, which ruleth all the reft; mine own affections, by,
"feeing the Queen's Majefty are doubled, and therefore I guefs
"what fight might work in others. But, if I might give advice,
"there fhould very few fubjects of this land have accefs to, or
"have conference with this Lady."

Hatfield Papers, Vol. I. p. 510.]

From the Queen of Scots to the Duke of Norfolk.

Mine own Lord,

I WROTE to you before, to know your pleafure if I fhould feek to make any enterprize; if it pleafe you, I care not for my danger; but I would wifh you would feek to do the like; for if you and I could efcape both, we fhould find friends enough; and for your lands, I hope they fhould not be loft; for, being free and honourably bound together, you might make fuch good offers for the countries, and the Queen of England, as they fhould not refufe. Our fault were not fhameful; you have promifed to be myne, and I yours; I believe the Queen of England and country fhould like of it. By means of friends, therefore, you have fought your liberty, and fatisfaction of your confcience, meaning that you promifed me you could not leave me. If you think the danger great, do as you think beft, and let me know what you pleafe that I do; for I will ever be, for your fake, perpetual prifoner, or put my life in peril for your weal and myne. As you pleafe command me, for I will, for all the world, follow your commands, fo that you be not in danger for me in fo doing. I will, either if I were out by humble fubmiffion, and all my fiiends were againft it, or by other ways, work for our liberties fo long as I live. Let me know your mind, and whether you are not offended at me; for I fear you are, feeing that I do hear no news from you. I pray God preferve you, and keep us both from deceitful friends. This laft of January.

Your own, faithful to death,

Queen of Scots, my Norfolk.

From the Same to the Same.

Myne own good Lord,

I HAVE forborn this long time to write to you, in refpect of
the dangers of writing, which you feemed to fear; but I muft
remember you of your own at tymes, as occafion ferveth, and let
you know the continuance of my truth to you, which I fee by this laft
look much detefted. But, if you mind not to fhrink at the matter,
I will die and live with you. Your fortune fhall be mine; therefore, let me know, in all things, your mind. The Bifhop of Rofs
writes to me, that I fhould make the offers to the Queen of England
now in my letter, which I write generally; becaufe I would enter
into nothing till I know your pleafure, which I fhall now follow. I
have heard that God hath taken your dear friend Pembroke, whereof
I am heartily forry; albeit that, nor other matter, trouble you to
your heart; for elfe you leave all your friends and me, for whofe
caufe you have done fo much already, that I truft you will preferve
you to a happyer meeting in difpite of all fuch raylers; wherein I
fufpect Huntingdon, for fuch like talk. But, for all their fay-
ings, I truft in God you fhall be fatisfied with my conditions and behaviour, and faithful duty to you, whenever it fhall pleafe God I be
with you, as I hope for my part the   maker fhall never have
the pleafure to fee, or hear my repentance or mifcontentment therein.
I have prayed God to preferve you, and grant us both his grace;
and then let them, like blafphemers, feel. So I end with the humble and heartieft recommendations to you of your own faithful to
death. This 19th of March.

From

From the Same to the Same.

I HAVE received, my own good conſtant Lord, your comfortable writings, which are to me as welcome as ever thing was,
for the hopes I ſee you are in to have ſome better fortune than you
had yet, through all your friends favour. And albeit my friends
caſe in Scotland be of heavy diſpleaſure unto me, yet nothing to
the fear I had of my ſon's delivery up to Queen Elizabeth, and
thoſe that I thought might be cauſe of longer delaying your affairs.
And, therefore, I took greater diſpleaſure than I have done ſince,
and that diminiſheth my health a little. For the Earl of Shrewſbury
came one night ſo merry to me, ſhewing that the Earl of Northumberland had been in rebellion, and was rendered to the Earl of Suffex, Lord Lieutenant of the North; which, ſince, I have found
falſe; but, at the ſudden, ſuch fear for friends combring me, I
wept ſo till I was all ſwollen three days after. But ſince I have
heard from you, I have gone abroad and ſought all means to avoid
diſpleaſure for fear of you; but I have need to care for my health, ſince
the Earl of Shrewſbury looks me to, and the peſtylence was in other
places. The Earl of Shrewſbury looks for Bateman to be inſtruſted
how to deal with me, becauſe he is ableſt and clean turned from
the Earl of Leyceſter; this I aſſure you, and pray keep that quiet.
I have no long leiſure; for I truſt to write by one of my gentlemen
ſhortly more ſurely. I pray you think and hold me in your grace
as your own, who daily ſhall pray to God to ſend you happy and
haſty deliverance of all troubles, not doubting but you would not
then enjoy alone all your felicities, not remembering your own
faithful to death, who ſhall not have any advancement or reſt without you. And ſo I leave to trouble you, but commend you to God.
This 17th day of May.

Your own Queen.

From

From the Same to the Same.

My good Lord,

IT has not been small comfort to me to have the mean to difcover at length, with our trusty servant the Bishop of Rofs, that
I might more plainly discover in all matters nor betray it, both for
the better intelligence of the State there to me, and of my heart to
him; but especially for the better intelligence betwixt us two; being means whom I have declared my opinion in all things to use
them by your advice, either to cover, as you please and shall best
serve your turn, for that will I have respect unto above all other
things, or to accept or refuse whatsoever conditions you think for both
our weale; for without yours I will not have any. And therefore
command him, as for yourself, and as your trusty servant; and believe him of all that he will assure you in my name: that is, in
effect, that I will be true and obedient to you, as I have promised,
as long as I live; praying you, if you be not, as you hoped you
should be, delivered, think no displeasure; but seek the best remedy,
and having amply communed with him, I will not trouble you with
long discourse but remitting all to him, I will, after my hearty commendations to you, my good Lord, pray God to send you your
hearty desire. From Chattesworth, the 14th of June.

Your own, faithful to death.

From.

From the Same to the Same.

SUNDAY I received a writing by Borthwick from you, whereby I perceive the fatisfaction you have of my plain dealing with you, as I muft do of my duty. Confidering how much I am beholden to you many ways, I am glad the grant of my good-will is fo agreeable to you. Albeit I know myfelf to be fo unworthy, to be fo well liked of one of fuch wifdom and good qualities, yet do I think my happe great in that, yea much greater than my defert. Therefore I will be about to ufe myfelf fo, that, fo far as God fhall give me grace, you fhall never have caufe to diminifh your good conceit and favour of me, while I fhall efteem and refpect you in all my doings fo long as I live, as you would wifh your own to do. Now, good my Lord, more words to this purpofe would be unfeemly to my prefent condition, and importunable to you, amongft fo many bufinefs; but this, truft you, as written by them that means unfeignedly. This day I received a letter from you by this bearer, whereby I receive the thought you take of my health, which, thanks to God, is much better than it was at his departing, but not yet very ftrong, nor quit of the forenefs of my fide. It caufes me to be more heavy and penfive than I would or need to be, confidering the care you have of me, whereof I will not thank you, for I have remitted all my caufes to you to do as for yourfelf. I write to the Bifhop of Rofs what I hear from the Duke of D'Alva, Governor of the Netherlands. Let me know your pleafure at length in writing, what I fhall anfwer. Now, my Norfolk, you bid me command you; that would be befides my duty many ways. But to pray you I will, that you counfel me not, to take patiently my great griefs, except you promife me to trouble you no more for the death of your ward. I wifh you had another in his room to make you merry, or elfe I would he were out
both

both of England and Scotland. You forbid me to write; be fure I E L I Z A-
will think it no pains, whenever my health will permit it, but plea- B E T H.
fure, as alfo to receive your letters, which I pray you to fpare not, 1570.
when you have leifure without troubling you; for they fhall fall in
no hands where they will be better received. The phyficians write
at length; they feem to love you marveloufly, and not miflike of
me. We had but general talk, and fome, of your matters; but not
in any body's name; therefore I anfwered nothing, but giving ear
foberly. When Borthwick goeth up, you fhall underftand all; in
this it is unintelligible; mean time I muft warn you, when I hear
any thing touching you. Argyle fends me word exprefsly, that
when he met at Stirling with Murray, the Regent of Scotland,
he affured him, I fhould never come home, and that he had intelligence for to be quit of me, remembered him of his promifes. Borthwick will write it to the Bifhop of Rofs, and my Lord Fleming.
Argyle prayed me, if you were my friend, to advertife you haftily:
Take of this what pleafes you, but I am fure they will be traytors to
you and me; and if they were in Turkey, you and I were never
the worfe; albeit I will not be importune. But, and this Summer
paft, I hope by the good all year. God preferve you from all traytors, and make your friends as true and conftant. From Wingfield
late at night this 24th.

Your affured,

MARY.

E L I Z A-
BETH.
1583.

From the
Originals in
the Paper
Office.

No. XIII.

Letters from Sir Edward Stafford, Ambaſſador in France.

[If one may judge from the remains of their correſpondence, Throck-morton and Stafford were the ableſt Ambaſſadors whom Queen Elizabeth employed in France during her long reign. The former was a deeper politician, and the more deſigning man; the latter had more of the courtier and the gentleman, and was particularly qualified for that Court, by having ſerved in the army, and having formed a general acquaintance in France, of both parties. Though he writes incorrectly, it is always with good ſenſe, and thorough knowledge of the world. In the affair of the Barricades, it ap-pears from Thuanus †, that the Duke of Guiſe behaved with par-ticular attention towards him, and Sir Edward, with equal ſpirit and politeneſs, refuſed to accept his protection.

His Lady was an extraordinary character, and, by her accom-pliſhments, equally fitted for the French court. She was niece to the Duke of Norfolk who was beheaded, and after the death of her firſt huſband the Lord Douglas Sheffield, was privately married to Leiceſter, by whom ſhe had the famous Sir Robert Dudley, The dread of the Queen's reſentment, and the favourite's malice, who diſowned the contract, was the occaſion of her ſecond marriage with Sir Edward Stafford; he was impriſoned for it, but ſhe appears to have made him, if not a very good wife, a very agreeable compa-nion; her conduct, indeed, not being defenſible. The ſuit which Sir Robert inſtituted, after the Queen's death, in the Star Cham-ber, to eſtabliſh the validity of his mother's marriage with the Earl, and the extraordinary manner in which the proceedings were ſtopped, are fully ſet forth in Dugdale's Baronage. By this act of injuſtice, the country loſt the ſervice of an able man in Sir Robert Dudley, who took refuge in Italy; and Charles the Firſt, during his troubles, was, for a ſum of money, induced to grant a patent of peerage to his daughter, by the title of Ducheſs Dudley, in the preamble to which patent the hardſhip of her caſe is fully acknow-ledged.]

† See alſo Satire Menippée, & Memoires de la Ligue.

Sir Edward Stafford to the Queen.

MAY it pleaſe your moſt excellent Majeſty, to give me leave to
advertiſe you what I find here, fit for your Majeſty, ſince I
writ laſt to Mr. Secretary. Still, of all ſides, and very credibly, I am
advertiſed, that there is a meaning and a good-will, to annoy your
Majeſty by all means, by the way of Scotland, and private Councils
had about it ; whereto, as I writ before to Mr. Secretary, Mannyng-
ville is called, and private conferences had with him, with a meaning to ſend him into Scotland, and to have men to go, to the number
of 1500, and to land at Dumbritton, and to fortify both the town
underneath, and the caſtle: and withal, that levies be already
making; but when I ſend to the places, I find nothing, but rather
things in ſhow, and given out by the Captains belonging to the Duke
of Guiſe, than otherwiſe.

This I am ſure of, that if there be any thing done, they muſt
embark them, and afore they embark, there muſt be ſome preparation
made for that, about which I hope I have given ſuch order, that it ſhall
be no ſooner in hand, but your Majeſty ſhall be advertiſed of it ; having
upon all havens, upon the coaſt of Normandy and Brittany, provided
to have preſent intelligence given; beſides that I have, to be ſurer,
ſent, both into Brittany and Normandy, men for the purpoſe.

I pray God keep his continual hand of his grace upon your Majeſty, as he hath done hitherto, and to preſerve you from all enterprizes againſt your perſon, which your Majeſty muſt be carefuller to
look to than ever, with more care of yourſelf, both for your own
ſake, and all your poor ſubjects: for, aſſure yourſelf, that I know for
a certainty, out of the bowels of your evil-diſpoſed ſubjects here,
and of them that are here furtherers of their naughty faſhion, that
they are out of hope of all ways and enterprizes to hurt you,
but

but only two; the one, by the way of Scotland, which they give out that they have affuredly at their commandment; the other, by the deftruction of your perfon, which they hope for.

As for Ireland, they ftick not to make a mock at it, and to fay, they practife there, but to keep your Majefty at the gaze, and to fpend your money, which they fay, they can make you fpend in great quantity, with a fmall charge of their part; and that it is the better way not any more to feek you, but at the fountain.

I know not whether your Majefty be advertifed of it; but I think, if it be fo, you fhould be fooner than we here, that the King of Spain hath fent a perfon of credit from him into Scotland, and treated with the King of Scots, and that there are fix hundred that are either gone, or upon the point of going, into Scotland, moft of them mufketeers. If it be fo, it is the beginning of a fire, that will burft out into fome great flame, which there are naughty people here look fhall not be long afore it come. There was never more of our naughty people in France than there is now, nor that fpeak fo villainoufly, nor fo plainly againft your Majefty, nor that feek every hole open, where there may be fome practices found againft you. I take a courfe of a fhow of mild dealing with every body, which maketh, that they that be leaft evil of them, are not afraid of me, and by that means I hope that there fhall no matter of ripenefs be, that can come to their hands, but I fhall have an inkling of it. I hope to do your Majefty fome kind of fervice with that courfe, and to keep it, without your Majefty give me commandment to the contrary. It may be a dangerous courfe for me, if any body that loveth me not, have power to do me harm with you; but, in the mean time, being the likelieft courfe to do you fervice withal, I will put mine own particular harm in a venture, to do the beft good I can to your public fervice.

Now to advertife your Majefty certainly of them that are likelieft to enterprize againft you here, or to favour it. For the houfe

of

of Guife, your Majefty knoweth their good-wills well enough. For the King, his courfe of dealing is fuch, and fo uncertain, that, by reafon of the uncertainty of his favours, there can never be affured judgment given which way he will bend himfelf; for, as long as Efpernon hath credit, he will hinder any thing the Duke of Guife doth, and fince thefe laft quarrels, private heart-burnings are, that be not fo hidden but men fee them, and it is greatly feared that he will not long laft, but that he will have St. Megrim's end: and certain it is, that Manningville had been difpatched long fince, if he, becaufe the Guife favoured the matter, had not hindered it: but ftill they prevail, for I hear it for certain, that Manningville fhall be difpatched, and embark at Eau. Whenfoever it be done, it will be fo fuddenly and fecretly done, that I fhall hardly have time to give your Majefty warning. And therefore, what your Majefty thinketh fit to be done in it, is to be done upon this warning, both for that your Majefty mindeth to do yourfelf of that fide; and for me, if it be your pleafure to have me do any thing in it, that you fend me your pleafure with all the expedition you may. The third, that I fear in the end, as much as any in France, is Monfieur. I fee his difpofition fuch, and fo flexible, to be brought to do any thing to feed his ambitious humour; and fince this laft quarrel of Efpernon and D'Aumale, he hath not let the opportunity fail, and fought upon the Duke of Guife in prefenting of him favour, which he hath often done afore, but they would never bite at it; but now it feemeth, they make fhow to hearken to it. The only hope that there is left of their not thoroughly agreeing is, that they know him. And this I am fure of, that no longer agone than yefternight, the Duke of Guife had private conference with a friend of his, about the matter, and afked him advice in it, being a thing, as he faid, he could not tell what to do in; the King's difpofition, to grace *Petits Valets* afore him, moving him; one way and Monfieur's nature another

6

another way, putting him in fear to have any thing to do with him. His friend's counsel was to him, to temporize, and to entertain Monsieur with as many courteous messages, and offers of service, as he could; but to take heed he committed nothing to writing, for fear lest time would give him cause to repent Monsieur's acquaintance, which was, and had been yet, dangerous to as many as had dealt with him, considering his little ability, and less disposition, to have regard to any men of quality that did him service. And besides his accustomed use to keep any thing he had in store, to cut men's throats that had offered him service, when he was once weary of them; which was hourly to be feared, his uncertainty being so great, as he, and every body knew it. And therefore, by any means, to keep that hand, that Monsieur should have cause for the present to be contented, and he in liberty to cleave either to him, or to remain fast to the King, which was the likelier of the two, considering his present state in the Crown, with the which he had ever held, and the other's nature, which he was to stand in awe of.

The Duke of Guise embracing him, resolved to follow his counsel, and upon that spake in such sort to Drow, that under colour of being sent to the King, was sent about that matter to the Duke of Guise, who used it so well, that Drow went away marvellous well satisfied; but when he required the Duke of Guise to write to Monsieur, he desired him to pardon him. So that I hope they will one entertain another, to serve the other's turn, without any thing at all, trusting one another.

Pinard, as I writ to Mr. Secretary the last day, is returned from Monsieur, marvelously discontented. He went for two special things, the one to bring Monsieur to the Court, according to his promise to the Queen Mother; the other, to get Cambray into the King's hand. For the first, Monsieur answered divers reasons why

he

he would not come to the Court : at the length he made a demand,
to have his guard lodged in the King's houfe, as well as the King's, which the King took in marvellous ill part. For the fecond, Pinard offered Monfieur from the King, that if he would put Cambray and the citadel into any man's hand that could fpend in France 25,000 Franks a year, to be the Governor of it, he would pay the garrifon and defend it upon his own coft and charge; or if he miftrufted that them that he fhould put in, might be too much at his devotion, he was contented to name unto him three of his own followers, that were men of quality; and if he would put any of them in, he would do the like; which were Rochepot, La Chaftre, and Bellegarde. But to be ftill at the charge to furnifh him whenfoever he would, to fpend his money, and wafte and fpoil his people, and to leave the government of a town of fuch importance in their hands, that have neither honefty to care for, nor goods to be careful of the lofs thereof, what treachery foever they committed, that he would not do. Which Monfieur refufing, was the caufe that Pinard came away dif- contented, and the King protefting that he fhould never be defired more to come to him, nor offered reafonable help, feeing he fo little fet by it.

Very wife men think here, that know Monfieur's humour very well, that when the King will no more intreat him to come, he will come of himfelf upon a fudden, and that he will be fain at length to defire that for Cambray that the King offereth.

Monfieur beginneth to be fomewhat more followed than he was, by means of the King's dealings in this affembly; for nei- ther the clergy is contented with him, nor the nobility. For he feeketh to draw more from the clergy than they will ever grant him, but by force; and feeketh to draw from the Nobility, part of their authority over their vaffals (as they term them), which will never be done without blows. And that maketh both forts to flock about Monfieur, more than they were minded; fo that

D d   the

the beft feers into the eftate here do think Monfieur's greatnefs will begin to rife again by the King's defaults. Some, as wife as they, think, that the King, finding it, will take up in time, and that though he do not, Monfieur hath fo evil ufed the reft of his fair offered fortunes heretofore, that any thing that can be offered him hereafter, will come but to wind, as the reft have done.

There came to me the laft day, late in the night, one apparelled like a Jefuit, defirous to come to me very fecretly; told me he was ready to do your Majefty all the fervice he might, affuring himfelf, that, according to your liberality accuftomed, you would recompence him; and that, for my part, I would keep his dealings fecret to myfelf; which affuring him, both of your part, for your liberality, and mine, for my fecretnefs, he declared to me firft, how he was often with the Spanifh Ambaffador, and now, by reafon of his coat, began to be great with the new-come Nuncio; that he found great amity contracted between them, which might be prejudicial to your Majefty. That he would difcover to me, from time to time, all their dealings; and that he gave me warning of one thing, that my wife was thought to be a Catholic in mind, though fhe made no fhew of it, and therefore I was to take heed what dealings fhe was acquainted withal. To the firft, I encouraged him all the ways I could, with affurance of my gratefulnefs, to the uttermoft of my power, and hope of your Majefty's reward farther. For the laft I thanked him greatly for it, told him it was a thing that I had always feared, and therefore defired him to have a fpecial eye to it, that I might be advertifed of it, and that, if I did once know it, I would keep her fhort enough. Which courfe I held with him, for two reafons, one, to have it given abroad that fhe is fo, which I have gone about, ever fince I came hither, to blow abroad, to make thofe women that be privateft about the Queen Mother, of the beft fort that come to fee her, to fpeak franklier to her. The other, to fee by the blowing of it abroad by him, whether he were a man fet

6   of

E L I Z A-
B E T H.
1583.

of purpofe to feel me or no. Which not only I have found out that way, being a thing by his means fpread round about the next days after; but alfo I prefently dogged him, and found that he went to the Duke of Guife's houfe prefently from me, and that he is one of the   belonging, and only depending upon him. I hope both to make his news he hath fpread abroad, and him, to ferve your turn, as I will make her handle the matter, and as I will ufe him, if your Majefty will fometimes make fome letters be written to me for the purpofe, that I may fhow.

And thus let me make an end, with making your Majefty to laugh, at one that came the laft day puffing to me in great hafte, affuring me, that it was certified that Segur's going into England was, to feek marriage of you for his mafter. And that he had carried a teftimony from all the churches, that confidering this laft accident of the Queen his wife's, he was at liberty to put her away, marry again, which they counfelled him to, and that your Majefty gave attentive ear to it. I anfwered him as coldly as I could, that was a thing I was not acquainted with, but that I knew your Majefty not fo hot to marry, but both you would have leifure to fee him free that fought you, and give us leifure to talk more of the matter afore it were done fo fuddenly.

Of the matters of the Queen of Navarre, I have written fo at large to Mr. Secretary, that my letter being already tedious enough, I leave troubling of your Majefty, and commit you to the tuition of the Almighty. This firft of December 1583.

I befeech your Majefty that this matter of my wife may not pafs yourfelf, for if it be given out any way at all, the play is marred, and your Majefty's fervice that way loft.

There was news came hither yefterday, that Monfieur was, with force, come from Chafteauthierry. Some fufpected he was come fecretly hither, to fpeak with the King and Queen Mother. And all his own folks here were in a marvellous dump. But the King

ELIZA- and Queen Mother were in greater, for they had advertifement he
BETH.
1583   was gone into Languedoc, and were greatly amazed. Yet the certainty is not known, but I had a lacquey from a friend of mine
there this morning, and letters, by the which I am affured, that
Monfieur is there ftill, but that he went about a little love matter
two or three leagues, and lay out but one night. To be more certain of all, I have, under colour of fending Monfieur a nag of mine,
that Monfieur hearing of had a mind to. I have fent one purpofely to prefent that nag, that will bring me the certainty.

Endorfed, copy of my letter to the Queen, by Painter, the firft
of December 1583.

Sir E. Stafford to Secretary Walfingham.

1583.   SIR,
Decemb. 1ft.
F IRST, to begin with fuch things as have paffed, or that I
omitted in my laft letter. The King fent for Clernaut after that
he was gone, and told him, that he had fent Bellievre to deal about
the matter of his fifter; that he was very forry with all his heart,
that evil reports had made him do that which he had done towards
her. That he defired him to be a means to the King of Navarre,
to have all things done to his fifter's honour; for, if he did not deal
well with her, all the wars for religion in France fhould be nothing
near unto that which fhould now be againft him with extremity;
that he would not have his blood difhonoured, and bid him go fpeak
with the Queen his mother, who fhould tell him more; which Clernaut did without any reply, to hear her afore he would make his
anfwer.

Thereupon he went to the Queen Mother, who delivered him the
fame thing the King did. And added withal, that for her own
particular,

particular, in dealing well with her daughter, fhe would be the King
of Navarre's agent in all his caufes, and Clernaut's for being the
mediator of it.

To her, Clernaut anfwered, that the King had ufed the fame
fpeeches to him; to whom he had forborne to anfwer; for the refpect
that he had, put him over to farther fpeech with her; but to her
he defired pardon, though he anfwered plainly, he would carry no
fuch anfwer to his Mafter. That the ground of her difhonour came
from hence, whence it was to be repaired. That if, the fault coming
from hence, they would, by ufing extremity, feek to make him do a
thing fo difhonourable, he was fure he had that courage, that he
would abide rather all hazards, and put himfelf in the protection of
God; and with that departed, and would have fpoken with the King
again, but he found him gone through the Queen Mother's chamber
a back way into the park, where in paffing he had fpoken with her;
and Villeroy fent for him an hour after, and told him, he was forry
for the fpeeches that had paffed from the King, and fo was the King
himfelf fince, being moved with an advertifement that came to him
from that country, that the King of Navarre meant prefently to
repudiate the Queen and take another. And defired him to be fo
difcreet as to make no word of that to the King of Navarre, the
King having fpoken it in choler, which he was very forry for.

To that Clernaut anfwered, that he never meant to deliver any fuch
meffage to the King of Navarre, whatfoever had come of it.

For the Queen of Navarre, Bellievre had made her advance herfelf to Cadillac by the laft news: fome fay now to Nerac, but the
King of Navarre goeth ftill farther from her, and there is yet no
news that Bellievre is come to him.

The King of Navarre is in Foix, and in going, furprized a town
of his own called Mont de Marfant, which, by the laft peace, fhould
have been put into his hands, and they ever kept it againft the
King's will, as the King affirmed by all meffages to the King of
Navarre,

Navarre, who prefently fent word to the King of it, that feemed to
be very well contented with it, though I know he ftorm marveloufly
at it, and know not whereabouts they are, fpecially by the King of
Navarre's going into Foix, which is within four leagues of Montreal,
and not far off D'Anville, with whom they fear marveloufly his conference.

The King is marveloufly offended with the Duke of Savoy, both
for the taking of Colmars, which he doth fufpect is done by intelligence between him and D'Anville, as alfo for this falling of the Five
Cantons of the Swiffers from him, which he layeth all upon him as
his practices: the King, as they fay, ftayeth but Bellievre's return, by
whofe hands all affairs of the Swiffers pafs; and it is thought he
meaneth to break league with them firft. The King hath fent for
the Ambaffador of Savoy, and hath been very earneft with him and
hot: the Ambaffador affureth the contrary, and ufeth mild fpeeches
and affurances to that intent.

I received letters to-day from Monf. de Beza, where he writeth,
that, for all the Duke of Savoy's preffing for this diet, he now flieth
the tilt, and delayeth the matter, and armeth himfelf, fo that the
affected cantons now affemble a diet, to provide for the worft, both
for their alliesand themfelves.

Alfo he affureth me, that the King of Spain hath drawn out
moft of his old garrifons out of Italy, and put in Bofognes, and that
both they and the reft of them that came from the Terceras, are already at Sanonne, and fhall go into the Low Country. Divers marvel
that being already fo ftrong there as he is, he bringeth in fo fuperfluous a number of all old foldiers, without it be for fome farther intent, than only the Low Country's reduction.

The King hath continued the *Grands Jours* for three months
longer. Truly juftice is done in them marvellous feverely. At the
firft it was thought that it was taken in hand to attrap them of the
religion; but truly it is come to all men, more to Catholics than
Proteftants.

Proteftants, Men of great quality have been executed in it. Buffi's father is condemned in it, and is fain to fly to Cambray to his fon-in-law Balagny, for fuccour; and his daughter, Balagny's wife, is come to this town to intreat for him, but the King refufeth pardon generally to all them that are condemned by the *Grand Jours.* And, in truth, there hath been marvellous great ordinary robberies committed, and murders by divers, that it is a fhame to hear.

I am credibly informed, that all Languedoc had been by this time in arms, if one Advignon, difguifed like a mariner, had not arrived fafely, with the King's packet hidden in a fachel of fand, and other fuch trafh, at Narbonne, to the Count of Joyeuze, in the laft month. His meffage was, to have a fpecial eye to all things, which, if it had not been done, divers places had been furprifed. The meffenger was laid for in divers places, and efcaped hardly, having exprefs charge from the King to go part by fea, if need were, and to caft away, if need were, the packet into the fea or fome puddle, the fame being made clofe up and heavy, of purpofe.

The caufe of Duke Joyeuze's going to Rome, (better known to your Honour, than to me it can be, being afore my time) was yefterday reported to me by a man of good credit, great knowledge, and a Catholick, as follows: To obtain difpenfation of the Pope, for the King to fell 100,000 crowns yearly revenue of church land. To procure the excommunication of Montmorency *tanquam fautorem hæreticorum,* according to the bull *In Cænâ Domini.* To buy the country of Avignon. To procure a red hat for the Archbifhop of Narbonne, his brother. But finding the opinion of his credit in France inferior to his own imagination, and the Pope and Clergy of Rome more ftately than he looked for, he was greatly difmayed and difcontented in himfelf; whereupon, it is thought, his difeafe is a melancholy that will make an end of him fhortly, as being increafed by that the Pope denied him in all.

The

The King feeketh in this affembly to have his gentlemen and gentlewomen that he made thefe laft years, to be brought to the kitchen * again, and all his new officers to be difcharged, with the authority of the affembly. And with this fimple conclufion, I commit your Honour to God. Paris, 1ft December, 1583.

Endorfed, copy of my letter to Mr. Secretary, by Painter, the 1ft of December 1583.

Sir Edward Stafford to the Queen.

1583.
Dec. 10th.

MAY it pleafe your moft excellent Majefty, to be advertifed, that hearing, as I writ in my laft to you, that Monfieur was departed from Chafteauthierry, whereof we had here a great alarm, upon divers bruits that came upon that, I fent a man thither, under the colour of prefenting him a nag, to fee what became of him: but I find that he was away but one night, and came again the next day, being only gone but to a gentleman's houfe thereby, with few company with him.

Monfieur taketh great pleafure in thinking, that they which were here were very much afraid of him, which in truth is true, and the King, as all they that be about him fay, groweth in more fear of him every day, than other. I cannot affure your Majefty that it is true, but that they may have better intelligence than outwardly they make fhow of; but if it be, they be the cunningeft carriers of it that ever was feen, and the wifeft of both religions are deceived in it, and they that be neareft about them both. On Sunday was the marriage between Ferragues's daughter and Anvilly; within two days after they be married, the father, the mother, and the wife

* Roturiers.

go back again, as they fay there. . The marriage was very private
without ceremony; and in truth, there was no great caufe why it fhould be otherwife, 'for fuch a man's daughter as Ferrague's, and fuch a man's fon as Anvilly was.

Surely, Madam, there were great troubles in likelihood to grow here, in men's opinions, and no fpeech was but of wars, of the which I have written more at large to Mr. Secretary, not to trouble your Majefty with the reading of too tedious a letter.

Monfieur has fent hither Rafont, very fecretly, to treat from him with the King of Navarre's and Prince of Condé's fervants here, to fee if they could make him certain how things in Languedoc and Guienne went; and to fee if there were not any way poffible, to bring to pafs a good truft between the King of Navarre, Monfieur, and the Prince of Condé, and them of the churches: and for to bring them the rather unto it, and to take all the doubts out of their heads, he offered them to put your Majefty for to anfwer for his good ufing of himfelf hereafter. And that, though they had caufe to fufpect Monfieur for what was paft, there were divers great and important reafons moved him; that hereafter, though for religion he would never take it in hand, yet if they would take arms for the *bien publique,* which had great need of it, that whilft he lived, he would take fuch part as they.

They made him a true account how things paffed there, which he firft demanded; but for the laft, they anfwered him very difcreetly, that the King keeping his promife with them, and letting them live in peace, they were to take it very thankfully, and to give God thanks.

As for your Majefty, they thought you would not counfel them any fuch thing. Rafont told them, that he had commandment to come and make me acquainted with it; but I hear not yet of him, yet it is four days agone; which hath made me to ftay fending, expecting to hear from his mouth, fome more particular matter than that which

E e   they

they had advertifed. Whereunto I had prepared a dilatory anfwer, with all the beft manner I could, if he had come; which courfe I mean to take in all fuch matters, but only to have a good ear, and a fmall tongue, till fuch time as I can advertife your Majefty, and know your pleafure.

He being not yet come, and, as I hear, going out of the town, I have thought good to ftay no longer, but to advertife your Majefty of it. They that gave me this advertifement, in following the matter, drew the wire fo well out of him, that he burft out that this league was propounded to the Duke of Guife, and that he had once agreed unto it; and, going to write his confent unto Monfieur, one of his friends pulled him from the paper, which almoft agreeth with that I writ to your Majefty in my laft letter; which brought them farther out of love with the matter, and more miftruft than before, to fee that he confeffed the feeking firft upon the Duke of Guife afore them, which two could fcarce hang well together.

At my firft coming hither, as my duty was to all Ambaffadors that have come to fee me, I have gone about ever to affure them, as they did me, on their Mafter's part, of the continuance of your Majefty's friendfhip towards their Mafters and States. Two days agone, the Ambaffador of Venice came to me, and fhewed me very earneft affection towards your Majefty, of that ftate, and a commandment from them to continue and increafe the fame, as a thing they defired, above all Princes of Chriftendom; and was very earneft with me to deliver it your Majefty, with great affurance on their part, in fuch kind as though, if it feemed your Majefty made account of them, that he might find it more than of ordinary compliments, he had fomething to fay farther. If your Majefty will have me to take knowledge of any thing more than of ordinary good will towards that State, having received commandment from you, I will obey it to the beft of my power. Likewife I writ to Monf. Chaftillion, as one of my old acquaintance at my coming firft, to renew

it, and to require his continuance of his good will towards your Majesty, which he had so often vowed to me. Last of all, to assure him,
of your good will towards him, as hereditable towards him for his
father's sake. I received answer from him with the greatest humility of service towards your Majesty, and offer to leave all causes in
France, to venture his life for the service of your Majesty, whensoever it shall please you to command him.

The Duke of Bouillon came the last day to the town, and sent to
me, that he would come see me that afternoon. I made an excuse
of business, because I would not have him come first to me; and presently after his man's departure, I went and saw him at his lodging;
where he acknowledged, as much as might be, his dutiful remembrance of your Majesty's honourable using of him in England, with
earnest protestations of his dutiful service, which he reiterated again
the next day that he came to visit me, and that very earnestly. So
did likewise Monsieur de la Vall, who came to visit me to that intent,
and I rendered him the next day his salutation, and likewise to the
Count Chasteauroux, who did the like to me in the honour of your
Majesty, to whom he protested his service.

The Pope's Nuntio sent his Secretary the last day to Monsieur,
who was received there with great kindness. I cannot hear by them
that come or write from thence, that it was any other than ordinary
compliments upon the Nuntio's first arrival. I shall hear more within
a day or two; they had both often and very secret conference.

I send your Majesty a letter which Monsieur sent me by a Courier, and withal I received from a friend of mine a letter with a little
in it, with a contrary hand in English. The words were,
The Ambassador that went to her Majesty is come again, and hath
brought nothing but words; whereat, what show soever we make, we
are not contented. I pray God it breed not some mischief. For my
part, Madam, I think nothing from thence can breed any great good,
without it be with doing somebody great harm, and therefore I think

E e 2 good

good words is your beft courfe, without any great deeds. I do keep
that hand with them (though I write plainly to your Majefty), that
they think not fo; and fo fhall do, if they hear not the contrary
from England.

Endorfed, Copy of my Letter to the Queen, by Chamberlain, the
10th of December 1583.

Sir Edward Stafford to Lord Burleigh.

1583
Dec. 19th.
I HAVE fent your Lordfhip the very words of Mr. Secretary's
letter to me, by Mr. Conftable, and leave to your Lordfhip's
judgment, whether any man that can fee farther than the end of
his own nofe, may not judge or think, that there is an evil meaning
in the writer *, and to fufpect that there is an intention, if it be not
already done, to make her that it is written from, in her name †,
to think as they mean.

" Sir, I am exprefsly willed by her Majefty to make this prefent
difpatch to you, thereby to require you in her name, that you do
carry a very watchful eye over the Lord Paget and Charles Arundel,
who have of late conveyed themfelves away without licence, feeking
very carefully to underftand what they may practife or deal in the
prejudice of this Crown, wherein her Majefty hath willed me to fignify to you, that fhe is affured that the alliance that my Lady, your
wife, hath with them, fhall not make you to be more remifs to perform your duty towards her, with that truft that fhe doth fpecially
repofe in you."

* Walfingham.   † The Queen.

Copy

*Copy of a private Letter to Mr. Secretary, about the An-
fwer of that he writ to me of my Lord Paget.*

SIR,

I RECEIVED the laft day a packet from your Honour, by
Mr. Conftable; in it a letter touching Paget and Arundell, and
the Queen's commandment for the diligent looking into their actions
here. Truly her commandment muft needs make me more diligent,
if it be poffible, not more careful; that my duty bound me to enough
afore, and therefore more I cannot.

I had, afore your letter, taken the fame fhow of carelefs courfe you
writ to me of, thinking it the beft; and truly I find fo by experience, for by that means they take lefs heed of me. I have had one
lodged by them, but I am fifhing for one that is daily with them,
and their fervant; I am not out of hope to have him. They have
yet dealt themfelves with nobody, nor feen any man of importance.
What Charles Paget doth for them I can hardly learn as yet, for he
is infeparable with Morgan, and Morgan is hand in hand with
the Bifhop of Glafcow; judge you what may be then moft likely,
and I muft have time to feek out; yet Paget, and his fellow, both
proteft, that neither they do, nor will do, any thing againft the
Queen's Majefty, nor hang upon the French King, the Pope, the
King of Spain, the Duke of Guife, nor any other, as long as neceffity for meat driveth not them to it, and that the Queen will let
them live to their confcience here, with reafonable favour, without
undoing. I fhall perchance come by their contrary dealings, ere
it be long, if they deal in any thing.

Paget hath received 4000 Crowns, as I am advertifed for certainty, by the hands of Bartholomew Martin here; the exchange
came

came from Mofley, a merchant in Cheapfide, to Roan, and from Roan hither.

Sure I am of one thing, that, as yet, they have fpoken with nobody of importance, nor any ftranger of value, without it be by the fecond hand, by Charles Paget's and Morgan's means, without fpeaking with any themfelves, for that yet the elder brother, nor his fellow, have not yet feen Morgan fince they came.

Now, Sir, give me leave to defire you to do me fo much favour, as that I may requeft you to tell the Queen that, what alliance foever any body had to my wife, there is ueither alliauce to her, to me, nor kindred to any of us both, not if it were mine own brother, that, if he enterprize any thing againft her, fhould fcape punifhment in extremity, as long as I had any handle. And therefore much lefs, I hope, fhe will doubt in thefe, who neither have kindred, alliance, or any other matter of value in them, to draw me a thought from my duty, though I were but a private man, much more being in a place of truft; which I befeech you to tell her, as there is nothing I can receive more wrong in, than to be in that point, never fo finally, doubted of.

I have the fooner fent you this bearer Afke, becaufe you may know of the fpeeches that are here of the French Ambaffador's going into Scotland; becaufe that, if you will, and think good, there are ways enough. The man that carrieth the difpatch being watched at Dover to fee what he carrieth, afore he come to London: his name is Harvey, the French Ambaffador's ordinary fervant.

Sir

Sir Edward Stafford to the Queen.

May it pleafe your moft excellent Majefty,

I RECEIVED four days agone this letter here inclofed from Monfieur to your Majefty, with another from him to myfelf, to fend it to you furely and fpeedily; which having kept four or five days in my hand, hoping of an ordinary poft, and finding the wind hath permitted none thefe three weeks and more, I durft no longer keep it, but to fend this bearer with it to your Majefty, moft humbly craving your pleafure to know, hereafter receiving any in fuch fort from him, whether I fhall fend it away prefently, to avoid opinion of negligence, or keep till a better opportunity, to avoid expence: and as I fhall know your Majefty's pleafure, fo will I direct myfelf in that, or any thing elfe.

For your Majefty's pleafure I received by Mr. Secretary, about my Lady, as in all things elfe, fo muft and will I fulfil your Majefty's will. I pray God, either for 500 marks of mine own, or as much of your purfe, I have as good intelligence, as I think that way would have gotten. For this your Majefty may affure yourfelf of, that there are four women in the Court, Madame Villeroy, Retz, Princefs of Condé and Nevers, that have all the news, and moft fecreteft devices of the Court; for there is never a one of thefe, or at the leaft amongft thefe four, one of them, that hath not either a lover, an honourer, or a private friend, of the fecreteft Council in the Court, that will almoft hide nothing from them. With thefe, fhe having conference, as they all defire her company, among women, (except Princeffes of your quality) few things but are ripped up; and the more bending they feel in religion, the more franknefs both in men

and

and women commonly there is; and the more they feel them bend, the more they ufe franknefs, hoping to make them full coming. I am fure of one thing, fhe could have done no harm; and it had been a great hazard, if by that means I had nôt done a great deal of good for your fervice. But as I havc my mind, while I am here, to feek no ways but to ferve you, fo feeing you like not of my way, I will feek no way but that·which may beft like you: and therefore I will feek fome way, the cleanlieft that I can, to take away the opinion I have already gone about to print, and find fome other the beft courfe I can, to do your Majefty the beft fervice I may *.

For'Monfieur, fince the Queen Mother went·thither, I hear nothing from thence; they here look daily for fomewhat.

Upon Friday laft, but then the Queen Mother was not arrived at Chafteauthierry, came Monfieur's Provoft from him, with letters to the King, to defire him to give him ftrong hand to attach the Abbot of Albene, as one, that the man apprehended, confeffed to be a partner in this confpiracy, and to defire the King prefently to fend him to him.

The King thinkéth ftrange to have fuch meffage from his brother within his realm; yet, feeming very willing to have any body to anfwer fuch fact, fent for the Abbot, and told him that he muft give him his faith and a furety fufficient, that he fhould keep Paris for his prifon, till he had anfwered to fuch things as his brother'had laid to his charge; which he called Monfieur's Provoft to affift unto, to fee what order he had taken with the Abbot; and therewithal fent his brother word, that he found this manner of his dealing with him ftrange, to fend to him that was his King, though his brother, to

* The Queen's declining to avail herfelf of the Lady Sheffield's turn for intrigue, proceeded either from a fcrupulous and laudable delicacy, to make ufe of fuch deceitful and hypocritical practices, or from her fufpicions of the Lady's fincerity and fidelity. She was niece to the beheaded Duke of Norfolk. Mr. Walpole has a portrait of her firft hufband, Lord Sheffield, at Strawberry hill.

†

fend

fend to him any that was remaining where he was, to be examined by him that had no juftice, and that he thought it had been
rather fit for him to have fent the foldier that he had, to him, to
have examined him, and confronted him with the Abbot, or any
other, he having only, by being King, the adminiftration of juftice in his hands, and not Monfieur. Yet he was contented to do
that he did, to fhow better nature, and more care over Monfieur,
than he looked Monfieur would do for him in that cafe; though in
the end, he thought it would fall out but practices of them about
him, to ftretch to farther matter, than any thing elfe of truth;
which a great many here are in fome opinion of: what will fall out
of it, I cannot judge yet.

The Abbot was with me here yefterday, and defired me to requeft
of your Majefty, with his humble duty, that you would, whatfoever
you heard of him, think of him as of an honeft man, and to remember, that though he be now away from Monfieur, your Majefty yourfelf once told him, that there was no place for an honeft
man to reft there, as long as Ferragues had any great credit about
him.

For the reft of that which is occurrent here, I leave it to Mr.
Secretary's letter, to whom I have written at large, for fear of
troubling your Majefty with too tedious a letter. Yet can I not end
without as plain dealing with you, to declare any good dealing of
Monfieur towards you, which I would be the gladder of the two I
might daily write, as I am by duty bound when I find the contrary.
I am very credibly informed, that when he heard of this villainous
act of Somerfield's confeffion, he grew in a great choler, and fwore
deeply, which he commonly doth not, that Jefuits only were the
fetters on of thefe enterprifes; and that, if he were a King, he would
rather hang them with his own hand, than fuffer any of them to live;
with many bitter words againft them, and many honourable and
loving fpeeches of your Majefty.

F f

No.

No. XIV.

From the Queen of Scots to Charles Paget.

[This Letter is printed as particularly pointed out by Mr. Hume in
the last quarto edition of his History.].

1586.
May 20th.

WITH an infinite number of other letters in cypher, I received five of your own, dated the 14th of January, 7th of
May, 24th and last of July 1585, and 4th of February 1586; but,
for their late arrival here and all at once, it hath not been possible
to make me yet see them all decyphered; so, wholly without any
intelligence of foreign affairs, it is very difficult for me to establish
any certain course for re-establishing of mine own on this side.   And
methink, I can see no other means to that end, except the King of
Spain, now being pricked, in his particular, by the attempt made on
the Low Countries, and the course of Drake, would take revenge
of this Queen; whilst France, occupied as it is, cannot help her.
Wherefore, I desire that you should essaie, either X——— during his
aboad in Spain, or by Bernandino Mendozo, to discover clearly if
the said King hath intention to set on this country; as to me it
seemeth to be the surest and readiest way for him, whereby to rid
himself altogether of the Queen's malice against him; so as now he
doth find himself constrained to come to the same remedies which, in
Don John D'Austria's time, were propounded unto him; which I
doubt he shall not find presently in these parts of such strength and
virtue, as if he had applied them in time and place; as to wit, whilst
that I had so well disposed Scotland to receive them, that the Catholic

party

party in this realm had the principals, which fince it hath loft. My relations in France were to have employed, therein, and the faid King not impeached in any other enterprize. I remember well that Don John was always ftiff of this opinion, that there was no other means in the world whereby to fet up again the King his brother's affairs in the Low Countries, and to affure his States in all other parts, then in re-eftablifhing this realm under God, and a Prince his friend; for fo much as he forefaw right well, that this Queen would not fail to break with him, and to give him, as fhe hath done, the firft blow. Now in cafe (as fayd is) that he deliberate to fet on this Queen, efteeming it moft neceffary, that he affure himfelf alfo of Scotland, either to ferve him in the faid .enterprize, or, at the leaft, hold that country fo bridled, as, it ferve not his enemy, I have thought good that you enter with E. in thefe overtures following: to wit, that I fhall travel by all means to make my fon enter in the faid enterprize: and if he cannot be perfuaded thereunto, that I fhall dreffe a fecret band and league amongft the principal Catholic Lords of that country, and their adherents, to be joined with the King of Spain, and execute at his devotion what, of their part, fhall be thought meet for advancing of the faid enterprize; fo being they may have fuch fuccours of men and money as they will afk, which I am fure fhall not be very chargeable, having men enough within the country, and little money ftretching far and doing much there. More-over, I fhall dreffe the means, for the more fecurity, to make my fon be delivered into the hands of the faid King, or in the Pope's, as by them fhall be thought beft; but with paction and promife to let and fet him at full liberty whenfoever I fhall fo defire, or that, after my death itfelf, being Catholic, he fhall defire to repair again to this ifle; without that ever the faid King fhall pretend nor attempt any thing to my prejudice or my fon's, if he yield himfelf Catholic in the fuc-ceffion of this crown. This is the beft hoftage that I and the faid Lords of Scotland can give to the faid King, for performance of that

which

which may depend of them in the said enterprize. But withal, must there be a Regent established in Scotland, that have commission and power of me and my son (whom it shall be easy to make pass the same, he being once in the hands of the said Lords), to govern the country in his absence; for which office I find none so fit as the Lord Claude *, as well for the rank of his house, as for his manhood and wisdom. And, to shun all jealousy of the rest, and strengthen him the more, he must have a council appointed him of the principal Lords, without whom he shall be bound not to ordain any thing of importance. I should think myself most obliged to that King, that it would please him to receive my son, to make him be instructed and reduced to the Catholic religion; which is the thing of this world I most desire; affecting a great deal rather the salvation of his soul, than to see him Monarch of all Europe. And I fear much, that so long as he shall remain where he is (amongst those who found all his greatness upon the maintenance of the religion which he professeth), it shall never lye in my power to bring him in again to the right way; whereby there shall remain in my heart a thousand regrets and apprehensions if I shall die, to leave behind me a tyrant and persecutor of the Catholic Church. If you see or perceive the said Ambassador to take hold of the said overtures, and doth put you in hope of a good answer thereunto, which you shall insist to have with all diligence, I would, in the mean while, that you should write to the Lord Claude, letting him understand, how that the said King is set on this country, and desireth to have the assistance of the Catholics of Scotland, to stop, at the least, that from thence this Queen have no succours. And, to that effect, you shall pray the said Lord, to found and grope the minds hereunto of the principal of the Catholic Nobility in Scotland, and others who, under other pretext, he might bring into their party; to the end you may make open light

* Hamilton.

whereby

whereby the said King may see, what he might look for in such
case at their hands, and also know what succours and supports both
of men and money they would require of the said King to hold Scotland at their devotion withal: moreover, that he declare unto you,
particularly, the names of those that are to enter into this band, and
what forces they are able to make together. And to the end they
may be the more encouraged herein, you may write plainly to the
said Lord Claude, that you have charge of me to treat in this matter
with him. But, for your first letter, I am not of opinion that you
discover yourself farther unto him, nor unto any other at all, until
you have received answer of the said King; which being conform
to this design, then may you open more unto the said Lord Claude;
shewing him, that to assure himself of my son, and to the end, (if it
be possible) that things be past and done under his name and authority, it shall be needful to seize his person, in case that willingly he
cannot be brought to this enterprize; yea, and that the surest were
to deliver him into the King of Spain's hands, or the Pope's, as shall
be thought best; and that, in his absence, he depute the said Lord
Claude, his Lieutenant-general and Regent of the government of
Scotland, which you are assured I may be easily persuaded to confirm
and approve: for, if it be possible, I will not, for divers respects, be
therein named, until the extremity. To persuade hereunto the
Lord Claude, it shall be good, that you assure him, by all means you
can, of my good will towards him and his house; that you promise
to travel to abolish all remembrance or grief of his brother the Lord
of Arbrothe's proceedings; and besides, that you indirectly put him
in hope, I shall make him be declared lawful heir to the Crown of
Scotland, my son failing without children; and that thereunto I shall
make the Catholic Princes of Christendom to condescend to maintain
him in that right. This is all, which, for that country of Scotland, I
can dress presently, upon so much as I know of the present estate

of

of the affairs of Chriftendom; charging you, very exprefsly, not to communicate this to any other at all, either Englifh, French, or Scottifh;
as alfo you fhall pray the faid Bernardino to do the like, and the faid
Lord Claude not to difcover by whom this motion is made unto him.
I have heard, that laft year there were 1200 *l.* appointed for my fon;
advife the P. S. to make them be arrefted, and preferved for the
negociation of this enterprize; for that which was before delivered, was right evil difperfed and employed. Chartley this 20th
of May, 1586.

I can write nothing prefently unto the Lord Claude himfelf, for
want of an alphabet between me and him; which now I fend you
here inclofed, without any mark on the back, that you may fend it
him. And if, by any nearer means, which I will effai to find on this
fide, I may write therein, I fhall not fail to remember, by the fame,
or the firft other I can find fitteft, the good teftimony and affurance
you give me of this dutiful affection towards me and my fervice.

Your letters dated the 10th of April, with the whole mentioned
therein, I received of late; but have no leifure to anfwer thereunto,
by reafon of the meffenger's hafte to be difpatched herewith, at this
day prefcribed for the purpofe. The want fhall be fupplied as foon
as I can. And whereas, here above, I promife to fend you an alphabet for the Lord Claude; I am even now put in hope of a mean
of convoy, direct from hence, to Scotland, whereby I do intend to fend
the faid alphabet, and fo retain the fame for that way, as the fureft
and fpeedieft. In the mean while, I would not omit to affure you,
that it is my intention your penfion be continued in ready payment; as I took good order therefore, and for his part, at de Che-
rolles being here, whereof he can well inform you, if he lift.

Gilbert

* *Gilbert Curll's superscription as followeth:*

THIS letter I had first written by the Queen my Mistress's own hand, and gave it her again; which was first written in French, and after translated by me,

GILBERT CURLL.

2d September,
1586.

Indorsed two different ways thus:

Copy of Charles Paget, his letter,

AND

Curll's transcript of the Queen's letter.

* These words are in the Lord Treasurer Burghley's hand-writing.

No.

No. XV.

Evidence againſt the Queen of Scots.

[This report of the evidence againſt the Queen of Scots at Fotheringay, and the confeſſions of her Secretaries afterwards in the
Star Chamber, is much fuller than *that* given by Camden in his
hiſtory, or the account printed in the State Trials; and the crime
of *compaſſing and imagining* Queen Elizabeth's death ſeems fully
proved againſt her.]

Die Martis, xxv. *Octobris* 1586.

From a Copy
of the trial in
the poſſeſſion
of the Earl of
Hardwicke.

THE Commiſſioners being all (except the Earls of Shrewſbury and Warwick, and Sir Amias Paulet), aſſembled within
the Star Chamber, a recapitulation was made by her Majeſty's
Privy Council, of all ſuch proofs as had been made againſt the Scots
Queen, before them at Fotheringay, &c. After which Nau and
Curle were brought perſonally before the Commiſſioners, and, in their
preſences, did avow and maintain all their confeſſions, examinations,
and ſubſcriptions to be true, in ſuch manner and form, as they have
written and made the ſame. And they did, then and there, expreſsly
affirm and maintain, that the Scots Queen had received and read
Babington's letters, and that, by her direction and expreſs commandment, the anſwer unto all the points thereof, was returned unto
Babington in her name, according as in the letter is ſet down.

Alſo, that, the ſame 12th of July, ſhe did write to the Lord Paget,
to Charles Paget, to Mendoza, to Sir Francis Inglefield, and to the
Archbiſhop of Glaſcow, concerning Babington's plot, &c. Whereupon the Lords and other the Commiſſioners, conferred together in
ſecret,

secret, and afterwards, as it is said, concluded upon their judgment.
And they called in the Queen's Serjeants, the Attorney and Solicitor,
and before them, as it is said, gave their sentences, by which all the
Commissioners present, except the Lord Zouch, pronounced, that
the Scots Queen was privy, &c. and that she had compassed and
imagined the death of her Majesty our Sovereign Lady, only the
Lord Zouch, as it is said, gave his sentence, that she was privy to
the compassing, practising, and imagining of her Majesty's death,
but he could not pronounce that she had compassed, practised, or
imagined the same, &c. And then Mr. Sanders was called for in,
to take notice of this sentence.

Note, That the Earl of Shrewsbury sent his judgment in writing, containing his consent unto the same; and so afterwards did
the Earl of Warwick.

The Commission reciteth the Statute made in the 27th year of the
Queen's Majesty's reign, and authoriseth the Commissioners to examine, whether Mary the Scots Queen, since the 1st of June, the
same 27th year, hath compassed or imagined any thing tending to
hurt the Queen's Majesty's person; or whether she hath been privy,
that any other person hath compassed or imagined any thing tending
to the hurt of her Highness's person, and thereupon to give sentence
or judgment, as upon good proof, the matter shall appear.

She was directly charged by the Queen's Serjeants, that she had
compassed and imagined the death and destruction of her Majesty,
and also was privy and consenting to the conspiracies and treasons of
Anthony Babington, and John Ballard, and their confederates, and
so was within the compass of both the said articles of the statute and
commission.

For declaration whereof, first, it was opened, that Ballard being
a seminary priest, and one that, by the space of five or six years, had
ranged through many parts of the realm, disguised in apparel, and
under sundry several names, seducing the Queen's subjects, and with-

drawing

drawing them from their due obedience, did go into France, in Lent last paft; and about a week after Eafter, had conference in Paris with Charles Paget, Thomas Morgan, and Bernardino de Mendoza, the Spanifh Ambaffador there, touching the invading of this realm, by foreign forces, rebellion to be ftirred amongft her Majefty's fubjects, and a ftrong party to be made to affift and join with the invaders, and the Scots Queen to be delivered. In which enterprize, Charles Paget affirmed, that there was no hope to prevail during her Majefty's life.

Hereupon, Ballard was fent into England, by direction from Charles Paget, and Mendoza, to folicit and practife the execution of this their complot.

He returned to London upon Whitfunday, being the 22d of May, and within four, or five days after, he conferred with Babington, and acquainted him with all the whole plot of thefe treafons.

In this conference, Babington and Ballard refolved, that all foreign power and invafion were in vain, unlefs the Queen's Majefty were taken away. Whereupon they concluded, that fix gentlemen fhould undertake the killing of her Majefty, and that Savage, who before that time was folicited at Rheims to execute that wicked action alone, and thereupon had vowed to perform that accordingly, and was come into England for that purpofe, fhould forbear to attempt it alone, and fhould be one of the fix; and at the time of the execution thereof, Babington, and certain others with him, fhould deliver the Scots Queen.

Thefe things, with many other material circumftances and parts of their treafons, were directly and voluntarily confeffed, by divers of the principal confpirators, both before and at their arrangement, as appears by the record; whereupon, to their deferts, and the juftice of the law, they were attainted and accufed.

After this declaration thus made, the proof againft the Scots Queen was entered into, and profecuted, as hereafter followeth.

Firft,

First, was read a confeffion made by Babington, written all with his own hand, and delivered to the Lord Chancellor, Lord Treafurer, and Mr. Vice Chamberlain, voluntarily and frankly, before he was committed to the Tower; wherein he fetteth down at large, about four years paft, being in Paris, that he did there grow acquainted with Thomas Morgan, who brought him to the Bifhop of Glafcow, Ambaffador Ledger in France for the Queen of Scots, and they both recommended their Miftrefs unto him, as a moft wife and virtuous Catholic Princefs, declaring the certain expectation of her future greatnefs in this land, by reafon of the undoubted title to this Crown, as next in fucceffion.

And after his return in England, they, by their letters, commended him to her fervice; whereupon, fhe wrote unto him a letter of congratulation.

After which he was folicited by other letters from Morgan, to be an intelligencer for her, and convey her letters and packets.

This courfe of fervice he continued for the fpace of two years; and about a quarter of a year before her remove from the Earl of Shrewfbury's keeping, left it off, and difcontinued the fame until July laft. At which time he received from her a fhort letter in cypher, by a boy unknown unto him, fignifying her difcontent for breach of their intelligence, requiring the fame to be renewed. And that fhe would fend fome packets unto him, which fhe had received from Thomas Morgan, in April laft before.

He doth alfo fet down at large, what conference paffed between Ballard and him, and the whole plot of the confpiracies and treafons.

He declareth further, that he did write a letter to the Scots Queen, touching every particular of this their plot, and fent it by the fame unknown boy.

Unto which fhe anfwered, twenty or thirty days after, in the fame cypher, by which he wrote unto her, but by another meffenger;

the

the tenor of both which letters he carried fo well in memory, that he reported and fet down fully all the principal points of the fame, as upon conference of his faid declaration, with the copies of the fame letters, it appeareth.

He affirmeth alfo, that he fhewed the letter of Queen of Scots to Titchborne, who did affift him in the decyphering of the fame; and that he fhewed a copy thereof to Ballard and others.

After the reading of Babington's declaration aforefaid, a part of Ballard's examination was likewife read, concurring with the fame; wherein he affirmeth, that Babington fhewed him a copy of the letter which he did write to the Queen of Scots; and alfo a part of the letter which the Scots Queen did write for anfwer to him, the whole not being then decyphered; and fetteth down, very certainly, divers material points of the fame.

Titchborne and Dunne, in their feveral examinations, do alfo affirm that Babington did impart unto them the fame letter from the Queen of Scots; and do likewife report fundry particularities of the fame, and Titchborne affirmeth farther, that he, at Babington's requeft, did write a great part of the fame, as Babington did decypher it, and read it unto him.

After this was read a copy of the letter written by Babington to the Scots Queen, wherein thefe material and effectual parts were, and are to be noted. Firft, he termed her his dread Sovereign Lady and Queen, and acknowledged all fidelity and obedience to her only.

He fignifieth unto her, that upon advertifement by Ballard from beyond the feas, of the purpofe of certain foreign powers to invade this realm, he hath now ftaid on purpofe to do her facred Majefty one day's good fervice.

That he communicated this his purpofe to fuch of the friends as he beft trufted; and faith, that upon conference with them, he hath found thefe things, firft to be advifed in this great and honourable action, upon the iffue whereof depended her life, and the weal and honour of our country.

Firft,

"Firft, for affuring of the invafion, fufficient ftrength in the, invaders, ports to be appointed for the foreign Princes to arrive at, with a ftrong party at every place to join with them, to warrant their landing. Then, the deliverance of the Scots Queen, and the difpatching of the ufurping competitor, the effecting whereof he doth vow and proteft, or elfe their lives to, be loft in the execution thereof.

"In all thefe particular points, he prayeth her direction, and for the avoiding of delay, that fhe by her princely authority would enable fuch as may advance the affair; feeing that it is neceffary, that fome there be that become heads, to lead the multitude, ever difpofed by nature, in this land, to follow the nobility: he offereth alfo, to recommend fome unto her, fit, in his knowledge, to be her Lieutenants in the Weft Parts, North Wales, and the countries of Lancafter, Derby, and Stafford.

He promifeth, that himfelf, with ten gentlemen, and one hundred of their followers, would deliver her from her keeper.

And for the difpatch of the Ufurper (from the obedience of whom he faith, that by the excommunication of her, they were made free), fix noble Gentlemen, all his private friends, would undertake that tragical execution.

He prayeth her, that by her wifdom it be reduced to method, and that her deliverance be firft, for that thereupon depended their only good, and all other circumftances fo to concur, that the untimely beginning of one, do not overthrow the reft.

He fubfcribeth

Your Majefty's faithful fubject,

and fworn fervant,

ANTHONY BABINGTON.

Then

Then was read a copy of the Scots Queen's letter to Babington, in answer of his, whereby she termeth him trusty and well-beloved; she commendeth his zeal and entire affection towards her; she accepteth and alloweth his offers; she declareth, that she hath long time dealt with foreign Princes touching these actions, always putting them in mind, how dangerous their delays were to the Catholics. She willeth him to assure their principal friends, that albeit she had not in this cause any particular interest, that which she may pretend, being of no consideration unto her, in respect of the public good of the State, she would be always ready and most willing to employ herein her life, and all that she hath, or may ever look for in this world.

To ground substantially this enterprize, she adviseth to examine deeply.

1st. What forces they could raise within the realm, and what Captains to be appointed in every shire, in case a chief General cannot be had.

2. Of what towns, ports, and havens, they could assure themselves, as well in the North, as West and South, to receive succours from the Low Countries, Spain and France.

3d. What places they esteemed most fit, and of greatest advantage, to assemble their forces at, and which way and whither to march.

4th. What foreign forces, as well on horse, as on foot, they required, and for how long pay.

5th. What provision of money and armour, in case they wanted, they would ask.

6th. By what means the six gentlemen did deliberate to proceed.

7th. And the manner how she was to be delivered out of hold.

She deviseth, that after they had amongst themselves taken their best resolution, that then they should impart the same to Mendoza, and she promiseth to write unto him of the matter, with all the

earnest

earneſt recommendation ſhe could; and alſo to any elſe that ſhould
be needful.

The affairs being thus prepared, and forces in readineſs both without and within the realm, ſhe ſaith, that then ſhall it be time to ſet
the ſix Gentlemen to work; taking order, upon the accompliſh-
ing of their deſign, that ſhe ſhould be ſuddenly tranſported from the
place of her reſtraint, and all their forces to be at the ſame time in
the field, and meet her, in tarrying for the arrival of the foreign aid;
which muſt be haſtened with all diligence.

And for that there can be no certain day appointed for the accom-
pliſhing of the ſaid Gentlemen's deſignment, ſhe willeth, that others
may be in a readineſs to take her from thence; that the ſaid Gentlemen have always about them (or at the leaſt at the Court), four ſtout
men, with ſpeedy horſes, to diſpatch by divers ways, ſo ſoon as the
ſaid deſign ſhould be executed, to bring intelligence to thoſe which
ſhould undertake her deliverance, ſo that ſhe might be taken from
the keeper, before he could hear of the execution of the ſaid deſign,
or at the leaſt, before he could remove her to any other place, or fortify the place wherein ſhe remained; and at the ſame inſtant to eſſay
to cut off the poſts ordinary ways.

She giveth earneſt warning not to ſtir on this ſide, before they be
well aſſured of foreign forces, nor to take her away, before they
were well aſſured, to ſet her in the midſt of a good army, or ſome
very good ſtrength, where ſhe might ſafely ſtay for the aſſembly of
their forces, and arrival of foreign Princes.

She referreth to Babington to aſſure the Gentlemen above mentioned, of all that ſhall be requiſite of her part, for the entire execution of their good will.

She promiſeth to eſſay, at the ſame time that the work ſhall be in
hand in theſe parts, to make the Catholics of Scotland to ariſe, and
put her ſon into their hands, to effect that, from thence, her enemies
here may not prevail of any ſuccour.

4

She

She willeth alfo, fome ftirring in Ireland were laboured, for to begin fome while before any thing were done here, to the end that the alarm might be given thereby, on the flat contrary fide that the ftroke fhould come.

· That for a General, it were good to found obfcurely the Earl of Arundell, or fome of his brethren: and likewife to feek upon the young Earl of Northumberland, if he be at liberty; and the Earl of Weftmorland, and the Lord Paget, fhould be brought home fecretly; and with them fome more of the principal banifhed men fhould return.

She directeth three means for her delivery; viz. fifty or threefcore to deliver her from her keeper, when fhe was riding to take air on the moors between Chartley and Stafford.

Or to fet fire in the barns and ftables at Chartley, in the night-time, and when her guardian fervants fhould go forth to quench the fire, then the others to enter and take her away.

Or to caufe fome of the carts, which came with provifion very early, to be overturned in the great gates, by practice with the cart-drivers, fo that the gates could not be fhut, and then thofe which were appointed for her delivery, to enter the houfe upon the fudden, and to take her away.

Finally, fhe requireth, for God's fake, that albeit they cannot com-pafs her delivery, yet notwithftanding they fhould not let to proceed in the reft of the enterprize.

She concludeth, what iffue foever the matter taketh, fhe will think herfelf obliged to Babington fo long as fhe liveth, for his offer to hazard himfelf (as he doth) for her delivery.

Both thefe copies of the two feveral before-mentioned letters, were advifedly perufed by Babington, and thereupon he did voluntarily confefs the fame to be the true copies of his letter to the Scots Queen, and of her anfwer to the fame, and for affirmation thereof, he fubfcribed his name to every page of both the faid copies with his own hand.

In

In doing whereof, he was fo circumfpect and careful, that finding two or three words miftaken in the writing of the copy of the letters, he ftruck out the fame, before he did fubfcribe it.

Hereupon, it was urged and inferred by her Majefty's learned Council, that if Babington's letter came to the Scots Queen's hands, then it was apparent that fhe was privy to the confpiracy for the taking away of her Majefty's life. And likewife, if fhe did write unto Babington to fuch effect, as in his declaration written with his own hand, and in the fame copy recognized and fubfcribed by him, is contained, then it cannot be avoided, but that fhe did not only compafs and imagine, but did alfo practife, the deftruction of her Highnefs, and fo was directly within both the parts of the commiffion and ftatute.

Hereunto, the Scots Queen, after her proteftation, anfwered, that fhe never faw nor knew Babington; and denied that fhe received any fuch letter from him, or that fhe wrote any fuch letter to him, or that fhe was privy to his confpiracies, or that fhe did ever practife, compafs, imagine, or was privy of any thing to the deftruction of her Majefty, or to the hurt of her perfon; confeffing neverthelefs, that fhe had ufed Babington as an intelligencer for her, and for the conveying of letters and packets.

And fhe added further, that fhe was not to be charged, but either by her word, or by her writing, and fhe was fure they had neither the one nor the other to lay againft her.

After which anfwer, fo by her made, divers other matters were alleged, and fhewed forth, to prove that fhe did receive the fame letters from Babington, and did alfo write anfwer unto him, as the before-mentioned copies did purport; with farther proof, as hereafter followeth:

Firft, it was inferred, that fince both the letters were written in the cypher ufed between the Scots Queen and Babington, and all the points of Babington's letter directly and effectually anfwered by

H h   the

the other, it cannot be, but that she received his letter, and so made the answer unto the same; and the alphabet of the same cypher being found amongst papers, and shewed to Babington, he acknowledged and thereupon subscribed his name to the same, as it appeared.

Also, the imparting of the same letter by Babington to Titchborne, who did help to decypher part of it, and to Ballard, Dunne, and others, when he was at liberty, and feared not the discovery of his treasons, but hoped then, within short time, to bring the same to his desired effect, is a stronger proof of the same letters.

Besides the voluntary declarations and confessions of the same letters by Babington, Ballard, Titchborne, and Dunne, after their apprehension, and their constant persisting in the same, before and after the time of their arraignment, and till their death, without retracting any part thereof, enforceth greatly the credit of the same.

And there is no likelihood or probability that Babington, or any one, would of himself devise and impute to others, a matter of so great importance and extreme danger.

Then it was added further, that besides the matters before mentioned, it was manifest, as well by the declarations and confessions of Nau and Curle, her servants and secretaries, subscribed with their own hands, without torture or constraint, and by their voluntary oaths verifying the same, that the Scots Queen did receive the same letter from Babington, and caused the same to be decyphered, and after advice, reading, and consideration thereof, caused the said answer to be written to Babington in her name.

And for proof thereof, it was alleged, that the copies of the same letters being shewed by some of the Lords of the Council, to Nau and Curle, they, upon reading and perusing thereof, subscribed their names thereunto, affirming the same, and acknowledging that the Scots Queen received the same from Babington, and thereupon she did give direction for the writing of the other unto him; which was verified, by shewing forth the same copies so subscribed by them.

And

And Nau fetteth down in writing with his own hand, the 6th of September, · that the Scots Queen did commonly hold this courfe, in receiving and writing of letters of fecrecy and importance, viz. that all letters written to her, were opened in her Cabinet, in her own prefence, and decyphered by her own commandment; and fuch letters as fhe did write to others, fhe did firft either write the fame in French with her own hand, or give direction to Nau to write the fame; after which, the fame being perufed by her, or read unto her, if they were to be written in Englifh, then did Curle tranflate them out of French into Englifh, and did eftfoons read them unto her, the fame being fo tranflated; which being done, Curle did put the fame in cypher, and fo they were fent away. He affirmeth farther, in his faid declaration, that the Scots Queen gave direction for the writing of the faid letter to Babington, and that in the writing thereof, the courfe aforefaid was holden.

There was alfo fhewed forth a paper written by Nau, containing fhort minutes and notes of the principal points of Babington's letter, and of the Scots Queen's letter to Babington, which was found amongft her papers at Chartley, which being fhewed unto Nau by fome of the Lords of the Council, he upon fight thereof confeffed it to be his own hand, faying, that upon reading Babington's letter to the Scots Queen, and her direction given for the anfwering of the fame, he did fet down the fame notes, to ferve as a memorial for him, for the writing of other letters; and this his confeffion, in that behalf, did he fubfcribe in the fame paper, with his own hand, in prefence of the faid Lords, and put his name thereunto; and after, in another examination, affirmeth the fame.

In this paper, amongft other points, is contained *Le Coup*, which can hardly be conflrued to be meant otherwife, than the blow or flroke for killing of her Majefty, being written upon fome occafion; and to fuch end, as Nau hath declared, as is aforefaid.

Alfo,

Alfo, Curle perufing an abftract of the principal points of both the faid letters, did confefs and affirm the fame, and thereupon, before the faid Lords, did with his own hand fubfcribe his faid affirmation, and put his name thereunto.

The fame points were put into French by Nau, and written all with his own hand, and by him likewife confeffed to be the matters contained in the fame letters, and thereupon alfo he did fubfcribe his name to the fame.

Befides, Nau being examined before the Lords aforefaid, the 21ft of September, touching the faid letters, faid that Curle did decypher Babington's letter to the Scots Queen, and after he (the faid Nau) did read it unto her, and fhe refolved to make anfwer unto the fame.

And faith further, that he took the points contained in the Scots Queen's letter to Babington, of her own mouth, from point to point, in the fame manner as he put in writing; whereupon he did draw the letter in French, and after brought it unto her, and fhe corrected it in fuch fort as it was fent to Babington. And faith, that the Scots Queen delivered unto him by her own fpeech, thefe points following, for anfwer of Babington's letter, upon confideration of the fame letter from Babington, wherein the fame points were contained, viz.

What forces were to be had here, what havens and ports, what places fitteft for the forces to affemble; what foreign forces they required; what provifion, money, and armour; by what means the fix Gentlemen meant to proceed; and the manner how fhe was to be delivered out of hold.

He faith alfo, that the claufe of the affociation upon pretence to withftand the Puritans, was devifed by the Scots Queen herfelf, and was by her direction put into the faid letter; and fo likewife, the other claufe that the fix Gentlemen fhould have fome ftout men well horfed, to give fpeedy intelligence when the defignment fhould be executed.

This

This examination of Nau was firſt ſet down in Engliſh, accord-
ing as he delivered it by ſpeech, and being read unto him, he did ſubſcribe his name unto the ſame, and after, upon peruſal and further conſideration thereof, he did ſet down in French with his own hand the ſubſtance thereof.

Curle being likewiſe examined before the ſaid Lords, the ſaid 21ſt September, faith, that he decyphered Babington's letter to the Scots Queen, and then the ſame was read unto her by Nau, whereupon ſhe directed Nau to draw an anſwer unto the ſame, which he drew in French, and read it unto her; which being done, Curle put it into Engliſh by her commandment, and after, read it unto Nau, and then, by her commandment, Curle put it into cypher.

He faith, that the ſame her letter to Babington had theſe parts, viz. What forces may be raiſed here; what havens and ports provided; what place fitteſt for the forces to aſſemble; what foreign forces they required; what proviſion, money, and armour, they would aſk; by what means the ſix Gentlemen meant to proceed, and how they meant to deliver her out of hold. And that the ſame letter contained a clauſe alſo, that the ſix Gentlemen ſhould have four ſtout men, well horſed, to give advertiſement ſo ſoon as the deſignment ſhould be executed; and contained three means for her delivery out of hold; and had alſo a device for an aſſociation to be pretended againſt the Puritans. He faith alſo, ſhe willed him to burn the Engliſh copy of the letters ſent to Babington.

Theſe examinations of Nau and Carle were ſubſcribed with their own hands, and affirmed upon their oaths, voluntarily taken before the Lords and Judges, and ſo ſome of the ſaid Lords and Judges did openly affirm.

All theſe confeſſions and declarations, examinations and ſubſcriptions, of Nau and Curle, were verified by the oath of Mr. Thomas Powell, Clerk of the Crown, who was preſent when they did write and depoſe the ſame, and being ſhewed to the Scots Queen, ſhe confeſſed

the

the fame to be the hands of Nau and Curle; albeit, as fhe faid, Nau
had not written his name as he did ufually accuftom to fign; but fhe
denied earneftly, that fhe did ever receive the fame letter from Babington, or write the other unto him, whatfoever Nau and Curle had
faid or depofed, faving fhe did take them to be honeft men; but fhe
did not know what apprehenfion, torture, fear, or hope of favour,
might make in them.

After thefe proofs thus produced and fhewed, it was alleged further, that the Scots Queen had not only intelligence by Babington of
Ballard's negociation in France, from the agents in France, and with
what direction, and for what purpofe he was fent from thence into
England, but had alfo the like intelligence out of France, from
her agents there.

And thereupon was fhewed forth a copy of a letter written to the
Scots Queen by Charles Paget the 26th of May 1586, *ftilo novo*,
which was decyphered by Curle, and being fhewed to him by fome
of the Lords, the 25th of September, he confeffed the fame, as well
by fpeech, as by his own voluntary fubfcription, and putting his
name thereunto. Whereby Charles Paget did fignify what conference Ballard had with him and Mendoza; and what plot they had
levied for the invafion of the realm, and ftirring of rebellion; and
what directions Mendoza had given unto Ballard.

It was alfo alleged, that after the Scots Queen had received the
faid letter from Babington, and had written anfwer, point for point,
to the fame, and given direction, touching the whole plot, promifing
withal to write to Mendoza, and to any elfe that fhould be needful,
fhe did, accordingly, the 27th of July, make difpatch of five feveral letters, all touching the fame action, viz. three into France,
one to Mendoza, another to Charles Paget, and the third to the
Bifhop of Glafcow; and two into Spain, one to the Lord Paget, and
another to Sir Francis Inglefield.

                   She

. She wrote to Mendoza, that fhe was fo difcouraged from entering
into any new purfuits, feeing the fmall effect of thofe in times paft,
that fhe fhut up her eyes to divers overtures and propofitions that
were made unto her by the Catholics within fix months paft, having
no means to give them found anfwer.

- But upon that, which of late again fhe underftood of the good
intention of the King of Spain towards thefe quarrels, fhe had written very amply to the principal of the faid Catholics, upon a defign
which fhe fent, with her advice upon every point, to refolve amongft
themfelves, for the execution thereof; and for fear of lofs of time,
fhe gave them order to difpatch unto Mendoza, with all diligence, one
from among them, fufficiently inftructed to treat with him, according
to the general propofitions which have been already made unto him,
of all things which they were to demand of him in that affair with
the King his Mafter.

Further, fhe anfwereth him on their behalf, upon their faith and
word given unto her, that they would faithfully and fincerely accomplifh, with the hazard of their lives, that which they fhould
promife by their Deputy, and therefore prayeth Mendoza to give
all credit therein, as if herfelf had difpatched him.

She faith further, that fhe would inform Mendoza with the means
of her efcape, which fhe would take upon her to perform, fo as a-
fore hand fhe may be affured of fufficient forces to receive and preferve her within the land, whilft all the armies may affemble.

The original draught of this letter written in French by Nau, and
by him fubfcribed and confeffed, was fhewed to the Scots Queen,
which fhe confeffed to be his hand, but faid, it was nothing to this
matter.

There is alfo a copy of the fame in Englifh, of Nau's hand, and
fubfcribed and figned by him.

She did write unto Charles Paget, that, upon return of Ballard, the
principal of the Catholics did impart unto her, their intention and

6 conference

conference to that which Charles Paget wrote, but more particularly
afking her direction for, the execution of the whole, and that fhe
made them a very ample, difpatch, containing the device, point by
point, in all things requifite, as well on this fide, as without the
realm, to bring their defignment to good effect.

That fhe directed them, that for lofing no time, having taken refolution amongft them, upon her difpatch, they would make hafte
to impart the fame to Mendoza, fending over therewith, either the
faid Ballard, or fome other the moft faithful and fecret they could
find. That fhe promifed to write to Mendoza, as fhe did prefently;
to give credit to the faid meffenger. So that if the Pope and King of
Spain had even intention to provide for the ifle, the occafion is prefently offered, very advantageous, finding all the Catholics therein
univerfally fo difpofed and forward, as there is more ado to keep
them back, than put them forward.

That for all difficulties which Mendoza could allege, as for getting her forth of hold, or otherwife, he fhould be thereof fufficiently cleared and fatisfied.

That it refteth only to purfue, fo hotly as can be, both in Rome and
Spain, the grant of fupport requifite, of horfemen, footmen, arms,
munition, and money.

That her opinion is, and that fo fhe hath written to the Catholics,
that nothing be ftirred on this fide, before they have fufficient promife and affurance of the Pope and King of Spain, for the accomplifhment of that which is required of them.

That fhe would have fent to Paget, a copy of her difpatch to the
Catholics, were it not that fhe is fure, that, by the meffenger, he fhould
know more thereof than fhe can write, he being to carry into thofe
parts the refolution of the whole, and for the fame refpect fhe referred the Lord Paget to be thereof informed by Charles Paget.

She thanketh him for the fixty crowns he gave to Ballard, promifing to make him reimburfed of the fame, by the Ambaffador.

She

She requireth to know how he hath proceeded with the Lord Claude, in the matter whereof she wrote unto him not long since, which being well effected, should well concur with the enterprize here.

Two original draughts of this letter were shewed forth, one in French, written by Nau, the other in English, written by Curle, which they confessed by their subscriptions, and affirmed by their oaths, before some of the Lords, as Mr. Thomas Powell did then depose.

She did write to the Lord Paget, that she doubted not, but he had understood by his brother, the overture which a deputy for the Catholics in this realm, had made on their behalf to Mendoza: whereupon, not long since she wrote very amply to the principal of the Catholics, for to have, upon a plot which she had dressed for them, their common resolution; and for to treat accordingly with the King of Spain, she addressed them to the Lord Paget.

She requireth him to confider deeply the said plot, and all the particularities necessary for the execution of it; namely, for the supporting of men, armour, munition and money; which must be obtained of the Pope, and of the King of Spain. She requireth to solicit the matter there, and to enter betime, because all negociations in that Court are drawn to great length.

This was also first drawn in French by Nau, and after put into English by Curle, and both the original draughts of their own hands were shewed forth, which they had confessed and subscribed before the Lords, and affirmed the same by their oaths, as Mr. Thomas Powell did also depose.

She did write to Sir Francis Inglefield, to give thanks to the King of Spain, for the 12,000 crowns; assuring him, that the same should be employed to none other use, but to the accomplishment of her escape.

I i   That

That she feareth the bruit which runneth, of a peace between the King of Spain and this Queen, shall retire many to pursue the designment of an enterprize of new dressed here.

That the principal Catholics of England having, about Easter last, made their complot together, to rise in Leicester's absence (myself not having wherewith to give them a substantial answer), sent one from amongst them to Charles Paget, who made their messenger to declare their designment to Mendoza, to know if his Master the King of Spain would hearken thereunto.

Whereupon all good hope being brought back again unto them, as they signified unto her, and, finding the same in manner confirmed by Inglefield's letter; she made then a very ample dispatch, by which, upon a plot which she had dressed for them, she gave them her advice, point by point, in every thing necessary for the execution thereof, and remitting them to take resolution thereupon.

That for to lose no time, without sending again unto her, they should dispatch, with all diligence, some one in their names, chosen, faithful, and sufficiently instructed, to Mendoza.

To impart unto him particularly the plot of their enterprize, and to require such support as is necessary of men on foot and horse, as also of armour, munition, and money; of which things, before they had sufficient promise and assurance, not to stir on this side.

That she had cleared the greatest difficulty, which has always been objected in the like enterprize, viz. her escape out of hold, and she hopeth to execute the same assuredly, as they shall design it.

That, if a peace be made in France, her cousin of Guise, having already great forces, may employ the same here, on a sudden, before the Queen be aware.

Of this letter there was also shewed for the two original draughts, one written in French by Nau, the other in English by Curle; which they had likewise confessed and subscribed before the Lords, and confirmed by their oaths, as Mr. Powell deposed.

She

She did write another letter to the Bifhop of Glafcow, which, for
that, in thefe points, it did in fubftance concur with the former,
containing alfo fundry other matters, not pertinent to this accord,
was not read, but the firft draught in French written by Nau, and
by him confeffed and fubfcribed before the Lords, was only fhewed
forth, for the verifying of the fame.

After that, the original draughts of thefe letters to Mendoza, and
Charles Paget, were fhewed to the Scots Queen, and were confeffed
by her, to be the hand-writing of Nau and Curle; fhe refufed to fee
the draught of fundry other letters hereafter mentioned, which were
likewife offered to be fhewed unto her, faying, fhe cared not whether
the fame were written by them or not, and acknowledging withal,
that about that time fhe made feveral difpatches, to fuch effects as
thefe letters did purport, which was, concerning aid to be procured
for her delivery, faying, that the fame was nothing touching the matter wherewith fhe was charged.

Hereupon it was urged, that this letter concurring directly, in matter and circumftances, with Babington's letter to her, and her anfwer
to the fame, did prove evidently that fhe received the one, and did
write the other, and fo was privy, and a compaffer and practifer of
the defign of the death of her Majefty, and on this behalf thefe particularities were fpecially voted.

She writeth to Mendoza, Charles Paget, and the reft, that the
Catholics did fignify unto her their intentions, and that fhe made
them an ample difpatch, giving her advice upon every point, point
by point, upon conference together of Babington's letter to her, with
her anfwer to the fame; this appeareth to be true, for by his, fhe
hath intelligence of their plot and intention; and by the other fhe
giveth her direction and advice, point by point.

In her letter to Charles Paget, fhe writeth, that upon the return
of Ballard, the principal of the Catholics had imparted unto her their
intentions, conformable to that which Charles Paget wrote unto her;

but

but more particularly upon conference of Babington's letter with that of Charles Paget of the 29th of May, it appeareth, that Babington fetteth down fundry particularities of the plot, more than are contained in Paget's letter.

In her letter to Babington, fhe promifeth to write to Mendoza, and others, and in thofe which fhe did write to Mendoza, Charles Paget, &c. fhe writeth, that fhe had given fuch direction; and accordingly Ballard was prepared and ready to have taken that journey, if he had not been prevented by his apprehenfion, as is confeffed by Ballard, Babington, and Savage.

She writeth to Charles Paget, &c. that the difficulty which hath been objected, touching her delivery out of hold, is cleared; and that fhe hopeth to have it executed affuredly, according to her defignment.

And accordingly, in Babington's letter to her, and her anfwer to the fame, the manner and means of her efcape is fet down at large.

In her letter to Charles Paget, fhe faith, fhe hath written to the Catholics, that no ftirring fhall be on this fide, before they have fufficient promife and affurance for the accomplifhment of that which is required of the Pope and King of Spain: and in this her letter of anfwer to Babington, it appeareth, that fhe did write to that effect.

In her letter to Sir Francis Inglefield, fhe writeth, that for Scotland, fhe is about to practife that her enemies may have no fuccour thence.

And accordingly, in her letter to Babington, fhe writeth, that fhe would effay, at the time that the work fhould be in hand in thefe parts, to make the Catholics of Scotland to arife, and put her fon in their hands, to the effect that from thence her enemies may not prevail of any fuccours; and withal willeth, that fome ftirring in Ireland were laboured for, to begin fome while before, to the end the alarm may be given on the flat contrary fide that the ftroke fhould come.

Both

Both which her devices have not failed of their fuccefs, for there have been ftirs and troubles both in Scotland and Ireland, the latter end of this Summer.

And where the Scots Queen confeffed, that fhe had written to procure invafion and rebellion, and feemed to juftify the fame as lawful, for to obtain thereby her delivery, it was faid, that being within the realm, and protected by the laws, and fo fubject to the fame, fhe might not ufe thofe means to compafs her delivery, whereby the Queen's life was apparently fought; for invafion and deftruction of her Majefty are fo linked together, that they cannot be fingle; for if the invader fhould prevail, no doubt they would not fuffer her Majefty to continue neither government nor her life; and in cafe of rebellion, the fame reafon holdeth.

It was further alleged, that, befides thefe feveral letters before mentioned, fhe did, about the time that thefe things were in hand, write divers letters to fundry other perfons beyond the feas, wherein fhe taketh herfelf to be the Sovereign of this realm, containing fundry matters very dangerous as well to our Sovereign the Queen's Majefty, as to the whole ftate of this realm. By which her intentions, in the matters wherewith fhe is now charged, may the better appear.

The 20th of May 1586, fhe did write to Charles Paget to practife with the Spanifh Ambaffador in France, to ftir the King of Spain to invade the realm, and to take revenge on the Queen's Majefty.

That the fureft and readieft way to rid himfelf altogether from this Queen's malice, is, by purging the fpring of the malign humours.

That by this long patience, he hath not prevailed any thing, and that there is no other means to fet up again the King of Spain's affairs in the Low Countries, and to affure his eftate in all other parts, than in re-eftablifhing this realm under a Prince his friend.

That if he deliberate, to fet in this Queen, he affureth himfelf of Scotland, either to ferve him, or to be fo bridled, as not to ferve his enemy.

That

That she will travel by all means, to make her son to enter into the enterprize, or, if he cannot be persuaded thereunto, then she will dress a secret league and bond amongst the Catholic Lords of that country, to join with the King of Spain.

That she will make her son to be delivered into the hands of the Pope, or King of Spain, with paction to set him at liberty whensoever she shall devise, or after their death, himself, being Catholic, shall desire, without that ever the King of Spain should pretend or attempt any thing to the prejudice of her son (if he yield him Catholic), in the succession of that Crown.

That a Regent should be established in Scotland, to govern in the absence of her son, and for that purpose named the Lord Claude Hambleton, alias Hamilton.

That she should write to the Lord Claude to procure him to draw the Catholic Lords of Scotland, to be at the King of Spain's devotion. That, after answer received from the King of Spain, conformable to this design, then Charles Paget to write plainly to the Lord Claude, that he hath charge from her to deal with the Lord Claude in this matter, shewing that it is needful to seize her son's person, if he cannot be willingly drawn to this enterprize, and that the next way were to deliver him in to the Pope or the King of Spain.

That Charles Paget should indirectly put the Lord Claude in hope, that she will make him to be declared lawful heir to the Crown of Scotland, her son failing without children, and that she will procure the Catholic Princes of Christendom to condescend thereunto.

She chargeth him not to communicate these things to any, either English, or French, or Scottish, and to pray Mendoza, and the Lord Claude, to do the like.

The letter was first drawn in French by Nau, and then translated in English, and after put into cypher by Curle, and an extract of the principal points thereof, was confessed and subscribed before some of the Lords the 25th of September, which was openly read and shewed forth.

Then

Then was read another letter, which the Scots Queen wrote to
Mendoza, the fame 20th of May, concurring with the former to Charles Paget, wherein she writeth, that Charles Paget had a large commiffion from her, to impart to Mendoza certain overtures on her behalf.

That there was another point depending thereupon, which she had referved to write to Mendoza himfelf, to be fent to the King his Mafter, on her behalf; no man elfe, if it were poffible, being privy thereunto, viz. That confidering her fon's obftinacy in herefy, and forefeeing the imminent danger like to enfue to the Catholic church, he fucceeding in this Crown; fhe refolved, in cafe her fon were not reclaimed to the Catholic religion. as fhe had title, to give and grant her right to the King of Spain, in fucceffion of this Crown, by her laft will and teftament, praying him to take into his protection, both her, and the ftate and affairs of this realm.

She willeth this to be fecret; forafmuch, if it fhould be revealed, it fhould be in France, the lofs of her dowry; in Scotland, the clear breach of her fon; and in this country, her total ruin and deftruction.

This letter was firft written in French by the Scots Queen's own hand, and then tranflated into Englifh, and put into cypher by Curle, as he confeffed and fubfcribed the fame the 25th of September laft.

Upon reading of thefe letters, it was noted, that the Scots Queen's intention was, to fubject this Crown and realm to the King of Spain, to the utter ruin and deftruction, both of the Queen's Majefty, and of all the antient nobility, which purpofe appeareth to be generally holden by the Englifh fugitives and traitors beyond the feas, as Babington and Savage fet down in their feveral confeffions and declarations; and that their intention is, to procure the King of Spain title to this realm, to be confirmed and invefted by the Pope, to take

away

away all objections againſt it. And, as Babington faith, Dr. Allen and Parſons ſtaid longer at Rome, to folicit the fame.

After this was read, another letter written to the Scots Queen, by Dr. Allen, the 5th of February, wherein he writeth unto her, Madam, my good Sovereign, for our refolution out of Spain, the whole execution is committed to the Prince of Parma.

That Father Parſons, Owen, and himſelf did bring the King's determination to the Prince, who feemed as glad as they, that he might have the effectuating of it; and gave great fign to do it, ſtrait upon the recovery of Antwerp, but harped ſtill upon this ſtring, that ſhe ſhould by money, or fome means, put herſelf out of their hands.

Then was read the Scots Queen's letter to Doctor Allen the 20th of May 1586, wherein ſhe called him Reverend Father, and faith, they have overſlipped many good occafions; and wiſheth, that they ſhould not withal omit this new offer, pinching near by this Queen.

Upon theſe letters were inferred, that Dr. Allen did acknowledge her to be his Sovereign, and to be the Queen of this realm in prefent poſſeffion, and ſhe accepting the fame, gave him the title of a Biſhop. Whereunto ſhe anſwered, that though Dr. Allen, and divers other foreign Princes, and the Catholics of this realm did fo take her, yet ſhe could not do withal; but for herſelf, ſhe did not claim to be fo.

It is alfo to be noted, that the refolution which was to be put in execution by the Prince of Parma, and which the Scots Queen was fo careful ſhould not be overſlipt, cannot be thought to be other but matter of great peril to her Majeſty's perſon and this ſtate. And fo it may alfo be gathered by a letter written by the Prince of Parma to the Scots Queen the 12th of January 1585, where he writeth, that touching the great fecret, he would keep it, as it becometh, and put to effect as much as ſhe ſhould command, and ſhould be in his power.

                              †   Alſo,

Also, the Scots Queen did write to Dr. Lewis, ult. April 1586, wherein she willeth him to impart her congratulations to the new elected Pope, and her affection towards him, chiefly for that she underfandeth his resolution bent, to follow, as near as he can, the traces and footsteps of good Pope Pius V. of whose memory she beareth a singular reverence, for the singular compassion he had of her present state, and his endeavour which he did manifest to relieve her.

Whereupon, it is to be noted, that her imaginations be against the Queen's person and state, since she exciteth the Pope to follow the steps of Pius V. who published the bull of excommunication against her Majesty, and thereby denounced her to be no lawful Queen, and discharged her subjects of their obedience and allegiance; out of which root hath sprung all the traiterous practices that have since been attempted against her Highness's person.

And for the verifying of these letters before mentioned, written by the Scots Queen; it is to be remembered, that the original draughts of all these letters, saving that only which she wrote to Babington, which, as Curle affirmeth, she commanded to be burned, as is before mentioned, were found amongst her papers at Chartley and put in a chest, sealed up by John Manners, Esq; Sir Walter Ashton, Knight, and Richard Bagot, Esq; which was first opened and unsealed, and the same draught taken out, by certain of the Lords and others of her Majesty's Privy Council.

After, on the 24th day of October, the Lords and other Commissioners being assembled at the Star Chamber at Westminster, to confer of the said matters, and touching their sentence, Nau and Curle were brought personally before them; and the papers, letters, and writings, which they had before confessed and subscribed, and affirmed by their oaths, as is aforesaid, being then and there likewise shewed unto them, they did then eftsoons voluntarily acknowledge and

K k   affirm

ELIZA- affirm all that to be true, which they had before fo confeffed and
BETH.
1586. fubfcribed, and that they had fo confeffed and fubfcribed the fame,
only in refpect of the truth, frankly and voluntarily, without any
torture, conftraint, or threatening.

And the faid Curle did then alfo further affirm, that as well the
letter which Babington did write to the Scots Queen, as the draughts
of her anfwer to the fame, were both burned at her command.

He faid alfo, after the decyphering of the faid letter written by
Babington, and the reading thereof to the Scots Queen, he admonifhed her of the danger of thofe actions, and perfuaded her not to
deal therein, nor to make any anfwer thereunto: and fhe thereupon
faid fhe would anfwer it, bidding him do that which he was commanded, and which appertained unto him.

No. XVI.

No. XVI.

*A letter from Sir Edward Stafford, Ambaſſador in France,
to the Queen, with one to Lord Treaſurer Burleigh, in-
cloſing it.*

[The importance of this diſpatch wants no recommendation. None
of the numerous Hiſtorians and Memoir Writers of this intrigue-
ing time, mention any ſuch propoſal of Henry III. or the confidence which he repoſed in the Engliſh Ambaſſador.

Henry IV. found himſelf obliged ſome years after to follow
this advice, which in a private letter to the Belle Gabrielle, he
calls "Faire le ſaut perilheux."]

Sir Edward Stafford to the Queen.

1587-8.
Feb. 25th.

May it pleaſe your Majeſty,

FEARING leſt you have loſt the cyphers that I ſent you, I
thought for avoiding that miſchance fit, to write to you in a
cypher I ſent my Lord Treaſurer at my coming away out of England, with one of the ſame that I ſent your Majeſty, with a few
more additions than was in yours. If it pleaſe your Majeſty, if you
have not your own in the way, to ſend to him for it; it will decypher this. I ſpake yeſternight with the French King, who ſent
for me, by a man quite unknown, to a houſe that I think I can gueſs
at again, though it were in the night, and that he brought me far
out of the right way to it, where I found nobody in the chamber
but himſelf. In the houſe I heard folks, but nobody ſaw me, nor I

From the
Original in
the Paper
Office.

K k 2   ſaw

faw nobody, for he that brought me tarried not in the chamber. The King began with me, that he had fent for me, according as he had fent me word the laft day, and upon the truft and confidence he had in me, and upon the faithful affurance I had given him, both in your Majefty and mine own, that whatfoever he delivered me, I would fend it directly to your Majefty's own hands, and that you would do what lay in you for the good of France, and keep it to your Majefty, fo that it fhould never be fpoken nor heard of, that he had dealt thus fecretly, or confidently with your Highnefs or any of yours. I told him, that when I made that offer unto him, upon fome fpeech that was ufed to me by fome of his, and that I durft promife your Majefty would keep it moft fecretly, if either I delivered it myfelf or fent it to your Majefty to your own hand; that, though I had then no commiffion to deal, becaufe your Majefty's fo often offers to do good had been little fet by; I had notwithftanding, prefently after I had faid the word, made a difpatch to fignify what I had done; that your Majefty had made anfwer unto me of avowing me, that your good will was, that it had ever been unto the King, that you would continue fo ftill; and that for the fecrecy of it, your Majefty did affure, that whatfoever he did deliver confidently to me, to write to you. that, I did affure him, and that whatfoever lay in your Majefty to pleafure him in any way that was within the compafs of your power, or with poffibility to do it with honour, that it fhould be done; that all things delivered to me, fhould never be fpoke or heard of; that all Princes did ufe counfel in all things of any weight, that your Majefty's cuftom was to do fo to, as reafon was, but that you had thofe faithful, wife, and fecret Counfellors, that whatfoever you did communicate to them (whereof there were not many that you ufed in thofe great matters of weight and fecrecy) that though you gave them no charge at all, they were fo difcreet, as they would eafily know what were fit to be done: but that I was fure, that if you did communicate it with any, you would give them

that

that particular charge, and take that affurance of them, as they neither would, nor durft but obferve; and withal, that if he would not,
I durft affure him that your Majefty would never deliver to any that
which he delivered to me, but to himfelf. And farther, that
whereas that fome ufed fome fpeech to me in the beginning, and
Pinard, the laft day that he came to me from his Majefty, had caft
out fuch a word, that your Majefty did make him thefe offers now
to him, to make profit of his dealing with your Majefty now, to
advance the treaty of peace with Spain, that you was in hands withal,
to make your Majefty gainer. That I did proteft to him from
your Majefty, that you never had fuch a meaning, nor fo much as
fuch a thought. That they were evil-difpofed people to break the
amity between France and England, that had thofe intentions, which
was their only drift; that I durft anfwer him upon my foul, that you
never had fuch a thought. He told me upon that, he would affure
himfelf upon my promife, that I and your Majefty would perform
it in all points; that he would deal plainly with me, and lay his
ftate more open to you than ever he did to any; that he was
very well contented you fhould take advice of any of your fecret
Counfellors whom it pleafed you; that he knew that you had them
that you did affure fhould do nothing paffing your commandment;
that he wifhed with all his heart to have given of his blood that he
had the like, that would depend upon nobody but upon his will, his
affairs fhould not (as he termeth it *pendre a la balance* as they do)
That whereas the laft day he fent me word by Pinard, the anfwer
he did, that it was the Queen Mother and his whole Council's peremptory advice, ftanding upon it, that it was not fit, that he fhould
defire your Majefty to meddle between him and his fubjects; that
thereupon he made the anfwer, and defired me to fend it away, as I
did by John Fourier, that nothing might be fufpected; that I hoped
of any thing from him, but that he would deal more plainly with
your Majefty, befeeching you with all his heart to do it, and without
making known to any, that any requeft came from him, becaufe
they

they of the religion, as he said, could keep nothing secret, and that your Majesty would persuade the King of Navarre to have a care of his estate, and to accommodate him with his Majesty in such sort as the league might have no pretence to ruin France and him both. Whereupon I replied unto him, the impossibility that it was for your Majesty to deal with the King of Navarre in religion, for the reasons that I had both told him, the other day, and after to Pinard, and which he, by himself in this action, might very well consider. That your Majesty, I durst answer, would do what you could any way, but to persuade the King of Navarre any more to change, than you had persuaded the King of Navarre to take it; that it was a thing you could not meddle in; that if his own judgment would make him do it for the good of his estate, that you would not meddle with his conscience, nor with his soul. He answered me again, that he would deal as plainly with me, as if I were his ghostly father; that as in truth he was so much addicted to his religion, as withal he would it had cost him a piece of his realm and part of his blood, that all the world, but specially France were of it, so he was not so much a *bigot*, as he termed it, which in English is *over-superstitious*, that he would rather let France ruin, and himself, than suffer liberty and exercise both, as he had both done, and would do again with all his heart; but it was now out of his power to do it, or to put France in peace, if he heard speak of religion as things stood; that he dealt plainly with me, that his last hope to have done it was, by the *Reisters* * means; who, if they had either valour or discretion, might have made the league, upon their knees, ask that which they had broken in arms, which was, that he expected and looked for, and was the only cause that he would take no knowledge of the many offers I made from your Majesty to stay them, if he had desired it; and that he had given them all the means they desired to have done it, if they could have taken it, and to have kept themselves far enough from

* German troops.

him,

him, as he kept himfelf from them, till they would needs come to
feek him, and by their own evil government had put him to that
plunge, that all the world marked him almoft with their finger; and
the league had almoft overthrown them quite, whereas they had afore
then, twice or thrice in their hands to have done the like with them,
and have ended all in a day, if they had judgment to have taken
it. And when they had failed of thofe occafions, if they had ra-
vaged Lorrain, and thofe places of Champaign and Burgundy that
were addicted to them, and left none unfpoiled, that were any way
adherents to them; they would have been glad to have prayed, and
he would have made them as much have prayed for peace, as they
had fought the contrary. But that, inftead of annoying them, they
came to feek him out, and let themfelves be fo low brought to his
hands, as either he muft have given the league the vantage they
defired over him, and have left them the honour of all; befides, that
he was conftrained to do as he did to take the honour out of their
hands. And yet let them lay (faid he) their hands upon their con-
fciences, thofe that were faved, owe him their lives, confidering the
ftate they had let themfelves be brought in by the others. And that
now all hope of any good that way, was taken away, for that they
had let them learn the way that was never thought on afore, to ruin
as many armies of *Reifters* as ever came into France, without fighting, and which he cannot impeach them of without he make himfelf
a party againft them, which cannot be, and that therefore it is not
any way poffible to have them do more good, but harm hencefor-
ward, by giving the contrary party, if they come to the help of
them, a colour to call in other * ftrangers, for their defence, that he
feareth worfe, and who fhall be good foldiers well governed, and
well paid, and that fhall have all the towns they have at the entry,
and in France, to back them, and at their devotion. So that now,
whofoever would be the caufe of their return, if they could be

* The Spaniards.

brought

brought to return (which he doth not believe), would be the cause of the utter subversion of the realm, and therefore the utter undoing of the King and the State; and therefore devised your Majesty to con- fider that, as one that loved him, as he assured, and had reason to do, in respect that the love of them, one to another, were profitable to both, and to be a means that the colour of maintaining of arms may be taken away, which cannot be, except the King of Navarre yield to him in religion, for keeping the league without colour of arming, did cut their throats; for they were brought into that beggary, as in peace they had not meat to put in their mouths, and every day, more and more, lost some of their affectionate servants.

I answered him as before, that I knew your Majesty would do what you could, and what was reason, to bring things to peace, and to keep them in it, but by that means I saw not how you could do it; for, first, to open your mouth to the King of Navarre of that point, I saw an impossibility; next, though the King of Navarre would do it, though your Majesty did speak to him of it, I know not how he could do it; for upon the Prince of Condé he had no power. And if the King of Navarre and Prince of Condé would both, there were great numbers in France of the religion, and great numbers of towns and strong holds, over whom if the King of Navarre did that, he should have no more commandment, and then were their colours of religion taken away no more, for the King of Navarre's and Prince of Condé's changing, than before. He an- swered again, that if the King of Navarre and Prince of Condé were changed, the rest would easilier be brought to think upon their con- sciences, and to dispose themselves to obey time; that though that were not, if the two next heirs were Catholics, but specially the King of Navarre, who was the next to fall (whom in the end, what brags foever any made, if it were not for religion, would ever, and should acknowledge him to be fo), these mischiefs that are happened now, under the colour they have taken, and the terror they have

put

put into mens minds, by that of the overthrowing of the Catholic
religion by the fucceffors that are Huguenots, fhould ceafe, and the
league brought back again into the fame ftate they were in, in
Monfieur's time, at which time they could not find means to have
this colour to put out their horns. And to that ftate they fhould be
put to again, to make them pull in their horns, if that caufe ceafed,
and to their utter overthrow. To the which I anfwered, that there
was a probability in the reafons, if there were a poffibility to bring
them to pafs; but if it pleafed him, as he had honoured me already,
to put his confidence in me, to give me leave to tell him my opinion,
I did affure him that I did find that probability in them, that if I
were of the King of Navarre's Council, and that he did command
me not to meddle with his confcience, but to counfel him the beft
way for the confervation of his ftate, and the prefervation of his
perfon, that it fhould be the firft counfel I would give him, to do
that which he defired; but if I were of his council, I would rather
be torn in pieces, than counfel him to defire it, but rather do what
I could to impeach it, if the King of Navarre had any fuch intent,
and would rather wifh him (feeing I had feen by proof that pretext
of religion could give them that had no intereft nor expectation to
the fucceffion, fuch an authority as they had gotten, as neither the
King by his poffeffion, nor the King of Navarre with the hope of
his fucceffion, could pull them out of it), to defire rather that the
King of Navarre fhould remain as he was, to have that religion to
be a bar to impeach him of attempting any thing in his time, than
in taking that away, to make him both the fun rifing clear, to make
him to be worfhipped, and to take the eclipfe quite away to ferve for
an object to darken his light. That I did proteft unto him, that I
did think it, and fo affuredly think it, that I durft hazard my life,
the King of Navarre neither had, nor ever would have fuch a thought,
what means foever he might have to do otherwife; yet I did think it
more wifdom to fhut up a treafure houfe with all keys and bars

L l   that

that could be found, to impeach them that would rob it, if they had
a mind to it, than to leave the doors negligently and wilfully open,
to fet a thief's teeth on edge, and to make him have a mind to it.
And fo in this, would rather counfel him to hazard the pulling down
of them, that had no intereft after him, and to permit, for fo neceffary a refpect, fo neceffary an inconvenience in France, than in taking
fo neceffary a thing away, which he fhould defire to be if it were
not, to incur the hazard of the greater in avoiding the leffer: that
I defired him to pardon me, for I protefted I faid no otherwife to
him, than I would advife your Majefty if you were in the like cafe,
with the like circumftances. I affure your Majefty, that he gave the
hearing at leifure, and was in a ftudy without anfwering me a good
while. At length, with thanks he told me, that every one could
rule a fhrewd wife but he that had her, and that he that had her
could tell worfe the way how to rule her; that that was his cafe;
but that he had rather hazard the pulling them down with the King
of Navarre, which he faw a poffibility in, and ftand upon thofe hazards, than in letting them have that colour ftill, to make it an impoffible thing to pull them ever upon their knees; but to fee them
ftrengthen in defpight of him daily, and which he cannot elfe remedy
as things ftand, but with the hazard of an utter overthrow of him
and France. That as for the King of Navarre, having once the pretence of his religion, and then forgone it, the pretence of Catholic
religion would never ferve the King of Navarre, to hurt him in his
time. And that though he would bring the league with all his heart
as low as he could, he would never fo utterly overthrow them; that,
if the King of Navarre fhould enter into any fuch intent, he could
quickly raife them to help him to impeach him of any fuch attempt.
I defired him to pardon me, that it was my zeal to have peace and
quietnefs that made me bold, and to have thofe things done for the
effecting of it, that were poffible, and to avoid all inconvenience that
might come to impeach fo good and fo neceffary an intent, for the
                                                                  good

good of both the realms. He told me, he had opened himfelf fo far,
as he never had done to any ftranger; and but to few of France, and
fo few, as if he did tell it me, I would fcarce believe it; that he
did truft upon my word, both of that I had given him from myfelf,
and in your Majefty's name, that if he were not kept promife withal,
he would never have dealing confidently with your Majefty, nor any
of yours. That he protefted to me, no living creature did know of
my coming, but he that brought me, nor he nothing of the matter, nor
never fhould any know more; that if ever it were heard of, he would
quite difown having feen me, and have caufe to do me all the difgrace that he could, and never to love your Majefty more, but to
hate you as much as he loved you. If you deal well with him in this,
and put your helping hand to the fetting France in quiet, and the
pulling it out of the mouth of them that make it a prey to ftrangers
on all fides, that he, being out of danger within France, may help
his neighbours without; which he protefteth to do in any need, and
never to fail them. That his enemies were your Majefty's, if it
were well looked into; that you may firft help him, becaufe you are
in quiet, and have means to do it if you would; and that, he bid
me affure myfelf he knew, and more than he could tell me, and
therefore defired you to put your helping hand to it. And that
though his Council, and fpecially Queen Mother, diffuaded him to
defire it at your hands, as a thing unhonourable to him to defire it,
that you fhould meddle between him and his fubjects; yet he did
fecretly by me defire, and befeech you; and that he fhould think
himfelf beholden to you for it, and moft of all, for doing it upon
his requeft, and keeping that fecret that he hath requefted you, as I
have promifed; for there was nothing would fo much vantage the
league againft him, as to have known that he had conference in this
fort with your Majefty, or any of yours. That his cafe, if it were
well weighed, were both to be regarded, pitied, and helped; that
he had not many to truft to, when his neareft failed him, and they,

that

that with all kind of bonds were moſt tied unto him; that he had gone farther with me than he had gone yet with any, or ever meant to do again, and therefore put me again, both of mine own promiſe, and my promiſe in your name, both for yourſelf, and your Counſellors, that if your Majeſty communicate it to any, you take aſſurance of them, that it ſhould never be heard of, which I did again promiſe, and proteſt to him, both in mine own name, and for your Majeſty. And I know you will, and ſo I humbly beſeech you to perform it, or elſe all confidence in you, and all means for me to do you ever any ſervice, is taken away for ever.

This being done, he fell with me into familiar ſpeech of many things of your Majeſty, of your government, of your Counſellors, all the which things I ſatisfied his demands in ſuch ſort, as was fit for me. Then of the Queen of Scots, which I was glad he fell into, becauſe I know there hath been great cunning uſed to keep that ſtill in his mind againſt your Majeſty, as he himſelf confeſſed; and particularly, for I think I left him ſatisfied better than he hath been, and ſpecially for your Majeſty's quite ignorance of it, and mere unwillingneſs to it; which at the firſt he ſmiled at, as not believing it, aſking whether it were poſſible for them? I gave him ſome reaſon that in my poor judgment I thought fit; that I dare aſſure you, he thinks better of it than he did, if he believe it not altogether. From that, how he was preſſed, and by whom, and among the reſt forgat not Queen Mother, that he ſtood upon his honour to revenge it, but ſpecially to help the King of Scots, and to egg him to it; whereunto I prayed him with ſuch reaſons as I could, to make him probably to ſee that their intents were nothing leſs than to care for that; his towns they took in the mean time, and other things they did daily, ſhowed that well enough. He confeſſed it, and ſwore by no ſmall oaths, that, if the King of Navarre be brought to that, that he may help the King of Navarre, or that he may have the King of Navarre to help him, that the marks ſhall remain of it. But that their colour was

ſuch,

fuch, and fo printed in mens minds by art, that the leaft ftir in the
world, that, not being taken away, cantoneth his towns, and putteth all his ftate in hazard ; that perchance the world might wonder at his manner of dealing hitherto; but his ftate was not as other men's, nor French humours as other people's; that as things ftood, he had no way to fave himfelf whole, but that; and if the King of Navarre do help him, will take another courfe, and be beholden to the King of Navarre, and his friends that fhall move him to do it. If not, he muft needs keep the fame courfe he doth, to fave the State, and to fwallow many things againft his ftomach, to win time, and do that way that, which he can elfe do no other way. From that, he fell into this peace treating with Spain, which I found he did not believe was meant of any fide; for of your Majefty's fide, he could not believe you believed it could be; and that he knew affuredly, that the King of Spain meant it not, or at the leaft if it do, it is but to ferve his prefent turn, and to be at quiet for the time to trouble France, where he hath begun. For he protefted by all the proteftations that could be, that fince this treaty began, he hath been continually preffed by the King of Spain, and is yet daily, and by others, to join to attempt againft your Majefty. I did anfwer him, that I could not tell what to think of that, but I knew it was extremely preffed by the King of Spain; which he afked me again if I were certain of it, and I affured him it; which I think he believeth; and withal, I affured him, that you would do nothing to the difadvantage of him and France, whatfoever you did elfe, which I think he believeth, but yet feareth this colour of treaty, whether it be in effect or no, will give the King of Spain leifure to trouble him, which as he faith, and hath reafon in it, is neither good for him nor your Majefty. And withal, told me fomewhat fhort, he had refpect to your Majefty; and that he, almoft alone, had held againft all the world in that, both at home and abroad, to do nothing might annoy you, and that in truth I know to be true; but that if your Majefty

I   had

had no refpect to him, in the end, natural reafon muft needs carry
him away to look the beft he can to himfelf, and draw him to that
which he will ever do unwillingly, whenfoever he is conftrained to it.
I affured him ftill of your good-will, and that the proof of it would
fhow it. He defired me it might be fo, for effects muft be that
which muft fhew it, and fware a great oath he would requite it.
From that, he complains of his merchants taken, and fpoiling, daily
by Englifhmen, and a thing that all the world cried out upon him
for, and that he bore as long as he could; that befides the fubjects
of France, whom he owed a care and refpect to, to preferve, it was
an indignity to him, which miniftred colour to the evil affected, to
pique him daily againft your Majefty.

To be fhort, he defired reafon for things paft, and order that they
may happen no more ; for he defired no caufe of jar, and that he
would give none. I affured him of it, that things paft could not be
remedied, but that juftice fhould be done, and order given that no
fuch inconveniences hereafter fhall happen. And withal, took occafion to tell him mildly, that the French Ambaffador made things worfe
than they were, which fhowed no good-will to maintain amity. He
told me in that, he did that, in that point, he had caufe given him ;
but in other things he told me plainly, *Il n'eft qu'un fot* ; and that, but
for Villeroy's fake, he would make him known fo, but that he would
not   Villeroy; and thereupon told me, that particularly the
Ambaffador fhould by no means have an inkling of this, no more
than any body elfe: I affured him of it, for all the world, and
defired him to be out of doubt of it. From that, he talked of the
Count Monbeliard's, and Wirtemberg's levying of men, to be revenged of that, the league had fpoiled in their country; but he is
not of opinion they have courage enough, and told me with thefe
words, *Ils ne font que des cocquins, qu'il ne ni e & qu'ils ne roma-
gent tout, le diable les emporte.* I caft out fome words to fee whether
he would be offended if a new army came into their frontiers to fpoil

†   them,

them, if fo they can no farther. I promife you, I cannot affure you of it, but I think he would not be difcontented at it, for thefe were his very words, *Le diable les emporte, qu'ils ny'ont demeuré dernier-ment, canaille quils font, & ne   chercher leur malheur, & qui ne les demandoint pas, fans faire rien de ce qu'ils   & pouvoynt aizement faire.* Thus he ended, repeating to me again the affurance that I had given him of the fecrecy of this, the affurance of his friendfhip to your Majefty, in fpite of any counfel or enticement, if you gave him caufe of your part, and means to that which were good for both, and that he might ftop them that meant nothing but deadly harm to them both.

Thus I have been long, but your Majefty muft pardon me, for it was my duty to make a plain relation to you, for to nobody elfe I could by promife. I did what I could to egg him to fpeak, and to open himfelf, and I think he hath done more than he hath done to many. I am not wife enough to advife your Majefty what to refolve upon in it, but I think he hath dealt truly in moft things, and according as he meaneth. I would wifh your Majefty to do what you you could well do to content him; for I am of that opinion, that there will hardly be ever in France, a King of a difpofition fitter for England; for furely he hath a defire, if he can live in peace, to attempt nothing againft England, or any elfe. But you had need to take advice of yourfelf, which is indeed the chiefeft of your Council; and of the wifeft elfe you can take advice of; for I am of that opinion, it is a ticklifh point to take counfel of; for if, in doing part of that which he defireth, your requeft were made a colour to the King of Navarre, to do more than you would have him do, and to take you at your word, and to make you to be the King of Navarre's excufe to the world; I am not wife enough to judge what good or harm it might bring your Majefty.

The King's words make me fufpect fomewhat, and other cir-cumftances make me fufpect more; and particularly feeking of

the

the King of Navarre's own folks, what they judge of his difpofition, maketh me doubt moft of all; and advertifements that I have from divers places confirm me more, whereof fome be certain, fome I cannot certainly affure you of, of both which forts I write plainly Mr. Secretary in a particular letter of that, becaufe I have kept your Majefty fo long, as I am afhamed to keep you longer, for troubling you, and therefore moft humbly taking my leave, I commit your Majefty to him that hath, and ever, I affure myfelf, will guard you in all your actions, and protect you from all your enemies. This 25th of February 1587.

Sir Edward Stafford to the Lord Treafurer.

MY very good Lord, I have fent your Lordfhip a book here that was brought me even now, which I have not yet read, and therefore cannot tell whether it be worth the fending to your Lordfhip or no, only to ferve for a colour that the copy of her Majefty's letter may not be thought upon ; which, if my packet of letters were greater than of one letter, might breed a fufpicion to have them opened, as I know others have been. I fpake with the King, and that at large, as by the copy of my letter to her Majefty you may fee. We had difcourfed of many things, and did what I could to make him fpeak, which in truth I think he hath done, more than he hath done to many. And of many things, I avow truly, he was very loath, at firft, her Majefty fhould communicate it to any. We had at length very familiar difcourfe of many things, and particularly of the Lord Treafurer, and them in his place: he knoweth every body's humour as well as I, and I think better. I found him have a found opinion of nobody's paffions there ; but Lord Treafurer

furer. I did not gainfay it. He was particularly contented that I fhould make Lord Treafurer acquainted with all, if I would; for he told me plainly, that though he took him to be more affected to Spain than to France, he knew him to be faithful to her Majefty, and affected to no paffion but her good only, and with thefe words, *fort homme de bien.* I anfwered him to his fatisfaction. For all other of his fellows I took oath, and faithful promife, to communicate nothing but only to her Majefty, that fhe might do after, as you may fee by the contents of the letter. I pray God fend her Majefty to take counfel of that which is beft for herfelf; for furely I cannot tell what to think of this world, nor well judge of the King of Navarre, and that fide, as you may fee by a particular letter I have written, of thefe things to Mr. Secretary; and alfo another of the news of the defeat, and taking of Maximilian by the Chancellor of Poland. And fo I commit you to the keeping of God. Paris, this 26th day of February, 1587.

M m   No. XVII.

No. XVII.

*A brief Difcourfe, containing the true and certain manner
how the late Duke of Guife, and the Cardinal of Lorraine his brother, were put to death at Blois, the 14th
of December 1588; for fundry confpiracies and treafons
practifed by them againft their Sovereign the French
King; wherein is farther declared the imprifonment of
fome other of the confpirators and leaguers, with divers
other circumftances and matters happening thereupon.
Written unto our late Queen Elizabeth, by Sir Edward
Stafford, at that time, her Ambaffador in the Court of
France.*

[This Narrative not being an original, nor the copy authenticated,
may not be thought to have thofe marks of genuinenefs, which the
other papers of Sir E. Stafford, inferted in this volume, have; and
it muft be owned, that fome of the circumftances differ from the
relations of De Thou and Davila..

It may not be improper to mention, that Stafford, when he came
home, was made Vice-Chamberlain of the Houfehold, and a Privy
Counfellor. He died in the beginning of King James's reign.]

From the
Harleian
Collection.
IN the time of Lewis XII. King of France, not above eighty years
ago, one Claude of Lorrain, or rather Vaudemout, a meer
ftranger, puffed up with riches and pride, began to fet foot, and feat
himfelf in France: who having a very fubtle and reaching head,
endeavoured to make his benefit of time, by warily and fpeedily laying

ing hold upon any occafion whatfoever, whereby to advance his mean eftate to fome place of honour and dignity. And, becaufe at firft he knew not how to fpeed himfelf better, he thought himfelf fairly promoted, when, with much ado, he was taken into the King's houfehold, and made Great Hunter; an office of but fmall and bafe account, in refpect of the honour which this ftranger gaped after. In procefs of time, after many revolutions and toffings, this ambition was ferved fo far, that he was created Duke of Guife and Aumale, Peer of France, and Governor of Burgundy; and fo deceafed. But the fucceeding offspring of this ftranger, not contented nor fatiated with the continual great and undeferved favours and honours, which they from time to time enjoyed, by the exceeding bounty and liberality of the King of France, although they were fo great, and fo many, as might have fatisfied to glut a moft ambitious and unfatiable gorge, bended and levelled their reftlefs defires to a more high and ftately fcope, than ever Claude of Lorrain durft prefume to think of, devifing and practifing how they might compafs the Crown of France: wherein, by their finifter and indirect practices, they have prevailed fo mightily, that they crept daily in credit more and more, and poffeffed the hearts of the Kings of France in fuch fort, that abufing their favours heaped moft plentifully upon them, and their houfe, they only, difpofed the chief offices both in Court and country, difplaced the Princes of the blood from the moft honourable offices, and governments of greateft truft, and in their rooms placed men of their own humour and faction, ruling and over-ruling all things in France at their own pleafure; infomuch that the gate of honour and promotion ftood open, in a manner, to none but fuch as depended wholly upon their devotion. Yet perceiving that all this was not enough to help them to the fupreme authority, without good right to it, or at leaftwife fome probable fhow and colour of right; and knowing that falfehood and lies can hardly have a plaufible paffage amongft

* Grand Veneur.

men,

men, except they mask disguised with a visage of truth (for all men
naturally do embrace that which they know, or think to be true),
they feigned to themselves a certain odd title to the crown; deriving
their pedigree from Charlemaine, but by such uncertain, false, and
counterfeit descents, yea, and such as, through extreme age, were
long ago worne out of date, that they may as well (and better) claim
to be monarchs of the whole world by lineal descent from Adam, as
to ascend to the crown of France by such worm-eaten, rotten, and
broken degrees. And to make this their title more plausible in the
ears of the simple, they suborned men of no small learning to print
and publish books in defence thereof. In which books this their
mishapen title, painted and shadowed with colours of rhetoric, was
slubbered over with some sorry arguments, and slender proofs, to
induce and settle in men's hearts a liking or good opinion of their
pretended right. But their proofs fell out to be so weak, and their
reasons so forceless, that no man in his right wits, except he were
their creature or beadsman, and so devoted to them that he would
believe any thing, though never so untrue, which made for the
Guisian greatness, could thereby be persuaded to like the better
either of them, or their forged title.

These things brought to this unlucky pass, the late Duke of Guise,
following the footsteps of his predecessors, by whom he had received an ambitious desire, and aspiring mind to the crown, in-
grafted in himself as hereditary in his own conceit; and being, from
his infancy, instructed by the late Cardinal of Lorraine, his uncle,
and armed with divers politic instructions, and subtle plots how to
carry himself in so dangerous an enterprise; amongst all the rest of
those cunning and deep devices, thought it fittest for his purpose, to
direct his chiefest endeavours to nourish and maintain, by all possible
means, the civil discord and long continued quarrel between the Protestants and Papists; that, in the midst of these domestical uproars, he
(by shewing himself very hot and forward, and somewhat extraor-
dinarily zealous in defence of the Romish Church, and in the sup-
preffing

preffing of the King of Navarre, and the Princes of the Blood, pro-
feffors of the reformed religion,) might eafily procure himfelf to be
the head of that faction, of which his predeceffors and he had been
fuch notable furtherers. And perfuaded himfelf, not without probable likelihood, that, by that means, he might gain, and firmly
unite unto himfelf, the hearts of the Catholics, and make himfelf
great with the forces of that faction, and with the King's powers
purchafe authority, whom (though half unwilling, and yet not daring
to do otherwife at that time,) he had drawn to call in his edicts of
pacification, and to denounce open war againft the King of Navarre
and thofe of the religion. Neverthelefs, perceiving that the King
profecuted the matter but faintly (in truth becaufe he durft not
truft the Guife, or any of his favourers with too great a power;
for fear left they fhould convert his own forces to his own overthrow and deftruction, as divers prefumptuous, and fome very apparent practices of the Duke, did give him juft occafion to fufpect),
he determined to take another courfe, though fomewhat more dangerous than the former, yet of more moment and affurance, for the
effecting of his conceived purpofe. Whereupon, the Duke dealing
with divers great Peers and States of France, efpecially fuch as either
kindred to himfelf, hatred to the King of Navarre, defire of inno-
vations, becaufe the prefent Government did not fatisfy their ambitious appetites, or fuperftitious zeal without knowledge, had made
partakers of his quarrel, told them openly that the King's careleffnefs, and cowardice in this religious and holy enterprize, was the
only caufe of the profperous fuccefs of the Proteftants, who began
in divers parts of France to grow very ftrong, and greatly to prevail, becaufe the King either would not, or durft not maintain a fufficient army in the field to impeach their proceedings; which mifchief (as he faid) was grown to that greatnefs, that it could not, by
any means, be redreffed, except thofe peers and ftates (to whom the
reformation of the commonwealth in fuch defperate cafes doth appertain,) did join together in an holy league (fo called, becaufe religion

ligion was the chiefeft caufe they did pretend in that action), where each fhould be bound to other by folemn and mutual oath, to fet to his helping hand, to the uttermoft of his power, for the removing of fuch corrupt minions (as he termed them) from the King, as favoured the King of Navarre, and laboured underhand to hinder the wholefome counfels, and politic platforms, agreed upon in Common Council by the Peers and States, for the benefit and honour of the King and Commonwealth, and the enlarging of the Catholic religion : and that they fhould fwear never to make any peace with the King of Navarre, or give over the war againft him, and his adherents, until they had utterly fubverted and overthrown them all. To which unholy league divers of the Peers, and other great men, were fworn, being feduced by thefe, and fuch like perfuafions.

The league being thus on foot, hath hatched, and brought forth a million of mifchiefs; and it cannot be denied but that all the chief doers therein, with their complices, favourers, and abettors, were to be judged and deemed no better than arrant traitors to the King, and enemies to the Commonwealth : for leagues are to be made only between abfolute Kings and Princes of Free States and Cities, for the maintenance of amity, and intercourfe of traffic to be had between either countries, and for the mutual help and fuccour the one is to afford the other againft dangerous enemies, or for fome fuch other public or private refpect, as may greatly concern the commodity and welfare of thofe countries, between whom the league is to be concluded. But, that fubjects fhould bandy themfelves againft their fovereign, or join in league without his confent, to reform and redrefs fuch things, as in the government of the ftate they fuppofe to be amifs, hath ever (and that defervedly) been counted a confpiracy or rebellion, and a point of moft dangerous and deteftable treafon. It hath always been an ufual practice for traitors to pretend reformation of the State, and of the King's court, from corrupt and bad humours, making this falfe fhow of zeal for their country's good, a fnare to blind and entrap the ignorant, and unlearned multitude

tude withal, and a cloak under which they fhroud their ambitious intents and treacherous drifts. No nation, almoft in any age, but can produce plentiful ftore of examples herein: but, inftead of all other, I will only deal with the Duke of Guife, the fequel of whofe cunning practices doth plainly prove, that he meant only, under colour of bettering, to difturb all things, that in the midft of thefe broils he might lay hold both of the King's life and crown, if oppor- tunity and his ability would ferve him thereto. In profecuting which his purpofe, he practifed underhand with the King of Spain, and procured from him fecretly 300,000 piftolets of gold yearly, to be diftributed to the chiefeft of the league, of which fum himfelf had each year 150,000 piftolets. But, no doubt, herein the King of Spain and the Duke had their feveral ambitious ends. The Duke made reckoning, that by this money, and by the French King's authority, he fhould be able to overmatch the King of Navarre, and in the end to fet himfelf above all others in the management of mat- ters of eftate; and to feize upon fo many of the greateft, ftrongeft, and richeft towns and fortreffes of the realm into his hands, that he might be able at his pleafure either to make away the King, or elfe to thruft him into fome abbey, there to live upon fome forry penfion, and fo to inveft himfelf with the long defired name of King, being then, and long before, *Dominus fac totum*, the chief commander both of the King and country. On the other fide, the King of Spain hoped, that, by this money, he fhould keep the Frenchmen fo bufied and troubled at home, that they fhould not have leifure to think upon the attempt of any thing in the Low Countries; the govern- ment and protection of which provinces, about that time, was offered unto the French King, by fome of the States of thofe Provinces. And alfo, that miniftring matter wherewith to continue the fire of this inteftine diffention, and unnatural difcord amongft them, he fhould fhake and weaken the eftate of France, whofe greatnefs and profperity was always an eye-fore to him, and his predeceffors.

And

And laftly, that by his bountiful liberality, he fhould bind many of the nobles unto him in fuch fort, that he might, one day, by their affiftance, make a prey of France, as he had done heretofore of Portugal, by the like corrupt and unking-like practice. And although the French King began to fufpect the unfortunate event of thefe traiterous and damnable drifts, and greatly to lament the mifery, wherein both himfelf and his whole country were like to be plunged, yet becaufe the Duke of Guife bore fo great fway over all France, and had the greateft part of moft vigilant and defperate noblemen at his devotion, he was enforced to fet a fair face on the matter, and wifely to diffemble, as if he had fufpected nothing, until time fhould afford him fit occafion to be revenged at the full. And, in the mean feafon, he determined to deny nothing abfolutely that the Duke of Guife fhould requeft, but withal to endeavour, as much as he could, fecretly to thwart and crofs his purpofes, and to draw fome of his enterprizes to fort to a more contrary event, than the Guife fhould either fufpect or imagine; wherein the Guife, or any man elfe was the eafier to be deceived, becaufe the world never thought the King to have half that politic wit, deep judgment, and undaunted courage, and admirable conftancy, which, by his refolute and rare attempts, luckily fince that time atchieved, he hath fhowed himfelf to have. Infomuch, that when the Duke of Guife and thofe of the league had 30,000 men in the field againft the King of Navarre, and very importunately folicited the French King to levy another army to the fame purpofe, the King yielded very willingly to furnifh, and fet forth 20,000 men; but yet, therewithal, he perfuaded the Duke of Guife, that it would be moft convenient for thofe prefent wars, to divide the whole army into three equal parts, that they might all, at once, invade the King of Navarre with fuch fury, and fo moleft him on all fides, that he fhould never be able to make head any one way, without imminent danger to lofe all another way. This carried a very fair colour of reafon. But the King did it efpecially to this end, that he might procure two parts of three to be guided by his own

efpecial

efpecial friends, whereas otherwife, fome one of the Duke of Guife's
houfe, fhould have been General of the whole 50,000, a thing too
dangerous for the King to endure. Wherefore he wifely, without any
fufpicion, brought to pafs, that the Duke Joyeufe, and the Duke of
Efpernon, both perfons to the King's efpecial favour and liking, preferred to honour, had the leading of the two armies ; and the
Duke of Mayne, the Guife's brother, commanded only the third
part. So that the King fending at firft but 20,000 to the field, had
about 33,000 at his devotion; and the Duke, with thofe of the league,
who fent 30,000, had at their commandment not 17,000. And
after that the Duke Joyeufe was flain, and his whole army defeated,
the King (who by agreement fhould have paid all the three armies)
fed the Duke of Mayne with delays in fuch fort, that for want of
victuals and pay, he was conftrained to diffolve and break up his
camp, and get him home. It cannot be denied, but that the King
wrought herein wonderfully politickly, the which notwithftanding
was not conveyed fo clofely, but that the Duke of Guife foon perceived the drift thereof; for it is hard to halt before a cripple.
The Duke therefore, half defpairing to atchieve the end of his unfatiable defires by thefe means, and relying much upon the favour of
the Parifians, accompanied only with eight gentlemen, that he might
be the lefs fufpected, entered into Paris, contrary to the King's exprefs pleafure and commandment, who diftrufting and fufpecting the
caufe of his coming, had given him to underftand that he was altogether unwilling to have him come thither, before he had appeafed the
troubles of Picardy, and quite taken away the caufes thereof. But
the Duke, notwithftanding the King had forbidden his coming thither, having laid fundry traiterous platforms for the feizing of the
King's perfon, and difpatching of him, being the only man that
ftood in his way ; and purpofing withal to pick quarrels with fome
of the wealthieft citizens in Paris, thereby to enrich himfelf with
their goods, and poffefs himfelf of the King's treafure, being at that
time kept in the Exchequer in Paris (for money was the finews and

　　　　　　　　　ftrength

ſtrength whereby he hoped to uphold this miſerable war), thought
he could not find out a fitter and more aſſured place, wherein to
execute his intended miſchiefs, than Paris, being a town always
affectioned to him, and ſwarming with multitudes of poor artificers,
porters, and peaſants, who, in hope of impunity and reward, are
ready at all times to attempt mutinies, murders, or any kind of vil-
lanies whatſoever, if they may but be egged on, encouraged, or coun-
tenanced by any man of authority or honour, that in ſuch actions
will undertake to be their head and ringleader ; as the miſerable and
more than barbarous maſſacre, moſt cruelly executed in that accurſed
town, upon the moſt renowned and worthy Admiral Chatillon, and
ſundry nobles, gentlemen, ſtudents, and other men and women of all
ſorts, ſo that they were ſuſpected to be of the religion, may give
ſufficient teſtimony.   And although the Duke, by reaſon of their
bad diſpoſition and deadly hatred that they always bore to thoſe of
the religion, did aſſuredly know that they would be ready at all
times to put in practice his cruel and bloody deſignments whatſoever; yet, that he might make himſelf ſtronger in Paris, and provide ſufficient ſtore of bloody and deſperate captains to govern and
lead the unſkilful multitude in thoſe troubleſome tumults, he cauſed
ſundry gentlemen and ſtrangers, that were his friends and retainers,
ſecretly to repair into the town, inſomuch as the city began to be
repleniſhed in divers places, and almoſt in all quarters, with Gui-
zards and leaguers.   But the King having ſecret advertiſements
before-hand, both of his coming and of his deviliſh intents, and tend-
ring greatly the quietneſs and welfare of the town, laboured what
he could to prevent all inconveniences that might ariſe.   And therefore cauſed twelve enſigns of Switzers, and eight enſigns of French
footmen, to be brought thither, having four enſigns of his guard
already there ; and cauſed his colonels and captains to ſeize upon
certain ſtrong and fencible places of Paris, that by that means they
might be the better able to ſuppreſs any ſudden ſtirs and uproars,
and retain the town in obedience and peace.   And to that end, he
cauſed

caufed fome of the Lords of the Council, and Knights of the Order of the Holy Ghoft, accompanied with divers officers of the crown and town, to make an exact fearch throughout all the quarters of Paris, to the end thereby to difcover and find out the ftate of the town, and alfo to avoid fuch ftrangers as fhould be found there, not to be avowed as they ought. But the Duke of Guife, like to the fpider, that fucketh poifon out of fweet flowers, took occafion hereof by divers of his efpials, that wandered up and down in every corner, to make the people (notwithftanding the King's great care to keep the town in perfect quietnefs, fufficiently appeared to all wife men, and dutiful fubjects) to betake themfelves to arms, and rebel, affirming that thefe forces, which the King had brought into the town, were purpofely provided for the facking of Paris, and putting divers of the chief and beft citizens to death. The giddy-headed multitude enraged with thefe falfe furmifes, animated by the prefence of the Duke, and ordered (or rather difordered) by the Duke's followers, made an alarum to arms, fortified themfelves in places of ftrength, affailed the King's forces with defperate fury, flew fifteen of the Switzers, wounded as many more, and unarmed the reft, fet upon certain companies of the King's guards unarmed, and caft them into prifon, and began to fortify and make trenches againft the Louvre, as if they would have befieged the King. But becaufe the Duke perceived that the King kept himfelf clofe in the Louvre, whither divers good fubjects reforted, to adventure their lives in defence of his Majefty, and alfo that this broil was haftened too foon, for he would have had the poffeffion of the King before thefe matters fhould have been broached, he durft not attempt any thing againft his Majefty's perfon. The King then feeing that there was no good to be done, and that he laboured in vain to appeafe this tumult, abandoned and forfook the town, rather than he would hazard the ftate of it by employing his forces againft the inhabitants thereof, and fo flying from thence, efcaped the fury of that brunt. When the King

was

was gone, the Duke laboured to make men believe that these broils
happened against his will; and to cause himself to be the less suspected, he released the Switzers and soldiers that were taken prisoners, restored them their arms, quieted the citizens, took all the
strong places of the city into his own hand, and sealed up the King's
coffers of his Exchequer (but took out the money first), protesting
that he did it not but to consign the whole into the King's hands,
when he should be at peace, or if need were, to employ it for the
preservation of the Romish religion and the Catholics, and to set
them at liberty from the persecutions which the hereticks, confederates (as he termed them) that were about the King, did prepare for
them. And although these insolent attempts, disgraces, and indignities,
preferred by the Duke against the King his Sovereign, did manifest
to all the world his treacherous and undutiful meaning, yet he took
upon him, by a letter sent unto the King, to excuse the matter (God
knows very barely), but with brave and high speeches, and afterward proffered unto the King certain articles of accord, much dero-
gatory to the King's Majesty, his honour, quietness, and safety, and
tending wholly to the honour and advancement of the Duke and his
complices: which articles I have here inserted, that the Duke's dis-
loyalty may thereby the better appear, in that he, being a subject and
vassal, dare presume to prescribe laws and conditions of peace unto his
sovereign liege Lord, which (no doubt) is to be reckoned a bold, presumptuous, and treasonable action. Some of the articles are these
ensuing.

· 1. That whereas the Duke had spent the greatest part of his
wealth and treasure in maintaining the wars against the King of
Navarre, and the hereticks, and was by that means grown very far
in debt, that the King, without any delay, should presently pay all
his debts out of the treasure of the crown.

2. Next, that the King should appoint and constitute the Duke
of Guise Lieutenant-general of all his forces, and refer all his wars,
                                                                      both

both against the heretics and others, to be ordered by his difcretion.

3. Thirdly, That the King should cause an assembly of the States to be forthwith summoned, to which assembly none should be admitted, but such peers, nobles, and burgesses of towns, as the Guise should make special choice of, for fear (as he pretended) left some heretic might slip in amongst the rest, which, by his provident care, he meant warily to look unto.

4. Lastly, That the King should renounce all leagues and amity with all protestant Princes and States whatsoever, but specially with the Queen of England and the town of Geneva; and should swear to maintain the Holy League, with other such like presumptuous, dangerous, and traiterous articles, unworthy and unbefitting a subject to offer to his King; which afterward you shall hear more largely, as they were propounded at the assembly of Blois. These articles the King could by no means brook, but because the time served him not to find fault withal, he condescended and promised, that he would submit himself to the counsel and advice of the Peers and States of France, and if by them these articles were thought convenient and necessary for the commonwealth, he would willingly bind himself to the observing them. In the mean season, the Queen Mother and others laboured so effectually between them, that the King and the Duke, in outward appearance, were reconciled again. The Duke being crept again into the King's favour (as he thought) began, after his accustomed manner, to urge the King very instantly, to send another army against the King of Navarre, whereunto he readily condescended, and sent an army of 20,000, of which he made the Duke of Nevers General, who sometime had been a Guisard, but was now become firm on the King's side, by reason of a marriage which the King had made between him and the Duke of Longueville's daughter. The Duke of Guise did much mislike that the army was not committed to the charge of some of his affinity or

faction.

faction. Neverthelefs, becaufe the Duke of Nevers was a Catholic and no friend to the King of Navarre, he durft not find fault with him, left, in fo doing, he fhould difclofe his ambitious humour too apparently. And therefore, feeming not to miflike the choice of fuch a General, he procured from the King, that a gentleman called La Chaftre, Governor of Bourges, a man wholly devoted to the Duke of Guife, might be appointed Marfhal of the Field; that, feeing he could not have the chief command of the whole army, yet, at the leaft, he might be privy to all the intendments of the General, and ftrike a great ftroke in difpofing the affairs of the camp, by reafon of this Marfhal.

This army, as fhall afterwards be declared, ftood the King in fuch and fo great ftead, as if it had been purpofely provided againft the Guifards. But the Duke having his eyes dazzled with gazing and gaping greedily over fovereignty, and his fenfes in a manner fo dulled with continual meditating thereon, and greedily thirfting to quench his unfatiable ambition, with no lefs than a whole king-dom, was fo carried away with vain conceits and imaginations of ruling and conquering, that he never thought upon the hidden hatred worthily conceived by the King againft him; but thinking the King to be void of all courage and care of his eftate, never offered to found the depth of his intents; whereas the King, on the other fide (wifely diffembling the matter, and feeming not to take notice of the Duke's difloyal meaning, becaufe at that time he knew not how to remedy it) lay hovering to take the Duke and his fellow con-fpirators at an advantage, when he might fafely, without any danger to himfelf, be revenged on their curfed bodies, which at length he moft happily performed, almoft beyond all men's expectation, to the great wonder and aftonifhment of the world. But all this not-withftanding, the Duke, profecuting ftill his intended mifchiefs, hammered daily new devices in his head, and at length fo far pre-

6　　　　　　　　　　　　　　　　　　　　　　vailed

vailed with the King, that he got him to fummon an affembly of the three eftates, to be forthwith holden at Blois, where, by him and his faction, were propounded certain fundamental and irrevocable laws, wholly tending againft the Majefty and fafety of the King, and the lawful title of the King of Navarre to the Crown. The effect of five of which laws were as followeth:

1. Firft, Becaufe the King was too backward and negligent, as he pretended, in profecuting the war againft the King of Navarre, the Duke of Guife, by common confent, fhould be made High Conftable of France, an office that by birth appertained to the Duke of Montmorency, and the managing of all the wars fhould be committed only and wholly to him.

2. Secondly, Becaufe the King was ever carelefs in fpending the treafures of the Crown, beftowing largely upon his favourites and minions, that he fhould be put to a penfion of 300,000 crowns by the year, to maintain his eftate withal; and two fuch treafurers fhould be named, and appointed to have the receiving, ordering, and difpofing of all the revenues and profits of the Crown, as the whole body of the affembly of the eftates fhould pleafe to nominate, which were in effect two fuch as the Duke himfelf fhould chufe.

3. Thirdly, whereas the King was greatly charged with a guard of forty-five penfioners, to whom, befides their daily diet in the Court, he allowed yearly 1200 crowns to each man; that thofe, and other fuperfluous officers, as he termed them, fhould be difmiffed, and the exceffive charge thereof faved. Here, by the way, it is to be underftood, that thefe penfioners are commonly called in France by the name of *Les quarant cinque*, and are, for the moft part, younger brothers of great houfe, or fuch gentlemen in whom the King repofeth fpecial confidence. Their order is, to go and ride always armed, either with cuiraffes of proof, partizans, fword and target, calivers, piftolets, or any other kind of weapon that they beft fancy. They always lodge in the next chamber to the King's bed-chamber, and

and, wherefoever he goes or rides, are next attendants unto his per-fon. The Duke did labour to have thefe men removed from the King, not for their great charge, but that the king being bereft of all fuccour, and left in a manner naked, might the eafier be fur-prized, and made a prey unto his mifchievous and devilifh treafons. But the Quarant Cinque (who, if this had gone forward, were like to lofe fo notable a penfion) did generally bear a deadly and unap-peachable hatred againft the Duke, which afterward ferved the King to very good purpofe.

4. Fourthly, that no peace nor pacification fhould be made with the Proteftants, but that they fhould be affailed on all fides, with fire and fword, until they were utterly extirpated and rooted out of France.

5. Laftly, that no heretic, nor any claiming from and by a he-retic, fhould be reputed capable of the Crown of France.

The fcope of thefe laws levelling directly to the advancing of the Duke to the Crown, and, by confequence, threatning to the King a headlong downfal from his high throne of Majefty, or elfe a fudden and unavoidable death fhortly to betide him, amazed the unfortunate King very much, and made him call all his wits about him, to devife fome one means or other to provide for his own fafety with all fpeed. And, to increafe his fear and vigilant care the more, he was, by fecret advertifements, given to underftand, that the Duke of Guife impatient of longer delay and ftrait, and full of damnable treafons and confpiracies, would attempt, as upon Chriftmas day laft, to murder him, as he fhould go to mafs in the night. For on that day the King goeth ufually to three maffes, one in the morning, another in the afternoon, and the third at midnight.

Though the fetreacherous calamities, huddling one upon another's neck, had been enough to fet fome men quite befide their wits, yet did the King, whatfoever he thought inwardly, make outward fem-blance as if he had fufpected nothing. And although his inward

thoughts

thoughts were undoubtedly cumbered with clouds of care, yet out- wardly he made fair weather of all, and bore himself fo wifely, fo conftantly, and fo quietly, that he fhowed not any more fign of dif-contentment by his countenance, behaviour, or otherwife, than in the quieteft and moft peaceable times of all his life before. And which is moft ftrange, he neither took advice, nor did communicate the matter with any creature in the world (though fome think he ufed the advice of his Secretary de Revol), but took counfel only of his pillow, and with mature deliberation contrived a plot in his brain, for the releafing of himfelf upon thefe dangerous calamities, and for the revenging of himfelf upon his hateful and accurfed enemies, which he put in practice, and did moft fortunately effect, according to his wifhed defire, after this fort, as followeth:

On Chriftmas Even's Even, with us the 13th of December laft, all the States being affembled at Blois for the caufes above fpecified, the King gave out that, the next morning betimes, he meant to go on Pilgrimage to Noftre Dame of Clere, a place eighteen miles dif-tant from Blois, and to that end he gave commandment, that the Quarant Cinque fhould make themfelves ready very early to attend upon him; and at night when he fhould go to bed, he willed one of the gentlemen of his chamber to bring him in pen, ink and paper, and then to fhut the door to him, faying, that he had fome affairs to write of, which when he had difpatched, he would go to bed of himfelf, without any help. But having his brains bufied with a thoufand cogitations, amongft fundry devices that came into his head, he thought no way fo good, as by making away with the Duke, and others of the confpiracy, to affure his own eftate and life. For he certainly perceived, that as long as the Duke did live, neither fhould himfelf live in quietnefs and fafety, nor France enjoy any refpite from troubles and calamities; whereas, by the Duke's death, himfelf fhould be delivered of a dangerous and deadly enemy, and his country of France of a pernicious plague. But fometimes fearing to

O o

attempt

attempt the Duke's death, becaufe he had fuch a multitude of friends
in town, fometimes determining to do it one way, fometimes another way, fometimes to defer it till another time. In the midft of
thefe and other ambiguous doubts, he could afford his wakeful eyes
no leifure to take their natural reft. But at length, confidering his
own death to be intended within two days, he thought it a point
of extreme folly to fpend too long time in deliberating, but refolved
prefently to prevent it if he could, by hazarding to kill the Duke
the next day, left the day after himfelf fhould go to the pot; and
if he failed to bring his purpofe to pafs, then to go on pilgrimage,
and by flight to feek fomewhere to fave his life. And therewithal
he thought it very requifite to appoint the means how fundry of the
confpirators, being far diftant in feveral places, might all at one
inftant drink of the fame cup, that there might none be left alive
in his kingdom that fhould dare to feek revenge of the Duke's death.
Whereupon, he fet himfelf to writing letters, warrants, commiffions
and inftructions, and appointed divers of his friends what parts they
fhould play in this tragedy; but in fuch fort, that none of them
fhould know to what end, or wherein they were to be employed,
until the very time they were to put in practice the thing that they
had in charge. In this wife he fpent the night, until it was four
of the clock in the morning, and then thinking it time to fet his
practice abroach, he called for one of his gentlemen, who coming
in, and perceiving the bed made, and many letters lying before the
King, imagined that there was fome great matters in the wind, but
of all other things he leaft fufpected that, which afterwards happened.
The King willed the gentleman to go to the lodging of one Laverdin
and to command him to come prefently unto him. This Laverdin
was nephew to the Duke of Nevers, and had a great charge of horfemen under his uncle, who fent him lately from the camp about fpecial affairs unto the Court. When Laverdin was come into the
King's bed-chamber, the King told him, that he had certain intelligence,

ligence, how the King of Navarre was determined to affail the Duke
of Nevers in his camp, and had devifed fo exquifite a ftratagem to entrap the Duke withal, that unlefs he was prefently advertifed of it, it would be very hard for him, or any of his whole army to efcape. And therefore he willed Laverdin upon his allegiance, and as he tendered the honour and welfare of his uncle, and the whole camp, to ride poft to his uncle with all poffible fpeed, and to deliver him a letter, which the King gave him, wherein the Navarre's policy and intent was fully difclofed, as he faid, and the means how to prevent it ; charging him further, not to difclofe this matter to any alive but to his uncle. The young gentleman humbly taking his leave of the King, promifed to foreflow no time in thefe affairs ; for, taking it for a great favour to have a matter of fuch importance committed to his truft and diligence, he made all hafte he could on his way, and fo much the rather becaufe his uncle's honour and fafety depended thereupon. But the King fearing left fome extraordinary caufe might ftay him too long in town, fent a gentleman after him to haften away, and to fee him on horfeback, and to fuffer him to have conference with nobody before his departure. This talk thus cunningly told by the King to Laverdin, made the gentlemen of this chamber affuredly to think that this was the only caufe of the King's writing all night. And thereupon every man held himfelf fatisfied, not feeking to difcourfe of any further caufes. But the King had written no fuch matter as he pretended ; for the true and certain effect of the letter was this, That the Duke of Nevers fhould prefently, upon the receit thereof, apprehend La Chaftre, Mafter of the camp, upon high treafon, and make him away by one means or other, without producing of him into public judgment, alleging, that he was of confpiracy with the Duke of Guife for murdering of the King. And further he certified him, that he meant that morning to difpatch the Duke, and therefore commanded him to retire with his army towards Blois, that he might have a power

about

about him in a readinefs to withftand any fudden attempt of thofe of
the league, who, as it was doubted, would prefently, after the Duke
of Guife's death fhould be once noifed abroad, betake themfelves to
arms. Laverdin made not fo great hafte, but that La Chaftre was
advertifed of the Duke of Guife's death, half a day at leaft before
Laverdin came to the camp, and advifed to fhift for himfelf, by a
meffenger fent exprefsly unto him for that only purpofe. Whereupon, perceiving it impoffible for him to efcape, fo many horfemen
being in the camp ready to purfue him upon the Duke's command,
if once he fhould attempt to fly, went prefently and fubmitted himfelf unto the Duke of Nevers, and fent his fon and heir unto the King
as hoftage and pledge of his good and dutiful behaviour. By which
means, and at the earneft fuit and intreaty of the Duke of Nevers
and others of La Chaftre's friends, the King gave him his pardon.
And becaufe the Duke de Mayne was a principal actor in all thefe
confpiracies, and was well known to be hot-headed and rafh, and
ready for any violent and defperate attempt, the King thought it
good, above all the reft of the leaguers, to make fure play with him,
and therefore fent an Italian gentleman in Poft to Guadagne, Governor of Lyons, to carry him a letter, in which letter the treafons
of the houfe of Guife were declared, but efpecially the intended
murder of the King, and Guadagne commanded to apprehend the
Duke de Mayne, then being in Lyons, and fecretly to caufe him to
be done to death. But the Duke de Mayne having intelligence of
his brother's death by a courier that came two hours before Guadagne received the King's letters, caufed his horfes to be bridled and
faddled, and his gentlemen to make themfelves ready to ride, and
fent for Guadagne and others of the chief of the city to come and
fpeak with him. When they were come, the Duke de Mayne in
few words declared unto them, that the King had murdered his brother the Duke of Guife, and that he fought the alteration of religion,
and fubverfion of the commonwealth, by murdering the chief Peers

and

and Nobles of France; and that, amongft the reft, himfelf was appointed to the flaughter. Wherefore, he exhorted them, for the love
they bore unto their mother the Holy Church, and to their native
country, that they would affift him to revenge this open tyranny, and
fight in defence of the Catholic religion. Behold the perfect pattern of a difloyal traitor, who feeks to arm fubjects againft their lawful King, and flanderoufly to term that by the odious name of tyranny, which in right cannot otherwife be called, than the due execution of juftice by the King's authority for treafon: But Guadagne
and the reft would by no means hearken to thefe difloyal perfuafions,
and yet bearing him in hand, that they would willingly adventure
their lives, either in defence of him or any of his. This they
perfuaded him, becaufe they knew not how the townfmen would
ftand affected in fuch a cafe; and that it was not fafe for him to ftay
there any while, but to get him to fome place of more affurance,
before the King fhould fend to apprehend him. This they fpake,
to the end they might be rid of his company, mifdoubting left his
abode in Lyons might draw a number of light-headed and needy
companions to take his part, and by that means raife a mutiny and
rebellion, and perhaps enforce the town to revolt from the King.
The Duke was as willing to be gone as they were defirous to have
him gone, becaufe he perceived that it was dangerous for him to ftay
there over long, being pent within the walls of Lyons, like a bird in
a cage, and amongft fuch friends as he knew not how he might
truft them; wherefore he prefently pofted away, and efcaped into
his government of Burgundy. Glad was Guadagne when he received the King's letter, that the Duke was departed, for he doubted
that he fhould not have been able to have executed the King's commandment, the Duke having intelligence thereof before hand;
and befides, he feared left, by his prefence, the quiet ftate of the
town might have been greatly endangered. Yet, fince that, Lyons is
revolted from the King, and joined with the traitors leaguers.

Thefe

These two meffengers being difpatched, the King fent for one Entragues, a famous captain, fome time a follower of the Duke of
Guife, but now grown into fpecial favour with the King, and told
him, that he would have him ride poft prefently to Orleans, and, by
any means (if he could) make himfelf mafter of the town, or, at the
leaft, of the citadel, and delivered to him a warrant, commiffion, and
inftructions, what he fhould do, when he had the abfolute command
of the town, written all with his own hand, and fealed with his own
fignet (as alfo were all the reft of the letters delivered to others), and
fo enjoining him to be fecret, fent him away. But what he had in
commiffion to execute is not known; for he getting poffeffion of the
citadel only, and not of the town, could not execute the King's commandment. It is very likely, that there were fome in Orleans that
fhould have affociated the Duke of Guife in this his laft journey,
but that they kept themfelves out of Entragues's hands.

Chevalier Breton underftanding that the Duke of Guife was flain,
pofted fo faft towards Orleans, and recovered the town in fo fhort a
fpace, that together with Chevalier D'Aumale and others of the Guife's
faction, they prevented Entragues of his purpofe, and kept the town
againft the King. So that Entragues was conftrained to betake
himfelf into the citadel, and there continued, being kept out of the
town perforce. The King thought it not requifite to write to any
other towns for the apprehending of any others of the league, until
he had difpatched the Duke of Guife, left having too many actors
upon the ftage at once, his intent might be difcovered before the
principal part was played. And to prevent all pofting and carrying
of news, he fent a ftrait commandment to the poft-mafter, charging
him upon pain of death to fuffer no man to have poft-horfes to ride
any whither, except he brought the King's own hand and feal for
a warrant. Thefe things thus feverally done, as if all his affairs
and bufinefs had been ended, he afked one of his gentlemen if the
Quarante-cinque were ready to attend him in his pilgrimage, who
answered,

anfwered, that they were, and waited his Majefty's coming. Then the King willed him to fee that all things were in readinefs, becaufe he meant not to ftay long ere he went. But firft he commanded him to go to his coufin the Duke of Guife, and to will him to come and fpeak with him before his departure, becaufe he had fome occurrence of great importance touching the King of Navarre to acquaint him withal. When the gentleman was gone for the Duke, the King called for eight of the Quarante-cinque to come to him into his bedchamber, to whom he declared, that the occafion why he had fent for them would admit no long difcourfe, becaufe the matter required prefent execution. But briefly he opened unto them, what manifeft and moft injurious difgraces and indignities he had fuffered at the Duke of Guife's hands, and how that the Duke was not content to have the government of the whole realm in a manner at his own difpofition, but that he alfo fought to defpoil him of his life and kingdom, and to hazard the utter fubverfion of the commonwealth by his moft traiterous, irreligious, and bloody practices. Then he fhowed them a letter of the Duke's intended treafons, adding, with a moft pitiful countenance, that the only means for him to be relieved in this extremity did reft upon their dutiful affections and refolute courage; that as foon as ever the Duke fhould enter into the chamber (for whom he had already fent, not doubting but that he would come prefently) they fhould all fet upon him, and kill him in that place, and he would bear them out, and be their warrant therein, and find a time to requite their faithful fervice to their feveral contents. He exhorted them to fhew themfelves dutiful and hardy in this cafe, urging them, that they, of all others, ought to be moft willing and ready to do it, becaufe the Duke was a heavy enemy of theirs, labouring, as much as he could, to have their penfions taken from them (which he himfelf thought it verily to be with the leaft for their deferts), and themfelves to be thruft out of the court and cafhiered. When he had faid this, he withdrew himfelf into an

inner

inner cabinet or clofet, and locked the door to him, having only a gentleman called Logniac in his company, leaving thofe eight gentlemen in the anti-chamber armed (as their manner was), and every one defirous to be revenged of the Duke, both in refpect of the treafons intended againft the King, as alfo of the injury proffered to themfelves. Neither had thefe gentlemen any time to deliberate of the fact, not being made acquainted with it before that inftant: for prefently after the King was gone into the cabinet, the Duke of Guife thinking he was fent for *bona fide* about fome news, with a cheerful countenance came into the King's bedchamber, for whom the eight gentlemen, without any fhow of anger or malice, made a ward, four on the one fide and four on the other, and fuffered him quietly to pafs into the midft of the chamber. But when he demanded for the King, they fhut the door, and prefently ftept to him with their poinards drawn: whereupon, he laid his hand upon his rapier, and proffered to draw, but one of them, with his left hand, gripped him by the arm fo ftrongly, that he could not, and calling him traitor, with his right hand gave him the ftab: with that, they fell all upon him, and poinarded him on all hands. The Duke ftruggled, but all in vain, and upon a brave courage proffered what refiftance he was able, but being over-preffed with a multitude of wounds, funk down in the midft of his enemies. And fretting, fuming, chafing, and fwearing, at laft uttered thefe words, " My fins have deferved " this;" and gave up the ghoft. Lo here untimely and unnatural death, the juft reward of monftrous treafon! Lo here the man whofe life had been often glutted with bloody maffacring of the children of God, doth now lie groveling in his own gore-blood, having felt the like punifhment (though defervedly) which caufelefs he had often inflicted, and that moft cruelly, upon others!

The King, who all this while liftened to what was done, perceiving the Duke to be difpatched, came forth of his cabinet, and ftedfaftly beholding the dead body, ufed thefe words, " I had rather

" thou

" thou fhouldeft die than I;" and caufed them to cover the body with a cloth of arras, greatly commending them, and giving them thanks for their good fervice.

It is credibly avouched, that not many days before the Duke of Guife was thus executed, he had warning given him by the Princefs of Lorraine and Chevalier Breton, that he fhould take heed to himfelf, becaufe they underftood by fome that were near to the King, that his death was intended to be brought to pafs, either by poifon or by outward violence, whenfoever occafion would ferve thereto. But he made flender account of their warnings, being ftedfaftly perfuaded that the King either faw not the clofe conveyance of his fecret confpiracies, or if he did fee them, that he durft not offer to feek revenge. Yea, that very morning that he was fent for to the King, as he paffed through a dark entry in the court, an unknown man delivered a letter to his page, requefting him to give it prefently to his Lord, becaufe it required great hafte, and concerned him very near. The Duke receiving this letter from the page, found therein written, that the King did intend fome mifchief towards him, and that he fhould forbear, at any hand, to come that day in his prefence, being a fatal, ominous, and unfortunate day unto him: affirming, with very confident terms, that the King, without all queftion, would that day attempt to take him away. When the Duke had read the letter, he called for pen and ink, and wrote underneath, *Il n'oferoit*, He dares not; and then very fcornfully threw it over his fhoulder, that any man might take it up, and fo proceeded towards the King's chamber, without enquiring after the party that wrote it, or fhowing any fign of aftonifhment or fear; whence may be gathered, that he was fully grounded and fettled in this opinion, that the King had not the heart to attempt any thing againft him. Thus did ambition blind and befot this fond and wretched Duke, being otherwife wife, and wary in all his actions that he thought he carried himfelf very covertly in his practices,

P p   when

when in truth they were fo apparent to all the world, that all the world might point them out with their fingers. He forgot that old proverb (which, having fo often and fo defervedly incurred the difpleafure of the King, he fhould daily have thought upon), That a reconciled adverfary is not to be trufted. Neither did he once remember the faying of Solomon, That the indignation of a Prince is death. But his appointed time was come, which he, by no means, could alter or defer : for it is not all the wit or policy in the world that can withftand or prevent what the Lord of Hofts hath once decreed. He taketh away wifdom from the learned and politic, and enfeebleth the ftrength of the courageous. He blindeth the underftanding of the moft circumfpect, when once they oppofe themfelves againft him and his Anointed, perfecuting Chrift in his members, and defpifing the lawful authority of Princes: yea, he caufeth evil to hunt fuch wicked men, and never to leave them, till carelefsly they run headlong into deftruction. Seeing this is the reward of wickednefs, ceafe, ye licentious worldlings, under colour of religion, to fatisfy the ambitious lufts of your heart. Ceafe, ye unbridled traitors, to lift up your arms againft the Lord's Anointed. Though the fear of God will not reclaim you, and keep you in awe, yet let this juft and inevitable chaftifement, defervedly inflicted upon the Guife, be a warning to ye all, by his example, not to delight in bloody perfecution, prophane atheifm, and ambitious treafon ; left, if you take not example by him, and fuch like, to leave your filthinefs and corruptions, wherein, like fwine, ye delight to welter, the Lord find you out in his fury, and make you to ferve as an example to others, of his moft juft punifhment.

But to return to our purpofe, the tragedy being thus begun with the death of the chiefeft, the King thought it very neceffary to omit no time, but immediately to appoint the other actors their parts; and thereupon, he fent for the Marfhal D'Aumont, and Larchant, one of the Captains of his guard, and fhowing them the dead

Duke,

Duke, briefly declared the caufe that moved him, in fo defperate a difeafe, to ufe fo violent a medicine; and commanded the Marfhal to take with him a fufficient company of his guard, and to command the gates of the caftle to be kept, and to appoint men in fuch other places as he fhould think meet for the quieting and fuppreffing of any fudden uproar that might happen, and to fuffer none to pafs up and down the caftle without the watch-word. Then was Larchant commanded to take with him fome forty or fifty of the guard, and to go with them into the great hall (which was, in a manner, directly under the King's chamber, where, by that time, the Peers and States were affembled, not hearing, or fo much as dreaming, of that which had happened), and there to arreft upon high treafon the two Cardinals of Lorraine and Bourbon, the Archbifhop of Lyons, the Duke d'Elbe, the Prefident de Nully, the Provoft of the Merchants of Paris, the Prefident of Orleans, the Lieutenant-colonel of Amiens, with divers Bifhops, Lawyers, and other great men, and to commit them all prifoners in feveral places of the caftle. The Marfhal performed his charge very orderly; and Larchant likewife, accompanied with a great many of the guard, every man with his match in the cock, and their pieces charged with the bullet, accomplifhed the King's command in all points, without any gain-faying or refiftance; for he came fo ftrong that they durft not difobey him, and fo unlooked for, that they wift not what to fay, but like fheep, or rather like goats, who are led to the flaughter, they were all carried away eafily. And, left fome bufy-headed fellows fhould take occafion thereupon to make a mutiny in the town, the King, at the very fame inftant that thefe matters were a doing in the great hall, had fent one Duchald, a notable captain, with fome bands of the Switzers of his guard, into the town, commanding to lock the gates; and to appoint watch and ward in convenient places, and to fuffer no man to ftir out of his doors, and then to repair, with a fufficient power, to the lodging of the Dutchefs of Nemours (mother to the Duke of

Guife,

Guife, and married, fince the death of her firft hufband, to the Duke
of Nemours), and commanded to keep as prifoners in their own
houfe, the Dutchefs, the young Duke her fon, and the Prince de Joinville, fon and heir to the Duke of Guife, who at that time were all
lodged in one houfe. The Prince de Joinville came to town for no
other purpofe at that time, but to marry the Princefs of Lorraine by
proxy, for and in the name of the Duke of Florence, to whom fhe was
betrothed. Moreover, the King, to take away all caufes of fufpicion,
and fear, from the townfmen, and others, that were not privy to the
confpiracy, caufed to be proclaimed, that this hurley-burley was
only to apprehend certain that had confpired the King's death, and
that there fhould be no violence or injury offered to any others;
commanding all men therefore, upon pain of death, to keep themfelves
quiet, and not to ftir abroad, until the King's commandment were
fully accomplifhed in apprehending the confpirators. Mean while,
the King was not idle, but having, before that, determined what
to do in every cafe, caufed the Duke of Guife's trunk and cafkets to
be broke open, to make fearch for letters and other news, and fent
for Pelicard the Duke's fecretary, unto whom the King fhowed the
dead corpfe of his mafter, the more to terrify him, charging him
that he was of counfel with the Duke in all his confpiracies, which
he muft now difclofe from point to point; and if he did refufe,
deny, or conceal any thing, it fhould be the worfe for him. But
becaufe, at that prefent time, his leifure ferved him not to examine
him at large, he commanded him to be committed clofe prifoner
until another time. Pelicard, being afterward examined, confeffed
many villanous practices agreed upon by the Duke and fome of the
leaguers againft the King, the leaft of which were fufficient to condemn his mafter of high treafon. And, if the King had not taken
that time, on Chriftmas midnight mafs, they had murdered the
King, the Prince of Condé, and the Count of Soiffons, his brother.
He confeffed likewife, that when the King fled from the Guife out

of

of Paris, there was a plot laid to have murdered the King, as he should have gone on proceſſion. A miſerable thing, that theſe men, who would needs be counted the very main pillars and only up-holders of religion, ſhould, in the temple of God, and at the ex-ercife of the higheſt point of their religion (as, falſely, they term that abominable idol of the maſs), offer to pollute their deviliſh hands in the blood of their lawful and anointed King, againſt whom, by the word of God (though he be wicked), they ought not, ſo much as once in heart, to conceive any hurt. But theſe are the fruits of that Prince-quelling profeſſion of Popery, which frames itſelf, in moſt points, to be contrary to God's word, that it may the better be known to be forged by Antichriſt : for whereas it is the expreſs commandment of God, that every ſoul ſhould ſubmit itſelf to the higher powers, as to the ordinance of God, this antichriſtian religion not only alloweth, but alſo, with rewards, enticeth and procureth vaſſals and ſubjects to bear arms againſt their Sovereign, and traiterouſly to de-poſe or murder him, without regard either of time, place, or duty, or religion, in contempt of God's ordinance, and the politic eſta-bliſhed laws of all nations. But to return to our purpoſe, from whence we are digreſſed : the Queen-Mother, who at that time kept her bed, through extreme ſickneſs and grief, for her eaſe, was lodged in the moſt quiet and remoteſt place of all the caſtle, far from the noiſe and concourſe of people, by reaſon whereof ſhe heard nothing of all this buſineſs. But the King having accompliſhed the moſt part of his deſires, thought good to make her acquainted with the matter, and to carry her the firſt news of it himſelf. Whereupon, accompanied only with eight gentlemen, that were in his chamber, he went to his mother's lodging, paſſing through the great hall, where the States remained ſtill, every man fearing that the caſe might be his own, and revolving in their troubled and diſquieted minds, what might be the ſequel of this ſtrange attempt; and, as he paſſed, they did all humble obeiſance unto the King, and he like—

wiſe:

wife very courteoufly faluted them again: neither could they perceive by his countenance, gefture, or otherwife, that he was any
thing moved or diftempered with what was done. Being come into his mother's chamber (after he had faluted her, and fome few
words had paffed between them, as touching her ficknefs, the hope
of recovery, and fuch like matters), at length he burft out into,thefe
words : " Madame, there is now no other King in France but my-
" felf." She anfwered, that fhe never knew it otherwife thefe
many years. But he replied, that he was now King of full years,
and out of his wardfhip. Whereto fhe anfwered, that fhe under-
derftood not his meaning; for fhe never heard of any that durft or
could deny it, fince he came firft to the crown, but that he was abfolute King, fubject to the command of none alive. He then, not
minding to hold her longer in fufpence, difcourfed to her, at large,
his morning's work, the Duke's treafons, and the caufes that moved
him to practice revenge in fuch fort as he had done. The Queen,
amazed to hear thefe ftrange and unlooked-for news, fetching a deep
figh, faid unto him, " It is well done (my fon), if it be well done.
" But I would you had made the Pope's Legate acquainted with it
" before you had taken it in hand, for fear leaft his Holinefs con-
" ceive ill of the manner of the doing it." " That had been the
" way to have marred all (quoth the King), and to have had my
" whole purpofe difclofed to the Guife. But now it is done, I mean
" to certify his Holinefs of it, who (no doubt) will approve my
" dealing herein, as being enforced by neceffity to take this, and no
" other courfe. And I am fure his Holinefs will the rather not miflike
" it, becaufe at his firft inftalment in the fee of Rome, in fomewhat
" the like cafe, he ufed a practice not much unlike to this." And
fo requefting his mother to be of good comfort, and to have fpecial
regard of her health, without troubling herfelf with matters of importance, which he requefted her to refer only to his vigilant care,
who would take fuch order therein as fhould be to her content, he

2   reverently

reverently took his leave, and went presently to dinner, where he fed as heartily, and looked with as chearful a countenance, as if he had, that day, attempted nothing but ordinary matters. After dinner, word was brought him, that the Cardinal of Lorraine took on grievously, and used divers reproachful words against the King, for the death of the Duke his brother, threatening to find the means to be revenged. The King, somewhat moved with these presumptuous and unadvised speeches, and calling to mind the disloyal pranks of this undutiful prelate, commanded the Captain of the Scottish guard to take some of his guard with him, and to dispatch the Cardinal out of the way: which commandment of the King he presently put in execution, and caused the Cardinal to be slain. Though this revenge did fully satisfy and appease the King's wrath and displeasure, conceived justly against the Guise, yet to the end those of the League might hereafter have no means to make reliques of his hateful body, he caused the same to be burned to ashes, and the ashes to be dispersed and thrown into the river. And because the King understood that the Archbishop of Lyons was the chiefest man to whom the Duke commonly used to commit the very secrets of his heart, and that he was also a principal deviser and contriver of all his damnable treasons, he determined to respite his life, and to reserve him in prison, that he might, at better leisure, fetch further matter out of him, and learn of him the very depth of the Duke's intents, together with the names of all his favourers, counsellors and abettors; and at length have him openly condemned by law. But the Cardinal of Bourbon being drawn into this action, by the importunity of those of the League, rather than by his own malice, hath his life granted him, at the earnest intreaty of some of his friends that are near about the King: and the rather, because, being very old, he is not likely to live long; and though he live, he is not likely, by reason of his imbecillity and weakness, to do any great hurt.

But,

But, as yet, he is detained in prifon, as are likewife the Prince de Joinville, the Dutchefs of Nemours, and the Duke her fon

When the King had finifhed this tragical enterprize upon two of the greateft perfonages in all France, and others of the Pope-holy league, he caufed the gates of the town, and caftle of Blois, to be fet open, that all might freely go in and out at their pleafure. That night, divers of the Duke of Guife's friends fled from the town of Blois, and other places, to Orleans, to the Chevalier Breton, and the Chevalier D'Aumale, who, as is before fpecified, hold the town, per force, againft the King. Entragues, having feized the citadel, kept it a while for the King's behoof, and, as much as he could, annoyed the town with his ordnance. But the leaguers trufting to their multitude, offered to batter the citadel, and to win it by affault. All day, and all night long, the bullets flew between them, as meffengers of affured·death, to whomfoever they talked withal. At length, the Duke of Nevers came thither, hoping to play the ftickler between them. But wherein the want was, I know he hath as yet done no great good.

Sir Edward Stafford, Ambaffador for her Majefty in the Court of France, at Blois.

No. XVIII.

No. XVIII.

Letters to and from Lord Leicester, in the Low Countries.

From the
Originals in
the Cotton
Library.

[These letters relative to the Earl of Leicester's administration in the Low Countries, are taken out of a much larger number, which, together with those about the Spanish Armada, and the concomitant Negociation in Flanders, would form a separate work, and not an uninteresting one. The character of Leicester is strongly marked in them, passionate and vindictive, but with more considerable talents for business, than Camden and other historians allow him.]

Lord Burghley to Lord Leicester.

My very good Lord,

1586.
Feb. 7th.

YOUR last letters, come to my hands, were by your Lordship written at the Hague the 29th of January, by which I was glad to perceive you had received my letters sent by Mr. Alye and my son; which were made old letters by the contrary winds, which of late have been so constant to hang long in our coast, as either your Lordship there have cause, or we here to wish it; for it holdeth strongly either West, which pleaseth us to send, but not to hear; or else in the East, which discontenteth either of us in contrary manner. By your Lordship's letters I find many things of my letters answered, and so I shall be able to satisfy her Majesty; but to be plain with your Lordship in a few words; I, and other your Lordship's poor friends, find her Majesty so discontent with your acceptance of the government there, before you had advertised, and had her Majesty's opinion, that although I, for my own part, judge this action

Q q

both

both honourable and profitable, yet her Majefty will not endure to hear any fpeech in defence thereof. Neverthelefs, I hope a fmall time fhall alter this hard conceit in her Majefty, whereunto I have already, and fhall not defift to oppofe myfelf, with good and found reafons, to move her Majefty to alter her hard opinions. But, to end this writing, I could not but to accompany this gentleman, Horatio Palavicine with my letter, whom, for his wifdom and all other good qualities, I need not to commend to your Lordfhip, being fo well known and approved to your Lordfhip as he is. From my houfe in Weftminfter,

Your Lordfhip's moft affured at command,

W. BURGHLEY.

Mr. Thomas Duddeley to Lord Leicefter.

I HAVE long forborne to write unto your Excellency, of the great diflike her Majefty hath conceived of your Honour's doing there, touching the acceptance of the abfolute government of thofe countries, having, long before this time, hoped your Excellency would have fent away Mr. Davifon to have fatisfied her Majefty, touching your whole proceedings in thofe caufes, as it pleafed your Excellency to write unto me, in your laft letter, dated the 10th of January, you would do. But forafmuch as neither Mr. Davifon is as yet come, neither hath your Honour hitherto written to her Majefty, fave of thofe caufes which her Majefty taketh in fo ill part, all your honourable friends here have much ado to fatisfy her Majefty, and to ftay her from fuch proceedings, to the overthrow of your Lordfhip's doing there, as would not only breed you great difcontentment, but alfo be the utter ruin of that fervice, and country, and withal, aggravate her Highnefs's diflikes of that action. It was

5   told

told her Majefty, that my Lady was prepared prefently to come over to your Excellency, with fuch a train of Ladies and Gentlemen, and fuch rich coaches, litters and fide faddles, as her Majefty had none fuch, and that there fhould be fuch a court of Ladies, as fhould far furpafs her Majefty's Court here. This information (though moft falfe) did not a little ftir her Majefty to extreme choler and diflike of all your doings there, faying with great oaths, fhe would have no more Courts under her obeyfance but her own; and would revoke you from thence with all fpeed. This, Mr. Vice Chamberlain firft told me in great fecret, and afterwards Mr.   ., and laft of all my Lord Treafurer. Unto them all I anfwered, that the information was moft falfe in every degree, and that there was no fuch preparation made by my Lady, nor any intention in her to go over, neither had your Lordfhip any intention to fend for her, fo far as I knew. This being told her Majefty by my Lord Treafurer, and Mr. Vice Chamberlain alfo, though not both at one time, did greatly pacify her ftomach; and truly I do know, by very good means, that my Lord Treafurer dealt moft honourably and friendly for your Lordfhip to her Majefty, both to fatisfy her Highnefs in this report, as in t'other great action, and fo hath Vice Chamberlain done alfo. But the long ftay of Mr. Davifon's company, your Honour's forbearing to write to her Majefty all this while, notwithftanding fo many meffengers as cometh from thence, doth greatly offend her more and more, and, in very truth, maketh all your friends here at their wits end, what to anfwer or fay in your behalf. Her Majefty hath, thefe ten or twelve days, devifed and been in hand with many courfes how and in what manner to overthrow that which your Honour, to your infinite toil, and her Majefty's greateft fafety and fervice, that ever any fubject did to their Sovereign, hath moft gravely and politickly begun, and hath fet down many platts for that purpofe, which I am fure your Excellency is not ignorant in. And truly the Lord Treafurer hath always befought her Majefty to

Q q 2   keep

keep one. ear, for your anfwer to her diflikes, and fo fufpend her judgment till Mr. Davifon come, or that your Honour did write unto her Majefty. The Lord Treafurer having been from the Court thefe eight days, her Majefty hath, four days agone, propofed to fend Sir Thomas Henneage unto you, with what commiffion I know not; but Mr. Vice Chamberlain and Mr. Secretary very honourably doth delay his difpatch, by all the means they can, and hopeth to put it off till Sunday next, at which time the Lord Treafurer will be at the Court, and then, by his help, they hope to qualify fome part of her Majefty's intentions; looking before that time that Mr. Davifon will arrive and fatisfy all furies. Mr. Vice Chamberlain hath of late told me of the letter, your Honour wrote unto him, which he acquainted Mr. Secretary withal, and took his opinion whether to fhew it to her Majefty or no; but finding her Majefty in fuch hard terms for your Lordfhip's not writing to herfelf, they thought it better then to conceal it; but yefterday, finding her Majefty difcontented, and hafting to fend away Sir Thomas Henneage to your Lordfhip, they conferred of the letter again, and blotting out fome things which they thought would be offenfive, and mending fome other parts as they thought beft, Mr. Vice Chamberlain refolved yefterday in the afternoon (I being with him) to fhew it unto her Majefty, hoping it will be fome fatisfaction to her Majefty in fome points, until further matter do come. All this they do to put off Sir Thomas Henneage's difpatch, and yet, if he do come, I hope he fhall bring no evil news, for I am fure her Majefty could not have fent any Gentleman of this Court that loveth you more dearly, and would be more loth to come with any unpleafant meffage unto you. Mr. Vice Chamberlain thinketh that your Honour's own letter to her Majefty will do more good, and better fatisfy her Majefty in all things, than all that they can do or fay; and wifheth withal, that you would beftow fome two or three hundred crowns, in fome rare thing for a token to her Majefty. There be divers of that fide, who, write to their friends

here

here at the Court, of such things as falleth out there, and so cometh to her Majesty's knowledge by the women, which breedeth some offence, and were better they wrote more wisely, or not at all. The Lord North seemeth to be a malecontent, and hath so written to her Majesty and also to my Lord of War, and, as it is said here, cometh away very shortly. Thus your Excellency seeth how your honourable friends of the Council doth make me acquainted with some of these secrets that concerneth your Honour, which I thought it my duty to advertise you, hoping your Excellency will take it in good part, and so praying the Almighty to bless all your doings, and send you most prosperous success in all your attempts.

Leicester House, this 11th of February 1585-6.

THOMAS DUDDELEY.

Mr. Davison to the Earl of Leicester.

My singular good Lord,

AFTER my departure from your Lordship, I was detained at the Brill some five or six days by the wind and weather. The Friday following I put to the seas, and, by God's goodness, had so happy a passage, as, the next morning, by ten or eleven of the clock, we anchored at the Reculvers within Margate, and the same night about midnight came to Gravesend, and from thence immediately with the tide hither, where I arrived the next morning early. Within an hour after, I sent to Mr. Secretary, to signify so much unto him, and to know his pleasure where I might wait on him, before my access to the Queen; that I might the better understand in what terms things stood in Court, and accommodate my course thereafter.

He

He returned me anfwer, that your Lordfhip's long detaining me there, had wounded the whole caufe; that he thought her Majefty would not fpeak with me; and yet wifhed me to come forthwith to the Court, left her Majefty, knowing of my arrival, before I prefented myfelf, might thereat take occafion to increafe her offence. The fame afternoon I repaired unto him; finding him utterly difcomforted with her Majefty's hard opinion and courfe againft the caufe. He let me underftand how heinoufly fhe took your acceptation of the government; how fhe had refolved to difpatch Sir Thomas Henneage to command you to refign it up, and to proteft her difallowance thereof to the States: that fhe had threatened Sir Philip Sidney and myfelf, as principal actors and perfuaders thereof, for which it feems we owe our thanks to fome with your Lordfhip. I was amazed at his difcourfe, as a thing far from that I looked for, and let him fee as clearly as I could, what reafons and neceffity had drawn both the States to prefs your Lordfhip's acceptance of the government, and yourfelf at length to yield unto it; affuring him that if her Majefty took the courfe fhe pretended, not only yourfelf fhould thereby be moft unhappily and unworthily difgraced, but the caufe withal utterly overthrown, with the perpetual ftains of her honour, and detriment of her eftate. Within a while after, he went up to her Majefty, and myfelf in the mean time to Mr. Vice Chamberlain, whither one of the grooms of her privy chamber came for me; I found her Majefty alone, retired into her withdrawing chamber, which I took for fome advantage. She began in moft bitter and hard terms, firft againft your Lordfhip for taking that charge upon you, not only without warrant, but (that which fhe urged greatly) againft her exprefs commandment (delivered unto you fundry times, as fhe faid, both by her own mouth, and confirmed by her Council), as a thing done in contempt of her, as if either her confent had been nothing worth, or the thing no way concerned her, aggrieving your fault herein by all the circumftances fhe might. And, for my particular,

ticular, found herfelf no lefs offended, in that I had not openly
oppofed myfelf againft it, wherein I had, as fhe pretended, greatly deceived the opinion and truft fhe had repofed in me. To all which, before I took upon me to make any anfwer, I humbly befought her Majefty, firft, to retain that gracious opinion of my poor duty, as to think, that no particular refpect whatfoever could carry me to deal otherwife with her than became an honeft and dutiful fervant, re-folved faithfully and truly to report unto her the true caufes and circumftances of your Lordfhip's proceeding in that behalf; and next, that it would pleafe her to lend me a patient and favourable ear, which obtained, I doubted not but that her Majefty would con-ceive more equally both of your perfon and proceeding, than fhe prefently appeared to do. And then fell to difcourfe unto her the eftate of the country before your Lordfhip's coming. The gene-ral difcomfort and difcouragemement conceived upon the length of your ftay. The doubtful terms wherein you found things at your arrival, not only fome towns of fingular importance, but fome whole provinces, inclining to a peace with the enemy, as defpairing of any found or good fruit to grow of her Ma-jefty's cold beginning. The general hatred and contempt of their government, taxed with corruption, partiality, and confufion. The continual profit and advantage the enemy made thereof, with the infinite hurt and peril of that eftate, by no means able to fubfift or ftand long, if it were not the more timely and difcreetly re-formed. That to help this, and fave themfelves, they found no way either fo fafe or fo profitable, as to fet fome perfon of wifdom and authority at the helm of their eftate. That, amongft themfelves, there was none qualified for fo great a charge. The Count Maurice being a child, poor, and of little refpect among them. The Elector, the Count of Hohenlo, and Huenar, ftrangers, and incapable of burthen. That thefe confiderations had moved the States by their Deputies, to infift fo earneftly and peremptorily upon that point with her Ma-

jefty,

jefty, befeeching her to vouchfafe fome principal perfon of hers, to take the charge, as the thing without which all the reft of her goodnefs, benevolence, and favours, was to little purpofe. That themfelves (howfoever the words of the contract appeared not, in full and plain terms, to exprefs fo much) did, and always had taken it as a matter granted; and thereupon not only intended the fame to your Lordfhip long before your coming, but plainly difpofed all their doings to that end, leaving their eftate, in manner, without all form of government, as your Lordfhip found it, till your arrival; and therefore did the more importunely prefs your Lordfhip to accept thereof. Wherein, though you had, under one pretext or other, long forborn and delayed to fatisfy them, neither flatly refufing it, for the danger's fake, nor willing to accept thereof, till her High-nefs's pleafure had been known, and yourfelf in the mean time thoroughly informed of their eftate; finding yourfelf at length wearied with their importunities, moved with their reafons, and compelled with neceffity, unlefs you would have lived there as an eye-witnefs of the difmembering and divifion of the whole country, not otherwife to be contained, and kept together, than by a repofed hope in her Majefty's found favour, which had not only been called in queftion, but utterly defpaired of by your refufal, you thought it better to take the courfe you did, carrying with itfelf increafe both of honour, profit, and furety to her Majefty, and good to the caufe; than by refufing thereof, to have utterly hazarded the one, and over-thrown the other. The neceffary confequence of which, I proved unto her, by a number of plain and particular circumftances; againft which, albeit fhe could in truth reply little, yet could I not leave her much fatisfied at this firft meeting, with any thing I could allege in your behalf; but perfifting ftill in her offence, broke many times forth into her former complaints, one while accufing you of con-tempt, another while of refpecting more your particular greatnefs,

than

than either her honour or service, and oftentimes digressing into old ELIZA-
grievances, which were too long and tedious to write. And because
she had often and vehemently charged myself to have forgotten my
duty, in that I had not dissuaded or opposed myself against your fact,
being there as her Ambassador, and knowing, as she pretended, her
pleasure and meaning. I let her see, that I never deemed so meanly
either of her own favour towards your Lordship, in the sending of
you, or of your own judgment in coming over, so meanly autho-
rized and backed, as to take the commandment of the reliques of
Mr. Norris his worn and decayed troops, as a charge very unfitting
to a person of your quality, and utterly disagreeing to the necessity
of the time and state, where you were; letting her see the dishonour
and peril must of necessity have grown, if either the action had been
longer suspended, or any other course taken to establish their government, than by your Lordship; both commanders, soldiers, and
subjects, refusing all other means, and protesting rather to run headlong to the sea, than to fall again into their former disorders and
confusions. And herewithal took occasion to remember unto her,
that being at the most part of the conferences the last year, between
my Lords her Majesty's commissioners, and their deputies, I had
heard some one of my Lords, if not her Majesty's self, answer the
deputies to that point, that albeit her Highness for her own part
intended not to take any further authority than was agreed upon,
yet would she not restrain them to give what authority and commandment they should find expedient and necessary for their
estate, to him that should by her Majesty be sent over to take
the charge of her own; a thing which, I told her, had been
confirmed unto me by some of their commissioners, since their
return home; adding withal, for my future justification, that
I never received line, either from herself, or any Counsellor she
had, tending to any such charge or commandment; without which,
I might have been accused of madness, to have dissuaded an action,

R r in

in mine own poor opinion fo neceffary and expedient, for her honour, furety, and greatnefs ; protefting unto her Majefty, that if·I
were yet there, and mine opinion demanded, I could not tell what
other advice to give your Lordfhip than that you had taken, efpecially having no contrary direction or commandment from her Highnefs. And thus, after long and vehement debate, for the firft night,
departed, leaving her, as I thought, much qualified; though in many
points unfatisfied.

The next morning notwithftanding, Sir Thomas Henneage was
difpatched in great heat, which fo foon as I underftood of, I repaired
again unto her; and (fo much was I perplexed) with tears befought
her to be better advifed, laying before·her the difhonourable, fhameful, and dangerous effects of fo unfeafonable and unhappy a meffage,
and humbly craving at her hands, that howfoever fhe ftood hardly
perfuaded of your Lordfhip's dealing, in confcience, as I told her,
without caufe, fhe would yet forbear to take a courfe fo violent, not
only to the utter difgrace and difhonour of one fhe had heretofore fo
highly efteemed, and now fpecially deferved better meafure at her
hands, but alfo, to the utter ruin of the caufe, lofs of her beft neighbours, and difcomfort of her good fubjects, with her own difhonour
and undoing. And·here fhe fell again into her former invectives,
aggrieving your fault the more, in that, all this time the matter was
on foot you had never vouchfafed to impart it with her, which I
excufed with all the art I had　And at this time took occafion to
prefs her Majefty to receive your Lordfhip's letters, which the day
before fhe utterly refufed, and now, after fhe had opened and began
to perufe, put up into her pocket, to read, as I think, at more leifure.
At length, having again, by many infinuations, prepared her to lend
me a more patient and willing ear than fhe had vouchfafed me the
day before, I renewed unto her my former day's difcourfe, in excufe
of your Lordfhip's action, which, if fhe did refpect either honour,
furety, or profit, fhe would rather efteem a fervice of fingular defert,

than

than any wife worthy of her difcountenance; letting her plainly un- derftand, that there was no mean courfe to be taken, either for them or for your Lordfhip, without a wilful hazard of all. That their miferies grew, efpecially for the lack of order and authority, and therefore driven to feek their cure from the contraries. That the fact, befides, did proceed from a fingular affection, confidence, and devotion to her Majefty, and therefore worthy her gracious conftruction.

That in your lordfhip's behalf, I could not in my poor judgment conceive what might juftly offend her. For if fhe would be pleafed to confider the neceffity, as well of her particular fervice as of the eftate of thofe poor countries, left defperate if your Lordfhip had refufed them, fhe fhould find you had no other remedy; if her honour, what greater might be done by a fubject, than, without increafe of her charge, to bind unto her the devotion and hearts of fo ftrong, rich, and populous countries, whofe good or ill neighbourhood might, of all others, moft profit or annoy her; if her furety, what might be greater, than to have the difpofition of that whole eftate, fo as fhe might give the law to the one fide and to the other, and either lengthen or fhorten the war at her own appetite? And here I urged her Majefty's fcope and end in this action, which, if tending to the relief and delivery of her poor neighbours, there was no other way: if to abate the greatnefs of a fufpected and dangerous neighbour, there could be no greater or more happy opportunity offered her: If to a peace, a thing (I told her) feared and fufpected, what other way had fhe to make a peace, either good for the poor countries, or fafe and honourable to herfelf; with a thoufand other things to like effect, againft all which fhe had little elfe to reply, than her alledged complaints againft the form and manner of your proceeding; confeffing that if you had taken the fame thing in fubftance (which, faid fhe, the contract offered you), without the title, fhe could have been for her own part better fatisfied, and her doings, if fhe fhould allow of your's, the better juftified. Whereto when I had replied, that it was not to be thought that the enemy

R r 2 might

might be more offended, or her cafe more impáired by the name than by the thing itfelf; fhe began to break off, letting me firft underftand how little fhe looked for fó peremptory, as fhe termed it, partial dealing, at my hands, of whom fhe had conceived a better opinion, and towaids whom fhe had intended more good than fhe now found me worthy òf. For the which, after I had given her Majefty, my mòft humble and dutiful thanks, taking herfelf to wit- nefs how far off I had been ever from affecting or feeking any fuch grace at her hands, I concluded with this humble fuit unto her Highnefs, that fhe would be pleafed, in recompence of all my tra- vails, to vouchfafe me her favourable leave to retire myfelf home, to beftow the reft of my days in prayer for her, whom, in all appear- ance, falvation itfelf was not able to fave, if fhe continued the courfe fhe was in, and therefore efteemed him happieft, that fhould have leaft intereft in the public fervice. And thus ended my fecond day's audience; which, howfoever fhe difguifed the matter, wrought thus much effect, that the fame night late, fhe gave order to ftay Sir Thomas Henneage, till he heard her further pleafure. The next morning early I repaired to my Lord Treafurer, whom I met upon the way, and followed down to the court, where I acquainted him with the whole courfe and reafons of your Lordfhip's proceeding, leaving him as little as I could unfatisfied, in any particular and neceffary circumftance. From me he went up directly to the Queen, and, as I certainly underftand, laboured very earneftly firft to revoke Sir Thomas, which failing of, he infifted upon the qualification of his meffage, whereof grew her Majefty's fecond letters to Mr. Hen- neage, to inhibit the delivery of the firft letters addreffed to the States, if he found it might hurt the common fervice; and that howfoever fhe refted offended without yourfelf, he fhould forbear your public and open difgrace. The fame afternoon, my Lord Treafurer procured my third audience, before whom I confirmed my former difcourfe, which I found her Majefty to conceive of fome-
                                                                    what

what better. And the fame night obtained leave to retire myfelf
home for fome few days. Since, I hear Sir Thomas is awaiting the
wind, intending to go forward, if the time yield not fome new occafion
of his ftay, which I have the better hope of, becaufe I find the heat
of her Majefty's offence towards your Lordfhip to abate every day
fomewhat, and herfelf difpofed both to hear and fpeak more tenderly
of you, and, when all is done, if things be well carried there, will, I
truft, deal more gracioufly, both with yourfelf and the caufe than
fhe hath of late feemed affected; which your Lordfhip may help
fomewhat by a more diligent entertaining her with your wife letters
and meffages, your flacknefs wherein hitherto appears to have
bred a great part of this unkindnefs. And albeit fome of your
friends, difcouraged with her Majefty's proceeding in your behalf,
do happily perfuade you to feek to withdraw yourfelf thence, and to
get leave for your return, as foon as you might, yet dare I not, under
your Lordfhip's correction, fecond their opinion, notwithftanding
I know it proceeds, on their parts, of an honourable affection to yourfelf and defpair of our found dealing here; becaufe I fee no other
fruit can grow of that courfe, than utter undoing to the caufe, and
difhonour to her Majefty, and difcredit to yourfelf. Whereas, on
the contrary, the time may work fome better effect in her Majefty's
difpofition, both towards yourfelf and your fervice.

The traffic of peace goeth on underhand, as I am advertifed, but
whether to ufe it as a fecond ftring to our bow if the firft fhould fail,
or of any fettled inclination thereunto I cannot affirm; however it
be, I have no let to tell her Majefty, that the difficulties, for any
thing I can obferve, will be infinitely great, to make any fafe or
honourable peace, either for them or herfelf, without an honourable war, which every man here apprehends not. Your Lordfhip's
fupply for men and money hath been cooled and hindred by the
other accident of offence taken at your proceedings, and yet live I in

9   good

good hope, that her Majefty will go through with her promife, and give order for your fatisfying, when this ftorm is a little more overblown. I have herein dealt exceeding earneftly, both with herfelf and my Lord Treafurer, letting them fee how greatly it importeth her honour and fervice, and have received his faithful promife to hold a good hand to the furtherance thereof.

Of Sir William Pelham's coming over, I wot not what hope to give your Lordfhip; he is now at his houfe in the country, afflicted both in body and mind. I have once or twice already heard from him, and find the gentleman exceedingly troubled, with the ftrange and hard meafure he hath received, enough to break the heart of any gentleman in the world, of his fort of deferving, that were not armed with his virtue and conftancy: but amongft all his other croffes, he doth proteft to me, there is no one that grieves him more, than by the malice of his enemies and unhappinefs of his fortune, to be kept and detained here from the perfon and caufe he fo much affecteth; as I think your Lordfhip fhall at more length perceive by his own letters.

For all other matters, leaving your Lordfhip to the report of fuch as be better informed than myfelf, and craving your pardon for fo long and tedious a difcourfe, I will here conclude with my moft humble prayers to God, to blefs your honourable labours with happy and honourable fuccefs. At my poor houfe, London, the 17th of February 1585-6.

Your Lordfhip's ever bounden and affured, do you humble fervice.

W. DAVISON.

Earl

Earl of Leicefter to Sir Francis Walfingham.

MR. SECRETARY, being loth to trouble my Lord with too
long a letter, maketh me thus bold to ufe fome addition to
you, being not only grieved, but wounded to the heart. For it is
more than death unto me that her Majefty fhould be thus ready to
interpret always hardly of my fervice, fpecially before it might
pleafe her to underftand my reafons for that I do. For my own
part, I am perfuaded hitherto, there could not any better fervice be
done unto her Majefty in thefe parts, and if fome other man had
done it, it could not be but it had been much better accepted. At
the leaft, I think fhe would never have fo condemned any man before
fhe heard him. And under her Highnefs's pardon and favour, I dare
refer the judgment of this matter, when it fhall be duly examined
and heard, to her Majefty's own felf, or to my worft enemies, wherefoever they be, much rather to any or to all her Privy Council. All
her Majefty can lay to my charge is, going a little further than fhe
gave me the commiffion for; if the matter be well confidered, the ftep-
forward is not fo great, if my authority, contracted before between
her Majefty and the States, be well perufed. And I thank God there
is no treachery nor falfehood in this I am blamed for. The Lord
grant her Majefty patiently to confider by this my doing, wherewith fhe is any way damnified, or farther engaged to the States
than fhe was before.

Her Majefty, I do remember well indeed, and fo may you, how
before all my Lords, fhe feemed to miflike that I fhould take any
other charge than as her General, or to make any oath to them
here, any manner of way. I told her Majefty likewife in the fame
prefence, it was then for no purpofe for me to go into thefe countries; for, if it were to be but her General only of 5000 men, Mr.
Norris had that charge already, and better able to difcharge it than I.

I did

Feb. 8th.

I did likewife put her both in remembrance of her contract with the
States, which had allowed me far more authority than that, and of
the dealing of my Lord Treafurer, and of yourfelf alfo, with them,
about a further entertainment for me, as in refpect I fhould be their
officer, as well as her Majefty's, in which I refer myfelf to both your
reports, being then prefent: for they always anfwered me, there was
no doubt but they would deal with me, as well as ever they did with
the Prince of Orange. But her Majefty indeed would not then hear
of it, though I made petition to be difcharged of the journey. Yet
afterwards in fpeaking with her, I found her very well content I
fhould receive any thing from their hands whatfoever, fo it might
not proceed from herfelf, but of themfelves. I did defire you, Sir,
at that time, to move her Majefty moft earneftly for my ftay at
home, telling you how much I fhould undo myfelf, and do her
Majefty no fervice, going after that manner. And if I be not for-
getful, it feemed then to you likewife that her Majefty was willing
enough that I fhould receive fuch charge and entertainment, as of
themfelves the Eftates would lay upon me, and give me. But I
will not ftand greatly hereupon, but admit me to be even according as her Majefty did contract with the Eftates: is it not there
agreed, I fhould be General of their wars and armies, as well as of
her Majefty's? Was I not placed there as Chief Counfellor of the
Eftate among them, and two nominated alfo by her Majefty to affift
me? I fuppofe in this place it was not meant neither for me nor
them, as counfellors for the wars only, for then I am fure there
fhould have been named more famous Captains to affift me. Befides, I am there authorifed to deal in money matters, and mints, and
fuch like, which are mere civil caufes: if then it be fo that this
authority was given me before, by her Majefty's and the Eftates'
contract, and that they would, partly from the honour borne to her,
and partly for that they would have the world know, they rely
wholly upon her, make choice of me, fo far interefted already
among them, and give me a title and place which fome other muft
                                                                    have

have had, as shall plainly appear to her Majesty by Mr. Davison; and that her Majesty is neither farther charged thereby, nor by any means drawn into any farther action or bond than she was before, and that of necessity some one must have had the place; I would fain know if any other had had it, but one wholly her Majesty's, whether she had not been disappointed of every part of that she looked for, specially for a good peace for herself and England? And whether the said payment of her waged soldiers by them, or the strength of all the garrisons placed by them, or the navy and mariners of these countries had been, without this authority to one of hers, at her Majesty's commandment or no? If then, by taking this place upon me, her Majesty being thereby no way to be charged, either by the King of Spain or otherwise, since it was the Estates' own election, and a matter merely done by themselves, to offer these great advantages to one of her own; methinks it should not receive so hard a construction, seeing, by the placing of me, the only benefit and greatest honour doth grow to her Majesty's self every way. For my own particular, I know it had been far better another had had it than I; but for her Majesty, if her gracious good opinion were not prejudiced already against me in this matter, both herself and all others must think it is much better for her service, in the hands of her own than of any other whosoever. But yet I am now very sorry that ever I was employed in this service: for if any man, of a great number else, had brought such a matter to pass for her, I am sure he would have had, instead of displeasure, many thanks. But such is now my wretched case, as for my faithful, true, and loving heart to her Majesty and my country, I have utterly undone myself; for favour I have disgrace, and for reward utter spoil and ruin. I could have taken warning of this before, if I would have doubted so much of her Majesty's goodness, or have cared more for my quiet and ease at home, than for her service abroad: and I am not so rich, but I might both well have spared my charge, and saved the labour of so dan-

S f   gerous

gerous a journey. But to conclude, if to make her Majesty to have the whole commandment of all these provinces, of their forces by sea and land, of their towns, and of their treasure, with knowledge of all the secrets of their Estate, yea, and to have brought over what peace she would, besides divers ways and means likely to have eased a great part of her charges, only by taking upon me the name of Governor, is so evil taken, as it hath deserved dishonour, discredit, disfavour, with all griefs that may be laid upon a man, I must receive it as deserved of God, and not of my Queen, whom I have reverenced with all humility, and whom I have loved with all fidelity. It shall end thus, that as I find myself most deeply wounded, and seeing her Majesty's good favour and good opinion drawn from me, that she conceiveth I have, or do belike seek rather my own glory than her true service, not forgetting that some such words were used of me, when I made suit to her Majesty to have a few Lords over with me, I do humbly beseech her Majesty by you (for I know my writing to herself, having these conceits of me, shall but trouble her) to grant me leave, as soon as she shall appoint one here, to supply my place for her better service, which I desire with all speed, and the sooner the better, to go live in some obscure corner of the earth, where I will end these grievous days in true prayer to God for her. And, as the Lord doth know, when she thought me any way touched with vain glory, I had no cause of vain glory to boast of. If I may glory in any thing, it must be, I see, in the crosses of this world, which Almighty God strengthen me unto. And so thinking every day a year, till I may receive order and dispatch of this place, I bid you heartily farewel. From the Hague, in Holland, the 8th of February, 1585.

Your loving friend,

R. LEYCESTER.

Earl

Earl of Leicester to the Lords of the Privy Council.

E L I Z A-
B E T H.
1585-6.
Feb. 8.

MY very good Lords, I have, to my very great difcomfort, received from you her Majefty's great miflike of my acceptance of this government, and that fhe will by no means avow, but rather difavow wholly, that which is done therein. I was fomeways a very unfortunate man, I muft confefs, that found fcant of her Majefty's wonted favour towards me before my going to take fo great and weighty a charge, as this in hand, not being ignorant of the infinite hazards, that I muft put my own poor eftate into, both life and all. Neverthelefs, the Lord God doth know, unto whofe mercy I do appeal, the very abundance of my faithful hearty love, borne ever to the prefervation of her facred perfon, and the care of her profperous reign, over our poor endangered country, was only caufe thereof. But, my Lords, thus much hope had I always, notwithftanding, in the great goodnefs of her Majefty, that in fo weighty a cafe as this is, her Majefty would, before fhe had condemned me fo far, have heard what reafons moved me to do this I have done, above her commiffion or commandment. And I doubt not but her Majefty, and you all, fhall well find, that I have adventured more, to do her Majefty acceptable fervice thereby, than to do myfelf either honour or good. And as your Lordfhips have had good experience heretofore, of the uncertainties of thefe paffages, fo was I here forty-three days before I did once hear word out of England. And for this matter, to fatisfy either her Majefty, or your Lordfhips, as it ought to do, muft ftand upon fundry reafons which neceffity brought forth at this time, to caufe me to accept of this government, which I had delivered to Mr. Davifon, to declare both to her and to your Lordfhips. I do moft humbly befeech your good Lordfhips to examine all thofe reafons but indifferently, if they feem to your wifdoms other than might

S f 2   well

well move a true and faithful careful man to her Majefty, to do
as I have done, I do defire, for my miftaken offence, to bear the
burden of it, which can be no greater than that which her Majefty
hath already decreed, to difavow me with all difpleafure and difgrace; a matter of great reproach and grief as ever can happen to any
man. And according to her will, which I perceive is meant by her
Majefty, I will be ready (feeing it not otherwife to be prefently ufed)
to obey her pleafure, if it were prefently to give it, without any
more ado, over again to them: but refpecting what hindrance it
may be to her Majefty's fervice at this time and to the whole caufe,
I truft I fhall not offend your Lordfhips, nor her Majefty, to give
this fimple advice, that it may pleafe her to fend fome nobleman
with all fpeed, whom it fhall like her, to fupply my place, according
to her firft meaning, and to revoke me, which I will humbly obey,
and take it as a matter from God, who can and will correct the ways
of finners, proiefting, in his prefence, and by the belief I have in
Chrift, that I have done nothing in this matter, but, to my judgment,
of fuch confequence for her Majefty's fervice, befides the furtherance
of the caufe here, as if life, land, and goods had lain upon it, I
muft have adventured it, as for an acceptable fervice. And yet
when I fet my foot on land, I no more imagined of any fuch
matter to be offered me, or more than was by her Majefty and
the Eftates contracted, than I thought to be King of Spain, nor
till I came to this town twelve days after: and yet was there fome
near affinity with this, by that contracted between her and the
Eftates. I have no caufe to have played the fool thus far for
myfelf; firft, to have her Majefty's difpleafure, which no kingdom
in the world could make me willing to deferve: next to undo
myfelf in my latter days, to confume all that fhould have kept
me all my life, in one half year: and fo much gain have I here
by it, as I have lived and fpent only of my own, fince I came, without ever having penny or groat from them, neither fhall get fo

4   much

much by them all here, if I had ferved them thefe twelve months,
as I have fpent fince I faw her Majefty and your Lordfhips laft: but
I muft thank God of all, and am moft heartily grieved for her Majefty's heavy difpleafure. I neither defire to live, nor to fee my
country with it. For if I have not done her Majefty good fervice at
this time, I fhall never hope to do her any, but will withdraw me
into fome out-corner of the world, where I will languifh out the reft
of my few too many days, praying ever for her Majefty's long and
profperous life; and with this only comfort to live an exile, that this
difgrace hath happened for no other caufe, but for my mere regard
for her Majefty's eftate, being driven to this choice, either to put
myfelf into her hands, for doing that which was moft probably beft
for her fervice, or elfe lofe her that advantage, which, at that prefent let flip, was not poffible to be gotten for her again. I doubt not
but, ere this, Mr. Davifon hath prefented to her Majefty my own letter, and acquainted all your Lordfhips with fuch reafons as have
moved me to deal as I have done, who was difpatched hence four
days before I received your Lordfhips letters, leaving me in opinion,
if her majefty had not thus conceived of it as fhe now doth, that I
would have thought my fervice had deferved more thanks. I fhall now
attend her Majefty's further pleafure, not daring to write to herfelf,
being thus offended. But will humbly defire your Lordfhips good
conftructions of my doings to her Highnefs, if you fhall find the
confideration worthy, with your Honourable and friendly means in
my behalf, being a man abfent, but moft faithful and loyal to my
moft dread Sovereign Miftrefs; and fo will be to my life's end, and,
to my power, humbly thankful to your Lordfhips all, for the good
favour you fhall fhew herein towards me. And fo will pray unto
God to keep you all in his fear, with long life.

    From the Hague, the 8th of February 1585.

                                    Earl

March 10th, 1585-6.

*Earl of Leicester's letter to Mr. Davison,
expostulating with him, and Mr. Davison's notes in the Margin upon it.*

Denied.

I appeal to the testimony of others.

The contrary appears,

He was difpatched the fame night I arrived.
Let Sir Philip Sidney and others witnefs.

I did my beft to fatisfy her Majefty,
wherein I appeal to her own confcience
and the teftimony of others.
This had been a trick of fupererogation more than I was fit to undertake.
As truly and particularly as himfelf or
any man there could have done.

His end in coming over, with fome
other circumftances, may decide this
queftion.

"IT hath not grieved me a little, that by *your
means* I have fallen into her Majefty's *fo deep*
difpleafure, but that you have alfo *fo carelefsly
difcharged your part,* in the due declaration of all
things as they ftood in truth. Knowing moft
affuredly, that *if you had* delivered to her Majefty
indeed the truth of my dealing, *her Highnefs
could* never have conceived as I perceive fhe doth.
For by the letters and meffages I have received
by Mr. *Henneage,* neither doth her Majefty know
how hardly I was drawn to accept this place before I had acquainted her, wherein no man living
knew fo much as yourfelf, to have fatisfied her,
as you faithfully took upon you, and promifed
you would, in fuch fort as you would not only
give her Majefty full fatisfaction, *but would procure me many great thanks.* Neither is *her Majefty informed rightly* what authority I have received, for if you had done it certainly as it
was, fhe would not be fo offended as fhe is.
For as *you did chiefly perfuade me* to take this
charge upon me, fo yet did I not deal fo vainly,
as it feems her Highnefs conceives, as though I
was fo glad of the place, I did not care how I
engaged her Majefty, contrary to her will and
pleafure, by my acceptance of the place, of which
no

For the clearing of some scruples depending on that charge, not for the thing itself.

All this while there was no note of any contrary commandment.

All this makes nothing to the purpose against me.

'As far for' as I was able.

As much as any private friend he hath.

A doubt bewrayed I confess, but no commandment to the contrary.

Standing with her Majesty's honour and service not against her express commandment.

As a man honestly affected to the cause, and more to himself, than this dealing meriteth.

Absolutely denied.

Though it were less than you make it, yet it is heavier than many men would bear for your sake.

no man knew better how to discharge me of that than yourself, who can remember *how many treaties* you and others had with the States before I agreed for all *your and their persuasions*, to take it sooner, and nothing did I seek more, as both the Dr. Clerks can also tell, than to have her Majesty clear from conclusions in this matter every way, and so did you all assure me, else had I never taken it as I did, which, when I found her Majesty no way bound, nor tied by my doing, and, by the acceptance of this place, I might so greatly, as I have indeed, advanced her service (if it be so considered) and withal help this country from the present imminent danger it stood in, made me the more willing to deal as 'I have done, and to adventure, *upon that assurance you gave to satisfy her Majesty;* but *I see not that you have done any thing;* specially I acquainting you with all my commissions and instructions before, *and did not hide from you the doubt* I had of her Majesty's ill taking it, except you did thoroughly make her know indeed both my care to please her Majesty before all things in the world, and the cause of her service chiefly, without engaging her any way, caused me to yield *to your persuasions here.* Therefore I conclude, *charging you with your conscience how* you do deal now with me; seeing *you chiefly brought me into it,* and to suffer me to rest misjudged of her Majesty, which could no way *have been heavy to you, though you had told the uttermost of your own doing,* as you faithfully promised me you would;

would, and rather than her Majefty fhould mif-
conceive of me; you would let her know the
whole truth indeed, for that I did *very unwillingly come to the matter*, doubting that to fall
out that is come to pafs, more *through lack of
good and fubftantial* making her Majefty truly
underftand the cafe, than for any offence in
reafon committed. And all this loft and falls
out by *your negligent carelefnefs*, whereof *I
many hundred times told you of, that you would*
both mar the goodnefs of the matter, and breed
me her Majefty's difpleafure. But *howfoever it
fall out, fhe fhall know all my reafons*, and Mr.
Henneage I truft will his knowledge, and then
refer all to God and her Majefty. Thus fare ye
well, and except your embaffages have better fuccefs, I fhall have no great caufe to commend them.
In fome hafte. At Harlem this 10th of March,
1585-6.

Your loving friend,

R. LEYCESTER.

The

Marginal notes:

It is done.
Hereof let the world judge.

Non caufa pro caufa.

You might doubt it, but if you had
uttered fo much, you fhould have employed fome other in the journey, which
I had no reafon to affect much, forefeeing well enough how thanklefs it
would be.

So let it be, fo the rules of truth and
juftice be kept.

*The answer of the Council of State to the Queen of Eng-
land's letter of the 13th of February 1585.*

1585-6.
March 18th.

T H E Y are very forry her Majefty is offended with the election
of the Earl of Leicefter, to be abfolute Governor; they confefs
her to have juft caufe of difpleafure, but yet hope when her Majefty is thoroughly informed of all the matter, fhe will then reft
better fatisfied of their proceedings. The authority is given him
no otherwife, than it was to other Governors heretofore: the
words, although they be abfolute, yet in their ufe there, the meaning is no other, than to give unto the faid Earl full power to execute
the contents of his commiffion, with refervation of fovereignty and
property of the country to the people, which commiffion cannot
without danger be called back again; and therefore they moft humbly befeech her Majefty to allow of their doings therein, which are
agreeable to her own advice, that the multitude of heads which breed
confufion in the government fhould be avoided, and fome courfe taken
for the redrefs of the fame.

Earl of Leicefter to the Lords of the Council.

My very good Lords,

1586.
March 27th.

A L T H O U G H I do expect her Majefty's good pleafure daily
for my revocation hence, yet will I no way in the mean time
neglect my duty to my fervice in the charge committed by her Highnefs to me, nor leave your good Lords unadvertifed what hath paft
fince my laft letters; which, as I remember, was from Harlem, upon
the arrival of Sir Thomas Henneage, before whofe coming I had
determined this journey to Utrecht, and was onward fo far in my

way; and, for that Sir Thomas Henneage would not proceed with
any refolution here with the States, touching his commiffion, till he
had received again her Majefty's pleafure, nor yet thought good I
fhould ftay my journey, becaufe it was of very great confequence,
and the affembly of all our foldiers that may be fpared out of the
garrifon, as well horfe as foot, appointed here by a certain day, I
did follow the former determination accordingly; the rather being
commanded by her Majefty to take my direction from Sir Thomas
Henneage, who in any wife wifhed me to proceed on, till I fhould
hear again from her Majefty. So I went to Amfterdam, and there
remained four or five days, and from thence hither to Utrecht,
where I am taking order for the prefent fervice now to be fet forth,
which is for the relief of a town called Grave, a place of very great
importance. We have other places to deal in like fort with, as alfo
to draw the enemy's force out of Brabant and Flanders hitherward,
which it is like they will, for the defence of fuch forts as they have
left guarded, and by which indeed they do befiege Grave, albeit they
have laid no battery to it; for there be five fkonces that they built
about it before I arrived here, yet have I, by ftealth, intelligence from
thence, and upon fome good opportunity, have caufed it to be both
victualled, and three hundred men put into it, notwithftanding their
fkonces. And now I hope it fhall be fully relieved, I have fent the
horfemen already onward, being 1500 very ftrong. The footmen
are alfo marching to the rendezvous, and will be there to-morrow
night all of them; being driven to feparate them for a time; and
till the fervice of Grave be paft, our horfemen lie at a village called
Nycarck, and our footmen at Amaron. Now I am moft earneftly
to recommend to your good Lordfhips the needful eftate of the
captains and foldiers here. I have been driven to borrow for their
relief, and for this journey to help them, 4000 l. of the merchants of Middleburgh. And what I have difburfed of mine own
purfe is not unknown here, I think, to all men. I would, the full

                                                                 eftate

estate of the disburfing of her Majesty's treasure heretofore were certainly known to your Lordships. I wish it for fundry respects, but it will require a very skilful man to examine it; her Majesty cannot lose by it, &c. and it would be a very good fatisfaction to me. And thus praying the Almighty God to preserve all your good Lord-ships, do take my leave. At Utrecht this 27th of March.

Your good Lordships always to command,

R. LEYCESTER.

Extract of my Lord of Leicester's Letter of the 5th of April 1586.

PRACTICES from hence to discredit his Lordship there.

It is greatly wondered at, that he receiveth no letters from her Majesty, nor fupply of men and money, so as men begin to doubt of her Majesty's purpose in the action.

The States wonted affection fomewhat altered, who of late begin to deal in strange fort.

A general mutiny likely to have followed by practice among the English foldiers *.

The States follow her Majesty's example in being strait laced.

Speeches given out that her Majesty hearkeneth after a peace.

Janfey taken.

Grave likely to be relieved.

* Probably that was the mutiny at Utrecht in the march to the relief of Grave.

Lord

Lord Burleigh to the Earl of Leicester.

My very good Lord,

ALTHOUGH of late many crosses and storms have happened
to trouble your Lordship's mind, to the hindrance of the common utility of the service of God, and of her Majesty in that country; yet since your conscience doth testify and warrant your doings to have been meant for the furtherance of the weal thereof, and the successes also, excepting the thwarts from hence, do make good proof that your actions do prosper; I wish your Lordship to continue your disposition, and to comfort yourself with your own integrity, which God will not have oppressed, though he may exercise your patience, and prove the fortitude of your mind, to continue well-doing, and suffer reproof for a time. Thus much for a small preface. And now to the matter; I doubt not but this bearer shall come with some better satisfaction, both for yourself and for the cause, than the enemies thereof have looked for. Since M. Vavasor came, we here, that meant well both to yourself and to the cause, found daily little comfort, and yet surely your friends here did not omit any opportunity; but, upon such conference as I had with them, of the doubtful state of that country, I, in presence of Mr. Secretary, used some boldness with her Majesty, and protested to her as a Counsellor, I could not forbear to let her know, that this course that she held against your Lordship was like to endanger her, in honour, surety, and profit; and that, if she continued the same, I prayed her Majesty that I might be discharged of the place I held, and, both afore God and men, be free from the shame and peril that I saw could not be avoided. I used boldly such bold language in this matter, as I found her doubtful whether to charge me with presumption, which partly she did, or with some astonishment of my round speech, which truly

was

was no other than my confcience did move me, even in *amaritudine
animæ.* And then her Majefty began to be more calm than before,
and, as I conceived, readier to qualify her difpleafure, and her opinion. And fo finding Sir Thomas Shirley ready to write about three
days paft, I willed him to advertife your Lordfhip that I doubted
not but that matters would not continue in that evil ftate they were;
and fo, as he can tell you, he did write, but ftaid the fending thereof
one day, in which time, to my great grief, looking for fo good refolution, I, and Mr. Secretary, found her gone backward, as one
that had been by fome adverfe, counfel feduced, to think that all
fhould do well in thofe countries, though your Lordfhip were difplaced. And fo he with grief ftaid his writing. But yet I did not
thus leave the matter; and fo yefterday Mr. Secretary and I adventured very boldly to declare our cenfures of peril to come, which no
counfel nor action fhould recover. And hereupon we obtained a favourable anfwer, though not to our full liking, but yet fuch as fhe
commanded to put in writing, and fo we were therein occupied.
And then, unlooked for, came a letter from your Lordfhip to Mr. Vice
Chamberlain, wherewith he made her Majefty acquainted, and fhe
told him, that fhe had declared her refolution to Mr. Secretary and
me, and fo willed him to come to my chamber, and fo he did, and
there we finding fome new occafion to feek a better refolution of her
Majefty, we all three went to her Majefty, and there I told her very
plainly, that I did fee that if fhe ufed not fpeed to content the States,
and the people of thofe countries, fhe would not only lofe them, but
her honour in the world, and fhe fhould find certainly as great danger
from thofe countries, as fhe had looked for comfort. Herewith, fhe
was greatly troubled, and fo, being thereunto moved, fhe affented to
do any thing that fhe might with her honour.

In fine, we moved her to affent, that your Lordfhip fhould continue your office for fome time, until the ftate of the matter might
be better confidered by her. And fo letters were appointed to be

fpeedily

fpeedily written, both to your Lordfhip and the Council of the States, and that Mr. Shirley might be fent away with all fpeed; and when the letters were ready written, came Pointz from Mr. Henneage, with letters from your Lordfhip to me, including a letter to her Majefty, which I fpeedily delivered with fuch good fpeeches as in honefty became me, for your excufe. She read your letter; and, in very truth, I found her princely heart touched with favourable interpretation of your actions, affirming them only offenfive to her, in that fhe was not made privy, not now mifliking that you had the authority. Surely I had caufe, and fo I did commend her princely nature, in this fort, of allowing both of you for your good intention, and excufing you of any fpot of evil meaning. And having her Majefty in this fort calmed, though it was not poffible to make your Lordfhip amends, yet I thought good to haften her refolution, which your Lordfhip muft now take to come from a favourable good Miftrefs; for fo truly fhe doth profefs. And you muft ftrive with your nature to throw over your fhoulders that which is paft. Thus your Lordfhip feeth I have been fomewhat long to fhow you the courfe to bring this honeft gentleman, Sir Thomas Shirley, to this meffage, who furely hath very honeftly behaved himfelf for your Lordfhip. And truly fo hath Mr. Vice Chamberlain *, and Mr. Secretary, and bidden many ftrange fpeeches. And now I will write no more hereof, but of fome other particular advices, the confideration whereof I leave to your Lordfhip as leifure may ferve you.

My Lord, until the ftate of the Queen's army, by mufter book, and her monthly charges, may appear more clear, here will be no further means for any more money. At this prefent there is paid 24,000 l. and that, added to her Majefty's former charge of 52,000, maketh 76,000, which fum her Majefty doth often repeat with great offence.

My Lord, I am very glad to fee a difpofition of fending fome fhips from thence, to impeach the Spanifh King, towards his Indies. It is

* Sir Chriftopher Hatton.

a matter

a matter that many years paft I did project to the Prince of Orange's Minifters, to have been attempted. We hear that Sir Francis Drake is a fearful man to the King, and that the King could have been content that Sir Francis had taken the laft year's fleet, fo as he had not gone forward to his Indies. We hear that he hath taken feven rich fhips on the coaft of the Indies. I wifh they were fafe in the Thames.

We are here troubled to underftand, that from Hamburgh and Dantzick, Lubeck, &c. there are a great number of hulks laden for Spain, and do mean to pafs about Scotland and Ireland, as fome of them did this laft year, which they do to avoid all ftays in our narrow feas. I would to God your fleet, now intended from thofe countries, could make a good prize of them; for fo fhould the King of Spain be unable to defend his feas, or to offend any other.

My Lord, where you write to me of that you hear of Champigny's errands, I will tell you what I know thereof; and what elfe is known to any other, I cannot write of. There is an Italian merchant in Antwerp that pretendeth acquaintance with Champigny, and he hath written hither to another merchant, to know whether her Majefty can be content to come to peace with the King of Spain. The anfwer is made, that, by the publication publifhed, it is to be feen, wherefore her Majefty hath fent her forces into the Low Countries. And, if the King of Spain fhall fatisfy her Majefty in honour, according to her proteftation, by reftoring to thofe countries liberty and peace, and to remove all men of war from thence, and reftore to her own fubjects their loffes, fhe can be content to hear any honourable offer from the King; and otherwife fhe mindeth to perfift in defence of her neighbours, and recovery of her fubjects loffes. This anfwer is made by words only, but not from her Majefty; and whether Champigny will any farther proceed I know not; but fure I am, he hath no caufe to make any vaunt hereof. And I truft their

need

need fhall make them fooner yield, than any caufe to come of this anfwer.

It may be, that there are other like motions made to her Majefty; but I think furely her Majefty mindeth not to fhow any yielding. For, God be thanked, fhe hath not caufe, but to expect the yielding to come from the King of Spain and his Minifters.

And where your Lordfhip writeth that the coming of my fon from Brill in this time, may breed fome doubts in men's conceits. Surely, my Lord, Sir Thomas Shirley can tell you, that, upon his report of his ficknefs, with danger not to recover without changing the air to come into England, the Queen's Majefty hearing thereof, without any motion of me, commanded Mr. Secretary to fend him her li-cence, with all poffible fpeed; and, as I underftand from himfelf, he is much injured with the noifomenefs of the place, where the water is not only brackifh, but, being heated on the fire, it ftinketh.

He alfo findeth the town in a manner utterly unfurnifhed of ord-nance, and without powder and bullets, fo as, in very truth, it was as as good out of her Majefty's hands, by reafon of the charge, as to have it only in a name. But how this fhould be remedied I know not, for her Majefty will not yield to any more charge, and I fee the States unwilling to pay that which they owe. And by a claufe in the treaty, they are bound to furnifh both the towns of Flufhing and Brill, upon your Lordfhip's demand, as her Majefty's Governor Ge-neral; and if there be any hope further, it muft proceed from your Lordfhip as Governor of the Provinces, with the Council of the States. I think Sir Philip Sidney hath alfo fome want of ordnance, but nothing like to that of the Brill, where there are not above feven pieces, few enough for one bulwark: but the danger is not to be feared, as long as your Lordfhip fhall profper in government. My fon alfo brought thither two hundred footmen and fifty horfe, but he could never get a penny for them, nor one penny to that gar-rifon fince he had the charge; and yet it may be, that he hath had

fome

some help of late; for the treasurer did write that your Lordship gave him order to help them with some money. I am now in doubt to write any further, for troubling of your Lordship, knowing how infinite your occasions be to write, and to read, beside continual actions.

By such letters as shall come from her Majesty, you shall find as much comfort from her Majesty, as you have received discomfort, though there be great differences in the effect; for the former I know hath deeply wounded your heart; and these cannot suddenly sink so low as the wound is; but your Lordship must add to this your own fortitude of mind. And so I most heartily wish you to be strengthened by God's special grace.

Your Lordship's most assuredly,

31 *Martii* 1586. W. BURGHLEY. *

* This resolute friendly behaviour of the old treasurer towards his rival Leicester during the Queen's displeasure, does him great honour; and strange it is, that Camden passes it over in silence; but indeed that historian's omissions are very unpardonable, considering the light he had.

No. XIX.

No. XIX.

Letters from Sir Philip Sidney, the Earl of Leicester.

[The Editor has several letters of Sir Philip Sidney; but these two may serve as a specimen. Had he lived, his uncle Leicester would, probably, have been more successful in his government. It is singular, that, amongst the different *Eloges* made upon him after his death, King James's verses are the most elegant: They are worthy of a scholar of Buchanan.]

Sir Philip Sidney to Lord Leicester.

Right honourable, my singular good Lord,

MY intent I have imparted to Mr. Lutty at large, to deliver to your Excellency. Now I am only to beseech your Excellency, and if I may prevail with your Excellency, to persuade you, that, if the journey into Frifeland be but upon such general grounds, as they were when I came away, which may as easily be done hereafter as now, that it will please you to send forces to the besieging of Steenberg, with 1200 of your footmen, besides them that these quarters may spare, and 300 of your horse, with them hereabout. I will undertake, upon my life, either to ruin it, or to make the enemy raise his siege from Grave; or, which I most hope, both. And it shall be done in the sight of the world, which is most honourable and profitable. For these matters of practices, I assure your Excellency, they are dainty in respect to their doubleness, which almost ever fails in them, and of the many impediments that fall in them, that, if notable reasons guide not, or some worthy person answer not for it, they are better omitted than attempted. Breda, un-

doubtedly,

doubtedly, at leaſt I think ſo, was but a trap; for our poor Eng-
liſhmen might have been ſuffered to take a place which they would
never have ſtriven to put them out of, till they might have cut both
them and us to pieces, who ſhould come to ſeize it. But, as for
Graveline, I will never ſtir till I have La Motte himſelf, or ſome
principal officer of his, in hand. Therefore, if it pleaſe your Excellency to let old Tutty and Read, with Sir William Stanley and Sir
William Ruſſel, with 200 horſe come hither, I doubt not but to ſend
you honourable and comfortable news of it; for I have good underſtanding thereof by this ſhew I made: and I know what the enemy
can do ſhall not ſerve. If this may be done, 500 pioneers with munition and victuals according, muſt be got; and, if God will, I
will do you honour in it. It grieves me very much, the ſoldiers are
ſo hardly dealt with in your firſt beginning of government, not only
in their pay, but in taking booties from them, as by your Excellency's letters I find. When ſoldiers grow to deſpair, and give up
towns, then it is late to buy that with hundred thouſands, which
might have been ſaved with a trifle. I think to write a French letter
to your Excellency, becauſe your Excellency wrote to me in that
language, which, if you pleaſe, may be ſhown to your Council;
for, by my troth, they are even in their old train, and may do that
ſafely under your colour now, which, before, they did the more
ſparingly, for fear of hatred. I humbly beſeech your Excellency, that
Morbais may find himſelf comforted for this ſervice he hath done
upon one of the beſt captains the Prince of Parma had. I am now
departing towards Eluſhing, and the tide calls me away. I will
therefore moſt humbly kiſs your hands, and refer the reſt to the next;
praying God to proſper your Excellency as I doubt not he will, and
ſo humbly take my leave. At Berghen.

Your Excellency's moſt humble and obedient,

PH. SIDNEY.

ELIZA-
BETH.
1586.

The Same to the Same.

Right Honourable, my fingular good Lord,

1586.
February 2d.

I HAVE fent this bearer, my Cornet, to your Excellency, whom I do moft humbly befeech you to difpatch again unto me, becaufe it ftands me much upon, to know what I fhall refolve on; becaufe my charges, divers ways, and particularly my horfemen, grow greater than I am able to go through withal. I had, of the Count Hollock, a patent for them of Somerdyke, to lodge me a number of horfe, till my company were fufficient to be muftered; there fome of them were, and now they have gotten, upon what caufe I know not, an act from your Excellency to be free from any. Whereupon, fo courteoufly thefe boors dealt, as to arreft my horfes, the very day that I had fent for them, thinking truly I fhould have have occafion to have ventured my life; and would not releafe them till I had paid them two hundred florins for the charges, as they pretended. I humbly befeech your Excellency, becaufe I know my Lieutenant hath been at the fea fide almoft this month, to my great expence, that I may have either a quarter affigned me, or elfe that to this place they may bring fuch provifion as the increafing of the number will require; for elfe, I being not to demand pay till they be muftered, nor to be muftered till my number be complete, it will be too heavy a burden for me to bear; who, I proteft to your Excellency, am fo far from defiring gain, that I am willing to fpend all that I can make; only my care is, that I may be able to go through with it, to your honour and fervice, as I hope in God I fhall.

For thefe men, they are of the richeft of thefe parts, and never touched with the war; but fo do the rich ftill put off all matters, by fending to fome friend or other of theirs in the Council, that may lighten them to burden others. I humbly befeech your Excellency my Cornet may return with fuch refolution as I may either go

4   through,

through, or give over my Cornet. For my part, I hope, and am almoft affured, to do you good fervice, and my heart burneth to do it,
if only my ability do not fail me in the way. For Roger Williams
alfo, I would it would pleafe your Excellency to difpatch his Ser-
jeant-majorfhip univerfally over all horfemen; and, in that nature,
you may better allow him fome good pension, than by being only
over the Englifh; and fo alfo for his Corner, the gentleman deferves
much.

Herewith I will no further trouble your Excellency, but humbly
take my leave, and pray to God for your long and profperous life
and victory. At Berghen.

Your Excellency's moft humble and obedient nephew,

PH. SIDNEI.

No. XX.

From the
originals in
the Cotton
Library.

No. XX.

Papers about a private Treaty with Spain.

[Lord Burleigh, as the pacific Minister, was the conductor of this private treaty, to which Walsingham and Leicester were, extremely averse. They appear, in this instance, to have judged better, and to have seen further into the designs of Spain than the wise Treasurer. However, it may be suggested, that Burleigh acted in this business rather in compliance with the Queen's humour, than his own opinion. In all his letters he appears very zealous for the common cause against Spain, and the League.

From the papers which the Editor has collected, Walsingham does not seem to have had that weight in the Queen's cabinet, which his abilities and fidelity deserved. The poverty in which he died is a reproach to the memory of his Mistress; if not to that of her Lord Treasurer.]

Lord Burleigh to Andreas de Loo *.

Signior Andreas,

IT is requisite for the matter of this intended treaty, that by frequent advertisements you should as well be acquainted with our proceedings, or with our stays, as you do diligently by your letters advertise us of your conceits and expectations there. And therefore, it is her Majesty's express commandment, that I should advertise you of her mind, and so also to answer your letters. There are come hither, since my last letters written from hence the last of August, and first of September, reckoning according to the old stile, two several packets from you, the first, of the 26th of August, dated at Brussels,

* A Flemish agent of the Duke of Parma.

which

which came whilft I was abfent from the court, having gone to my houfe at Theobalds the 2d of September. The fecond of your's, was of the laft of Auguft, written alfo from Bruffels, which came alfo about the 9th of this month in my abfence, for I came not until the 11th. All which your letters being brought to Mr. Comptroller, were feen by her Majefty, and yet by her fent to me, and therewith I was commanded to come to the court; and upon conference with her Majefty, upon your letters, fhe feemed in fome fort forry to fee you troubled with the conceit you had of the long delays of the coming of our Commiffioners thither; confidering that, although indeed their coming may feem to you to be more delayed than were meet, yet, in very truth, the caufe thereof proceedeth not of any difpofition of her Majefty to have the fame deferred, not fo much as for one day, but that the caufe proceedeth of lack of refolutions and anfwers, from my Lord Leicefter, who hath had charge a good time paft to have induced the States to like of her Majefty's intention for treaty of peace, both for herfelf with the King of Spain, and alfo to procure a univerfal peace in thofe Low Countries; without which, you well know, that her Majefty can make no account of long continuance of any peace that fhall be made betwixt her Majefty and the King of Spain; neither can there be any certainty of the intercourfe for the fubjects of this realm and thofe of the Low Countries and the houfe of Burgundy, and this reafon is of fuch force as no man can deny, but that the intercourfe for Prince's fubjects, is the proper, and almoft the only fruit of peace betwixt Kings; and without it, the private amity and friendfhip betwixt Princes for their own perfons, doth fmall good; otherwife than that thereby they may appear in the fight of God void of malice. But to enlarge this argument needeth not, for you know the effect thereof. And although, by your letters of the laft of Auguft, you feem fearful left the Duke of Parma, and the King's Counfellors there, fhould conceive finifterly of this delay, as though her Majefty might mean to

abufe

abuse the Duke, yet her Majesty hopeth that my letters written from hence, the same day that yours were written from thence, being come to your hands long before this, have satisfied both your own fear, and altered a conceit of the Duke, if he had so conceived any thing amiss of her Majesty for this delay. For by those my letters I did, by her Majesty's commandment, advertise you, according to the very truth of the whole matter, how my Lord Leicester had, by her Majesty's commandment, proceeded there, and what difficulties he found there to persuade the States and people, to allow of her Majesty's intention, to obtain a peace for them. And that her Majesty expected daily to hear of some better success therein, by the travail of the said Earl, who did show himself as willing to have a good peace made, for her Majesty's satisfaction, as the Duke of Parma had showed his disposition. So as at the time of my said letters, we did look to have had some good answer, tending to the acceleration of this treaty, within a short time. And so her Majesty hopeth that, if you have acquainted the Duke, with the contents of my said letters, he should rest satisfied for any sinister conceit of her Majesty. But now I think it needful to advertise you, how the case presently standeth, that the Duke knowing the truth of the state thereof, you well see that the delay of the coming of our Commissioners proceedeth not of her Majesty, the same being in very truth greatly misliked of her Majesty, so as she presently omitteth nothing in her power to further it. For, in very truth, my Lord of Derby, who had been lately sick in his own country, came hither on Saturday last, the rest of our commissioners being, afore that, ready to take their journey, and their commissions made ready. And now even on the same Saturday, came my Lord of Leicester's Secretary, Mr. Atye, from the Earl, hither, with letters to her Majesty, declaring in what earnest sort my Lord of Leicester had travailed with the States to induce them to allow of her Majesty's purpose; but altogether to a mischievous contrary course, there was a seditious practice used in those countries, by a most false invented untruth, to put into all the

people's

people's heads, that her Majefty had already made a fecret conclu-
fion of peace for herfelf, with the King of Spain, and that the fafe-conduct fent hither from the Duke of Parma (whereof the copies were common amongft them), was only to warrant the coming of the Queen's Commiffioners to confirm the fame peace, and not to treat thereof. To this falfe and feditious report, was added, that my Lord of Leicefter was directed from her Majefty, to get into his poffeffion as many towns as he could, with intention to deliver them to the Duke of Parma, upon payment to be made to her Majefty of her Majefty's charges of all her aid given to the States of the country. And hereupon the Earl of Leicefter knowing thefe reports to be falfe, and yet finding how, by fundry practices, both many of the States, and a great number of the people, have been feduced to believe the fame, he hath been greatly troubled, and ufed no fmall labours to ftay thefe falfe reports, and to make it manifeft, fpecially to the Council of State, and to the States themfelves, how falfely thefe reports have been invented and fpread abroad. And herein hath his Lordfhip been occupied from day to day, this long time, and as he writeth to her Majefty, he hath fo prevailed with fome principal perfons, that are lovers of their country, and do defire peace, as he hopeth to overcome this wicked attempt, being the worft of fome fuch as care not for the public weal of their country, fo they may continue their private authority and profit, which by peace, and without the war, they cannot have. And to the end it fhall not be thought that thefe things are alledged by the Earl of purpofe to prolong time for fome other purpofe, I am fure that the Duke of Parma cannot be ignorant, if it fhall pleafe him to caufe fuch as ferveth him for intelligence amongft the States, and the towns of Holland and Zealand, to inform him, as I am fure he hath no lack thereof, but that he fhall be largely advertifed hereof, and perchance more largely, infomuch, for this falfe opinion conceived againft the Earl, there hath been great controverfy betwixt the States and the

X x   Earl,

Earl, they oppofing themfelves againft his authority, and maintaining both the Counts Maurice and Hohenloe, to withftand the placing
of any Englifhmen in any of the towns where they have credit.
Surmifing to the towns that the Earl of Leicefter hath inftructions
from her Majefty, to get into his hands all the towns that he can, to
deliver them to the Duke of Parma, according to the conclufion
which they fay is already fecretly made for a peace between her
Majefty and the King of Spain. And where the Earl hath, by his
letters and meffages to divers towns, declared thefe reports to be
merely falfe, there was one of the States named Barnevelt, that went
to certain affemblies, and moft impudently declared thefe to be true,
and that he had feen the copies of the Queen's Majefty's letters to
the Earl, containing that fhe had made peace already, though
fecretly, and therefore the Earl fhould, upon colour of continuing
fuccours to them, put into their towns Englifh forces, fo as the fame
towns might be delivered to the King of Spain, upon payment of
her charges, according to her fecret covenant. Of this Barnevelt's
feditious, malicious, and falfe dealings, the Earl hath complained to
the States, and hath required that he might be charged to fhow forth
thofe letters, that he feigneth himfelf to have feen. And fo the
Earl, at the time of Mr. Aty's coming from thence, which was about
the 2d of September, hoped, by the difcovery of this falfe treacherous
practice of Barnevelt, and of his condemnation afore the States,
that he fhall fhortly after this mifchievous courfe practifed againft
the weal of the country, and againft her Majefty's bleffed purpofe, to
bring the whole country to an univerfal peace. And fo we now hope
fhortly to hear of good fuccefs of the Earl's travail with them, which
being certified to her Majefty, I can affure you, the Commiffioners
being in full readinefs, fhall not ftay one day longer than fhall be
needful. By this my large writing you may well perceive in what
plain fort I do deal with you, to the intent that if you fhould find
any fcruple to remain in the Duke's mind, notwithftanding thofe
                                                        reafons

reafons that you had to declare to his Highnefs, by my letters of the laft of Auguft, you might, with the largenefs of this my letter, ftay him from any doubt of her Majefty's fincerity. And fo to continue his purpofes rather to make peace, than to follow any further provifions for increafe of hoftile actions. As in truth we hear fo much thereof by the works at Antwerp, about maritime matters, and of the daily affemblies and calling together of mariners and fhipwrights to Dunkirk, Newport, and Graveling, out of France and other places, befides his meffengers fent into Germany and Italy, to hafte the new forces from thence, fo might thefe things in very truth move her Majefty to doubt, that in the end, though our Commiffioners fhould come thither, and treat of peace, yet there fhould be devices ufed to break off the treaty, and fo in a fort to take her Majefty and the Low Countries unprovided. But notwithftanding thefe likely conjectures to move doubts, her Majefty mindeth to continue her godly purpofe to contract a peace, if fhe may have it with reafonable conditions for her furety, and the univerfal weal of all thofe Low Countries, the Provinces United; a matter not to be neglected by her Majefty for many refpects, maintainable both afore God and the world. I pray you remember to fend anfwer to the points of my laft letters of Auguft, concerning a new fafe-conduct, with a general claufe for fuch as her Majefty may chance to change before their coming thither, if any that are already named fhould fall fick, afore they fhould be fent from hence. And alfo concerning the commiffion by which the King of Spain's Commiffioners fhall treat; whether it fhall not be in the King's name, as reafon requireth ? Likewife remember the other points contained in a later letter, dated *primo* September, fent with the other of the laft of Auguft, for a fafe conduct to be fent from the Duke of Parma to Embden, for the King of Denmark's Ambaffador. And in penning the new fafe-conduct, it is required for ours, to omit in the fame, a certain fentence, breeding a fcruple in her Majefty, as though this matter for peace had been originally fought by her Majefty,

X x 2

contrary

contrary to the truth of the proceeding, as yourself doth well know.

And so I wish you to enjoy the end of your long labour, wherein no small numbers are to be partners with you, whereof I will account myself to be one, that shall hope of more rest by peace, than I have of long time felt by these troubles.

Earl of Leicester to Lord Burleigh.

My Lord,

I WILL trouble you at this time the less, for that I hope before this long, your Lordship hath understood at large my whole proceedings here, as also how the state of things stood at the departure of my Lord North and Mr. Beale. Then do I trust her Majesty is better satisfied for my honest service done for her, than appears by the letters to me she doth conceive. God and my conscience doth know, that I have done her Majesty careful and true service, and she doth blame me (when she shall understand all her own commandments to me, as Mr. Beale hath them), without my due desert. For, touching the peace, it shall appear, before I had any direct warrant from her Majesty, I did take a course with the Council of State (for the States General came not to me in fifteen days after I arrived), to make them know, that her Majesty should have just cause to deal for a peace, for I saw they were not able to maintain war. I laid all her Majesty's great and infinite charges afore them, and so did I both more largely, and more earnestly when the States came to me. Then immediately fell out the false slander of her Majesty's contracting and dealing with the Duke of Parma, without their knowledge. Yet before that, as Mr. Beale can tell, I sent Bardesius into Holland, to declare to the States, that I found their dealings so strange, as I, finding her Majesty many ways pressed from the King of Spain, to

hearken

hearken to a peace, which she would not do all this while in respect of them, but to make them first acquainted withal, and would, I knew, offer first to join and deal with them, before she would make any resolution for herself; therefore I wished them, their estate appearing to be so weak as it was, whereof I must advertise her Majesty, that they would take such a course as both her Majesty and they might jointly enjoy a peace, to avoid their insupportable charge, and loss of so many people as daily were lost by the wars. This message was grievously taken, and they did send Bardesius back with a most lamentable answer, testifying their utter undoing if her Majesty should take that course; and the poor man, upon his knees, in the presence of the Council, desired me to be a mean to persuade her Majesty to stay some time longer, to see what means the States could find to satisfy her otherwise. That he durst not declare my message to all the States, but to two or three of the wisest, who returned him in that sort. And that he would go back again to press them to look better about them, confessing her Majesty had reason to take some such course: but he hoped, the cause had moved her to do that good she had done, and if she should alter from it, they were all undone. All this while had not I received any such letters from her Majesty to will me directly to move the matter of peace, as now I find she takes it. But within two days after this dealing last with Bardesius, there came a letter signed by her Majesty, to deal with the States for the peace, finding them not able to maintain their war. Your Lordship may see, that before this letter, which was the most absolute of all, I had dealt to the same effect; but because Bardesius had not done my message to the whole States as I willed him, I sent Mening and Valke to them, with more plain instructions, as may appear by their own declaration. In which meantime, grew forth these false lewd bruits of her Majesty's dealing, and that I had both private instructions and letters from her Majesty, to treat a peace, either by fair means, or by force, and that my seeking the absolute

govern-

government at this time, was only to have power in my hands, if
they refufed her Majefty's offers, then to compel them. This matter was prefently publifhed to all quarters, as I then advertifed her
Majefty, and fome of your Lordfhips, whereupon it behoved me to
deal carefully for the fatisfying the world in honour of her Majefty's
dealing in this matter, and thought at that time the courfe both
honourable and convenient which I took, for fatisfaction of all men,
as no doubt it hath proved, and yet no whit hindered her proceeding to peace, if it pleafed her, but with more honour every way.
Now touching my commiffion to have done this fooner, it muft reft
upon my inftructions, and upon her Majefty's prefent directions by
her letters; if it fhall not appear by Mr. Beale's declaration, that I
have obferved both, let me receive blame, and fhame too; as, in the
letter her Majefty hath written to the States, I muft receive fhame;
for in the beginning it is fet down, that I was ftraitly commanded
by her Majefty to make the overture to them, at my firft arrival, and
that fhe wonders how I can anfwer it.   Firft, my Lord, let it be confidered when I came away, whether any fuch intention was meant,
or not.   If it be faid it was, why was my Lord of Buckhurft's proceeding fo far therein mifliked by her Majefty, and us all then ; and
why might not his proceeding therein have ferved, without my going
over for the fame alfo ? Befide, to what end was there 5000 men
fent more over with me, after the miflike had of his dealing ? Was
it, to be at fuch charge, either for her Majefty's felf or the States, to
come over to make immediately this overture of peace ? Why was
the increafe of her Majefty's part fet down to 30,000 l. if I would
have ftrained my inftructions, but to 50,000 l. by my Lord Buckhurft's offer before it was, and the States to augment their part
to a 100,000 l. to levy an army for the field ? Was all this
that I fhould immediately move the peace ? A matter which not
only myfelf delivered from them to her Majefty, at my return
into England, but the Commiffioners themfelves in England affirm-

                                                     ed

ed the fame, both to your Lordſhips and to her Majeſty alſo. By my Lord of Buckhurſt likewiſe it appeared, how far they were off, and what danger it was likely to breed to this Eſtate, they moving thereof in ſuch ſort as her Majeſty did ſeem to ſurceaſe that courſe, and to encourage them immediately, cauſed my going with a contrary ſhow, to comfort and animate them here all I could: ſo that I truſt, theſe things called to remembrance, it will not be thought that I was preſently to make this overture; neither would I have taken that office upon me, as I am ſure your Lordſhip, and others my Lords can remember, not for a 100,000 l.; her Majeſty's diſpleaſure ſet aſide. But, my Lord, as I take it, it was both her Majeſty's pleaſure, and all your reſolutions at that time, for my going, to be firſt to reduce the State to the former courſe it was in, being then much altered, and drawn into faction, as indeed it, was, and is; that, that being done, which it pleaſed you all to conceive then, was not like to be, without my own being here, with her Majeſty's thorough favour and countenance; and that if I could do that, whereby her Majeſty's party might be the ſtronger, and the enemy thereby the more greedy and deſirous to ſeek a good peace in time, and that by the ſhow of a ſtrong war between her Majeſty and them, the enemy was like to come to the better conditions. And that theſe things being brought to paſs, the country firſt ſettled, and a ſtrong preparation in the field againſt the enemy, I ſhould then take occaſion to perſuade theſe people to hearken to a treaty of peace, and if they would refuſe ſo godly, and ſo reaſonable a matter, that her Majeſty might and would uſe her own wiſdom for her own affairs, &c. Or if, after my arrival, I ſhould, after all proofs and trials made, find theſe men obſtinate, and withal unable to bear out the charge of the war hereafter, and not pay ſuch debts as were due both to her Majeſty, and to her people in their pay, as alſo pay for the charge of theſe laſt numbers brought over by me, that then alſo, I ſhould not only move the matter of peace, but alſo, if they ſeemed to refuſe her offer,

that

that I fhould let them know, that fhe will not be at any further
charge here, for their caufes. This, as far as ever I could conceive,
was her Majefty's and all your Lordfhips determinations: for better
proof, examine my inftruĉlions, let her Majefty's letters be feen, the
notes of which, concerning that point, I have delivered Mr. Beale, to
put her better in mind thereof; and among which, one fpecial
matter for my comfort, and leads from this, her Majefty doth promife, as alfo fent me fundry the like meffages, that I fhould not in this
fervice lack any thing in the world, to further it withal. And if
all they agree with that I have done, and that I have not proceeded
againft thefe, I truft her Majefty will alter her heavy conceit, as
well of my negligence as careleffnefs in her fervice. And withal,
that it will pleafe her to remember her promife for my abode, which
fhe faid earneftly fhould not be above three months. But now I
perceive her Majefty is perfuaded that I am here to my own defire,
and that it was fecretly my own motion to come hither, and to have
this place. For that, I will defire no other witneffes, befides what I
protefted to her Majefty's felf, but your Lordfhip, and all the reft of
my good Lords and friends there, whether I ever feemed to defire,
or could in reafon wifh it. Firft, the abfence from her Majefty; next
mine own poor eftate, in what terms it refted, and doth yet, I think,
is made known to you, and others my friends. The hindrance I
had by my laft journey; the ingratitude I found in the States, and
little hope of any good; befides my years, and decay of health, to
lofe all thefe by my journey; and the greateft of all, the fear of
her Majefty's difpleafure, which I got in the laft voyage, with the
lofs, I proteft to God, of 25000l. clear of expences, befide all I received, being before at leaft 8000l. in debt, and yet never fo near
out of debt, fince the firft year I ferved. I truft thefe be reafons for
her Majefty not to think I am here at my own liking, for neither do
I like the place, nor would have taken it upon me, to have received
in gift 40,000l. but for the perfuafion of your Lordfhips all, and the

fervice

fervice was thought I only might do here, for her Majefty and the
common caufe; and this, I take God to record, I fpeak from my
heart according to truth, and even fo, I pray you, my good Lord,
anfwer for me, and be a mean, if ever I may requite it, to help me
fpeedily home. And I fee no caufe of ftay, the anfwer had of thefe
men, but her Majefty fending, fuch one, or appointing one here to
take the charge of her army. As for the authority of my government, I have not accepted of it, becaufe I did altogether follow her
Majefty's expectation for the peace, and fought to drive as many
advantages for her to take her own courfe by, as I could. And
now to haften their anfwer, I have fent them, her Majefty's mind by
Mr. Killegrew, although for my own fhame I forbear the delivery
of the letter, till I hear again. For truly her Majefty's felf fhall be
as greatly touched as I, for thereby will thefe froward firft begin-
ners of her Majefty's flander take hold, to affirm it to be true, as
they may, and by the manner of our proceeding hitherto. Her
Majefty may deal as fhe doth, and yet draw the caufe from the
States, and fo moft honourably may fhe go forward, if as fafely,
which God grant. For it is wonderful to hear how the States are
hated, for giving her Majefty caufe thus to deal, for now, all blame
is laid upon them; and this is alfo the beft and next way for all the
people to commit themfelves to her Majefty's order, as I believe it
will fall out fo. Whereas, otherwife, it will hardly be believed
there, the great alteration of all men's minds it would make. But
all as fhall pleafe her Majefty; for my part, I have ferved her as I
would to anfwer to God for it. I commit your Lordfhip to God,
having no paper left.

At Utrecht, this 30th September, 1587.

Your Lordfhip's, &c.

R. LEICESTER.

Earl

Earl of Leicester to Lord Burleigh.

October 30.

My very good Lord,

I WAS in good hope that I should have heard out of England, e'er I should have had any cause to write any more than I
have done heretofore. But howsoever I am respected; I will not
omit my duty in advertising her Majesty and my Lords, how matters pass here in the mean while. The States proceed still, after one
sort; for the establishment of their government, as I have already
declared. And if these men hold their authority as they do, they
will shortly bring their purposes to pass, specially using the matter
of peace so greatly to their advantage as they do; whereof I have
written both to her Majesty and your Lordship at large. And although it will hardly be believed, but by those that be here present among them, that so holy and honest a cause should be so misliked, yet so doth it fall out now, that the hearts of all men are
greatly daunted, and the devices of practising heads hath the more
way given them to take effect. And nothing doth argue to me
greater cause to mistrust the meanings of these men, than the jolity
they make upon this motion of peace, as men glad and contented to
have men's minds altered from her Majesty; using all the practices
and devices they can, to further it. For they are not ignorant
that if her Majesty shall leave them, that they have no Prince to
trust or lean unto, and yet do they what they may, to make her
Majesty forsake them. For no men can take more dishonourable
or spiteful courses, since the motion her Majesty hath made unto
them, for so good a matter, than they have done. They have delivered out in the worst sort, and with an interpretation of their
own, that her Majesty hath always had no better intention toward
them, than to get a peace in the end for herself. That I have been

9

fent

sent over, this last time chiefly, for that purpose, under colour of my authority and government here; and have secretly, and some ways openly enough, sought to hinder my credit with the people, all they can possibly: whereby they might the more easily settle their government as they would have it. And in truth they have chosen a fit time for it, and have gotten a good ground for them to work on. For the people they persuade one way, that by a peace there is no way but destruction for them, and hereupon they descant upon her Majesty in the highest note, to alienate their hearts. The soldiers they persuade another way, that having peace they must be discharged, and if they will continue their service with them, they will entertain them still, and agree to no peace, whatsoever the Queen of England shall do; who, they assure themselves, will have peace. This is a persuasion your Lordship can consider very substantial, both to hold them with them, and to alter them from her Majesty. Beside, if they had never so good devotion to serve under me, they must now doubt, or rather be out of doubt, that if her Majesty leave them, it is not like that I shall remain among them, or have any authority to do them any good. And therefore, if they should now seem to lean to me for her Majesty's service, it must be too weak a pillar, seeing there is no assurance for any maintenance for them. The like reason must needs fall into the minds of others, that have been, and are well affected, both to the cause and to her Majesty, that if she be minded to treat for peace, and these men do refuse to join with her, it is like she will take offence and leave them; if it so fall out, whom have they to trust unto, or what cause shall they have to stand with me, or to declare openly any affection to her Majesty? They find the States already, how they are bent by the persuasions they use in all places, and what constant protestations they have made of late, specially all those of Holland and Zealand, to go through with this cause, both for religion or their liberty, to the last drop of their blood; whereby they have enchanted many well meaning men,

who

who do not look thoroughly into their doings, nor obferve diligently their manner of proceeding; for if they did, they would take it, as I am perfuaded it is, the Syren's charm Wherein for my further conceit of their intent, I will refer your Lordſhip to my letter to Mr. Beale; for being but my own collection, I dare not incenfe her Majefty, for it may be fo different from wifer mens judgments, as I will rather firſt offer it to their examination and confideration For if they have no deeper fetches here, than by their prefent proceedings it appears, there can be no wife man that beholdeth it, but fee manifeſtly they run headlong to their own deſtruction, and overthrow of religion, liberties and all. The reafons I refer you to Mr. Beale's letter; but if there were no more but thefe two, they be fufficient; the firſt is, to reject or neglect the aid of fuch a Prince as her Majefty is, before they had made all the proffers in the world, to have won, and perfuaded her to have compaffion on them, as loft people without her, as they will be certainly, without God's miracle. The other is, the fmall care they have of their conjoined friends and united confederates, as Utrecht, Guelders, Overyffel, and Brabant, with whom they mean to deal moſt hardly and ſtraitly withal, and even to make them defperate, feeing it likely that her Majefty will leave the caufe. So that your Lordſhip may hereby perceive the eſtate prefently, which at more large particularly you ſhall know by Sir Richard Bingham, whom I mean to fend forthwith over, who is a wife and worthy gentleman, and a man of great judgment. And for the alterations here, you may fee the caufe, being taken only upon the motion of a godly and good matter, to drive honeſt men to defpair, and to take themfelves the full fway of their own will, to bring what they will to pafs. That the people, and well difpofed, are choaked by their perfuafions, and difcouraged, as they dare not ſhow to her Majefty that, they would gladly have caufe to do, nor to me, her Miniſter, fearing my ability, as indeed they have caufe to do.

                                                    :   Therefore,

E L I Z A-
B E T H.
1587.

Therefore, my Lord, touching this flate, there is but one of these ways, either for her Majefty to concur with thefe mens new plot of government, and yield them her wonted affiftance withal, or to withdraw her forces, and break utterly off with them, upon their unthankful and bad dealings with her, befide the altering their government without her knowledge, and ufing her Lieutenant as they have done; or elfe to qualify her late motion of the peace, if with her honour fhe may do it, and to fend an Ambaffador to perfuade the people here, by promife of her favour, and countenance of her longer fupport, if they be able, upon further conference with them, to fhow to her Majefty that they be able to hold out the war with fufficient contributions; which, if her Majefty fhould find this way good, would alter all thefe confederacies here, as quite as if they had never been; and upon my life, have all thefe fellows changed that now rule, and do with them what fhe will. And it had been fo done by the people upon my firft arrival now, but that craftily they began, by times, to caft out the matter of peace, and the caufe of my coming to be for none other, and this they begun with before Sluys was loft; and they knew it would make a ftay at leaft among men, to fee what would become of her Majefty's dealing, and mine here in that matter, having good advertifement out of England to maintain their bruit, as I did write both to her Majefty and your Lordfhips. In which time, as they loft no time, fo fell it out, that this motion of peace was profecuted as you know from her Majefty, which hath greatly confirmed thefe men, and condemned me much with the people, fpecially of Holland and Zealand. Neverthelefs how careful I have been to difcharge my duty towards her Majefty, to ftay mens minds, and devotions every where, until her doings fhall give juft caufe to the contrary, I will refer me to all that ferve her Majefty here, and do not doubt but your Lordfhip, and the reft about her there, will have regard of this weighty caufe, to think what is like to be the fequel of it, if it quell, as it muft needs as the cafe

ftands,

ftands, and as thefe men proceed with it. For if it were poffible for, them to hold and maintain a war againft the enemy, without her Majefty; for my part I would fear the lefs any danger to her Majefty or the realm; but feeing it manifeft, that without her Majefty's aid, or fome fuch Prince, it is not poffible for them to ftand, no not any long time, I muft needs think that the King of Spain muft fhortly have them again, in the worft fort, and with greateft peril for her Majefty. The matter is fo far carried already, as there can be no long delays for her to ufe, for fuch remedy as fhe fhall think meet. I have been told to fet you down three ways, for my capacity can think of no other, and they be hard all; wherefore I will refer them, and any other to God, her Majefty, and your Lordfhip's prudent advices. For I muft fay it again, thefe countries once gone, you fhall never fee the like fecurity for England again. A few here, and a few elfewhere, hath brought all this ill to pafs. For my own part, if the lofs of my blood and life could advance her Majefty's fervice, it hath been, and fhall be to my laft hour ready. And as one of the three ways I fpeak of, is the way moft feared, of all the good fort; fo if her Majefty's courfe fhould light that way, which is utterly to leave them, all would then fall to prefent diffolution. And I am greatly deceived if thefe that would appear to be the only patriots, do not defire that way, before the other. Amongft other things of late, they have, in two or three principal matters, flatly broken the treaty; but of that, and divers other particular doings of theirs, you fhall underftand more by Sir Richard Bingham, who fhall not be long after this, and truft you will help myfelf to be one of the next after him; the fooner the better, for I have no means to continue me twenty days here. And I fee now no fervice for me to do, except her Majefty take the laft way, and it muft afk a prefent charge, as I have alfo fet down to the faid Sir Richard Bingham, which I can hardly think of but it were the only fure way, and moft honourable way, and the beft way to bring a good peace about, though not

fo

fo hafty, and fpeedy a way, as you are in hand with now; but it is ~~E L I Z A-~~
an old faying, the fureft way is always the neareft way. God fend ~~B E T H.~~
her Majefty, I befeech him, to take the fureft way, though it were ~~1587.~~
the longer and the farther way. And fo end, committing your
Lordfhip's health and long life to his fafe protection. At Utrecht,
going to-morrow to Dort, this 30th of October 1587.

Your Lordfhip's, &c.

R. LEICESTER.

Good my Lord bear with my fcriblings, for I am many waya
troubled, and impeached, even whilft I write.

Earl of Leicefter to the Lords of the Council.

My good Lords,

I AM forry that in refpect of my place amongft yourfelves, and   1587.
my hard fervice here, I can receive no more comfort, or be more   Nov. 6th.
regarded than I find hitherto I am. But I am far more grieved to
fee thefe weighty caufes that toucheth not only the well or ill doing
of thefe countries committed to my charge, but that fo deeply concern her Majefty, and the whole realm of England, to be fo paffed
over as they be. As for my own perfon, I know it worth not much
confideration, the more fault on thofe that have made no better
choice; but to lay fo great a charge upon a man fo little cared for, is
not well. For it is hardly feen, that fuch a charge fhould go without better countenance, or more credit than I have received, to further this fervice withal. I truft I have not failed to make known,
both to her Majefty and fome of your Lordfhips, from time to
time, the ftate of thefe countries, and of my charge; but how feldom
I have received either her pleafure or direction, I know beft, that
have fo often craved it. Only for the motion of peace, which as

foon

soon as I had her Majesty's commandment, I did propound it to the States, and yet was greatly blamed that I had not done it sooner, though without so good warrant as I take it. Yet what care I had to do it, according to such instructions as I had, that might be most to her Majesty's honour, and the safety of the cause here, I refer me to my general declarations, as well to her Majesty's self, as to others, and specially Mr. Beale, who was privy, and acquainted with the whole; but what effect hath followed the alteration of that course, and the want of supply of that, which I did humbly give my advice to her Majesty for, doth now appear; which was, to send over some man of credit, to have dealt with these men at large, and substantially, as well touching their ill dealing with her Majesty, as to proceed with the motion for the treaty of peace, in such sort as might withal retain the hearts and good affections of the people toward her. I did not desire this, for that I was not both willing and ready to do it myself, or any other service her Majesty would command me, but I did truly set down unto her, how unfit I was of all others, to use that kind of service, being so greatly suspected, or rather detracted by the State's dealing as I was, wherein also they did her Majesty no little wrong, in the public reports they made; unto which I thought myself bound in duty to make answer, as I did; and did send it over to your Lordships by Atye. A thing which I am sure gave great satisfaction here to all the better sort, and no hindrance at all to that purpose which her Majesty intended, but very great furtherance, as I can well prove; albeit it was here given out, and brought from England, that her Majesty reproved it, saying, that I had absolute commandment to have broken the matter of treaty, upon my first arrival to the States, and did rest in great offence toward me therefore; which opinion yet remains, and is given out by such as would have my credit stand in suspence. But touching this matter, I have both declared to her Majesty by writing, what effect it hath taken, as also by Sir Richard Bingham, who hath been an ear and eye-witness of it. The

matter

matter I fear hath not bred more confusion among men here, than it will cause of great trouble ere long to her Majesty, and as also there. For as peace, no doubt, of itself, is a most happy and blessed gift of God to all people on the earth, so yet in these days, all circumstances considered, between such Princes, where so great differences are, specially for the church of God, and the consciences of men, it must be deeply weighed, whether, to defend the enemy by such a war, or be reconciled to him by a dangerous peace, be better. But chiefly to examine the likelihood of the peace thoroughly, before we be too far lulled with the name and hope of it, lest it bewitch us, and bring us to a dangerous and most senseless security. And that we may look very precisely into the charmers, both abroad and at home. For, most assuredly, there be great treasons and treacheries in hand, at this present. And as England hath been long, to her Majesty's great peril, infected with such, so do I greatly fear that they had never greater affinity with these abroad, than at this hour. I have not spared to write my opinion of some in these parts, nor to declare the presumptions I have gathered of some notable revolt here, not in the generality, but by the subtle practice and secret conjuration of a few, that are (no doubt) bought by the King, and they will sell their country. I have, heretofore, described the nature and condition of these men, they be covetous, they be without religion, and the chief of them strangers. They love not the good people of the country, and they know the people doth hate them. For the better confirmation of my conceit, they have made no officers nor magistrates these seven years, but the lewdest and worst disposed persons, both in religion and otherwise, that they can find out. They seek, all ways that may be, to deface all her Majesty's doings to the people, and to withdraw their good minds from her. They show open mislike and hate to our nation, that, with loss of their blood, and long serving them, hath made sufficient proof of their well deserving. Their small account they make of her Majesty's favour and aid to

them,

them, which would more flatly appear, but for fear of the people; and yet be they, affured that without it they cannot ftand; the little or no preparations, indeed, that they make to refift, or annoy the enemy; the appointing fuch to have the command of their men of war, that are wholly at their devotion, making the colour of it, as though it were done only by the Counts Maurice and Hol-lock, for private diflike of me, which I know they have no caufe at all at my hands to do fo; and alfo their keeping the payment of all foldiers to themfelves, and to be the more fure of them; the care-lefsnefs for the fuccour of Sluys, or providing any place befide to refift the enemy; the continual information I have from well-willers on the other fide, who affirm certainly, that there be of the States reconciled to the King, and hath offered all fervice to render the countries again, and to help to drive out the Englifh. Thefe be of the States of Holland, and fome of Zealand, I fpeak of, who do not only impeach all the reft that are well affected, by reafon of their credit and their numbers, being the greater, but do what they can to difcourage the reft of the provinces united with them: info-much as of late they have taken a refolute order, that all their con-tributions, which is two parts of three, fhall go only to the payment of their own garrifons, and defence of their own towns. They have made profit of this motion of peace, as I have told you, to difcredit her Majefty if they can, and to difgrace me with the people, that they may the better proceed in their devices and practices. For, in this mean while, is the enemy grown very mighty, both by land and water. He never yet had that ftrength by much. He hath all pre-parations ready, as well by water as land, to befiege or attempt any place. He is near 40,000 men for certain. The States prepare yet no refiftance; befide they have given it out, that all was for France, till now that they be ready to march. I have fent for as many men as are within my commandment, to furnifh Bergen-op-Zoom, a place very like they will feek, which will afk at the leaft 3000 men, to de-

fend

fend such a siege as the Prince will make; which if I can see so
furnished, as may probably be kept, we will defend it, otherwise I
will deliver it to the States, and save our people, and let them either
defend it or lose it. And I doubt not we shall have enough to do
to defend these other towns in her Majesty's charge, if the forces be
such as I hear, and any of the States traitors, as is to be greatly suf-
pected. For my part, since you have left me here all this while,
and all our English forces, which were almost 6000, besides the ordinary, revoked and discharged, I will leave my bones here also, if
there be any attempt made to this place; and do trust your Lordships
will consider, what importance it is of for her Majesty, as well for
her money, as to procure a treaty, and it must be as well defended
by sea, as by land, or else, if the country revolt, it will surely be put
in great hazard. For myself, I am at this present, and a good while
have been less regarded, and worse left than Sir John Norris was.
For I left him not only all the captains and officers, that were under
me, both noblemen and others, but 2000 English soldiers in the
States pay. I am not only left without those I brought, and those
in the States pay, but all officers discharged, and such able men as
are fit now, at such a time, to take charge, and give direction. I
have now staid Sir William Pelham, till I hear from your Lordships,
whom I had once discharged fully, and Sir William Reid had his
passport to go over, whom I yet stay also; not doubting but you will
all have that due care over these countries generally, and these places
of her Majesty's particularly, that shall be meet for so great and
faithful Counsellors to her Majesty, and to your country. For myself, it is no time now to complain, or to stand upon mine own
causes. I am here, as you have known, and may perceive by this
declaration, with small honour to her Majesty, and less credit to myself. I beseech you now weigh me, as a poor man in her service,
and as but a governor of Flushing or Brill. I would be sorry to be
lingering on this long, to receive now the dishonour of loss within

Z z 2 my

my charge, of any place of her Majefty's, as I muft think them in great danger. But whatfoever fhall go, my life fhall be loft withal. There be fome captains there, I would they were fent over in hafte, as Sir Roger Williams, Sir Har. Norris to the Brill, and his brother, whofe company is at Oftend. Thus I commend the ftate of this place fpecially to your Lordfhips, that there may be victual in readinefs prepared, for we muft not truft to thefe countries help now, and your navy with all fpeed, for therein will confift our chief furety. And fo I commit your Lordfhips all, to the fafe protection of the Almighty. In much hafte this 6th of November 1587.

Your Lordfhip's affured poor friend,

R. LEICESTER.

I will not fail to take the beft order I can devife for the defence of this ifle of Walckeren, and have fent to the States again, to fee their care. Sir William Pelham I fent to Bergen-op-Zoom, to give order there, and look for him this night again. I forgot to move your Lordfhips alfo, to have five or fix thoufand men in readinefs, neareft the coaft, for all events; and to keep Sir Richard Bingham ready, if need be, that he may return.

Sir

Sir Francis Walfingham to the Earl of Leicefter.

My very good Lord,

IN the midft of my diet I fell into a fever, and fince my recovery of the fever, I am troubled greatly with a defluction of an humour into one of mine eyes, which hath been the caufe why your Lordfhip hath not heard from me thefe many days. I hope your Lordfhip, confidering it groweth from the hand of God, will excufe me.

I doubt not but that your Lordfhip is thoroughly acquainted with our Court proceedings, fince the return of the Lord North, and my brother Beale. From him, and other your Lordfhip's honourable friends in Court, I know you are informed, how offenfively it is taken, that the matter of peace goeth flowly forward there. It is reported that both Mr. Herbert the Mafter of the Requefts, and Mr. Ortell, fhall prefently repair over, to deal effectually with the States, for the advancement of the faid peace. And it is alfo faid that our Commiffioners fhall put themfelves prefently in a readinefs to depart into thofe countries, to the end, that when the States have given their affents to yield to the treaty, there may be no time loft. There is the more hafte made in this matter, for that Andreas de Loo doth write, that the Duke of Parma thinketh he is but mocked and dallied withal; and that he doubteth greatly, that, if the Commiffioners fhall not be prefently fent over, the faid Duke will break off, and not proceed to the treaty, which we do believe here to be mofttrue; and will, by no means, be perfuaded that the King of Spain and the faid Duke do but dally with us; fo ftrong a conceit are we grown to have of both their fincerities, contrary to the opinion of all men of judgment, feeing the great preparations made both by fea and land.

Sir

Sir Edward Stafford hath advertifed hither, that the French King hath efpecially fent unto his agent in Spain, to learn there, whether the King of Spain meant foundly to proceed in this treaty of peace with the Queen, from whom he hath received undoubted anfwer, that the King doth it only to win time, and to abufe the Queen of England. This, notwithftanding that Mr. Stafford hath gotten it from one of good account about the King, is offenfively taken here; fo much do we miflike any thing that may hinder the faid treaty of peace.

Your Lordfhip hath done very well to caufe Monfieur Averley that came from Monfieur Segure to make report unto me only, of that he had to fay; for otherwife great inconveniences might have grown thereby, to the prejudice of the common caufe. I think he fhall return, without imparting the matter to any other.

Such news as I have received out of France, touching the King of Navarre*, and the Reifters camp†, I fend herewith unto your Lordfhip. And fo moft humbly take my leave.

From my houfe in London the 9th of October 1587.

Your Lordfhip's to command,

FRANCIS WALSINGHAM.

---

* The battle of Coutras was fought the 20th of October.
† The Reifters were overthrown by the Duke of Guife.

Sir

Sir Francis Walsingham to the Earl of Leicester.

My very good Lord,

ALTHOUGH it hath pleafed God to quit of my fever, yet is not my body reftored to that ftate of ftrength, as that either my hand or head can endure the ufe of my pen; and therefore I am humbly to pray your Lordfhip to excufe me, in that I write not with mine own hand. Touching the refolution taken, both for your Lordfhip's return, and the caufes of thofe countries, fince the arrival of Sir Richard Bingham, I can fay nothing. I pray God they may fall out to your Lordfhip's contentment, who hath received as hard meafure as ever nobleman, or any other meaner minifter, that hath at any time been employed in foreign fervice. I fear there is not care taken in the manner of your Lordfhip's revocation, both of her Majefty's honour, and your Lordfhip's, as appertaineth. But good my Lord, let nothing ftay you there (unlefs fome extraordinary caufe fall out, as your return may breed fuch a change there, as may en-endanger this eftate), for your continuance will but work you increafe of difhonour and difgrace. A letter from the Duke of Parma to her Majefty, hath bred in her fuch a dangerous fecurity, as all advertife-ments of perils and danger are neglected, and great expedition is ufed in difpatching of the Commiffioners, Sir James Crofts * being now appointed to fupply Sir John Herbert's place, unto which I fear that, if my ficknefs had not been the lot, I had been preferred, which would have drawn her Majefty's difpleafure upon me, being fully refolved, in no fort, to have accepted thereof, for that I would be loth to be employed in a fervice, that all men of judgment may fee apparently (in refpect of the handling of the matter) cannot but work her Majefty's ruin. I pray God, I, and others of my opinion, may prove in this falfe prophets.

* Comptroller of the Houfhold.

Scotland

Scotland is altogether neglected, from whence all our mifchief is like to come, where the employment of 2000 men by the enemy, with fome portion of treafure, may more annoy us, than 30,000 men landed in any part of this realm. No one thing more doth prognofticate an alteration of the eftate, than that a Prince of her Majefty's judgment, fhould neglect, in refpect of a little charges, the ftopping of fo dangerous a gap, as that is like to prove. What practices have this laft year been fet abroach in that realm, tending to the annoyance of this realm, your Lordfhip, by the enclofed extracts (which I pray you may be referved unto yourfelf) fhall perceive. Monfieur Junius, fent from the Duke Cafimir, is now returned with fome weak fatisfaction, fuch as I fear will breed no great contentment; for we have not fkill here, neither of timely, nor thorough doing. The manner of our cold and carelefs proceeding here, in this time of peril and danger, maketh me to take no comfort of my recovery of health, for that I fee apparently, unlefs it fhall pleafe God in mercy, and miraculoufly, to preferve us, we cannot long ftand. And fo, recommending your Lordfhip unto his protection, and wifhing your fpeedy return, I moft humbly take my leave. From my houfe in London the 12th of November 1587.

Your Lordfhip's to command,

FRANCIS WALSINGHAM.

Sir Richard Bingham doth acknowledge himfelf greatly bound unto your Lordfhip for your honourable account of him. For the which he leaveth nothing undone that may exprefs his thankfulnefs.

No. XXL.

No. XXI.

Letters from Sir Francis Walsingham to Sir Edward Stafford, Ambassador at the Court of France.

[These dispatches are given as specimens of the ordinary correspond-
ence of Secretary Walsingham with the Queen's Ministers
abroad. He was once deceived; and that was by the crafty
Charles IX. and his more crafty and profligate mother Catherine
of Medicis, in 1572. He thought them sincere with regard to the
Protestants. It made that impression on him, that he took care
never to be over-reached again. He delivered himself up entirely
to his business; was so frank as often to displease a Mistress, who,
with great qualities, was capricious and dilatory.—This collection
shews, what no other gives the least intimation of, that he was
sometimes left out of the secret, as in the previous negociation
with the Duke of Parma; and was on the point of resigning.—
His connection with Leicester is strongly marked in the letters
between them.]

Sir Francis Walsingham to Sir Edward Stafford.

SIR,

HER Majesty's pleasure is, you shall, at such time as may seem
best unto you, repair to the King, and, with some shew of
conceived unkindness, declare unto him, that she hath great cause to
find herself very much grieved; for that having most constantly embraced and entertained his friendship, and thereof, from time to time,
yielded manifest proofs and testimonies; namely, of late, that she
sent two ministers of her's, one after another, expresfly unto him,
to make offer unto him of neighbourly aid and assistance, upon the
accident that fell out of the outrage and revolt committed by the
Duke of Guise; he seemeth now to yield her a very unkind requital
thereof in divers things; among which her Majesty's pleasure is,

September
8th.

you fhould firft make mention of the Galeaffe*, which, being entered and won by her fubjects, with the lofs of their blood, and
divers of their lives, fhe cannot but think it a very.hard point, that
the ftrictnefs of law fhould fo far prevail againft good debts, and the
refpect of profeffed friendfhip and good neighbourhood, as that reftitution of the ordnance of the fame fhould be made unto the enemy,
becaufe the faid Galleaffe ran on ground within gun-fhot of Calais.
Adding thereunto alfo, the ftrange demeanour towards her, of his
fubjects of Newhaven, in the road whereof, one of the enemy's veffels of the number of their fleet, being affailed by one of her fhips,
the Lieutenant of the Town, as her Majefty is informed, making
himfelf in a manner a party againft her with the enemy, planted his
ordnance upon the fands, and difcharged the fame upon her faid
fhip. Furthermore, fhe would have you alfo take knowledge in
her name of a fpecial meffenger fent unto the Pope, to fue unto him
for a difpenfation with his oath taken for obfervation of the alliance and treaties that have been heretofore paffed between both
their progenitors; and to let him underftand, that if he have any fuch
meaning to break off the faid alliance with her, he fhall do honourably to make it in plain fort known to her.

Laftly, Her Majefty's pleafure is, you fhould, to the fame purpofe, acquaint him with the words printed in the Spanifh Ambaffador's oration, of his pretended renouncing of her alliance and amity,
wherein fhe conceiveth that he cannot, in honour and due regard of
her fatisfaction, but juftify himfelf to the world, by fome public
writing. This do I write by her Majefty's commandment, and yet
can I not but advife you, if you fee the delivery thereof unto the
King, in fuch fort as the fame is fet down, will do any harm, to ufe
your difcretion; for it is hard here to prefcribe what is fit to be done
there. It behoveth her Majefty greatly to continue amity with that
crown; and therefore it is not convenient that any breach fhould
grow between us upon light quarrels. This intended affembly† at

* A Spanifh man of war taken off Calais.   † Of the States.
                                                    Blois

Blois will difcover what is to be looked for from thence. If there
were true magnanimity in the French King, I fhould hope well; but when I look into his weaknefs, I rather defpair than hope.

Her Majefty findeth it ftrange, that you fhould make any doubt touching the matter of the pique and jealoufy between the Duke of Parma and the Spaniards, being that the continuance thereof cannot but advance her fervice; and therefore fhe would have you, by all means poffible, to nourifh the fame.

We hear, out of the Low Countries, that the faid Duke* is at Bruffels, and hath drawn all his forces up into Brabant, with a pur- pofe, as it is thought, to attempt fomewhat againft Bergen-op- zoom.

How things do ftand in Scotland, you fhall perceive by the in- clofed copy of a letter from Sir Robert Sidney.

For the Spanifh fleet, fince the news of their doubling the north ifle of Scotland, we have not certainly heard of their courfe, and yet do in reafon fuppofe, that they are, e'er this time, at home. Some report is given out, that they had loft a great number of their fhips towards the back fide of Ireland in the laft ftorm, and were returned home but forty fail; but we have no fufficient ground to give credit thereto. And fo I commit you to God. At St. James's, 8th Sep- tember, 1588.

Your's, &c.

Fra. Walsingham.

Sir

Sir Francis Walfingham to Sir Edward Stafford.

SIR,

I DO make this difpatch unto you, to let you underftand of fuch
advertifements as we have lately received out of Ireland; which
it is thought meet to fend unto you, to the end you may be able to
fatisfy fuch as fhall be defirous to know thereof, which cannot be
conftructed to be delivered of any cunning on our part, confidering
that they are the confeffions and teftimonies of our adverfaries themfelves, and therefore it hath been thought convenient to commit them
to the print *. For the particularities I refer you to the printed
book. We do look fhortly to hear from thence of other fhips to
fall into the like diftrefs, for the fouth-weft winds have blown fo
hard, as, in the judgment of our feamen, it hath not been poffible
for them to return into Spain. It is likewife meant, that within a
while, the fubftance of the whole proceedings of the Spanifh navy,
and ours, fhall be publifhed both in French and Italian †.

Touching that you writ to me in your laft letters, if you had
authority to put the French King in   you would hope to do
fome good: the Queen hath willed me to let you underftand, that
fhe marvelleth you fhould expect any fuch commiffion, confidering
that, in a matter tending fo much, to the benefit of her fervice, you
may, without further authority, do all good offices that occafion fhall
require.

Other matter we have nothing here meet for your knowledge, but
that, upon advertifement received, that the Duke of Parma hath
brought his forces about Bergen-op-zoom, and drawn the cannon
thither, intending to employ his whole power againft that place,
her Majefty meaning not to give over the honour fhe hath already

---

* This is republifhed in the Harleian Mifcellany.
† There were two accounts publifhed by authority, one called a letter to D. B. Mendoza,
the other faid to be tranflated from the Italian.

gotten,

gotten, hath given order for the fending thither of 1500 men from hence, of her own fubjects, and 500 Walloons of the ftrange churches, which, together with the ftrength that is already in the town, we hope fhall be able to hold the place, and to repulfe the Duke.

From the Court at St. James's, the 30th of September, 1588.

Your's, &c.

FRA. WALSINGHAM.

Sir Francis Walfingham to Sir Edward Stafford.

S I R,

October 19.

HER Majefty confidering how much it importeth the quietnefs and fafety of the Princes of this part of Chriftendom, to ufe advantage of the late victory it hath pleafed God to give unto her, in the conflict with the Spanifh navy, by keeping the King of Spain unable to redrefs and fet up the like forces to difquiet his neighbours withal; as fhe doth mean for her part to do that, which her means may ftretch unto, and occafions fhall require; fo finding, by experience in thefe laft preparations made by the faid King, that without fuch helps of victuals, munition, and other neceffaries, as he hath received out of other Princes' dominions, he had never been able to fet out the late army, and namely, without great relief of victuals, fpecially corn, out of divers parts of France; her High-nefs hath therefore willed me to direct you to move the French King, from her, and in her name, to make fuch a general reftraint, that no corn be tranfported out of any part of his dominions into Spain. Which as he may take a juft colour to do, for the furnifhing of his army now ready to march into Poictou *; fo do there not.

* Againft the Hugonots.

Want

want sufficient reasons to induce him to do it, as a matter beneficial
as well unto himself as to others, if he shall consider (as he hath
been often heretofore put in mind thereof by her Majesty's Ministers, though with little fruit), how those of the League, who have
so long disquieted his realm, and so often and insolently done disgrace to his own person, are maintained and supported in their
actions by the King of Spain's purse, and without him were not
able to subsist. And further, how now of late the Duke of Savoy
hath seized the Marquisate of Saluffes, which it is not to be thought
he would have attempted, without affurance of the King of Spain's
affiftance, in maintaining his said attempt, being no ways of himself
able to bear out such an action against a King of France. But if the
King shall not be moved by these reasons to yield unto the said restraint, tending as it doth, as well to his own good as to her Majesty's, she shall have cause to think that the King doth not make
that account of her friendship that he hath made show of, and as
she doth merit, considering the honourable and friendly offers she
made unto him, at such time as he was forced to retire out of Paris.
Which, as she hath already in part cause to think very evilly requit-
ed, in respect of the late speedy delivery of the King of Spain's
ordnance, taken in the Galleaffe at Calais, and the ship at Newhaven; so, if the King shall refuse her this request, being for the
common good, as well of them both as of all Chriftendom, she shall
have a plain proof that he doth neither respect her amity, nor weigh
his own eftate, and the affairs of Chriftendom, as appertaineth. And,
as a further matter of unkindnefs, it is thought meet that the King
should be let underftand, upon some apt occasion to be taken by you,
as of yourself, but not by direction, that her Majesty hath reason to
take it unkindly, that his Ambaffador here, hath had no direction to
congratulate the good succefs she hath had against the Spanish army,
as in the like cafes is accuftomed between Princes being in such terms
of amity, as the world taketh them to be.

Her

Her Majesty's further pleasure is, that you should inquire very carefully, by all such good means and instruments as you shall think meet, to learn how the King of Spain doth take the loss his army hath sustained, as well in the conflict, as otherwise by the hand of God; and whether he carry any disposition to take a revenge thereof, or by what means. As, on the other side, her Highness's meaning is, to use the benefit of the victory, by the employing of Sir John Norris, and Sir Francis Drake, in such sort as this bearer shall declare unto you.

For the matters of Scotland, Sir Robert Sidney is of late returned, with a very good answer from the King, who giveth great assurance to maintain good amity with her Majesty, and to stand constantly in the maintenance of the cause of the religion. The copies of the said King's letters omitted in the last dispatch, you shall receive herewith.

And so having nothing else for this time, I bid you heartily farewell. From the Court at St. James's, the 19th of October 1588.

Your's, &c.

FRA. WALSINGHAM.

SIR,

AFTER the signing of my other letter, I received advertisement from a friend of mine at St. John de Luce, that there is great scarcity of corn in Spain this year; and that their hope is to be relieved out of France, without the which, they are like to endure great extremity. If the King there shall not assent unto a restraint, it is meant, that such of our ships as lie upon the coast of Spain, shall impeach all those that they shall find laden with grain, or any other kind of victual, from repairing thither, of what nation soever they be.

It were good the King were let know so much by way of discourse. There is some information already made to those of the East Countries;

tries, that in cafe any of them fhall be found upon the feas laden·
with corn, munition, or other warlike-furniture, for Spain, they
fhall be held for good prize.

If it fhall pleafe God to blefs Sir John Norris and Sir Francis
Drake, in their enterprizes, I hope all Chriftendom fhall receive good
by it.   And fo, in hafte, I commit you to God.

\Your's, &c.

FRA. WALSINGHAM.

———————————

Sir Francis Walfingham to Sir Edward Stafford.

S I R,

THE return of this bearer giveth me occafion to acquaint
you with fuch things as have paffed of late in our affairs.
The Duke of Parma hath of late retired his fiege from Bergen-op-
zoom, finding the place fo well provided, and thofe within to make
fo good countenance, as he had no hope to win it without exceeding
lofs.   Himfelf is retired to Bruffels, and his forces partly into garrifon, and partly, as we hear, are fent into Spain, by direction from
the King, doubting of fome attempt to be made by her Majefty upon
Portugal.

To the end you may underftand how things are between Scotland
and us, I have fent you a copy of Mr. Afhby's letter, whereby you
fhall perceive what great proteftation the King maketh of both his
conftancy in religion, and fincerity in the amity of this crown.

I am informed that the French Ambaffador here hath received
order to ftay here, and that his wife returneth to him, and that he
is in hope that Villeroy fhall be reftored to the execution of his place,
which giveth us occafion to doubt, the Ambaffador being known to
be fo greatly affected to thofe of the League, and the Duke of Guife

3   enjoying

enjoying the favour of the court, that the King will refolve to run that courfe. But of thefe things we fhall hear more certainty from you. And in the mean time I bid you heartily farewel. From the Court at Greenwich, the 10th of November 1588.

Your's, &c.

FRA. WALSINGHAM.

Sir Francis Walfingham to Sir Edward Stafford.

SIR,

THE Ambaffador of France is greatly offended, that the King's Nov. 28. requeft for his repair into France is denied. To be plain with you, confidering in what terms France now ftandeth, and how the King feemeth to be affected towards her Majefty, I fee no reafon but that fhe might have affented thereunto. It is true, that your friends here, in refpect of the peril that they doubt might have befallen to yourfelf, have prevailed fo far (notwithftanding her Majefty did affent to his departure upon the firft motion), as he is ftaid, until there fhall come fome anfwer from you, touching the matter you have in charge to deliver unto the King about the faid Ambaffador. Her Majefty would have you ufe fome diligence in returning anfwer to thefe letters, for that the Ambaffador is marvellous importunate, and impatient, pretending that his utter undoing dependeth upon this ftay. I wifh, confidering how ill affected he ftandeth to this State, that fome better-minded man were fent hither to fupply his place; but I doubt greatly of any change, for that fuch as are employed in like charges, are fo ill paid, as every man is glad to be exempted from public charges.

Her Majefty is very careful to receive particular information of the proceeding in Spain, and therefore I pray you be earneft with

your

your friend, from whom you receive your chief advertisements from those parts, to deal effectually with his correspondent in Spain, to inform him frequently how things do pass, as well both in court, as also of the maritime preparations in that realm.

There came advertisement from Paris about ten days past, that the King of Spain was very sick, and without hope of recovery; but because it cometh not confirmed from you, we do not believe it here., It is hard to keep the death, or dangerous sickness, of a Prince, long secret, and therefore it cannot be, if it had been true, but that the French King's Agent would have advertised thereof; the death of the said King importing his Master so much as it doth. The Duke of Parma, since his repulse received at Bergen, attempt-eth nothing, nor meaneth to do, before the next Spring, unless it be by way of surprize. And so do I commit you to God. From my house at the Savoy, the 28th of November, 1588.

Your's, &c.

FRA. WALSINGHAM.

Sir Francis Walsingham to Sir Edward Stafford.

SIR,

THE principal cause of the dispatch of this bearer groweth of the use I know you have of his service there.

Her Majesty resteth very greatly contented with the King's friendly answer touching the restraint *; which if the same shall be duly performed, the King of Spain shall not be well able either to annoy us, or defend himself; for that realm hath already more people than they can well feed; and therefore, if he shall draw thi-ther foreign forces, without the which that kingdom will not be well

* Of Corn.

defended,

defended, he fhall more annoy his fubjects there by famine, than the enemy by force.

It is greatly marvelled here, that the King doth put up fo quietly the wrong done unto him by the Duke of Savoy. It is an unequal match when the Duke proceedeth with the cannon, and the King only with the ufe of meffengers. If he take not a more refolute and princely courfe in government (and that fhortly), his kingdom will be cantoned in his own days.

There was never a more apt occafion offered unto him to have been revenged of the heads of the League, than in the prefent affembly of the States, to have laid before them the miferable and dangerous ftate that France is caft into, through their ambitious pretexts and defigns, under the vizor of religion: and although perhaps there be many of the prefent affembly there, that ftand affected toward them, yet no doubt of it, the generality, through the natural affection they bear to the prefervation of their country, would eafily be drawn to take revenge, if they might find in the King a princely refolution to go through with the matter.

The prefent difeafes of France will not be cured with that temporizing courfe that he now holdeth. For while he feeketh to recover a few towns, that are in the hands of thofe of the League, he will hazard his whole kingdom. But I fear there hangeth a fatal deftiny over that realm, which will not be avoided.

The conferring the government of   upon Nemours doth breed a jealoufy, that the diflike between the Guifes and his partizans, and the King, is but a matter diffembled; for who, fay they, would give any countenance to that houfe, that is already grown to over great ftrength, and that in reafon ought to be difcountenanced, or rather utterly to be overthrown. And fo I recommend you to God. From the Court at Greenwich, 10th of December, 1588.

Your's, &c.

FRA. WALSINGHAM.

3 B 2   No. XXII.

No. XXII.

From a
Copy in the
poffeffion of
the Earl of
Hardwicke.

*Letter of Henry Cuffe, Secretary to Robert Earl of Effex,
to Mr. Secretary Cecil, declaring the Effect of the Inftructions framed by the Earl of Effex, and delivered to
the Ambaffador of the King of Scots, touching his title to
the Crown of England, which letter was written after
Cuffe's condemnation.*

[Had this curious confeffion of Cuffe's been known to that accurate
and intelligent compiler Dr. Birch, it would have been inferted
in his Memoirs of Antony Bacon. From that excellent collection,
we are as well acquainted with the Earl of Effex, and the Court
of Queen Elizabeth, as if we had lived in it. Happy would it be
for all Courts, if they reflected a little more on the figure they are
to make in hiftory. " Whatever may be faid of me, faid the 1ft
Duke of Ormond, I am refolved to lie well in the Chronicle."
Vide Carte, Vol. II.]

IT is now high time, that he, whom a public juftice hath condemned *, and pronounced the child of wrath, fhould, with the
fooneft, lay afide all cares of this life, referving himfelf only for that,
which the only author of life hath honoured with this teftimony, that
unum eft neceffarium.

For the better attending whereof, and avoiding all future diftrac-
tions, I have refolved, of your Honour's commandment, to perform
this laft duty, by writing what of late I have often wifhed to have
tendered to your Honour by word of mouth.

* He was condemned the 5th of March 1600-1, and hanged at Tyburn on the 13th of that
month, being then about forty years of age.

At

At the time of my laft examination in this houfe, it pleafed your
Honour to demand of me the fum of thofe inftructions, which my
late Lord and Mafter had made ready againft the coming of the Scottifh Ambaffadors, whom he daily expected. Being at that time wholly
poffeffed with exceeding grief, I could yield your Honour and the
the reft of their Lordfhips very fmall fatisfaction; in regard whereof
I have ever fince defired fome private accefs to your honour, but being utterly out of hope of fo great a favour, and being now called
on by Mr. Lieutenant to perform my promife made unto your Honour at the time of my condemnation, I have thought it neceffary to
prefent to you the effect of thofe inftructions, obferving, as far as my
memory will ferve me, the very words and method of the original
itfelf.

Inftructions for the Earl of Mar.

That the King his Mafter thought it neceffary to befeech her Majefty to declare the right to the fucceffion of this Crown; not becaufe
he obferved in her Majefty any want of princely favour and affection
towards him; but becaufe he hath found, by infallible proof, that
fome very gracious with her Majefty, being of extraordinary both
power and malice, will not fail one day (if God prevent it not) to
make their advantages of the uncertainty of fucceffion, not only to
the prejudice, but alfo to the evident hazard and almoft inevitable
ruin of the whole ifland. For proof of their power there needeth
no long difcourfe, all means, in all parties and quarters of the realm
being in a manner wholly in their hands.

In the Weft, Sir Walter Raleigh commanding the uttermoft province, where he may affift the Spaniards in their firft invafion, if
that courfe be held fitteft; being alfo Captain of the ifle of Jerfey,
there to harbour them upon any fit occafion.

In

In the Eaft, the Cinque Ports, which are the keys of this realm, are in the hands of Cobham; and likewife Kent, the next and directeft way to the imperial city of this realm.

The treafure, the finews of the ftate, and the navy, the walls of the realm, being commanded by the Lord Treafurer [*] and the Lord Admiral, both thefe great Officers of State, and the reft abovenamed, being principally loved by the principal Secretary, Sir Robert Cecil, who, for the farther ftrengthening of himfelf, hath eftablifhed his own brother the Lord Burleigh in the government of the north parts; and in the Prefidentfhip of Wales, now void, will undoubtedly place fomebody, who fhall undoubtedly acknowledge it of him; as likewife in Ireland he hath accordingly procured for Sir George Carew that province, which, above all others, is fitteft for the Spanifh defign, in whofe hands, if the commander himfelf may be believed, there is a greater army than he needeth. To omit, that the faid Sir George Carew is fhortly in expectation to fucceed in the government of that whole kingdom, upon the recalling of the now Lord Montjoy.

That their malice towards the King was no lefs than their power, it appeareth,

Firft, That fome of them had given direct proof of their ill affection by ill offices: and this point was left to the Ambaffadors, becaufe the Earl of Effex was informed, that the King was able to procure clear evidence thereof.

Secondly, Becaufe all their counfels and endeavours tended to the advancement of the Infanta of Spain to the fucceffion of this crown; which point was confirmed by nine arguments.

1. Their continual and exceffive commending of the Excellencies of the Infanta, and feeking, by all means, to breed both in her Majefty, and in all others, an extraordinary good opinion of her.

2. The earneft feeking to revive the treaty lately broken, notwithftanding it was interrupted by the Spaniard, not without fome difadvantage offered to the Crown.

* Lord Buckhurft.   † Munfter.

3. The

3. The speech of the principal Counsellor (and, as I remember, he said he meant it of your Honour) to an honourable Personage, that he knew there could no sound peace be made betwixt us and Spain; yet for the better compassing of some purposes, he could be willing to entertain the treaty again.

4. The slack and easy hand, that hath been lately carried towards the priests of the jesuitical faction, of all others the most pernicious; which can have no other interpretation, than that the Popish faction favouring the Infanta, which are as many as the Jesuits can prevail with, might depend on them, as on their chief protectors.

5. The speech of the Lord Treasurer, who upon news that the Archduke was hurt, and, as some thought, slain, in the last year's battle at Newport, answered, that if he were slain, he thought her Majesty had lost one of her best friends.

7. The alteration of their proceeding with Alabaster and one Rolston, who have ever found more favour since they professed themselves of the Spanish faction.

Two more reasons were there, which I cannot now call to mind.

Whether, among so many other matters of importance wherewith he lately acquainted your Honour, and the rest of their Lordships, any of these reasons and instructions were by him remembered, I know not; only, because your Honour and their Lordships did, at that time, earnestly press me to deliver some of them, I have endeavoured to give your Honour the best satisfaction I could, being verily persuaded, that this abstract, in sense, very little differs from the first draught.

Of my own particular, being no less destitute of hope than comfort in this world, I dare say nothing; only I beseech your Honour, let it not be thought presumption to add thus much in general, that if the King of Kings thought it fit for his glory, where he found least merit, to extend his greatest grace, your Honour will account it no small resemblance of that divine pattern, if his Royal Lieutenants

5   • and

ELIZA-
BETH.
1600-1.

and their Minifters upon earth, having laid proftrate humble offenders at the feet of juftice, fhall be content to furrender up the fword of juftice into the hands of mercy.

Thus, moft humbly befeeching your Honour, to vouchfafe me your favourable opinion at my laft farewell out of this miferable world, I reft,

Your Honour's moft humble

and moft diftreffed fuppliant,

HENRY CUFFE.

No. XXIII.

No. XXIII.

Two letters of Sir Dudley Carleton (afterwrds Viscount From the Wharton Papers.
Dorchester), concerning Sir W. Raleigh's plot ; inclosed
in the following letter from Mr. Dudley Carleton, to
Philip Lord Wharton.

My noble Lord,

THE two letters inclosed are those, of which, when I told your Lordship, you shewed yourself very desirous to have sight, and therefore I have sent them to you. That Dudley Carleton, whose name you will find subscribed to them, was my uncle, who died Secretary to his late Majesty, who had likewise honoured him with the title of Viscount Dorchester; and I suppose you knew him. He was, at the time he wrote them, Secretary to my Lord of Northumberland's father, and both an ear and eye witness of most that passed in the arraignment and execution at Winchester, in *anno* 1603. I wish they may serve your Lordship to such use as you desire; and if I could give you any farther light, I should be most ready to serve you, as being

Your Lordship's, &c.

DUDLEY CARLETON.

London,
Feb. 14th, 1651.

Sir

Sir Dudley Carleton, to Mr. John Chamberlain.

S I R,

Nov. 27th.   I WAS taking care how to fend unto you, and little looked for fo good a means as your man, who came to me this morning; and though he would in all hafte be gone, I have ftayed him this night, to have time to difcourfe unto you thefe tragical proceed-ings.

I was not prefent at the firft or fecond arraignment, wherein Brooke, Markham, Brookefby, Copley, and the two Priefts were condemned, for practifing the furprize of the King's perfon, the taking of the Tower, the depofing of Counfellors, and proclaiming liberty of religion. They were all condemned upon their own con-feffions, which were fet down under their own hands, as declara-tions; and compiled with fuch labour and care, to make the matter they undertook feem very feafible, as if they had feared they fhould not fay enough to hang themfelves. Pirra was acquitted, being only drawn in by the Priefts as an affiftant, without knowing the pur-pofe; yet had he gone the fame way as the reft (as it is thought), fave for a word the Lord Cecil caft in the way as his caufe was in handling, that the King's glory confifted as much in freeing the in-nocent, as condemning the guilty.

The Commiffioners for this trial were, the Lord Chamberlain, Lord of Devon, Lord Henry Howard, Lord Cecil, Lord Wotton, the Vice Chamberlain, the two Chief Juftices, Juftice Gawdy, and and Warburton. Of the King's Council, none were employed in that, or the arraignment, but the Attorney *, Heale, and Philips; and in effect, none but the Attorney. Sir Walter Raleigh ferved for a whole act, and played all the parts himfelf. His caufe was dif-

* Coke.

joined

joined from the Priefts, as being a practice only between himfelf and
the Lord Cobham, to have brought in the Spaniard, to have raifed
rebellion in the realm, by faftening money upon difcontents, to
have fet up the Lady Arabella, and to have tied her to certain conditions; as to have a perpetual peace with Spain; not to have beftowed herfelf in marriage but at the direction of the Spaniard; and
to have granted liberty of religion. The evidence againft him, was
only Cobham's confeffion, which was judged fufficient to condemn
him; and a letter was produced, written by Cobham the day before,
by which he accufed Raleigh as the firft practifer of the treafon betwixt them; which ferved to turn againft him; though he fhewed, to
countervail this, a letter written by Cobham, and delivered to him
in the Tower, by which he was clearly acquitted. After fentence
given, his requeft was, to have his anfwers related to the King, and
pardon begged; of which, if there were no hope, then that Cobham might die firft. He anfwered with that temper, wit, learning,
courage and judgment, that fave that it went with the hazard of his
life, it was the happieft day that ever he fpent. And fo well he
fhifted all advantages that were taken againft him, that were not
fama malum gravius quam res, and an ill-name half hanged, in the
opinion of all men, he had been acquitted.

The two firft that brought the news to the King, were Roger
Afhton and a Scotchman; whereof one affirmed, that never any man
fpoke fo well in times paft, nor would do in the world to come; and
the other faid, that whereas when he faw him firft, he was fo led
with the common hatred, that he would have gone a hundred miles
to have feen him hanged, he would, ere he parted, have gone a thoufand to have faved his life. In one word, never was man fo hated,
and fo popular, in fo fhort a time. It was thought the Lords fhould
have been arraigned on Tuefday laft, but they were put off till Friday and Saturday; and had their trials apart before the Lord Chancellor * (as Lord Steward for both thofe days), eleven Earls, nineteen

* Ellefmere.

3 C 2

Barons.

JAMES I. Barons. The Duke *, the Earl of Marr, and many Scottish Lords
1603. stood as spectators; and of our Ladies, the greatest part, as the Lady
Nottingham, the Lady Suffolk, and the Lady Arabella, who heard
herself much spoken of these days. But, the arraignment before,
she was more particularly remembered, as by Sir Walter Raleigh,
for a woman, with whom he had no acquaintance, and one, whom,
of all that he ever saw, he never liked; and by Serjeant Hale, as one
that had no more right to the Crown than himself; and for any
claim that he had to it, he utterly disavowed it. Cobham led the
way on Friday, and made such a fasting day's piece of work of it,
that he discredited the place to which he was called; never was seen
so poor and abject a spirit. He heard his indictment with much
fear and trembling, and would sometimes interrupt it, by forswearing
what he thought to be wrongly inserted; so as, by his fashion, it was
known ere he spake, what he would confess or deny. In his first
answer, he said, he had changed his mind since he came to the bar;
for whereas he came with an intention to have made his confession,
without denying any thing, now seeing many things inserted in this
indictment with which he could not be charged, being not able in
one word to make distinction of many parts, he must plead to all
not guilty. For any thing that belonged to the Lady Arabella, he denied the whole accusation; only said, she had sought his friendship,
and his brother Brooke had sought her's. For the other purposes, he
said, he had hammered in his brains some such imaginations; but
never had purpose to bring them to effect. Upon Raleigh, he ex-
claimed as one who had stirred him up to discontent, and thereby
overthrown his fortunes. Against him he said, that he had once propounded to him a means for the Spaniard to invade England, which
was, to bring down an army to the Groyne, under pretence to send
them into the Low Countries, and land them at Milford Haven:

* Of Lenox, then the only one of that degree.

                                                              that

that he had made himſelf a penſioner to Spain for 1500 crowns by the year, to give-intelligence; and, for an earneſt of his diligence, had already related to the Count D'Aremberg, the particularities of what paſſed in the States audiences at Greenwich. His brother's confeſſion was read againſt him, wherein he accuſed him of a contract made with Aremberg for 500,000 crowns to beſtow amongſt diſcontents, whereof Raleigh was to have had 10,000, Grey as much, and Brooke 1000; the reſt, as they ſhould find fit men to beſtow it on. He excepted againſt his brother as an incompetent accuſer, baptizing him with the name of a viper; and laid to his charge (though far from the purpoſe) the getting of his wife's ſiſter with child; in which it is thought he did young Coppinger ſome wrong.

A letter was produced which he wrote to Aremberg for ſo much money; and Aremberg's anſwer, conſenting for the furniſhing of that ſum. He then flew to his former retreat, that in this likewiſe he had no ill meaning, and excuſed Aremberg as one that meant only thereby to further the peace. When particularities were farther urged, that, in his intended travel, he meant to have gone into the Low Countries to the Archduke; from thence into Savoy; ſo into Spain; then have returned by Jerſey; and there to have met Raleigh, and to have brought ſome money from the Well Spring, where it was to be had, he confeſſed imaginations, but no purpoſes; and ſtill laid the fault upon his own weakneſſes, in that he ſuffered himſelf to be miſled by Raleigh. Being aſked of his two letters to different purpoſes, the one excuſing, the other condemning Raleigh; he ſaid, the laſt was true, but the other was drawn from him by device in the Tower, by young Harvey the Lieutenant's ſon, whom Raleigh had corrupted, and carried intelligence betwixt them (for which he is there committed, and is likely to be arraigned at the King's Bench). Having thus accuſed all his friends, and ſo little excuſed himſelf, the Peers were not long in deliberation what to judge; and after ſentence of condemnation given, he begged a great while for life and

favour,

favour, alleging his confeſſion as a meritorious act. Grey, quite in another key, began with great aſſurances and alacrity; ſpake a long and eloquent ſpeech, firſt to the Lords, and then to the Judges, and laſtly to the King's Council; and told them well of their charges, and ſpake effectually for himſelf. He held them the whole day, from eight in the morning till eight at night, in ſubtle traverſes and ſcapes; but the evidence was too perſpicuous, both by Brooke's and Markham's confeſſions, that he was acquainted with the ſurprize*; yet the Lords were long ere they could all agree, and loth to come out with ſo hard cenſure againſt him. For though he had ſome heavy enemies, as his old antagoniſt, who was mute before his face, but ſpake within very unnobly againſt him; yet moſt of them ſtrove with themſelves, and would fain (as it ſeemed) have diſpenſed with their conſciences to have ſhewed him favour. At the pronouncing of the opinion of the Lords, and the demand whether he had any thing to ſay why ſentence of death ſhould not be given againſt him, theſe only were his words, "I have nothing to ſay;" there he pauſed long; "and yet a word of Tacitus comes in my " mind, *Non eadem omnibus decora:* the houſe of the Wiltons had " ſpent many lives in their Prince's ſervice, and Grey cannot beg his. " God ſend the King a long and proſperous reign, and to your " Lordſhips all honour."

After ſentence given, he only deſired to have one Travers †, a Divine, ſent for to come to him, if he might live two days. If he were to die before that, then he might have one Field, whom he thought to be near. There was great compaſſion had of this gallant young Lord; for ſo clear and fiery a ſpirit had not been ſeen by any that had been preſent at like trials. Yet the Lord Steward condemned his manner much, terming it Lucifer's pride, and preached much humiliation; and the Judges liked him as little, becauſe he

---

* Of the Court.   † A Puritan, the antagoniſt of Hooker

diſputed

disputed with them against their laws. We cannot yet judge what will become of him or the rest; for all are not like to go one way. Cobham is of the surest side, for he is thought least dangerous, and the Lord Cecil undertakes to be his friend. They say the priests shall lead the dance to-morrow; and Brooke next after; for he proves to be the knot that tied together the three conspiracies; the rest hang indifferent betwixt mercy and justice, wherein the King hath now subject to practise himself. The Lords are most of them returned to the court. The Lord Chancellor and Treasurer remain here till Tuesday, to shut up the term. My Lord goeth from hence to Petworth; but I pick quarrel to stay behind, to see an end of these matters. The Court is like to Christmas at Windsor; and many plays and shews are bespoken, to give entertainment to our Ambassadors.

The French King doth winter at Fountainbleau, and is fallen into a new delight of the Italian comedians, of which I send you a conceit put upon Monsieur Rosny. The Queen is there made *Chef du Conseil*, and grows very expert in dispatch of affairs. The Marquis is quite retired from Court. Rosny and Soissons go up and down like two buckets; for they are not so reconciled, but as one comes to the court, the other is ever going away. They say we shall have here from thence, ere long, Mr. Zamet *; I know not to what other purpose, unless it be to teach us to make good sauce, and to show their variety of excellent men in all crafts. The Marquis de Luttin, Ambassador of the Duke of Savoy, is at Brussels, and so far on his way hitherwards. The Grand Chaoux is arrived at the French court, and will likewise come hither to congratulate with our King from the Turk. The Venetian Ambassadors had audience at court on Sunday last. They were brought from Southampton to Salisbury, by Mr. Allen Percy, with two of the King's coaches, and four pad horses, and were welcomed with the foulest day that came

---

* A French financier, gamester, and *bon vivant*. Henry IV. often eat with him.

this

this year; and at night (as they came late), found but feven beds prepared for feven fcore. The day they were had to their audience, there was an embargo of coaches before the court gate, to bring them thither; but as foon as they were arrived, every man departed with his own coaches, for fear of the like arreft; fo as the greateft part of them were forced to go home on foot, and fome of the beft fort to ftay till midnight, for the return of their coaches. The knavifh Frenchmen laugh at their diforders, and fay they are ferved like right Pantaloons; but they deferve to be better ftiled, for they are come in beft fhew and fafhion of any I faw yet; and do all things with as great magnificency. As to their Captain that wafted them over, they gave forty crowns; befides petty prefents; whereas the Spanifh Ambaffador gave Sir Robert Mansfield a leather jerkin, and the Count D' Aremberg, a Parmefan cheefe.

A fortnight fince, there was a petty Ambaffador at Court, from the State of Stade, who came when no man looked for him; and took the King as he found him, prefently after fermon, and in the open prefence fet upon him with a long Latin oration. The King made him no long anfwer; but gave the honour of entertaining him to Secretary Herbert *. The Agent of Geneva hath obtained a collection to be made in all the churches of England and Scotland, for the fpace of three months; his Mafters, in the mean time, have fairly fcaped another furprize on a Sunday as they were at fervice. The fiege of Bolduc is raifed, and the two Generals retired to Bruffels and the Hague. I fend you a letter I received from Mr. Winwood, of this Summer's fervice in thofe parts; wherein I think you will marvel, as well as I, that the States are grown fo curft hearted to give away Grave, becaufe they cannot take Bolduc. The Spanifh Ambaffador hath been with the King to expoftulate fome words he heard to be fpoken at thefe arraignments, in prejudice of his Mafter;

* Called fecond Secretary, but the bufinefs was engroffed by Cecil.

and

and to pleafe him, the Attorney took occafion to make an open apology. The laft week he feafted the French Ambaffador's * wife, with many of our ladies; and had mufic and dancing; at which the French Ambaffador and he were at half falling out, who fhould lead the dance. They all returned very ill fatisfied, for cheer or entertainment.

The French Ambaffador, at his laft audience, brought his companion D'Auval, to take his leave; who is gone for good and all. The King knighted him, and gave him a jewel of 150 crowns.

Our Ambaffador in France † (they fay) is bufy in making a new French grammar and dictionary. One Walton, a man of his, that has remained with him ever fince his going over, is turned Monk, and hath put himfelf into a cloifter at Compiegne.

Fitzherbert, whom he took into my place, is come over hither to feek a new fortune. Out of Ireland, here are come many captains and cafhiered officers, with their pockets full of brafs, and fue to have it made good filver; but the Lord Treafurer's fkill is not that of alchymy. The coffers are fo empty, that houfehold officers are unpaid, and the penfioners and guard are ready to mutiny. There was, a fortnight fince, near Salifbury, a defperate combat, betwixt Douglas the Mafter of the King's Horfe, and Lee, brother to the Avenor; who began their quarrel at Windfor. Douglas was left dead in the field, with three hurts, and was buried three days after in Salifbury church, with a kind of folemnity, at which the Duke, the Scottifh Lords, and all other Scot and Lot were prefent. Lee was hurt in four places; but lives, and is like to efcape. He is not much followed by the Scots, becaufe they hold there was fair play between them. The younger Douglas has his brother's place, which doth fomewhat help to appeafe the quarrel. Sir Thomas Germyn hath got the reverfion of Jerfey, after Sir John Painton.

---

* Mr de Beaumont, a punctilious character.   † Sir Thomas Parry.

Sir

Sir Philip Herbert and Sir James Hayes have got betwixt them a grant of Tranfport of Cloths, worth 10,000 l. at the leaft. I do call to mind a pretty fecret, that the Lady of Pembroke hath written to her fon Philip, and charged him, of all her bleffings, to employ his own credit, his friend's, and all he can do, for Raleigh's pardon; and though fhe does little good, yet fhe is to be commended for doing her beft, in fhewing *veteris veftigia flammæ*. And thus being come round where I began, it is time to leave you, defiring you to excufe me to my coufin Sir Rowland Litton, for not writing; and fo you well may, for you have enough for yourfelf and all my kindred and friends, to make you all weary. My brother Carleton and brother Williams are both here, and have left all well from whence they came; fave only the little gentlewoman in Northamptonfhire; who is fo woe-begone for lack of good company, that fhe thinks the plague in London would not have hurt her fo much, as melancholy in the country. I fupped this night with Sir Henry Fanfhaw, where you were kindly remembered. Sir Walter Cope is in this town, and Sir Hugh Befton likewife, who often afks for you as your friend, and therefore you are the more to lament that he is untimely come to a night-cap. Many marvel at his fudden breaking, but moft afcribe it to a thought he took at a word which Sir Walter Raleigh fpoke at his examinations; who afked if Sir Hugh Befton was not apprehended and tortured, becaufe he was always of his chiefeft council. I fhall never end, unlefs I abruptly bid you farewel.

From Winchefter, the 27th of November, 1603.

Your's, &c.

DUDLEY CARLETON.

The

The Same to the Same.

SIR,

I KNOW not when or how to fend to you; yet here happening. December an accident worth your knowledge, I cannot but put it in record, 11. whilft the memory of it is frefh; and for the reft, ftand to the venture.. But becaufe I have taken a time of good leifure, and it is likely this letter will take his leifure, ere it come at you; I may as well leap in where I left, when I wrote to you by your man, and proceed in an order by narration; fince this was a part of the fame play, and that other acts came betwixt, to make up a tragical comedy.

The two Priefts that led the way to the execution, were very bloodily handled; for they were both cut down alive; and Clarke, to whom more favour was intended, had the worfe luck; for he both ftrove to help himfelf, and fpake after he was cut down. They died boldly, both; and Watfon (as he would have it feem) willing; wifhing he had more lives to fpend, and one to lofe, for every man he had by his treachery drawn into this treafon. Clarke ftood fomewhat upon his juftification, and thought he had hard meafure; but imputed it to his function, and therefore thought his death meritorious, as a kind of martyrdom. Their quarters were fet on Winchefter gates, and their heads on the firft tower of the caftle. Brooke was beheaded in the Caftle-yard, on Monday laft; and to double his grief, had St. Croftes in his fight, from the fcaffold, which drove him firft to difcontent*. There was no greater affembly than I have feen at ordinary executions; nor no man of quality more than the Lord of Arundel and young Somerfet; only the Bifhop of Chichefter, who was fent from the Court two days before, to prepare him to his end, could not get loofe from him; but, by

---

* Miffing, I fuppofe, the Mafterfhip.

3 D 2   Brooke's

Brooke's earneſt entreaty was fain, to accompany him to the ſcaffold, and ſerve for his ghoſtly father. He died conſtantly (and, to
ſeeming, religiouſly); ſpake not much; but what he ſaid was
well and aſſured. He did ſomewhat extenuate his offences, both in
the treaſons, and the courſe of his life; naming theſe rather errors
than capital crimes; and his former faults, ſins; but not ſo heinous
as they were traduced; which he referred to the God of Truth
and time to diſcover; and ſo left it, as if ſomewhat lay yet hid,
which would one day appear for his juſtification. The Biſhop went
from him to the Lord Cobham; and, at the ſame time, the Biſhop of
Wincheſter was with Raleigh; both by expreſs order from the
King; as well to prepare them for their ends, as likewiſe to bring
them to liberal confeſſions, and by that means reconcile the contra-
dictions of the one's open accuſation, and the other's peremptory
denial. The Biſhop of Chicheſter had ſoon done what he came for,
finding in Cobham a willingneſs to die, and readineſs to die well;
with purpoſe at his death to affirm as much as he had ſaid againſt
Raleigh; but the other Biſhop had more to do with his charge;
for though, for his conſcience, he found him well ſettled, and reſolved to die a Chriſtian, and a good Proteſtant, for the point of
confeſſion, he found him ſo ſtrait-laced, that he would yield to no
part of Cobham's accuſation; only, the penſion, he ſaid, was once
mentioned, but never proceeded in. Grey, in the mean time, with
his miniſter Field, having had the like ſummons for death, ſpent his
time in great devotions; but with that careleſs regard of that, with
which he was threatened, that he was obſerved neither to eat or
ſleep the worſe, or be any ways diſtracted from his accuſtomed
faſhions. Markham was told he ſhould likewiſe die; but by ſecret
meſſage from ſome friends at Court, had ſtill ſuch hope given him,
that he would not believe the worſt news till the laſt day; and
though he could be content to talk with the preacher which was
aſſigned him, it was rather to paſs time, than for any good purpoſe;

for

for he was catholickly difpofed; to think of death no way difpofed.
Whilft thefe men were fo occupied at Winchefter, there was no fmall
doings about them at Court, for life or death; fome pufhing at the
wheel one way, fome another. The Lords of the Council joined in
opinion and advice to the King, now in the beginning of his reign,
to fhew as well examples of mercy as feverity, and to gain the title
of *Clemens*, as well as *Juftus*; but fome others, led by their private
fpleen and paffions, drew as hard the other way; and Patrick Gal-
loway, in his fermon on Tuefday, preached fo hotly againft remiff-
nefs and moderation of juftice, in the head of juftice, as if it were
one of the feven deadly fins. The King held himfelf upright, betwixt two waters; and firft, let the Lords know, that fince the law
had paffed upon the prifoners, and that they themfelves had been their
judges, it became not them to be petitioners for that, but rather to
prefs for execution of their own ordinances; and, to others, gave as
good reafons, to let them know, that he would go no whit, the fafter
for their driving; but would be led as his own judgment and affections would move him; but feemed rather to lean to this fide than
the other, by the care he took to have the law take his courfe, and
the execution hafted.

Warrants were figned, and fent to Sir Benjamin Tichborne, on
Wednefday laft at night, for, Markham, Grey, and Cobham; who in,
this order were to take their turns, as yefterday, being Friday, about
ten of the clock. A fouler day could hardly have been picked out,
or fitter for fuch a tragedy. Markham being brought to the fcaffold,
was much difmayed, and complained much of his hard hap, to be
deluded with hopes; and brought to that place unprepared. One
might fee in his face the very picture of forrow; but he feemed not
to want refolution; for a napkin being offered by a friend that ftood
by, to cover his face, he threw it away, faying, he could look upon
death without blufhing. He took leave of fome friends that ftood
near, and betook himfelf to his devotions, after his manner; and
                                                                      thofe

JAMES I.
1603.

thofe ended, prepared himfelf to the block. The Sheriff, in the mean time, was fecretly withdrawn by one John Gib, a Scotch Groom of the Bedchamber; whereupon the execution was ftayed, and Markham left upon the fcaffold to entertain his own thoughts, which, no doubt, were as melancholy as his countenance, fad and heavy. The Sheriff, at his return, told him, that fince he was fo ill prepared, he fhould yet have two hours refpite, fo led him from the fcaffold, without giving him any more comfort, and locked him into the great hall, to walk with Prince Arthur. The Lord Grey, whofe turn was next, was led to the fcaffold by a troop of the young courtiers, and was fupported on both fides by two of his beft friends; and coming in this equipage, had fuch gaiety and cheer in his countenance, that he feemed a dapper young bridegroom. At his firft coming on the fcaffold, he fell on his knees, and his preacher made a long prayer to the prefent purpofe, which he feconded himfelf with one of his own making, which, for the phrafe, was fomewhat affected, and fuited to his other fpeeches; but, for the fafhion, expreffed the fervency and zeal of a religious fpirit. In his confeffion, he faid, though God knew this fault of his was far from the greateft, yet he knew, and could but acknowledge his heart to be faulty; for which he afked pardon of the King; and thereupon entered into a long prayer for the King's good eftate, which held us in the rain more than half an hour; but being come to a full point, the Sheriff ftayed him, and faid he had received orders from the King, to change the order of the execution, and that the Lord Cobham was to go before him; whereupon he was likewife led to Prince Arthur's hall, and his going away feemed more ftrange unto him, than his coming thither; for he had no more hope given him, than of an hour's refpite; neither could any man yet dive into the myftery of this ftrange proceeding.

The Lord Cobham, who was now to play his part, and by his former actions promifed nothing but *matière pour rire*, did much

cozen

cozen the world; for he came to the scaffold with good assurance, and contempt of death. He said some short prayers after his Minister, and so outprayed the company that helped to pray with him, that a stander-by said, *he had a good mouth in a cry, but was nothing single.* Some few words he used, to express his sorrow for his offence to the King, and craved pardon of him and the world; for Sir Walter Raleigh, he took it, upon the hope of his soul's resurrection, that what he had said of him was true; and with those words would have taken a short farewel of the world, with that constancy and boldness, that we might see by him, it is an easier matter to die well than live well.

He was stayed by the Sheriff, and told, that there resteth yet somewhat else to be done; for that he was to be confronted with some other of the prisoners, but named none. So as Grey and Markham being brought back to the scaffold, as they then were, but nothing acquainted with what had passed, no more than the lookers-on with what should follow, looked strange one upon the other, like men beheaded, and met again in the other world. Now all the actors being together on the stage (as use is at the end of a play), the Sheriff made a short speech unto them, by way of the interrogatory of the heinousness of their offences, the justness of their trials, their lawful condemnation, and due execution there to be performed; to all which they assented; then, saith the Sheriff, see the mercy of your Prince, who of himself, hath sent hither a countermand, and given you your lives. There was then no need to beg a *plaudite* of the audience, for it was given with such hues and cries, that it went from the castle into the town, and there began afresh, as if there had been some such like accident. And this experience was made of the difference of examples of justice and mercy; that in this last, no man could cry loud enough, *God save the King;* and at the holding up of Brookes's head, when the executioner began the same cry, he was not seconded by the voice of any one man, but the Sheriff. You muſt think, if the ſpectators were ſo glad, the actors were not ſorry; for even thoſe that went beſt reſolved to death, were glad of life. Cobham vowed openly, if ever he proved traitor again, never ſo much as to beg his life; and Grey, that ſince he had his life, without begging, he would deſerve it. Markham returned with a merrier countenance than he came to the ſcaffold. Raleigh, you muſt think (who had a window opened that way), had hammers working in his head, to beat out the meaning of this ſtratagem. His turn was to come on Monday next; but the King has pardoned him with the reſt, and confined him with the two Lords to the Tower of London, there to remain during pleaſure. Markham, Brookſby, and Copley, are to be baniſhed the realm. This reſolution was taken by the King without man's help, and no man can rob him of the praiſe of yeſterday's action; for the Lords knew no other, but that execution was to go forward, till the very hour it ſhould be performed; and then, calling them before him, he told them, how much he had been troubled to reſolve in this buſineſs; for to execute Grey, who was a noble, young, ſpirited fellow, and ſave Cobham, who was as baſe and unworthy, were a manner of injuſtice. To ſave Grey, who was of a proud inſolent nature, and execute Cobham, who had ſhewed great tokens of humility and repentance, were as great a ſolecifm; and ſo went on with Plutarch's compariſons in the reſt, till travelling in contrarieties, but holding the concluſion in ſo indifferent balance, that the Lords knew not what to look for, till the end came out, *and therefore I have ſaved them all.* The miracle was as great there, as with us at Wincheſter, and it took like effect; for the applauſe that began about the King, went from thence into the preſence, and ſo round about the Court.

I ſend you a copy of the King's letter, which was privately written the Wedneſday night, and the meſſenger diſpatched the Thurſday about noon. But one thing had like to have marred the play; for the letter was cloſed, and delivered him unſigned; which the King

remembered

remembered himſelf, and called for him back again. And at Wincheſter, there was another croſs adventure; for John Gib could not
get ſo near the ſcaffold, that he could ſpeak to the Sheriff, but was
thruſt out amongſt the boys, and was fain to call out to Sir James
Hayes, or elſe Markham mig t have loſt his neck. There were
other by-paſſages, if I could readily call them to mind; but here is
enough already for *un petit mot de lettre*, and therefore I bid you
heartily farewel. From Saliſbury this 11th of December 1603*.

Your's, &c.

DUDLEY CARLETON.

* There are in the Saliſbury Collection,
ſeveral letters from theſe priſoners during
their confinement, which probably would
throw light on their reſpective caſes, if they
were publiſhed.

3 E

No. XXIV.

Mr. Chamberlain to Sir Dudley Carleton at Turin.

My very good Lord,

From the
Paper Office.
1614
March 15th.

I AM newly returned from Cambridge, whither I went some two days after I wrote you my laſt. The King made his entry there the 7th of this preſent, with as much ſolemnity and concourſe of gallants and great men, as the hard weather and extreme foul ways would permit. The Prince came along with him, but not the Queen, by reaſon (as it is ſaid) that ſhe was not invited; which error is rather imputed to their Chancellor, than to the ſcholars, that underſtand not theſe courſes. Another defect was, that there were no Ambaſſadors, which no doubt was upon the ſame reaſon; but the abſence of women may be the better excuſed for default of language, there being few or none preſent, but of the Howards, or that alliance; as the Counteſs of Arundel, with her ſiſter, the Lady Elizabeth Grey; the Counteſs of Suffolk, with her daughters of Saliſbury and Somerſet; the Lady Walden and Henry Howard's wife; which were all that I remember. The Lord Treaſurer kept there a very great port and magnificent table, with the expence of a thouſand pounds a day, as is ſaid; but that ſeems too large an allowance; but ſure his proviſions were very great, beſides plenty of preſents; and may be in ſome ſort eſtimated by his proportion of wine, whereof he ſpent twenty-ſix tun in five days. He lodged and kept his table at St. John's college; but his Lady and her retinue at Magdalen College, whereof his grandfather Audley was founder. The King and Prince lay at Trinity College, where the plays were repreſented; and the hall ſo well ordered for room, that above 2000 perſons were conveniently placed. The firſt night's entertainment was a comedy, and acted by St. John's men, the chief part conſiſting of a counterfeit Sir Edward Ratcliffe, a fooliſh tutor of phyſic; which proved

but

but a lean argument; and though it were larded with pretty shews
at the beginning and end, and with somewhat too broad speech
for such a presence, yet it was still dry. The second night was a
comedy of Clare Hall, with the help of two or three good actors
from other houses, wherein David Drummond in a hobby horse,
and Brakin the recorder of the town, under the name of Ignoramus,
a common lawyer, bare great parts. The thing was full of mirth
and variety, with many excellent actors (among whom the Lord
Compton's son, though least, was not worst), but more than half
marred with extreme length. The third night was an English
comedy, called Albumazar, of Trinity College's action and invention; but there was no great matter in it, more than one good
Clown's part. The last night was a Latin Pastoral of the same house,
excellently written, and as well acted, which gave great contentment, as well to the King, as to the rest. Now this being the state
of their plays, their acts and disputations fell out much after the
same manner; for the divinity act was performed reasonably well,
but not answerable to the expectation; the law and physic acts stark
naught; but the philosophy act made amends, and indeed was very
excellent; insomuch that the same day, the Bishop of Ely sent the
moderator, the answerer, the varier or prevaricator, and one of the
repliers, that were all of his house, twenty angels a piece. Now,
for orations and *confcios ad clerum*, I heard not many; but those I
did, were extraordinary; and the better, for that they were short.
The university orator, Netherfole, though he be a proper man, and
think well of himself, yet he is taxed for calling the Prince *Ja-
cobiffime Carole*; and some will needs add, that he called him *Jaco-
bule* too; which neither pleased the King nor any body else. But
sure the King was exceedingly pleased many times, both at the plays
and disputations; for I had the hap to be, for most part, within hearing; and often at his meals he would express as much. He visited
all the colleges save two or three, and commends them beyond

Oxford, yet I am not fo partial, but therein I muft crave pardon not to be of his opinion. Though I endured a great deal of penance by the way for this little pleafure, yet I would not have miffed it, for that I fee thereby the partiality of both fides; the Cambridge men pleafing and applauding themfelves in all, and the Oxford men as faft condemning and detracting all that was done; wherein yet I commended Corbet's modefty whilft he was there; who being ferioufly dealt withal by fome friends to fay what he thought, anfwered, that he had left his malice and judgment at home, and came thither only to commend.

Paul Tomfon the gold-clipper hath his pardon, and not only fo, but is abfolved *a pœna et culpa*, whereby he keeps his livings, and never came to trial; and I heard he had the face to appear in the town, whilft the King was there.

Sir Arthur Ingram is, in a fort, *defurranné*, for Sir Marmaduke Dorrell is appointed to keep the table, and difpatch the bufinefs of the cofferer, and he only to retain the name till Michaelmas, that the accompts may be made up, and in the mean time order taken, that he may be reimburfed of fuch monies as he hath lawfully laid out, or can challenge in this caufe.

Old Sir John Cutts is lately dead, and here is fuch a fpeech of the Lord Roffe, but there is no great credit given to it, becaufe it comes only out of the Low Countries. Your nephew Carleton is arrefted with the fmall-pox, which hindered his journey to Cambridge.

I had almoft forgotten, that almoft all the Courtiers went forth Mafters of Arts, at the King's being there; but few or no Doctors, fave only Younge, which was done by a mandate, being fon to Sir Peter, the King's fchool-mafter. The Vice Chancellor and univerfity were exceeding ftrict in that point, and refufed many importunities of great men, among whom was Mr. Secretary, that made great means for Mr. Weftfield; but it would not be; neither the King's intreaty for John Dun would prevail; yet they are threatened
with

with a mandate, which, if it come, it is like they will obey; but JAMES I.
they are refolved to give him fuch a blow withal, that he were better 1614.
be without it.   Indeed the Bifhop of Chichefter, Vice Chancellor,
hath been very ftiff, and carried himfelf very peremptory that way,
wherein he is not much to be blamed, being a matter of more confequence than at firft was imagined.   He did his part every way, as
well in moderating the Divinity Act, as in taking great pains in all
other things, and keeping exceeding great cheer.

I have here fent you the queftions in brief, for otherwife they
would bear too great a bulk.   And fo I commend you to the protection of the Almighty.   From London the 16th of March 1614.

Your Lordfhip's to command,

JOHN CHAMBERLAIN.

JAMES I.
1617.

No. XXV.

From a copy
taken by Mr.
Sawyer, edi-
tor of Win-
wood's Me-
mours.

The Earl of Buckingham to Mr. Secretary Winwood.

[Sir Walter Raleigh accufed King James of having difclofed the whole
defign of his voyage to Gundomar. How far the following letter confirms this charge, is left to the reader's judgment. Winwood, who was a great enemy to the Spanifh interest, must
have executed this commiffion with reluctance.]

S I R,

I HAVE acquainted his Majesty with your letter, and that which
came inclofed from Sir Henry Wotton, of whofe opinion his
Majesty is, touching the advertifement given therein, that this
difcovery is like to unite the Duke and the Venetian clofer together,
and bring on better conditions for a peace with Spain. His Majesty perceiveth by a letter he hath received from the Spanifh Ambaffador, that you have not been yet with him to acquaint him
with the order taken by his Majesty about Sir Walter Raleigh's
voyage; and therefore would have you go to him as foon as you can
poffible, to relate unto him particularly his Majesty's care of that
bufinefs, and the courfe he hath taken therein.   And fo I rest.

                                    Your very loving friend,

                                                BUCKINGHAM.

Lincoln,
March 28th, 1617.

No. XXVI.

Papers relative to the Spanish Match.

[The *Pro* and the *Con* about the Spanish Match, has been suffici- From the Harleian MSS. in the British Museum. ently difcuffed by the Hiftorians. The letters that now follow, will throw additional lights on that impolitic tranfaction, and on the characters of a doating Monarch, an unexperienced heir appa-rent, and a favourite, intoxicated not only by his power, but by the familiarity in which he lived with his Royal Mafters. It is fufficient to add, that the Spanifh Court at laft were fincere and earneft for the Match; that it was broke off, in no very handfome manner, by the Englifh Miniftry; and that it was abfurd in King James and his Council ever to expect, that the Spanifh Cabinet fhould engage in a war againft the other branch of their family, for the reftitution of the Palatinate. The expedient propofed by that Court, of educating a young Proteftant Prince in fo Catholic a Court, as that of Vienna, though recommended by the Earl of Briftol, was certainly impracticable. That Nobleman, though a man of honour and ability, was difappointed in his hopes of mak-ing his fortune at home by the marriage, and points very darkly at fome fecrets relative to it, in a defence prefented to King James after his return; the copy of which hereafter follows].

King James to the Prince, and Duke of Buckingham.

MY fweet Boys, and dear ventrous Knights, worthy to be put Feb. 26th. in a new Romanfo.

I thank you for your comfortable letters, but alas, think it not poffible, that ye can be many hours undifcovered, for your parting

was

was fo blown abroad that day ye came to Dover, as the French Ambaffador fent a man prefently thither, who found the ports ftopped; but yet I durft not truft to the bare ftopping of the ports, there being fo many blind creeks to pafs at, and therefore I fent Doncafter to the French King, with a fhort letter of my own hand, to fhow him that refpect, that I may acquaint him with my fon's paffing unknown through his country; and this I have I done, for fear that, upon the firft rumour of your paffing, he fhould take a pretext to ftop you: and therefore Baby Charles, ye fhall do well, how foon ye come to in Spain, to write a courteous excufe of your hafty paffage to the French King, and fend a gentleman with it, if by any means ye may fpare any. Vacandarie is come from Spain, but brings no news, fave that Sim Digby is fhortly to be here, with a lift of their names, that are to accompany your Miftrefs hither; only Briftol writes an earneft letter, to have more money allowed him for his charges at that folemnity, otherwife he fays, he cannot haften the confummation of the marriage; but that ye two can beft fatisfy him in, when ye are there. Your houfhold, Baby, have taken care to fave a good deal of your ordinary charges in your abfence. Kirke and Gabriel will carry Georges and Garters to you both with fpeed, but I dare fend no jewels of any value to either of you by land, for fear of robbers, but I will haften all your company and provifion to you by fea: Noblemen ye will have enow, and too many; Carlifle and Montjoy, already gone; Andover goes prefently; and Rocheford by land; Compton goes by fea, and I think Piercy, Arran, and Denbigh, go by land. I have fettled Sir Francis Crane for my Steenie's bufinefs, and I am this day to fpeak with Fotherby, and by my next, Steenie fhall have an account both of his bufinefs, and of Kitt's* preferment, and fupply in means; but Sir Francis Crane defires to know if my Baby will have him to haften the making of that fuit of tapeftry that he commanded him.

* Duke of Buckingham's brother.

                                                          I have

'I have written three confolatary letters already to Kate †, and received one fine letter from Kate; I have alfo written one to Sue ‡, but
your poor old Dad is lamer than ever he was, both of his right
knee and foot, and writes all this out of his naked bed; God Almighty blefs you both my fweet boys, and fend you a fafe, happy
return. But I muft command my Baby to haften Steenie home, how
focn ye can be affured of the time of your home-coming with your
miftrefs, for, without his prefence, things cannot be prepared here;
and fo God blefs you again and again.

JAMES R.

The Prince and Duke to King James.

Dear Dad and Goffip,

ON Friday laft we arrived here at 5 o'clock at night both in per- .March 10th;
fect health; the caufe which we advertife you of it no fooner
was, that we knew you would be glad to hear as well of the manner
of our reception, as of our arrival. Firft, we refolved to difcover
the woer, becaufe, upon the fpeedy opening of the ports, we found
pofts making fuch hafte after us, that we knew it would be difcovered within twelve hours after, and better we had the thanks of it,
than a poftilion. The next morning we fent for Gondemar, who
went prefently to the Condé of Olivares, and as fpeedily got me
your Dog Steenie, a private audience of the King; when I was to
return back to my lodging, the Condé of Olivares himfelf alone
would accompany me back again to falute the Prince in the King's
name. The next day we had a private vifit of the King, the Queen,
the Infanta, Don Carlos, and the Cardinal, in the fight of all the
world, and I may call it a private obligation hidden from no body;
for there was the Pope's Nuncio, the Emperor's Ambaffador, the
French, and all the ftreets filled with guards and other people: be-

† Wife to the Duke of Buckingham. ‡ Sifter to the Duke of Buckingham

3 F

fore

fore the King's coach went the beſt of the Nobility, after followed'.
all the Ladies of the Court: we fat in an inviſible coach, becauſe
nobody was ſuffered to take notice of it, though ſeen by all the
world: in this form they paſſed three times by us, but before we
could get away, the Condé of Olivares came into our coach and conveyed us home, where he told us the King longed and died for want
of a nearer ſight of our woer. Firſt, he took me in his coach to go
to the King; we found him walking in the ſtreets, with his cloak
thrown over his face, and a ſword and buckler by his ſide; he leaped
into the coach, and away he came to find the woer in another place
appointed, where there paſſed much kindneſs and compliment one to
another. You may judge by this, how ſenſible this King is of your
ſon's journey, and if we can either judge by outward ſhows, or general ſpeeches, we have reaſon to condemn your Ambaſſadors for rather
writing too ſparingly than too much. To conclude, we find the
Condé Olivares ſo overvaluing of our journey, that he is ſo full of
real courteſy, that we can do no leſs than beſeech your Majeſty to
write the kindeſt letter of thanks and acknowledgment you can unto
him: he ſaid no later to us than this morning, that if the Pope
would not give a diſpenſation for a wife, they would give the Infanta
to thy ſon's Baby, as his wench, and hath this day written to the
Cardinal Lodovicio, the Pope's nephew, that the King of England hath put ſuch an obligation upon this King, in ſending
his ſon hither, that he intreats him to make haſte of the diſpenſation, for he can deny nothing that is in his kingdom. We muſt
hold you thus much longer to tell you, the Pope's Nuncio works
as maliciouſly, and as actively as he can againſt us, but receives
ſuch rude anſwers, that we hope he will be ſoon weary on't: we
make this collection of that the Pope will be very loth to grant a
diſpenſation, which, if he will not do, then we would gladly have
your directions how far we may engage you in * the acknow-

---

* When Steenie writ this he was not in his right mind, as it would have been a breach of
all the laws againſt the Pope's power.

ledgment

ledgment of the Pope's special power, for we almost find, if you will be contented to acknowledge the Pope, chief head under Christ, that the match will be made without him.   So craving your blessing, we rest

Your Majesty's humble and obedient son and servant,

CHARLES.

Your humble slave and dog,

Madrid the 10th of   STEENIE.
    March 1623.

For the best of fathers and masters.

The Prince and Duke to King James.

Dear Dad and Gossip,

WE are now got into Spain, free from harm of falls, in as per-
    fect health as when we parted, and undiscovered by any Mon-
sieur.   We met Greslie a post beyond Bayonne, we saucily opened
your letters, and found nothing either in that or any other, which
we could understand without a cypher, that hath made us repent
our journey; but by the contrary, we find nothing but particulars
hastened, and your business so slowly advanced, that we think ourselves happy that we have begun it so soon ; for yet the temporal articles are not concluded, nor will not be, till the dispensation comes,
which may be God knows when, and when that time shall come,
they beg twenty days to conceal it, upon pretext of making preparations : this bearer's errand was answered by our journey thither,
yet we have thought it fit he should go forward to bring you certain
news of your boys, that craves your blessing, and rests

Your Majesty's humble and obedient son and servant,

CHARLES.

And your humble slave and dog,

STEENIE.

For the King.

3 F 2

King

King James to the Prince and Duke.

My fweet Boys,

GOD blefs you for the welcome cordial that Grifley brought me from you yefterday: The Spanifh Ambaffador, and Boifchotte, from the Archdutchefs, are now agreed with me, for the depofiting of Frankendale in the King of Spain and the Archdutchefs's hands, without any mention of my treating with the Emperor, for that cannot now be done with my honour, he having thrice broken all his promifes unto me: all the other conditions are very reafonable, but I hear a whifpering ftill, that the King of Spain would have a match between my grand-child and the Emperor's daughter; but if either that way, or any other, this bufinefs be brought to a good end, it muft now be done by the King of Spain's mediation betwixt the Emperor and me, whom he hath fo far wronged and neglected, whereas before I did mediate the Emperor and my fon-in-law. As to my Baby's own bufinefs, I find by Briftol's cyphered letter, two points like to be ftucken at, that ye muft labour to help by all the means ye can. The one is a long delay of finifhing the marriage; for that point, I doubt not but you will fpur it on faft enough, for though there is no other inconvenient in it, but the danger of your life, by the coming on of the heats, I think they have reafon there, if they love themfelves, to wifh you and yours rather to fucceed unto me, than my daughter and her children; but for this point, I know my fweet Goffip Steenie will fpur and gall them as faft as he did the poft horfes in France. The other point is, that they would, if not leffen, at leaft protract the terms for payment of the dowry; this were a bafe thing, and a breach of their promife made many years ago, which the Condé of Gondemar, I am fure, will bear witnefs unto me, and if your travel thither have not earned it, as they fay, God

fend

fend that ever it do me or you good. I hear they there would be at a general peace, and comprehend alfo the Low Countries; for my part, fo that the bufinefs of the Palatinate were at a good end, I wifh it were fo; but if the bufinefs of your match be once fully concluded, I would be glad, fweet Goffip, that ye feel their pulfes anent the thing ye know concerning Holland *, which will be fitteft for you to found, being my Admiral; but I am afhamed to tell you, by the way, how many prizes belonging to you, your knavifh and un- thankful fea captains have meddled with, and fhared amongft them- felves, which are not fo few as three or four, as John Coote informs me, but within few days ye fhall, with God's grace, have a good account of that bufinefs. In the mean time, I have fully fatisfied the French Ambaffador of my Baby's care to difcharge honeftly his promife unto him.. I fend this poft in hafte, for preparing and fa- cilitating the paffage from the coaft of Spain to the court thereof, for my Baby's fervants and baggage, my fhip being now ready to make fail, and yet will I write with her again within two or three days, with grace of God, this being the fixth letter I have written to you two, five to Kate, two to Sue, and one to my mother Steenie, and all with my own hand. And thus God blefs you both, my fweet boys, and grant you, after a fuccefsful journey, a happy and joyful return. to your dear Dad.

Newmarket, the
15th of March.

JAMES R.

* This muft have been fome hoftile act againft the Dutch. .

King James to the Prince and Duke.

My fweet Boys,

March 17.

I WRITE this now, my feventh letter, unto you, upon the 17th of March, fent in my fhip called the Adventure, to my two boys adventurers, whom God ever blefs. And now to begin with him, *a Jove principium*, I have fent you my Baby, two of your chaplains fitteft for this purpofe, Mawe and Wrenn, together, with all ftuff and ornaments fit for the fervice of God. I have fully inftructed them, fo as all their behaviour and fervice fhall, I hope, prove decent, and agreeable to the purity of the primitive church, and yet as near the Roman form as can lawfully be done, for it hath ever been my way to go with the church of Rome *ufque ad aras*. All the particularities hereof I remit to the relation of your before named chaplains. I fend you alfo your robes of the order, which ye muft not forget to wear upon St. George's day, and dine together in them, if they can come in time, which I pray God they may, for it will be a goodly fight for the Spaniards to fee my two boys dine in them: I fend you alfo the jewels as I promifed, fome of mine and fuch of yours, I mean both of you, as are worthy the fending. For my Baby's prefenting his miftrefs, I fend him an old double crofs of Lorrain, not fo rich as ancient, and yet not contemptible for the value; a good looking-glafs, with my picture in it, to be hung at her girdle, which ye muft tell her ye have caufed it fo to be en-chanted by art magic, as whenfoever fhe fhall be pleafed to look in it, fhe fhall fee the faireft Lady that either her brother or your father's dominions can afford; ye fhall prefent her with two fair long diamonds, fet like an anchor, and a fair pendant diamond hanging at them; ye fhall give her a goodly rope of pearls; ye fhall give her a carquant or collar, thirteen great balls rubies, and thirteen knots

or

or conques of pearls, and ye fhall give her a head-dreffing of two
and twenty great pear pearls; and ye fhall give her three goodly
peak pendants diamonds, whereof the biggeft to be worn at a needle
on the midft of her forehead, and one in every ear; and for my
Baby's own wearing, ye have two good jewels of your own, your
round broach of diamonds, and your triangle diamond with the
great round pearl; and I fend you for your wearing, the three
brethren, that ye know full well, but newly fet, and the mirrour of
France, the fellow of the Portugal diamond, which I would wifh
you to wear alone in your hat, with a little black feather; ye have
alfo good diamond buttons of your own, to be fet to a doublet, or
jerkin. As for your I, it may ferve for a prefent to a Don. As for
thee, my fweet Goffip, I fend thee a fair table diamond, which I
would once have given thee before, if thou would have taken it,
for wearing in thy hat, or where thou pleafes; and if my Baby will
fpare thee the two long diamonds in form of an anchor, with the
pendant diamond, it were fit for an Admiral to wear, and he hath
enough better jewels for his miftrefs, though he's of thine own thy
good old jewel, thy three pindars diamonds, the picture-cafe I gave
Kate, and the great diamond chain I gave her, who would have
fent thee the leaft pin fhe had, if I had not ftaid her. If my Baby
will not fpare the anchor from his miftrefs, he may well lend thee
his round broach to wear, and yet he fhall have jewels to wear in
his hat, for three great days. And now for the form of my Baby's
prefenting of his jewels to his miftrefs, I leave that to himfelf, with
Steenie's advice, and my Lord of Briftol's; only I would not have
them prefented all at once, but at the more fundry times the better,
and I would have the rareft and richeft kept hindmoft. I have alfo
fent four other croffes, of meaner value, with a great pointed diamond in a ring, which will fave charges in prefents to Dons, according to their quality; but I will fend with the fleet, divers other

9   jewels.

jewels for prefents, for faving of charges, whereof we have too much need; for till my Baby's coming away, there will be no need of giving of prefents to any but to her. Thus you fee, how, as long as I want the fweet comfort of my boys converfation, I am forced, yea, and delight to converfe with them by long letters. God blefs you both, my fweet boys, and fend you, after a fuccefsful journey, a joyful and happy return in the arms of your dear Dad.

JAMES. R.

* From Newmarket, on St. Patrick's day, who, of old, was too well patronized in the country you are in.

The Prince and Duke to King James.

Dear Dad and Goffip,

THAT your Majefty may be the more particularly informed of all, we will obferve our former order, to begin ftill where we left, which was, we think, at the King's private vifit in the night. The next day, your Baby defired to kifs his hands privately in the palace, which was granted, and thus performed. Firft, the King would not fuffer him to come to his chamber, but met him at the ftair foot, then entered into the coach, and walked into his park. The greateft matter that paft between them, at that time, was compliments, and particular queftions of our journey, then, by force, he would needs convey him half-way home, in which doing, they were both almoft overthrown in brick pits. Two days after, we met with his Majefty again in his park, with his two brothers; they fpent

* There cannot be a ftronger proof of the trifling, goffiping turn of King James than this letter; and one is not furprifed, that, when his fon and his favourite returned home, they did what they pleafed.

their

their time in feeing his men kill partridges flying, and conies running, with a gun. Yefterday, being Sunday, your Baby went to a monaftery called St. Jeronimo's, to dinner, which ftands a little out of the town. After dinner came all the Counfellors in order, to welcome your Baby; then came the King himfelf, with all his nobility, and made their entry, with as great triumph as could be, where he forced your Baby to ride on his right hand, which he obferves always; this entry was made, juft as when the Kings of Caftile come firft to the crown: all prifoners fet at liberty, and no office nor matters of grace falls, but is put into your Baby's hands, to difpofe. We trouble your Majefty more particularly with thefe things of ceremony, that you may be better able to guide yourfelf towards this nobleman, who is fent of purpofe to advertife you of your fon's fafe arrival here, for fooner than he was received in the palace, they took no notice of his coming. We had almoft forgotten to tell you, that the firft thing they did at their arrival into the palace, was the vifiting of the Queen, where grew a quarrel between your Baby and Lady, for want of a falutation; but your dog's opinion is, that this is an artificial forced quarrel, to beget hereafter the greater kindnefs.

For our many and chief bufinefs, we find them by outward fhows, as defirous of it as ourfelves, yet are they hankering upon a converfion; for they fay, that there can be no firm friendfhip without union in religion, but put no queftion in beftowing their fifter, and we put the other quite out of queftion, becaufe neither our confcience nor the time ferves for it, and becaufe we will not implicitly rely upon them. For fear of delays (which we account the worft denial), we intend to fend, with all fpeed, Mihill Andros, to come to bring us certain word from Gage, how he finds our bufinefs profper there, according to which we will guide ourfelves. Yet ever refolving to guide ourfelves by your directions; fo craving your bleffing we end.

Your Majefty's humble and obedient fon and fervant,

CHARLES.

3 G

I be-

* *I befeech your Majefty advife as little with your Council in thefe bufineffes as you can.* I hope in writing jointly as we do, we pleafe you beft, for I affure your Majefty, it is not for faving pains. This King did intreat me to fend your Majefty a great recautho, in his name (which is a compliment), for which, in my poor opinion, it will not be amifs for your Majefty to write him a letter of thanks, for all the favours he has done me fince I came hither, with that of the Condé of Olivares.

CHARLES.

Madrid,
the 17th of March 1623.

Your Majefty's humble flave and dog,

STEENIE.

Duke of Buckingham to King James.

Dear Dad and Goffip,

THE chiefeft advertifement of all we omitted in our other letter, which was to let you know how we like your daughter, his wife, and my lady miftrefs: without flattery, I think there is not a fweeter creature in the world. Baby Charles himfelf is fo touched at the heart, that he confeffes all he ever yet faw, is nothing to her, and fwears, that if he want her, there fhall be blows. I fhall lofe no time in haftening their conjunction, in which I fhall pleafe him, her, you, and myfelf moft of all, in thereby getting liberty to make the fpeedier hafte to lay myfelf at your feet; for never none longed more to be in the arms of his Miftrefs. So craving your bleffing I end.

Your humble flave and dog,

STEENIE.

* This is in the Prince's own hand, and fo is the date.

I have

I have inclosed two or three letters of the Condé of Olivares, to JAMES I.
Gondemar, whereby you will judge of his kind carefulness of your 1623.
son.

For the best of Masters.

King James to the Prince and Duke.

My sweet Boys,

GOD bless you both, and reward you for the comfortable news March 25.
I received from you yesterday (which was my coronation
day), in place of a tilting; and God bless thee, my sweet Gossip, for
thy little letter all full of comfort. I have written a letter to the
Condé d'Olivares, as both of you desired me, as full of thanks and
kindness as can be devised, and indeed he well deserves; but in the
end of your letter, ye put in a cooling card, anent the Nuncio's
averseness to this business, and that thereby ye collect, that the Pope
will likewise be averse; but first ye must remember, that in Spain
they never put doubt of the granting of the dispensation; that themselves did set down the spiritual conditions, which I fully agreed unto, and by them were they sent to Rome, and the Consulto there concluded, that the Pope might, nay ought, for the weal of Christendom, grant a dispensation upon these conditions; these things may
justly be laid before them; but I know not what ye mean by my
acknowledging the Pope's spiritual supremacy. I am sure ye would
not have me renounce my religion for all the world; but all that I
can guess at your meaning is, that it may be ye have an allusion to
a passage in my book against Bellarmine, where I offer, if the Pope
would quit his godhead, and usurping over Kings, to acknowledge
him for the Chief Bishop, to which all appeals of churchmen ought

JAMES I.
1623.

to lie *en dernier refort* *; the very words I fend you here inclofed, and that is the fartheft that my confcience will permit me to go upon this point; for I am not a Monfieur who can fhift his religion as eafily as he can fhift his fhirt, when he cometh from tennis.

I have no more to fay in this, but God blefs you, my fweet Baby, and fend him good fortune in his wooing, to the comfort of his old father, who cannot be happy but in him. My fhip is ready to make fail, and only ftays for a fair wind, God fend it her; but I have, for the honour of England, curtailed the train that goes by fea, of a number of rafcals. And my fweet Steenie Goffip, I muft tell thee, that Kate was a little fick within thefe four or five days of a head-ach, and the next morning, after a little cafting, was well again. I hope it is a good fign, that I fhall fhortly be a goffip over again, for I muft be thy perpetual goffip; but the poor fool Kate, hath, by importunity, gotten leave of me, to fend thee both her rich chains; and this is now the eighth letter I have written to my two boys, and fix to Kate. God fend me ftill more and more comfortable news of you both, till I may have a joyful, comfortable, and happy meeting with you, and that my Baby may bring home a fair lady with him, as this is written upon our Lady-day.

JAMES, R.

* And for myfelf, if that were yet the queftion, I would with all my heart give my confent, that the Bifhop of Rome fhould have the firft feat. I being a weftern King, would go with the Patriarch of the Weft. And for his temporal principality over the Signiory of Rome, I do not quarrel it neither; let him, in God's name, be *primus epif-copus inter omnes epifcopos, et princeps epifcoporum,* fo it be no other-wife but as St. Peter was *princeps apoftolorum.*

The Prince and the Duke to King James.

Dear Dad and Goffip,

ACCORDING to our promife in our laft, we write to you this March 27. day again, for our poft is not yet parted, and that this may not altogether be empty, we think it not amifs to affure you, that neither in fpiritual nor temporal things, there is any thing preft upon us more than is already agreed upon; fain would they, in this time of expecting the difpenfation, have treated upon the ends and effects of friendfhip, but we have avoided it with fo many forcible arguments, that they now reft fatisfied. They were likewife in hope of a converfion of us both, but now excufes are more ftudied than reafons for it, though they fay their loves fhall ever make them wifh it. To conclude; we never faw the bufinefs in a better way than now it is. Therefore we humbly befeech you, lofe no time in hafting the fhips, that we may make the more hafte to beg that perfonally, which now we do by letter; your bleffing.

Your Majefty's humble and obedient fon and fervant,

CHARLES.

Madrid, the 27th of March 1623;

Your Majefty's humble flave and dog,

STEENIE.

King James to the Prince and Duke.

My fweet Boys;

GOD ever blefs, and thank you for your laft fo comfortable let- April 10. ters; it is an eafe to my heart now that I am fure you have received fome of my letters. As for the fleet, that fhould, with

God's

God's grace, bring my Baby home; they are in far greater readi-nefs than you could have believed, for they will be ready to make fail before the firft of May, if need were; and the fmalleft of fix, befides the two that go for Steenie, are between five and fix hun-dred tons, their names and burden, Dick Grame fhall bring you, who is to follow two days hence; it is therefore now your promife to advertife by the next poft, how foon ye would have them to make fail, for the charge and trouble will be infinite, if their equi-page ftay long aboard, confuming victuals, and making the fhips to ftink. My Goffip fhall come home in the George, and the Ante-lope wait upon him, and of their readinefs Dick Grame will bring you word. The Treafurer * likewife made that money ready, which my Baby defired: I muft bear him witnefs, he fpares not to engage himfelf, and all he is worth, for the bufinefs.

The 10th of April.

JAMES, R.

The Prince and Duke to King James.

Dear Dad and Goffip,

WE are forry that we are not able to continue the advertifement of the difpenfation's arrival: it is certainly granted, and is as certainly upon the way hither, and although clogged with fome new condition, yet fuch as we hope with eafe to remove. They are thefe: two years more to the education of the children; no other oath to be miniftered to the Roman catholic fubjects, than that which is given to the Infanta's fervants, and that they may all have free accefs to her church. We hope in granting the firft, yet mak-

* Cranfield Earl of Middlefex.

6

ing

ing it hard, we shall not only facilitate the other two conditions, but, in a little time hereafter, bring more years back again with the two; to this we will both recommend secrecy here, and to you there. If we receive your directions in time to this, we will punctually follow them. To the second, our answer will be, the oath was made by act of parliament, and that you cannot abrogate it, without the whole consent of your people. In the last, we hope to let them see, as it will bring but a pester and an inconvenience to the Infanta herself, so it will less satisfy the Catholics, because it will make the act more public, and less useful to their ends, than to have the exercises of their consciences freely, in their own houses; for all meeting in one centre, the number will seem greater, and so make the State jealouser, and consequently make their security more uncertain, this being no less than in covered words, to ask liberty of conscience, which you have neither mind nor power to grant; many other reasons we have, and so powerful, that we make neither question to speed the business, nor to end it to your own liking; which sweet Jesus grant, and your blessing to

Your Majesty's humble and obedient son and servant.

CHARLES.

Madrid, the 22d of April 1623.

Your Majesty's humble slave and dog,

STEENIE.

The Prince and Duke to King James.

Dear Dad and Goffip,

April 27th. MIHILL Andros is now come back from Rome, but the Difpenfation got hither before him: that you may the better judge
of the conditions it is clogged with, we have fent you Gage's letters;
this comfort yourfelf with, that we will not be long before we get
forth of this labyrinth, wherein we have been entangled thefe many
years: we befeech your Majefty be fecret in the conditions, and
be affured we will yield to nothing, but what you may perform, both
with your honour and confcience: if you fhould not keep them
fo, it will beget difpute, cenfures, and conclufions there to our prejudice. The chief end of fending this poft is to tell you, that the
Groyne is refolved on, to be the fitteft port for your fhips, and us
here; wherefore we pray your Majefty to make no delay, but to fend
them with all fpeed thither. Sir, I Steenie am commanded by my
wife, to trouble you with a deed of honour and charity, to have a
care of the widow, miftrefs Murrey, whom you promifed, in her hufband's time, to provide for, and her feven children. We have been
both much comforted with the return of Dick Grame, who hath
made to me your Dog in particular, fuch a relation of your Majefty's
conftant care and love of me, in my abfence, that now I fhall follow your fervice with a chearful heart, though not with a more truft-
ful nor affectionate one; for he hath told me your carriage hath been
fuch, that it hath calmed the mad malice of all my enemies, which
was no fmall grief to me to hear they were of fo great a number; and
for that honour *, which your Majefty tells me my Lord Treafurer
hath been an importunate fuitor for, though not a fecret one, give

* A Dukedom.

me

me leave, out of the pride of my heart to fay, whenfoever any thing proceeds otherwife than immediately from your own heart and affection, I fhall kifs it, and lay it down at your feet again, for hitherto you have accuftomed me to no other. Out of a certain report here, that you had done it, I fent Edward Clarke purpofely to intreat you to undo it, or to add one more for my fake; but now that it is undone, which I thank God heartily for, I befeech your Majefty humbly on my knees to let it remain fo, till I have the happinefs to fpeak with yourfelf, which is infinitely defired by your two boys that crave your bleffing.

P. S. By Prince Charles.

We fend this poft with fuch fpeed, that we have no time to write this better.

Your Majefty's humble and obedient
fon and fervant,

CHARLES.

Madrid,
the 27th of April, 1623.

Prince Charles to King James.

S I R,

I DO find, that if I have not fomewhat under your Majefty's hand to fhow, whereby that ye engage yourfelf to do whatfomever I fhall promife in your name, that it will retard the bufinefs a great while; wherefore I humbly befeech your Majefty to fend me a warrant to this effect: April 29th

We do hereby promife, by the word of a King, that whatfoever you our fon fhall promife in our name, we fhall punctually perform.

3 H

Sir,

Sir, I confefs that this is an ample truft that I defire, and if it were not mere neceffity, I fhould not be fo bold, yet I hope your Majefty fhall never repent you of any truft you put upon

Your Majefty's humble and obedient
fon and fervant,

Madrid,
the 29th of April, 1623.

CHARLES.

Duke of Buckingham to King James.

Dear Dad and Goffip,

April 29th. THIS letter of your fon's is written out of an extraordinary defire to be foon with you again; he thinks if you fign thus much, though they would be glad (which yet he doth not difcover) to make any farther delay, this will difappoint them: the difcretion of your Baby you need not doubt, and for the faith of myfelf, I fhall fooner lofe life, than in the leaft kind break it. And fo in hafte I crave your blefling *.

Your Majefty's moft humble
flave and dog,

Madrid,
the 29th of April, 1623.

STEENIE.

* There cannot be a ftronger proof of the reliance which the Prince and the favourite had on the King's weaknefs, than thefe two letters.

King James to the Prince and Duke.

My fweet Boys,

YESTERDAY in the afternoon I received two packets from you after my coming hither, by two feveral pofts, and the day before I wrote to you my opinion from Theobald's, anent the three conditions annexed to the difpenfation: I now fend you, my Baby, here inclofed, the power you defire. It were a ftrange truft that I would refufe to put upon my only fon, and upon my beft fervant. I know fuch two ye are, will never promife in my name, but what may ftand with my confcience, honour, and fafety, and all thefe I do fully truft with any one of you two: my former letter will fhow you my conceit, and now I put the full power in your hands, with God's bleffing on you both, praying him ftill, that after a happy fuccefs there, ye may fpeedily and happily return, and light in the arms of your dear Dad.

JAMES, R.

Greenwich,
the 11th of May, 1623.

The Prince and Duke to King James.

Dear Dad and Goffip,

THE Pope having written a courteous letter to me your Baby, I have been bold to write him an anfwer, without your Majefty's leave, the copy whereof is here inclofed: we make no doubt but to have the opinions of thefe bufily Divines reverfed (for already the Condé of Olivares hath put out ten of the worft), fo your Majefty will be pleafed to begin to put in execution the favour towards your

June 6th,

3 H 2

Roman

Roman Catholic fubjects, that ye will be bound to do by your oath, as foon as the Infanta comes over, which we hope you will do for the haftening of us home, with this proteftation to reverfe all, if there be any delay of the marriage. We fend you here the articles as they are to go, the oaths private and public, that you and your Baby are to take, with the Councils', wherein, if you fcare at the leaft claufe of your private oath (where you promife that the Parliament fhall re-voke all the penal laws againft the Papifts within three years) we fought good to tell your Majefty our opinions, which is, that if you think you may do it in that time (which we think you may), if you do your beft, although it take not effect, you have not broken your word, for this promife is only as a fecurity that you will do your beft. The Spanifh Ambaffador, for refpect of the Pope, will prefent unto you, the articles as they came from Rome; as likewife for to require, that the delivery of the Infanta may be deferred till the Spring. his commiffion is to prefs for this, but to be fatisfied with what we have yielded to here. We both humbly beg of your Majefty, that you will confirm thefe articles foon, and prefs earneftly for our fpeedy return. So craving your bleffings we reft,

> Your Majefty's humble and obedient
> fon and fervant,
>
> CHARLES.
>
> Your Majefty's moft humble
> flave and dog,
>
> STEENIE.

King James to the Prince and Duke.

My fweet Boys,

YOUR letter by Cottington, hath ftrucken me dead; I fear it June 14th.
fhall very much fhorten my days, and I am the more perplexed
that I know not how to fatisfy the people's expectation here, neither know I what to fay to our Council, for the fleet that ftaid upon
a wind this fortnight. Rutland, and all aboard muft now be ftaid,
and I know not what reafon I fhall pretend for the doing of it *, but
as for my advice and directions that ye crave, in cafe they will not
alter their decree, it is in a word, to come fpeedily away, and if
ye can get leave, and give over all treaty. And this I fpeak without
refpect of any fecurity they can offer you, except ye never look to fee
your old Dad again, whom I fear ye fhall never fee, if you fee
him not before Winter. Alas, I now repent me fore, that ever I
fuffered you to go away. I care for Match, nor nothing; fo I may
once have you in my arms again; God grant it, God grant it, God
grant it, amen, amen, amen. I proteft ye fhall be as heartily welcome, as if ye had done all things ye went for, fo that I may
once have you in my arms again, and God blefs you both, my
only fweet fon, and my only beft fweet fervant, and let me hear
from you quickly with all fpeed, as ye love my life; and fo God fend
you a happy and joyful meeting in the arms of your dear Dad.

JAMES, R.

From Greenwich, the 14th
of June, 1623.

* Here follow five lines blotted fo as not to be read.

Prince Charles and the Duke to King James.

Dear Dad and Goffip,

June 26.   THOUGH late, yet at laft, we have gotten the articles drawn up in form, which we fent you by the Lord Rochford, without any new addition or alteration. The foolery of the Condé of Olivares hath been caufe of this long delay, who would wilfully againft thee have pulled it out of the Junto's and Council's hands, and put it into a wrangling lawyer's, a favourite of his, who, like himfelf, had not only put it into an odious form, but had flipped in a multitude of new, unreafonable, undemanded, and ungranted conditions, which the Council yielded unto, merely out of fear; for when we met with the Junto, they did not make one anfwer to any of our objections, but confeffed, with bluſhing faces, we had more than reafon of our fides; and concluded with us, that the fame oath ſhould ferve, which paſſed between Queen Mary and King Philip, being put to the end of every article which is to be fworn to. By this you may a little guefs with what favour they proceed with us, firſt, delaying us as long as poffibly they can, then, when things are concluded of, they throw in new particulars, in hope they will pafs, out of our defire to make hafte; but when our bufinefs is done, we ſhall joy in it the more that we have overcome fo many difficulties; in the mean time we expect pity at your hands. But, for the love of God, and our bufinefs, let nothing fall from you to difcover any thing of this, and comfort yourfelf that all things will end well, to your contentment and honour. Our return now, will depend on your quick difpatch of thefe; for we thank God we find the heats fuch here, as we may very well travel both evenings and-mornings. The Divines have not yet recalled their fentence, but the Condé tells us, he hath converted very many of them, yet keeps his old form,

in

in giving us no hope of any thing, till the bufinefs fpeaks it itfelf. But we dare fay they dare not break it upon this, nor (we think) upon any other, except the affairs of Chriftendom fhould fmile ftrangely upon them, which will at all times, and in all cafes, guide them. So craving your bleffing we end.

SIR,

In the midft of our ferious bufinefs, little pretty Toby Matthews comes to intreat us to deliver this letter to your Majefty, which is, as he calls it, a picture of the Infanta's, drawn in black and white. We pray you let none laugh at it but yourfelf, and honeft Kate; he thinks he has hit the nail of the head, but you will find it the foolifheft thing that ever you faw.

Your Majefty's humble and obedient fon and fervant,

CHARLES.

Your Majefty's moft humble flave and dog,

STEENIE.

Madrid,
the 26th of June, 1623.

Prince Charles and the Duke to King James.

Dear Dad and Goffip,

OUR other letter was written before William Crofts came; he hath brought with him letters to our heart's defire; we have June 27. thus far made ufe of them already. This morning we fent for the Condé of Olivares, and, with a fad countenance, told him of your peremptory command, intreating him in the kindeft manner we could, to give us his advice how we might comply with this, and not deftroy the bufinefs. His anfwer was, that there was two good ways

2   ways.

ways to do the bufinefs, and one ill one; the two good ones was, either with your Baby's converfion, or to do it with truft, putting all things freely, with the Infanta, into our hands; the ill one was, to bargain, and ftick upon conditions as long as they could. As for the firft, we abfolutely rejected it, and for the fecond, he confeft, if he were King, he would do it, and, as he is, it lay in his power to do it; but he caft many doubts left he fhould hereafter fuffer for it, if it fhould not fucceed; the laft he confeft impoffible, fince your command was fo peremptory. To conclude, he left us with a promife to confider of it, and when I, your dog, conveyed him to the door, he bad me chear up my heart, and your Baby's both. Our opinion is, that the longeft time we can ftay here, will be a month, and not that neither, without bringing the Infanta with us. If we find not ourfelves affured of that, look for us fooner. Whether of thefe refolutions be taken, you fhall hear from us fhortly, that you may in time accordingly give order for the fleet. We muft once again intreat your Majefty to make all the hafte you can, to return thefe papers confirmed, and in the mean time to give order for the execution of all thefe things, and to let us here know fo much.

Sir, let the worft that can come, we make no doubt but to be with you before you end your progrefs; therefore we intreat you to take comfort, for in your health depends all our happinefs. So craving your blefling we end.

I your Majefty's Dog befeecheth you to tell Cottington that I love him, and I pray you to do the like, for he is an honeft man and deferves it, or elfe call me knave.

Your Majefty's humble and obedient fon and fervant,

CHARLES.

Your Majefty's moft humble flave and dog,

STEENIE.

Madrid,
the 27th of June, 1623.

Duke of Buckingham to Secretary Conway.

Dear Friend,

I PRAY you deliver this inclofed to his Majefty: it contains no June 29.
more than that on Wednefday at the fartheft, we fhall have our
laft anfwer. I hope it will be good; if it be not, we fhall be foon
with you, fo farewel.

Your affectionate friend and fervant,

Madrid,
the 29th of June, 1623. G. BUCKINGHAM.

Prince Charles and the Duke to King James.

Dear Dad and Goffip,

BY Killegrew's difpatch, you underftand how we intreated the June 29.
Condé of Olivares to give us his advice how we might comply with your peremptory command, and not deftroy that bufinefs
our hearts was fo much fet on; to give an anfwer to which he
required fome time. The next day, at night, we fent for him again,
and preffed him for his opinion and counfel; to which he anfwered,
on Monday the Divines fhould meet and give in their opinions, and
upon Tuefday or Wednefday at the fartheft, his Majefty fhould fend
us his laft and final anfwer; but perceiving that we all looked fadly,
and was at a refolution to return fpeedily upon it, if it were not to
your Majefty's fatisfaction and ours, which could not be, except they
refolved prefently to give her without any new or farther conditions,
he concluded, that he would do his beft, and bid us be of good
comfort, for he was in no doubt himfelf but all would end well.
This we have thought good to advertife your Majefty of, to the end

3 I you

JAMES I.
1623.
you may not grieve yourfelf, nor think the time long; and confidering till our coming, nothing was done, or intended, you may be the better fatisfied with this our ftay. They fhall no fooner declare themfelves to us, but you fhall have it; fo we crave your bleffing, and end.

Your Majefty's moft humble and obedient fon and fervant,

CHARLES.

Madrid, the 29th of
June, 1623.

Your Majefty's moft humble flave and dog,

STEENIE.

Prince Charles and the Duke to King James.

Dear Dad and Goffip,

July 15.

YOU have underftood by this time, how we were forced to refort to your laft letter, fent to us by Crofts: they continue ftill the fame expreffions of joy which we then advertifed you of. We have thought it fit again, at this time, to intreat you to put all thofe things in prefent execution, in the favour of your Roman Catholic fubjects, that you're bound hereafter to do by the articles; for we are in good hope, if that be, to bring the Infanta at Michaelmas with us. We have given them thefe reafons to perfuade them to it; the lengthening of your Majefty's days; the honour of your fon; the fatisfaction of your whole people in general; and the eafier and fooner performance of what is promifed, with the charge you have been this year already at, and how much it will be increafed more by her ftay till the Spring. We have fhowed them three ways to do it; firft, by alledging the Infanta's love to your fon, which will ferve to take off the blame of the act from the Condé of Olivares, if the people fhould diflike it, which he feems much to fear, and for which,

4

which, we find, he hath little reafon; but becaufe he gives fo ill, and fo unlikely a reafon, we philofophy upon the worft on his part, than to make another trial with the Junto of Divines, where they may make ufe of the advertifement they received laft, concerning the execution, from their own Ambaffadors; but that, I hope, will be better ftrengthened by what they fhall write hereafter; and laftly, while this is working, to fend to Rome, to perfuade the Pope to difpenfe with this King's oath, fince your Majefty, your fon, and your Council, hath agreed to that, for which that oath was required.

Sir, We do not know whether this will take effect or not; if it do not, we will be the fooner with you; we know you will think a little more time will be well fpent to bring her with us, when, by that means, we may upon equaller terms treat with them of other things. Do your beft there, and we will not fail of ours here. You fhall do well to fee the Ambaffadors letters, and fend them in your own packets. Of all this we muft intreat you to fpeak nothing, for if you do, our labour will be the harder here, and when it fhall be hoped there, and not take effect, they will be the more difcontented. I your Baby have, fince this conclufion, been with my miftrefs, and fhe fits publickly with me at the plays, and within thefe two or three days fhall take place of the Queen, as Princefs of England. I your Dog, have alfo had a vifit of her, to deliver your letter, and to give her the *par bien* of this conclufion. As this profpers, you fhall hear from time to time. So we crave your bleffing, and end.

Your Majefty's humble and obedient fon and fervant,

CHARLES.

Madrid,
the 15th of July, 1623.

Your Majefty's moft humble flave and dog,

STEENIE.

King James to the Prince and Duke.

My fweet Boys,

July 21.

EVEN as I was going yefterday in the evening to the Ambaffador's to take my private oath, having taken the public, before
noon, with great folemnity, Andover came ftepping in at the door
like a ghoft, and delivered me your letters. Since it can be no better I muft be contented; but this courfe is both a difhonour to me,
and double charges, if I muft fend two fleets; but if they will not
fend her till March, let them, in God's name, fend her by their own
fleet. The Ambaffadors fpeak broadly againft this delay, and plainly
fay that it is fenfelefs, and fwear they will write earneftly with Cottington, to perfuade the change of that refolution; but, if no better
may be, do ye haften your bufinefs, the fleet'fhall be at you fo foon
as wind and weather can ferve, and this bearer will bring you the
power to treat for the Palatinate, and the matter of Holland; and,
fweet Baby, go on with the contract, and the beft affurance ye can
get of fending her next year; but, upon my bleffing, lie not with her
in Spain, except ye be fure to bring her with you, and forget not
to make them to keep their former conditions anent the portion,
otherwife both my Baby and I are bankrupts for ever. And now I
muft tell you miracles; our great Primate* hath behaved himfelf
wonderful well in this bufinefs, infomuch as my Lord Keeper † fays,
he will love him the better while he lives for it; and my Lord
Chamberlain hath gone beyond all the Council, in clear and honeft
dealing in this bufinefs; as all other things I remit to the fufficiency
of this bearer, whom Steenie hath fo earneftly recommended unto
me. And fo God blefs you, my fweet children, and fend you a happy, joyful, and fpeedy return in the arms of your dear Dad. Amen.

Whitehall,   JAMES, R.
the 21ft of July, 1623.

* Abbot.   † Williams.

Secretary Conway to the Duke of Buckingham.

Gracious Patron,

VOUCHSAFE that firſt with which I am fulleſt, my unexpreſ- July 23d.
ſible thankfulneſs for the honour and favour of your letter by the
Lord of Andover, who arrived to his Majeſty's preſence on Sunday the 20th of July, unheard of till he preſented himſelf, in the withdrawing chamber, to his Majeſty. His Lordſhip delivered the packet
to the hands of his Majeſty, who, when he had read the letters, gave
them to Sir Francis Cottington, and afterwards gave me your Grace's
directed to me, which I received with as much joy, and more humble
acknowlegement, than ever I applied to words directed from the
hands of a miſtreſs. And to the buſineſs, your letters came as ſeaſon-
ably; his Majeſty having feaſted the Ambaſſadors, the Lords of the
Council having received his Majeſty's warrant under the Great Seal,
and taken their oaths without diſpute, ſo many as was there; the Lord
Chamberlain being then extremely ill of the ſtone, and the Lord
Brooke ſo too, the Earl of Arundel gone into Flanders to viſit his ſon
then ſick there, Zouch at Dover, Southampton in the country, Sir
Robert Naunton at his houſe not called.

His Majeſty called, into his bed-chamber, Mr. Secretary Calvert,
Cottington, and myſelf, communicated to us the contents of your
letters, by which appeared the condition of the affairs with you, and
what you required hence. The contentment began there, which
quickly ran through Court and city, and will fly through the kingdom, that his Highneſs and your Grace would ſhortly be at home; a
point much queſtioned and feared. All you expected hence was in
ſuch forwardneſs, as there was not much to be ſaid to it. The deli-
berations were the ſtaying of that part of the fleet laſt deſigned into
Scotland, and ſending them, with the reſt, to the port you deſired
(St Anderas); and how to move the Spaniſh Ambaſſadors to write, that
the favour intended to the Roman Catholics was already put in execution;

cution.; which feemed not uneafy, the Council having advanced fo far, and his Majefty attending only the Ambaffadors repofing a little, before he paffed to his part. The Ambaffadors being brought from their rooms of reft unto the lodging next to the ftone table chamber, his Majefty found them there, and they having with them only their prieft, Mr. Secretary Calvert, Sir Francis Cottington, and myfelf were called in, and had the honour to be witneffes to as dainty an introduction to a bufinefs of that confequence as ever I heard, which freely foreffiowed the impoffibilities of the exact performance of the literal part concerning the Parliament, but in the fenfe of doing his beft; and in the underftanding of that part, which gives freedom and immunity to the Roman Catholics from all laws. His Majefty's reading on that text, *faving in violent cafes, according to reafon of ftate*, to that part the Ambaffador gave all approbation; but, gently and modeftly, by acknowleging his Majefty's abfolute power, feemed to call for and depend upon fatisfaction in that point. But all thofe paffages for your more eafe, I leave them to Sir Francis Cottington's more clear relation. Upon his Majefty's motion for the Ambaffadors letters into Spain, that favour to the Roman Catholics was already put into execution, they faintly accorded; but withal prayed to have fome acts done, which might be public and authentical.

His Majefty accorded that, and folemnly fatisfied all on his part to be done.

The Ambaffadors took their leaves, contented to the full. And although greater aftonifhment could not furprize men, than the contemplation of the iffue of thefe laft actions; yet, conceiving the point to be the redemption and fatisfaction of the Prince, they are comforted, beyond the poffibility of their difcourfe, by the confidence they have of the noble, conftant, pious refolutions of his Highnefs and your Grace; of which the beft fort of the people are not only very full, but withal well affured concerning religion.

Notwithftanding all the fearful rumours fpread and figns conceived, it will truly be a work worthy of the Prince and yourfelf, to

make

make your return as foon as poffible, and either to bring the Princefs ·JAMES I. with you, or the Piince as free ·as his affection, and the general paft _{1623.} demonftration, will, admit; if the neceffity of the affairs, or the power of deftiny, will have it otherwife, there is nothing but a fad fubmiffion. But for my part, there is nothing that I cannot hope from the venture and good fortune of his ·Highnefs and your Grace.

After refolution taken by his Majefty 'to haften the Lord of Rutland to you with the fleet, and that his Majefty had refolved upon fome limitation for the difpatch of Sir Francis Cottington in matter and time, and had given order to Mr. Secretary Calvert to make the difpatch back to Spain, I took the boldnefs to get leave of his Majefty to go to Greenwich on the Monday, to folemnize a marriage between a daughter of mine and Sir Robert Harley. I returned hither yefterday to fee the profecution of the fleet's difpatch, have fpoken with the Lord of Rutland, and find all things well advanced; and this night I hope to find his Majefty at Andover, and to return to the Lord of Rutland his Majefty's warrant to carry the fleet to St. Andera, and that is all his Lordfhip attends; at leaft, by that time he will be ready to go the fleet. Your noble Lady, the unmatchable pattern of a wife, and your daughter as exceedingly fair, are both well; and the confidence of your fpeedy return hath wrought a great advantage of the complexion and good looks of your reverenced lady and honourable fifter.

If I were not jealous of myfelf, that I look upon the public good with the fpectacles of felf-love, I fhould a thoufand-times beg of you to haften his Highnefs's return and yours. But I will pray to the Almighty to make you way to his glory, and your own honour. And I do beg of your Grace to prefent my fervice acceptably to his Highnefs, and that you will be pleafed to keep in your intentions to command. Your Grace's, &c.

EDWARD CONWAY.

P. S. The acts of favour are gone this day to the King's fignature, which known, will create cold fweat and fear, until the return of his Highnefs and your Grace.

Prince Charles and the Duke, to King James.

Dear Dad and Goffip,

July 29th.   AFTER a long expectation of Grifley, he arrived yesterday
morning, with the good news of your health, and the difpatch
of our bufinefs: we are forry that there are arofe in your confcience
any fcruples, but we are very confident, when we fee your Majefty,
to give you very good fatisfaction for all we have done; and had we
had lefs help, we had done it both fooner and better, but we leave
that till our meeting. Sir, we have not been idle in this interim,
for we can now tell you certainly, that, by the 29th of your Auguft,
we fhall begin our journey, and hope to bring her with us; but if
they will not fuffer her to come till the Spring, whether we fhall be
contracted or not, we humbly befeech your Majefty to leave it to our
difcretions, who are upon the place, and fee things at a nearer diftance, and a truer glafs than you and your Council can there; for
marriage there fhall be none, without her coming with us, and in
the mean time comfort yourfelf with this, that we have already convinced the Condé of Olivares in this point, that it is fit the Infanta
come with us before Winter. He is working underhand with the
Divines, and, under colour of the King' and Prince's journey, makes
preparation for hers alfo; her houfhold is a fettling, and all other
things for her journey, and the Condé's own words are, he will
throw us all out of Spain as foon as he can. There remains no more
for you to do, but to fend us peremptory commands to come away,
and with all poffible fpeed: we defire this, not that we fear we fhall
have need of it, but in cafe we have, that your fon (who hath expreffed much affection to the perfon of the Infanta) may prefs his
coming away, under the colour of your command, without appearing an ill lover. I your Baby give you humble and infinite thanks,

for

for the care you have expreffed, both to my perfon and honour.
And I your flave and dog, who have moft caufe, give you none at
all, becaufe you have fent me no news of my wife, and have given
her leave to be fick, and I conclude it the more dangerous, becaufe
you dare not write me news of it. We hope you have fent the reft
of the navy towards us, by this time; if you have not, we befeech
you to ufe all the fpeed you can, as we fhall do, to caft ourfelves,
with an increafe of your fleet. So we crave your bleffing.

Your Majefty's moft humble and obedient fon and fervant,

CHARLES.

Your majefty's moft humble flave and dog,

Madrid,
the 29th of July, 1623.

STEENIE.

Duke of Buckingham to King James.

Dead Dad and Goffip,

IF I fhould give you due thanks for all you have done for me, I   July 30th.
fhould fpend my time in nothing elfe, and fo want to give this
account of your fon's bufinefs, which you have moft reafon now to
hearken after. When you fhall have moft leifure to receive thanks,
and I thought beft how to give them, as heretofore fo then, your part
will be to back and run from them. In the mean time, Sir, know,
that upon the King's Council, and Court's expreffion of joy, that
the Prince had come into, and accepted of their own offers here, to
be contracted, and ftay for the Infanta's following him at the beginning of the Spring, that we thought it a fit time in the heat of their

3 K   expreffions,

expreſſions, to try their good-natures, and preſs the Infanta's preſent going. Whereupon the Prince. ſent me to the Condé of Olivares, with theſe reaſons for it, that firſt, it would lengthen much your days, who beſt deſerved of them in this, and many other buſineſſes; It would add much to the honour of the Prince, which otherwiſe muſt needs ſuffer; The Infanta would thereby gain the ſooner the hearts of the people, and ſo conſequently make her deſires and their ends ſooner and eaſier to be effected in favour of the Catholics; That otherwiſe we ſhould compaſs but one of thoſe ends for which we came, for marriage, and not friendſhip, and ſo it would prove but like the French alliance; That the affairs of Chriſtendom would eaſilier and ſooner be compounded; That if he had any reaſons of ſtate in it, which he hoped to gain at the Spring, I would ſhow him how he would better compaſs it now, than when their diſtruſt would beget the ſame in us; How your Majeſty had been this year at a great charge already, and how this delay would but be of more, to both kingdoms: With this I intreated him to think of my poor particular who had waited upon the Prince. hither, and in that, diſtaſted all the people in general; How he laid me open to their malice and revenge, when I had brought from them their Prince a free man, and ſhould return him bound by a contract, and ſo locked from all poſterity, till they pleaſed here; How that I could not think of this obligation, if he would relieve me in it, without horror or fear, if I were not his faithful friend and ſervant, and intended thankfulneſs. He interrupted this with many grumblings, but at laſt ſaid, I had bewitched him; but if there was a witch in the company, I am ſure there was a devil too. From him I repaired to his Lady, who, I muſt tell you by the way, is as good a woman as lives, which makes me think all favourites muſt have good wives, whom I told what I had done; ſhe liked of it very well, and promiſed her beſt aſſiſtance. Some three or four days after, the Prince ſent to intreat him to ſettle her houſe, and to give order in other things for their journey; he aſked what

day

day-he, would go away, but himfelf named the 29th of your Auguft, which the Prince accepted of. Some two days after, the good Coun- tefs fent for me, the moft afflicted woman in the world, and told me the Infanta had told her, the Prince meant to go away without her, and for her part, fhe took it fo ill, to fee him fo carelefs of her, that fhe would not be contracted till the day he was to take his leave. The Countefs told me the way to mend this, was to go to the Condé, and put the whole bufinefs in the King's hands, with this proteftation, that he would rather ftay feven years, than go without his Miftrefs, he fo much efteemed her; and if I faw after, that this did not work good effects, that the Prince might come off, upon your Majefty's command, at pleafure. With this offer I went to the Condé, he re- ceived it but doggedly; the next day I defired audience of the In- fanta, to tafte her. I framed this errand from your Majefty, that you had commanded me to give her a particular account of what you had done, and that you had overcome many difficulties to perfuade the Council to come into thefe articles, and that you yourfelf was come into them, merely in contemplation of her, and that you had given order for prefent execution, and fince you had done thus much to get her, you made no queftion but her virtues would perfuade you to do much more for her fake. When I had done this, I told her of the Prince's refolution, and affured her, that he never fpoke of go- ing, but with this end, to get her the fooner away; but that here- after he durft ufe no diligences for her and himfelf, fince he was fubject to fo ill offices, except fhe would take this for granted, that he would never go without her, which fhe liked very well of. When I had done this, I told her, fince fhe was the Prince's wife, all my thoughts was bent to gain her the love of that people whither fhe was to go, and I fhowed her how the articles contained no more than for the time to come; but there was many Catholics, who at this day were fined in the Exchequer, and though it would be fome lofs to your Majefty (though I think it would be none), yet, if fhe

3 K 2   would

would make a requeſt to the Prince for them, your Majeſty would quit it. I hope I have not done ill in this, but ſure I am, it hath not done ill to our buſineſs; for what with this, and that news of the ſending the four ſhips to Leith, this morning the Counteſs hath ſent the Prince this *recautbo*, otherwiſe called meſſage, that the King, the Infanta, and the Condé, are the beſt contented that can be, and that he ſhould not now doubt his ſoon going away, and to carry the Infanta with him.

Sir, I cannot end this letter without recommending this bearer your ape, to your care, as any thing falls; Porter that came with us, will ſtand in great need alſo of your help, and in helping theſe two, you help me, who humbly crave your bleſſing.

Your Majeſty's ſlave and dog,

The 30th of July.

STEENIE.

Secretary Conway to the Duke of Buckingham.

Moſt gracious Patron,

Auguſt 5.
SINCE my laſt to your Grace by Mr. Killegrew, there hath fallen ſome miſunderſtandings or diſputations, which have varied the ſtate of proceedings touching the execution of grace intended by his Majeſty to the Roman Catholics, and the ſatisfactory letters promiſed by the Ambaſſadors. By the copy of Mr. Secretary Calvert's letter to me, bearing date the 2d of this month, which I ſend herewith, your Grace will ſee what were the difficulties; and by the copy of the Ambaſſador's letter, you will ſee thoſe dry and cold paſſages which his Majeſty found to differ far from thoſe large and zealous offers they had made, of writing unto Spain, declared by a letter of Mr. Secretary Calvert's, of the laſt of July, whereof I now ſend your Grace a copy; though I conceive I ſent you one before, by Mr. Killegrew,

7

legrew,

legrew, who went from hence the 2d of this month, with an intention to take those effectual letters with him. The third of this instant, I received from Mr. Secretary, his letter of the second, by which his Majesty, finding that those effectual letters were not written, nor intended to be prepared, but new disputes raised, his Majesty commanded me to write to stay Mr. Killegrew, which I instantly did, but whether those letters came time enough to stay him or no, I know not yet. The same day Killegrew went from hence, the Ambassadors set forth hitherward, and arrived here the fourth, at two of the clock. Immediately, his Majesty sent my Lord Carlisle and myself, to them with instructions (after the compliment of welcome performed), to show them the reasons of the validity of the performance his Majesty made of his promise, and of the weakness and invalidity of that they desired: and then the inconvenience to his Majesty, for reason of state, to satisfy them in that kind, the proof of which was delivered thus.

His Majesty having undertaken to give an immunity unto the Roman Catholics for the time to come, was afterwards drawn by the importunity of the Spanish Ambassadors (and by desire and opinion to make a speedy return of his son, with the accomplishment of the marriage, and in the company of her Highness the Infanta), to give order for a pardon for all things past, that stood to the advantage of the King, and in his power to release. And for the time to come, to give likewise (under his Majesty's seal) a dispensation and immunity from all penal laws, statutes, or ordinances whatsoever they were subject to, for their consciences. And this, for the care his Majesty had of the accomplishment of his royal promise, which he would make sure against himself, and his successors, at all events. Which the Ambassadors having refused, propounding a proclamation, which was but a suspension of the law, might be made void by another proclamation, and did not bind a successor; and therefore his Majesty knew not by what counsel they were carried

to

to refuſe a full and good ſecurity, and in place thereof to propound a
defective one.   His Majeſty being very unwilling to make a con-
ſtruction that the Ambaſſadors ſought delays here, to the end that,
upon them, they might form delays in Spain, or that the Ambaſſadors would be carried with the variety, vain-glory, or malice of the
Roman Catholics, to require things unſafe for them, and unproper
for his Majeſty to grant, who beſt knew what were the beſt ſecuri-
ties for the making good of his word and oath, and what was moſt
ſuitable with the peace of his government.

To this the Ambaſſadors anſwered, with ſuch doubts and arguments as they had gathered up from the ignorant, fearful, diſtruſt-
ful Roman Catholics that had ſought them.

The reply to this was, that, if the Ambaſſadors knew the ſtrength
of our laws, the authority, and inviolable dignity of a Great Seal,
the roundneſs and integrity of his Majeſty's proceeding, and would
but truly underſtand the unproperneſs of a proclamation, in point of
government, they would be ill ſatisfied with thoſe that had caſt them
upon that counſel: and then they might judge how much cauſe his
Majeſty had to be diſpleaſed with thoſe that had puſhed at ſo great
inconveniences, and been authors of ſo great a delay.   And the
better to rectify the Ambaſſadors' judgments and knowledge in this,
it was propounded to them, that there were wiſe and judicious
lawyers, that were well known to be Roman Catholics; that it
was not doubted but that his Majeſty would be contented to permit
one ſufficient man of thoſe (to be choſen by them) to look into the
validity of the pardon for the things paſt, and of the diſpenſation of
the things to come: and that it ſhould be lawful for that lawyer to
attend his Majeſty's Attorney, and to give aſſiſtance and force, with
all legal terms and proviſions, for their better ſecurity.   And that
concerning the proclamation, they might be pleaſed to know, that
it was the judges, juſtices, and inferior officers, in whoſe power it
was to proceed againſt, or to queſtion, or moleſt the Roman Catho-
                                                                    lics;

lies; and to all thofe officers, the pardon, difpenfation, and prohi-
bition further to moleft them, was to be directed: a proclamation was
only to the vulgar people, who had no intereft in the bufinefs, nor
were capable of any thing but fear and rumour. And the Ambaffadors were prayed (as men of eftate) to judge whether it were
more feafonable, the Prince away, the marriage not made, the temporal conditions not publifhed, to intimate this grace by proclamation, or to let it flide in by this more filent way of pardon and difpenfation.

Here the Ambaffadors gave a ftop to themfelves, began to proteft
their care of the peace of the ftate, and to recount the orations they
had made to the Roman Catholics, to receive this Grace thankfully,
as a mere grace of the King.

And here they let fall the pretence for a proclamation, and laid
hold upon the offer of the fecurity by pardon with the infpection of a
Counfellor; prayed that they might appoint one to folicit that Counfellor, and that the Counfellor, and the perfon to be fent to him,
might have warrant, by a letter from a Secretary of State, that his
Majefty would take well their endeavour in that bufinefs. And there
remained no vifible exception, on the Ambaffador's part, but the
charge of a pardon, to which they had anfwer to fatisfy them. And
they being fully fatisfied, the opportunity was not loft to require
them then to write prefently to the King of Spain, the full performance, on his Majefty's part, and to folicit the fpeedy accomplifhment
of the bleffed marriage, and the fpeedy return of the Prince in the
company of the excellent and happy Infanta.

To this we found a ready preparation in Don Carlof and, it may
not be faid a backward, but a cautious enquity by the Marquis of
Ignioza, for an anfwer to his propofition, who, in conclufion, took
occafion to propound a paper drawn, of certain limitations, to which
if his Majefty would explain his confent, under the hand of his Secretary, he would prefently write, to the uttermoft extenfion, for the
juftifying

juſtifying of his Majeſty's real and royal accompliſhment, and for the haſtening the concluſions in Spain. This paper was brought in by Mr. Gage, and withal, the form of the proclamation, and another paper of requeſts deſtined to be delivered to his Majeſty. The form of the proclamation was undoubtedly one of the moſt impertinent pieces that could be ſhewed.

For the paper of requeſts, it concerned Scotland, and Ireland, and received ſuch anſwers, as the Ambaſſadors ſeemed in very large meaſure to approve.

Since, we have heard nothing of it. For the paper of propoſitions, for his Majeſty to approve by his Secretary, my Lord Carliſle very judiciouſly ſuffered it to be received, to be preſented to his Majeſty, and approved by him, and in the mean time a proviſional promiſe made, that Mr. Gage ſhould be diſpatched to ſolicit the execution of the pardon, and an effectual letter written, if his Majeſty did approve of the propoſitions; which propoſitions (at their requeſt) were left in their hands, to be tranſlated into Engliſh, and delivered this morning; of which propoſitions I ſend your Grace a copy herewith. I inſtantly repreſented them to his Majeſty, who commanded me to wait upon my Lord Carliſle again to the Ambaſſadors; and to us his Majeſty gave inſtructions upon theſe two exceptions: the one concerning the compoſition made with recuſants for forfeitures, and given away by patent to others, and was not now in the power of his Majeſty no more to take from them, than to take back any land he had granted by patent, or than that it ſhould be poſſible for him to make void theſe pardons and acts of grace to the Roman Catholics, to be paſſed under the Great Seal. But his Majeſty was well pleaſed, that, ſince he took off them all the penal ſtatutes, by which they were made liable to theſe things, if they could by pleading by law prove, that the cauſe being taken away, the effect ceaſed, they ſhould have equal juſtice. With this they quieted themſelves.

The

The other point was, concerning the declaration, that fcholars fhould be admitted into fchools and colleges, without having any oaths adminiftered unto them.

To this, his Majefty excepted, as a thing of a tender and dangerous interpretation for his honour and conftancy, that he fhould not only at one inftant give unexpected grace and immunity to his fubjects the Roman Catholics, but feem to endeavour to plant a feminary of other religion than he made profeffion of. But it was enough that his Majefty took off all penalties from them, fo as they ftood in poffibility to be admitted by grace, if they would not take the oaths, or otherwife they might forbear entering into univerfities; but fuch as could gently pafs in by favour, according to the example of many that do fo now.

The Marquis of Ignioza anfwered, that all penalties were not taken off them, for the penalty of fhame remained upon them, that they could not be capable of offices equally with other men.

The reply to that was, that there was no fhame but what the laws had impofed: that the laws, by the King's grace, were taken away, and taken away with more advantage to them, than the Proteftants were left in.

For if a perfon capable of any preferment, defired a place or office, if the King, or other perfon that had power to beftow the place accepted him, he could not be refufed for not taking the oaths; for grace hath fufpended them for the Roman Catholics, but not to the Proteftants.

This, and the reft, coft many more arguments, the clearing of which received good affiftance by the difcretion and moderation of Mr. Gage, who fometimes affifted the clearing of points by good interpretation, fometimes by bearing witnefs to the truth of the allegations concerning formalities, and condition of our ftate and law. But with all the aids, the Marquis of Ignioza found himfelf troubled, his reafon convicted, that his Majefty did accomplifh to the full, whatfoever he was obliged to by the articles, or his royal promife;

3 L

and

and yet that was fhort of what the Marquis defired to gain, to magnify himfelf by, in the way of fupererogation. But being finally
preffed judicioufly to examine how punctually his Majefty had accomplifhed all that he was tied to by the articles and more, for the
contemplation of haftening the conclufion of this bleffed bufinefs,
and the joyful coming of thofe excellent Perfonages hither; and
that he would in goodnefs think this delay too long, and juftly write
that his Majefty had fully accomplifhed all his part to be done; and
add to it this good office of preffing a fpeedy confummation of the marriage in Spain, and fpeedy coming of their Highneffes together; to
this he anfwered with an earneft (almoft a choleric) franknefs, that he
ought and would write, that the King had fulfilled every jot of that
he was bound to, and more; but wherein more (though he would
write into Spain) he would not tell us; but added withal, that he
would write, that though the King had performed all, yet the Catholics were left by the negligence committed by the Council of
Spain, without poffibility to be poffeffed of offices.

The reply to this fhowed him, from the arguments before, that
judgment was ill grounded, and that if he fhould write fo into Spain
(whereof there was no neceffity), it might be a mifinformation, and
yet caufe queftion and delay in the proceedings.

From hence the Marquis took occafion to breath out many proteftations of his roundnefs, purenefs in this bufinefs, and equal faith
to both Kings; profeffing it to have been, before he came out of
Spain, his judgment and his counfel (wherein he was now more
fortified), that the advantage of Spain, was to confummate the match
fpeedily, and alike to haften the return of their Highneffes into
England.

And although he waved the difpatch of his letters into Spain from
hence, by an argument of what ill fpirits may philofophy upon it,
yet he vowed upon the crofs of the Lord Carlifle's fword, and by all
the rights and bounds of heaven and honour, that he would hafte to

7   London,

London, hafte the difpatch of the pardon, fend a copy of it, and
with it his letters of celebration of his Majefty's royal performance in every tittle; and warrants there fhould be no delay, concurring with his many former letters to that effect.

This narration his Majefty hath commanded me to make thus particularly and largely, that his Highnefs and you might, by fight of the whole frame, judge of the perfection or imperfection of the building. And I have forborn the form, of this my Lord of Carlifle faid, or this I faid, not of ambition to flide myfelf into equality with him; but well knowing whatfoever I fhould call his, would not look like his, wanting both life and his polifhing. But this I truly fay, whatfoever is good and effectual, is his, and mine nothing but the faults.

And this I will as truly fay, this caufe is dear to all England, and as precious I believe to us two, as to any two in England.

Your Grace may be pleafed, even of your grace, to prefent my fervice to his Highnefs, to whom that I never write, is only of reverence; and alike to vouchfafe my acknowledgment of what I am, is by you, and for you, as I am by humble affection and faith,

Your Grace's, &c.

Salifbury,   EDWARD CONWAY.
Auguft 5th, 1623.

3 L 2

Secretary Conway to the Duke of Buckingham.

Gracious Patron,

THE Lord Carlisle being appointed to marshal the train of the Ambassadors in this day's hunting, required me to present his service to your Grace, and in his name to beseech you to reserve from the eyes and knowlege of all men but his Highness, the post-script of his Majesty's letter, as you tender an humble, faithful, active servant of yours, until you shall have ample knowledge of all the circumstances of that information.

Since the finishing of my exorbitant narration, Mr. Gage hath been with me to propound a meeting between the Ambassadors, the Lord Carlisle and myself, to accord upon some limitations of the matters to be comprehended in the pardon and dispensation, which being done, and put under our hands, the Marquis will write the effectual letters so often mentioned, for the assurance of the full accomplishment of all on his Majesty's part, and hastening of the match.

I have acquainted his Majesty with the proposition, and his Majesty readily approves it, and your Grace may be confident, all possible to be done, shall be done, that may hasten his Highness's return, and yours, in which my interest is no less, than happy, or unhappy.

I have not time to clear myself to your Grace; but, thus, I am sometimes perplexed, not being able of your friends to conceive which is to be preferred. I must believe all that profess it, and love them for that; but want trials to discern farther, having less commodity to do that, than others; because I never use a mask to shadow whose I am, and desire not to know, under the seal of friendship, that which I cannot conceal with mine own integrity. And that all pro-

fess

fefs to you, is no marvel, for the conftancy of our mafter's affection
to you, is enough to keep the crooked ftraight.

When your Grace fhall think it fit to inftruct my faith and induftry, there is nothing fo longed for as your commandments.

It feems, upon the marriage, it will be fit, that fome qualified perfon be fent to give the *Parabieu*; and it is poffible the Lord Carlifle
his eye is upon it, and for ought I can fee, there is none more proper for your fervice; if it be not fo, the faireft way (by your Grace's
pardon) is, to find it fuperfluous to fend any. If thefe kind officiouf-
neffes be too much, God and your Grace forgive it, for it comes of
humble faith and duty, from

Your Grace's, &c.

Salifbury,   EDWARD CONWAY.
the 6th of Auguft, 1623.

King James to the Prince and Duke.

My fweet Boys,

I WRITE to you now upon the good fifth day of Auguft *, in the
afternoon. Secretary Calvert's moving the Ambaffadors to have
a fight or copy of what they wrote, hath produced this effect, that
I find their letters leaner and drier than either I expected or deferved.
What courfe I have taken with them hereupon, at their coming
hither to this feaft, Secretary Conway's letter will inform you at
large. To be fhort, I have given order to put in execution, all that
I have promifed, and more; as themfelves confefs, and had been done
before this time, if themfelves, by new unreafonable motions, had
not hindered it. And thus much more than I promifed have I
granted unto them; at their earneft fuit, which is, a difcharge of all
debts already owing to me by recufants; and therefore, if they caft
up now the great dowry that they are to give, remember that, by

---

* James honoured the 5th of Auguft, with his efcape from Earl Gowrie, at Perth, on
a folemn annual thankfgiving, on account of that day, in 1600.

this

this deed, I quit fix and thirty thoufand pounds of good rent, in England and Ireland; which, in good account, will ftrike down the third part at leaft of their dowry. If Killegrew be not already gone, he will deliver this letter unto you; but if he be gone, Clark will give you it, who fhall immediately be difpatched after the fealing of that pardon and privy feal which is prefently to be drawn up. I have no more to fay, but if you haften you not home, I apprehend I fhall never fee you, for my extreme longing will kill me; but God blefs you both, my fweet boys, upon this good day; and he that delivered me from fo great a danger upon it, preferve you, and grant you a fpeedy, happy, and comfortable return in the arms of your dear Dad. Amen. Amen. Amen.

JAMES, R.

Carlifle hath told me a tale of this Marquis, that fhews him to be a flim man, and my Steenie's fmall friend; and the Devil take them all that are fo, except my Baby, who I know can never love Steenie; but in earneft he broke off a crafty difcourfe to Carlifle, but he choaked him fo foon; therefore keep this to yourfelves till ye hear more of it.

Secretary Calvert to Secretary Conway.

SIR,

I HAVE at this inftant received from you a new *reveille-matin* about the fleet, and would be glad to know of you in particular what I am to do more than I have done, which if I knew, I were unworthy to live, if I did not give his Majefty all contentment, by my humble and diligent endeavours. I have told you often, that I cannot learn from the commiffioners of the navy here, that any thing is demanded for her fetting forth, except victuals; and that I had

fpoken

spoken with Sir Allen Apsley, who assured me that all should be ready and aboard by to-morrow; so as there shall not need any other course to be taken now by making provisions out of the merchants ships.

I have also spoken again this morning with Mr. Coke, who tells me that the commissioners of the navy had Sir Allen Apsley before them on Wednesday last, and then assured them the like, that longer than to-morrow the ship of victual should not stay, unless the wind hindered her, which I hope shall not. To be surer, he shall be called upon again this day. It is not possible to do more, for any thing I can see. When this victual comes about to Portsmouth, then will there be no cause for the fleet to stay an hour, for any thing I know, unless you hear any new complaints from my Lord of Rutland, which we know not here, being nearer to you than us.

8th August.

King James to the Prince.

My dearest Son,

I SENT you a commandment long ago, not to lose time where ye are, but either to bring quickly home your mistress, which is my earnest desire, but if no better may be, rather than to linger any longer there, to come without her; which, for many important reasons I am now forced to renew; and therefore I charge you, upon my blessing, to come quickly, either with her or without her. I know your love to her person hath enforced you to delay the putting in execution of my former commandment. I confess it is my chiefest worldly joy that ye love her; but the necessity of my affairs enforceth me to tell you, that you must prefer the obedience to a father, to the love ye carry to a mistress. And so God bless you.

August 10th.

Cranbourn,
the 10th of August, 1623.

JAMES, R.

Prince Charles and the Duke to King James.

'Dear Dad and Goffip,

THE caufe why we have altered our Secretary is, that I your
Laby will not let your Dog trouble himfelf with writing, becaufe he has been of late troubled with a great cold, with a little fit of
an ague, for which he was drawn blood, but now, thanks be to God,
he is perfectly well. Cottington arrived here the fifth of this month
late at night, whofe coming, we hoped, would have made a great
alteration to the better in our bufinefs; but we find that they here
believe the Marquis Inoyofa's intelligence, better than all your Majefty's real proceedings; but we befeech you take no notice to the
Marquis of Inoyofa of his juggling (for he has written hither, contrary to his profeffions), until we wait upon you. The caufe why
we have been fo long unwriting to you, fince Cottington's coming,
is, that we would try all means poffible (before we would fend you
word), to fee if we could move them to fend the Infanta before winter. They, for form's fake, called the Divines, and they ftick to
their old refolution; but we find by circumftances, that confcience is
not the true, but feeming caufe, of the Infanta's ftay. To conclude,
we have wrought what we can, but fince we cannot have her with
us that we defired, our next comfort is, that we hope fhortly to kifs
your Majefty's hands.

Sir, We have been informed by my Lord of Briftol, that, by the
French Ambaffador's means, the Spanifh Ambaffador has feen all the
letters that we have written to you, and that you are betrayed in
your bed-chamber. So craving your bleffing, we reft,

Your Majefty's moft humble and obedient fon and fervant,

CHARLES.

Sir,

Sir, I have been the willinger to let your fon play the Secretary at this time of little need, that you may thereby fee the extraordinary care he hath of me, for which I will not intreat you not to love him the worfe, nor him that threatens you, that when he once gets hold of your bed-poft again, never to quit it.

Your Majefty's moft humble flave and dog.

STEENIE.

Prince Charles and the Duke to King James.

Dear Dad and Goffip,

THIS day we take our leaves; to-morrow we begin our journey; we leave our bufineffes thus. This Pope being fick (as they fay here), hath not yet given power for the delivery of the difpenfation, upon the capitulations agreed upon, wherefore they not being able (though many Divines fay the contrary) to contract me your Baby, until that power come from Rome, and they not having ufed us with thofe realities, as to encourage us to rely longer upon uncertainties, I your Baby have thought fit to leave my promife to the King in my Lord of Briftol's hands, to deliver it when that power comes from Rome. As for the bufinefs of the Palatinate (now that we have preft them to it), we have difcovered thefe two impediments; firft, they fay, they have no hope to accommodate it, without the marriage of your grandchild with the Emperor's daughter; but though we know you will like the propofition of the marriage, yet we know not how either you, or your fon-in-law and daughter *, will like it with this condition, that your grandchild be bred up in the Emperor's court. The fecond is, that though they are content to reftore him to all his lands, and his fon to both lands and honour,

August 30th.

* King and Queen of Bohemia.

3 M

yet

JAMES I. yet they will not engage themfelves to reftore himfelf to honours,
1623.   but have it left to their mediation and courtefy; and how the firft
point will be obtained of the father, when they will difcontent him
in the latter, we leave you to judge. For the jointure and temporal articles, we will be able (when we fhall be fo happy as to kifs
your Majefty's hands) to give you a perfect account; in the mean
time we crave your blefling, and end.

Your Majefty's humble and obedient fon and fervant,

CHARLES.

Your Majefty's moft humble flave and dog,

STEENIE.

Madrid,
the 29th of Auguft 1623.

The Infanta to King James.

S I R,

Auguft 30th. I WAS very glad to receive the letter your Majefty hath
been pleafed to fend me, by which your Majefty fhoweth a
good-will and affection to me: and although in both thefe things I
do correfpond with equal degree and meafure, yet I do acknowledge
the favour, and with a defire to have fome occafion to fatisfy (as far
as is in my power), to fo great an obligation; being alfo anfwerable to
this, the good pleafure of the King, my Lord and Brother, who loveth
and efteems your Majefty fo highly, as alfo all that belongeth to
your Majefty. God fave your Majefty, as I defire.

Madrid,   Your Majefty's moft affectionate,
the 30th of Auguft, 1623

MARIA.

Duke of Buckingham to King James.

Dear Dad and Goffip,

THIS bearer hath ftaid for the Infanta's and other letters, a day Sept. 1ft. longer than was refolved of, which hath given me this occa- fion, by ftealth from your Baby, to affure your Majefty, by this laft night's reft, of my perfect recovery. Nothing dejected me fo much in my ficknefs, as my abfence from you; nor nothing was fo great a cordial to me in my recovery, as this thought, that in a few days we fhall ftep towards you; yet I befeech your Majefty to believe this truth, that I fo far prefer this bufinefs, and your fervice, before any particular of my own, that this refolution hath not been taken with precipitation, but when we faw there was no more to be gained here, we thought it then high time with all diligence to gain your prefence. Sir, my heart and very foul dances for joy; for the change will be no lefs than to leap from trouble to eafe, from fadnefs to mirth, nay, from hell to heaven. I cannot now think of giving thanks for friend, wife, or child; my thoughts are only bent of having my dear Dad and Mafter's legs foon in my arms; which fweet Jefus grant me, and your Majefty all health and happinefs; fo I crave your bleffing.

Your Majefty's moft humble flave and dog,

The 1ft of September.

STEENIE.

SIR,

I'll bring all things with me you have defired, except the Infanta, which hath almoft broken my heart, becaufe your's, your fon's, and the nation's honour is touched by the mifs of it; but fince it is their fault here and not ours, we will bear it the better; and when I fhall have the happinefs to lie at your feet, you fhall then know the truth of all, and no more.

3 M 2

Prince Charles to the Pope.

Sanctiffime Pater,

LITERAS S^{tis}. V. vigefimo Aprilis 1623 Romæ datas, tantâ
animi gratitudine et obfervantiâ accepimus, quantâ cum bene-
volentia pioque affectu videntur exaratæ: nobifque imprimis grata
fuere illa, quibus uti placuerit S^{ti}. V. incitamenta à nunquam fatis
laudatis nobiliffimorum majorum noftrorum exemplis petita, qui
anteactis feculis nunquam parati magis exitere advitæ capitifque dif-
crimen adverfus hoftes Chrifti nomini infeftos ultro fubeundum, quo
facro fanctum ipfius cultum latius propagarent, quam nos hoc tem-
pore (quo inveterata Satanæ, difcordiarum patris, malitia obtinuit
tantum, ut diffidia admodum infelicia inter illos ipfos, qui religionem
Chriftianam profitentur, longè latèque diffeminaverit), ad omnem
opem atque operam fedulò adhibendam, ut ecclefia Dei aliquando
reconcilietur, atque ad priftinam pacem et unitatem denuò reduca-
tur: quod pro primo femper gradu ac paffu tantique momenti effe
habuimus, ut vel maximè conferat ad facrofanctum Domini et Sal-
vatoris noftri Jefu Chrifti nomen ac gloriam fœlicius in terris pro-
movendam : quod non minori nobis honori futurum ducemus, pro-
genitorum noftrorum veftigiis prementes, in tam piis et religiofis fuf-
ceptis eorundem imitatores extitiffe, quam ab iifdem genus noftrum et
originem deduxiffe: ad quod nos plurimum hortantur præcepta domini
noftri regis, ac patris mei propenfio, et vehemens admodum quo flagrat
defiderium huic tam fancto operi manum porrigere auxiliatricem :
nec non intimus animi dolor, quo commovetur, dum fecum con-
templatur deplorandas ftrages et calamitates, quæ a fimultatibus et
diffenfionibus inter principes Chriftianos exortis paffim producuntur.
Nec illud porro judicium, quod S^{ti}. V. vifum eft facere de eo, quod
nos tenemur defiderio, cum Principe Catholica Romana matrimo-
nium contrahendi, a S^{ti}. V. fapientiâ atque charitate diffonum omnino
eft

eft aut alienum, fiquidem, uti a S. V. rite obfervatum eft, vix aut ne vix quidem tanto, quo fruimur, ftudio cuperemus tam arĉto et indiffolubili propinquitatis vinculo cum cujufdam perfonâ conjungi, cujus religionem odio et deteftationi haberemus. Sed S. V. hoc fibi perfuafum habeat, eam noftram effe, femperque in pofterum futuram, moderationem; ut non folam quam longiffimè à nobis fufpicionem omnem removebimus, atque ab omni demum aĉtu temperabimus, qui aliquam præ fe fpeciem ferat nos à Romanâ Catholicâ religione abhorrere, fed omnes potius captabimus occafiones, quò leni benignoque rerum proceffu finiftræ omnes fufpiciones è medio penitus tollantur : ut ficut omnes unam et individuam Trinitatem, et unicum Chriftum crucifixum publicè profitemur, ita in unam tantummodo fidem, in ecclefiam unam unanimiter coalefcamus. Quod ut effeĉtum demus, labores omnes et vigilias, et quodcunque itidem periculum, quod inde rebus noftris aut perfonæ poterit imminere, fi faĉto opus erit, parvi pendemus. Quod reliquum eft, S^{tt}. V. gratias, quas poffumus maximas, pro literis veftris, quas infignis muneris loco habemus, referentes, S^{tt}. V. profpera omnia, æternamque fælicitatem comprecamur *.

---

* There are feveral copies of this remarkable letter in the hiftorians ; the above was tranfcribed from the original draught. Lord Clarendon fays very properly of it, writing to Secretary Nicholas from Jerfey, "The letter to the Pope is, by your favour, "more than compliment ; and may be a "warning that nothing is to be done or faid "in that nice argument but what will bear "the light."
See Lord Chancellor Clarendon's State Papers, vol. ii. p. 337.

* *Duke of Buckingham to King James.*

Dear Dad and Goffip,

IT cannot but have been an infinite trouble to have written fo long a letter, and fo foon, efpecially at this painful time of your arms; yet wifh I not a word omitted, though the reading forced blufhes, deferving them no better, neither is it fit I fhould ever diffemble with my mafter. Wherefore I confefs truly I am not a jot forry for the pains you have taken; this might argue I love myfelf better than my Maker, but my difobedience in this, with my humble obedience in all my future actions, fhall witnefs the contrary; and I can boldly fay it is not in the power of your large bountiful hand and heart ever hereafter either to increafe my duty and love to you, or to overvalue myfelf as you do, by thinking it fit I fhould be fet fo far above my fellows †. There is this difference betwixt that noble hand and heart, one may furfeit by the one, but not by the other, and fooner by yours than his own; therefore give me leave to ftop, with mine, that hand which hath been but too ready to execute the motions and affections of that kind obliging heart to me. As for that argument that this can be no leading cafe to others, give me leave to fay, it is true only in one (but that is a great and the main) point; for I grant that I am more than confident, you will never love none of your fervants, (I will be faucy here) better than Steenie; thus it will be no leading. But you cannot deny but it may be a precedent of emulation hereafter, to thofe that fhall fucceed you, to exprefs as much love as you have done to me; and I am fure they may eafily find many fitter fubjects. So if it be unfit in refpect of the number, this way it will be increafed; but I maintain it is unfit in refpect there is not here, as in other places,

---

* This letter, plainly relating to Buckingham's being made a Duke, was certainly writ from Spain. His ducal patent bore date May 18th, 1623.

† Here follows a line and a half blotted out

a difa distinction betwixt Dukes and King's children; and before I make a, or a step to that parity between them and other subjects, I'll disobey you, which is the most I can say or do. I have not so much unthankfulness, to deny what your Majesty saith, that my former excuse of the disproportion of my estate is taken away, for you have filled a consuming purse, given me fair houses, more land than I am worthy of, to maintain both me and them, filled my coffers so full with patents of honour, that my shoulders cannot bear more; this I say is still a great argument for me to refuse, but you have not been contented to rest here, when I thought you had done more than enough, and as much as you could * but hath found out a way, which to my heart's satisfaction, is far beyond all; for, with this letter, you have furnished my cabinet with so precious a witness of your valuation of me, as in future times it cannot be said, that I rise, as most courtiers do, through importunity. For which character of me, and incomparable favour from you, I will sign, with as contented, nay as proud a heart,

Your poor STEENIE,

as Duke of Buckingham.

---

† Prince Charles to the Duke of Buckingham.

STEENIE,

I SEND you here inclosed the interrogatories that the King thinks fit should be asked concerning the malicious accusations of the Spanish Ambassador. As for the way, my father is resolved (if you do not gainsay it, and show reason to the contrary) to take the oaths himself, and to make Secretary Calvert, and the Chancellor of

---

* Follows half a line blotted
† The following letters were writ after the return of the Prince and the Duke to England.

the

the Exchequer, to take the examinations in writing under their hands that are examined; thus much is by the King's command. Now for my opinion, it is this, that you can incur no danger in this, but by oppofing the King's proceedings in it, to make him fufpect that you have fpoken fomewhat that you are unwilling he fhould hear of; for I cannot think that any man is fo mad, as to call his own head in queftion, by making a lye againft you, when all the world knows me to be your true friend, and if they tell but the truth, I know they can fay but what the King knows, that you have avowed to all the world, which is, that you think, as I do, that the continuance of thefe treaties with Spain might breed us much mifchief; wherefore my advice to you is, that you do not oppofe, or fhow yourfelf difcontented at the King's courfe herein, for I think that it will be fo far from doing you hurt, that it will make you trample under your feet, thofe few poor rafcals that are your enemies. Now, fweetheart, if you think I am miftaken in my judgment in this, let me know what I can do in this, or any thing elfe, to ferve thee, and then thou fhalt fee that all the world fhall daily know more and more, that I am and ever will be,

Your faithful loving conftant friend,

April 26th, 1624.   CHARLES, P.

Prince Charles to the Duke of Buckingham.

STEENIE,

THIS day the Lower Houfe has given the King a fubfidy, and are likewife refolved to fend a meffage, humbly to entreat him to end this feffion before Chriftmas. I confefs that this that they have done, is not fo great a matter, that the King need to be indulgent over them for it; yet on the other fide (for his reputation abroad at this time), I would not wholly difcontent them : therefore my opinion is,

that

that the King fhould grant them a feffion at this time, but withal I would have him command them not to fpeak any more of Spain, whether it be of that war, or my marriage.

This, in my opinion, does neither fuffer them to encroach upon the King's authority, nor give them juft caufe of difcontentment: I think you will find that all thofe of the Council that the King trufts moft, are likewife of this mind. Sir Edward Cecil writ me a letter from the army, of much ftuff, but it was of fafhion; the moft of the letter was of reafons why the King fhould enter into a war for the defence of the Palatinate, and truft no more treaties, but the end of it was, that he might be employed in it. Now, in earneft, I wifh the gentleman well, but yet I would not have Sir Horace Vere (who has both endured fo much mifery, and done fo good fervice there), either to be difcouraged or difgraced: therefore I think the King fhall do well to employ Cecil, but I would not have him come over the other's head. So praying you to commend my humble fervice to the King I reft,

Yours more than can be expreffed,

and as much as can be thought,

CHARLES, P.

King James to the Duke of Buckingham.

My fweet dear child, fcholar, and friend,

ST. Paul thou knoweft commands us to examine ourfelves, before we go to the facrament, but yet he commands to go and receive it; fo though I put thee in mind to fpeak as thou promifed to the Spanifh Agent, yet did furely expect thy coming here this night. Thou may make the big rich man bring him hither to thee, or thou may

take

take occasion to go any day in this week to dine at London, and meet with him there, if he cannot be brought to thee to-morrow morning. Alas, sweet heart, I find by this how precise thou art to keep thy word to me, when thou prefers it to thy own greatest comfort in coming to me; God reward thee for it, but I must quarrel thee, that though in both my former letters I prayed thee to bring the

with thee, thou hast not so much as sent me word whether they can come or not; I would gladly have them here, but howe'er it be, fail not to be here thyself to-morrow, before supper-time. And so God bless thee and all thine to the comfort of thy dear Dad.

JAMES, R.

Your old Purveyor sends you a kid for your dinner to-morrow, and thou shall find another here.

Prince Charles to the Duke of Buckingham.

STEENIE,

HIS Majesty likes the last letter better than the first, only it has two faults where the other has but one. In the first it has only this, that it binds his Majesty to a promise, that if any of his Majesty's Popish subjects offend, he must let the Pope know of it before he punish them, which ye may remember upon the inditing of the letter his Majesty says he stuck upon; and the second error in the new letter is, that his Majesty wishes the Pope to expel the Jesuits by order. Now, his Majesty leaves the ordinary form of doing it to the Pope, by his own ordinary ways; his Majesty hath nothing ado to teach him by what order to do it; he has likewise put in the last letter before the subscription, *S. V. devotissimus*; whereas, in his Majesty's letter to the former Pope, there was nothing written but his

Majesty's

Majefty's name. He likewife, in one place at leaft of the fecond letter, omits to put in *Romanos* after *Catholicos*. Now, ye know, my father has ever ftood upon it, both by word and write, that he is as good a Catholic as the Pope himfelf; therefore fince they take to themfelves the ftile of Catholic Roman, let them brook it a God's name, he will not fcant them of a fyllable of it. I will fpeak to Secretary Conway for a pafs for Robert Watfon, but by this ye may fee, that, of neceffity, the letter muft be written over again before his Majefty can fign it, which he prays you that it may be done with all fpeed poffible; and as for your letter to the Cardinal, he likes very well of it. As for the requeft ye make his Majefty to delay his journey to Royfton; he fays ye play the part of a crafty courtier, that where an inch is given you, ye would fain win a fpan; for, in earneft, he fays it will be far againft his heart to ftay at Theobalds, where he can have no reception, but to doil up and down the park, for there is no kind of field-hawking there; and befides, while the feafon is yet fweet and hares of breath, his Majefty can with eafe begin that exercife, which he cannot do fo well when it is later in the year; and as for your part, if ye fhall not be ready to go with him to Theobalds, according to his many warnings of you, and your promife to him, he can take no pleafure to be there, and he fays that ye abfolutely promifed to go with him at his back coming. As for my part, I hope to be able to follow him quickly, howfoever I fhould be loth that he fhould ftay for me; his Majefty intends likewife to write to you to-morrow morning. So in hafte I reft

Your faithful conftant loving friend,

CHARLES, P.

Duke of Buckingham to King James.

Dear Dad and Goſſip,

NOTWITHSTANDING this unfavourable interpretation I find made of a thankful and loyal heart, in calling my words crude Catonic words, in obedience to your commands, I will tell the Houſe of Parliament, that you having been upon the fields this afternoon, have taken ſuch a fierce rheum and cough, as not knowing how you will be this night, you are not yet able to appoint them a day of hearing ; but I will forbear to tell them, that, notwithſtanding of your cold, you were able to ſpeak with the King of Spain's inſtruments, though not with your own ſubjects. All I can ſay is, you march ſlowly towards your own ſafety, thoſe that depend of you. I pray God at laſt you may attain to it, otherwiſe I ſhall take little comfort in wife or child, though now I am ſuſpected to look more to the riſing ſun, than my Maker.

Sir, hitherto I have tied myſelf to a punctual anſwer of yours; if I ſhould give myſelf leave to ſpeak my own thoughts, they are ſo many, that though the quality of them ſhould not grieve you, coming from one you wilfully and unjuſtly deject, yet the number of them are ſo many, that I ſhould not give over till I had troubled you; therefore I will tie myſelf to that, which ſhall be my laſt and ſpeedy refuge, to pray the Almighty to increaſe your joys, and qualify the ſorrows of your Majeſty.

Duke of Buckingham to King James.

Dear Dad and Gossip,

AS necessity enforces me, instead of repairing to you, according to your command, and my promise, to go many miles from you another way, and consequently from myself; all my perfecteſt joys and pleaſures chiefly, nay ſolely conſiſting in attending your perſon; ſo methinks duty and good manners command me, on the other part, to give you an account under my own hand, though it be yet ſomething unſteady and weak. But before I give the reaſons of the change of my former reſolution; there is a thing not much in exerciſe now in the world, called thankfulneſs, that calls ſo faſt and earneſtly upon me, that I muſt firſt, though I have already done it by the aſſiſtance of a young Nobleman called Baby-Charles, whom you likewiſe by your good offices made my friend, who, without all doubt, hath already perfectlier made my thanks, than I ſhall my-ſelf; yet having the pen in my hand, I muſt needs tell you what I obſerve in your late abſent and public favour, but ancient manner of obliging your poor unworthy ſervant, whereby I find you ſtill one and the ſame dear and indulgent maſter you were ever to me, never being contented to overvalue, and love me yourſelf, but to labour all manner of ways, to make the whole world do ſo to me. Beſides, this aſſures me, you truſt me as abſolutely as ever, largely expreſt in this, that you have no conceit of my popularity; otherwiſe, why ſhould you thus ſtudy to endear me with the Upper and Lower Houſe of Parliament, and ſo conſequently with your whole kingdom? All, and the leaſt I can ſay is this: That I naturally ſo love your perſon, and, upon ſo good experience and knowledge, adore all your other parts, which are more than ever one man had, that were not only all your people, but all the world befides, fet together on one fide, and you alone on the other, I fhould, to obey and pleafe you, difpleafe, nay defpife all them; and this fhall be ever my popularity. Give me leave here, to ufe your own proverb, *For this the devil cone me no thanks* *. The reafons of my going to Newhall are thefe, Firft, I find bufinefs and the fight of bufy folk does me much harm, and though your extraordinary care and watchful eye over me, would keep them from fpeaking to me, yet in a court I muft needs look many of them in the face. Then Theobalds houfe is now very hot, and hath but few change of rooms; both inconvenient to a fick body. Then my Lord of Warwick tells me, that, by experience, he hath found Newhall air as good a one to ride away an ague, as any in England, and that lately he loft one, by the benefit of that air: I mean near hand, which I think will be all one. By this time, I fear I have troubled you, and were it not that I write to you, I am fure I fhould have wearied myfelf. I have now only one requeft to you; as you firft planted me in your Baby Charles's good opinion, if you think it fit for your fervice, in my abfence continue me in it. And fo give me your blefling.

Your Majefty's moft humble flave and dog,

STEENIE.

---

* This is a very different ftyle, from that in a fubfequent letter, where he takes the popular fide againft the King's.

Duke of Buckingham to King James.

Dear Dad and Goſſip,

THOUGH I writ laſt night, yet I think it not amiſs to add one word more, to expreſs myſelf more particularly. My Lord Maxwell is arrived, and hath aſſured me, having had it out of the Pope's own mouth, that the diſpenſation is granted free, and unclogged. He further adds, that after he had, in a rough manner, ſpoke with the Nuncio at Paris, inſomuch that he told him he would complain of him preſently in a letter to his Holineſs, he anſwered him calmly thus, and with ſome expreſſion of fear, That he ſhould do it; that if he would but have a little patience, he would quickly go through the buſineſs, and have no cauſe to complain. All this I have told Fiatt, but under the roſe. I likewiſe told him you reproached to me, where is your glorious match with France and your royal frank Monſieurs? I told him alſo, I had order to ſet a ſhort day for the aſſembling of the Parliament, and that you had commanded me, if the Spaniſh Agent came to viſit me, that I ſhould, upon pain of your diſpleaſure, not only uſe him civilly, but kindly. He anſwered me impatiently and confuſedly, What, cannot one make a trial of gaining better and more advantageous conditions, without an intention to break? Whereupon I told him I did not think there was one occaſion, beſides the ties of honour or honeſty, would give them leave; but I was ſorry and aſhamed, that ſo unſeaſonably, after all things was performed to their deſire, nay more than they could have imagined, witneſs the aſſiſtance of ſhipping, the hearty profeſſions of my maſter, as well by letter, as thoſe verbal compliments he ſent by Monſieur La Riviere, and now, at the time when acknowledgements at the leaſt, if not requitals, ſhould come, with greedy gluttonous appetites to ſeek to ſurfeit on the forbidden tree, can re-

7   ceive

ceive no cleanlier an interpretation, than to have come from an unreafonable, unjuft, falfe and unmannerly appetite; and thus you
have ended *avec bone bouche:* but I thought in my mind fhitten
mouths. I pray you, Sir, do not kifs that word, nor bewray, for
want of bold and abfolute language, a good bufinefs. I ended with
Monfieur thus, your mafter acknowledges he hath already the fubftance of what he defires, though I know the contrary. The Pope
is to receive fatisfaction, not from my mafter but yours. Now
then let every man act his own natural proper part. Spain muft
really be cozened; let the Pope do that, fince he can as well
pardon himfelf, as all the world. The Pope feemingly muft be
cozened; let France do that, who hath the title of the moft Chriftian
King, and fo may the eafilier obtain a pardon: my mafter will neither be cozened, nor cozen. Wherefore the moft Chriftian King muft,
moft confcionably, undertake to his Holinefs, for as much as may cozen
Spain, France, and Rome; who may not, for their union, be called
the Father, the Son, and the Holy Ghoft. Sir, I will weary your
patience with one word more, if you pleafe: treat as little as may be,
and roundly let the Ambaffador know, you fo much prize your honour, that neither in a circumftance, nor form, will you make an
alteration, and fet your Ambaffadors a fettled, fhort, peremptory
day, for an anfwer; if it prove good, I fhall be as foon ready to go
from hence, as it can be to come hither; if ill, then let your Ambaffadors as fpeedily come away; for never admit of new journies to
Rome, neither doth it need. I will end with Mall's compliment to
me; Lord Father, I love you well. Lord Father I will die for you.
So I crave your blefling, as

Your Majefty's moft humble flave and dog,

STEENIE *.

* It would be endlefs to tranfcribe more
letters in this naufeous ftyle betwixt the King
and his favourite, there are feveral in an in-
decent one. The negociation with France
was then depending, and conducted with as
little regard to dignity and true policy, as
that with Spain.

Duke of Buckingham to King James.

Dear Dad and Goffip,

I HAVE fent Watt Montague this morning into France, with the copy of thofe things you refolved of with the French Ambaf-fador, that our Ambaffadors may no more complain for want of timely advertifements. The Spanifh Agent will be with me, before I can have well ended this letter. Gundemar's man was with me this morning; the difcourfe I had with him, I am fure will not only be pleafing to you, but make you laugh. The moft part of the morning I fpent with the French Ambaffador, and yet could not make an end; wherefore he hath earneftly intreated me to ftay this day in town, as likewife to fee the difpatch he will fend into France. He makes no queftion of an anfwer from thence anfwerable to your heart's defire. I confefs I believe it, and the rather becaufe I know they dare do no otherwife, and am fure you now begin to laugh in your fleeve, to fee yourfelf fo courted of all fides, that all their actions turn to your advantage.

Dear Dad, fince I cannot come to-night, let this hafty letter give thanks for that true, favourable, and moft affectionate interpretation of my ftaying here: and God never relieve me when I have moft need, if it be not a feparating of myfelf, when I am from you, and in lieu of having comfort, and my heart's eafe by you to ferve you, I give myfelf nothing but trouble and vexation.

Your Majefty's moft humble flave and dog,

STEENIE.

Duke of Buckingham to King James.

Dear Dad and Goſſip,

HAVING more buſineſs than was fit to trouble you with in a
letter, I was once reſolved to have waited on you myſelf, but
preſently came to me the news of the Spaniſh Ambaſſador's going
to you, which hath diverted this reſolution at this time, becauſe I
will not increaſe that in you of which I have already found too
much; and that I will not let the Ambaſſador himſelf think, that
you are diſtruſted, though this gives enough and too much to your
people. I have, to eaſe your labour, writ ſome things to my Lord of
Arran, by whom I likewiſe expect my anſwer. Only I will trouble
yourſelf with this, that I beſeech you to ſend me your plain and re-
ſolute anſwer, whether, if your people ſo reſolve to give you a royal
aſſiſtance, as to the number of ſix ſubſidies and fifteenths, with a promiſe after, in caſe of neceſſity, to aſſiſt you with their lives and fortunes; whether then you will not accept it, and their counſel, to break
the match with the other treaties; and whether or no, to bring them
to this, I may not aſſure ſome of them underhand, becauſe it is
feared, that when your turns are ſerved, you will not call them
together again to reform abuſes, grievances, and the making of laws
for the good government of the country, that you will be ſo far
from that, that you will rather weary them with it, deſiring nothing more than their loves and happineſs, in which your own is
included. Sir, I beſeech you think ſeriouſly of this, and reſolve
once conſtantly to run one way. For ſo long as you waver between
the Spaniards and your ſubjects, to make your advantage of both,
you are ſure to do it with neither.

I ſhould for my own contentment (though I am ſure I do you
ſome ſervice here, and would be able, if you would deal heartily

and

and openly with me, to do more), wait upon you oftener, but JAMES I.
that you going two ways, and myfelf only one, it occafions fo
many difputes, that till you be once refolved, I think it is of more
comfort and eafe to you, and fafer for me, that I now abide away.
For to be of your opinion, would be flattery, and not to fpeak
humbly mine own, would be treachery; therefore I will, at this
time, with all the induftry of my mind, ferve you here, and pray
for the good fuccefs of that, and the lengthening of your days, with
all the affeâions of his foul, that will live and die a lover of you.

JAMES I.
1624.

Your Majefty's moft humble flaye and dog,

STEENIE *.

*What follows is all written with the Duke of Buckingham's own
hand.*

That you did not mean to put a fcorn upon them, to call for their
advice, and then to rejeâ it, if they give royal affiftance with it.

Fuft, to give them thanks for their uniform offer of advice.

Then to take notice of their careful proceedings in the Lower
Houfe.

That you do not defire to engage them in their gift, till you be
declared anent their advice.

And if you be engaged into a war by their advice, you mean not
to hearken to a peace, without firft hearing them.

And that they may fee your fincere dealing with them, you will
be contented that they chufe a committee to fee the iffuing out of
the money they give, for the recovery of the Palatinate, in cafe you
accept their advice.

* This is a remarkable letter, and the only   been writ about March or April 1624. It
one in the popular ftrain I ever met with of   fhews the old King's averfenefs to a quarrel
the Duke of Buckingham's. It muft have   with Spain.

Then

Then to fhow them that this is the fitteft-time that ever prefented itfelf to make a right underftanding between you and your people†.

And you affure yourfelf, their behaviour will fo continue as they have begun towards you; that they fhall fee, by proof, how far you will be in love with parliaments for making of good laws,, and reforming of abufes.

Duke of Buckingham to King James.

Dear Dad and Goffip,

BECAUSE the fenfe and thankfulnefs of my heart, for your excellent melons, pears, fugared beans, and affurance of better fruit planted in your bofom than ever grew in Paradife, will beft appear in my humble obedience of your commands, I thought it fitteft to delay the anfwer of your kind letter, till I might give you a full account of all it contained. By this time, I hope, Mr. Secretary hath told you, I miftook not the Ambaffador, but he his own language; but before I could difpatch with him, the day was fo far fpent, that night accompanied me to Newhall: but this morning I have firft agreed with Mr. Jennings, who is the fitteft man we could have chofen for this bufinefs, and hath affured me that what is projected, I dare not fay in this, but as in all other things, refolved of, till you fay content, will be foon done, eafy, cheap, and without hindering deer, fow, or man, of free paffage. The particulars I referve till I may demonftrate it, upon the map or place; but in the mean time, Mr. Jennings will be preparing the ground, the trees, and all other neceffary things, fo that there fhall be no time loft, till you be acquainted with all, and pleafed with it. Now for my own park,

† Here follows two lines blotted out.

I have

JAMES I.
1624.

I have found this morning another fine wood that muſt go in with the reſt, and two hundred acres of meadows, broom, cloſes, and plentiful ſprings running through them; ſo that I hope Newhall park ſhall be nothing inferior to Burleigh. My ſtags are all luſty, my calf, bald, and others are ſo too. My Spaniſh colts are fat, and ſo is my jovial filley. Mall, Great Mall, Kate, Sue, and Steenie, ſhall all wait of you on Saturday, and kiſs both James's and Charles's feet. To conclude, let this letter aſſure you, that the laſt words I ſpoke to you are ſo true, that I will not only give my word for them, ſwear upon the Holy Evangeliſts, but take the bleſſed ſacrament upon them. So craving your bleſſing I reſt

Your Majeſty's moſt humble ſlave and dog,

STEENIE.

Baby Charles, I kiſs thy warty hands.

Duke of Buckingham to King James.

Dear Dad and Goſſip,

I DO not know what fault I have made of late, that you ſhould take ſo cruel a revenge of me, as to put me in the fear your laſt but one letter did. I am too far behind-hand to let the quarrel reſt ſo, though in your laſt you made a propoſition full of affection, if I may call it by ſo ſaucy a name. You are now in the place I love, therefore, for that reſpect, I will now forbear you, but when off of that ground, look to yourſelf. I hope to have the happineſs to-morrow to kiſs your hands, therefore I will not ſend you the letter you writ to the Pope, which I have got from Secretary Calvert. When he delivered it to me, he made this requeſt, that he hoped your Majeſty would as well truſt him in a letter you were now to

write

wiite, as you had heretofore in the former. I did what I could to diffemble it; but when there was no means to do it, I thought beft to feem to truft him abfolutely, thereby the better to tie him to fecrecy [*]. If this be a lie, as I am fure it is, then you may begin to think, that, with a little more ftock, I may cry quittance. So I crave your blefling.

Your Majefty's moft humble flave and dog,

STEENIE.

A million of thanks for your good melons and pears.

Duke of Buckingham to King James.

Dear Dad and Goffip,

IN one of your letters you have commanded me to write fhortly, and merrily. I fhall ever, and in all things, obey you. I humbly thank you for making your commands eafy to be obeyed in thefe two particulars; and fo you preferve the laft fo, ftill the firft hath been fo rivetted with what is paft, that no time to come can alter it. How can I but write merrily, when he is fo I love beft, and beyond all the world? I fhall love the poor fellow's face the better for it while I live, for relating it with fuch joy. And for my writing fhort, why fhould I ever write otherwife, when all I can fay muft be fhort of what I fhould fay and do, you have fo infinitely obliged me? therefore I will, nay I muft be fhort. I have left off phyfic; I will wait of you by the day appointed. I had Jennings with me about Theobalds park. All is well, and goes on bravely;

----

[*] Secretary Calvert refigned foon after, and turned Papift, his fucceffor was Sir A. Morton. No wonder he fhould wifh to be   entrufted with a fecret correfpondence between his Mafter and the Pope.

and

and fo is your Baby Charles, whom I hope to wait of down. This
inclofed will give you an account of the Dunkirker's fhips. By
this little paper you will underftand a fuit of fine Hollands. By the
other parchment, a fuit of my Lord Prefident's. Of all do but what
you pleafe, fo you give me your bleffing, which I muft never be denied, fince I can never be other than

Your Majefty's moft humble flave and dog,

STEENIE.

Duke of Buckingham to King James.

Dear Dad and Goffip,

THOUGH I have received three or four letters from you fince
that I writ laft to you, yet as Tom Badger fays, I am not
behind-hand with you, for I have made a hundred anfwers to them
in my mind; for kinder letters never fervant received from mafter;
and for fo great a King to defcend fo low, as to his humbleft flave
and fervant to communicate himfelf in fuch a ftile of good fellow-
fhip, with expreffions of more care than fervants have of mafters,
than phyficians have of their patients (which hath largely appeared
to me in ficknefs and in health), of more tendernefs than fathers
have to children, of more friendfhip than between equals, of more
affection than between lovers in the beft kind, man and wife,
what can I return? Nothing but filence; for, if I fpeak, I muft be
faucy and fay thus, or fhort of what is due: my purveyor, my
good-fellow, my phyfician, my maker, my friend, my father, my
all; I heartily and humbly thank you for all you do, and all I
have. Judge what unequal language this is in itfelf, but efpecially
confidering

confidering the thing that muſt ſpeak it, and the perſon to whom it muſt be ſpoken. Now tell me whether I have not done diſcreetly to be ſilent all this while. It is time I ſhould be ſo again, or elſe commit a fault in wearying him that never wearies to do good. Then thus I'll end. I begin my journey to-morrow. I ſhall have the Prince to wait of. We ſhall be at Theobalds. The one will hunt hinds and does; the other ſurvey the trees, walks, ponds, and deer. The next day after, lay ourſelves at your feet, there crave your bleſſing, then give an account of Theobalds park to the beſt of man, though not of the kind of man, yet made by man more than man, like a man, both artificial man, and my moſt natural ſovereign, who by innumerable favours hath made me

Your Majeſty's both humble ſlave and dog,

STEENIE.

No. XXVII.

The Spanish Match continued.

The Earl of Bristol's Letters.

From the
originals in
the Paper
Office.

[So much pains was taken by the Duke of Buckingham and his party, both at the end of King James's reign, and the beginning of his fucceffor's, to throw blame on the Earl of Briftol's conduct, that it is but juft to lay before the Public, what that Nobleman had to offer in his own vindication. The Reader will find a manly and clear ftyle in his difpatches, far fuperior to that of his correfpondents in office; and will not hefitate to pronounce him much better qualified for a firft Minifter, than the infolent and capricious Favourite, or the infufficient Secretary. The Reader may compare the private apology of Lord Briftol to King James, with the articles he gave into the Houfe of Lords againft the Duke of Buckingham, and his anfwer to the articles preferred againft himfelf by the Attorney General. The abrupt diffolution of that Parliament put an end to the procefs.]

Earl of Briftol to Secretary Calvert.

Right Honourable,

ON Monday the 29th of September, *ft. vet.* my Lord Ambaffador, and the Cardinal Capata, and the other Counfellors of State, together with all the whole houfehold which had waited on the Prince to St. Andero, returned hither; having received all great content in the entertainment which was given there aboard, and much admiring the fhips, but taken with nothing more than with the

Octtober 24.

3 P   princely

princely carriage of his Highnefs towards them; which I can fafely fay unto you, without flattery, hath been generally fuch, as never any Prince that went out of his country, gained fo much upon the affections of a ftrange people, as his Highnefs hath done here; whereof the extraordinary great liberality and bounty which he hath ufed, hath not been the leaft-caufe; which he was pleafed, at his embarking, much to enlarge, by giving order, that the gifts and rewards of all thofe which had attended him in his journey, fhould be double the value of what was firft appointed for them; a note of all which, when I fhall have perfected the lift, I will fend unto his Highnefs, and to yourfelf. We have found fome difficulty in taking up of monies; but I fhall, God willing, fee it punctually performed to his Highnefs's honour.

The King, fince his Highnefs's departure, hath many ways expreffed his love and affection towards him, of which, in my particular, I have had experience; who, upon occafion of bufinefs, have not need, according to the ufual manner, and as all other Ambaffadors do, to crave audience of him, but, by a fpecial and unufual favour, have at all times free accefs unto him, giving only notice to fome gentleman of the chamber, of my being there, and of my attendance; the which grace and favour my Lord Ambaffador Sir Walter Afton likewife, fince his return, enjoyeth. On Tuefday the 7th of this prefent month, *fl. vet.* my Lord went hence to the Efcurial, whither it pleafed this King, upon occafion of fome bufinefs which offered in the treaty of the Palatinate, to fend for us, who had removed thither fome few days before *a la brama*, it being ufual with him at this feafon, when the ftags come down to rutt from the mountains, to pafs fome time in hunting there. We were no fooner come thither, which was the next day before dinner, but we were prefently carried by the Condé of Olivares, up to the King in his bed-chamber, where we found him without his cloak, and in the fame manner as he ufeth to be feen of fuch of his fervants only as

are

are near about his perfon, and were received of him with extraordinary freenefs and affability: he being pleafed to fay, that now, for that he accounted the Prince's Highnefs to be his brother, he would not treat us as Ambaffadors, but as of his houfehold. We were feafted at dinner by the Mayor Domo, and accompanied by divers gentlemen of the chamber. After dinner, the King took us abroad in his own coach, in which he had no other with him, but only Don Carlos his brother, and the Condé of Olivares, and fo carried us to the Campillo, a place well-known to his Highnefs, where we faw him kill four-ftags, and afterwards returned fomewhat late, well nigh an hour within night, to the Efcurial, where we were entertained and lodged in the King's houfe. The next morning, it was the King's pleafure that we fhould go forth by ourfelves to hunt in the woods not far diftant from the houfe, where we killed each of us a ftag, and coming back to the Efcurial, were admitted that day to fee the King dine. Which particulars, although they will feem no great matter in England, where they are things of ordinary courfe, yet I can affure you, they are thought ftrange here, and efteemed extraordinary graces, fuch as of which, I dare boldly fay, they have not feen any former examples.

This being only to acquaint you with thefe particulars, deferring all matter of bufinefs to the other difpatches, I commit you to God's bleffed protection, and with the remembrance of my love and fervice to you, I reft,

Your's, &c.

Madrid,
October 24th, ſ⁹ vet.

BRISTOL.

Earl of Briftol to the King.

May it pleafe your moft excellent Majefty,

Augt. 29th.   ALTHOUGH, by my other letters, I have given your Majefty
a full account of all things that paffed exteriorly betwixt this
King and his Highnefs upon his departure; yet fince the further
purfuing of your Majefty's bufineffes is now left unto myfelf and Sir
Walter Afton, I think it my duty to reprefent truly unto your Majefty, in what ftate they now ftand; to the end that hereafter I may
give your Majefty a more juftifiable account of my proceedings, and
your Majefty, being truly and rightly informed of the truth, may the
better direct and command what fhall be fitteft for your fervice.

Firft, concerning his Highnefs's Match, thus it ftandeth. Upon
the arrival here of this Pope's approbation of thofe few articles which
were laft fent into Rome, this King is by powers left with him by the
Prince to marry *per verba de præfenti* the Infanta, which he is contented to capitulate fhall be within ten days after the arrival of the
faid approbation; and, in the *interim*, the Infanta is here ftiled by
the name of *Princeffa de Ingaltierra*, and in all things efteemed as
his wife betrothed; and in that quality carrieth herfelf towards all.

As touching the temporal articles; they were begun to be treated
of fo near the departure of the Prince, that there had been but only
one meeting and conference concerning them fince the Prince his
arrival, which was only two days before his highnefs's going. And
then there was on all fides fo much to do, that it was not poffible to
bring any of them to a conclufion; but, God willing, prefently upon
the return of the King and his Minifters to the town, we will refume the treaty where I had formerly left it, and hope to give his
Highnefs fome good account of it before his going out of Spain (if
it be not hindered by his Highnefs carrying fome of the Commiffi-

oners

oners along with him to the fea-fide), or unto your Majefty, fpeedily after the return to Madrid.

As touching the bufinefs of the Palatinate; there have been feveral conferences and meetings about it, and it feemeth to be brought to this iffue, that, upon your Majefty's condefcending that the Prince Palatine's eldeft fon may be bred in the Emperor's Court, with the other conditions of fubmiffion which have ever been offered, they are contented that there be a full reftitution made of all his territories, both of the Upper and Lower Palatinate, together with the Dignity Electoral; but hereunto they would fufpend his prefent admiffion, not by way of abfolute exclufion, but to be reftored thereunto, upon his future good behaviour, and your Majefty's and the King of Spain's farther interceffion. But againft this there hath been abfolute proteftation made, for the reafons which I have prefumed to fet down in writing, and have now fent them unto Mr. Secretary Calvert, to prefent them unto your Majefty. But, God willing, we fhall prefently refume his treaty, and your Majefty fhall have a faithful account thereof.

Concerning the bufinefs of Holland, wherein I received fome late directions by your Majefty's letters of the 20th of July, directed unto my Lord of Buckingham and myfelf, I conceive it is not yet feafonable any way to ftir in it; and I muft here, like a faithful and much obliged fervant unto your Majefty, prefume to deal freely and clearly with you, that if your Majefty's great and high wifdom find not means to compound and accommodate what is now out of order, although I conceive it not to be doubted, but that the match will; in the end, proceed, yet your Majefty will find yourfelf fruftrated of thofe effects of amity and friendfhip, which by this alliance you expected. For the truth is, that this King and his Minifters are grown to have fo high a diflike againft my Lord Duke of Buckingham, and, on the one fide, to judge him to have fo much power with your Majefty and the Prince, and on the other fide, to be fo ill affected to

them

them and their affairs, that, if your Majefty fhall not be pleafed in your wifdom, either to find fome means of reconciliation, or elfe to let them fee and be affured that it fhall no way be in my Lord of Buckingham's power to make the Infanta's life lefs happy unto her, or any way to crofs and embroil the affairs betwixt your Majefties and your kingdoms; I am afraid your Majefty will fee the effects which you have juft caufe to expect from this alliance to follow but flowly, and all the great bufineffes, now in treaty, profper but ill. For I muft, for the difcharge of my confcience and duty, without defcending to any particulars, let your Majefty truly know, that fufpicions and diftaftes betwixt them all here, and my Lord of Buckingham, cannot be at a greater height. This I fet down unto your Majefty, only to lay truth before you, which, if any refpect in the world fhould make me forbear, I fhould judge myfelf unworthy of life, efpecially in a bufinefs of fo great confequence; in the profperous and fuccefsful conclufion whereof, I conceive the greateft part of the quiet and happinefs of your Majefty's life is like to confift. So, having given unto Mr. Secretary Calvert an account of all your Majefty's bufineffes, I prefume not to trouble you any farther; but, with my humble prayers to God for your Majefty's health and profperity, I recommend your Majefty to his moft holy protection. And reft,

Your Majefty's moft humble, and moft
faithful fervant and fubject,
BRISTOL.

Madrid,
Auguft 29th, 1623. <i>f^o. v.s.</i>

The Same to the Same.

May it pleafe your moſt excellent Majeſty,

Sept. 9th.

I Prefumed, in a former letter, in the difcharge of the duty of a faithful fervant, to fet down unto your Majeſty, how much prejudice I conceived might come unto your Majeſty's fervice, by the high diſtaſtes grown betwixt them here and my Lord Duke of Buckingham, if by your Majeſty's wifdom it were not prevented.

That letter I wrote upon his Highnefs's departure from Madrid; fince I followed the Prince unto the Efcurial, being left behind a day for the difpatch of bufinefs. There I found the former diſtaſtes betwixt the Duke and the Condé of Olivares grown to a publick profeffed hatred, and an irreconcilable enmity; but for the Prince, I cannot but let your Majeſty underſtand, that, from the higheſt to the loweſt, he hath left all men's hearts fet upon him; and the leave taking betwixt the Prince and the King was with as great profeffion of love and affection as could be, whereof I was a witnefs, being interpreter betwixt them; and prefently fet down the effect of their fpeeches in writing, which I have fent unto Mr. Secretary Calvert, together with the copies of the King of Spain's letter, written that night unto the Prince, all with his own hand, in confirmation of what he had faid, and the Prince his anfwer thereunto; whereby your Majeſty will fee how their hearts ſtand one towards another, and how likely it is, that all your great affairs will in the end have good fuccefs, if they be not, by the paffions of the Miniſters of the one fide or the other, interrupted. I ſhall not prefume to lay blame on any, but I ſhall faithfully labour and take care that other men's faults and errors may not have fuch reflection upon your Majeſty's affairs, as that thereby they may be hazarded.

2

I well

I well know how long your Majefty hath treated this bufinefs, and how great things your Majefty hath done for the bringing of it to effect.   And queftionlefs, the fame motives and conveniences for making of this alliance and friendfhip with Spain, which were, are ftill on foot; and to them is added the fatisfaction which I fuppofe his Highnefs hath of the Infanta's perfon, and the good fuccefs of them more affured than ever, and the time prefixed.   So that I hope all thofe accidents which ordinarily fall out at the interview of Princes, wherein difference of cuftom or religion may raife diftaftes, the emulation which groweth between their chief fervants and Minifters, whereby often the affairs of their Mafters are difordered and hazarded, will, by your Majefty's great wifdom and prudence, be fo tempered and moderated, that they may caufe no difturbance either in the alliance, or the effects which are to be expected from it.   I prefume to write thus much unto your Majefty, for that I conceive through the fcarcity of the place, the negligence of officers, and the humour of the Spaniards, the Prince his fervants may return home with little fatisfaction; yet, as on the one fide, thefe omiffions have little relation to your Majefty's great affairs, fo I dare fay, that the King of Spain, (who I hope will, in the match and all other things, give your Majefty good fatisfaction) cannot but be forry to fee it wanting in thefe petty circumftances, wherein I know there hath not been wanting in this King, all poffible care for the preventing of them; although the faults of officers, and the fterilnefs of the country by which the Prince is to pafs, I guefs will fend the whole company home, with many juft caufes of complaint, but I am confident that neither that, nor any other perfonal mifunderftandings whatfoever, will be of power to put any difturbance in your Majefty's high and important affairs.

For all other particulars, I have given an account of them unto Mr. Secretary Calvert, fo that I fhall not prefume to give your Majefty any further trouble, but with my humble prayers to God

for

for the increase of all happiness and prosperity unto your Majesty,
I humbly recommend your Majesty to God's holy protection, and
rest,

Your Majesty's, &c.

Madrid, the 19th of Sept.
1623, *st°. vet.*

BRISTOL.

The Same to the Same.

May it please your Majesty,

BY my cousin Simon Digbye I gave your Majesty an account of all that passed here, upon the Prince's departure, and that, according to what was capitulated, his highness had left powers for the marrying of the Infanta, *per verba de præsenti*, which powers were made to the King and his brother Don Carlos, but left with me, to be delivered upon the arrival of the Pope's approbation, and so declared to be his Highness's pleasure before all the King's Ministers that were present at the solemn acts of passing the Prince his powers unto the King. Since his Highness's departure, I have received commandment from his Highness, not to make delivery of the said powers, until his Highness shall be satisfied what security may be given him that the Infanta will not become a religious woman, after the betrothing, and that I expect his further pleasure therein, as your Majesty will see by the copy of his Highness's letter unto me, which I presume to send unto your Majesty, as likewise the answer which in that point I make unto his Highness, to the end your Majesty may have perfect information of the whole estate of the business. For that I conceive the temporal articles are so far agreed, that I hope to give your Majesty an account of them within few days, and to your content; and the business, after so

3 Q   many

many rubs, brought to that eſtate, that, I am confident, there will
not be any failing in any point capitulated betwixt your Majeſty or
his Highneſs, but all will be punctually performed. I conceive
your Majeſty (continuing your deſire of the match) would be loth
to have the fair way it is now in to be clogged or interrupted by any
new accident or jealouſy that may be raiſed; for queſtionleſs there
is no ſecurity in that particular, that can on his Highneſs's part be
required, that they will refuſe him. And I muſt further let your
Majeſty underſtand, that the firſt of the temporal articles is, that
the *deſpoſorios* ſhall be within ten days after the arrival of the Pope's
approbation, which is hourly expected : ſo that I muſt deal like a
faithful ſervant with your Majeſty. If upon the coming of the Pope's
approbation, it being capitulated that the *deſpoſorios* ſhall be within
ten days after the arrival of it, I ſhould withhold the powers, and
they underſtand that it is by a ſecret order of the Prince's, there
being a clauſe in the ſaid powers, that the Prince ſhall no ways,
either in part or whole, revoke the ſaid powers, or detract from
them, but that they ſhall be in force until Chriſtmas; I fear your
Majeſty will find your buſineſs much diſturbed and retarded by it.
And therefore I am an humble ſuitor unto your Majeſty and the
Prince, if you would have things go on in that fair way (I now
ſuppoſe them to be in), that a poſt may be inſtantly diſpatched
back unto me, authorizing me to deliver the ſaid powers upon the
arrival of the approbation, and, having taken fitting ſecurity, in this
particular point, of the Infanta's not entering into religion after her
betrothing. And I hold it infinitely convenient that this be done
with all poſſible ſecrecy and ſpeed, and that the Spaniſh Ambaſſadors come not to any knowledge that ever any ſtay was made
of the delivery of the powers. And if, in the interim, the approbation
come, I doubt not but, for twenty or twenty-four days, to find other
fair pretexts of deferring the *deſpoſorios*; and herein I beg your
Majeſty's reſolution with all ſpeed poſſible.

I hope

I hope that in two days Mr. Secretary Cottington will be able to begin his journey towards England. He will give your Majesty an exact account of all your busineffes here, and such a one, as I conceive, your Majesty will be glad to hear. Your Majesty may therefore be pleafed to fufpend any refolution in them until you have heard him. And fo with my prayers for the increafe of all happinefs unto your Majefty, I humbly, &c.

J AMES I.
1623.

Your Majefty's, &c.

Madrid, the 24th of Sept. BRISTOL.
1623, 4°. vet.

The Same to the Same.

May it pleafe, &c.

I HAVE received your Majefty's letters of the 8th of October, on the 21ft of the fame, fome hours within night, and have thought it fit to difpatch back unto your Majefty with all poffible fpeed, referring the anfwer to what your Majefty hath by thefe letters commanded me, to a poft that I fhall purpofely difpatch when I fhall have negociated the particulars with this King and his Minifters; wherein, God willing, all poffible difpatch fhall be ufed.

Oct. 24th

But forafmuch as I find, both by your Majefty's faid letters, as likewife by letters which I have received from the Prince's Highnefs, that you continue your defires of having the match proceeded in, I held it my duty that your Majefty fhould be informed, that although I am fet free, in as much as concerneth the doubt of the Infanta's entering into religion, for the delivering the powers left with me by his Highnefs, yet by this new direction I now receive from your Majefty, that the *defpoforios* fhould be deferred until Chriftmas, the faid powers are made altogether ufelefs and invalid, it be-

3 Q 2 ing

ing a claufe in the body of the faid powers, that they fhall only remain in force till Chriftmas, and no longer, as your Majefty will fee by the copy of them, which I fend here inclofed. Your Majefty, I conceive, will be of opinion, that this fufpending of the execution of the powers, until the force and validity of them be expired, is a direct and effectual revoking of them, which not to do, how far his Highnefs is in honour engaged, your Majefty will be beft able to judge, by viewing the powers themfelves. Further, if the date of thefe powers do expire (befides the breach of the capitulations), although the match itfelf fhould not by jealoufies and miftrufts be hazarded, yet the Princefs's coming at the Spring into England, will be almoft impoffible. For by that time new commiffions and powers fhall be (after Chriftmas) granted by the Prince, which muft be to the fatisfaction of both parties, I conceive fo much of the year will be fpent, that it will be impoffible for the fleets and other preparations to be in a readinefs againft the Spring. For it is not to be imagined that they will here proceed effectually with their preparations, until they fhall be affured of the *defpoforios*, efpecially when they fhall have feen that, feveral times, deferred on the Prince's part, and that, upon pretexts that are not new, nor grown fince the granting of the powers, but were before in being, and often under debate, and yet were never infifted upon to make ftay of the bufinefs; fo that it will feem that they might better have hindered the granting of them then, than the execution of them now, if there were no ftaggering in former refolutions, the which although really there is not, yet cannot it be but fufpected, and the clearing of it between Spain and England will coft much time. I muft humbly crave your Majefty's pardon if I write unto you with the plainnefs of a truehearted and faithful fervant, who have ever co-operated honeftly unto your Majefty's ends, if I knew them. I know your Majefty hath long been of opinion that the greateft affurance you could get, that the King of Spain would effectually labour the entire reftitu-

tion

tion of the Prince Palatine was, that he really proceeded to the JAMES I.
effecting of the match; and my inftructions under your Majefty's 1623
hand were, to infift upon the reftoring of the Prince Palatine, but
not fo as to annex it to the treaty of the match, as that thereby the
match fhould be hazarded; for that your Majefty feemed confident,
they here would never grow to a perfect conclufion of the match,
without a fettled refolution to give your Majefty fatisfaction in the
bufinefs of the Palatinate. The fame courfe I obferved in the carriage of the bufineffes by his Highnefs and my Lord Duke, at their
being here; who, though they infifted on the bufinefs of the Palatinate, yet they held it fit to treat of them diftinctly, and that the
marriage fhould precede as a good pawn for the other. Since their
departure, my Lord Ambaffador Sir Walter Afton, and myfelf, have
much preffed to have this King's refolution in writing, concerning
the Palatinate, and the difpatches which your Majefty will receive
herewith concerning that bufinefs, were written before the receipt
of thefe your Majefty's letters, and doubtlefs it is now a great part
of their care that that bufinefs may be well ended, before the Infanta's coming into England; and his Highnefs will well remember,
that the Condé de Olivares often protefted the neceffity of having
this bufinefs compounded and fettled before the marriage, faying,
otherwife they might give a daughter, and have a war within three
months after, if this ground and fubject of quarrel fhould be ftill
left on foot. The fame language he hath ever fince held with Sir
Walter Afton and myfelf, and that it was a firm peace and amity,
as much as an alliance, which they fought with his Majefty. So
that it is not to be doubted, but that this King concluding the match,
refolveth to employ his utmoft power for the fatisfaction in the reftitution of the Prince Palatine. The queftion now will be, whether
the bufinefs of the Prince Palatine having relation to many great
Princes, that are interefted therein (being at great diftance), and
being indeed for the condition and nature of the bufinefs itfelf, im-

poffible

poſſible to be ended, but by a formal treaty; which of neceſſity will require great length; whether the concluſion of the match ſhall any way depend upon the iſſue of this buſineſs; which I conceive to be far from your Majeſty's intention, for ſo the Prince might long be kept unbeſtowed, by any averſeneſs of thoſe that might have particular intereſt in the Prince's remaining unmarried, or diſlike of his matching with Spain. But that which I underſtand to be your Majeſty's aim is, only to have the concluſion of this match accompanied with as ſtrong engagements as can be procured from this King; for the joining with your Majeſty, not only in all good offices, for the entire reſtitution of the Prince Palatine, but otherwiſe, if need require, of his Majeſty's aſſiſtance. Herein I have, theſe days paſt, laboured with all earneſtneſs, and procured this King's public anſwer, which, I am told, is reſolved of, and I ſhall within few days have it to ſend to your Majeſty; as likewiſe a private propoſition which will be put into your hands; and ſhall not fail further to purſue your Majeſty's preſent directions of procuring this King's declaration in what ſort your Majeſty may rely upon this King's aſſiſtance, in caſe the Emperor, or the Duke of Bavaria ſhall oppoſe the entire reſtitution of the Prince Palatine. But I conceive, if it be your Majeſty's intention that I ſhould procure here, firſt, this King's peremptory anſwer in the whole buſineſs, and how he will be aſſiſtant to your Majeſty, in caſe of the Emperor's or Duke of Bavaria's averſeneſs, and that I ſhould ſend it unto your Majeſty, and receive again your anſwer, before I deliver the powers for the *deſpoſorios*; the match would thereby, if not be hazarded, yet I conceive the Infanta going at Spring would be rendered altogether impoſſible. For if upon the arrival of the Pope's approbation, which is hourly expected, the powers be demanded of me, according to the Prince's declaration, and the agreement in the temporal articles, by which the *deſpoſorios* are to be within ten days after the coming of the ſaid approbation, I cannot refuſe them but upon ſome grounds.

If

If I alledge your Majefty's defire of having the *defpoforios* deferred until Chriftmas, they know, as well as myfelf, that his Highnefs's proxy is then out of date (befides the infringing of the capitulations), and they will judge it as a great fcorn put upon this King (who, ever fince the Prince's granting of his powers, hath called himfelf the Infanta's *Defpofado)* and to that effeﬅ the Prince hath written unto him, in fome of his letters; befides, it will be held here a point of great difhonour unto the Infanta, if the powers called for by her friends, fhould be detained by the prince's part; and whofoever elfe may have deferved ill, fhe certainly hath neither deferved difrefpeﬅ nor difcomfort. Further, upon my refufal to deliver the powers, all preparations which now go on chearfully and apace, will be ftayed, and there will enter in fo much diftruﬅ, and fo many jealoufies, that if the main bufinefs run not hazard by them, at leaft much time will be to clear them. I muft therefore, in difcharge of my duty, tell your Majefty, that I conceive that all your Majefty's bufineffes here, are in a fair way. The match, and all that is capitulated therein they profefs punﬅually to perform. In the bufinefs of the Palatinate they profefs, that they infinitely defire, and will, to the utmoft of their powers, endeavour to procure your Majefty fatisfaﬅion. The Prince is likely to have a moft worthy and virtuous lady, and who fo much loveth him; and all things elfe depending on this match, are in a good and a hopeful way.

This is now the prefent eftate of your Majefty's affairs, as it appeareth unto me and to Sir Walter Afton, with whom I have communicated this difpatch, as I do all things elfe concerning your Majefty's fervice. And I muft clearly let your Majefty underftand, that I conceive, by retaining the powers, when this King fhall call for them, and offering to defer the *defpoforios* until Chriftmas, that your Majefty's bufineffes will run a great hazard, what by the diftaftes and diftrufts that will be raifed here, and what by the art and induftry of thofe which are enemies to the match; whereof every court of

Chriftendom

JAMES I.
1623.
Chriftendom hath plenty. That therefore which I prefume, with all
humility, to offer unto your Majefty is, that you would be pleafed to
give order with all poffible fpeed, that when the bufinefs fhall come
cleared from Rome, and that the powers for the marriage fhall
be demanded of me on the behalf of this King, that I may deliver
them, and no ways feek to interrupt or fufpend the *defpoforios*,
but affift and help to a perfect conclufion of the match; and that for
the bufinefs of the Palatinate, I continue my earneft and faithful
endeavours to engage this King as far as fhall be poffible, both for
the doing of all good offices for the Prince Palatine's entire reftitution, as likewife for this King's declaration of affiftance, in cafe
the Emperor or Duke of Bavaria fhall oppofe the faid reftitution.
Herein I will not fail to ufe all poffible means, and, I conceive, that
the difpatch of the match will be a good pawn in the bufinefs; and
the help and affiftance which the Princefs being once betrothed
would be able to give in this court, to all your Majefty's bufinefs,
would be of good confideration. So fearing I have already too far
prefumed upon your Majefty's patience, I humbly crave your Majefty's pardon, &c.

                                   Your Majefty's, &c.

Madrid,
the 24th of October 1623.   BRISTOL.

The Same to the Same.

May it pleafe, &c.

Nov. 26th. ON the   of November *ft*. *vet.* arrived here Mr. Killegrew, Mr.
Wood, and Mr. Grifley, all with your Majefty's difpatches, and
the duplicates of them; which fhall be exactly and punctually obeyed.
And for that the difpatches I fent from hence on the 24th of this
                                             month,

month, in which I specified the nomination of the 9th of December
_st_. _nov._ for the defpoforios, I conceive your Majefty may be in
fome perplexity. until you know the arrival of thofe your directions,
and the exact obedience that fhall be given to what you are pleafed
to command; I held it fit to leave your Majefty as few hours as was
poffible in any doubt, and therefore have, the very fame night, fent
away Peter Killegrew; by him to let you know, that that part of
your Majefty's commands which concerneth the deferring of the
defpoforios, Sir Walter Afton and myfelf have intimated unto the
Condé de Olivares; and fo likewife is the reft concerning the Palatinate; which, to-morrow, Sir Walter Afton and myfelf will draw into
writing, and deliver to this King.

As for my departure from this court, it fhall be with all fpeed, to
caft myfelf at your Majefty's feet, where I am no way diffident to
appear an honeft and faithful fervant. Though being engaged for
more than fifty thoufand crowns for the Prince, and all my wife's
jewels at pawn, and having no means nor credit on this fide of the
fea, for a quarter of the money which is neceffary for my journey,
I humbly befeech your Majefty to take it into your confideration, that your Ambaffador's going from this court, may not be
like a running away in debt, and leaving his wife and children in
pawn; but rather than fail punctually to obey your Majefty's
commandments, I will come home on foot. In the interim, for
that I find my proceedings blamed by a letter that faith it was of
your Majefty's dictating, with order to fhew it me, I moft humbly
befeech your Majefty to pafs your eyes on the inclofed paper, which
is, what, on fo great a fudden, I can fay to juftify my proceedings;
which, if it fatisfy not your Majefty, I muft have recourfe unto your
Majefty's grace and goodnefs, and to the integrity and fidelity of
mine own intentions; for my confcience beareth me witnefs, that I
have committed no error through want of zeal or affection to your
3 R honour.

honour and fervice. And fo wifhing unto your Majefty all increafe of happinefs, &c.

Your Majefty's, &c.

Madrid, the 26th of Nov.
1623, f°. vet.

BRISTOL.

Earl of Briftol and Sir Walter Afton to the Same.

May it pleafe, &c.

Dec. 26.

BY our letters of the 6th of December we gave your Majefty an account of what anfwer we had then received in writing; unto that which had been formerly propounded by us in your Majefty's name, in the bufinefs of the Palatinate. Since, we received another anfwer upon the memorial we delivered according to your Majefty's directions, fignified to me the Earl of Briftol, by your letters of the 13th of November, which falleth out to be fuch, as, in our above-mentioned letters of the 6th of December, we told your Majefty we feared it would be, much worfe, and much more referved than any we had formerly received; it being rather indeed an expoftulation than any direct anfwer to any point by us propounded.

Hereupon we held it fit to have recourfe unto the Condé de Olivares, and the reft of the Council of State, reprefenting unto them, what had been fignified unto us, to have been the refolution of the Council the 22d of November, viz. That this King was refolved to procure your Majefty entire fatisfaction; and that the Condé de Olivares had wifhed us to fignify fo much to your Majefty in this King's name, and intreated us to empawn our honours and our lives, if need were, for the faithful performance of it, and that he had affured us we fhould receive fo much in writing before the *defpoforios*: that we had accordingly, as we were defired, given your Majefty fuch affurance: that we now defired that we might be able

to

to let your Majefty know the true caufe of this alteration, and whether this King had changed his former refolution of procuring your
Majefty fatisfaction, and upon what ground. They plainly let us
know, that this King, out of his love and defire of friendfhip with
your Majefty, was refolved to employ his utmoft endeavours for the
procuring your Majefty entire fatisfaction; but, to have it extorted
from him by way of menace, or that it fhould now be added to the
marriage by way of condition; and that his fifter muft be rejected
unlefs the King would' undertake to give fatisfaction, and that, by
declaring that he would make a war againft the Emperor, if need
were; whatfoever the King's refolutions might be in the bufinefs itfelf, he could neither with his honour, nor with the honour of his
fifter (whom he would no way force or thruft upon the Prince),
make any other anfwer for the prefent, than what he had done.
We then let them underftand that we conceived that they much
miftook the manner of your Majefty's and Prince's proceeding;
firft, for any menace, we knew of none more than what the nature
of the bufinefs itfelf implied, which was, that there was no great
likelihood of continuance of much love and friendfhip betwixt your
Majefties, whilft this King fhould remain with the eftate * of your
children, or whilft indeed this bufinefs fhould not be fully accommodated ; but for your Majefty's manner of proceeding, as it was with
great freenefs and reality, fo it was with much love ; for your Ma-
jefty-being, in nature and honour, obliged to procure the reftitution
of your children, defired that therein you might rely upon this
King's friendfhip without being conftrained to feek other courfes,
wherein being of late fomewhat difcouraged, by reafon of the giving
away of Beckftrott, and this King's giving the title of Elector unto
the Duke of Bavaria, your Majefty had thought it fit to bring this
bufinefs to fome certain iffue, and to know how far you might rely
upon this King's friendfhip herein; to the end that, at the fame

* The Palatinate.

time

time that your Majesty contracted. alliance with this King, you
should not be forced to make leagues and confederation with all the
enemies of the House of Austria; but that, jointly with a marriage,
your Majesty might make a perfect and sincere friendship betwixt
your crowns and posterities, and remove all occasions which might
interrupt it.

After many several debates, this King hath been contented to
make unto your Majesty the same full answer which was intended.
before the deferring of the *desposorios*; and we have procured it to
be under this King's hand, by way of letter unto your Majesty; although, in point of honour, the Council of State will not let the
original letter be sent unto your Majesty, until it may be delivered
by way of answer unto some letter of your Majesty's; but it is
firmed by this King, and so deposited, with promise to be delivered
unto us upon the first letter we shall procure from your Majesty
touching the business of the Palatinate. In the mean time, I have
the said letter, attested by the Secretary of State, delivered unto us as
this King's answer to our propositions, which we here send originally unto your Majesty, together with the translation of it. And
we assure your Majesty, it hath not been the easiest part of our negociation, to procure it in this form, for they here judged it strange,
that your Majesty having written nothing to this King, we should
press to have this King's answer, by way of letter unto your Majesty, or otherwise than by act of Council, which is the usual form
to all memorials, and especially in this conjuncture.

Your Majesty may therefore be pleased to command such a letter
to be drawn and sent, as may justly occasion such an answer; the
which, we humbly conceive, if it be merely a letter of credence for
us, in the businesses of the Prince Palatine, will be fittest; for that
all things contained in this King's present letter, are in answer of
the particular points of our memorial; and I the Earl of Bristol was
sent unto, to know if I had any blank of your Majesty's; for that,

upon

upon any letter I would deliver from your Majefty in this bufinefs, the King's original letter fhould be delivered by way of anfwer.

So that the eftate of the bufinefs of the Palatinate we conceive to be the fame it was before the deferring of the *defpoforios*, only with the lofs of fo much time, and that we yet want the affiftance and interceffion of the Princefs.

We have likewife moved this King that, in conformity of that which he now hath promifed unto your Majefty, he difpatch prefently unto the Emperor, and write effectually unto him for to come to a fpeedy conclufion of the bufinefs, which is promifed unto us, and we will be careful to fee the poft difpatched away. Though, as your Majefty's faithful fervants, we cannot but prefent unto you our humble opinions, that the way to come to a fpeedy conclufion of this bufinefs is, fpeedily to conclude the marriage; for if that fhall not really be proceeded in, it is not to be fuppofed that the friendfhip between this King (whofe Minifters ftick not to declare, that he cannot but judge his fifter not well ufed) will eafily find means to fruftrate any effects your Majefty may expect from his mediation or friendfhip; but the match being really and fpeedily brought to a conclufion, we cannot but be very hopeful that all things elfe will follow to your content. And fo, moft humbly wifhing unto your Majefty all increafe of happinefs and profperity, we recommend your Majefty to God's holy protection, and reft

   Your Majefty's moft humble and moft
     faithful fervants and fubjects,

Madrid, the 26th of Dec.
1623, *ft. vet.*

         BRISTOL.
         WA. ASTON.

JAMES I
1624.

Harleian
Collection.
No. 6798.
No. 43.

The Answers of the Earl of Bristol to certain Interrogatories intended for His Majesty's private satisfaction, with a reserve for a permission of making recourse to such other things as may be farther necessary to his clearing.

Interrog. I. WHETHER did you think yourself really dealt withal by the Emperor and his Ministers, when you were his Majesty's Ambassador in Germany?

Answ. He saith, that he guided himself by public and avowed answers which were given him by the Emperor under his hand, and the Imperial Seal; and conceiveth that it becometh him with great modesty and caution, to censure the thoughts and intentions of so great a Prince, but referreth himself therein, to his dispatches of that employment, wherein he dealt honestly and faithfully with his Majesty, by advertising truly what he understood or thought then upon the place; and hath many great testimonies of the extraordinary satisfaction which his Majesty expressed to have of his fidelity and industry in the said employment. And at his return gave an account thereof first to his Majesty and the Lords, and afterwards to the Parliament. He saith further, that he then moved his Majesty, that he would not rely upon single treaties, but that he would actually declare himself, and maintain an army under his own standard, for the defence of the Palatinate, which resolution his Majesty was pleased to take. He likewise addeth, that not only his actions mentioned in the next article, but his letter unto his Majesty, and the Lords, bearing date the 26th of July 1621, wherein he beseecheth them that they would not, upon any hopes, lay aside the care of all fitting preparations for a war, in case a peace might not

6   honourably

honourably be had, are sufficient testimonies on his behalf, that though he dare not give any censure upon the Emperor's thoughts, nor cast any aspersion of indirect proceeding upon so great a Prince, yet his care, industry and advice was to have the worst prevented.

Interrog. 2. Whilst the affairs of Bohemia and Germany had a face of strength on the King's son-in-law's side, did you press the King of Spain's Ministers to particular resolutions; and if you did not, why did you give such large and confident assurances of their real dealing, as many of your letters speak?

Answ. To the said interogatory, he answereth to the first part thereof, that while the affairs of Bohemia and Germany had a face of strength on the King's son-in-law's side, the King of Spain and his Ministers were, by Sir Francis Cottington, and Sir Walter Aston, (who then resided in the Court of Spain) pressed with all earnestness to particular resolutions, as all occasions required; which he knoweth, for that he was acquainted with his Majesty's directions and their dispatches, which are ready to be produced, by which it will appear, that like good Ministers they omitted nothing in that kind, that was to be done.

To the second clause of the interrogatory he saith, that by the distinguishing of times he conceiveth, that it will appear that the business is much mistaken, both concerning his letters, or any assurances given by him. For it is most certain that all was lost, before his letter out of Spain beareth date; by which it will be apparent, that he hath been very unfortunate to have the loss of things attributed to the hopes he gave from Spain, when there was nothing left when his letters came unto his Majesty's hands, which are pretended should (through hopes given by them) have detained his Majesty from taking some other course than what he did, for the defence of the Palatinate; as it will be made manifest by that which followeth. In the year of God 1619, the Prince Palatine took the Crown of Bohemia; the Summer following, the Marquis Spinola took all that

which

which he holdeth on the Lower Palatinate. In the month of November next enfuing, the battle of Prague was loft. In the month of
February 1620-1, the Princes of the Union difbanded, and expofed the
Palatinate to the enemy, which, by the induftry of the Earl of Briftol,
was for that time faved by the fufpenfion of arms he then procured
at his being at Bruffels, which he will fhow was by his Majefty, the
Prince Palatine, and the Duke of Deuxponts, acknowledged. In
the year 1621, the Upper Palatinate was abandoned by Mansfelt,
and taken by the Duke of Bavaria. In the month of July, the fame
year (the war being revived) the caftle of Stien was taken by Don
Gonzales de Cordova; and Sir Horatio Vere held it fit, in regard of
the inequality of power, to leave the field, and put all his forces into
three towns, Heidelburgh, Manheim, and Franckendale, which was
all that was then left. At the fame time he faith, that he was earneftly requefted by the Council of Heidelburgh to come unto them
from Nurembergh, where, at his coming, he found all things in
miferable confufion and want: he then fuccoured and relieved them,
and Franckendale, which was then befieged, by the troops which
were brought down by his procurement. And the Council of Heidelburgh, the Prince Palatine himfelf, and his Majefty have been
pleafed (as he can well fhow) to acknowledge a fecond time of the
faving of the remnant of the Palatinate, to his care and induftry.
Hitherto he conceiveth nothing excepted to, againft any of his letters or proceedings. In the year 1622, he began his journey towards Spain, and arrived about July 1622, but it was Auguft before
he did negociate, by reafon of the expectance of the Condé de Gondemar; about which time the Duke of Brunfwick and the Marquis
of Baden received their overthrows; and prefently after Heidelburgh
was loft with little refiftance; fo that there remained only Manheim
and Franckendale; for the faving whereof, he procured the King of
Spain to write his letters, not of mediation, but to command his
forces to be affiftant to the Englifh, and not to permit them to be
                                                         wronged,

wronged, or assailed by any other. These letters bear date the 29th of October; and his Majesty is pleased to write of them in his letters of the 24th of November, as followeth: " That howsoever the order given unto the Infanta for the relief of Manheim arrived too late, and after the town was yielded into the hands of the enemy Tilly, yet we must acknowledge it to be a good office of your nego-ciation, and an argument of that King's sincere and sound intention." So that he doubteth not but that he will appear to the world, that neither any thing hath been lost by the hopes which his letters gave, nor hath he neglected any duty, that by a faithful servant in this could be done, as his Majesty is pleased to acknowledge by his letters of the 1st of January 1622-3, a few days before the Prince began his journey towards Spain, in express terms; viz. " concerning that other " unfortunate knotty affair of the Palatinate, to say the truth, as " things stand, we cannot tell what you could have done more than " you have already."

Interrog. 3. Whether did you judge that the King of Spain would have had a change in religion in England with the match, or some advantageous conditions concerning the Low Countries, or else no Match?

Answ. To this interrogatory he saith, he never heard of any such intention or proposition from the King of Spain, or any of his Mini-nisters: for if he had, he would have rejected it with scorn and in-dignation, as he did the proposition that was made in 1611, for Prince Henry's being a Catholic; and afterwards other conditions in the year 1614, propounded by the Duke of Lerma, which he would not so much as promise the sending of them unto the King, as will appear by his several dispatches of those times. But of this par-ticular, he never heard any thing. And as for any advantageous conditions, that by the match should have been procured for Spain, touching the Low Countries, he never knew any act was in treaty, or in speech, concerning the Low Countries, that had any relation to this

3 S match.

JAMES I. match.   He craveth leave to make anfwer thereunto, when he fhall
  1624.   have the happinefs to await upon his Majefty in perfon *.

   Interrog. 4. Whether did you find that the Minifters of Spain with
your treaty with them, did endeavour to keep you in generalities,
and to avoid particulars?

   Anfw. He faith that it is true, that the ftile of negociation in Spain
is flow, and they are hardly put from generalities.   But when the
bufinefs he treated were ripe, he found them not avoid the coming
to particulars; and that on the 12th of December 1622, they agreed
to all the points of religion for the match; that then, in the King of
Spain's anfwer in writing, of   date, he particularly promifeth
the procuring of the difpenfation in March or April laft, at the
farther; and that in the *interim*, all the temporal articles fhould be
agreed, and in conformity thereof, the faid articles were treated and
agreed : viz. That the proportion fhould be that which fhould appear
to have been in the King's father's time agreed of; viz. That the
defpoforios fhould have been within forty days after the arrival of the
difpenfation, and the Infanta to have begun her journey twenty days
after that.   And that Don Duarte of Portugal fhould have been the
perfon that fhould have attended her, with all other particulars, as
will appear by his difpatch.

   Interrog. 5. Whether did you take any difcontent at the Prince's
coming into Spain, or did you hold it indifferent whether he had the
Princefs with him, or that fhe fhould come after him?

   Anfw. He faith, he did not take any difcontent at the Prince's
coming into Spain, but was infinitely joyed to fee him fafely arrived;
although it is true that he wrote unto his Majefty in his firft letter †
after the Prince's arrival, that he was glad he was not acquainted
with the intention of that journey, for if he had, he fhould have

---

   * This alludes probably to fome overture about the Low Countries, thrown out by the
Duke of Buckingham, when he was in Spain with the Prince.
   † This letter is printed in Sir D. Dalrymple's Collections, 1762.

protefted

protested against it; and that, although he hoped things might end as happily as they had begun hopefully, yet if they did .so, he should attribute it to a particular grace of God, beyond human prudence : for knowing that by the interview of Princes (what through the distastes that commonly arise amongst their Ministers, and other accidents which happen) that friendship and amity is seldom bettered or increased; knowing likewise the dispensation not to be then granted, and fearing left his Prince's person being in their power, they might make use of it to their advantage in pressing farther points in religion than had been formerly settled; for these, and for divers other greater and more important reasons, which he shall declare unto his Majesty when he shall attend him, he seemed not to approve the journey, out of his judgment and zeal to the King's service and the Prince's safety, but no way out of any dislike or discontent of his own. And for the second clause of this interrogatory, he saith, he did not hold it indifferent whether his Highness had the Princess with him, or that she should come after him; but infinitely desired and laboured, that they might have come together. And he conceiveth the Spaniards that were the cause to hinder it, did extremely ill, and imprudently.

Interrog. 6. Whether did you find more forwardness or affection in the King of Spain and his Ministers towards the Match, before the Prince's coming thither, or afterwards?

Answ. He saith, that before the Prince's coming, he found all forwardness and affection in the Spaniards to the match, and all assurances of their real desiring of it, which could pass betwixt Princes and Christians: and he conceiveth no man will doubt thereof, that shall read his dispatch unto your Majesty, of the 9th of September 1623, wrote then upon an occasion of a rumour that had been raised, that nothing should be really intended in the Match before the Prince's coming into Spain. But he saith, he conceiveth, that after the Prince's arrival in Spain, their desires to the Match were

much

much increafed, by the knowledge of the Prince's perfon, and by his conftant, virtuous, and princely behaviour, by which he won the hearts of all forts of people unto him, although it be true that fome perfonal diftaftes did then put the bufinefs in much diftraction. But the time when he conceiveth the Match was by the King and all men in Spain moft defired, was, after the Prince's departure out of Spain. For the Prince having left fo great a renown behind, and the King and he having parted upon fuch affectionate terms, which were continued and much increafed by the daily exchange of courteous letters betwixt them, and thofe difgufts and harfhnefs which had formerly happened by the diftaftes of their Minifters, being now by abfence removed; the King of Spain and the whole Court feemed never fo much to defire it, as then. And the King made upon all occafions conftant and public profeffions, that he would, for no earthly regard, fail in one tittle, either in fubftance or circumftance, of what he had capitulated or promifed unto the Prince's Highnefs. And he had caufe to guide himfelf according to the oaths and proteftations of fo great a King. And if he had not really and honeftly intended as he profeffed, he is anfwerable for it, betwixt God and his own confcience.

Interrog. 7. Why did you fo confidently inform his Majefty, from time to time, of their real and fincere proceeding in Spain, having been acquainted before with the affront put upon his Majefty with the breach of the treaty concerning the Match of Prince Henry?

Anfw. To the firft part of the 7th interrogatory, he faith, he never gave his Majefty any hopes of their real proceedings in Spain, but the fame that were then given him, without adding or diminifhing; neither could he have done otherwife with honefty and fafety. Further, the hopes he gave, were never upon conjectures, or vain intelligence, but upon all the affurances both in word and writing, that could pafs between Princes and Chriftians. And if the difpatch he wrote to his Majefty, bearing date the 9th of September 1623, may

but

but be perufed, he no way doubteth, but it will appear that he was not deceived, but ferved his Majefty with no lefs care and vigilancy, than with truth and fidelity. Laftly he faith, he had reafon to give ·fuch hopes as he did, of that which he never doubted but that it would take effect, until after the ftay of the *defpoforios.* As for the infe- rence concerning the match of Prince Henry, it being ten or twelve years fince, we have many frefh examples, that ftates alter their re- folutions in their defigns, and many times their alliances, in much fhorter time. But for that the giving a due anfwer unto this point, by deducing bufinefs from Prince Henry's time unto this prefent, would be of greater length than befitteth this anfwer, he will in a paper apart fet down the whole progrefs of the bufinefs, from the year 1611, unto this prefent time, wherein he no way doubteth but to make it appear to his Majefty, that he hath ferved him like a good and faithful fervant.

Interrog. 8. Whether did not Mr. Porter at his being in Spain tell you, that the Condé of Olivares faid, that it was a prepofterous de- mand for the King of Spain to take arms againft his uncle, againft the Catholic league, and the Houfe of Auftria; and that of the Match he knew nothing, nor what it meant?

Anfw. He faith, that not long before Mr. Porter's departure out of Spain, Sir Walter Afton told him, that he had heard that Mr. Porter fpeaking with the faid Condé Olivares, he fhould deny that there was ever any intention that the King of Spain fhould affift his Majefty with his arms, in cafe by other means he could not pro- cure him fatisfaction in the bufinefs of the Palatinate. And that thereon, he fpeaking with Mr. Porter, Mr. Porter told him as much in effect. But concerning the fecond part of this interrogatory, that the Condé of Olivares fhould tell him, that touching the Match he knew nothing, nor what it meant; he faith, he (Porter) never faid any fuch thing to him as he remembereth, but if he be not much

deceived,

deceived, the clean contrary; and that the Condé fhould tell him, that for the bufinefs of the Match he held it concluded : and this he fuppofeth to be much more probable, for that he did not only underftand, that Mr. Porter went away in that point fully fatisfied, having often not only fpoken himfelf with the Lords of the Spanifh Council, but alfo been made acquainted with the good anfwers he carried back : but he is likewife farther confirmed in that belief, for that, it fhould feem, Mr. Porter, at his return into England, did not raife any doubt, neither in the Prince nor Duke, but that all was really proceeded in, in Spain; for befides the Prince's journey that enfued thereon, which doubtlefs would not have been to try experiences; and if that be infifted upon, the contrary will be made apparent. The King is pleafed, in his letters of the 7th of   to write as followeth : " Right trufty, &c. The difpatch brought us by Endymion Porter, " doth give us fufficient affurance of your faithful endeavours and " diligence, to expedite thofe great bufineffes you have in charge; " for which we are pleafed to return you both our gracious accept- " ation and thanks." And fo wifheth him to proceed and confummate the whole bufinefs of the Match, according to the commiffion he had. And touching the Palatinate * he writeth, viz. " To fay the " truth, as things ftand, we cannot tell what you could have done, " more than you have already." And the Prince in his letters of the 6th of January 1622, all written in his own hand, in anfwer of thofe he fent by Mr. Porter, is pleafed to write, viz. " Briftol, this is to " give you thanks for the fuccefsful pains you have taken in all your " bufinefs, but efpecially in that of my marriage, &c." and concludeth, " Now I muft end as I began, with thanks, for your pains " hath deferved that, and much more. And I affure you, you have " made good, and, if it were poffible, increafed the good opinion I " had of you."

* At that time, and till the Prince's return from Spain, the Palatinate was a very fecondary confideration.

And

And the Duke of Buckingham in his letters of the 5th of January 1622, to the Condé of Gondemar, in anfwer of thofe which Mr. Porter had brought him (which letter was written in the hand of Mr. Cottington, and a long poftfcript in the Duke's hand) writ in fuch fort, as did appear, that Mr. Porter had raifed little fcruple that the Match was in ill terms. And my Lord Duke in his letters at the fame time to the Condé of Olivares, which letters I conceive will prove to have been drawn in Spanifh by Mr. Porter himfelf, faith, he hath underftood by the relation of Mr. Porter of the offices he doth, for the continuing amity, and an entire union betwixt their Majefties and their Crowns, and particularly how much he doth labour to effect the Match, and to accommodate the affairs of the King's fon-in-law, and that thereby he findeth himfelf obliged to a full refolution, not only to ferve the King of Spain in all that he can, but to comply in all things with his Excellency, as his friend and true fervant. And as for that the Condé of Olivares fhould fay, he knew nothing of the Match; he would not meddle with what may have paffed between the Condé of Olivares and Mr. Porter, but the truth thereof will eafily be made apparent by divers letters which he hath, under the hand of the Condé Olivares, in which will be feen, that he both treated, and knew of the Match, before Mr. Porter's arrival. Befides the difcourfe of the Condé of Olivares, which hath been fo much fpoken of in the world, for the transferring of the Match for the Prince unto one of the Emperor's daughters, beareth date while Mr. Porter was at Madrid, and thereby it will appear, that he had formerly heard of the Match.

As for the other point concerning the Palatinate, he affirmeth, that all he had faid of the profeffions, to affift his Majefty with armies, is true, and he caufed as much to be affirmed to Mr. Porter, at his being in Spain, by the Condé Gondomar and Sir Walter Afton; and fending to the Condé of Olivares to expoftulate with him of that which he underftood he fhould have faid to Mr. Porter, he anfwered him concerning Mr. Porter, that, which he willingly omitteth, but

3

for

for the bufinefs he fhall have ample fatisfaction, for that the King's intentions were ftill the fame, and that whenfoever he would come to the King, he would not make nice to fpeak again whatfoever he had promifed; whereupon having audience appointed him within two or three days, there being an infection at that time in his houfe, of which divers of his fervants had died, on that very night before he fhould have had audience, he intreated Sir Walter Afton to go alone to the King, who was pleafed, upon his moving the bufinefs of the Palatinate, to make unto him, in the fame form of words, the fame anfwer, which he made to them both at the Efcurial, wherewith Sir Walter Afton acquainted Mr. Porter, in his prefence, and fome others. And if he be not miftaken, Mr. Porter accompanied Sir Walter Afton that day, and kiffed the King's hands, and feemed rather to be very forry that the Earl of Briftol had preffed the bufinefs fo far, than that he any way remained unfatisfied: herein he humbly befeecheth, that Sir Walter Afton's difpatches may be produced, which he conceiveth muft bear date about the 12th or 13th of December 1622.

Interrog. 9. Why did you not prefs, before the Prince's coming into Spain, the reftitution of the Palatinate, to the perfon of the King's fon-in-law and his fucceffor, in all particular points, both in matter and form?

Anfw. He faith, that before the Prince's coming into Spain he did prefs the reftitution of the Palatinate to the perfon of the King's fon-in-law and his fucceffor, in all particular points both in matter and form, as will appear by his feveral difpatches, and is acknowledged by his Majefty, by his letters of the 7th of January 1622-3, it being but few days before the Prince's coming into Spain, wherein he faith, concerning the affairs of the Palatinate, "To fay the truth as things "fland, we cannot tell what you could have done, more than you "have already."

Interrog. 10. Did you, upon all occafions, as you had ample caufe, reprefent the merit of his Majefty, or did you at any time let it fall or undervalue it?

Anfw.

Anfw. He faith, he did, upon all occafions, as he had ample caufe, reprefent the merit of his Majefty; neither did he at any time let it fall, or undervaluc it, as will amply appear by fundry of his difpatches, aad many memorials in that bufinefs, ready to be produced.

Interrog. 11. When the breeding of his Majefty's grand-child with the Emperor was propounded, (which implied a converfion of him,) did you reject it, or did you think it advantageous and counfellable for his Majefty?

Anfw. He faith, that the breeding of his Majefty's grand-child with the Emperor, as he remembereth, was never propounded to him, but in the prefence of fuch * as befitted not him to reject, or accept of it; but when the Match for him, with the Emperor's daughter, hath been fingly at any time propounded to him, he hath faithfully reprefented it to his Majefty. But for the inference, that by the parenthefis is made (that his converfion was thereby implied) he never imagined it, nor feeth ground for it. For if the meaneft Princefs in Chriftendom, matcheth with the greateft Monarch, capitulateth for the full ufe of her confcience, he knoweth not upon what ground it is fuppofed, that it fhould have debarred the King's grandchild; neither ever underftood he but he fhould have had his family fuch as his Majefty, and his father, had appointed for him; and this may lefs be inferred, as he fuppofeth, in the Emperor's Court, than in any Court of Chriftendom; for that he remembereth the young Prince of Anhalt being the Emperor's prifoner, and after being fet at liberty, but with condition to continue in the Emperor's Court, the free ufe of his religion was not denied; fo likewife two of the Dukes of Saxe, who were in the Emperor's fervice, and divers others, both counfellors, and of his bed-chamber, and of his chief commanders in the wars, are avowed Proteftants; and in Vienna itfelf there is a congregation of fourteen or fifteen thoufand, which publicly and avowedly have the free ufe of their religion. And as for the fecond caufe, whether

* *i. e.* The Prince, and the Duke of Buckingham.

3 T   he

he thinketh it advantageous or counfellable or not, he judgeth it more
or lefs counfellable, and advantageous, according as the ftate of affairs fhall ftand, and as the conditions fhall be made better or worfe,
by the treaty of them.

Interrog. 12. Whether did you think it the way for the greatnefs
of England, to have the King thereof, under the obedience of the
church of Rome; or did you ever judge it convenient and requifite for
the Prince himfelf, in contemplation of that Match, to conform himfelf to the Roman Catholic religion?

Anfw. He faith, he never did, nor doth think it the way, for the
greatnefs of England, to have the Kings thereof under the obedience
of the church of Rome; and he is very much grieved that any fuch
interrogatory fhould be afked him, having all the days of his life,
and in all places, lived and approved himfelf a Proteftant, and never
having done, publicly or privately, any act that was not fuitable to the
fame profeffion. He further faith, that, in all his foreign employ-
ments, for the fpace of fourteen years, of more than five hundred
perfons, of all qualities, that have attended him, there was never any
one perverted in his religion, fave two Irifh footmen, who in England had been bred Papifts; and if his Majefty be pleafed to take further information, he humbly befeecheth his Majefty to fend for not
only Dr. Mew and Dr. Wren, the Prince's chaplains, which were
with him in Spain, but for Mr. Sandford, one of the Prebends of
Canterbury, Mr. Bofwell, Parfon of St. Lawrence London, and
Frewyne, deputy reader in Magdalen College in Oxford, who have
all been his Chaplains in Spain; as likewife fuch Catholics as are
known to have been long his ancient acquaintance and friends, and
to examine them upon oath, whether, either publicly or privately,
either in Spain or England, they have known him, in any kind, to
make fhow, or fo much as to forbear upon all occafions avowedly to
declare the religion he profeffeth; and therefore he humbly befeecheth, if that out of any difcourfe or argument he held *pro* or *con*, upon
misunderftanding

misunderstanding or mistaking of arguments, any information hath been given, or any assertion made, whereupon that interrogatory may have been grounded, his Majesty will cause the said accusations to be set down in writing, and he will not fail therein to give his Majesty full and entire satisfaction. To the second part of this interrogatory he saith, he did never either invite, by persuasion of his own, or by procuring conference of others, the Prince to be a Roman Catholic; nor did he judge it convenient and requisite for his Highness (in contemplation of that Match) to conform himself to the Roman Catholic religion, or to any part belonging to it.

Interrog. 13. When the Prince found it convenient for his affairs, and his duty to his father, to return, did you oppose it or no, and if you did, then upon what grounds?

Answ. He saith, when the Prince found it convenient for his affairs, and his duty towards his father, to return, he did never oppose it; but he remembereth, four or five days before Mr. Secretary Cottington was sent out of Spain into England, there was some serious debate before the Prince, about his going or sending Sir Francis Cottington; at which time he spoke that which, in his judgment and conscience, he thought fittest for the King and Prince's service, as befitteth a Minister and Counsellor of the King to do; and this was about the 25th of May, some months before any thing was concluded, and divers months before the Prince's departure out of Spain; and all things after this were approved and ratified by the King and Prince.

Interrog. 14. When there was an addition of articles, and a distinction between public and private articles, did you then persuade the Prince to come into those articles of addition, did you assure or persuade him, that the oath was required only to the public articles, and not to the private, and did you deal plainly with him in that or no?

Answ. To the first clause he saith, that in the articles of addition he never persuaded the Prince to any, but unto such as he had order

from

from the King fufficiently to warrant him ; and he faith, that all the
faid articles of addition were fettled in a junto of the commiffioners on
both fides, where the Prince was pleafed to affift himfelf in perfon,
where all things, as they were concluded, were drawn up into a formal
kind of journal, by the Secretary Cirica, and Mr. Secretary Cottington,
out of which all the particular articles were to be drawn, as well thofe
that were to be fworn, as thofe which were only to be figned or promifed, for which the faid journal ferved as a rule. All the articles
and all things elfe, which the King of Spain was to promife, were
afterwards drawn up into the body of one entire treaty, whereof he
knew nothing. But the Prince fwore not all contained in the faid
volume, for much thereof belonged not to him, but to the King of
Spain, and he fwore only to thofe particulars, which were agreed he
fhould fwear to, and fo it was expreffed by the Secretary at the taking
of his oath, in thefe very words, *V. A. juro to que a de jurar, prometto
que a de prometer.* That the Prince fhould fwear that which it was
agreed he fhould fwear, and promife what was agreed he fhould promife. And indeed, in the body of every article, it is punctually fet
down whether it be to be fworn, or figned, or to be promifed; and
this is the truth of that which really paffed, wherein, as he under-
ftandeth it, there hath been committed no kind of error, neither did
he ever hear it queftioned until now. And he faith, that he did then
deal plainly with his Highnefs, as he doth now truly with his Majefty.

Interrog. 15. Did you not find by the Prince, that he took himfelf
neglected, and attempted on to be oppreffed, by the Spanifh Minifters,
in their demands ?

Anfw. To the firft part of this interrogatory he faith, that he doth
not remember that ever he found by the Prince, that he took himfelf
to be neglected, neither ever faw he caufe for it, during the Prince's
being there; for it was not poffible that there could be an higher eftimation and value fet upon the worth and perfon of any man, than he
underftood

underftood 'ever to be in that Court, of the Prince's perfon and virtue. Petty omiffions in matter of fervice or entertainment, it may be there were many, but other neglects he never remembereth to have obferved the Prince to take notice of, neither doth he believe that the Prince ever did; in which belief he is confirmed by his Majefty's letters bearing date the 18th of October, written fince the Prince's coming home, in thefe words following, " We will that you repair " prefently to the King, and give him knowledge of the fafe arrival " of our dear fon to our Court, fo fatisfied and taken with the great " entertainment, perfonal kindnefs, favour, and refpect he hath re- " ceived from that King and Court, as he feems not able to magnify " it fufficiently; which maketh us not to know how fufficiently to " give thanks; but will that you by all means endeavour to exprefs " our thankfulnefs to that King and the reft, to whom it belongeth, " in the beft and moft ample manner you can." The Prince, by his letters of the fame date, commandeth him to affure that King, that he will never forget the favours he did him whilft he was in his Court; fo that he conceiveth he hath no caufe to judge that the Prince held himfelf neglected. For the fecond point, it is true, that, under colour that the King of Spain was to take an oath to the Pope, for the performance of all that was by his Majefty promifed in point of religion, they infifted, as it were for a counter-fecurity, upon many things which were never before fpoken of; but it was well known that he dealt freely with the Condé of Gondemar, and the Condé of Olivares, letting them know, that it was an unworthy and a difcourteous proceeding with his Highnefs, to make his condition the harder for the great obligation he had put upon them, by fo freely putting his perfon into their hands. For they well knew that the bufinefs was fettled and agreed with the Earl of Briftol before the Prince's coming. And therefore, now to infift upon any thing further, was neither noble nor fair proceeding. Hereupon they grew very difcontented with him, and laboured, as much as was poffible, to avoid him,

him, of all men living, in their further negociation; and that this was really so, and not now alleged by way of answer, will appear by his letters unto his Majesty, of the 9th of September 1623; so that in this particular he then did, and still doth, much blame the course they held with his Highness.

Interrog. 16. Whether had you ever any information given you (as rising from faith to his Majesty) that the Match was not intended but to win time, except his Majesty would grant an absolute toleration of religion in his dominions, and a restoration of the rebels and fugitives of Ireland to their estates; and of any attempts to be made against any of his Majesty's dominions, if the Match should break?

Answ. To the 16th he saith, that if any particular person, or the time, had been specified in the interrogatory, he would have made a clear answer, which now he only can do by conjecture; for that divers (some by way of intelligence, some to cozen him, and to raise distrust, set on by the Ministers of other Princes, that desired to cross the Match), have spoken to him somewhat towards the effect of this Interrogatory. But the party that he remembereth to have spoken unto him, nearest to all the points of this interrogatory, was one Mr. Lascelles at Brussels; but there was no kind of ground or probability in any thing that he said; only, being in want, he desired to have got some money of him, and pretended to serve the King, by way of giving intelligence, so that he might have an entertainment, which he promised to acquaint the King withal, as he did at his return; but, as he remembereth, the King said, he was an idle cozening fellow, and would not give way to have any thing given him. Divers others may have spoken to him something tending to this purpose, whereof he remembereth not the particulars, but he used not to make such kind of men's frivolous or fancied adventures, a rule for the guiding of his actions and judgment: that which he relied on was, the solid judgment and advertisement of Sir Francis Cottington, and Sir Walter Aston, out of Spain, as will appear by

their

their several difpatches; and his laft embaffage into Spain was grounded upon the affurances and profeffions which were made in Spain unto them, that this young King meant really to purfue the treaties, which were on foot with his father, and to proceed with his Majefty in the fpeedy effecting of them.

Interrog. 17. Whether did you give advice to the Prince to ftay till Chriftmas, and fo confequently to the Spring, in hope to bring the Infanta with him?

Anfw. He doth not remember pofitively to have given the Prince any fuch advice, to ftay till Chriftmas or the Spring; but thinketh, that, by way of pondering and debating the cafe, he may have held difcourfe with the Prince tending to that effect.

Interrog. 18. When the Prince was returned, and his Majefty expreffed to you, by his letters, his refolution to couple the proceedings of the Match, and reftitution of the Palatinate together, and you had taken knowledge of it, why did you change your counfels, and appoint a certain day for the *defpoforios*, and that fo fhortly, as it was no ordinary diligence that could or did prevent it?

Anfw. Firft, he faith, For his proceedings to confummate the Match, he hath warrant and inftructions under the King's hand. Secondly, It was the main fcope of his embaffage. Thirdly, He was enjoined it by the King's and Prince's commandments under their great feals. Fourthly, He hath pofitive orders under the King's hand by letters fince. Fifthly, It was agreed by capitulation to be within ten days after the coming of the difpenfation. Sixthly, The King and Prince had fworn unto the treaty. Seventhly, They fignified to him, by their letters at the very fame time, that they intended to proceed in the marriage, and renewed the Prince's powers. Eighthly, The powers were to that end left in his hands. Ninthly, The Prince's royal word, being in the body of the powers engaged, that they fhould have due execution until Chriftmas, without revocation or impeachment, he could not ftop them without exprefs order,

which,

which, as foon as he had, he obeyed. Tenthly, He had overthrown the marriage without order, for the King of Spain protefted to be free of the treaty, if the *defpoforios* fhould be deferred. Eleventhly, He durft not, without a precife warrant, put fuch a fcorn upon a lady whom he then efteemed the Prince's wife, or fpoufe at leaft, for as fuch he was commanded to ferve her. Twelfthly, He was himfelf fworn to the treaty. Laftly, He would not, in honour and honefty, but endeavour to perform that public truft which was repofed in him, when the powers were depofited in his hands, with public and legal declaration, taken into an inftrument by the Secretary of State, leading and directing the ufe of them, and this being now *Inftru- mentum ftipulatum*, wherein the King of Spain was interefted, as well by acceptation of the fubftitutes, as the Prince by granting the powers, he could not in honefty fail that public truft, without clear and undoubted warrant: and indeed that was to be public, and with confent, or at leaft with notice given of it to the King of Spain. The Earl of Briftol now defireth, that all countermands may be produced, not in generalities, but in the formal words, and then it will appear if they be fuch as might warrant againft the above-fpecified orders and reafons; for he findeth (under favour) that what he hath been charged withal, formerly by letters, and now is alleged to have been directed him, is far differing from any fenfe he could ever make out of the fuppofed direction; and fo likewife what is affumed out of his difpatches, will appear to be mifunderftood. But herein he defireth that no regard may be had to general allegations, by words of mouth; but that the original papers may be produced and examined, and that by them the caufe may be truly ftated and judged. But he further faith, that if the refolution fpecified in the interrogatory had been an abfolute and direct command, as it was far from it (as will be after fhewn), yet he had incurred no kind of blame, for he had an abfolute anfwer in the bufinefs of the Pala- tinate, as will appear by the joint difpatch of Sir Walter Afton and himfelf,

himfelf, of the 23d of November; and the Condé of Olivares wifhed them, upon their honours and their lives, to anfwer his Majefty, that he fhould have entire fatisfaction: and fo much was in a formal anfwer to have been delivered in writing, which was the anfwer afterwards fent the 8th of January, before he could have delivered the Prince his powers: and both he and Sir Walter Afton were fo confident that they had complied with his Majefty's defire herein, that they gave him the *Parabien* thereof by their faid letters of the 23d of November, writing as followeth: " We hope that your
" Majefty may, according to your Majefty's defire fignified to me
" the Earl of Briftol, by your letters of the 8th of October, give as well
" unto your Majefty's royal daughter, this Chriftmas, the comfortable
" news of the near expiring of her great troubles and fufferings,
" as to the Prince, your fon, the congratulation of being married to
" a moft worthy and excellent Princefs;" by which it will appear
that he intended not to have left the bufinefs of the Palatinate loofe,
when he meant to have proceeded to the marriage. But he muft
confefs, that he was of opinion ever, that the beft pawn and affurance his Majefty could have for the real proceeding in the bufinefs of
the Palatinate was, that they proceeded really by the effecting of
the Match. And this was ever the opinion of my Lords the Commiffioners, and of his Majefty himfelf, as will appear by his inftructions of the 14th of March 1621, figned with the King's hand, viz.
" We conceive if the King of Spain hath not a real and fincere in-
" tention of giving fatisfaction in that which concerns our fon-in-
" law, he would never proceed to a conclufion of the Match. And
" we fhall judge it is an undoubted argument of his meaning to
" gratify us in the bufinefs of the Palatinate, in cafe he fhall go
" on with the Match." And this opinion ftill continued in his
Majefty and my Lords; for in the King's letter of the 7th of
January 1622, his Majefty is pleafed to write: " This was the
" reafon that moved us, at the inftance of our Council, to urge the

3 U " bufinefs

" bufinefs of the Palatinate, fo as to bring it to a fpeedy point."
Not but that the very precifeft of them were always of opinion,
that if the Match were once concluded, the other bufinefs would be
accommodated to our fatisfaction: fo that he conceiveth, that had
this refolution been a precife commandment, he had made no fault,
but had complied fully with it, in coupling the two bufineffes together; and had produced ample warrants for the directing of his
judgment therein: but he faith, the caufe is far different, for this
refolution of his Majefty was only fignified unto him by his letters
of the 8th of October, by which he is required fo to endeavour, that
his Majefty may have the joy of both at Chriftmas; which had been
effected, had he not been interrupted. And there was no other
way in the world but by proceeding to the marriage, jointly with fo
real a promife as he had in the bufinefs of the Palatinate, whereby
there was any poffibility of fatisfying his Majefty's defire of having
the joy of both at Chriftmas, but that both muft otherwife be overthrown, for the Match was, by this direction, for feveral refpects, rendered impoffible. Firft, a marriage being a reciprocal act, the day of
celebration cannot be appointed but by a common confent of both
parties; but the King of Spain would by no means condefcend to
the prolonging of the day beyond the term limited by the capitulation, which was within ten days after the coming of the difpenfation, but made it formally to be protefted, That in cafe the Earl of
Briftol fhould infift upon the deferring of the *defpoforios*, he would
hold himfelf freed from the treaty, the Earl of Briftol infringing the
capitulations. Secondly, although the King of Spain fhould have
condefcended to have had the *defpoforios* prorogued until Chriftmas,
yet was there another impoffibility, by reafon of the expiring of the
Prince's powers before; befides the fcorn which would have been put
upon the King of Spain and his fifter, by nominating a day for the
marriage, when the powers are out of date; and this is by his Majefty himfelf acknowledged, in his letter of the 13th of November

5   1623,

1623, as followeth: " We have received your letters of the 8th of
" October, and the copy of that power which was left by our dear
" son; we have examined and approved your reasons, and do assure
" you, that if we had seen the power left by our son, before our last
" letter, we had not written to you in the form we did, in our letters
" of the 8th of October, touching the time of Christmas." So that
it is apparent that the Earl of Bristol is no way to be charged with
any inferences out of this letter, which the King himself acknow-
ledgeth to have been grounded upon want of due information. So
that all the fault that herein hath been committed, was certainly the
concealing of the expiration of the powers from the King, which
can no way be attributed to the Earl of Bristol. But pre-supposing
there had been no such error or mistaking, as his Majesty is pleased
to take notice of in his said letters before, of the 8th of October, yet
the Earl of Bristol saith, he might not have done otherwise than he
did, for there was nothing expressed in the said letter, but a desire
of his Majesty's, that the marriage should be at Christmas, but no
positive order that it should not be before. Nor in the business of
the Palatinate was there any order to make it a condition of the marriage or to be annext unto it, as without it to break the marriage;
whereas his main instruction, bearing date the 4th of March 1621,
under the King's hand, directeth him as followeth: " We would
" have you by all means to press the restitution of the Palatinate,
" but not so as to make the treaty of the marriage any way de-
" pendent thereon." And his Majesty in his letters of the 30th of
December, expressing his meaning in the former letters of the 8th
of October, saith, " We have received your joint dispatch in the 6th
" of December; (viz.) our words, that ever express our meaning,
" were, that both our affection and our dear son's did constantly
" pursue, with all earnestness, the marriage with that excellent
" Princess; our interpretation to you in direct terms was (as we
" declare it to be our meaning) not to press the restitution of the

3 U 2   " Pala-

" Palatinate and electoral dignity as a condition of the marriage."
Now the cafe ſtanding thus, he referreth it humbly to his Majeſty's
wiſdom not only whether he be free from fault herein ; but whether,
without great fault and imprudence, he could have done otherwiſe ;
for he muſt, upon inferences and collection (and theſe ſuch as were
acknowledged to have been upon wrong information), have gone
againſt his poſitive and clear orders and inſtruction, under the King's
own hand. It is true, that an Ambaſſador may ſometimes take inferences of warrants, but it muſt be only when apparently it effecteth
or helpeth forward that which he is employed about, but not when
it overthroweth or croſſeth the main drift and ſcope of his employment, as it was in this cafe ; for the King of Spain requiring the
Earl of Briſtol to proceed, or to free him from the treaty, he had
been highly faulty to have gone againſt his Majeſty's inſtructions,
and to have overthrown the errand he was employed in, without clear
direction and *mandato ſpeciali.*

To the ſecond clauſe he ſaith, he did not change his counſels, and
that, under correction, his diſpatches have been much miſtaken in
that point, for the cafe ſtands as followeth : Sir Walter Afton and the
Earl of Briſtol had uſed all induſtry that was poſſible to diſcover how
the motion of the deferring of the *deſpoſorios,* upon the coming of the
diſpenſation, would be taken there, and finding an abſolute reſolution
in the King, to proceed punctually according to the capitulations,
within ten days after the coming of the diſpenſation ; and at the fame
time likewiſe getting advertiſement from Rome, that the diſpenſation
was granted, and would preſently be there ; upon this occaſion, and
no alteration of his reſolution (to the end that in ſo great a cafe he
might have a clear and undoubted underſtanding of his Majeſty's
pleaſure), he diſpatched away with great diligence, letting his Majeſty know, that it would not be poſſible for him to protract the
marriage above twenty-four days, unleſs he ſhould hazard the breaking

ing of it, for which he had not warrant; but that this was no refo-lution, nor that the King was no ways fo ftraitened in time, as is pretended, will appear by the difpatch of the Earl of Briftol's of the 24th of September 1623. In which, upon the fcruple that was made of the Infanta's entering into religion, he writeth the fame which he did in the difpatch of the 1ft of November, viz. That if the difpenfation fhould come, he knew no means how to detain the powers above twenty or twenty-four days; fo that although this difficulty happened not until the middle of November, yet it was forefeen that it muft of neceffity happen, whenfoever the difpenfation fhould come, and there was warning of two months time given thereof, viz. from the 14th of September until the 29th of November, which was the day appointed for the *defpoforios*, which were prevented by the arrival of his Majefty's letters, commanding the ftay of them, bearing date the 13th of November 1623, *fto. vet.* So that he fhall moft willingly fubmit himfelf to his Majefty's cenfure, which was the fafer, or the dutifuller way, to have, upon inferences, overthrown fo great a bufinefs, (for to that iffue it was brought), and he required either to proceed to the *defpoforios* according to capitulations, or to have fet the King of Spain free from the treaty; or, on the other fide, firft to have reprefented unto his Majefty, with truth and fincerity, as he did, the true ftate of his affairs, with his humble opinion, viz. That it fhould be judged a great difgrace to the perfon of the Princefs, to have the marriage deferred : That the King of Spain would efteem it a great fcorn put upon him, to have a day nominated for the marriage, when the powers fhould be expired : That the engagements by oaths, and otherwife, on both fides, are great : That the detention of the powers without fome emergent caufe, would be fubject to conftruction : That this Match fo much defired by his Majefty would be overthrown, or at leaft much time loft : That the conclufion of the Match would in all likelihood fecure the reftitution of the Palatinate. And in cafe thefe reafons fhould not perfuade

his

JAMES I. his Majefty to proceed, the Earl of Briftol intimated, that, for the
1624. honeft difcharge of the public truft that was repofed in him, when
the powers were by the King and Prince in truft depofited in his
hands, and for his fufficient warrant in fo great a cafe, he defired
clear and exprefs order which he yet had not, and in the *interim*
whilft his Majefty might take into confideration thefe great inconveniences, the faid inconveniences were all fufpended by the faid Earl of
Briftol keeping the bufinefs in fair terms, that his Majefty might have
his way and choice, clear and unfoiled before him. To the end that
if he fhould command a ftay of the bufinefs, he might be obeyed; if
he fhould have thought fit that the Match fhould have proceeded (as
was by the Earl of Briftol believed), he might not have found his
bufinefs difordered; and in this difpofition were the King's affairs
upheld, until by his Majefty's and the Prince's letters of the 13th
of November, the Earl of Briftol had exprefs command not to proceed to the *defpoforios*, which he readily and exactly obeyed. So
that the objection againft the Earl of Briftol dependeth upon no act
or fault committed, but merely upon an intention which was never
reduced into act: in which if there had been any obliquity or fault,
as there was none, the fault certainly was removed by his obedience,
before the intention was put in execution, for fo it is in cafes towards
God himfelf; befides this is for fuch an intent as (is divulged and
pretended as a fault, againft him) was never meant. And for the
other fault of appointing a day, he faith, he never appointed any day
but was therein merely paffive, in admitting the day nominated by
the King of Spain, according to the capitulations, as will appear by
Secretary Alvis his letters of the 3d of December.

Interrog. 19. Whether had you a refolution for the reftitution of
the Palatinate, and eftablifhment for the temporal articles, before
that day?

Anfw. For the firft part of this interrogatory, he conceiveth to
have fully fatisfied it, in his anfwer to the precedent article. Touching

-ing the second part thereof, concerning the temporal articles, he faith, that when the *defpoforios* was appointed to have been (as he remembereth) on Friday the 29th of Auguft before the Prince's departure out of Spain, which was only hindered becaufe the difpenfation came not, the Prince appointed Sir Walter Afton and himself, to meet with the Spanifh Commiffioners, and they drew up the heads of the temporal articles, wherewith the Prince and the Duke of Buckingham were made acquainted; and in cafe the difpenfation had come, and the *defpoforios* been performed on that day, there had been no other provifion made for them before the marriage. But prefently upon the Prince's departure, he caufed them to be drawn into a form, and fent them to his Majefty on the 27th of September 1623, defiring to underftand his Majefty's pleafure with all poffible fpeed, efpecially in cafe he difapproved any thing, but never received notice of his difliking of any of them, until he recovered thofe letters which put off the *defpoforios*. Yet notwithftanding, Sir Walter Afton and he were very careful to have fettled the temporal articles, and they were not only to have been figned before the day of the *defpoforios*, but they had begun to treat upon points of conveyance and confederation, as he fhall more particularly make known unto his Majefty, when he fhall have the happinefs to wait upon him.

Interrog. 20. When the approbation of the difpenfation came from Rome (which, by a conditional article, was to come clear), why did you accept of it without ftanding upon the juft exceptions, and fo feem to redeem the King and his Minifters from the breach of the treaty, and caft colour of fault upon his Majefty and the Prince, who were wholly innocent, and had been clearly apparent fo, if you had made right ufe of it?

Anfw. He faith, that when the difpenfation came from Rome, it no way belonged to him to take exceptions unto it, neither did he

accept

accept of it, for it was an article agreed, that his Majefty fhould have nothing to do with the difpenfation; but it being only for the fatisfaction of the King of Spain; he was to procure it in fuch fort, as was to fatisfy his own confcience; neither was it any thing to his Majefty, whether there were any difpenfation or not. That therefore the difpenfation could not but be judged clear, when the King of Spain refted fatisfied, and defired to proceed to the effecting of the marriage, without infifting upon any further demands. And this was truly the cafe, for the Condé de Olivares, the very night the difpenfation arrived, fent him word thereof, requiring to proceed to the *defpoforios* according to the capitulations; but he replied, that he would take no notice of the difpenfation to be come, nor clear, until it were in the King's hands, whereupon the next day divers Commiffioners came, defiring fome declaration, in fome points agreed of, and the mending of fome words according to the journal of the treaty, which was agreed fhould be the rule for the drawing of the articles, but he abfolutely denied them all, refufing fo much as to change or add any one word or tittle; and this he did only to gain time, as he did for twelve days, to the end he might receive directions in the mean time from his Majefty, ere he would fee any one condition or article inftanced, in which was added for the clearing the difpenfation by him; and the Nuncio feeing he could get no more, delivered in clearly the difpenfation to the King; for his order indeed was to affay the getting of thofe alterations, but not fo to infift upon them, as any way to retain the bufinefs for them. Now when the difpenfation was thus in the King's hands, and he, by his Secretary, advifing as much, and that he was ready to proceed to the marriage, he conceiveth there neither could, nor can queftion be made of the clearnefs of it, that is to fay after it was in the King's hands; for before, he admitted not of it, as will well appear, for that he would not fuffer the ten days, within which, by the capitulations, the *defpoforios*, were to be after the coming of the difpenfation, to be accounted from the arrival

3   of

of it in Madrid, but from the time that it was clear in the King's
hand. On the other fide he faith, he was careful to do nothing that
might clog the bufinefs; for knowing how much his Majefty had
defired the Match, and being, by his Majefty's letters of the 8th of
October, commanded to proceed to the marriage at Chriftmas, and
the Prince faying in his letter of the fame date, that he was induced
to yield to the deferring of the marriage till Chriftmas, becaufe the
King might have an anfwer before that time, in the bufinefs of the
Palatinate, and fo no time need to be loft in a bufinefs he defired fo
much; and afterwards in the faid letter he faith, " I have written
" this, that you may know from me, as well as from the King my
" father, the intent of this direction, which I affure you is no way
" to break the Match;" he leaveth it to his Majefty's juft and wife
judgment, whether it fhould not have been on the one fide, an undutiful, unwife, and unfafe courfe for him to have raifed any fuch
difficulty, as fhould not have been in his power always to allay it,
or as could not have been poffible to have been cleared from England, before the time defired by his Majefty, which was Chriftmas,
in cafe the King of Spain fhould have been perfuaded to have prorogued the *defpoforios* until then; and on the other fide, to have done
or omitted any that might have given the Spaniard juft colour or pretext of delay, or drawn the default on myfelf. It having been then
made an objection againft the bufinefs and himfelf, that all had been
treated only to gain time, and entertain his Majefty, without any real
intention of making the Match; and therefore it ill befitted him to
be the raifer of any new delays, but to bring the bufinefs to a fpeedy
iffue; and yet he feemeth to remain under cenfure, for that it hath
not fucceeded, fo that at one time he is queftioned to have proceeded,
and blamed becaufe he fucceeded not. As for the redeeming of the
King of Spain, and his Minifters, from the breach of the treaty, for
cafting any colour of fault on his Majefty or Highnefs, he conceiveth
he cannot but be abfolutely free from it; for until after he was taken

3 X

from

from the employment,. he never underftood the treaty to be broken,
but only fufpended until the bufinefs of the Palatinate were fettled;
for by all his Majefty's and the Prince's letters, even until he was
recalled, he never knew any other intent but to proceed therein; and
to that end likewife the Prince's powers were renewed unto him; and
fince the taking of the bufinefs. off his hands, he faith, he hath fo
much defired the having nothing to do therewith, that he ingenuoufly confeffeth, that he knoweth not how, or wherefore it was broken, on the one fide or on the other.

.. This is the moft humble anfwer of the Earl of Briftol, intended for
his Majefty's private fatisfaction, together with fuch things as he
referveth to be delivered by word of mouth to his Majefty, when he
fhall be permitted to wait on him: but if his Majefty, fhall be
pleafed to call him to any further trial, he then declareth, for brevity
fake, and many other reafons, he hath referved the greateft and moft
important part of his defence, from which he defireth he may not
hereafter be debarred; neither giveth himfelf for concluded by this
anfwer, unlefs his Majefty be clearly and fully fatisfied, as he hopeth
he will. He further humbly befeecheth, that he may not be charged
with any error in this his anfwer, either for defect in words, or for
any thing that was not of fault before, or that can only be gathered
out of fome defect or error of his anfwer, and not out of things not
charged; fince he knoweth his Majefty's moft pious intent was, by
thefe queftions, to have fuppofed paft faults examined, and not occafion to be adminiftered by them of committing new. . .

No. XXVIII.

Papers relative to the French Match.

From the originals in the possession of the Earl of Hardwicke.

[King James pursuing the same weak system of policy, that his son could not be honourably matched but with a Catholic Princess, opened a treaty for a marriage with France, as soon as that with Spain was dissolved. He employed in the negociation two of his principal courtiers and favourites, whose names and characters are sufficiently known from the histories of that time. It is proper to observe, however, that the Earl of Carlisle (Hay) appears to have been a Minister of a more generous spirit, and less tractable disposition, than his colleague Holland.

The following documents are published, for the first time, from the originals, and as they open some of the secret passages of that negociation, are thought not undeserving the public notice. The terms granted to the Papists in favour of this marriage, were as little compatible with the laws of the kingdom, or with sound policy, as those agreed to in the treaty with Spain. However engaging and amiable the French Princess was in her person and accomplishments, her fatal influence in the Councils of her husband, and her constant attachment to the Popish interest at home and abroad, are too notorious to be enlarged upon here.]

From Secretary Conway to Lord Carlisle and Lord Holland.

Right Honourable, Rufford, 12th Aug. 1624.

YOUR joint letter of the 17th of this present, *st. novo*, I received the 11th late at night, by the hands of Cook. I did this morning represent it to his Majesty, who found it very strange that

3 X 2 his

his good brother fhould make fo ftrange ufe of his difpleafure to his Minifter* the Marquis *de Vieuville*, as to make his ambition or inordinate actions reflect upon his Majefty, and change, or give ftop to fo happy a negociation.

His Majefty's pleafure is, that you jointly addrefs yourfelves to that King, and that you declare to him, that his Majefty cannot believe that his good brother the French King means to take up the fafhion of Spain to intangle this bufinefs, of fo high and clear condition, with advancements and retractions, to fpin out time and expectations unprofitably; nor can his Majefty underftand it for reafon, to change the ftate and degree this treaty was in, by difavowing his Minifter, who being, according to public faith, in his general calling and practice, and further authorifed by a letter of credit, with which alfo hath concurred the overtures and affurances of that King's Extraordinary Ambaffador the † Marquis de Fiatt.

Further, his Majefty's pleafure is, that you declare to his dear brother, that he expects that King, for his own honour as well as for refpect to his Majefty, and for the good faith which he repofeth in that King's Minifters, fhould make good their overtures and promifes to him, and not fuffer him to partake of the wrong and punifhment, which is but that which his Majefty would make good to his dear brother in the like cafe, howfoever he fhould punifh the Minifter; for it is eafy to fee, how unfafe it is to treat at all, if the difavowing of a Minifter fhould be a juft fatisfaction to the treaty, and a difcharge to that King that fhould fo difavow his Minifter.

Further his Majefty's pleafure is, that you declare to that King, that in cafe he fhall refolve, by the difavowing of the Marquis de Vieuville, after his Majefty's proteftation, that he cannot agree to any article, nor go further than the letter which was required, and which he hath confented to, and fhall prefs his Majefty to further articles, which the government and reafon of ftate of his kingdoms and

* Juft removed from being Surintendant des Finances.
† Ambaffador here.

people

people will not permit, he can make no other conftruction of it, but
that the moft Chriftian King his brother feeks occafion to break the
treaty; and fo his Majefty wills that you declare that neceffarily to be
an end of the treaty, which his Majefty hath purfued with fo paf-
fionate affection, and for fo good ends, both for Chriftendom and
thefe two crowns. His Majefty's pleafure is, you prefs earneftly
that King upon thefe points, and lay down to him in writing, both
what the Marquis de Vieuville faid to you of the fatisfaction fhould
be taken by a letter, and that not to leave that King fuch a gap to
fcape out by; as alfo the affurances given to his Majefty by the
Marquis de Fiatt, which, added to your own arguments, will be fufficient to reduce him to the conditions propounded, or bring it to a
refolution, that the treaty is wholly ended.

And if you fhall not find that before this come to you, or upon
thefe remonftrances, that King fhall not have retracted that ftrange
drawing off, but refts upon his power to decline the accord upon the
difavowing of his Minifter. His Majefty's pleafure is, that you
require of that King permiffion (in the company of fome confident
fervant of that King), to have accefs to the Marquis de Vieuville,
to the end to demand of him, by what warrant he moved the Lord
Kenfington to affure his Majefty that a letter * only under his Majefty's hand fhould be fatisfactory, that fo Vieuville's condemnation
wholly, and his Majefty's fatisfaction in part, may come out of
Vieuville's own mouth.

And this is that which I have in charge, which, for obedience
to your commandments, I have hafted fo, as you find abundance of
errors; excufe it for his fake that fubmits all he may be valued by
otherwife, to the mere affection of being efteemed, &c.

Your Lordfhip's, &c.

---

* This letter related to fome terms for the Papifts, which the King did not chufe to avow
publickly.

From Walter Montague to the Earl of Carlisle.

My Lord,

THIS day being Saturday, fince the arrival of Monfieur de la Riviere, Monf. de Fiatt came to court, bringing the inftructions he had received out of France to prefent to the King the alteration of many words in the King's laft explanation, which they pretended to be prejudicial to the Pope, and the alteration of them to be no ways to us. He alledged this reafon for this laft demand, that they had treated with the Nuncio to procure the delivery of the difpenfation, letting him know the neceffity of making the marriage, and the impoffibility of obtaining their laft demand; how far the King of France had preffed them to the hazarding of the bufinefs, fo that there was no more to be expected but the King's laft explanation, which he (the Nuncio) confidering, took exceptions at many words that tended, he faid, more to the neglect than the fatisfaction of the Pope, which words he advifed them to endeavour to change, and copied over the laft explanation, with many omiffions and additions, which of themfelves can no longer endanger us, but by the ill confequence any change now may bring with it: this laft alteration of theirs they would have figned and dated, as the firft are, to avoid the inconvenience of any new treaty; and upon the grant of this they pretend the difpenfation may be delivered; and * Ville aux Clercs writes, that you will fecond this their requeft; for the King of France's letter to De Fiatt, commands him to obey Ville aux Clercs' order. De Fiatt, to fweeten this, told my Lord, that this was not in the way of treaty, but of a civil requeft from the King of France to the King of England, to defire his favour in that which might import him his peace with the Pope, and no way difturb our King

* French Secretary of State.

5　　　　　　　　　　　　　　　　　　　　　　　with

with any essential alteration: so that since the King of England might purchase to himself so great an obligation, and so important a security to the King of France at so easy a rate, he did not doubt of his chearful embracing it.

My Lord * at first was startled at the name of changing, but at last went up to the King with both the copies, the King's own explanation, and the new one that came out of France, and came down with this answer; That the King wondered much that the King of France his brother would persuade himself, that since this agreement he would be brought to alter the least tittle agreed upon; that he might as well alter all the treaty as this particular; and that it concerned him only to satisfy *him*, not the Pope; and since he was satisfied, he might find some other means to content the Pope; and being it was but in the way of a request, he could answer him no way, but by a request to pardon him for the refusal of it: and that when he shall hear from his Ambassadors accordingly, he would make his answer by them. De Fiatt then undertook to counsel my Lord, as a friend, to refer it to the Ambassadors; that they, if they found it no ways prejudicial to the King, might assent to it; if they did, to refuse it. My Lord answered again, that he could refer nothing to them which he had not received from them, therefore he ought to pay them that respect, as to determine of nothing without their advice, which he expected shortly: so Fiatt was very well satisfied, and resolved to expect your letters, and upon them to send his answer. My Lord hath writ to you, by this bearer, his mind in this point, pressed you much to dispatch. De Fiatt's business, which, we expect by Goring's † journey, depends all upon that, and the raising of 40,000 l. which will take some days, do we what we can. Your Lordship will have sent away concerning this, before this come to you; this relation I made bold to trouble you with, as having the honour to be present at it. You both know the

* Conway.   † Sir G. Goring.

heart

heart and the head; the former will excufe this, and all the reft of my prefumptions. The Lord Steward's * place, the King fays, fhall be no more difpofed of.

The Prince being inquifitive concerning your differences with the Minifters, I made him the trueft relation my memory could furnifh me with; in all particulars his Highnefs juftified you fo much, that he faid if you had done lefs you might have paffed for kind men, but not for wife, and this I will make good upon him.

I have made him in love with every hair in Madam's head, and fwears fhe fhall have no more powder, till he powder her himfelf.

My Lord Duke vowed to-day before De Fiatt, to do all he could to bring Holland the garter; how much that is you know.

My fuit is, that if ever you have occafion to fpeak to the bleffed Queen ‡ of any ill thing, that you exprefs it by naming me, for that's the only way I can hope fhe fhould care to hear of me again.

Thus hoping I have been fufficiently troublefome to your Lord-fhip, I reft, &c. &c. &c.

I know not the day of the month †.

From Lord Carlifle to the Duke of Buckingham.

Our moft noble Lord,   Paris, Oct. 2, 1624.

IF Mr. Packer's of the 16th had brought the wound without the cure, we mean his Highnefs's mifchance §, without his recovery, we had been fwallowed up in forrow and confufion; but the affu-

---

* Duke of Richmond, who was dead.
‡ Queen-mother of France.
† Walter Montague, the writer of this letter, afterwards turned Papift, and died Abbot of Pontoife, after the reftoration. He was fecond fon to the Earl of Manchefter.
§ A fall from his horfe.

rance

ance he gives us, that he is now well and merry, minifters to us that abundance of joy, as we cannot contain from multiplying in humble thanks to your Lordfhip, who have been pleafed fo carefully to derive unto us the greateft happinefs that could be, from the brink of the greateft mifery and affliction; of this duty therefore we acquit ourfelf firft, and in the next place efteem it an effect of much noblenefs and favour, that you carry fo free and open an heart to us, as to communicate all that paffes betwixt this King and your Lordfhip, out of whofe letter we collected, what was carefully concealed from us before, Pere Hyacinth's overtures to the Minifters of this State touching the Palatinate; which gave us occafion to found the Cardinal * in that point; who finding it ftrange, that we fhould come to have any notice thereof (the friar having ftipulated an oath from them to conceal it from us, out of a pretended conceit of our averfenefs to his propofitions, and a hope to find a more fatisfactory anfwer from the King himfelf; who (faid he) had heretofore in a manner agreed to the motions) after that he had underftood from us, that we had received fome touch thereof from England (as now freed from his oath), he ingenuoufly related to us the whole ftory; letting us know the offers to be, the reftitution of the Lower Palatinate in prefent, the reftitution of the Upper upon the reimburfement of twelve millions towards the expence, which the faid Duke pretends to have made in thofe wars; but with condition of quitting the Electorate for ever, or at leaft (and upon a modefter fuggeftion of this State), till it might defcend upon a Catholic branch of the Prince Palatine's own ftock. Whereupon we let him know the falfehood of the friar, in alledging that facility in the King our mafter to fuch unreafonable conditions, and then how acceptable a thing it would be to his Majefty, if this King and State would be pleafed henceforth to fhut their ears to fuch impertinent intercourfes: Whereupon the Cardinal replied, That they had not liftened thus

* Richlieu.

3 Y

far

far to any other end, than by amufing the Duke with fome hopes,
to conceal the better their more fecret intentions and refolutions;
and that from henceforth they would put him over to us, whom he
wifhed to entertain friendly, that it might help likewife the better
to cover their defigns, which (faid he) fhall be rather with the fword
than pen or tongue; and to that purpofe affured us that there were
new commiffions forth for the raifing more forces towards an army
of 16,000 men, which the King meant to put forth in the Meffin, and
to conduct the fame in his own royal perfon. In the other bufinefs
which your letten touches upon, we have ftirred nothing, neither
do we intend, till we receive a new commandment upon noble
Goring his relation, whom we expect daily; and fo we defire your
Lordfhip to do Monfieur de Botru from hence, whom this King
means to poft away, to congratulate the Prince his happy deliverance
from fo defperate a danger. He will come in a private quality, but
merits the entertainment of the greateft Ambaffador, both for that
height of favour he is in with the King and Queen-mother, his
intimatenefs with the Cardinal, and fingular good offices he hath
done in our bufinefs, which alone will make him welcome to your
Lordfhip, whofe hands we here moft humbly kifs, refting in all
humble devotion, &c.

P. S. That of Botru we humbly befeech your Lordfhip to impart unto his Majefty and Highnefs in great fecret, and fo to keep it
till you hear further from us; for with this caution were we made
privy to it. Your Lordfhip likewife will pleafe to reprefent how
cordially they proceed here in Mansfield's bufinefs; who has not
only his money paid him, but his troops here are ready to march.
So faith the Cardinal, and therefore defires a like quick and effectual
difpatch of him in England, which your Lordfhip is intreated to
procure *.

* This Botru went not, but his brother, a witty gentleman, and favourite of the Queen-
mother's.

In the Earl of Carlisle's Hand-writing:

IT will be neceffary his Majefty's pleafure fhould be expreffed in the inftruftions, in what form he will be content the marriage fhall be folemnized by *procureur* in France. In the treat * for Madame Chriftienne, his Majefty did allow of the form which was ufed in the marriages of the laft French King with Queen Marguerite and of that King's fifter with the Duke of Bare; but his Majefty then required, that after the coming of the Lady into England there might be fome new aft performed before fome of our Bifhops, for the ratifying of what had been done by *procureur*, by the declaration of the perfons themfelves. and that thereupon they fhould receive the bleffing of our church.

The French Commiffioners difliked this demand, as derogating from the rights of their own church; and laft of all required to know what the form of the aft fhould be, which was to be repeated in England. It will be in vain to expeft a marriage without a renunciation; for befides that all their treaties with other States run upon that ftrain, they hold it moft neceffary to be ftipulated with us in regard of our other pretenfions, which they will not admit fhould be fortified by a new title, not fo much as to the collateral fucceffions: befides, the two elder fifters having made renunciations, the youngeft muft not expeft to be treated with more favour, and abfolutely it will be labour in vain for us to expeft it. It is alfo to be remembered, that in the treaty with Madam Chriftienne, his Majefty did admit of the renunciation for the direft line, refufing only the collateral.

The like may be faid for the reimburfement †, which is a general condition expreffed in all treaties for the daughters of France; and

---

* In 1616.   † Of the portion.

was

JAMES I.
1624.

was not forgotten in the treaty his Majesty made for his own daughter with the Elector Palatine, and it seemeth to be grounded upon reason and justice; for otherwise, if the Lady survive her husband, and have a desire to return into her own country and marry again, either she must be endowed the second time, or else in second marriage must depend wholly upon another state for her maintenance, and their portion, having nothing to prefer her but her jointure, which may be made so much the less, according to the custom of France, if you admit of a reimbursement.

Touching the charges of the transportation, they offer to defray her till she embarked, and you to transport her in your ships. After she is arrived in England, will you think fitting the French should bear her charges to London? Touching the jewels which are demanded to the value of 15,000 l. sterling, it is an article which is expressed in all treaties, and is of so small a proportion, as is not to be stood upon.

From Secretary Conway to the Ambassadors.

Octob. 5th, 1624.

Right Honourable,   London, Oct. 5th, 1624.

IN a part of my last to your Lordship, I gave you an account how his Majesty had put in deliberation with his Council Conte Mansfelt's propositions, as also the advice the Lords had given for his Majesty to comply in every part of them; but with condition, First, To see the French King's hand both for ratification of the articles and conditions of the whole action; as also for approbation of the rendezvous of the English to be made in France, their quartering, marching, and conjunction with the French, and ease and favour in retreat, either in particular articles or general terms; but howsoever,

to

to be affured and confirmed by that King's fignature made authentic. His Majefty hath now fo far approved of the Count Mansfelt's pro-pofitions, and the advice of his Council, yet with refervation of this unmovable pofition, That the hand of his dear brother the French King muft declare his conjunction in the action, before he put into execution any thing.   Yet thus far his Majefty hath moved, he hath figned a warrant unto his Council of war to pay unto Count Mans-felt, fo foon as the French King's hand fhall be feen, to the effect above fpecified, 15000 *l.* in affifting of his charge and arming of his troops; and 2000 *l.* a month, fo long as the action fhall laft to the ends to be directed.

His Majefty hath further confented to the levy of 12000 men by prefs, to be tranfported at his coft to the rendezvous in France; letters for the mufters are in hand, and commiffions to be expedited, wherein, for the honour of our nation, and as a good prefage, we hear by Count Mansfelt, that the young Lord Hay's * good fortune fhall guide a fourth part of the troop. His Majefty hath written his let-ters of moft gracious and ferious recommendation unto the Prince of Orange, my Lords the States, and thofe of Embden, for favour to the perfon, freedom and equity to be fhewed to Count Mansfelt in his pretences, paffage, rendezvous, and accommodation, with an intima-tion of the merit of his paft and future actions, done and to be done, for the public good, and particular intereft and fervice of his Ma-jefty's dear children.

His Majefty hath commanded me to fhew your Lordfhip how far he is advanced upon this work; the rather for your confidence, en-couragement, and recommendation, and to the end that he may not extend himfelf further in a work of oftentation, that may fucceed vain, nor make fruitlefs expences, which the prefent condition of this ftate hath leaft need of; he commanded me to make this exprefs difpatch to you, of which he requires an anfwer with all the expedition you

* Son to Lord Carlifle.

may,

may, and there cannot appear a better ground for your Lordfhip's
preffing a clear underftanding in this point, than the firft motions of
this coming from France; the fhortnefs and neceffity of time requiring fpeedy execution, which challengeth, of neceffity, an expreffion under that King's hand of his confent for the landing, quartering, and marching of the Englifh, to keep it from being an act of
hoftility, and is confonant with the league of defence which, by your
inftructions, you are to treat for before the alliance, but was remitted,
for comelinefs' fake, until the treaty of the marriage had an iffue.

   This is the charge that I have received, to which I can add nothing, but the eftablifhment of a noble perfon, Sir Robert Naunton
into the Mafterfhip of the Wards; and the effects of an outrageous
ftorm which caft a fhip of his Majefty's into a great deal of danger
upon a land called the Brake, from whence fhe was hardly faved;
a fmall pink of my Lord Admiral's funk, and all the fhips difordered, and thirteen or fourteen caft away, with all their men. One
of the Dunkirk fhips efcaped by plain failing, and another attempted
it in that great ftrefs of weather, but whether efcaped or funk we
know not yet, but a great diforder happened upon her attempt to
go; for a Hollander falling upon her, the King's fhip came in to
part them, and letting fly equally at them both, with blows of the
cannon equally diftributed, perfuaded them to peace. How the
King will take that faucinefs at the Hollander's hands I know not.
And now like a gentle and fweet calm after this ftorm, give me leave
to·tell you the King at Royfton, thanks be to God, and the Prince at
Hampton Court, are both in good health, and the moft excellent Duke,
gracious Buckingham, is feeking after health, in Wallingford houfe,
with a cheaiful mind and glad countenance, which makes him hope
he is in the way to find it. And if I knew in what way to put myfelf to find your commandments, and obey them to your advantage,
I would travel to any part for them; from whence I befeech you to
judge that I attend them here with the devotion of

                Your Lordfhip's moft humble and
                   obedient fervant, &c. &c.

From Lord Carlisle to the Prince.

May it pleafe your Highnefs,   *Paris, Oct. 7th,* 1624.

A S your Highnefs will perceive by our letters to Mr. Secretary,
we have preffed, by all the arguments and inftances we were able,
firft the acceptance of his Majefty's letter inftead of the *efcrit particulier,* and afterwards that they would join with us in a real affociation, for the reftoring of the Palatinate, and patrimonial dignities
of his Majefty's children, *en leur premiere eftre,* after fuch time as
the marriage fhould be concluded and confummate, offering in the
mean while to content ourfelves with a promife in writing, to be
figned by this King and his Commiffioners, for the real performance
thereof, with affurance alfo, that in the mean while they would not
defift to purfue their preparations and actual expeditions, fuitable to
their fo frequent promifes and pretences. But we have received a
flat negative to our faid propofitions, which gives us occafion to fufpect either their fidelity, or elfe that the Marquis D'Effiat doth from
time to time give them fuch affurances of our facility in England, as
doth traverfe all our negociations here. It may therefore pleafe your
Highnefs to give your humbleft fervant leave, out of his zeal and
devotion to your Highnefs's fervice, to reprefent unto your Highnefs, that our endeavours here will be fruitlefs unlefs you fpeak unto
the French Ambaffador in a higher ftrain, and that my Lord of Buckingham alfo hold the fame language unto him. It is true that they
do offer unto us this King's word for their affiftance, and that their
Ambaffador fhall give his Majefty the like affurance; but what affurance can be given to the verbal promife of this people, who are fo apt
to retract or give new interpretations to their former words (efpecially
in a bufinefs of this high nature and importance), your Highnefs, out
of your excellent wifdom, will eafily difcern; neither will there be

any

any hazard in fpeaking to the Ambaffador in a high language, confidering how we have them here locked up, and engaged to conclude
the marriage, whenfoever we fhall condefcend to their demands,
touching the *efcrit particuher*; and we are confident that if we may
be vigoroufly affifted in England, we fhall draw them to better reafon touching our fecond propofition, wherein it will be too much
hazard, and lefs honourable to leave them loofe, and to engage ourfelves. And we are the rather of opinion that, notwithftanding the
countenance they make, they will be brought into reafon rather than
they will break off this matter, wherein they receive fuch full fatisfaction to all their demands. The Queen Mother having openly
declared " qu'il meriteroit d'eftre lapidé qui s'y oppoferoit;" but I
leave all to be weighed in the balance of your Highnefs's incomparable judgment, and with all humility, attend your Highnefs's further commandments. As being, &c. &c.

From Lords Carlifle and Holland to Secretary Conway.

Right Honourable,   *Paris, Oct. 18th,* 1624.

Octob. 18th. ACCORDING to your order, that yours of the 25th brought
us, we firft prefented to the Commiffioners here his Majefty's *
letters to be figned only by his own royal hand, and preffed it by all
the arguments that either you fuggefted or our own reafon miniftred
unto us; but we did fing a fong to the deaf, for they would not endure to hear of it. In the next place we offered the fame to be further figned by his Highnefs and a Secretary of State, wherein we
pretended to come home to their own afking; but this would not

* This related to fome favours to the Catholics, which were not to be made public.

ferve

ferve the turn neither (though long and earneftly contefted by us), for out of a confidence they had, that his Majefty would not fcrupu-loufly infift upon the formality of an *Efcript*, they had fent that to Rome, and made it the bafis of all their work towards the Pope's dif-penfation, and therefore if they fhould now go about to change the foundation, they fhould hazard the whole fabrick, and leave the Pope poffeffed of jealoufies that the King our Mafter did but feek ways of more eafe how to elude the Catholics expectation. And when they per-ceived that we continued to make new replies againft this allegation, they endeavoured to cut all fhort by telling us, they wondered much to fee fuch ftiffnefs in us; when, as Monfieur de Fiatt had written to them from the King our Mafter's own mouth, his Majefty had accord-ed whatfoever they fought both for matter and form. We then offered to become the Marquis's interpreter, which was, by fhewing all that fulfilled in this letter, fo figned as was meant; but when they went further to affure us, that the grant was even to their own prefcribed form, we pretended much ftrangenefs at the matter, fince we had received letters of a far other tenor; but here fitly inferred, upon his confidence of theirs, that if the King our Mafter was pleafed to come fo thoroughly home in all and every point of their demands, we hoped they would meet us by as frank and punctual obfervance of thofe promifes, which they might remember to be folemnly made at the beginning of this treaty, that no fooner fhall the articles of marriage be accorded, but before ever they preffed the figning of them, they would enter into another treaty of league, not only de-fenfive but offenfive, for the Palatinate, and to prepare thefe articles alfo to be figned with the former. We found them not a little fur-prized by the motion; for Monfieur de la Ville-aux-Clercs had caufed a fair draft of the articles for the marriage to be made, in hopes to fee all our hands to them before we parted. Their anfwer was, that, for a defenfive league, there was one already, and if we thought that any force might be added to it by renewing it, they were very ready fo to

do; but, for the offensive one, they never promised any till the marriage should be consummated, and then meant it not under writing,
but by such a real and actual performance, as they presumed would
be more satisfactory than all the articles in the world. We then shewed their own sense to them, and convinced their consciences, by a precise repetition of their own words, first in general to enter upon a
treaty of the league, and then every one's in particular, shewing
what league; " donnez nous des prestres, quoth the Cardinal, et
" nous vous donnerons des Colonels ; donnez nous du faste pour con-
" tenter le Pape, (says le Vieuville,) et nous nous jetterons dans vos
" interests à corps perdu; and suitably spake the Chancellor, nous
" espouserons touts vos interests comme nos propres." All which
they confessed, but pretended to have sufficiently satisfied by the
actual concurrence of this King, which they commended further, by
promising it in as large a latitude as his Majesty's heart could desire
it. But to capitulate with us in writing, would but cast rubs in the
way of their dispensation, and make it altogether impossible, since it
must needs highly offend the Pope to hear they should enter into an
offensive league with Heretics against Catholics, and was like so far
to scandalize the Catholic Princes of Germany, as this King should
lose all credit with them, whom yet he hoped to win to their better
party. But in this point we silenced them by propounding this question to them, Whether they would chuse rather to incur the unjust
offence of uncertain friends, or the just offence of him that was likely
to be the best friend they had in the world ? And then the difficulty
of the dispensation we removed, by complying with them thus far,
that the public treaty should be suspended till that was obtained, provided that, for the present, they would procure a promise under this
King's hand and their own, that when that danger should be once
avoided, they would give his Majesty that full satisfaction which is
now required, and in the *interim* would actually perform, on their
part, towards Mansfeld's expedition, as much as the King our Master

should

should do on his. Their anfwer was, That they could not conde- scend to any thing in writing; but if the King's faith and promife would ferve the turn, that fhould be renewed to us here, and to his Majefty-likewife by their Ambaffador in England, in as full and ample manner as we could defire it. We told them, that Princes were wont to build great defigns, fuch as were thofe of peace and war, upon furer foundations than bare words. And why, quoth Count Schomberg, fhould you call into doubt the King's word, efpe- cially in a matter wherein his honour and intereft are as far engaged as thofe of the King your Mafter's? You do not hear us, anfwered we, call the King's word in queftion; but if he be fo far interefted as you pretend, give us leave to find it fo much the more ftrange, that he makes fuch great difficulties, to oblige himfelf to them by writing. The final conclufion of this conference was, that they would confult the King's further pleafure herein, and let us know a full refolution the day following. But then likewife we received a flat negative to either of our demands; neither availed it ought to allege unto them the King's own promife *totidem verbis* to the contrary, no more than it did to refound in their ears the reafon and equity of our mo- tion otherways; befides the good grace wherewith he might eternally oblige the King our Mafter, in an occafion that tended equally to his own honour and profit, and which being loft, there was no appear- ance of ever meeting with the like to endear his cordial affection to him. To all which they had nothing to reply but to inculcate their former offers of the King's verbal affurance ftill, and to make a buckler of their forwardnefs in Mansfeld's bufinefs, to whom they had not only advanced their own monies, but that which the State of Venice was quoted to likewife, fo to remove the inconvenience that might happen in the levies of his troops through their flacknefs. They had no will to tell us the reafon that the Venetian Ambaffador plainly delivered to them, of this their flow pace in a matter of fo high im- portance; which therefore we refrefhed their memory with, by tell-

ing

ing them, how that flate had, thefe fix or feven years together, offered
fuch fecurity, and been fo plain in all their proceedings, as they muſt
not think ſtrange if now they kept centinel to defcry thoroughly into
thofe myſtical ways of theirs, that fo they be not anew decoyed.
The Cardinal's anſwer was, how they were not to become refponfible
for their predeceſſors faults; that the world ſhould fee them walk
another and more conſtant courfe; and, to purfue to a concluſion his
argument which we had interrupted, told us, that fixteen hundred
horfe were ready to march, and fo were the companies of foot likewife, which the faid Mansfeld was to receive from thence. But is
this all the anſwer, quoth we, which we are like to receive from the
propofitions we make you? We have no other to return, faid they.
Why then, quoth we, let us give you an expedient of compounding
all this difference; give us the *eſcrit ſecret*, which we defire; and to
let you fee what little inconvenience the King your Maſter ſhall incur
thereby, we will oblige ourfelves, upon our honours, nay upon our
falvations, to procure that care in your concealing it, as (the
contents thereof being obferved by this King) it ſhall never pafs
the knowledge of his Majeſty, his Highnefs, the Duke of Buckingham, and our Secretary of State. But when we found this notice
likewife rejected, upon no other pretenfions than this, that it was extremely unfeafonable at this prefent time to hazard the offence of the
Pope under the truſt of other men's fecrets; we then thus parted
with them; " Well, fince we can obtain no better reafon from you,
" this we will do, we will truly and plainly reprefent unto the King
" our Maſter, our propofitions and your anſwers, with all the cir-
" cumſtances on either part, and when we have ſhewed how ſtiff you
" continue in thefe your own ways, we will endeavour the beſt we
" can, that this may be no bar to that part of our felicity which con-
" fiſts in enjoying that incomparable Lady, Madame; but with this
" *Item* by the way, which, for deeper impreffion fake, we twice re-
" peated, that we knew not whether, when the King our Maſter
                                                        " ſhould

" fhould hear of this their proceedings, he might not open his ear to
" new councils, and embrace fuch offers as might come to him from
" other parts, and leave them perhaps to feek place for repentance when
" it would be too late." And with this we, fomewhat abruptly, took
our leaves, and immediately, with the countenance of difcontented perfons, went to Paris, as conceiving this the beft way left, to bring them
unto reafon; and here we expect fome better refolutions from them,
or a new commandment from his Majefty (if fo he can content himfelf with verbal affurances), before we dare adventure to fign the articles. But this we are perfuaded, that the Queen-Mother and the
Cardinal are fo paffionately affected to the Match, as they will leave
nothing untried to work the King to whatfoever is poffible, rather
than the bufinefs fhould thus mifcarry in the very haven.

To their care likewife, we afcribe the quick difpatch of the Pere
Hyacynth; who returned towards Baviere fome three or four days fince,
very badly edified in the bufinefs he came about. The Secretary des
Embaffadeurs, who conducted him to his coach, took his farewel of
him by this pretty compliment, " Je prie dieu (mon Pere), qu'il vous
" conduife bien en votre pays, et que je ne vous voye jamais plus fi
" ce n'eft en paradis, dont il nous faffe jour touts deux; mais que
" ce foit le pluftoft pour vous, et le plus tard pour moy, que faire fe
" pourra."

But though he and his companion be gone, yet there are two befides, that will (howfoever without that vifor of holinefs) carefully
act their part, viz. the two agents of the Emperor and the Duke of
Baviere. The former whereof fought audience, the very day following our laft conference, but with liberty to be covered before the
King, as a thing due to the greatnefs of his Mafter; who therefore
had his pacquet accordingly, that unlefs he would come with cap in
hand, he might keep himfelf fairly where he was.

From Mr. Lorkin to the Lords Carlisle and Holland.

October 11th, 1624.

Octob. 11th.   Right Honourable and my most singular good Lords,

THOUGH I can hardly command my eyes to direct my hand (so ready are they to close, upon every line that drops from my pen), yet have I forced this obedience from them to give your Lordships a brief account of my journey hither, my safe arrival here, and the index I find of the crisis of the business.

· Upon Saturday, in the evening, I arrived at Boulogne in good hour (as your Lordships will have understood from Mr. Carre), and would, the same night, have continued my journey to the gates of Calais, but that the wind turning fair invited me to embark there; which, after some five or six hours refreshing myself, in expectance of the tide, I did, and put forth to sea, where we had not advanced above two leagues, but, we were so becalmed, for nine or ten hours together, as there was no moving one way nor other. Against heaven it was a folly to be impatient, and yet I was almost so foolish. At length, by signs and becks to a fishing-boat, which we descried a great way off, I found means to put myself ashore, and so took post to Calais, where finding the weather calm, and that little wind (that was stirring) turned quite contrary, I had no means to pass unless I ventured myself to a shallop, which I did at sun-set on Sunday evening, and arrived at Dover, half-starved with cold, on Monday morning betwixt four and five of the clock, and entered into London just as the clock struck three. Here I understood that his Majesty was gone to Royston, but that his Highness, my Lord Duke, and Mr. Secretary Conway were, or would be, all here the same evening. By four I waited upon Mr. Secretary, from whom one of the first questions was, Whether he expressed himself unto your Lordships clearly enough, yea or not? I was loth to make my mouth the first witness of his obscurity,

rity,

rity, and therefore declining the direct anfwer, reftrained myfelf to
his laft letter, and told him, that it put your Lordfhips to fome ftand,
to fee his Majefty come fully home to the French King's demands
for the Match, and yet reftrain the figning of the articles to a
condition, of firft procuring others for the league, or at leaft an act
in writing. Whereunto he prefently replied, that he then obeyed
his Majefty's commandment, who had no intention that one fhould
be done without the other, and both his Majefty and his Highnefs,
and my Lord Duke, had had the perufal over thofe letters more than
once. And added, that your Lordfhips had already favoured that
King beyond your commiffion, which enjoined you firft to treat of
the league and then of the alliance, or at leaft to make things go hand
in hand together. But refumed again his firft queftion, Whether his
difpatches were at any time intricate? Whereunto, finding myfelf
preffed either to fpeak truth, or lie, I thus helped to difguife the
former to him; that fometimes he fo cautioufly and prudently in-
volved his meaning, in a clofe and covered ftile, as forced your Lordfhips to affemble your wits together to pick it out. By his truth he
fwore there was no fuch prudent confideration in it, but if there
were any darknefs, it was unwitting, and contrary to his defire,
which was to give the perfect light, and that he referved copies of all,
which I fhould fee, that I might inftance in fome particulars, that
fo he might know the better how to mend the fault hereafter. This
ftruck me dumb, and gave him leifure to read over the difpatch;
wherein he often interrupted himfelf by fuddenly uttering forth thefe
words, " Before God, I fear all is fpoiled, and that we fhall fuddenly
" break upon this difference." I defired his Honour to have the
patience to finifh it, which he did, not without fome other fuch-
like repetitions; and in the end of all, confirmed to me his aforefaid
fears, that we were like to come to a fudden rupture; and that, within
this month, Gondemar would be here with new offers, powerful
enough, in the Spanifh party's conceit, to prevail. Here I delivered
him

him your Lordſhip's letters of credence, which prepared his ear to liſten to the relation of the offers, which, by Mr. Gourden's means, without nominating the perſon, were conveyed to you; and theſe I commended by all thoſe motives and reaſons which your Lordſhips furniſhed me with, or my own underſtanding could ſuggeſt to me. But the ſame voices of deſpair ſounded ſtill, unto me, that all this would not ſerve the turn, nor deliver his Majeſty from juſt appre-henſions, that this Match ſo offered (not only with a ſimple refuſal of a league, but a flying back from their own word and promiſe) was rather out of a deſign to ruin him, than to ſtrengthen him; and that it was an ordinary practice amongſt many great Princes, to think their daughters or ſiſters well beſtowed, if they might thereby be able to compaſs their own ends. He here aſked me, whether I had letters for his Highneſs and my Lord Duke? I anſwered yes. He further enquired of me, whether I brought not a double of this diſpatch to them? but yet I had brought the foul copy with me, becauſe if the King and Prince ſhould be at different places, your Lordſhips were deſirous I ſhould make lecture thereof to his Highneſs likewiſe; the rather, that if any occaſion of queſtion might ariſe upon any par-ticular, I might be able to reſolve it. He thereupon replied, that he would go preſently and perform that himſelf, and would call upon the Duke, that, if his Grace thought fit, he would make the lecture to both together, and that I might be preſent to deliver to either my letters likewiſe. I feared to offend, if I had, by any different motion gone croſs to this demand, and therefore I obeyed, and had the ho-nour to go along with him in his own coach. But the diſpatch was firſt read to them in private; and I only admitted afterwards to de-liver my letters, which was after long attendance, to me eſpecially, that had not taſted one morſel of meat ſince I came from Bologne. Theſe being delivered, I returned to ſcribble this account, and intend to-morrow, to ſee whether I may have acceſs to acquit myſelf more particularly of your Lordſhips commands to both; and ſtrive (as in this)

this, fo on all other occafion, to let your Honours fee, that I have
no greater ambition than to be approved

Your Lordfhips, &c. &c.

From the Same to the Same.

Oct. 21ft, 1624.

Right Honourable and my moft fingular good Lords,

MY former letter contains a true relation of all that paffed be- October 21.
tween Mr. Secretary Conway and me; I referved that which
followed upon my admittance into the Prince and Duke, for another
letter a-part, that if your Lordfhips thought fit to fhew the other to
any, they might therein read no other characters but thofe of defpair. Being therefore admitted into their prefence, his Highnefs
commanded me to deliver what your Lordfhips had been pleafed
to commend to me in truft, which I did fo fully and effectually, as
the Duke interrupting me, told the Prince, that this was much better than that which Fiatt had told him, and his Highnefs confirmed
it by an affirmative. After I had ended all, I added, that if his
Majefty pleafed to condefcend to thofe conditions (in cafe he fhould
find an impoffibility of getting better), your Lordfhips would be
then fo much the bolder, to prefs all things home to their utmoft
extremity, as having a prefent remedy at hand to folder up that
breach which eagernefs of difpute might otherwife occafion. His
Highnefs and my Lord Duke (both) applauded the courfe, if fo be
his Majefty fhould like of it; and agreed (on Wednefday) to go
exprefsly to Roifton, to communicate thefe things with them, and
to know his pleafure therein. I have craved leave to interpofe this
caution, that, if his Majefty confented to the motion, yet that a quite
contrary countenance might be put on, and the Marquis de Fiatt

4 A   carefully

carefully entertained in defpair, becaufe otherwife your Lordfhips' endeavours would be quite fruftrate: and befides, it would have a far better grace, that the fweetnefs of the conclufion might flow directly from his Majefty, by his own inftruments (your Lordfhips) than by a ftranger, who, perhaps, might draw the greateft honour and thanks thereof unto himfelf, as having extorted it by the induftry of his own wit. This his Highnefs and my Lord Duke prefently affented to, and promifed me carefully and punctually to obferve, but with *an if ftill*, if it might once be brought to the point.

I cannot deduce things more particularly; for the meffenger parts early in the morning, and I am now too much oppreffed with fleep.

Copy of the Secret Efcrit prefented by the French Ambaffadors, and avowed to be the fame agreed on between them and his Majefty's Ambaffadors in France.

18th November, 1624.

Nov. 18. LE Roy de la Grande Bretaigne donnera au Roy un efcrit particulier figné de luy, du Sereniffime Prince fon fils, & d'un Secretaire d'Eftat; par lequel il promettra, en foy & parole de Roy, Qu'en contemplation de fon tres cher fils, & de Madame Sœur du Roy tres Chreftien, qu'il permettra à tous fes fubjects Catholiques Romains de jouir de plus de liberté & franchife, en ce qui regarde leur religion, qu'il n'euffent fait en vertu d'articles quelconques accordès par le traité de mariage fait avec l'Efpagne: ne voulant, pour cet effect, que fes fubjects Catholiques puiffent eftre inquietés en leurs perfonnes & biens pour faire profeffion de la dite religion & vivre en Catholiques, pourveu toutesfois qu'ils en ufent modeftement,

ment, & rendent l'obeisance que de bons & vrays subjects doivent à leur Roy, qui par sa bonté ne les restreindra pas à aucun serment contraire à leur religion.

Ce que dessus a eté accordé par Messieurs les Ambassadeurs du Roy de la Grande Bretaigne ce 18 Novembre 1624, à Paris.

Ainsi signé

CARLILE,
HOLAND.

Collat. par moi,
    DE LOMENIE.

From Secretary Conway to Lords Carlisle and Holland.

Right Honourable,   London, 23d Dec. 1624.

I MUST now acknowledge the receipt of two of your letters, the one of the 5th, the other of the 17th of December. I see now, that, before I received your Lordships of the 5th, you had received mine in answer to those brought by the noble gentleman Sir James Auchterlony.

On the 12th of this present at Cambridge, the ratification of the treaty, agreed on and signed by your Lordships, was signed by his Majesty; and, at the same time, the *escrit secret*, and the confirmation of the 9th article, were likewise executed and signed by his Majesty and the Prince severally. The ratification of the treaty is since exemplified under the Great Seal. And, in the demands concerning the Roman Catholics, the French Ambassadors have received full satisfaction; only some legal formalities are to be done, which Monsieur de Ville aux Clercs desires to see before he goes, and for that puts off his journey till Monday. The greatest difficulty hath been concerning the passage of Mansfelt's troops, and the restraint given by his Majesty to Count Mansfelt, not to attempt any act of hostility

4 A 2

upon

JAMES I.
1624.

upon any the lawful dominions or poffeffions of the King of Spain or the Archduchefs. The Ambaffadors here have ufed the fame arguments at Cambridge, we now receive from you. Whereupon his Majefty was pleafed to make a declaration, grounded upon the words of the Ambaffadors, in which, after fome former declaration, his Majefty concluded with the qualifying of his reftraint; indeed taking it away, by permitting them to fecond their companions, or fecure themfelves, if they were affaulted, and fo make their way by arms, if paffage be denied them. The copies of thefe things were prepared to be fent to you, but being not accepted by Monf. de Ville aux Clercs, till they fhall be otherwife altered, I forbear that, till they be agreed on; and I have held up this account, from the 13th to this day, in expectation to have had leave confented to, for a few days return for you the moft noble Earl of Carlifle. But until yefterday, I had no certain refolution, and then I received fignification of his Majefty's pleafure, that, the difpenfation being accorded according to the information of Monf. de Ville aux Clercs, who exprefsly went to court for that purpofe, my Lord Duke's journey would be fo fudden, and the time every way fo fhort, as that his Majefty could not permit your return, for which I am forry, being deferred from the hope of kiffing your hands; a great honour and contentment taken from me.

Every meffenger that comes from Dover will tell you, that the troops march to the rendezvous daily. The reft of the circum- ftances belonging to this, and whatever elfe my affection and my duties might think proper to deliver to you, as well as the magnificent feaft the Duke gave yefternight to the Ambaffadors, defer to the next opportunity; to which yet I muft not leave this commandment of his Majefty's, to fignify his pleafure to your Lordfhips, that you put yourfelves out of your defraying at the charge of that King; nor can I conclude this without the acknowledgment of my infinite

7

obligations

obligations to your Lordſhips favours, and the preſentation of my duties and ſervice, in which I remain

Your Lordſhips, &c.

From Lords Carliſle and Holland to Secretary Conway.

Right Honourable,

WE have forborn to trouble you with the ſeveral bruits which have run here of the commotions of thoſe of the religion, till we ſhould ſee what certain form they would take, yet we have not been wanting upon every occaſion to entreat this King, the Queen-mother, and the Miniſters, not to give too eaſy credit thereto to the prejudice of the good reſolutions now in hand. But we do now underſtand, from certain aſſurance, that Monſieur De Soubize, with ſome companies of thoſe of the religion, hath ſeized upon the Iſland of Rhé, near Rochelle, hath left 500 men there with arms, to fortify and defend it, and is himſelf gone with five ſhips on ſome expedition, which is not yet diſcovered. We are extremely ſorry that we muſt believe that Monſieur De Soubize hath ſo unadviſedly and unſeaſonably engaged himſelf in this deſperate action; but we are aſſured, that the body of thoſe of the religion do not participate therein; but that it is only ſome private diſcontented gentlemen, who, pretending a deſire and neceſſity to procure a better obſervation of the public faith, and the edicts (which they generally complain are too often violated), have animated Monſieur De Soubize to undertake the reformation, hoping withal to repair their own neceſſitous fortunes thereby. The laſt night, having attended the King at a comedie, upon the riſing of the company, he came unto us of himſelf, and in a free and chearful manner entreated us to aſſure the King our maſter from him, that theſe inſolences of thoſe

of

of the religion should alter nothing in the resolutions he had taken for the public good, nor in the particular promises he had made unto his Majesty. Whereupon we rendered unto him special thanks, for so frank a declaration of the constancy of his good affections; and we besought him, that though some indiscreet gentleman had incurred his displeasure, yet that he would still be pleased, for the interest of the commonweal of Christendom, to temper his chastisement with clemency, and not drive the body of those of the religion, by a rigorous proceeding, to the extremity of a general despair; which he promised to do. We have this day, upon this occasion, spoken with the ministers of the State, who have confirmed the same assurance which we received from this King; and more particularly, by the mouth of the Cardinal de Richlieu, they did inform us, that it was true they had taken orders for the present arming of the ships for the recovery of the Island of Rhé, as also for the raising of three little armies, whereof one, consisting of 6000 foot and 400 horse, should remain in Poictou, and those parts about Rochelle; another of 8000 foot and 500 horse, should be raised in Languedoc; and a third of 6000 and 400 horse, about the confines of Champagne; the two first to repress any further tumults or combinations in those provinces, the latter to make head against any incursions of Calalto's or Tilly's troops, if they should attempt it. Yet that, nevertheless, they had newly, by an express courier, renewed the order to the Constable for the hastening of his passage over the mountains; and that they had more money ready for Mansfelt than they had promised, and renewed their former instance, and advise, that Mansfelt should make his passage by the way of Berghen, and not by France; in respect of the hazard he should run of endangering the main enterprize, encountering, at his very entrance, a puissant army of Calalto's and Tilly's troops, with the forces of the country, which they say were joined upon the confines to withstand his proceedings. We opposed to this reason the strength of Mansfelt's

army,

army, the known courage and abilities of the General, and efpecially the impoffibility of tranfporting their 2000 horfe by fea. Whereunto they made anfwer, that they had underflood from Mansfelt, that he would have taken order for it. We are affured by the Ambaffador of Savoy, that he is not only ready, in his Mafter's name, to give affurance for the payment of his portion of money for the entertainment of Mansfelt's troops; but that the Venetian Ambaffador hath alfo newly received order from that Seignory to give. fatisfaction for their proportion; fo, as they pretend, there now remaineth no other difficulty but the refolution of the paffage. We promifed the Minifters to make a true narration of their allegations, which we have faithfully done; but as, at our conference, we held them ftrictly to the firft agreement for the paffage by France; fo we have altered nothing in that behalf, for the reafons particularly alledged in our former letters; and for that we fuppofe, this new defire of theirs here proceedeth rather from the intereft of their own affairs, than from any new extraordinary affection to the bufinefs; conceiving that the refolution will be beft guided by his Majefty's incomparable wifdom, with the opinion of the General.

From Lord Carlifle to the Duke of Buckingham.

My moft noble dear Lord,   Paris, 16th Feb. 1624-5.

IN the care and ftudy which I have to maintain that friendfhip inviolable, which I have profeffed to your Lordfhip, I cannot obferve a more fafe and faithful rule than to follow your Lordfhip's both precept and example, in ufing a cordial and fincere liberty, which is the cement and foul of true friendfhip. I will, therefore, my moft dear Lord, prefume, by my own hand, to communicate

municate my heart to your Lordſhip, and to your Lordſhip only, by
remonſtrating unto you, that this unworthy people, neglecting the
honour and reſpect which they owe to the greatneſs of our gracious
Maſter, the obligation which they have to his Highneſs's tran-
ſcendent merit, quality, and affection, and the gratitude which belongeth to your Lordſhip's noble favours, are grown ſo indiſcreetly
and unreaſonably preſumptuous, as to impoſe a new treaty upon us,
after a perfect treaty concluded, ſigned, and ſworn by his Majeſty,
wherein, by the Pope's borrowed name, they would exact not only
all the diſhonourable and prejudicial circumſtances which, with much
labour and conteſtation, we had avoided or rejected in the whole courſe
of our former conferences and treatings; but would inforce no leſs
than a direct and public toleration, not by connivance, promiſe, or
eſcrit ſecret, but by a public notification to all the Roman Catholics,
and that of all his Majeſty's kingdoms whatſoever, confirmed by his
Majeſty and the Prince his oath, and atteſted by a public act, whereof a copy to be delivered to the Pope or his Miniſter, and the ſame
to bind his Majeſty and the Prince's ſucceſſors for ever. This holdeth proportion, I muſt confeſs, with the whole courſe of their former
proceedings. For firſt, in the point of aſſiſtance, which we required
for the reſtoring of his Majeſty's children to their ancient patri-
mony and dignities, they would not enter into any formal aſſociation, but undertake that this King ſhould give us a promiſe, which
ſhould become equivalent thereunto by their real performance; but
when, upon the ſigning of the treaty of marriage, we came to receive it, we found them to be ſo imperfect, as for the ſaving of his
Majeſty's honour, we rather choſe to have none; and now, when it
cometh to the performance, we underſtand they are fallen ſhort, by
the one half, of the aſſiſtance of cavalry promiſed to the Count Mansfelt; and it is notorious to all the world, how flatly and falſely they
are fallen from the public faith, which they had given for the de-
ſcent of Mansfelt's troops in France, and the paſſage to be made
from

from hence, after they had difcovered the advantage which we had gained upon them in that point.

Touching the treaty of marriage, after his Majefty had admitted of their full demand of the temporal articles, they infifted that, after the example of the treaty with Spain, fomething muft be granted in favour of our Catholics, for the facilitating of the difpenfation, which they then pretended fhould only be fhewed to the Pope, and afterwards withdrawn, and whereof the execution fhould ftill remain in our power, and that they required it only for form fake and their own juftification; which, when we had agreed with the Marquis de la Vieuxville, fhould pafs only by way of letter from his Majefty to this King, Vieuxville was difgraced, and difavowed; and when afterwards the *efcrit fecret* was admitted, and framed upon the expence of much time and confultation both here and in England, the infamous word Liberty, was, by the falfe fuggeftions and artifice of Ville-aux-Clercs foifted in (which I befeech your Lordfhip we may have commandment to caufe to be altered, as a thing which was furreptitioufly gotten without our thought or confent), and now laft of all, by pretence of the Pope's authority, they would impofe upon us real alterations, and new additions, extravagant in themfelves, and incompatible with his Majefty's honour, and the peace of his kingdom. Do but remember, my moft noble dear Lord, how much your noble and generous proceedings in Spain did endear you to the loves and hearts of his Majefty's people, all which you will lofe (I befeech your Lordfhip to pardon my liberty, proceeding from a faft and fincere friendfhip) if you give way in this; the world will now conclude it was nothing but a particular paffion, and animofity, and not care of the public, which excited you thereunto. Nothing can more juftify and advantage Digby, than the admiffion of the laft of thefe new conditions, which carry with them more prejudice and difhonour than the conditions of the Spanifh Treaty, which might feem, out of necef-

4 B

fity

fity, to be extorted, the Prince's precious perfon being in their hands; but now there being no fuch neceffity, the envy will be wholly caft upon the negociators. I befeech your Lordfhip to give your humble faithful fervant, who hath made a league offenfive and defenfive with your frienfhip, leave to affure you, that you will find little faith or faft friendfhip in any but the true Britifh hearts; much lefs in thefe, inconftant and perfidious monfters, who will make little fcruple to ruin their beft friends, fo as they may not fail to compafs their ends. Shall I give your Lordfhip a demonftration thereof? But I muft firft conjure your Lordfhip, by all that is holy and inviolable, to keep it moft fecret; for I have it from a dear friend, who was the firft perfon in the whole world acquainted with it, whom I had rather lofe my life than ruin, and that cannot be avoided if this fecret be difcovered. I have only imparted it to my dear colleague, from whom I conceal nothing; and now am going to tell your Lordfhip, that upon the late news which was brought hither of the death of the King of Spain, there was a projeét framed, that Madame, for whom we have been fo long in fuit, fhould be given in marriage to Don Carlos (they having offended the State of Spain, not daring to ftrike, and unwilling enough to reaffure them), and that they would endeavour to content his Highnefs with the Queen of Spain, as being their daughter, and fomewhat more fuitable to his years. But I fear to abufe your Lordfhip's patience too much. The conclufion of all is this, that, by a round fharp negative, you will fhew your refentment of the indignity which is offered, by thefe new extravagant demands, to his Majefty, and the fweet Prince's honour, to the honour of England, and to your Lordfhip's favour and friendfhip; whofe honour and fortune they would make little difficulty to facrifice to the obtaining of their own ends and defires. But, my dear Lord, you muft then rejeét the whole, elfe you will fuffer their prefumption to encroach too far upon the honour

of

of our great Mafter, and will give more courage to their infatiable appetite, and this, I dare maintain, is not the way to break, but to facilitate and fecure the marriage; the prefent conftitution of their affairs, both at home and abroad, being fuch, as they will not care to offend his Majefty, if they fhould difcover his refolution. Quarrel with the Marquis D'Effiat; not with his perfon, for that is worthy of all favour and efteem; but quarrel with his charge, with his commiffion, and with his Minifters arts; who when they find 'tis inflexible, fet him a-work. If any thing be granted him, that they ftop our mouths withal; if he promife any thing, that they difavow, as having no commiffion to treat; whereof we have found the experience three or four times. In other paffages, heretofore, I have had much patience for your Lordfhip's fake; but now that I find, that, without any fenfe either of honour or gratitude, they care not how they wound their beft friends, I can endure it no longer, for your Lordfhip fhall ever find, that *contra gentes,* I am ever conftant

JAMES I.
1624-5.

Your Grace's, &c. &c.

From Mr. Thomas Lorkin to the Lords Carlifle, &c.

London, February 12th, 1624-5.

Right Honourable and my fingular good Lords,

I HAD difpatched away this account, two or three days fooner, but that I was partly in expectation of fome further order from Court; and partly in hope of preventing the fpeed of any other by mine own diligence. But as the former is like to be fruftrate, by the order La Riviere pretends to have received of delivering his Majefty's letters to the French King himfelf, which, together with the copy

4 B 2

inclofed,

inclofed, being put into my hands by Mr. Secretary Conway late laft night, comes now demanded by him this morning in Mr. Secretary's name, though I refufe to give it, till I receive an exprefs commandment from his Honour's own mouth; fo in the latter I find myfelf deceived by being caft into fuch an intricate labyrinth about your Lordfhip's fupply, as I can fee no fudden iffue out. For though his Majefty hath, upon my Lord of Buckingham's recommendation, carefully follicited by Mr. Secretary, been pleafed to grant a warrant for 12000 *l.* which the Lord Treafurer feconded by another to the Attorney; and he made his draught for the Signet and Privy Seal; yet this ftops a little at the King's fignature; and I find, befides, the Exchequer fo empty, and the difficulties of getting money fo great, as (notwithftanding all the fair language my Lord Treafurer gives me, and that cordial I think, and fuch as deferves your Lordfhip's thankful acknowledgments) I fear fomewhat the expedition. Yet, to redeem by Providence as much time as may be, I am bufy in the *interim* with the merchants to ftipulate for the return, which requires a new care; fince (as the exchange goeth), and efpecially for the quick remitting fo great a fum, I apprehend much lofs.

This being promifed by way of excufe, I leave your Lordfhip's particular, and come unto the public. Wherein, firft, for Mansfeld's bufinefs, you may pleafe to underftand, how his Majefty was content with a very fhort account, becaufe it was fully determined before I came; fo that all that remains for your Lordfhip to do in this point is, as far as I can learn from his Grace, to prefs, what is poffible, the haftening away of the cavalry to join with the infantry; fince, till it be, how well foever the family fhall be compofed and their difpenfation cleared, which will be your Lordfhip's fecond tafk, the noble Duke intends not to ftir from hence.

For the word Liberty (in the *Efcrit particulier)*, his Majefty is pleafed to leave that to your Lordfhip's difcretion, and will think it a

good

good piece of fervice, if you can obtain that it be razed out. Yet would not, by any means, that it fhould be preffed, to caufe any ill blood, or bad correfpondence betwixt the two Crowns; for that were to deftroy one part of his defign, which aims, not only at the marriage, but an amity. And this will do well to be cherifhed by a friendly clofure of the bufinefs, fo to fweeten a little any harfhnefs that may have paffed in the precedent negociation. And to this refolution his Majefty is rather fwayed, by the judgment he makes of the value of the word, which being merely relative to what was meant in contemplation of the treaty with Spain, carries with it a great deal more fhow than fubftance. It is, in effect, the charge I received from his Majefty's own mouth to derive unto your Lordfhips. And to fpeak truth, much cannot be expected from any thing that is concluded in that relative form, fince your Lordfhips can remember, that the Commiffioners pleaded for it by this argument, that they knew not how little they obtained thereby, the bounds being locked up in his Majefty's own breaft, and defired it rather as a colour to content the Pope, than for any great tye they thereby pretended to faften upon the King.

The fpeedy accomplifhment of Monfieur D'Effiatt's bufinefs will give great contentment, and is efpecially recommended by his Grace to your Lordfhip's care. I think there cannot be a more powerful argument to enforce it, than from that tranfcendent expreffion of kindnefs which his Majefty's letter imports, to perfuade to a reciprocal demonftration of affection; and that, as in other more effential points, fo in this, of fending the ribbon to his Majefty, that he may gratify the Ambaffador therewith.

There yet remains one commiffion, which I am to deliver from my Lord Duke, to both your Lordfhips jointly; and that is, in his name to defire you to quicken (as far as cleanly and handfomely you may) the performance of a purpofe, which he is informed, that King (and

9   either

either Queen-Mother or the Cardinal) hath, of prefenting his Grace with pictures, which will be much more welcome if they come before his journey, than if they follow after.

I fhall add only this for news, that Sir Albertus Morton is now fworn Secretary; that the Cardinal denies (in a letter to Monfieur D'Ffiatt) what your Lordfhips advertifed about the confultation and refolution, touching the Prince's reception (in cafe his Highnefs fhould pafs over into France), and defires to know the author of that impofture; that is his term. What further paffed betwixt the Ambaffador and me upon this fubject, I fhall referve till I have the honour to attend your Lordfhips, when I fhall acquit myfelf of a great many other particular commands to either. In the *interim*, I moft humbly befeech your Lordfhips to confirm me ftill in your favourable good opinion, and to honour me with the quality, whereby I pretend to value myfelf moft, of being

Your Lordfhips, &c. &c.

P. S. I had almoft forgot, to let your Lordfhips know, how infinitely fatisfied his Majefty and Highnefs were with Madame's kind reception of the prefent, and the demonftrations of her affection upon that occafion. I come now from Mr. Secretary, with whom, pleading againft the delivery of the letter to La Riviere, he filenced me by fhewing me a commandment under the Duke's own hand, won thereto (as it is like) by the fuit of the Ambaffador, that thereby he might the better facilitate his own affair. From Denmark there came news yefternight as good as his Majefty's own heart can wifh, the particulars I cannot learn. I may not omit one thing which both my Lord Duke and Mr. Secretary ferioufly recommended, that in any future negociations with the Minifters, your Lordfhips truft not to words only, but procure it under their hands in writing.

From Secretary Conway to Lord Carlisle.

Right Honourable,   Chesterford, Feb. 24th, 1624.

I PUT your Lordships dispatch of the 19th of this instant into
his Majesty's hands this day, which he graciously read, and then
commanded me to give your Lordship for answer, that, by a dispatch
made yesterday to you, which will be with you before this can come
to your hands, your Lordships will see the resolution his Majesty hath
taken, following your wise advices, and the reason of the cause as it
was laid before him.   And that very dispatch itself will likewise be
with you almost as soon as this; it being held up for the cause, and
short time in that dispatch expressed, so as his Majesty cannot see how
he may grant the propositions you make for the Lord Carlisle's leave
of coming hither, without giving a great delay to the great business
in hand, and offering subject of much jealousy to that King and his
Ministers; the rather for the shadows taken at you the Lord Carlisle's
person already.   Neither doth his Majesty think it seasonable, in this
conjuncture of affairs, to seem to surprize or affright them: nor can
his Majesty see how this coming away of you my Lord Carlisle
can be suitable with the stile practised by Ambassadors in the ancient and modern times (except in like case as my Lord Holland's
coming by consent of that King, and for the use and advantage of
that King's service from whom he came).   But if the advantage lie
only for the service of his Majesty, his Majesty conceives that you
Lord Carlisle are not unfurnished with Gentlemen of worth to whom
you may trust the relations of things of great consequence.   And if
the secrets might be such as a knowledge of a third from you two,
could not be chosen to bring it to his Majesty, your Lordships might
at least by that confident person write that greatest secret.   And now

all

all this is laid before your Lordſhips, his Majeſty, not to deny to your
wiſdoms, nor to the truſt, experience, and approved faithfulneſs and
judgment, he hath ever found in you, and particularly in my Lord
of Carliſle, the latitude which is fit for a King to leave to his truſty
Ambaſſadors, his Majeſty is gracíouſly pleaſed that you the Earl of
Carliſle may come according to your deſire, if upon this debate with
you by this preſent diſpatch, you the Earl of Carliſle ſhall be pleaſed
to find it good, for the ſervice of his Majeſty, and advancement of
the buſineſs, to come; provided you make that King acquainted with
it, and that he give a conſent to it as for his ſervice, at leaſt that it
give him no offence, and that you warrant yourſelf by the cauſes
known to you, through all theſe difficulties which appear to his Majeſty. Notwithſtanding all which he will not prejudge of you, but
that you may know ſomething, that may juſtly move and authorize
your deſire to come, and your coming. But for the propoſitions of
Denmark, come to you by way of Sir Robert Anſtruther; notwithſtanding ſome things to that point already ſent you, his Majeſty hath
commanded me to advertiſe your Lordſhips, that the King of Denmark was not come ſo far as a declaration, by the induſtry and ſolici-
tations of the Marquis of Brandenbourg; but that ſince, in contemplation of his Majeſty, he hath come to the propoſitions herewith
ſent you, upon which his Majeſty (upon good grounds) hath made
diſpatch to the King of Denmark, agreeing to the King of Denmark's propoſitions, and hath turned the negociation of Sir Robert
Anſtruther, and Sir James Spens, his Majeſty's Miniſters in thoſe
parts, to accommodate all jealouſies between the Kings of Denmark
and Sweden, and form the army under the conduct of the King of
Denmark, or to loſe no aid to deſire from them their ſeveral aſſiſt-
ances by ſeveral ways, upon knowledge given, and direction from
his Majeſty, which way they ſhall take.

His Majeſty likes well the hope that is given of the places that
will be taken in Milan within ſix days. But (I conceive) will
be

be bettter pleafed when he fhall hear that they took them fix days ago.

I muft obferve my duty to make this a fudden difpatch; and I fhall fpeed it the better to let your Lordfhips know, that his Majefty hears you willingly, efteems you much, and trufts you accordingly; and like a great King to worthy Minifters, is unwilling to refufe you any thing. When your Lordfhip ftands thuswith the greateft King, and my bleffed Mafter, what can I offer you, but praifes and prayers for you, and the affection, faith, and duty of

Your Lordfhip's, &c. &c.

The Duke of Buckingham to Lord Carlifle.

My Lord,   Theobalds, March 15th, 1624.

I GIVE your Lordfhip many thanks for your letter, and for the advertifements you give me therein, whereof I fhall not be fparing to make good ufe. And in the mean time, I defire your Lordfhip ftill to have your eyes open, and to ftop any courfe, as much as you can, which may hinder the bufinefs of the Palatinate, and affairs of Germany, and of the religion, until I come; for which I cannot yet appoint a day, till I hear from your Lordfhip, that all is done touching the fettling of Madame's houfe; and then I defire you to fend away Sir George Goring with all fpeed; upon whofe coming, I will refolve on the time of taking my journey, and I purpofe to come with fuch ftore of materials and propofitions, as I fhall make them willing to hearken to me. In the mean time I reft

Your Lordfhip's, &c. &c.

4 C

From Secretary Conway to the Same.

Right Honourable,   Theobalds, March 16th, 1624.

IN all things you are pleafed to honour me more than I am worthy; and in your laft difpatch, you vouchfafe to lay a fault upon hafte, that you do not account the paffage of feveral directions you have received from his Majefty. And yet in the fame you fulfil all that could be advifed from hence, or hoped for there. And although it be not imagined, that you have been put to the trial of your uttermoft powers; yet it is attributed to the ftrength of your noble virtues, that none other could have done fo much. And indeed the praife of your Lordfhip, the joy in the thing, and the furprize, in time and manner, had been inexpreffible, but that all human things have fomething of earth and defect. So this coming in the time of my gracious Mafter's ficknefs, was fubject to that allay of a careful accident, without abatement in itfelf, or any of the circumftances.

It feems your Lordfhip did purpofe to have fent the original, which you require to have returned to you by the Duke's Grace; but you changed your council and fent but a copy; which I remember to your Lordfhips for my difcharge, when the Duke fhall come, the copy you fent, by faith, being as effectual as if you had fent the original. And I muft not conceal from your Lordfhips the chearfulnefs that fhewed itfelf through the double fadnefs of every face, firft for the little hope they had for fo entire a good fuccefs, and then for the extreme grief that every one fuffered for the fharp and fmart acceffes of his Majefty's fever, though a pure intermitting tertian, whereof this day early he had his feventh fit; but, thanks be to God, lefs intemperate than the reft, and hath left more clearnefs and chearfulnefs in his looks than the former; and I know I fhall join with your Lord-

ſhips

ſhips in this prayer, that God, of his goodneſs to his Majeſty, and JAMES I. mercy to us and the reſt of his ſubjects, would reſtore him to his 1624-5. perfect health.

Your Lordſhips cannot but believe that, in the acceſs his Majeſty was in when your letters came, he could not expreſs what he would have done, if his ſtate of health had anſwered his affections; but he left not undeclared his contentment in the act you procured from that King, and his ſatisfaction in ſuch ſervants, as did not only happily do the thing, but did wiſely foreſee and foretel the way to do it, for which the praiſe and thanks is yours.

Give me leave to tell your Lordſhips, the excellent Prince, and the gracious Duke, could not hide their contentment in your Lordſhips, and in your works; and their own letters will tell you the reſt, from ſo certain knowledge, and with ſo much a better grace, as I would not detain you by any thing of mine from that content.

Here is now no ſpeech, but of the ſpeed of the Duke going, which I ſhall join with your Lordſhips in haſtening of, for the reaſons I have from you.

By this diſpatch I ſend to my noble friend, Sir George Goring, from whom I received the demands, the *reglement* of the moſt excellent Princeſs, her houſehold; and becauſe I know how communicable all things are between you, I will not importune your Lordſhips with repetitions; nor will I give leave to the extremity of my aſſertion to your ſervice, to breathe itſelf out in the large expreſſions it longs to manifeſt itſelf by, but, with due reſpect to your patience and greater affairs, conclude this, with this perfect truth, that I am

Your Lordſhips, &c. &c.

STATE PAPERS.

From the Same to the Same.

Right Honourable; Theobalds, March 24th, 1624.

YOUR Lordship will eafily judge the perplexity the Prince, the principal perfons of this Court, and the affairs are in, when you fhall underftand the ftate of his Majefty's health, of which my particular letter to that purpofe, will give your Lordfhips an account.

This is, by the commandment of the Prince his Highnefs, according to the mind of his Majefty, to fignify his pleafure to you, that your Lordfhips let that King and his Minifters know, that it cannot be fuitable with the good nature of a fon, in fo dangerous a ftate of his father's health, to entertain fuch jollity and triumph, as duly belong to fo acceptable a marriage; nor can it be congruous with the thankfulnefs, and faithful love of the Duke of Buckingham, to leave his Majefty in fuch a condition as he now is. Your Lordfhips muft therefore be pleafed to acquaint that King and his Minifters with the fad ftate of his Majefty's health, and withal that, amongft the continual thoughts, that his Highnefs hath of that excellent Lady and that happy Match, he is not without an examination of that King's promife, and the exact terms in it. And although his Highnefs makes interpretation, that if, upon fuch an extraordinary occafion as this is, his proxy and powers fhould not come thither by the precife time of the 31ft day after the fignature of that King's promife, that King would, upon the poffible convenient coming of his powers, pafs, according to the conditions, to the folemnization of the marriage; yet, in a cafe which his Highnefs purfues with fuch paffion, he would not fuffer any point of omiffion to be on his part. And therefore, he prays and requires your Lordfhips to procure from that King, a categorical anfwer, how he underftands and means to ftand upon

that

that limitation of time of thirty-one days, and whether he intends any reafonable time after the thirty-one days. For if that King fhall bind his Highnefs precifely to the 31ſt day, his Highnefs will refolve to entreat the Duke de Chevreufe, to perform the office for him, and fend him his powers. So that the points your Lordſhips muſt clear are, to explain the thirty-one days, whether intended precifely, or as not to be fooner, but at any convenient time after; and where it is faid (when the Duke of Buckingham or fome other fhall be fent from the King, and bring power from the Prince) whether, in this necef-fity, it will not be as acceptable, or at leaſt admitted, that a Duke there be intreated on the part of the Prince. For your Lordſhips may be pleafed to be affured, that if God, according to our hope and prayers, fhall reſtore our gracious Maſter to his health, the Duke will be with you with all poffible fpeed.

And this being the charge I have, your Lordſhips will fee how needful it is you return a fpeedy anfwer; and I fee how fit it is for me to end your trouble, with the prefentation of my fervice to your Lordſhips commandments, at which I remain, in all humble affeΓΌon,

Your Lordſhips, &c. &c.

From the Same to the Same.

Theobalds, March 24th, 1624, late at night.

Right Honourable,

THAT your Lordſhips may know the caufe we have of filent fadnefs, and bear fuch a part in it as your noble fweet powers will contribute, I muſt deliver to you, that this laſt night was the tenth night of his Majeſty's fever, which exercifed much violence upon

upon a weak body, which being reverenced and loved with fo much caufe as his Majefty hath given, ftruck much fenfe and fear into the hearts of his fervants that looked upon him. Yet, to deliver to you the ftate clearly, this day his Majefty hath taken broths, hath had large benefit of nature, and hath flept well. And, more to your comfort, his Majefty did, with life and chearfulnefs, receive the facrament in the prefence of the Prince, the Duke, and many others, and admitted many to take it with him; and in the action and the circumftances of it, did deliver himfelf fo anfwerable to his writings and his wife and pious profeffions, and did juftly produce mixt tears between comfort and grief; and this day, and now this night, he recovers temper, refts, in appearance to us, ftrength, appetite, and digeftion; which gives us great hope of his amendment, grounded not only upon defire, but upon the method of judicious obfervation.

To your ears and affection I know this difcourfe is paffionately acceptable, but to your hearts and tender love wounds and grief; and therefore I will enlarge this part of the ftory no further; but will tell your Lordfhips that Mr Lorkin is ftaid a little by the Duke of Buckingham to affift in the preparation of the Prince's powers, that he may bring them unto you as clear as is poffible, and upon any thing that hath been debated here, may furnifh your Lordfhips with the arguments, if the things be drawn fo far, or that your wifdoms may think fit to make ufe of them. This letter I had intended for your Lordfhips before I had order for that of the fame date which comes with it. When God fhall fet open the windows of his mercy unto us, by reftoring to our bleffed Mafter his perfect health, I will then, with more chearfulnefs, and all fpeed, give you that accefs of joy, and withal continue the acknowledgment of my obligations, the offer of my humble fervice, and the fame fuit I make now to be valued

Your Lordfhips, &c. &c.

From the Same to the Same.

Right Honourable, Whitehall, April 12th, 1625.

THE proxies being ready to go under feal, and the reft of the Peers agreed, and upon the point of difpatch, and his Majefty's letters written to come towards you fome time to-morrow by Mr. Coburne, fervant of his Majefty's, I receive order to difpatch this exprefs to your Lordfhips, with advertifement to you that his Majefty hath underftood, that an Ambaffador of quality is intended to be fent hither from that King, which is a work of more folemnity and coft to both fides than well befits this conjuncture, and the ftrong alliance and friendfhip betwixt the two Kings, which challengeth rather familiarity, and mutual care of each other's coft and convenience. And that there is not any thing which an Ambaffador can perform, which may not be better done by the Marquis D'Effiatt. And therefore his Majefty hath commanded me to fignify his pleafure unto your Lordfhips to do your beft endeavours to ftop his coming, which his Majefty will take for a very acceptable office done to him.

Thanks be to God, his Majefty is in health; the Duke in phyfic, for health's fake. The King of Denmark hath, by much importunity, fent Sir Robert Anftruther hither, with fo fingular a teftimony of ftrong affection and gallant refolution, that, without any other affurance than the words of his Majefty's Ambaffadors, he hath met in perfon with the Lower Saxe Courts, and fome other Princes, to fatisfy whofe fears, he hath raifed, put into armies, and holds in readinefs, 10,000 foot, and 4000 horfe. And if his Majefty will comply with him, according to the promifes given him, he purpofes to be in the field by the 16th of May, with 25,000 foot, and 7000 horfe. I go too far in your Lordfhips trouble, confidering I fhall to-morrow

trouble

trouble you again, and for this I beg pardon now, and, with affurance
of the continuance of them, even for your own virtues fake, I prefent you my humble fervice, continuing in the condition of

Your Lordfhips, &c. &c.

From the Same to Lord Doncafter.

Right Honourable,　　　　　　Whitehall, April 28th, 1625.

HIS Majefty hath commanded me to accompany this worthy
　gentleman Sir Francis Netherfole (Secretary to his dear fifter,
and Refident for his Majefty for the affairs of Germany) with letters
of direction to your Lordfhips to induce that King, by all the convenient ways that may be poffible, to continue his aids for the recovery
of the Palatinate, but with fuch a declaration, as may anfwer the
fpirit of the end for which thofe forces are employed, which is, to
put his Majefty's dear brother into fuch authority or nomination, as,
how fpecious foever it be, yet it may not leave him like a forgotten
or unknown man in the army; which part his Majefty recommends
to your judgments fo to negociate, as may turn moft to the advantage of the end propounded.

His Majefty hath added one commandment more, that your Lordfhips folicit that King for the company of Gens D'Arms to be conferred upon the Prince Edward, one of the King of Bohemia's fons.
I did mean to have put this letter into Sir Francis Netherfole's hands,
to deliver to your Lordfhips; but defire to accommodate you, for your
own particulars, hath put me off that; the relation whereof, I
recommend to your trufty and diligent Mr. Lorkin; only my duty
enjoins me to inform you, that upon a conference to-day at my Lord
Treafurer's houfe, at which was prefent the Lord Treafurer, the

7　　　　　　　　　　　　　　　　　　　　Duke

Duke of Buckingham, the Chancellor of the Exchequer, and myfelf (affifted with Burlamachi and Van Lore), we, in fine, difcovered, that there was no order come from France for the payment of one penny, which hath much difordered the bufinefs here. And your Lordfhips muft think of caufing the money to come in fpecie; or I fee not how that article concerning the portion can be accomplifhed in any reafonable time; for when one day is broken, I know not what day will be kept.

Mr. Lorkin doth ufe miraculous diligence concerning your Lordfhips arrears. I hope to get affignation to Burlamachi to pay fo much in Paris out of the portion; but if your Lordfhips can raife it thence, his Majefty is pleafed to give order for the repayment of it. Even here I break off my letter, and fought out his Majefty to have a warrant figned to the Treafurer for your Lordfhips 4000 l., which I have procured, and doubt not but that Mr. Lorkin will get you the money, and follow this. And to fatisfy your Lordfhips of every pace we go, I difpatch this to you, having written it by fnatches, and having given way to many interruptions, befides two or three long ones in your Lordfhips fervice, for which caufe I befeech you forgive every disjointed part of this, and vouchfafe the humble prefentation of my fervice, which fhall ever be performed to you with fuch faith and duty, as fhall juftify my affurance to ftile myfelf

Your Lordfhips, &c. &c.

P. S. Francis Netherfole brings with him the copy of Count Mansfelt's commiffion to communicate to your Lordfhips.

From the Same to Lords Carlifle and Holland.

Right Honourable,   Whitehall, May 5th, 1625.

IT is impoffible for fo dull an expreffion as mine to fet out to life, the general contentment and applaufe that all faces and voices made for the joyful news your Lordfhips gave of the happy knot tied between the moft excellent perfons of the King and Queen of England, and the hearty prayers formed by every man, and Amen to each other.

But when I fhould obferve the diftrefs his Majefty was in, to pay the facrifice of joy to his Miftrefs, and duty of gravity to his kingly wifdom, I want the art to divide that hair; only I muft tell you, he difcovered what he fought to hide, and all learnt to increafe their joy by his.

The next is to let your Lordfhips know, that his Majefty is well pleafed that you return with the Queen, and by this doth give you leave. But becaufe, even as I am writing this, I conceive it were fit you had a letter for that King from his Majefty, I will enquire better, and, if need be, move for it; and difpatch it to you by an exprefs, continuing for ever according to my infinite obligations,

                  Your Lordfhips, &c. &c.

P. S. If I could be filent, I would fay nothing of this gentleman, whofe good affection leads him to defire this journey. And being fo well known unto your Lordfhips as he is, and your noble courtefies being fo free to all men, I fhall not need to move your Lordfhips to take knowledge of his merit, yet wifh him the happinefs of your favour.

57ī

CHARLES
I.
1625.

From the
Harleian
Collection.

*Account of the vaſtly rich cloaths of the Duke of Bucking-
ham, the number of his Servants and of the noble Per-
ſonāges in his train, when he went to Paris, A. D. 1625,
to bring over Queen Henrietta Maria.*

[This is a ſingular ſpecimen of the luxurious magnificence of
that great favourite.]

My Lord Duke is intended to take his journey towards Paris, on
Wedneſday the 31ſt of March.

H IS Grace hath for his body, twenty ſeven rich ſuits embroidered, and laced with ſilk and ſilver pluſhes; beſides one rich
white ſatin uncut velvet ſuit, ſet all over, both ſuit and cloak, with
diamonds, the value whereof is thought to be worth fourſcore thouſand pounds; beſides a feather made with great diamonds; with
ſword, girdle, hatband and ſpurs with diamonds, which ſuit his
Grace intends to enter into Paris with. Another rich ſuit is of
purple ſatin, embroidered all over with rich orient pearls; the cloak
made after the Spaniſh faſhion, with all things ſuitable, the value
whereof will be 20,000 *l.* and this is thought ſhall be for the wed-
ding-day in Paris. His other ſuits are all rich as invention can frame,
or art faſhion. His colours for the entrance are white pwatchett,
and for the wedding crimſon and gold.

Three rich ſuits a-piece,
Twenty Privy Gentlemen; ſeven Grooms of his chamber; thirty
Chief Yeomen; two Maſter Cooks.

Of his own ſervants for the Houſehold,
Twenty-five ſecond Cooks; fourteen Yeomen of the ſecond rank,
ſeventeen Grooms to them; forty-five Labourers Selletters belonging
to the kitchen.

8   Twelve

Twelve Pages, three rich fuits a-piece; twenty four Footmen, three rich fuits, and two rich coats a-piece; fix Huntfmen, two rich fuits a-piece; twelve Grooms one fuit a-piece; fix Riders, one fuit a-piece; befides eight others to attend the ftable bufinefs.

Three-rich velvet coaches infide; without with gold lace all over; eight horfes in each coach, and fix coachmen richly fuited; eight-fcore muficians richly fuited; twenty-two watermen, fuited in fky-coloured taffety, all gilded with anchors, and my Lord's arms; all thefe to row in one barge of my Lord's. All thefe fervants have every thing fuitable, all being at his Grace's charge.

Lords already known to go,

Marquis Hamilton,	Mr. Villars,
Earl Dorfet,	Mr. Edward Howard,
Earl Denbigh,	Lord Prefident's * two fons,
Earl Montgomery,	Mr. William Legar,
Earl Warwick,	Mr. Francis Anflowe,
Earl Anglefea,	Mr. Edward Goring,
Earl Salifbury,	Mr. Walter Steward.
Lord Walden,	

Befides twenty-four Knights of great worth, all which will carry fix or feven Pages a-piece, and as many Footmen. This whole train will be fix or feven hundred perfons at leaft. When this lift is per-fect, there will appear many more than I have named.

* Lord Manchefter.

END OF THE FIRST VOLUME.

A P P E N D I X.

No. I.

Letter of Richard III. *to the Bishop of Lincoln.*

From the
Harleian li-
brary.

[This letter is an additional proof of the falshood of the traditional
story about Jane Shore, and confirms Sir Thomas More's account
of her, *in his pitiful history.*—That Lord Hastings had succeeded
Edward the Fourth, in her affections, is well known; but perhaps the reader now learns for the first time, that after her
penance, she had another admirer, who *made a contract of matrimony* with her.]

BY THE KING.

RIGHT Reverend Father in God, &c. Signifying unto you,
that it is shewed unto us, that our servant and follicitor, Thomas
Lynom, marvelloufly blinded and abufed with the late wife of William Shore, now being in Ludgate by our commandment, hath
made contract of matrimony with her, as it is said, and intendeth,
to our full great marvel, to proceed to effect of the fame. We, for
many caufes, would be forry that he fo should be difpofed; pray
you therefore to fend for him, and in that ye goodly may exhort
and stir him to the contrary. And if ye find him utterly fet for to
marry her, and none otherwife would be advertifed, then, if it may

　　　　ftand

RICHARD ſtand with the law of the church, we be content the time of mar-
III.
1484.   riage be deferred to our coming next to London ; that, upon ſufficient ſurety found of her good abearing, ye do ſend for her keeper,
and diſcharge him of our ſaid commandment, by warrant of theſe,
committing her to the rule and guiding of her father, or any other,
by your diſcretion, in the mean ſeaſon.   Given, &c.

To the Right Reverend Father in God,

The Biſhop of Lincoln, our Chancellor.

No. II.

The Earl of Leicester to Queen Elizabeth.

From the original in the Paper-office.

[This letter, which produced the memorable and popular visit of Queen Elizabeth to her camp at Tilbury, was omitted in its proper place; and it is hoped, the subject will justify the inserting it here.]

July the 27th, 1588*.

MY most dear and gracious Lady! It is most true that these enemies that approach your kingdom and person, are your undeserved foes, and being so, hating you for a righteous cause, there is the less fear to be had of their malice or their forces; for there is a most just God that beholdeth the innocency of your heart; and the cause you are assailed for is his and his church's; and he never failed any that faithfully do put their chief trust in his goodness. He hath, to comfort you withal, given you great and mighty means to defend yourself; which means, I doubt not but your Majesty will timely and princely use; and your good God that ruleth all, will assist you and bless you with victory.

It doth much rejoice me, to find, by your letter, your noble disposition, as well in present gathering your forces, as in employing your own person in this dangerous action. And because it pleaseth your Majesty to ask mine advice touching your army, and to acquaint me with your secret determination for your person; I will plainly and according to my poor knowledge, deliver my opinion to you. For your army, it is more than time † it were gathered, and

---

* The Earl died in the beginning of the September following.

† Sir John Smith, an old soldier, in his curious treatise of the tactics of this time, gives but an indifferent account of the formation and discipline of this army, which he saw encamped; so it was very fortunate the veteran troops in the Low Countries did not land.

about

about you, or fo near you, as you may have the ufe of it upon few hours warning; the reafon is, that your mighty enemies are at hand, and if God fuffer them to pafs by your fleet, you are fure they will attempt their purpofe in landing with all expedition. And albeit your navy be very ftrong, yet, as we have always heard, the other is not only far greater, but their forces of men much beyond your's; elfe were it in vain for them to bring only a navy provided to keep the fea. But, fo furnifhed, as to both keep the feas with ftrength fufficient, and to land fuch a power as may give battle to any Prince; as, no doubt, if the Prince of Parma come forth, their forces by fea fhall not only be greatly augmented; but his power to land fhall the eafier take effect, wherefoever he will attempt; therefore it is moft requifite for your Majefty to be provided for all events, of as great force every where as you can devife. For there is no dalliance at fuch a time, nor with fuch an enemy; you fhall hazard your own honour, befide your perfon and country, and muft offend your gracious God, that gave you thefe forces and power, and will not ufe them when you fhould. Now for the placing of your army; no doubt but I think, about London, the meeteft for my part; and fuppofe others will be of the fame mind; and that your Majefty do forthwith give the charge thereof, to fome fpecial nobleman about you; and likewife do place all your chief officers; that every man may know what he fhall do; and gather as many good horfes, above all things, as you can, and the oldeft, beft, and affuredeft Captains, to lead; for therein will confift the greateft hope of good fuccefs, under God. And as foon as your army is affembled, that they be, by and by, exercifed, every man to know his weapon; and that there be all other things prepared in readinefs for your army, as if they fhould march upon a day's warning; efpecially carriages, and a commiffary of victuals, and your mafter of ordnance. Of

thefe

thefe things, but for your Majefty's commandment, others can fay more than I, and partly there is orders already fet down.

Now for your perfon, being the moft dainty and facred thing we have in this world to care for, much more for advice to be given for the direction of it, a man muft tremble when he thinks of it; fpecially finding your Majefty to have that princely courage, to tranfport yourfelf to the utmoft confines of your realm, to meet your enemies and to defend your fubjects. I cannot, moft dear Queen, confent to that; for upon your well doing confifts all the fafety of your whole kingdom; and therefore preferve that above all. Yet will I not that, in fome fort, fo princely and fo rare a magnanimity fhould not appear to your people and the world as it is. And thus far, if it pleafe your Majefty, you may do, to draw yourfelf to your houfe at Havering; and your army being about London, at Stratford, Eaft Ham, and the villages thereabout, fhall be always not only a defence, but a ready fupply to thefe counties, Effex and Kent, if need be. And in the mean time, your Majefty, to comfort this army, and people of both counties, may, if it pleafe you, fpend two or three days to fee both the camp and the forts. It is not above fourteen miles at moft from Havering, and a very convenient place for your Majefty to lie by the way, and fo reft you at the camp. I truft you will be pleafed with your * Lieutenant's cabbin; and within a mile there is a gentleman's houfe, where your Majefty may alfo be. You fhall comfort not only thefe thoufands, but many more that fhall hear of it. And thus far, but no farther, can I confent to adventure your perfon. And by the grace of God, there can be no danger in this, though the enemy fhould pafs by your fleet. But your Majefty may without difhonour return to your own forts being but at hand; and you may have two thoufand horfe, well to be lodged at Rumford and other villages near Havering; and your footmen to lodge near London.

* The Earl himfelf

Laftly,

Laftly, for myfelf, I fee, moft gracious Lady, you know what will moft comfort a faithful fervant; for there is nothing in this world I take that joy in, that I do in your good favour; and it is no fmall favour to fend to your poor fervant, thus to vifit him. I can yield no recompence, but the like facrifice I owe to God, which is a thankful heart, and humbly next my foul to him, to offer body, life and all, to do you acceptable fervice; and fo will pray to God, not only for prefent victory over all your enemies, but longeft life, to fee the end of all thofe that wifh you evil, and make me fo happy as to do you fome fervice.

From Gravefend, ready to go to your poor, but moft willing foldiers. This Saturday the 27th July.

Your Majefty's, &c.

R. Leycester.

P. S. I have taken the beft order I can poffibly with the Lieutenants of Kent, to be prefent at Dover themfelves, and to keep there three or four thoufand men to fupply my Lord Admiral, if he come thither, and with any thing elfe that there is to be had. I wifh there might be fome quantity of more powder fent to lie in Dover, for all needs.

STATE PAPERS.

ELIZA-
BETH.
1588.

From the ori-
ginals in the
Paper-office.

No. III.

Letters from the Commanders of the Fleet, about the Spanish Armada.

[The zeal and activity which these great seamen exerted at this important crisis, will always endear their memory to the nation.]

From Sir Francis Drake to Secretary Walsingham, from aboard the Revenge.

June the 24th, 1588.

ALTHOUGH I do very well know, that your Honour shall be at large advertised by my very good Lord, the Lord Admiral, that the Spanish forces are descried to be near at hand, in several companies, on our coast, as it is reported for certain by three barks, unto whom they gave chace and made shot; yet have I thought it good also to write these few lines unto your Honour, nothing doubting but that (with God's assistance) they shall be so fought out, and encountered withall, in such sort, as I hope will qualify their malicious and long pretended practices. And therefore I beseech your Honour to pray continually for our good success in this action, to the performance whereof we have all resolutely avowed the adventure of our lives.

2

From the Lord Admiral † *to the Same.*

SIR,   July the 6th, 1588.

B EIN G here in the midft of the Channel of the Sleeve, on Friday being the 5th of this month, I received your letter of the 28th of June, and another of the fame date, which was written after you had made up your packet.

The caufe of the long time that thefe letters were in coming unto me was, becaufe the purfuivant embarking himfelf upon the Monday at Plymouth, was fain to beat up and down the fea with a contrary wind until Tuefday, before he could find me.

By your firft letter, I find how greatly you ftand affured, that neither the French King, nor the havens and port towns, that ftand for the King, will give any help or affiftance unto the Spanifh army. As for New Haven, it is not a place that can ferve their turns.

By your other letter you perceive, by an advertifement you have from my brother Stafford, that there is money fent down to Breft and Conqueft, for the relief and affiftance of the Spanifh fleet, if they arrive there. I wifh with all my heart, that they were with the beft * * * * * ‡ they could give them. It fhould not be long after, but that I would give them another welcome. For if it be they mean to touch there, then affuredly they have a meaning to join forces with the Duke of Parma. I have no doubt, but that Lord Henry Seymour, being fo ftrong as he is, will have a care, that he fhall not ftart any whither to meet them. And it fhall be very well that you have fome trufty efpial there, to give certain intelligence when the Duke's forces fhall be ready, that then my Lord Henry

† Lord Charles Howard, afterwards Earl of Nottingham
‡ This and feveral other fuch gaps, in this letter, could not be filled up, the original being much decayed.

Seymour

Seymour may lie in the mouth of their haven to intercept their
coming forth.

I am forry to perceive by your letter, that her Majefty hath no more care to have forces about her; confidering the great peril that may come by negleﬁing that which fhould be done in time. I have written unto her Majefty very earneftly about it; and, I hope, that God will put into her mind to do that which may tend moft to her fafety.

I am fure you have feen the letter which I fent unto her Majefty, of the difcovery of certain of the Spanifh fleet not far off Scilly, which made me to make as much hafte out to fea as I could; for upon Sunday our viﬁuals came to us, and having the wind at north-eaft, I would not ftay the taking in of them all; but taking in fome part of them, I appointed the reft to follow with me, and fo bore to Scilly, thinking to have cut off thofe Spanifh fhips feen there, from the reft of their fleet; but the wind continued not fixteen hours there, but turned South South-Weft, that we were fain to lie off and on in the Sleeve, and could go no farther.

Then did I fend Sir Francis Drake, with half a fcore fhips and three or four pinnaces, to difcover. In his way, hard aboard Ufhant, he met with a man of mine, whom I had fent in a bark, ten days before, to lie off and on there for difcovery, who had met with an Irifh bark, and ftaid her, which had been on the 22d taken by eighteen great fhips of the Spanifh fleet, fixteen leagues South South-Weft of Scilly. They had taken out of the faid bark five of her moft principal men, and left in her but three men and a boy. One of the greateft Spanifh fhips towed her at her ftern by a cable, which in the night time, the wind blowing fomewhat ftiff, broke, and fo fhe efcaped in the ftorm. This did affure us greatly, that the Spanifh fleet was broken in the ftorms afore; and, by all likelihood, we conjeﬁured, if the wind had continued northerly, that they would have

returned

returned back again for the Groyne; but * * * * * wind hath served thefe fix or feven days * * * * muft look for them every hour if they mean to come hither.

Sir, I fent a fine Spanifh carvell on, eight days agone, to the Groyne to learn intelligence, fuch a one as would not have been miftrufted; but when fhe was fifty leagues on her way, this foutherly wind forced her back again unto us. Therefore I pray you, if you hear or underftand of any news or advertifements by land, that I may hear of them from you with expedition.

I have divided myfelf here in three parts, and yet we lie, within fight of one another; fo as if any of us do difcover the Spanifh fleet, we give notice thereof prefently the one to the other, and thereupon repair and affemble together. I myfelf do lie in the midft of, the channel with the greateft force. Sir Francis Drake hath twenty fhips and four or five pinnaces, which lie towards Ufhant; and Mr. Hawkins, with as many more, lieth towards Scilly. Thus are we fain to do; or elfe, with this wind, they might pafs by, and we never the wifer. Whatfoever had been made of the Sleeve, it is another manner of thing than it was taken for. We find it by experience, and daily obfervation, to be an hundred miles over: a large room for me to look unto. And whereas it is thought that we fhould have regard * * * * * forces of the Spanifh fleet, if they fhould bend for Scotland, they would in their way thither keep fo far away weftward of Cape Clear, as they would be farther from us at any time than it is betwixt England and Spain; fo that the beft advertifements, that we muft hope for, muft be from you, by the knowledge that you fhall have overland from Scotland, if they be difcovered there; and then our beft and neareft courfe will be unto them through the narrow feas, where I have no doubt but we fhall defeat them of their fleet, whatever they do with * * * *. But, for my own part, I cannot perfuade myfelf but their intent is * * * * * * * * *. Where
there

there are fo many doubts we muft work by the likelieft ways, and leave unto God to direct for the beft. And fo I bid you moft hearty farewell. From aboard her Majefty's good fhip the Ark, the 6th of July 1588.

Your affured loving friend,

HOWARD.

Sir Francis Drake to the Lord Henry Seymour.

Right Honourable and my very good Lord,   July 21.

I AM commanded by my good Lord, the Lord Admiral, to fend you the carvel in hafte with thefe letters, giving your Lordfhip to underftand, that the army of Spain arrived upon our coaft the 20th of the prefent, and the 21ft we had them in chace; and fo coming up to them, there had paffed fome common fhot between fome of our fleet and fome of them; and as far as we can perceive, they are determined to fell their lives with blows. Whereupon his Lordfhip hath commanded me to write unto your Lordfhip and Sir William Winter, that thofe fhips ferving under your charge fhould be put into the beft and ftrongeft manner you can, and ready to affift his Lordfhip, for the better encountering of them in thofe parts where you now are. In the mean time, what his Lordfhip, and the reft following him, may do, fhall be furely performed. His Lord-fhip hath commanded me to write heaity commendations to your Lordfhip and Sir William Winter. I do falute your Lordfhip, Sir William Winter, Sir Henry Palmer, and all the reft of thofe ho-nourable gentlemen ferving under you, with the like; befeeching God of his mercy to give her Majefty, our gracious fovereign, always victory againft her enemies. Written aboard her Majefty's good

4 F 2

fhip

E L I'Z A-
BETH.
1588.   fhip the Revenge, off of Start, this 21ft, late in the evening

1588.

Your Lordfhip's poor friend ready to be commanded,

FRANCIS DRAKE.

P. S. This letter my honourable good Lord is fent in hafte. The fleet of Spaniards are fomewhat above a hundred fails, many great fhips. But truly, I think not half of them men of war. Hafte.

Your Lordfhip's affured,

FRANCIS DRAKE.

From the Same to Secretary Walfingham.

Moft Hononourable,   July the 31ft, 1588.

I AM commanded to fend thefe prifoners afhore by my Lord Admiral; which had, ere this, by me been done, but that I thought their being here might have done fomething, which is not thought meet now. Let me befeech your honour, that they may be prefented unto her Majefty, either by your honour, or my honourable good Lord my Lord Chancellor, or both of you. The one, Don Pedro, is a man of great eftimation with the King of Spain, and thought next in this army to the Duke of Sidonia. If they fhould be given from me unto any other, it would be fome grief to my friends. If her Majefty will have them, God defend, but I fhould think it happy.

We have the army of Spain before us, and mind, with the grace of God, to wreftle a pull with him. There was never any thing pleafed better, than the feeing the enemy flying with a foutherly wind to the northwards.

God grant we have a good eye to the Duke of Parma; for, with the grace of God, if we live, I doubt it not, but ere it be long, fo to

handle

handle the matter with the Duke of Sidonia, as he fhall wifh himfelf. at St. Mary port, among his vine trees.

God give us grace to depend upon him; fo fhall we not doubt victory; for our caufe is good. Humbly taking my leave, this laft of July, 1588.

> Your honour's faithfully to be commanded ever,
>
> FRANCIS DRAKE.

I crave pardon of your honour for my hafte, for that I had the watch this laft night upon the enemy.

> Your's ever,
>
> FRANCIS DRAKE.

From the Same to the Queen.

Auguft the 8th, 1588.

THE abfence of my Lord Admiral, moft gracious fovereign, hath emboldened me to put my pen to the paper. On Friday laft, upon good confideration, we caft the army of Spain fo far to the northwards, as they could neither recover England nor Scotland; and within three days after, we were entertained with a great ftorm confidering the time of year, the which in many of our judgments hath not a little   the enemy way.

If the wind hinders it not, I think they are forced to Denmark, and that for divers caufes. Certain it is, that many of their people were fick and not a few killed; their fhips, fails, ropes and wafte, needeth great reparations, for that they had all felt of your Majefty's forces. If your Majefty thought it meet, it were not amifs you fent prefently to Denmark, to underftand the truth, and to deal with that King according to your Majefty's great wifdom. I have not written this whereby your Majefty fhould diminifh any of your forces. Your

5 Highnefs's

Highnefs's enemies are many; yet God hath and will hear your Majefty's prayers, putting your hand to the plough for the defence of his truth, as your Majefty hath begun. God, for his truth's fake, blefs your facred Majefty now and ever. Written aboard your Majefty's good fhip the Revenge, this 8th of Auguft, 1588.

Your Majefty's faithful vaffal,

FRANCIS DRAKE.

From the Same to Secretary Walfingham.

Auguft the 10th, 1588.

REASONS why he thinks, that the Spanifh fleet is gone to Norway or Denmark; that the King of Denmark can beft help their wants.

The Prince of Parma, I take him to be as a bear robbed of her whelps; and no doubt, but being fo great foldier as he is, that he will prefently, if he may, undertake fome great matter, for his reft will ftand now thereupon. It is for certain, that the Duke of Sidonia ftandeth fomewhat jealous of him, and the Spaniards begin to hate him, their honour being touched fo near, and many of their lives fpent. I affure your Honour not fo little as five thoufand men lefs, than when we firft faw them near Plymouth; divers of their fhips funk and taken; and they have nothing to fay for themfelves in excufe, but that they came to the place appointed, which was at Calais, and there ftaid the Duke of Parma's coming above twenty-four hours, yea, and until they were fired out. So this is my poor conclufion, if we may recover near Dunkirk this night, or to-morrow morning, fo as their power may fee us returned from the Channel, and ready to encounter them, if they once fally, that the next news you fhall hear, will be the one to meeting againft the other; which when it fhall come to pafs, or whether they meeting or no, let us all

with

with one confent, both high and low, magnify and praife our moft gracious and merciful God, for his infinite and unfpeakable goodnefs towards us.

Written with much hafte, for that we are ready to fet fail to prevent the Duke of Parma, this foutherly wind, if it pleafe God, for, truly, my poor opinion is, that we fhould have a great eye upon him.

P. S. Since the writing hereof, I have fpoken with an Englifhman, which came from Dunkirk yefterday; who faith, upon his life, there is no fear of the fleet. Yet would I willingly fee it.

END OF THE FIRST VOLUME.